Official Google Cloud Certified Professional Cloud Security Engineer Exam Guide

Become an expert and get Google Cloud certified with this practitioner's guide

Ankush Chowdhary and Prashant Kulkarni

‹packt›

BIRMINGHAM — MUMBAI

Official Google Cloud Certified Professional Cloud Security Engineer Exam Guide

Authors: Ankush Chowdhary and Prashant Kulkarni

Reviewers: Hector Diaz, Assaf Namer, Lanre Ogunmola, and Holly Willey

Managing Editor: Arun Nadar

Development Editor: M Keerthi Nair

Production Editor: Shantanu Zagade

Editorial Board: Vijin Boricha, Megan Carlisle, Alex Mazonowicz, Aaron Nash, and Ankita Thakur

First published: August 2023

Production reference: 1220823

Published by Packt Publishing Ltd.

Grosvenor House

11 St Paul's Square

Birmingham

B3 1RB

ISBN 978-1-83546-886-9

www.packtpub.com

Foreword

We are digitizing the planet at an increasing pace. Small and large businesses, governments, and other public institutions, and the daily fabric of our lives increasingly depend on reliable and secure systems.

More of these systems are now operating in one or more hyperscale cloud providers. Such cloud providers continue to invest in security as a reflection of their importance to customers in critical infrastructures and of their own desire to manage risk for large numbers of organizations. With increasing security, resilience, reliability, and compliance in the cloud, many organizations are moving more data and workloads to get these benefits.

At Google Cloud, we are committed to providing our customers with the most secure and reliable cloud platform possible and we have invested significantly in secure by design and secure by default approaches to provide higher assurance to help customers operate securely.

While our goal is to make Google Cloud as easy to secure as possible, we also know that designing, configuring, and operating large cloud deployments for real workloads requires solid expertise and experience. We also know that security is not just about technology. It's also about people.

At Google, we have been focused on developing the cybersecurity workforce through our cybersecurity certificate programs and many other resources that not only grow the number of people available to organizations to improve cybersecurity, but also increase their depth and specialism in important fields like cloud security. Our Professional Cloud Security Engineer certification is one of the most comprehensive and respected cloud certifications in the industry. It is a valuable credential for professionals to demonstrate their expertise, and for organizations to know they're working with someone who has validated expertise and is committed to the right security practices as encoded by Google Cloud security experts.

Ankush and Prashant, in developing this *Official Google Cloud Certified Professional Cloud Security Engineer Exam Guide*, are providing an immensely useful resource for professionals to learn and ready themselves for this important certification in a growing field with huge demand for such skills. The guide serves as the authoritative source aligned with the exam blueprint and offers professionals an easy way to study not just what's relevant to the exam, but further reading material and paths to additional Google Cloud-provided training courses.

Well-configured cloud services represent a significantly increased level of security for many organizations that will bring continued societal benefits. We hope with the expertise gained from your Google Cloud Certified Professional Cloud Engineer status, you will be part of this security evolution.

Phil Venables

Chief Information Security Officer, Google Cloud

"One who can see that all activities are performed by the body, which is created of material nature, and sees that the self does nothing, truly sees".

– Bhagavad Gita 13:30

Contributors

About the authors

Ankush Chowdhary, Vice President – CISO, HPE

With an unwavering focus on technology spanning over two decades, Ankush remains genuinely dedicated to the ever-evolving realm of cybersecurity. Throughout his career, he has consistently upheld a deep commitment to assisting businesses on their journey towards modernization and embracing the digital age. His guidance has empowered numerous enterprises to prioritize and implement essential cybersecurity measures. He has had the privilege of being invited as a speaker at various global cybersecurity events, where he had the opportunity to share his insights and exert influence on key decision-makers concerning cloud security and policy matters. Driven by an authentic passion for education and mentorship, he derives immense satisfaction from guiding, teaching, and mentoring others within the intricate domain of cybersecurity. The intent behind writing this book has been a modest endeavor to achieve the same purpose.

I want to express my deepest gratitude for the completion of this book. This accomplishment is not solely my own; it is the result of the collective contributions and support from many individuals in my professional and personal life.

To my family, friends, and all who have supported me, thank you for being the guiding forces and pillars of strength throughout this journey. Your unwavering support, encouragement, and belief in my abilities have fueled my determination and kept me grounded.

I am grateful for the wisdom and insights shared by my colleagues and mentors. Your contributions have added depth and richness to the content of this book.

I dedicate this book to all of you, for your invaluable presence and the influence you have had on its creation. Your collective efforts have shaped its realization and made it a reality.

Prashant Kulkarni, Cloud Security Architect, Google Cloud

In his career, Prashant has worked directly with customers, helping them overcome different security challenges in various product areas. These experiences have made him passionate about continuous learning, especially in the fast-changing security landscape. Joining Google 4 years back, he expanded his knowledge of Cloud Security. He is thankful for the support of customers, the infosec community, and his peers that have sharpened his technical skills and improved his ability to explain complex security concepts in a user-friendly way. This book aims to share his experiences and insights, empowering readers to navigate the ever-evolving security landscape with confidence. In his free time, Prashant indulges in his passion for astronomy, marveling at the vastness and beauty of the universe.

I would like to thank my loving family and friends, including my supportive wife, my two wonderful children, my parents, and our goofy labradoodle.

I would like to dedicate this book to all the passionate learners and seekers of knowledge who embrace the joy of learning. It is a tribute to those who see challenges as opportunities for growth and relish the journey of acquiring new skills and insights. May this book serve as a guiding light, empowering you to overcome hurdles and unlock the boundless potential within the world of Google Cloud security engineering. Your unwavering dedication to learning inspires us all!

Last but not least, I would like to thank our publisher, Packt, and the whole editing team who worked tirelessly to make this book the best we could!

About the reviewers

Hector Diaz is a Cloud Security Architect at Google, partnering with highly-regulated organizations to design and operate secure and compliant cloud environments. Before joining Google, Hector spent 15 years architecting security and Cloud solutions for customers in the financial, retail, and telecommunications industries to achieve their business goals.

Assaf Namer is a Cybersecurity leader, Principal Cloud Security Architect, security patent holder, and mentor. He has worked on a few startups as well as industry giants such as Intel, AWS, and Google. Assaf is the creator of a few security blueprints and has led some of the largest cloud agreements, and offers governments security advice. He holds a master's degree in Cybersecurity, MBA, and a professional program in AI/ML from MIT.

Lanre Ogunmola is a Cloud Security Architect at Google Cloud and has more than 15 years of work experience with a strong focus on data protection, cryptography, threat modeling, and risk assessment. He holds an MS in Cybersecurity from the University of Nebraska and has earned CISSP, CCSP, CISA, CISM, CKA, CKS, and other Google Cloud certifications. Outside of work, he loves watching soccer and experiencing new cultures.

Holly Willey is a Cloud Security Architect who helps organizations craft secure, scalable, and resilient systems in the cloud that address their business needs. She has worked as an architect for Google Cloud, ServiceNow, and AWS, as well as in engineering roles at Splunk and F5 Networks. Her early career included more than a decade spent designing, building, and supporting mission-critical databases for financial services, telecommunications, and e-commerce companies. Holly holds an M.A. in Teaching Mathematics and Science from Seattle Pacific University and a B.A. in Business Administration from the University of Washington.

Table of Contents

6

Google Cloud Identity and Access Management   91

7

Virtual Private Cloud   135

10

Cloud Data Loss Prevention   259

11

Secret Manager   301

12

Cloud Logging   317

13

Image Hardening and CI/CD Security   341

14

Security Command Center   365

15

Container Security   397

Preface

Organizations are increasingly adopting cloud migration for several reasons, including scalability, cost-efficiency, and agility. Cloud platforms offer the ability to scale resources on demand, reduce infrastructure costs, and quickly adapt to changing business needs. As a result, businesses are seeking to leverage the benefits of cloud computing, leading to rising demand for cloud security. Cloud security plays a crucial role in cloud computing, and so cloud service providers such as Google Cloud invest heavily in security measures such as encryption, access controls, threat detection, and incident response. By migrating to the cloud, organizations can leverage the expertise and infrastructure of cloud providers to enhance their overall security posture, protecting against data breaches, unauthorized access, and other cyber threats. As a result, there is growing demand for skilled professionals who can ensure the security of these cloud environments.

Data breaches and security incidents have become a major concern for businesses. The role of a Google Cloud security engineer involves implementing robust security measures, designing secure architectures, and managing access controls to safeguard data from unauthorized access, breaches, and other security threats. The Google Professional Cloud Security Engineer Certification acts as a testament to your proficiency in securing cloud environments and demonstrates your commitment to professional development. It enhances your credibility and opens up new career opportunities in the field of cloud security.

This book will introduce you to a range of essential topics. It will provide an understanding of cloud security fundamentals and the shared responsibility model. The book will go in-depth into the security features and services offered by Google Cloud, such as IAM, network security, container security, and Security Command Center. It will also address secure cloud architecture and design, data protection and encryption, security operations compliance and governance, and best practices. Additionally, the book has two full mock exams to aid in exam preparation. By covering these topics thoroughly, the book prepares you to excel in the certification exam and thrive as a cloud security practitioner using Google Cloud.

By the end of this book, you will have gained the knowledge and skills required to pass the Google Professional Cloud Security Engineer Certification exam and implement architectural best practices and strategies in your day-to-day work.

Who this book is for

This book is for IT professionals, cybersecurity specialists, system administrators, and any technology enthusiasts aspiring to strengthen their understanding of Google Cloud security and elevate their career trajectory. We delve deep into the core elements needed to successfully attain the Google Cloud Professional Security Engineer certification—a credential that stands as a testament to your proficiency in leveraging Google Cloud technologies to design, develop, and manage a robust, secure infrastructure. As businesses increasingly migrate their operations to the cloud, the demand for certified professionals in this field has skyrocketed. Earning this certification not only validates your expertise but also makes you part of an elite group of GCP Security Engineers, opening doors to opportunities that can significantly advance your career. Whether you're seeking to gain a competitive edge in the job market, earn higher pay, or contribute at a higher level to your current organization, this book will guide you every step of the way on your journey to becoming a certified Google Cloud Professional Security Engineer.

What this book covers

Chapter 1, *About the Google Professional Cloud Security Engineer Exam*, focuses on the Google Professional Cloud Security Engineer Certification and provides guidance on how to register for the exam. This chapter also covers the outline of the exam.

Chapter 2, *Google Cloud Security Concepts*, covers how Google secures its cloud infrastructure. You will learn how shared security responsibility is applied to the different Google Cloud services, the defense-in-depth model that Google deploys in securing its infrastructure at various layers, and how the isolation and security of data are achieved. Other areas covered include threat and vulnerability management, security monitoring, and data residency.

Chapter 3, *Trust and Compliance*, looks at two essential aspects of cloud architecture. The first part of the chapter focuses how Google builds security and privacy and provides customers with full transparency. Data security is all about control, and you will learn about how Google Cloud empowers its consumers to own, control, and protect their data. The second part of the chapter covers the different compliance standards and programs that Google Cloud is compliant with and how you can gain access to compliance reports. It also gives an introduction to some advanced topics that will be discussed later in the book when covering continuous monitoring and continuous compliance.

Chapter 4, *Resource Management*, covers Google Cloud Resource Manager and how resources are organized. It also covers of IAM policies, organizational policy controls, Cloud Asset Inventory, and firewall rules that can be applied and inherited via the resource hierarchy.

Chapter 5, *Understanding Google Cloud Identity*, introduces Google Cloud Identity. You will learn how to design and build your authentication strategy on Google Cloud using Cloud Identity. The topics include user lifecycle management, device security, cloud directory, account security, app management, identity federation, and single sign-on.

Chapter 6, Google Cloud Identity and Access Management, takes a deep dive into Google Cloud Identity and Access Management. It covers IAM roles, permissions and conditions, service accounts, how to manage service account keys, and IAM policy intelligence, along with best practices and design considerations.

Chapter 7, Virtual Private Cloud, covers network security concepts within Google Cloud. You will look at what a VPC is and the different types of VPC models, as well as how to do micro-segmentation using subnets, custom routing, and firewall rules. Furthermore, you will also look at DNSSEC in Google Cloud and different types of load balancers.

Chapter 8, Advanced Network Security, teaches you how to secure your content by using the advanced network security features that are available on Google Cloud. This chapter also covers Identity-Aware Proxy, Private Google Access, VPC Service Controls, DDoS, and the web application firewall.

Chapter 9, Google Cloud Key Management Service, lays the foundation for understanding the key hierarchy in Google Cloud **Key Management Service** (**KMS**) and how envelope encryption works. In this chapter, you will look at different types of encryption keys, their purpose, and how Google does encryption and key management, including coverage of the underlying cryptographic operation. The chapter also covers concepts such as bringing your own key to the cloud.

Chapter 10, Cloud Data Loss Prevention, guides you on how to use Google Cloud **Data Loss Prevention** (**DLP**) to secure sensitive data. It covers techniques used to scan for sensitive data by creating scan jobs and also how to enforce DLP rules to redact sensitive data using techniques such as masking, redaction, and tokenization.

Chapter 11, Secret Manager, guides you on how to use Google Cloud Secret Manager to create secrets that are used during runtime by your applications.

Chapter 12, Cloud Logging, covers how Cloud Logging works on Google Cloud. You will look at the different log types and key components for logging and learn how to build a centralized logging system for continuous monitoring.

Chapter 13, Image Hardening and CI/CD Security, teaches you how to harden compute images for both virtual machines and containers. It covers how to manage, secure, patch, and harden images, and how to build image management pipelines. Furthermore, you will look at building security scanning of the CI/CD pipeline. Finally, this chapter covers some Google Cloud Compute Engine security capabilities such as Shielded VMs and confidential computing.

Chapter 14, Security Command Center, explores the capabilities offered by Security Command Center and teaches you how to configure and use Security Command Center's capabilities to detect threats, vulnerabilities, and misconfigurations. You will also look at how Security Command Center can be used to build automated incident response and ingest its findings with third-party security information and event management tools such as Splunk.

Chapter 15, *Container Security*, covers how to design, develop, and deploy containers securely on Google Cloud. The topics covered include various aspects of container security, such as image hardening, isolation, implementing a security policy, scanning containers, and Binary Authorization. It also covers various security features of **Google Kubernetes Engine** (**GKE**) and some best practices.

Mock Exam 1 is a full-length exam covering all certification areas. Pay attention to the language of the questions.

Mock Exam 2 is another full-length exam covering all certification areas. This exam should increase your confidence in passing the exam.

To get the most out of this book

To get the most out of a certification book like this, follow these strategies:

- **Set clear goals**: Define your objectives and what you aim to achieve by studying the certification book. Identify the specific areas you want to strengthen your knowledge in and the skills you want to acquire.

- **Plan and allocate time**: Create a study schedule that fits your routine and allows for consistent learning. Allocate dedicated time each day or week to focus on the book's content. Consistency is key to retaining information effectively.

- **Active reading**: Approach the book with an active mindset. Take notes, highlight important concepts, and jot down questions for further exploration. Engage with the material actively to enhance comprehension and retention.

- **Hands-on practice**: Supplement your reading with practical exercises and hands-on labs whenever possible. Apply the concepts and techniques described in the book to real-world scenarios. This will solidify your understanding and help you develop practical skills.

- **Review and reinforce**: Regularly review the topics covered in the book to reinforce your knowledge. Make use of review questions or quizzes provided in the book or seek additional practice exams to test your understanding and identify areas that require further study.

- **Seek additional resources**: While the certification book serves as a comprehensive guide, supplement your learning with additional resources such as official documentation, online tutorials, video courses, and practice exams. Use these resources to gain different perspectives and reinforce your understanding.

- **Join study groups or communities**: Engage with others pursuing the same certification. Join online study groups or communities where you can discuss concepts, share insights, and clarify doubts. Collaborating with peers can enhance your learning experience.

- **Track your progress**: Keep track of your progress by setting milestones or checkpoints throughout your study journey. Celebrate achievements along the way, and identify areas that require more attention to ensure a well-rounded understanding.

- **Practice time management**: Efficiently manage your time during the exam preparation phase. Allocate sufficient time for reviewing and practicing sample questions or mock exams to simulate the actual exam environment and improve your test-taking skills.

- **Stay motivated**: Maintain a positive mindset and stay motivated throughout your certification journey. Remember your goals and the benefits that achieving the certification can bring. Reward yourself for milestones reached and stay committed to the process.

By implementing these strategies, you can maximize your learning experience with the certification book, deepen your knowledge, and increase your chances of success in the certification exam.

Download the color images

We also provide a PDF file that has color images of the screenshots and diagrams used in this book. You can download it here: https://packt.link/Wmiqu.

Conventions used

Code words in text, database table names, folder names, filenames, file extensions, pathnames, dummy URLs, user input, and Twitter handles are shown as follows: "The lifecycle state is displayed as ACTIVE or DELETE_REQUESTED."

Words that you see on the screen, for example, in menus or dialog boxes, also appear in the text like this: "Navigate to **Billing** from the console menu on the left."

A block of code is set as follows:

```
{
  "creationTime": "2020-01-07T21:59:43.314Z",
  "displayName": "my-organization",
  "lifecycleState": "ACTIVE",
  "name": "organizations/34739118321",
  "owner": {
    "directoryCustomerId": "C012ba234"
  }
}
```

When we wish to draw your attention to a particular part of a code block, the relevant lines or items are set in bold:

```
{
  "type": "service_account",
  "project_id": "project-id",
  "private_key_id": "key-id",
  "private_key": "-----BEGIN PRIVATE KEY-----\private-key\n-----END
```

```
PRIVATE KEY-----\n",
  "client_email": " prod-service-account@project-id.iam.
gserviceaccount.com ",
  "client_id": "client-id",
  "auth_uri": "https://accounts.google.com/o/oauth2/auth",
  "token_uri": "https://accounts.google.com/o/oauth2/token",
  "auth_provider_x509_cert_url": "https://www.googleapis.com/oauth2/
v1/certs",
  "client_x509_cert_url": "https://www.googleapis.com/robot/v1/
metadata/x509/service-account-email"
}
```

Any command-line input or output is written as follows:

```
git secrets --add 'private_key'
git secrets --add 'private_key_id'
```

New terms and important words are shown like this: "The aim of this book is to help cloud security professionals pass the **Google Cloud Platform** (**GCP**) Professional Cloud Security Engineer exam."

> **Tips or important notes**
> Appear like this.

If you are using the digital version of this book, we advise you to type the code yourself. Doing so will help you avoid any potential errors related to the copying and pasting of code.

Get in touch

Feedback from our readers is always welcome.

General feedback: If you have any questions about this book, please mention the book title in the subject of your message and email us at customercare@packtpub.com.

Errata: Although we have taken every care to ensure the accuracy of our content, mistakes do happen. If you have found a mistake in this book, we would be grateful if you could report this to us. Please visit www.packtpub.com/support/errata and complete the form.

Piracy: If you come across any illegal copies of our works in any form on the Internet, we would be grateful if you could provide us with the location address or website name. Please contact us at copyright@packt.com with a link to the material.

If you are interested in becoming an author: If there is a topic that you have expertise in and you are interested in either writing or contributing to a book, please visit authors.packtpub.com.

Share your thoughts

Once you've read *Official Google Cloud Certified Professional Cloud Security Engineer Exam Guide*, we'd love to hear your thoughts! Scan the QR code below to go straight to the Amazon review page for this book and share your feedback.

https://packt.link/r/1835468861

Your review is important to us and the tech community and will help us make sure we're delivering excellent quality content.

1

About the GCP Professional Cloud Security Engineer Exam

The rate of migration to the cloud is growing exponentially. The cloud is something of a *Masai Mara* right now, and we don't expect that this will slow down. New projects are often now born in the cloud and end up staying there.

> **Note**
>
> The Masai Mara is an iconic African savanna landscape characterized by an annual wildebeest and zebra migration of over 1.5 million animals.

This growing trend has created new opportunities, specifically for cloud security. There is now soaring demand for cloud security professionals. It is not news to those in the field of cybersecurity that cloud security skills are not only in demand but scarce. Cybersecurity professionals with cloud security skills are now very sought after. Security used to be the number one obstacle to organizations moving to the cloud. Now, security is the top reason that organizations want to move to the cloud. This only increases the demand for cloud security professionals.

> **Note**
>
> For more details see *13 Cloud Computing Risks & Challenges Businesses Are Facing In These Days* by *Bernardita Calzon*, published on June 6, 2022 on the datapine website (`https://packt.link/xlnX6`).

The aim of this book is to help cloud security professionals to pass the **Google Cloud Platform** (**GCP**) Professional Cloud Security Engineer exam. The topics covered in this book not only include exam-specific content but also extend to some optional GCP cloud security topics.

This chapter covers why you should take this exam, how to register, and what to expect in the exam.

In this chapter, we will cover the following topics:

- The benefits of being a certified cloud security engineer
- How to register for the exam
- What to expect and some helpful tips

Benefits of being certified

As per Burning Glass, a leading labor market analytics firm, there is 115% projected growth for cloud security in the next five years. Not only are cloud security skills in demand, but it's also a very lucrative field. For Google Cloud security skills more specifically, there is 113% growth expected. This makes having GCP cloud security knowledge a must for cybersecurity professionals. What's more, earning the Professional Cloud Security Engineer certification will be a resounding endorsement of their skills.

Gaining a new skill or certification always helps boost your profile and increase your chances of being hired. The Google Cloud Professional Security Engineer certification validates a person's proficiency in designing, developing, and managing a secure infrastructure that leverages Google Cloud Platform technologies. This globally recognized certification can offer various benefits, including the following:

- **Increased employability**: This certification is recognized by many employers globally. It proves your skill set and makes you a desirable candidate for roles that involve Google Cloud security.

- **Higher earning potential**: On average, certified Google Cloud professionals have a higher salary compared to non-certified professionals in similar roles.

- **Skill validation**: The certification validates your knowledge and skills in Google Cloud Platform security. This can boost your confidence and credibility when dealing with projects or discussing solutions with clients or colleagues.

- **Professional development**: The preparation process for the certification exam can significantly enhance your current understanding of Google Cloud Platform security features and best practices. This knowledge is critical for those who want to excel in the cloud security domain.

- **Keep up-to-date**: The field of cloud technology is constantly evolving. The process of getting certified requires you to study and understand the latest Google Cloud security services, tools, and best practices.

- **Expand your professional network**: When you become certified, you can join groups and communities of other certified professionals. This provides opportunities to network, learn, and share experiences.

- **Company benefits**: If you're a part of a company that's a Google Cloud partner, your certification can contribute to your company's partner level, which can offer additional benefits, resources, and recognition for the company.

Overall, being a certified Google Cloud Professional Security Engineer is a valuable credential that can open significant career opportunities and benefits in the rapidly growing field of cloud computing.

Whether you're looking to get certified or just acquire new skills, the aim of this book is to help you understand GCP's cloud security capabilities.

Registering for the exam

The GCP Professional Cloud Security Engineer exam is two hours long and consists of multiple-choice questions. The exam can be taken at a testing center, or you can choose to have an online-proctored exam from a remote location. The cost of the exam is USD$200 plus tax and is only available in English. You can register for the exam by following these steps:

1. Navigate to the GCP Professional Cloud Security Engineer landing page at `https://packt.link/PZx8D`, where you can find more detailed information about the exam.

    You will find many useful resources here, such as an exam guide, sample questions, training options, and links to community learning and the certification hub.

2. Select the option to book the exam by clicking on **Register**, which will take you to the Webassessor Google Cloud certification landing page at `https://packt.link/2FmkY`. You will need to create an account with Webassessor in order to book your exam.

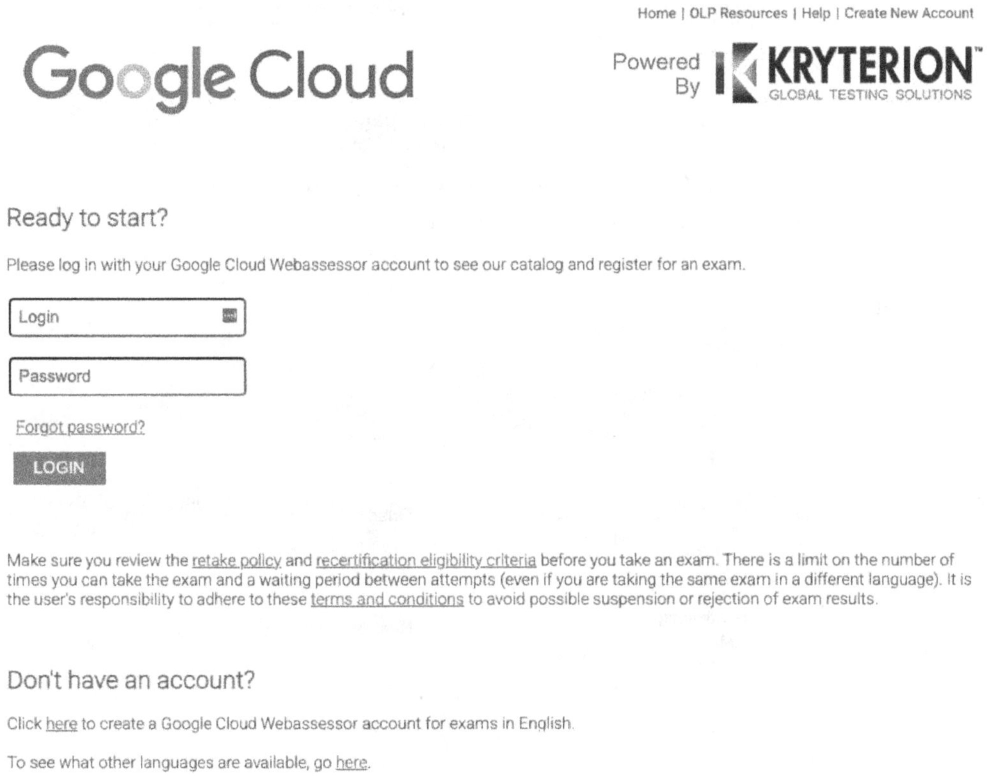

Figure 1.1 – Logging in to Webassessor

3. Once you have created an account and logged in, you will need to select the exam you would like to register for. Here you will also be able to select whether you would like to sit the exam at a testing center or via the online-proctored method.

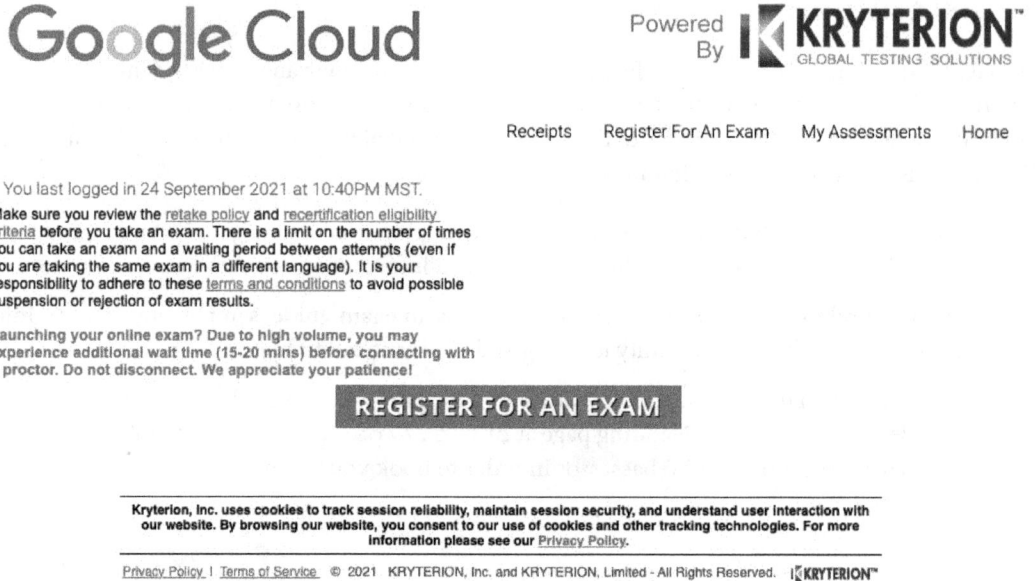

Google Cloud

Powered By **KRYTERION** GLOBAL TESTING SOLUTIONS

Receipts   Register For An Exam   My Assessments   Home

You last logged in 24 September 2021 at 10:40PM MST.

Make sure you review the retake policy and recertification eligibility criteria before you take an exam. There is a limit on the number of times you can take an exam and a waiting period between attempts (even if you are taking the same exam in a different language). It is your responsibility to adhere to these terms and conditions to avoid possible suspension or rejection of exam results.

Launching your online exam? Due to high volume, you may experience additional wait time (15-20 mins) before connecting with a proctor. Do not disconnect. We appreciate your patience!

REGISTER FOR AN EXAM

Kryterion, Inc. uses cookies to track session reliability, maintain session security, and understand user interaction with our website. By browsing our website, you consent to our use of cookies and other tracking technologies. For more information please see our Privacy Policy.

Privacy Policy | Terms of Service   © 2021   KRYTERION, Inc. and KRYTERION, Limited - All Rights Reserved.   **KRYTERION**

Figure 1.2 – Registration page

4. Note that for every exam, there is a + sign. By expanding that, you will be able to choose between the options of testing center and online-proctored.

Google Cloud Certified - Professional Cloud Security Engineer (English)	This is the Google Cloud Certified - Professional Cloud Security Engineer exam. Please refer to the exam guide for current topics that may appear on the exam. You may attempt an exam at a test center or online and each attempt regardless of delivery method or language counts toward the total permissible attempts and the waiting period between attempts still applies (see our Retake Policy here).		*multiple*		
Google Cloud Certified - Professional Cloud Security Engineer (English)	Pre-requisites:: Retake Policy :		Onsite Proctored	USD 200.00	Buy Now
Google Cloud Certified - Professional Cloud Security Engineer (English)	Pre-requisites:: Retake Policy :		Remote Proctored	USD 200.00	Buy Now

Figure 1.3 – Exam selection

5. Next, you will be allowed to select a testing center.

Choose options below to narrow down the list of testing centers displayed.

Country:	United States	Province/State:	New York	City:	New York	OR

Postal Code		Range	10 miles			Search

Select the Testing Center where you wish to take the test.

AVAILABLE TESTING CENTERS

☐

☐	Alliance Computing Solutions_New York City	545 8th Avenue, #1210	New York	New York	United States	Map

Select   Cancel

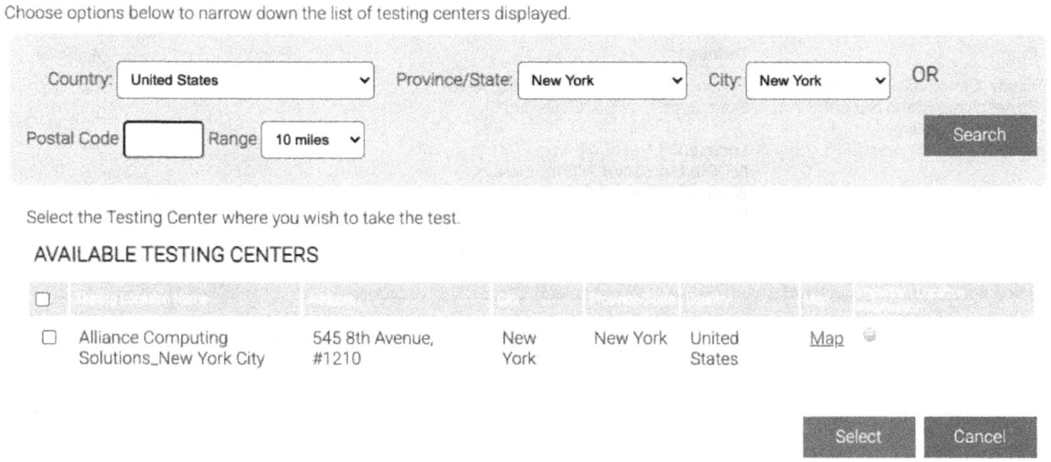

Figure 1.4 – Select a testing center

6. Next, you will need to select a date and time when you wish to sit the exam at your preferred center.

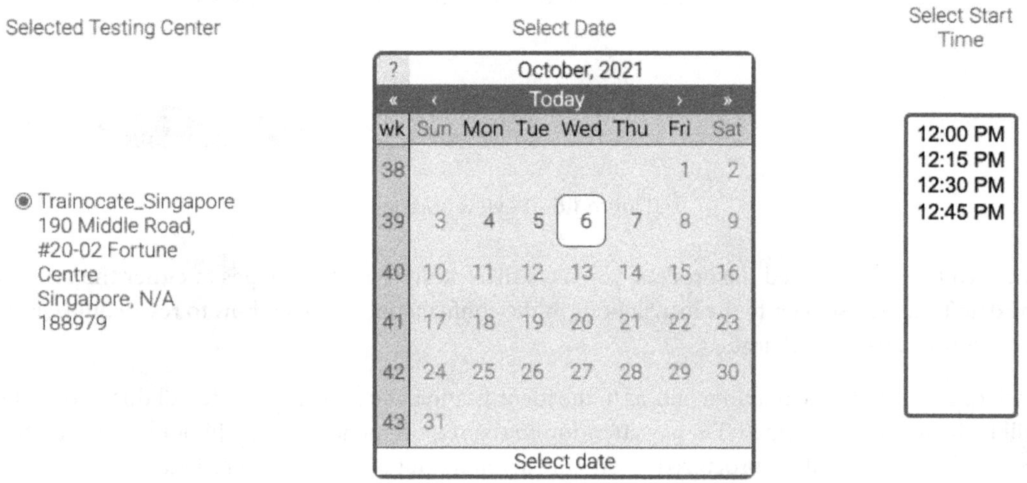

Selected Testing Center	Select Date		Select Start Time

October, 2021

«	‹	Today	›	»

wk	Sun	Mon	Tue	Wed	Thu	Fri	Sat
38						1	2
39	3	4	5	6	7	8	9
40	10	11	12	13	14	15	16
41	17	18	19	20	21	22	23
42	24	25	26	27	28	29	30
43	31						

Select date

◉ Trainocate_Singapore
190 Middle Road,
#20-02 Fortune
Centre
Singapore, N/A
188979

12:00 PM
12:15 PM
12:30 PM
12:45 PM

Figure 1.5 – Book a date and time for the exam

7. Proceed to checkout and complete the transaction by either paying the fees or using a voucher, if you have one.

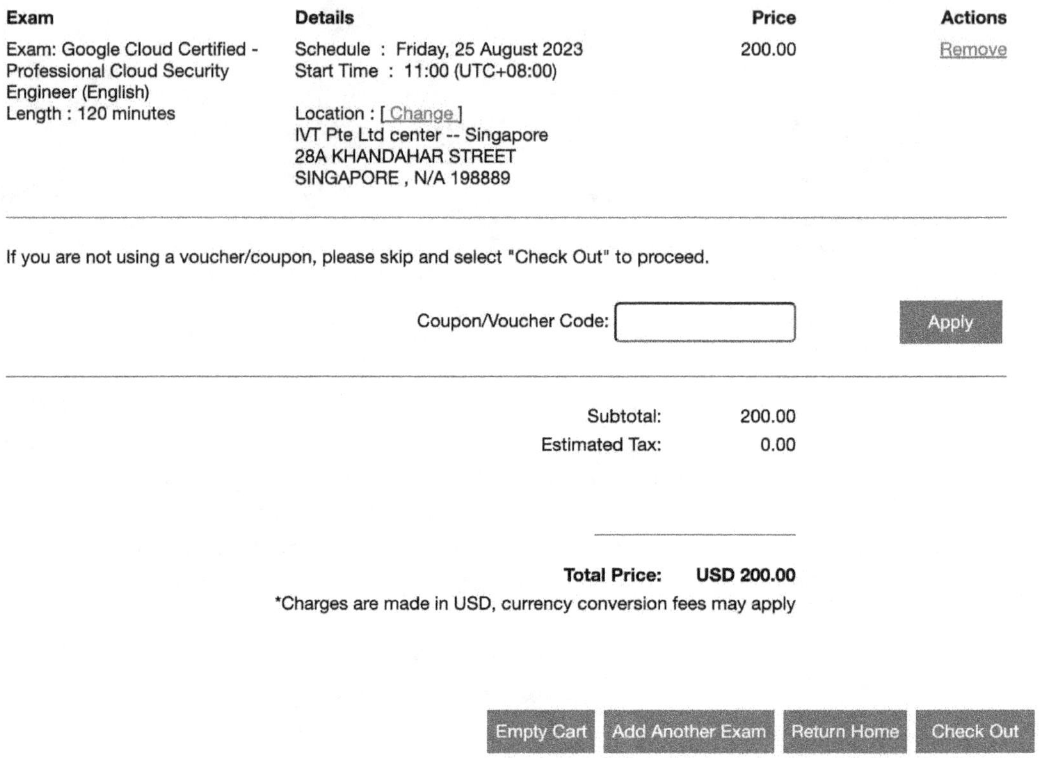

Exam	Details	Price	Actions
Exam: Google Cloud Certified - Professional Cloud Security Engineer (English) Length : 120 minutes	Schedule : Friday, 25 August 2023 Start Time : 11:00 (UTC+08:00) Location : [Change] IVT Pte Ltd center -- Singapore 28A KHANDAHAR STREET SINGAPORE , N/A 198889	200.00	Remove

If you are not using a voucher/coupon, please skip and select "Check Out" to proceed.

Coupon/Voucher Code: [   ]   Apply

Subtotal:	200.00
Estimated Tax:	0.00

Total Price: USD 200.00

*Charges are made in USD, currency conversion fees may apply

Empty Cart   Add Another Exam   Return Home   Check Out

Figure 1.6 – Review and pay

Once you have completed the process, you have the option to make changes to either the center or the date/time. Please refer to the instructions in the confirmation email on how to reschedule without incurring cancellation charges.

Each center has specific requirements as to the identification you need to provide. All this information will be included in the email. Do pay attention to the requirements as you will not be allowed to sit the exam, whether online-proctored or on-site, if you do not have the proper identification.

Some useful tips on how to prepare

Cloud security exams are different from those for other security certifications. They require both depth and breadth of knowledge in multiple security domains. Most vendor security certifications focus on the product, but the GCP Professional Cloud Security Engineer exam focuses on domains such as identity and access management, data protection, network security, logging and monitoring, and security operations. It is important for those attempting the exam to have a sound understanding of the foundational security concepts. This book assumes that you already have basic knowledge of these concepts; if you don't, it's highly encouraged that you gain that knowledge before attempting the exam.

Every individual has a different way to prepare and study, but it's advised that you follow the structure laid out in this book and build knowledge in the areas covered. If you are familiar with GCP security, you can skip chapters and/or read them in any order. For those who are new to GCP, it is highly recommended that you follow the sequence of chapters.

The GCP certification page (`https://packt.link/WlaJJ`) for the Professional Cloud Security Engineer exam contains some helpful details on the exam syllabus, an exam guide, and sample questions. Do take the time to read those as they offer insights. The content of this book is based on the exam blueprint.

The exam questions are multiple-choice and based on real-world scenarios. The test is based on your knowledge of GCP security products and technology. The topics and options can range from cloud security best practices and security configuration to product-specific security controls and how you would meet compliance objectives. The exam is geared toward what cloud security engineers experience day to day while performing their roles.

This book will help you prepare for the range of questions in the exam, and each chapter has a section to test your knowledge. Nothing compares to having hands-on experience; therefore, it is highly encouraged that you create a free GCP account if you don't already have one and spend some time playing around with GCP's security products. Google Cloud Skills Boost has a great collection of GCP security labs, and that collection is recommended for you to get some hands-on experience. In each chapter, there are links to whitepapers and relevant Google Cloud Skills Boost for you to complete. Please note that Google Cloud Skills Boost is a paid service; you can either buy a subscription or pay for each lab.

Another useful resource is courses offered by Google Cloud Skills Boost. In the *Further reading* section of each chapter, you will find links to Google's official courses that are offered through Google Cloud Skills Boost. For those who are new to GCP or familiar with another cloud provider, it is highly recommended that you do some introductory GCP courses from Google Cloud Skills Boost. They will help you build a sound understanding of how GCP is different and what capabilities are offered.

Finally, some key things to remember for the exam. Many of you will already know this, but remember to read the questions very carefully. Most questions have a scenario to paint a picture, but the actual question that is asked is usually in the last line. For example, a question may describe how developers in an organization are building an application that stores sensitive data and how developers and end users access it. It is important to focus on aspects such as who the user is (*the developer*), how they access the application (*by identity and access control*), and what needs to be protected (*the sensitive data*). Extracting such information will help you identify the solution that addresses all those areas.

Always use the option of marking the question for later if you are not sure. Sometimes, the next question is asked in a way that answers the previous question. In that case, you can mark both questions to come back to later and then revisit them before you hit submit. Do keep some time at the end to revisit the questions. Often, when you do 60+ questions, you tend to overlook certain things. Giving yourself an opportunity to check your answers will help.

Summary

In this chapter, we looked at how the GCP Professional Cloud Security Engineer certification is distinguished from others by the kinds of security domains it concerns. We also covered the benefits of getting certified and how to register for the exam.

The next chapter will cover aspects of Google Cloud security at the infrastructure level to help you understand how Google secures its cloud footprint and the various compliance programs and standards it is compliant with.

Further reading

Refer to the following links for further information and reading:

- Google Cloud Certification: `https://packt.link/9hV9a`
- Professional Cloud Security Engineer: `https://packt.link/knxFi`
- Google Cloud Skills Boost: `https://packt.link/gyaJD`

2

Google Cloud Security Concepts

In this chapter, we will cover Google Cloud's security and compliance fundamentals. We will take a look at how Google Cloud secures its cloud infrastructure using strategies such as defense in depth and zero trust. On the compliance side, we will look at different compliance standards and frameworks that Google Cloud is compliant with. Google has a unique approach to shared security responsibility and recently adopted the *shared fate* concept. We will look at these ideas to get a better understanding of Google's responsibility and the customer's responsibility when it comes to security.

After that, we will look at the key pillars of security that Google applies to build a trusted infrastructure that doesn't rely on a single technology but has multiple stacks. We will get a better understanding of each of those stacks and how and where they are applied. Finally, we will briefly cover aspects such as threat and vulnerability management from a Google infrastructure perspective.

The key topics in the chapter include the following:

- Overview of Google Cloud security
- Shared security responsibility
- Addressing compliance with Google Cloud
- The key pillars of security by design
- Threat and vulnerability management

Overview of Google Cloud security

The concepts in this chapter don't appear in the exam and are not part of the exam blueprint. As a Google Cloud security professional who will be responsible for securing enterprise workloads and making them compliant, it's important that you gain a sound understanding of how Google secures its infrastructure. As a security practitioner myself, I have seen many customers who like to understand aspects such as how the underlying infrastructure is secured, how the hypervisor is secured, how Google achieves multi-tenancy, and which compliance objectives are and are not met. To be able to advise your customers or internal teams, it's essential to know about these topics.

Google Cloud provides a very comprehensive set of security documentation on these topics and it's highly recommended that you take the time to read them. This chapter is a summary of some of the key topics that you must know. There are links at the end of this chapter for you to refer to these documents.

Google has the mission to build the most trusted cloud. In order to achieve this, Google has implemented multiple layers of security to protect its infrastructure, the data, and its users. Let's further understand how Google Cloud doesn't rely on single technologies to make it secure, but rather builds progressive layers of security that deliver true defense in depth.

Google, from the beginning, built its infrastructure to be multi-tenant, and the hardware is Google built, managed, hardened, and operated. All identities, whether they are users or services, are cryptographically authenticated, and only authorized application binaries are allowed to run. Google applies zero-trust principles whereby there is no trust between services, and multiple mechanisms are applied to establish trust. As a Google Cloud user, you have the option to use the Google-operated, -owned, and -managed end-to-end private encrypted network. Google enforces **Transport Layer Security** (**TLS**) for its externally exposed **Application Programming Interfaces** (**APIs**) across its network, and any data stored on Google Cloud is encrypted by default. This makes things much simpler for organizations as it removes the overhead of managing encryption infrastructure and the lifecycle management of the encryption keys. You can find more on encryption and key management in *Chapter 9, Google Cloud Key Management Service*. The scale of Google's network allows it to absorb the largest of DDoS attacks; protection from volumetric attacks (Layers 3 and 4) is applied by default. Last and most importantly, Google operates 24x7 security operations to detect threats and respond to security incidents.

In order to further strengthen its security posture, Google has end-to-end provenance. Google servers are custom-built for the sole purpose of running Google services and don't include unnecessary components such as video cards that can introduce vulnerabilities. The same applies to software, including the **operating system** (**OS**), which is a stripped-down, hardened version of Linux. Google has also built Titan, a custom security chip that offers first-nanosecond boot integrity and allows for both server and peripherals to establish a hardware root of trust. Titan uses cryptographic signatures to validate low-level components such as the BIOS, bootloader, kernel, and base OS image during each boot or update cycle. Titan is embedded across Google's hardware infrastructure, servers, storage arrays, and even Pixelbooks and the latest Pixel phones. Google has developed its own network hardware and software to enhance performance and security, resulting in custom data center designs that incorporate various layers of physical and logical protection. Moreover, by maintaining end-to-end control over its hardware stack, Google minimizes the risk of third-party vendors interfering. In the event of a vulnerability, Google's security teams can promptly create and deploy a solution without relying on external parties.

Titan

Google's purpose-built chip to establish
hardware root of trust

Purpose-built
chips

Purpose-built
servers

Purpose-built
storage

Purpose-built
network

Purpose-built
data centers

Reduced "vendor in the middle" risk

Figure 2.1 – End-to-end provenance and attestation

Data privacy is an important aspect for many customers using the cloud. A key Google Cloud differentiator is how Google Cloud has built-in privacy controls to earn customer trust. One of those services is **Access Transparency**; this service allows customers to gain visibility if and when Google engineers try to access a customer environment. A typical use case would be when a customer contacts Google Cloud support and an engineer is assigned to work to resolve the case and requires access to customer cloud components. In this case, Google can provide full transparency logs to the customer. All these cloud privacy commitments are backed by contractual agreements and commitments, including third-party independent assessments.

The data privacy commitments include the fact that as a customer you own and control your data; Google does not access your data or move it to another location. As a customer, you are responsible for securing and controlling access to your data. Furthermore, Google does not sell or use your data for advertising. There is no backdoor access to Google services for government or law enforcement. As covered earlier, Google encrypts all communications across physical boundaries and encrypts data at rest automatically without customer intervention, adding a further layer of security by default. Lastly, a unique and key differentiation of Google Cloud is how transparent Google is in sharing the logs of any activity that may have led to a Google engineer accessing customer data. This is done by a service that Google offers called Access Transparency. We will cover more on this in the coming chapters.

Shared security responsibility

Google offers a range of services on its cloud platform, including traditional **Infrastructure as a Service (IaaS)** services such as Google Compute Engine, **Platform as a Service (PaaS)** services such as managed databases, and also **Software as a Service (SaaS)**. Besides these, Google Cloud offers a rich set of security products and services that customers can use to secure their workloads on Google Cloud. Broadly, when we talk about security on the cloud, we divide it into two parts: security *of* the cloud and security *in* the cloud. These are standard industry terms, where security *of* the cloud refers to what the cloud service provider is responsible for and security *in* the cloud is about the customer having the responsibility to use security products and services offered natively in the cloud or third-party products. As shown in *Figure 2.2*, the boundaries of responsibility between the customer and the cloud provider change based on the services selected. If the customer is using IaaS to host their workload, then the customer is responsible for protecting the virtual infrastructure, data, users, and monitoring. The responsibility shifts based on the type of service being used.

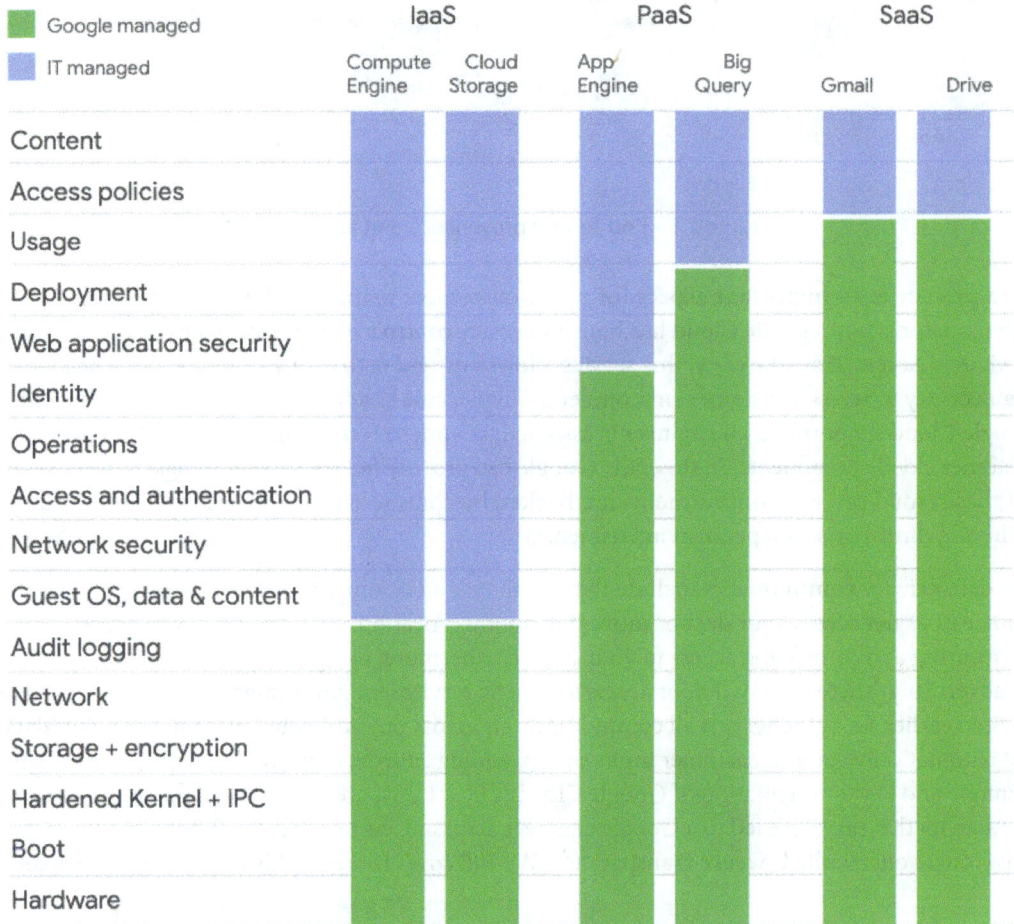

Figure 2.2 – Google Cloud's shared security responsibility (IaaS)

Google has more recently adopted a *shared fate* rather than *shared responsibility* mindset. The premise of this is to operate using a shared fate model for risk management in conjunction with customers. Google believes that it's their responsibility to be active partners as their customers deploy securely on Google Cloud, not to be delineators of where Google's responsibility ends. Google is committed to standing with customers from day one, helping them implement best practices for safely migrating to and operating in a trusted cloud. This is a big step, with Google extending help to customers using

Google Cloud and providing assurance that they will help customers not only when they are adopting the cloud but also if and when there are security incidents that require collaboration between Google and the customer. There is a great whitepaper on how Google responds to incidents and how the responsibility model works; do check out the link in the *Further reading* section for more details.

Addressing compliance on Google Cloud

Google is committed to building trust with customers through certifications and compliance across Google Cloud. A full list of compliance badges can be found here: `https://packt.link/abHuN`. As part of Google's compliance commitments, all of Google's products undergo various third-party independent assessments against compliance controls in order to achieve certifications for standards such as PCI-DSS, ISO, SOC 2, and so on. A full list of all compliance certifications and their relevant reports can be found on the Google Cloud website.

As a customer who is looking to adopt Google Cloud, compliance is key. In order to be compliant, Google implements hundreds of security controls to meet those compliance objectives. As a customer, when you move to Google Cloud, whether you host a single virtual machine or hundreds, you end up inheriting all of these security controls. This not only makes your security posture better but also takes the cost and complexity out of your project scope, making things much simpler from a compliance perspective.

Similar to security being a shared responsibility, compliance is also shared. Google is compliant with a number of international and local standards and privacy guidelines, such as the **Personal Data Protection Act** (**PDPA**), for various countries. Let's take a look at PCI-DSS as an example of how shared responsibility for compliance works. As a customer, if you have the requirement to be PCI-DSS compliant, you can use Google Cloud to run your compliant workloads, by consuming Google Cloud services that are PCI compliant. A list of PCI compliance services can be found here: `https://packt.link/nZhGL`. From an infrastructure perspective, Google Cloud is compliant with PCI-DSS. Your responsibility as a customer includes securing and making your applications and services compliant. These applications and services are not part of Google's core infrastructure, so they fall under the customer's set of responsibilities. It should not be assumed that just because Google Cloud is compliant with PCI-DSS, you will automatically be compliant; although you do inherit compliance-specific controls, they are limited to Google infrastructure.

The next section will further explain how Google's security and compliance controls are built into its cloud infrastructure.

Security by design

Google's approach to security by design is to ensure that multiple technology stacks are deployed to secure the infrastructure, identities, services, and users. *Figure 2.3* highlights the different layers of security that are built into the Google Cloud infrastructure.

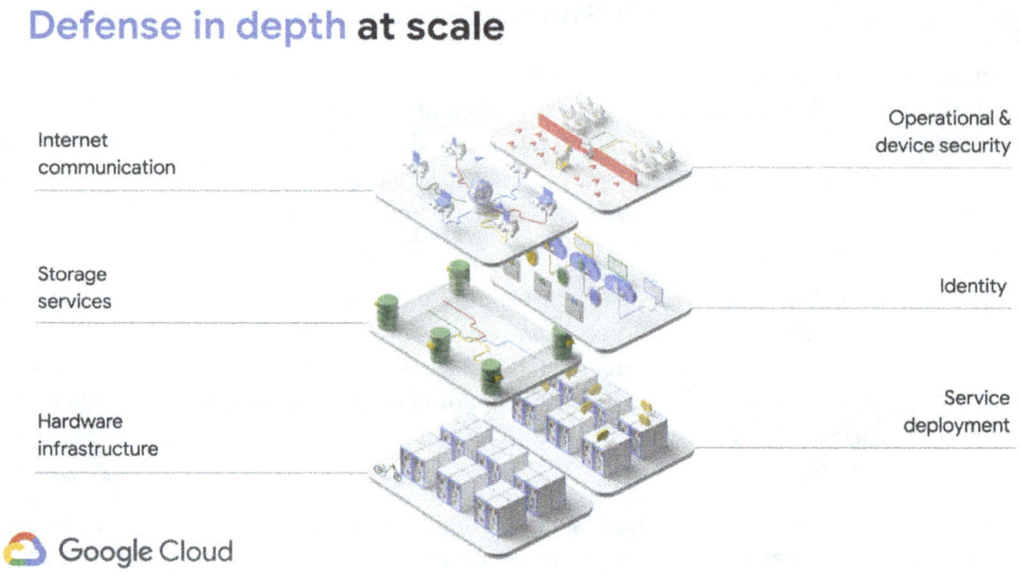

Defense in depth at scale

Figure 2.3 – Google defense in depth

In this section, we will cover the key concepts, from operational security to physical security, that Google uses to deliver true defense in depth and at scale.

Operational security

Google's operational security covers aspects such as how Google deploys software services, secures devices and credentials, addresses insider threats, and manages intrusion detection. Let's look at each of these concepts briefly.

In order to securely deploy software services, Google has a secure central control and conducts two-way reviews. Furthermore, Google also provides libraries that prevent developers from introducing certain vulnerabilities such as XSS attacks in web applications. In addition to using automated tools for source code static analysis and identifying bugs, manual security testing is also conducted. These manual tests are run by experts covering areas such as web security, cryptography, and operating systems.

Google also runs a Vulnerability Rewards Program where they pay anyone who discovers and discloses bugs in Google's infrastructure or applications.

Google implements robust security measures to protect employee devices and credentials. In fact, Google leverages a service accessible to all cloud users to safeguard its own devices and user credentials. Through BeyondCorp Enterprise, Google ensures that appropriate users have timely access to designated applications. This approach involves continuous monitoring of devices and users, regular patching and updates, enforcement of strong authentication measures, and utilization of **two-factor authentication (2FA)** at Google. Additionally, application-level access controls restrict access to internal applications solely for authorized users accessing the service from managed devices and from network addresses or geolocations that align with the established policy.

To address insider risk, all privileged user access is actively monitored. To further limit employee access, any privileged action that can be safely performed using automation is done so. All users who have access to end-user data have their activity logged and monitored by the security team for access patterns and to investigate anomalies. More details on how Google Cloud does this can be found here: `https://packt.link/PuBbM`.

Google uses very sophisticated intrusion detection techniques, where all data processing pipelines integrate with both host- and network-level signals. These signals are combined with detection rules and machine learning to identify potential threats that are monitored and actioned by security operation teams around the clock. Google also conducts an active Red Team exercise to improve security and its overall effectiveness.

Network security

We have already covered how Google owns, operates, and manages its own global private network, which is fully encrypted and has TLS enforced. This not only delivers lower latency but improves security. Once customers' traffic is on Google's network, it no longer transits the public internet, making it less likely to be attacked, intercepted, or manipulated in transit. Besides this, Google also secures its **Google Front Ends (GFEs)**. When a service wants to make itself available on the internet, it can register itself with the GFE. The GFE performs a number of functions, such as ensuring that the correct certificates are used for terminating TLS and applying best practices such as perfect forward secrecy. GFEs also provide protection against DDoS attacks. Google has multi-tier and multi-layer protection for DDoS to ensure that the services behind GFEs are protected from such volumetric attacks. Besides GFEs, there are multiple layers of hardware- and software-based load balancers that are both network- and application-aware. All these security controls, together with Google's global-scale infrastructure, ensure that the largest of the DDoS attacks can be absorbed and mitigated.

Besides these network-based security controls, Google further enforces user authentication before it allows any access to its network. The user authentication goes beyond a simple username and password and also intelligently challenges users for additional information based on risk factors. These risk factors include information about the device the user is logging in from, such as the IP address and geographical location of the device. Once past these controls, the user is then prompted for a second factor before access is granted.

Data security

Google ensures that data in motion and data at rest are both secured. We've already covered how Google enforces TLS for all data in motion and encryption by default for data at rest. In addition to the default encryption of data at rest, as a Google Cloud user, you also get the option to select a variety of different options for how you can encrypt data. Recall the previous section on data privacy and Google's commitment to establishing itself as a trusted cloud provider; you as a Google Cloud customer have full control and ownership over your data, meaning you can choose to use the default encryption or use Cloud Key Management Service, which can perform the entire key lifecycle management. Alternatively, you can use Cloud Key Management Service and import your own key material, or you can go the **Bring Your Own Key** (**BYOK**) route or use multi-tenant Cloud HSM, which provides FIPS 140-2 Level 3 protection for your keys. If you operate in a highly regulated environment and need to retain full control of the keys and the infrastructure, you do have the option to use a Google-partner-provided external HSM that is integrated with an external key management service and is accessed via Google's Cloud Key Management Service. More on this in *Chapter 9, Google Cloud Key Management Service*.

The challenge with data security is that the data has to remain secure throughout its lifecycle. Whether the data is being created, shared, stored, analyzed, archived, or deleted, it has to be secure. This brings us to how Google manages the data deletion side of things. A key concern from customers is that when you stop using a service that you've used to store sensitive data, even when you have deleted the data, how can you be sure that the data will be wiped from physical media as well? Let's take a quick look at the controls and compliance side of data deletion. When you want to delete data on Google Cloud, it's not immediately deleted but is marked as *scheduled for deletion*; so, if you have accidentally deleted your data, you have the option to recover it. After the data is scheduled for deletion, it is deleted in accordance with service-specific policies.

Google details the entire data handling and data governance as part of their whitepaper called *Trusting your Data with Google Cloud Platform*; a link to this resource can be found in the *Further reading* section of this chapter. We will be covering the data management side of things in more detail in the next chapter on trust and compliance on Google Cloud.

Services and identity

For human-to-system interaction or for calls between systems (such as inter-service access), Google applies cryptographic authentication and authorization at the application layer before any access is granted. Although there are network-perimeter-based controls and network segmentation and firewall rules, Google does not rely solely on that and applies zero-trust principles. Each service that's running also has an associated service account, including the cryptographic credentials that are used for authenticating and authorizing when a remote procedure call is initiated to access other services. Besides this, there are a number of techniques used, such as isolating and sandboxing in order to protect services that might be running on the same machine. Some of the techniques used are language- and kernel-based sandboxing, hardware virtualization, and Linux user separation.

Besides the techniques discussed here, Google's infrastructure also provides strong privacy and integrity for the data that traverses its networks. All protocols for applications such as HTTP are encapsulated inside the remote procedure call infrastructure. To provide greater control, every service owner has the ability to configure the crypto-based protection level required for remote procedure calls; for example, service owners can enable integrity-level protection for data that is of low sensitivity inside data centers. As part of Google's encryption capability, all data is automatically encrypted, including the data that goes between the **wide area network** (**WAN**) and data centers. There is no additional configuration required to enable this and it is configured as default.

Physical and hardware security

In this section, we will look at how Google provides the physical security of its facilities, hardware design, and provenance, and finally, we will look at boot-level security. Together, all these components cater to what we call low-level security controls for Google Cloud.

All Google data centers that cater to Google Cloud services are designed and built as per Google's stringent physical and access controls. Through the *security by design* principle, Google also implements redundant security layers for physical security.

Google employs a range of controls to ensure secure access to its data centers, limiting it only to those who require it to do the job. In terms of physical security, Google has implemented multiple layers of protection across its global data center facilities. These measures include the use of **Closed-Circuit Television** (**CCTV**), vehicle barricades, biometric identification systems, access restrictions for authorized personnel, thorough background checks for employees with facility access, as well as the deployment of laser-based intrusion detection and metal detectors.

At some sites, Google operates some of its servers inside a third-party data center. In those situations, Google ensures that all additional physical security controls mandated by Google are deployed on top of what the data center already has in place. These physical security controls also form part of many compliance programs. Therefore, it's important for Google, in order to stay compliant, to adhere to consistent physical security controls for each of its facilities.

Google has a complex infrastructure consisting of thousands of servers and plenty of network equipment in each of its data centers. Google custom-designs its equipment, which includes the server infrastructure and the network equipment.

In order to eliminate supply chain risks, Google has a process in place to vet every component vendor and audit and validate the security of the components. As covered in earlier sections on end-to-end provenance, all of Google's server and network infrastructure components have a hardware security chip built in; these custom chips are designed by Google. With the deployment of these chips, security is further enhanced and Google is able to not only securely identify the hardware but also authenticate approved devices.

Secure boot stack controls are becoming increasingly common, and more and more customers are expecting their cloud service providers to have them in place. Google is leading the space in securing the boot stack and machine identity. A secure boot chain is built into servers to ensure that the right software is running. In order to ensure this, Google applies techniques such as cryptographic signatures in its low-level components, including the kernel, BIOS, bootloader, and base operating system. Every time the server boots or updates, these signatures are validated. In order to establish a hardware root of trust, every server in the Google data center has an identity bound to the root of trust and the software. When using an API, the same authentication credentials are used for all calls made in order to manage the underlying systems and perform administrative tasks. To manage a large fleet of servers and to ensure they are updated and patched in a timely manner, Google has created automation systems to detect and diagnose both hardware- and software-related issues where, if required, machines are removed from the respective service.

Threat and vulnerability management

The reason for covering threat and vulnerability management at this point is that the components that form this domain, such as vulnerabilities, malware protection, incident response, and security monitoring, are key for customers adopting the cloud. Questions relating to how a cloud service provider manages threats and vulnerabilities are some of the top concerns of customers. Therefore, as security practitioners and engineers, it's important to understand and be able to articulate how Google Cloud provides capabilities to manage threats and vulnerabilities.

As part of its vulnerability management program, to keep its infrastructure secure from cyber threats, Google has technological controls, techniques, and processes to address a multitude of attack vectors. Google actively scans for security-related threats and has manual and automated penetration testing, security assurance programs, and a very mature software security system that includes automated source code scanning and manual reviews. The aim is to ensure that if and when a security vulnerability is identified, it is proactively managed, contained, and controlled. Each identified vulnerability is assigned a priority based on its severity, and the respective team and owners are assigned to mitigate and fix the vulnerability.

Similar to vulnerability management, malware protection controls are built into the Google Cloud infrastructure. Malware attacks can lead to a variety of risks, such as account compromise, data theft, and unauthorized access to the network. Malware continues to increase both in variety and in number. Therefore, it is important for any organization to build strong controls and processes to address malware. Google has higher stakes when it comes to protecting its infrastructure as it has thousands of customers who use its cloud infrastructure to run their business-critical workloads. Hence, Google has built a strategy to manage malware infection, and it applies both automated and manual tools to detect malware. Google has automated scanners that look for websites that host malware and flag them in its search for potential malicious websites used for malware and phishing. The Google Safe Browsing solution scans billions of URLs every day in order to find unsafe websites and then flag them to warn users. This technology is also built into Chrome browsers to warn users of potentially malicious websites. Besides Google Safe Browsing, another of Google's products is VirusTotal, which is a repository for viruses, Trojans, backdoors, worms, and other malicious software. Many adversaries modify their virus signatures to avoid detection by anti-virus tools; therefore, Google uses multiple anti-virus engines in products such as Google Drive and Gmail to effectively identify malware that may be missed by a single engine.

Google has built an effective and robust security monitoring program. Google security monitoring tools gather a variety of information, such as telemetry from its internal network, user actions such as those taken by employees who may have privileged access, and external vulnerabilities, to further enrich the data.

At different points in Google networks, technologies are implemented to monitor and flag anomalous behavior using a variety of techniques, such as detecting the presence of traffic that might indicate botnet connections. Google uses a combination of proprietary and open source technologies for its security monitoring. Google's Threat Analysis Group and its security research arm, Project Zero, work by identifying security threats and making organizations aware of them, such as by placing alerts on public data repositories. Furthermore, like any other security analytics and intelligence unit, Google scans multiple security-related reports on the internet, including blogs, wikis, and mailing lists. For unknown threats, Google conducts automated analysis of the network, and further investigation is conducted to understand how it operates and whether a flag is a false positive or not.

We've already covered aspects of incident response and how Google effectively manages security incidents. Google's incident management response process is aligned with NIST (NIST SP 800-61). Not only is this a rigorous and tested process, but aligning with NIST also helps Google in its compliance program. The incident management process covers the entire lifecycle from detecting and responding to containing, resolving, and then applying the learnings from the incident.

This might be helpful to many customers using Google Cloud, as there are many organizations that adopt the NIST model for handling incidents, meaning the entire end-to-end process is further streamlined for them. Google's security incident response team is available 24x7 to address incidents. For an incident that may have impacted a customer, Google responds to the customer and/or its partners based on the nature of the incident and then helps and supports the customer throughout the process to ensure the incident is resolved. The entire end-to-end process for how Google manages its incident response process is documented and the whitepaper is available and highly recommended for further reading. The following diagram is from that whitepaper. It illustrates the workflow of how Google responds to security incidents and manages the lifecycle.

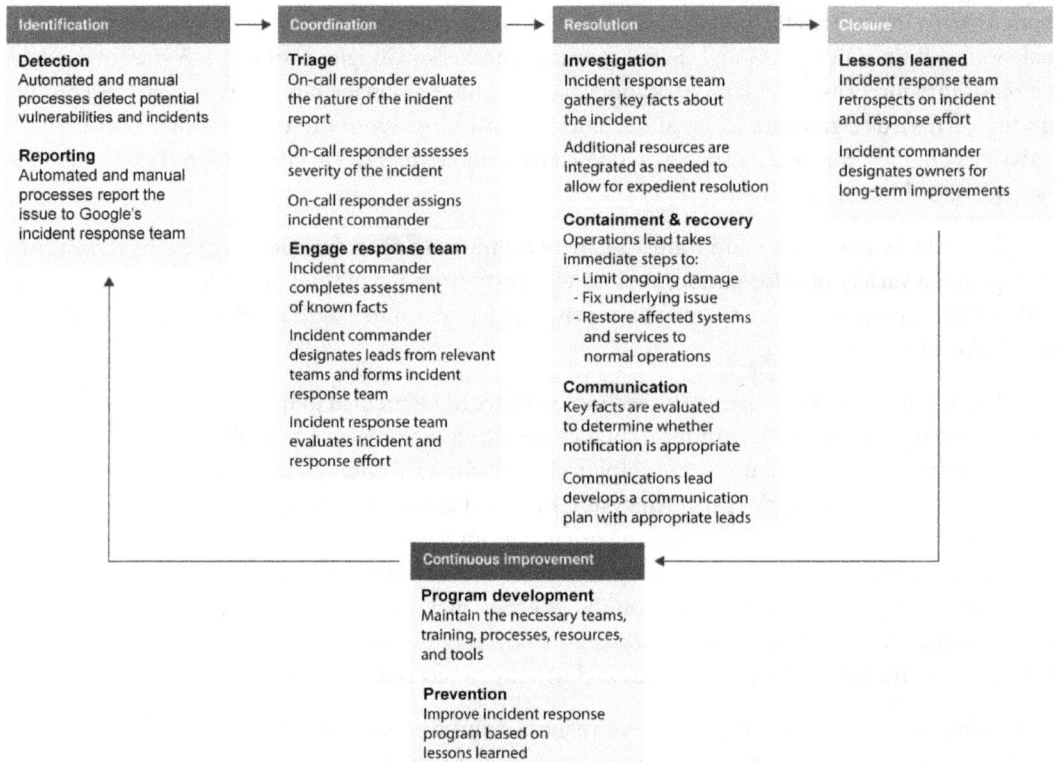

Identification	Coordination	Resolution	Closure
Detection Automated and manual processes detect potential vulnerabilities and incidents	**Triage** On-call responder evaluates the nature of the inident report	**Investigation** Incident response team gathers key facts about the incident	**Lessons learned** Incident response team retrospects on incident and response effort
Reporting Automated and manual processes report the issue to Google's incident response team	On-call responder assesses severity of the incident

On-call responder assigns incident commander

Engage response team Incident commander completes assessment of known facts

Incident commander designates leads from relevant teams and forms incident response team

Incident response team evaluates incident and response effort | Additional resources are integrated as needed to allow for expedient resolution

Containment & recovery Operations lead takes immediate steps to: - Limit ongoing damage - Fix underlying issue - Restore affected systems and services to normal operations

Communication Key facts are evaluated to determine whether notification is appropriate

Communications lead develops a communication plan with appropriate leads | Incident commander designates owners for long-term improvements |

Continuous improvement

Program development Maintain the necessary teams, training, processes, resources, and tools

Prevention Improve incident response program based on lessons learned

Figure 2.4 – Google Incident response workflow

The incident response process can be complex, and it's important that as a customer you understand what responsibilities fall under your scope. Google will help guide and support as required, but the final responsibility does sit with the user, who is the owner of the system, to take action and remediate.

Summary

In this chapter, we gave an overview of Google Cloud's core security infrastructure. We looked at how Google secures and makes its infrastructure compliant, and we covered what the shared security responsibility model and shared fate on Google Cloud are. Next, we looked at some *security by design* building blocks, covering operational security, data security, service and identity, and low-level security controls, such as physical security and boot stack security. Finally, we learned about threat and vulnerability management and how Google Cloud runs its malware protection, vulnerability management, security monitoring, and incident response.

In the next chapter, we will look at trust and compliance, which is an extension of the core security and compliance infrastructure of Google Cloud.

Further reading

For more information on Google Cloud security, read the following whitepapers:

- Google security whitepaper: `https://packt.link/uQ9Oq`
- Google Infrastructure Security Design Overview: `https://packt.link/Bf8JM`
- Trusting your data with Google Cloud: `https://packt.link/4hV6r`
- Data incident response process: `https://packt.link/zKPNf`
- Encryption in transit: `https://packt.link/PPPxJ`

3
Trust and Compliance

In this chapter, we will look at the very important aspects of trust and compliance. The first part of the chapter focuses on trust, including how Google enables security and privacy and provides customers with full transparency. We will walk through examples of how you can access transparency logs and how they are used. The last part of the chapter covers the different compliance standards and programs that Google Cloud is compliant with, and how you can gain access to compliance reports. We will look at ways to access compliance reports using Compliance Reports Manager.

In this chapter, we will cover the following topics:

- Security and data privacy
- Building trust using access transparency and access approval
- Understanding compliance on Google Cloud

Establishing and maintaining trust

Data privacy and the protection of customer data are critical in establishing trust. There is no shortcut to it: time and experience are the only two factors that help in maintaining and establishing trust. Translating that to the cloud means that customers don't have the luxury of spending time testing whether a **cloud service provider** (**CSP**) can be trusted. Therefore, CSPs such as Google Cloud use *compliance* in order to demonstrate and establish *trust*.

Google creates trust by means of transparency. The Google Cloud Enterprise Privacy Commitments dictate how Google Cloud protects the privacy of its customers. Let's take a look at the privacy principles that Google defines:

- As a customer, you control and own your data. You define and control where you want to store your data (in terms of geographical location), and only you can decide where you want to move/copy your data to. Google does not have any control over copying or replicating data outside of the region that you have selected. Google only processes the data as per the various agreements.

- Customer data is not used for any ads or targeting other users for ads. Customer data does not belong to Google, which is very clearly stated by Google's policies and principles. Google Cloud will never use customer data in other Google products, including ads, or use customer data for any purposes not described in mutual agreements with customers.

- As part of the many different compliance programs that Google Cloud is compliant with, Google transparently collects data that it requires to perform necessary business functions and is aligned with compliance standards such as ISO 27001, SOC 2, GDPR, and other privacy best practices.

- None of the data hosted on Google Cloud is sold by Google to any partners or third parties for any purpose. Google's policies on data handling are very well defined and have both procedural and technical controls built around them. Google has set a very high bar for how customer data is stored, hosted, and served. Furthermore, Google's compliance reports and legal agreements with customers provide details on Google Cloud's compliance with regard to using customer data in accordance with legal, compliance, and regulatory requirements. Google never sells or uses customer data outside of the scope of the aforementioned obligations.

- Every Google product has both security and privacy built into it from the beginning. There are well-defined policies and controls that dictate how the security and privacy of each product are managed and designed. These aspects are considered of the highest importance.

As we can now see, building a trusted cloud environment that customers rely on for their business-critical information requires security, transparency, and privacy to be built into it. Google Cloud's principles ensure that these are addressed. It's difficult to establish trust in the absence of these principles and independent audits to demonstrate adherence to the compliance standards.

In the next section, we will look at how transparency is provided by Google Cloud. We will walk through a common scenario to help you understand how transparency logs and access approval work on Google Cloud.

Access Transparency and Access Approval

Before we discuss the Access Transparency and Access Approval products, let's understand why they are so important. We discussed in the previous section how transparency plays a key role in establishing trust, and it also helps Google to differentiate its security posture. At the time of writing, other major **cloud service providers (CSPs)** do not offer transparency logs. Customers who are highly regulated or have compliance requirements need to view and share logs of activities performed by their CSPs. Analysts such as Gartner have highlighted transparency logs as a key feature for CSPs.

Now that we have established the importance of transparency for CSPs, we will look at the product capability that Google offers. Google has two products for transparency: **Access Transparency**, which provides near real-time logs whenever Google administrators access your Google Cloud environment, and **Access Approvals**, where you can control administrative access to your data.

Access Transparency

Access Transparency logs are a feature provided by Google Cloud that offer customers visibility into the actions performed by Google employees when they access customer data. These logs provide a detailed record of any access made by Google's support and engineering teams to customer content or data stored within Google Cloud services. Access Transparency logs help customers meet regulatory compliance requirements, security audits, and internal governance policies. By providing a comprehensive record of access activities, these logs contribute to building trust and ensuring the integrity and privacy of customer data within the Google Cloud platform. Google follows a set of best practices to control access to customer data. These best practices include the following:

- **Least privilege**: All access by Google employees is denied by default. If and when access is granted, it is both conditional and temporary and limited to only what is necessary for a user to perform their role and function.

- **Limit singular access to data**: It is extremely difficult for Google employees to singularly access customer data without another individual being involved. Therefore, quorum-based access control for data is enforced.

- **All access must be justified**: Google personnel, by default, do not have access to customer data. When Google personnel have privileged access, they must have the required permissions, business justification, and consent. Again, quorum-based controls apply to ensure that there is oversight of the task being performed.

- **Monitoring and alerting**: Monitoring and response processes exist to identify, triage, and remediate violations of these access controls.

As you can see, there are a number of procedural and technological controls and policies in place to ensure that insider risk and administrative privileges are managed and controlled. When any of these activities happen due to business requirements for a customer environment, Google logs the activities and shares them when the customer requests the transparency logs. Customers request Access Transparency logs by enabling the service through the **Identity and Access Management** section of the Google Cloud console.

Adding transparency logs to purpose-built tools has a clear intent: to establish trust and help customers in gaining visibility of their data and demonstrate adherence to compliance requirements with auditors.

A key distinction to note between Access Transparency logs and admin activity logs is that admin activity logs are limited to recording the actions of the users or administrators of your Google Cloud organization, whereas Access Transparency logs record actions taken by Google employees. Access Transparency logs include details such as the impacted resource and the relevant action taken, the time of the action, the reason, and information about who accessed it.

There are many reasons why you want to have access to transparency logs. Let's take a look at some of them:

- To verify that the Google personnel who accessed your content did so with a valid business justification, such as support requests

- To verify that Google support engineers have not made an error while performing instructions you as a customer provided them with

- To verify and track compliance with legal or regulatory requirements

- To collect and analyze transparency logs and ingest them in a security information and event management tool

Transparency logs and the products that support them are listed on Google Cloud's website: `https://packt.link/R03rx`.

In order to enable Access Transparency, you need to have either the Premium, Enterprise, Gold, or Platinum support level. If you are not sure what support level you have, you can check that by accessing the following link: `https://packt.link/m0rhf`. Once Google has validated that you have the relevant support level, they can enable transparency logs.

Enabling Access Transparency

Using these instructions, Access Transparency can be either enabled or disabled. Before proceeding, you need to check your permissions at the organization level. Navigate to the Google Cloud Console page using this URL: `https://packt.link/9iuM4`. Select your Google Cloud organization when prompted to do so and check that the correct IAM admin role related to Access Transparency has been set (`roles/axt.admin`):

1. Select the Google Cloud project that you would like to use:

   - It's important to note that although Access Transparency is configured at the project level, once it's enabled, it will be available for the entire organization.

   - If you have a requirement where you need to only enable project-level Access Transparency, you will need to contact Google Cloud Support. This function can be configured from the console.

You can only configure Access Transparency inside a project where the project is already associated with a billing account. If your project is not associated with a billing account, then you will not be able to enable the Access Transparency service.

2. Navigate to **Billing** from the console menu on the left. If you see the message **This project is not associated with a billing account**, you will need to select a different project or associate the project with a billing account. Refer to the help on the page for guidance on how to change the billing account for a project.

3. Next, navigate to the **IAM & Admin | Settings** page and then click **ENABLE ACCESS TRANSPARENCY FOR ORGANIZATION** button shown in *Figure 3.1*.

If you are unable to see the **ENABLE ACCESS TRANSPARENCY FOR ORGANIZATION** button, it is due to one of the following reasons:

- You do not have a billing account associated with your project
- You do not have the IAM admin permission to perform the function
- The required support package is missing

Access Transparency

Access Transparency can be enabled for your Organization.

ENABLE ACCESS TRANSPARENCY FOR ORGANIZATION

Figure 3.1 – Access Transparency enabled confirmation

Access Approval

Next, we will look at what Access Approval is and how it works. Access Approval ensures that you as a customer give your consent to Google support engineers to access the content in your environment. If you decide, for whatever reason, that you don't want to give that permission, access will be denied. Irrespective of whether you approved access or denied access, a transparency log activity entry will be created.

We will look at an example of a customer support workflow to better understand how the approval process works.

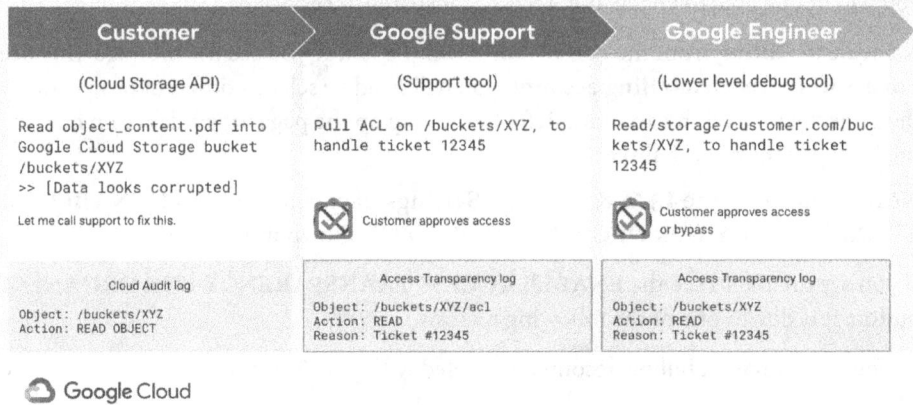

Figure 3.2 – Access Approval workflow

In this example, the customer tries to access a file stored in a Google Cloud Storage bucket and is unable to access it. The customer then opens a support ticket. At this stage, admin activity logs are created for the API call that was made to read the object. Next, the Google support engineer, using the support tool, attempts to retrieve the **access control list** (ACL) for the particular bucket that the customer is trying to access. The Google support engineer does not have access, so a request is sent to the customer to either approve or deny the request. Once the customer approves the request, the Google support engineer can retrieve the ACL that was inaccessible earlier. At this stage, a new transparency log entry is created that captures the **object**, which is bucket/XYZ/acl, the associated **action**, which is READ, and the **reason**, which is the ticket number, #12345. In the last step, the Google support engineer needs to open the file that the customer was trying to access. The reason for this is to establish that the file is now accessible, so the ticket can be resolved. Again, the support engineer will be denied access to the document and another Access Approval request will be routed to the customer to take action. At this point, the customer can either allow or deny the request, which depends on a number of factors, such as whether the document is sensitive. If the data inside the document is generic and not sensitive and there are no other concerns, the customer then approves the request. Once the request is approved, the Google support engineer can access the document and a corresponding transparency log is created: **OBJECT bucket/XYZ ACTION Read and REASON is the ticket number #12345**.

The point of explaining the entire process of how Access Approval works is to demonstrate how customers can have control over their data, which is one of the key principles we discussed in the previous section, that is, how Google ensures that trust is established.

You have the ability to enable Access Approval for the services you want to use it for. A list of supported Google Cloud products can be found here: https://packt.link/f5MDC.

Access Approval requires your consent only for requests for the content stored in the services you select. When you enroll for Access Approval, the following options are available to you:

- You can automatically enable Access Approval for all supported services. This is the default option.
- You can selectively enable Access Approval for services with GA-level support. When you select this option, it automatically enrolls all the services that Access Approval will support in the future with GA-level support.
- Finally, you can also choose the specific services you want to enroll in Access Approval.

Using Access Approval gives you increased control over the implementation and usage of this feature, allowing you to determine how and for which services you enable it. It provides flexibility in tailoring access approval processes according to your specific requirements.

However, it's crucial to note that there are certain exclusions that apply to Access Approval. These exclusions refer to specific scenarios or services where the feature may not be applicable or available. It's important to familiarize yourself with these exclusions to ensure you have a clear understanding of the limitations and can make informed decisions regarding the use of Access Approval in your organization.

By understanding and considering these exclusions, you can effectively utilize Access Approval in a manner that aligns with your security and compliance needs while adhering to any applicable restrictions or exceptions. Here are a few scenarios in Access Approval that are exceptions:

- Non-humans have programmatic access that is allowed and reviewed by Google processes. A compression task that runs on content is one example, as is disk destruction during the content deletion process. When binary authorization checks for accesses, it ensures that the job came from code that was checked into production.
- Manual access, such as legal access, is used when Google accesses customer content to meet legally binding requirements; in these instances, the Access Approval process is bypassed.
- When Google looks at customer content to fix a service outage, this is called a *service outage*.
- An Access Approval request will not be generated if any other Access Transparency exception is logged and if any activity fails to generate an Access Transparency log.

Similar to Access Transparency, for Access Approval you need to have either the Premium, Enterprise, Gold, or Platinum support level. If you are not sure what support level you have, you can check by accessing the following link: `https://packt.link/II1xE`.

Once you have validated that you have a required support level, you can enable Access Approval by following the steps in the next section.

Configuring Access Approval

To enroll in Access Approval, follow these steps:

1. In the Google Cloud console, navigate to the project, folder, or organization for which you want to enable Access Approval.

2. Go to the **Access Approval** page: `https://packt.link/o84Ct`.

3. To enroll in Access Approval, click **ENROLL**.

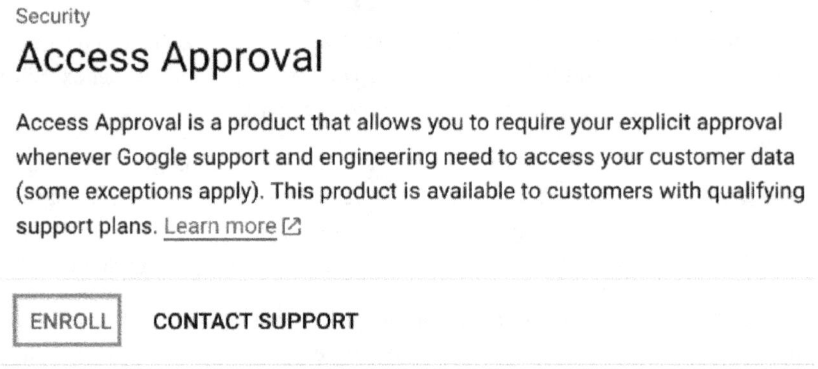

Security

Access Approval

Access Approval is a product that allows you to require your explicit approval whenever Google support and engineering need to access your customer data (some exceptions apply). This product is available to customers with qualifying support plans. Learn more ↗

| ENROLL | **CONTACT SUPPORT**

Figure 3.3 – Access Approval enrollment

4. In the dialog box that opens, click **ENROLL**.

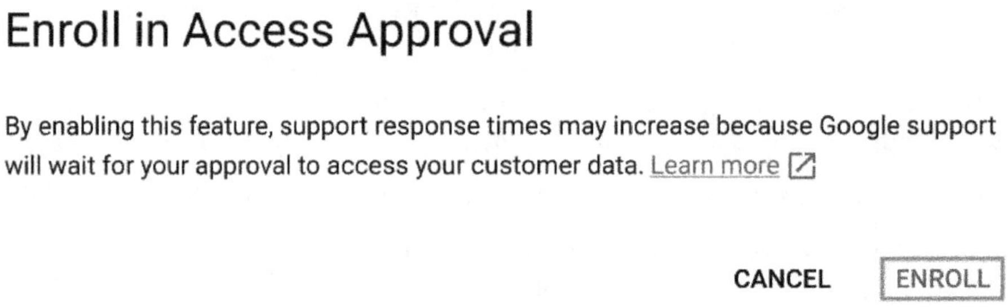

Enroll in Access Approval

By enabling this feature, support response times may increase because Google support will wait for your approval to access your customer data. Learn more ↗

CANCEL | ENROLL |

Figure 3.4 – Access Approval enrollment success

Understanding Access Transparency and Access Approval helps you understand how trust is established using transparency. If you need to build an environment on Google Cloud that is regulated and has access to transparency logs, these products will help you achieve the goal. Google has also built its Assured Workloads product, which utilizes transparency logs. Assured Workloads is out of scope for the Google Cloud Professional Security Engineer exam, but if you wish to read more about it, you can refer to the links in the *Further reading* section at the end of this chapter.

Security and privacy of data

Earlier in the chapter, we covered the data privacy principles adhered to by Google. In the previous chapter, we also covered how Google Cloud enforces the security of data by default, such as by encrypting data in transit by default. When you store your data on Google Cloud, you will read and write data; thus, there will be times when data will be out of Google-enforced security boundaries. Enforcing the encryption of data in transit ensures that data is secure.

When data is stored in any Google Cloud Storage products, the encryption of data at rest is enforced by default. This improves the security posture for any organization adopting Google Cloud, as you don't have to manage the underlying encryption technology to manage the key lifecycle or encrypt data because these controls are fully managed by Google Cloud.

Google Cloud provides flexible options to help you align with Google privacy principles and control your data. You can choose the level of control you want for your keys. For example, you can use Google Cloud **Key Management Service** (**KMS**) to create and manage your own keys, or import your own keys and store them in software, which would be KMS, or in Cloud **Hardware Security Module** (**HSM**), which is a FIPS 140-2 Level 3 certified appliance.

Many customers who have stringent compliance and regulatory requirements have the option of using an **external key management** (**EKM**) system. EKM systems are hosted by Google partners and are integrated with external HSMs. Google has built partnerships with selected EKM vendors, who integrate their EKM solutions with Google Cloud KMS. With this option, customers can use the existing key store, which can be HSM-based, and use the EKM solution to point to the keys. This gives customers the greatest control over their keys as Google does not persist them. At the time of writing, only Google Cloud provides such a capability to customers via its partners: Equinix, Fortanix, Ionic, Thales, and Unbound.

On the topic of data privacy and security, another key area that is a requirement for many customers and is also a growing regulatory requirement is **data residency**. Google is committed to meeting customer needs with regard to data residency. There are several capabilities and assurances that Google provides to help customers meet this requirement. Data residency can only be provided for the services listed here: `https://packt.link/ENTe8`. Let's look at some of the capabilities that Google Cloud offers for data residency:

- You can control where you store your data. This applies to ensuring that your data stays in a physical geographical location, also known as a Google region. Google provides assurance, in the form of compliance reports, that Google will under no circumstances move or copy your data to another region. This can only happen if you decide to move your data. You can also apply an organization policy at the folder or project level, whereby the resource location constraint is applied to enforce that only approved regions can be used to launch new services. This can be further combined with Cloud IAM, where you can enable or disable certain services for users so that they do not move data to locations outside of the approved geographical regions.

- While restricting data to a certain location is important, another control that is available to further enforce data localization is Cloud KMS. Cloud KMS has data regionalization assurances in place. Therefore, as a customer, in order to maintain the data residency of your keys and data, you need both your keys and your data to be within the boundaries of a specific Google Cloud location. This can be achieved by creating a key ring in Cloud KMS that is bound to a specific location.

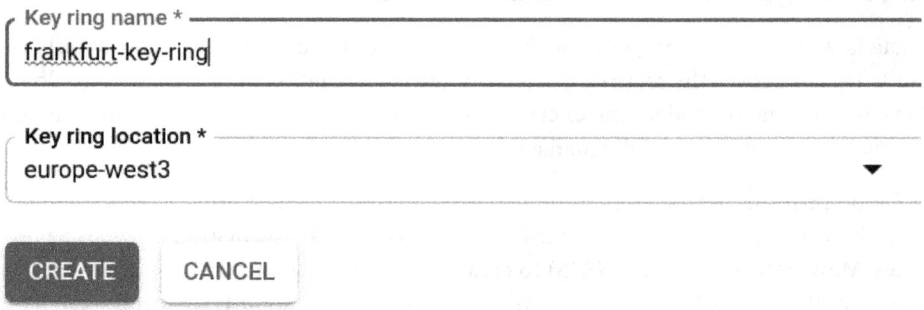

Key ring name *
frankfurt-key-ring

Key ring location *
europe-west3   ▼

CREATE   CANCEL

Figure 3.5 – Google Cloud KMS geo-location configuration for key ring

Customer-Managed Encryption Keys (**CMEKs**) provide additional data security controls. They also ensure that resource creators can choose the appropriate locations for their resources.

- Another Google Cloud product that can help ensure that only users from a certain location can access data is VPC Service Controls. This product allows you to enforce egress and ingress policies as well as to define IP address ranges and geo-locations from which you want users to access services and data. Combined with a Cloud IAM policy, you can allow only authorized users from locations that you define. All Google Cloud services inside the *service perimeter*, a virtual boundary inside the Virtual Private Cloud, can be accessed based on a defined policy. This ensures that data is not moved to locations that are not allowed.

Google recently also announced a new feature, **Key Access Justifications** (**KAJ**). Every time there is a request to decrypt data using Cloud KMS or an external KMS, a detailed justification is provided including details such as which key was requested to decrypt the data. This is combined with a mechanism where you can approve or deny key access using an automated policy that you can configure. Using these controls, you can also limit Google's ability to decrypt your data. As the owner of the data, you are the arbitrator of who has access to your data and not the cloud provider.

Third-party risk assessments

A third-party risk assessment or vendor risk assessment is often a requirement for many regulated customers who want assurance from Google Cloud about specific controls. An example of this would be a financial institution such as a bank that wants to host workloads on Google Cloud and needs Google Cloud to complete a vendor questionnaire. Google Cloud provides self-assessment questionnaires. These are complimentary documents that cover Google Cloud's security controls and can help customers assess the security of their service. These self-assessments are available via Google Compliance Manager, which can be accessed here: `https://packt.link/B15d7`.

Some of the available assessments are as follows:

- Google Cloud's **Cloud Security Alliance (CSA) STAR** self-assessment is available here: `https://packt.link/rnqoe`.

- The **Standardized Information Gathering (SIG)** core questionnaire can be accessed by customers to perform an initial assessment of third-party vendors to help determine how security risks are managed across 18 different risk domains. This report is accessible here: `https://packt.link/6fTSQ`.

- The IHS Markit KY3P due diligence questionnaire can be downloaded from `https://packt.link/syPOz`.

- Google Cloud's data processing and security terms (`https://packt.link/qQMu6`) are also available to customers, covering how Google processes customer data.

Besides these resources, Google Cloud also provides security whitepapers on topics ranging from data encryption and privacy to incident response and compliance, which can be used to understand Google Cloud-specific security controls. The whitepapers can be accessed here: `https://packt.link/c0aIn`.

Compliance in the cloud

In this section, we will cover two topics: how you can access the compliance reports that are made available by Google Cloud, and some of the tools and capabilities that are available to achieve continuous compliance in the cloud.

Google products undergo compliance reviews by independent third parties, and the relevant compliance reports are made available to customers. There are two sets of compliance reports: one set can be downloaded from the Google Cloud website and is generally available to anyone; the other set can be requested by a Google **Technical Account Manager (TAM)** if the Google customer has a TAM assigned to their organization. You can find Google Cloud's compliance reports here: `https://packt.link/eaDuj`. New Google Cloud products often have a delay of a few months before they are added to the compliance scope. Google has a scheduled review cycle, and new products are added based on that. Each product undergoes SOC 2 and ISO audits first, followed by market-specific certifications.

Google is compliant with international standards such as ISO 27001, ISO 27017, ISO 27018, SOC 2, and SOC 3. Besides these, there are some country-specific compliance frameworks, such as FedRAMP for the US and MTCS for Singapore. Similarly, for other countries, such as Germany and Australia, Google Cloud is compliant with their respective in-country privacy and compliance requirements. It is important to note that every Google Cloud region is compliant with a consistent set of compliance standards. Even though FedRAMP may not be relevant to customers in some parts of the world, Google Cloud regions are compliant with its standards. This is one of the key advantages to customers having all these compliance standards built into Google Cloud. While Google Cloud is committed to compliance with standards across all its regions, certain regions may not be compliant with certain standards due to local laws and regulations. This means that specific regulations that are applicable in the region must be taken into consideration when assessing compliance with any particular standard. For example, some regions may not be compliant with certain security standards, or a region may have specific data protection laws that must be adhered to. In these cases, it is important to ensure that the region where you are using Google Cloud's services is compliant with the applicable standards before committing to any particular service. The following is a diagram of the compliance standards and frameworks that Google Cloud is compliant with. The full list of compliance standards can be found here: `https://packt.link/fJr39`.

Figure 3.6 – Third-party certifications and regulatory compliance

We'll now take a brief look at some of the key international standards that Google Cloud is compliant with. The intent is not to cover them in depth but at a high level for your understanding of the scope of these compliance standards. From an exam perspective, you will not be tested on your knowledge of compliance standards:

- **ISO 27001**: This is an **Information Security Management System** (**ISMS**) framework, consisting of 14 groups, 35 control objectives, and 114 controls. ISMSs are documented based on ISO 27001 standards, which provide guidelines for setting up, implementing, operating, monitoring, reviewing, maintaining, and enhancing them. As one of the core compliance programs, ISO 27001 encompasses all types of organizations (commercial businesses, government agencies, and non-profit organizations). Google Cloud undergoes a yearly third-party audit to certify individual products against this standard.

- **ISO 27002**: The ISMS controls the implementation details. This is not a certification standard but rather an advisory document containing a list of best practices and guidelines that organizations can use to meet the controls listed in the ISO 27001 standard. It recommends information security controls to mitigate risks to the confidentiality, integrity, and availability of information. Since this is an advisory document, organizations can choose to use these controls, a subset of them, or a completely different set to certify against the ISO 27001 standard.

- **ISO 27017**: This framework is an extension of ISO 27001 and focuses specifically on information security relating to cloud computing beyond the general guidelines in the preceding document. This standard advises both cloud service providers and cloud service customers to create a matrix of individual and shared responsibilities.

- **ISO 27018:** This is a set of security guidelines that specifically focus on the processing and protection of **Personally Identifiable Information** (**PII**). It extends the control objectives of ISO 27002, which is a broader standard for information security management systems. Security safeguards for public cloud service providers operating as PII processors are the primary emphasis of this standard.

In the next section, we will take a look at how you can download these compliance reports using Compliance Reports Manager.

Compliance reports

Compliance Reports Manager provides Google Cloud customers with the ability to download selected compliance reports directly from `https://packt.link/C6JRN`. New reports are launched at the end of every month.

You can access Compliance Reports Manager via this link: `https://packt.link/yBhnU`.

Let's do a quick walk-through of how you can download these reports:

1. Using the filter, you can select what report you want to download. The options in the filter include **Industry**, **Region**, **Report Type**, and **Product Area**. **Industry** has two options: **Industry-agnostic**, such as the ISO, SOC, and CSA reports, and **Government/Public** sector, which refers to reports relevant to government agencies such as IRAP for Australia. Please work with your Google Cloud representative to help you locate those reports.

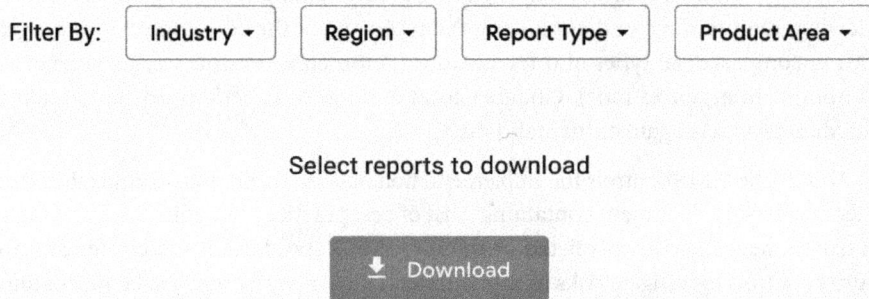

Filter By: Industry ▾   Region ▾   Report Type ▾   Product Area ▾

Select reports to download

⬇ Download

Figure 3.7 – Compliance Reports Manager

2. Next, you specify using the filter what report you want, and you will see the option to select and then download the report from Compliance Report Manager. In this example, we have left **Industry** as the default, **Region** is **Global**, **Report Type** is **Audit Report**, and **Product Area** is **Google Cloud**.

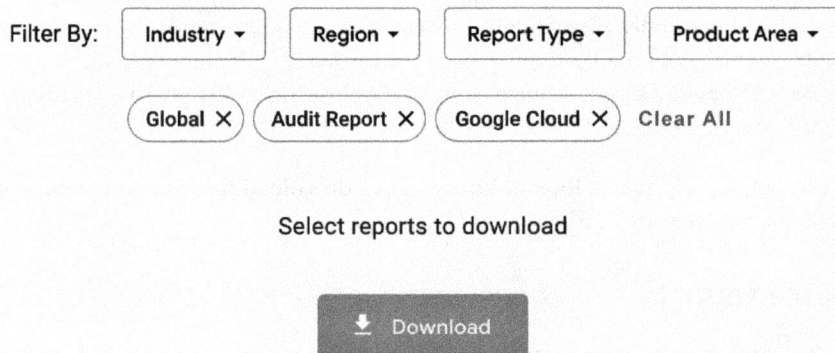

Filter By: Industry ▾   Region ▾   Report Type ▾   Product Area ▾

(Global ✕) (Audit Report ✕) (Google Cloud ✕)   Clear All

Select reports to download

⬇ Download

Figure 3.8 – Google Cloud Compliance Report Manager filter

3. Next, you can select the report you want and click **Download**. In our example, we have a PCI-DSS report selected to download.

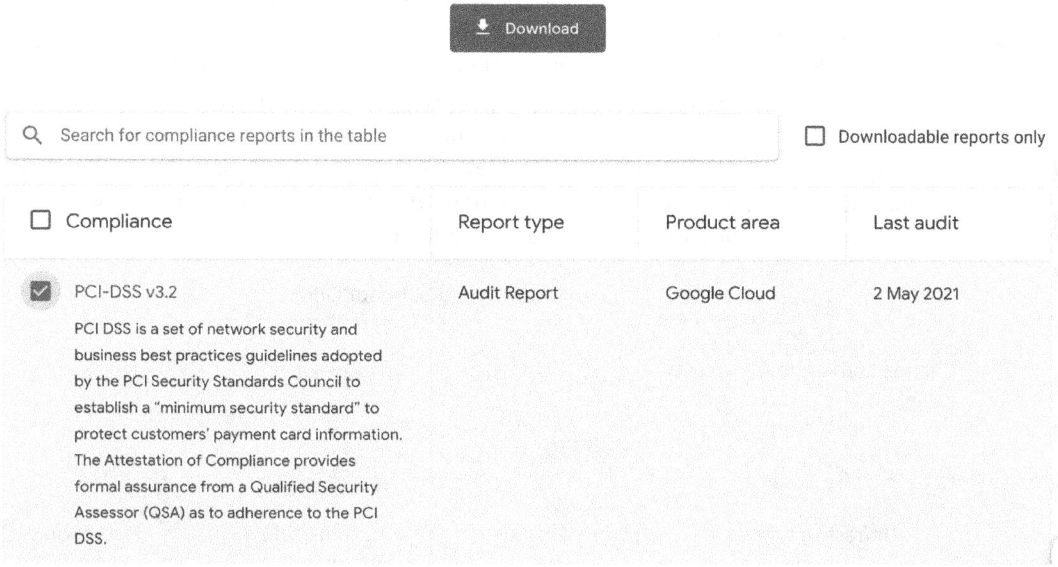

Figure 3.9 – Compliance manager: PCI-DSS report download

After this, you can download and view the PCI-DSS audit report. In a similar way, you can download other reports.

Continuous compliance

All the benefits that the cloud has to offer, specifically, capabilities such as automation and orchestration, make compliance in the cloud much easier to achieve. One of the key advantages that many customers gain when moving from traditional on-premises data centers to the cloud is the ability to achieve compliance in a more automated way. The cloud helps you achieve compliance and audit objectives in an automated and on-demand fashion rather than waiting on quarterly manual audits. This reduces the time needed to resolve security-related issues, thus improving your overall security posture. Google Cloud offers an elegant solution to meet compliance objectives.

In this section, we will look at cloud-native capabilities that are available on Google Cloud that can help you to achieve continuous compliance. Continuous compliance means that you can run your compliance checks on your cloud assets against the policy that is being implemented. Whenever an asset changes its state, such as a running Google Compute Engine resource with new known vulnerabilities, the compliance-as-code policy executes to check the state and returns a result to indicate compliance or non-compliance. If compliant, no action is required; however, depending on your organizational maturity, you can take different actions. For example, you may just want a notification to be sent to your security and compliance teams to take action and review the finding, or you can build an automated process that means that once an asset is found to be non-compliant, a Cloud Functions script will execute and take corrective action to make the asset compliant again.

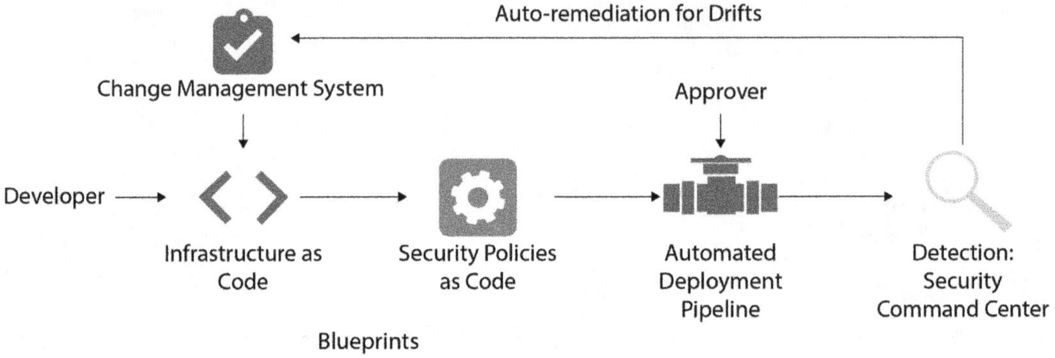

Figure 3.10 – Continuous compliance pipeline

Google Cloud offers a comprehensive set of tools and services that help organizations ensure that their systems and applications remain in compliance with laws and regulations. This includes automated compliance checks, continuous monitoring, and alerting capabilities to help organizations respond quickly to potential issues.

Summary

In this chapter, we looked at how Google Cloud establishes trust using transparency and applies privacy principles backed up by independent audits and compliance. We also covered two key products that help customers establish trust: Access Transparency and Access Approval. In terms of ensuring the security and privacy of data, we covered the controls available, such as encryption and KMS. Furthermore, we looked at the importance of data residency and how Google Cloud provides capabilities, features, and products to support the localization of data. We covered third-party and vendor risk assessments and the support that Google Cloud extends in helping customers to be compliant with regulatory requirements. Finally, we covered aspects of compliance in the cloud such as how you can download Google Cloud compliance reports, standards, and an overview of achieving continuous compliance in the cloud.

In the next chapter, we will cover the resource hierarchy in Google Cloud.

Further reading

For more information on Google Cloud security, trust, and compliance, refer to the following links:

- Trusting your data with Google Cloud: `https://packt.link/mEnMK`
- Compliance offerings: `https://packt.link/k7PMI`
- Resource on risk and compliance vendor due diligence: `https://packt.link/ugIhD`
- Data residency, operational transparency, and privacy for European customers on Google Cloud: `https://packt.link/I9lgg`
- Overview of Assured Workloads: `https://packt.link/BgkjA`

4

Resource Management

In this chapter, we will look at resource management and understand some of the key components, such as projects, folders, and organizations. When building your environment on Google Cloud, these components can help you do segmentation at a macro level. We will also look at organizational policy constraints, some of the pre-built constraints that are available, and how the inheritance of policy works for **Identity and Access Management** (**IAM**) and firewall rules. We will also cover Cloud Asset Inventory, which is an essential part of resource management, and its role from a security perspective. We will end the chapter with some best practices and design considerations for resource management.

In this chapter, we will cover the following topics:

- Overview of Google Cloud Resource Manager
- The resource hierarchy
- The Organization Policy Service
- Organization Policy constraints
- Policy inheritance
- Hierarchical firewall policies
- Cloud Asset Inventory
- Design considerations and best practices

Overview of Google Cloud Resource Manager

Google Cloud Resource Manager acts like a container for your cloud resources, allowing you to group your resources in a hierarchical way within the project, folder, or organization. Think of Resource Manager as a high-level way to perform macro-level segmentation. This not only helps you define the entire organization's structure but also the implementation of security guardrails that can be inherited. More on this in the *Policy inheritance* section.

Figure 4.1 is an example of how you can structure your organization on Google Cloud. The top-level organization is where all your other components such as folders and projects are created. Organizing your resources in a hierarchical way lets you manage aspects such as access control and other configuration settings. The same applies to IAM policies, which can be applied at different levels and are then inherited top-down.

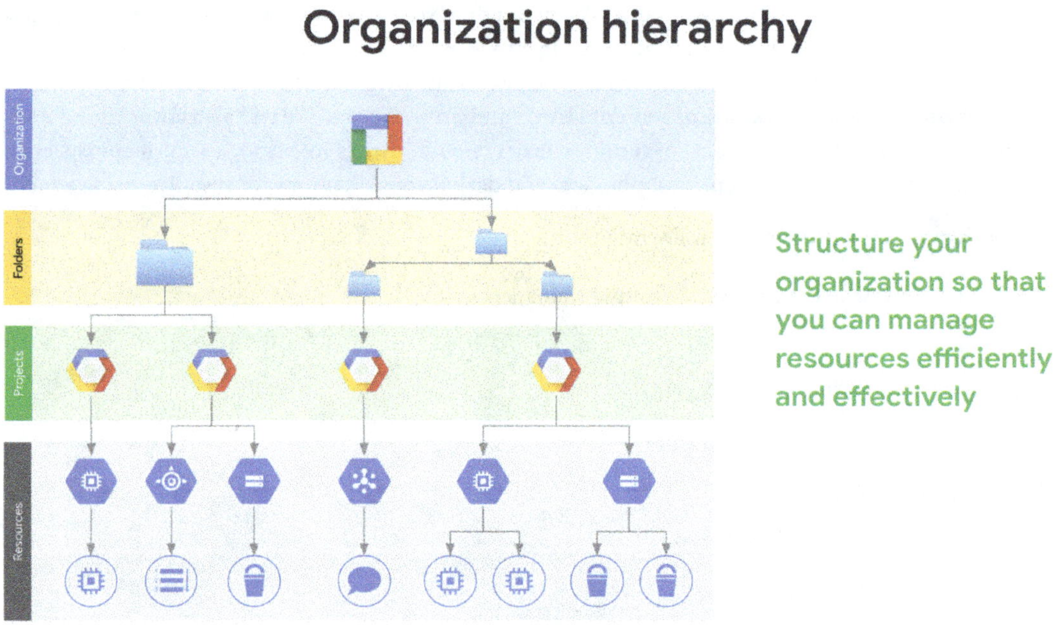

Figure 4.1 – Organization hierarchy

Let's take a look at the key components that make up the organization hierarchy and further explore how policies are applied and inherited and also some best practice examples for organization structure.

Understanding resource hierarchy

The key components that make up the resource hierarchy are as follows:

- **Organization**: The top-level component—all other components are linked to this.

- **Folders**: Used to group similar projects to consistently apply policies. These are optional but highly recommended.

- **Projects**: Where all the resources, such as your compute instances, databases, and others, exist.

Now, let's look at each of these components in detail. From a certification standpoint, you will be tested on resource hierarchy and the topics covered in this chapter. It's important to understand how to manage and create resources and apply access policies and organizational constraints. We will cover all these topics in this chapter.

Organization

This is the root node and hierarchical super-node of the project. It is closely associated with the Workspace / Cloud Identity account. It's a single directory containing the organization's users and groups. The organization is created from the Cloud Identity account. After creating a Cloud Identity account, you need to manually create an organization through the console to provision the GCP organization. The organization doesn't contain users or groups but rather holds GCP resources. Users and groups are part of Cloud Identity, but they receive IAM permissions in GCP. The organization at the top-level node represents, for example, a company in the resource hierarchy. Google Cloud Identity and Workspace are provisioned within one organization. When a user creates a project in Google Cloud, only then is an organization automatically created. Organizations are also needed to manage the resource lifecycle. They act as central resource management for all projects that are created. All members of the organization belong to the organization by default. With an organization, you can also apply policies across all resources, such as IAM policies and organization policies. We will cover this in the *Policy inheritance* section later in this chapter.

In the following figure, let's understand the link between Cloud Identity and Workspace. The link between Google Cloud Identity and Google Workspace is that Google Cloud Identity provides the foundation for user authentication and access management, which is used by Google Workspace to manage and secure user accounts and access to its suite of productivity tools. You cannot have an organization without Cloud Identity (which is a prerequisite). It's important to note that the Cloud Identity / Workspace super admin is the overall owner of the domain verification and also has the right to create any IAM role in Google Cloud.

> **Note**
>
> You can read more about Cloud Identity in *Chapter 5, Understanding Google Cloud Identity*, and *Chapter 6, Google Cloud Identity and Access Management*.

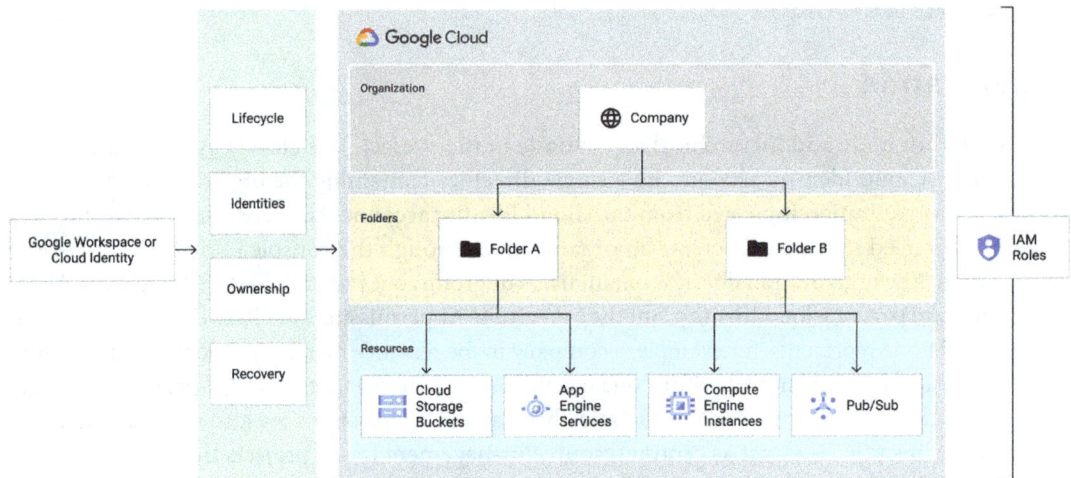

Figure 4.2 – Organizations

The organization resource that is exposed via the Resource Manager API has the following construct:

```
{
  "creationTime": "2020-01-07T21:59:43.314Z",
  "displayName": "my-organization",
  "lifecycleState": "ACTIVE",
  "name": "organizations/34739118321",
  "owner": {
    "directoryCustomerId": "C012ba234"
  }
}
```

In the preceding snippet, the number 34739118321 represents the unique identifier, which is the organization ID; my-organization is the display name that is generated by the Cloud Identity domain; the creation time and the last modified time are also recorded; and the `owner` field is set by Workspace and cannot be changed—it is the customer ID that is specified in the Director API.

Folders

The main function of the folders is to group and segment your projects. You can define boundaries when designing your organization structure. Similar to organizations, the folders have certain parameters and principles to follow, which will be discussed in this section. Folders are the nodes in the organization hierarchy and are used to model a workflow and access pattern. Let's take a look at *Figure 4.3* to understand how you can use folders in your GCP organization.

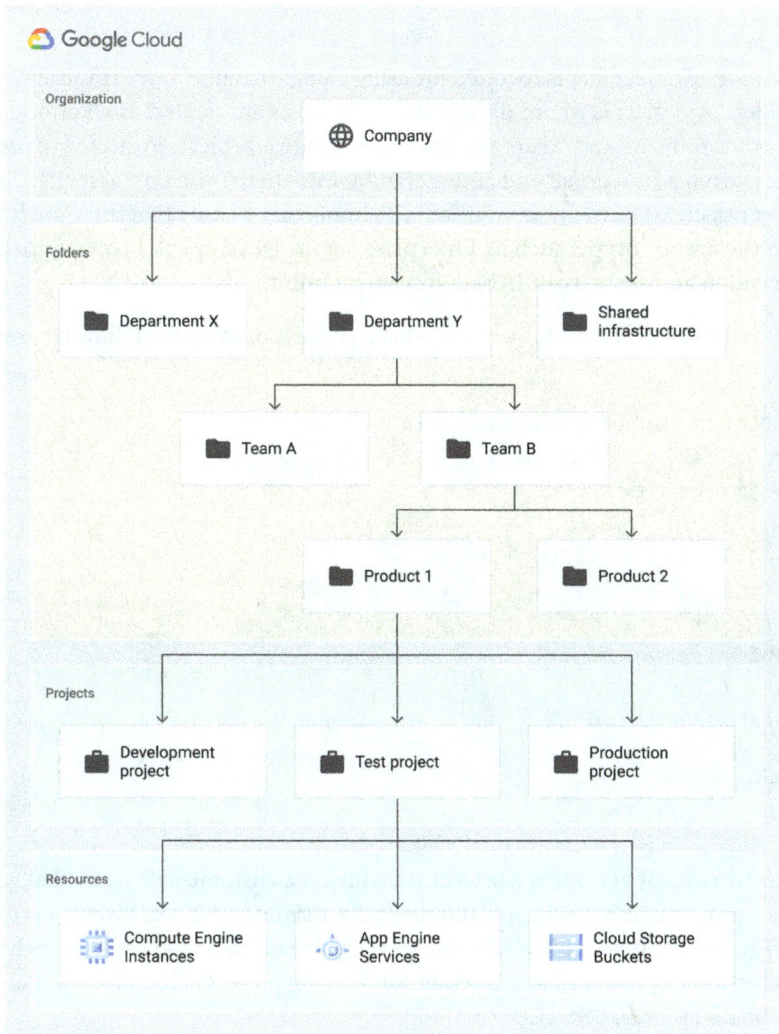

Figure 4.3 – Example enterprise organization

In this example enterprise organization structure, the first level of folders represents a company's departments, such as **X** and **Y**. As folders have the capability to go up to 10 levels deep (a hard limit), you can create more folders, which could represent different teams, and then further segment them into different products. This gives you the ability to define access control and permissions at the department level, team level, or product level. Note the policy inheritance applied is top-down. There is flexibility in modifying the folder tree and it's also possible to move projects, but you have to be mindful of policy inheritance, as that could potentially impact you moving one project from, say, **Team A** to **Team B**. An important design criterion is to decide on a folder structure that is in line with how your policies should be applied.

Projects

A project is a base-level object that is required for using Google Cloud. Your organizations can contain projects and folders. A project is where all your cloud resources are created. Each project is completely separate from other projects and so are the resources inside a project. Projects are useful to group specific resources from a functional and access standpoint. There is no cost associated with creating projects and you can create as many as you want (it's important to note that there are limits that may apply based on the account type, such as Enterprise versus Developer). Projects are not bound to geographical location and serve as an IAM enforcement point.

Let's take a look at the construct of a project and what it consists of using the following example snippet:

```
{
  "createTime": "2020-01-07T21:59:43.314Z",
  "lifecycleState": "ACTIVE",
  "name": "my-project",
  "parent": {
    "id": "634792535758",
    "type": "folder"
  },
  "projectId": "my-project",
  "labels": {
    "my-label": "prod"
  },
  "projectNumber": "464036093014"
}
```

Each project has two identifiers: one is a project ID, which is a customizable name that you can create, and the other is a project number, which is automatically assigned by Google when a project is created and is unique. This project number is read-only. You can also add labels to projects such as if a project is used for production (represented as `prod`) or for filtering projects. The lifecycle state is displayed as `ACTIVE` or `DELETE_REQUESTED`.

The project ID and project name are used when you are interacting with cloud resources. For every request to manage your cloud resources, you need to specify the project information.

Understanding how IAM policy inheritance works

We will cover cloud IAM in depth in *Chapter 6, Google Cloud Identity and Access Management*. In this section, we will understand how hierarchical IAM policy inheritance works in organizations. Cloud IAM allows you to configure fine-grained access to your Google Cloud resources. It lets you configure who (users) have access (permissions/roles) to what (resources) by means of an IAM policy.

The following figure depicts how IAM policy inheritance works, which is top-down, meaning you can configure an IAM policy at the organization level, folder level, or project level, and even at the resource level. If you recall from previous sections, we looked at how an organization hierarchy can be created based on your access boundaries.

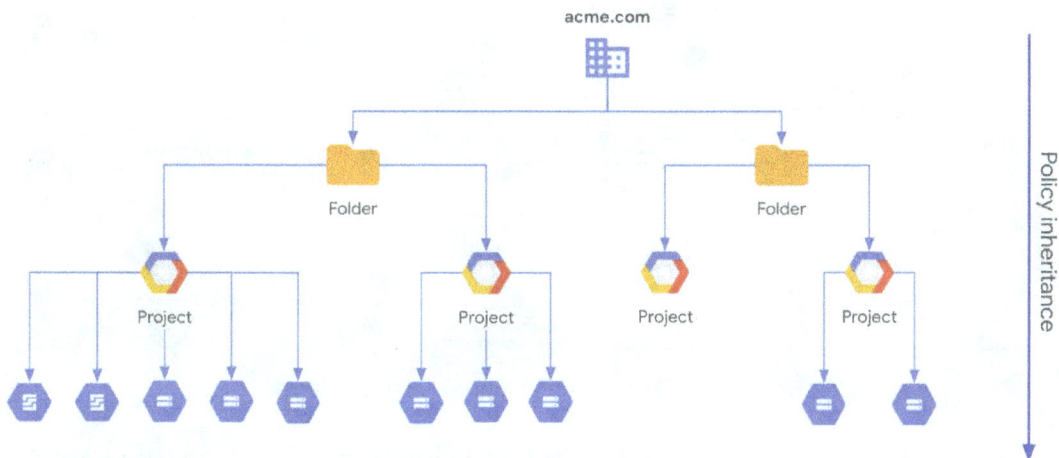

Figure 4.4 – IAM policy inheritance

> **Note**
>
> The effective policy for a resource is the union of the policy set at that resource and the policy inherited from its parent.

Essentially, what this means is that resources inherit the policy from the project, and the project inherits the policy from the folders and the organization. From the preceding figure, if you give Alice, the user, the role of Project Editor at the folder level, then Alice will have access as Project Editor for all the projects that are under the specific folder. If you assign Bob the role of an instance admin at the resource level for a given project, then Bob will only have access as an instance admin for the compute instance in that particular project.

Another aspect to remember is while you have the ability to migrate projects from one folder to another, IAM policy inheritance will apply, meaning when you move the project, it will inherit the IAM policies for that particular folder, and permissions applied on the project will be kept. The permissions associated with the previous folder will no longer be applied and the new folder permissions will be inherited.

Let's further look at an example of how IAM policy inheritance works; we will look at policy inheritance for Compute Engine, as illustrated in *Figure 4.5*.

Policy inheritance: Compute Engine example

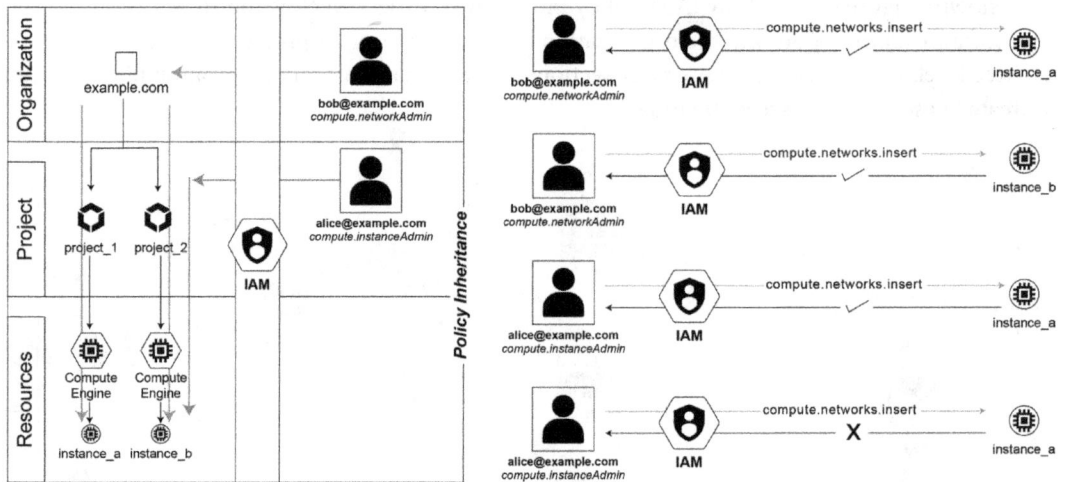

Figure 4.5 – IAM policy inheritance—Compute Engine

In *Figure 4.5*, Bob is granted access at the organization level as `compute.networkAdmin`; therefore, Bob will have access to perform IAM admin functions as governed by the policy for both `instance_a` and `instance_b`. Another user, Alice, is assigned `compute.instanceAdmin` at the `project_2` level. In this case, Alice can perform the `compute.instance.insert` function for `instance_b`, which is grouped under `project_2`, but will not have the permissions to perform the `compute.networks.insert` function for `instance_a` as Alice does not have the permissions at the project level for `project_1`.

Next, we will look at how you can apply Organization Policy Service constraints to your resources in Google Cloud.

Applying constraints using the Organization Policy Service

The Organization Policy Service provides you with a centralized and programmatic method to apply constraints across your organization and the respective cloud resources. We often dictate requirements that need to be applied organization-wide; these constraints are non-negotiable and every resource in your cloud environment has to adhere. This is where Organization Policy Service constraints come in, giving you the ability to centrally apply these policies to avoid or mitigate misconfigurations downstream in your projects and cloud resources. This helps you create guardrails that you can define, which can be based on regulatory requirements or internal compliance. The development teams who are consuming Google Cloud services do not have to worry about applying these policies and duplicating the effort. This further reduces the number of errors that may happen as you are now centrally in control of applying organization-wide constraints.

It is important to know the difference between IAM and Organization Policy Service constraints. While IAM focuses on who can take an authorized action on a particular resource, policy constraints focus on the what, meaning what restrictions are enforced on the resources dictating how they can be configured. An example would be giving access to a user called Bob to perform administrative functions on Compute Engine using an IAM policy, but by defining a constraint of not allowing external IP addresses to be assigned to the compute engine, you can restrict Bob from configuring an external IP address for any instance under the organization.

Let's further understand how an organization policy is applied, as per *Figure 4.6*.

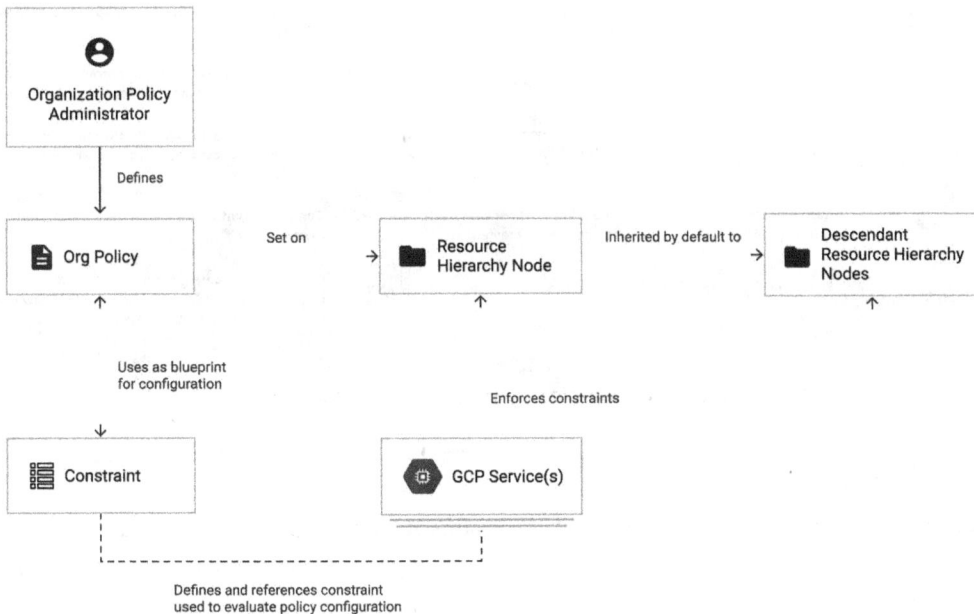

Figure 4.6 – Organization policy

As per the preceding illustration, an **Organization Policy Administrator** can apply an **Org Policy** at the organization, folder, or project level. An **Org Policy** must define a set of constraints that enforce restrictions as part of the policy. Once the constraints are defined, the policy can then be applied at the level decided by the administrator. Note that an **Org Policy** can be overridden at a lower level if needed by an **Organization Policy Administrator**. Next, we will take a look at the different types of constraints that can be applied.

Organization policy constraints

Constraints, simply put, are nothing but restrictions that can be applied to a resource. You have the ability to apply these constraints at different node levels, such as organization-wide or at the folder or project level. Google Cloud defines these constraints as a guardrail that defines what can and cannot be done for a particular resource.

Every constraint is defined by a set of attributes and these include a unique name such as `constraints/compute.disableSerialPortAccess`, a human-friendly name with a description of what the constraint is, followed by the default behavior of the constraint.

Figure 4.7 shows a list of a few constraints that are highly recommended for every GCP cloud environment to enforce.

Services	Constraints	Description	Useful for
Google Compute Engine	External IPs for VM instances	Defines a set of VM instances allowed to use external IP addresses.	Ensuring **minimal external surface**. VMs should normally get internal IPs only.
	Skip default network creation	Skips the creation of the default network and related resources during project creation.	Enforcing usage of **centrally managed and secured VPC networks**.
	Require OS Login	Enables OS Login on all newly created projects.	Ensuring SSH access to VMs is **centrally managed by IAM**, and not SSH keys stored as project/VM metadata.
Cloud IAM	Domain restricted sharing	Defines the set of members (domains) that can be added to Cloud IAM policies.	Protect against **malicious acts and human mistakes** by **ensuring access** only for users in **whitelisted domains**.
GCP	Resource location restriction (**Beta**)	Defines the set of locations where location-based GCP resources can be created.	**Compliance with regulations** that restrict resources location.
Cloud Storage	Enforce bucket policy only	Requires buckets to use Bucket Policy only where this constraint.	**Object-level access** policies don't consider bucket-level policy. They are hard to get visibility into, and can become a **security risk**.

Figure 4.7 – Example organization policy constraints

> **Note**
> You can find a complete list of supported constraints at `https://packt.link/Onku2`.

Policy inheritance

Organization policy inheritance works by applying the policy at the node level (organization/folder/project), where the policy will be inherited by the resources. You can also create custom policies at child nodes, and these can either merge or overwrite the inherited policy.

Let's further understand the policy inheritance rules to better understand how policies are evaluated and applied:

- The first rule applies when no policy is defined. If a resource doesn't inherit or have a policy defined anywhere in the hierarchy, then the constraint's default behavior is enforced.

- The second rule states that if a resource node has a policy set, it will override any parent policy set for that node. However, there is an exception to this rule. If the node policy has the `inheritFromParent` attribute set to `true`, the resource node will inherit the policy from the parent node. In this case, the node-level policy will be merged with the inherited policy, and the two will be reconciled and evaluated.

- The third rule is if a resource node has `inheritfromParent = false` set, the resource node will not inherit the policy from the parent node. If a policy is configured at the resource node level, it will take effect; if no policy is configured, then the default behavior of the policy will be enforced as defined in the first rule.

- The fourth rule is about managing conflicting policies. Let's consider an example where you have a policy constraint defined at the folder level that allows the value `project/123`, and you have another policy constraint at the project level under the folder that denies the value `project/123`. In such circumstances, when a parent policy allows an action and the project level denies the same action, `DENY` will always take precedence. This is how policies are merged. It is also highly recommended as a best practice to not create policy conflicts where one policy contradicts another. This results in confusion about the actual purpose of the policy.

An important note on exceptions that applies to policy merges: for all organization policies that are derived from Boolean constraints, do not merge. For example, say you have defined a policy constraint at the folder level and set enforcement to `true`. Another policy constraint for the project under the folder is set to `false`. In this case, the most specific policy action, `false`, will take effect.

Google Cloud documentation uses the illustration in *Figure 4.8* to explain how policy evaluation works. Let's summarize based on the preceding rules what policy actions are taken on each resource:

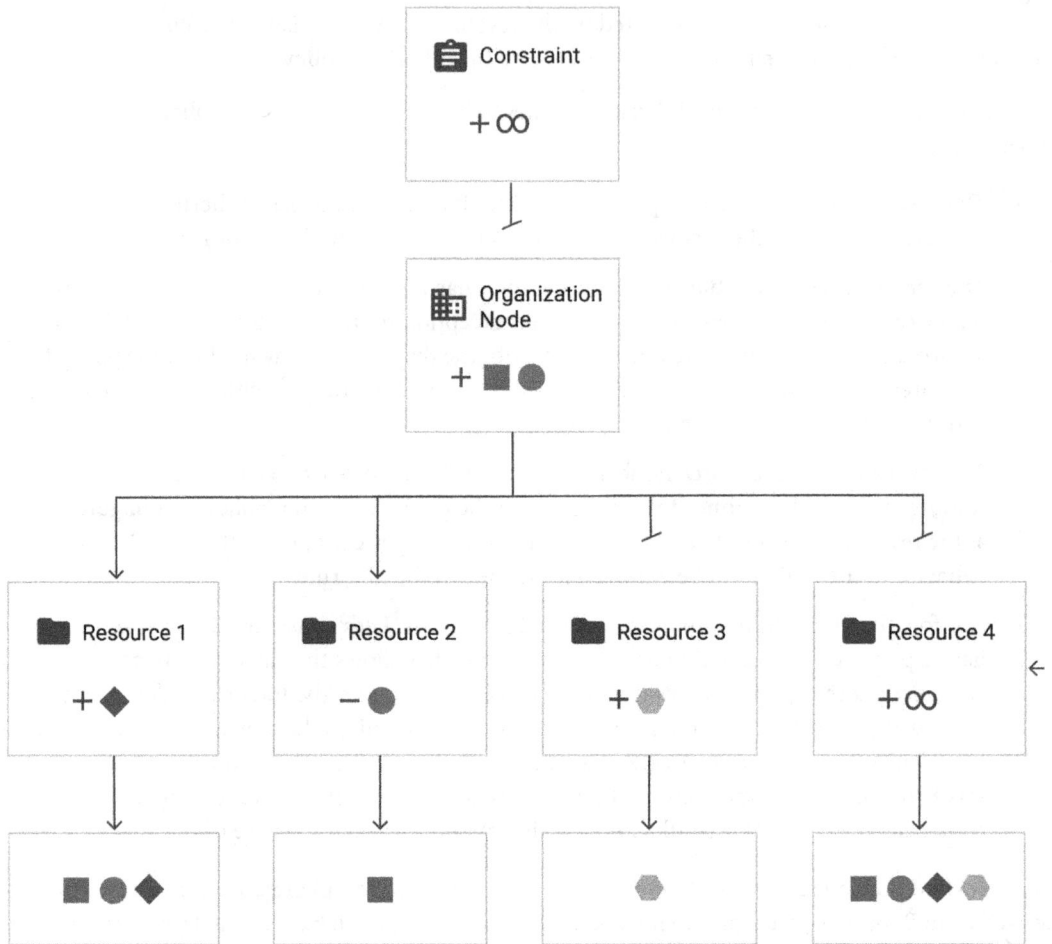

Figure 4.8 – Organization policy constraints evaluation criteria

In this example, we see at the **Organization Node** level a red square and a green circle defined. For **Resource 1**, the arrows represent inhertitfromParent = true; therefore, the first resource will inherit a red square and green circle and add a blue diamond as a node-level resource policy.

Similarly, for **Resource 2**, inhertitfromParent = true; therefore, it will inherit the policy from the parent but it defines another policy at the resource node level to remove the green circle. This means the reconciled policy will only include the red square.

The next two resources are set to `inheritfromParent = false`; therefore, for **Resource 3**, a yellow circle is added as defined by the node resource policy, and for **Resource 4**, `restoredefault` is defined. This means all default policy constraints will be defined.

This concludes the resource management topic. In the next section, we will cover hierarchical firewall policies and how they are applied and evaluated.

How hierarchical firewall policies work

Although hierarchical firewall policies are out of scope for the exam, they are included here for completeness and awareness. Hierarchical firewall policies are applied in a similar way to how you apply IAM policies and constraints for an organization. You can enforce these policies at the organization root node or folder level. This lets you create a consistent set of network policies across the entire organization.

Hierarchical firewall policies are similar to how VPC firewall rules work, where you can create allow or deny rules. The only difference is that hierarchical firewall rules do allow you to delegate rules by applying a `goto_next` action. Also, lower-level rules cannot override higher-level rules that are defined by the network administrators and are applied organization-wide.

There are some specifications defined for hierarchical firewall policies. Let's understand them, including the evaluation criteria:

- You can only create hierarchical firewall policies at the organization and folder level.
- Creating a policy does not enforce it, unless you apply it at the level you want to, such as at the organization or folder level.
- Rule evaluation is based on the resource hierarchy. All rules at a given level are evaluated before moving to the next level.
- The `goto_next` action lets you delegate the evaluation of the policy to a lower-level policy at the next level.
- Using resource targets such as virtual machine instances, subnets, or specific services such as **Google Kubernetes Engine** (**GKE**) clusters, you can create hierarchical policies for specific VPCs and VMs. This can help you manage exceptions for certain VM groups.
- You can include either an IPv4 or IPv6 address as part of the policy but cannot include both in the same policy.

Next, let's take a look at how policy inheritance works for hierarchical firewall policies.

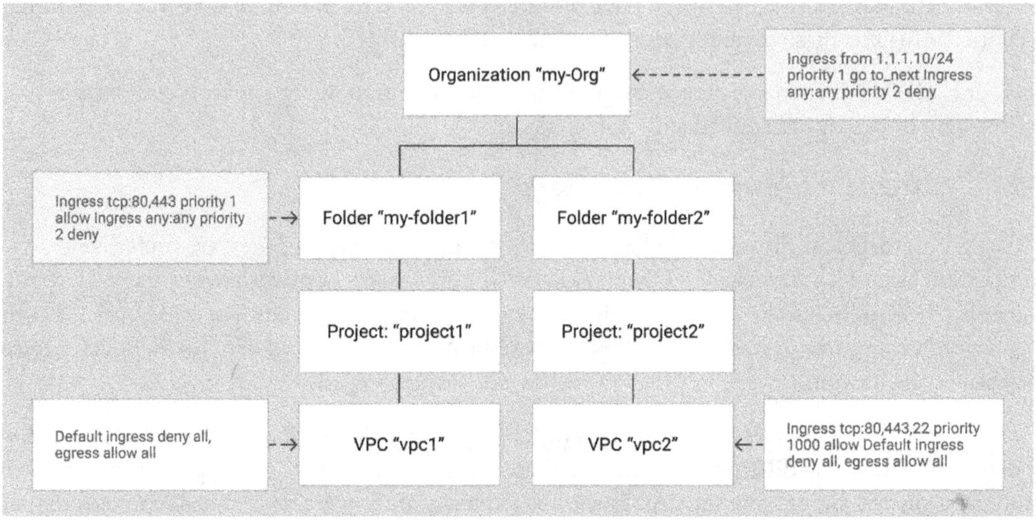

Figure 4.9 – Hierarchical firewall policy inheritance

In *Figure 4.9*, you can apply hierarchical firewall policies at the organization level or folder level. When applied at the **Organization "my-Org"** level, all policies are inherited by the folders and their respective projects and VPCs. In the case where policies are applied only at the folder level, such as the one in the preceding figure applied at the **Folder "my-folder1"** level, these policies will only apply to **project1** and **vpc1**. Also, note that lower-level policies cannot override higher-level policies, as mentioned earlier. However, you have the ability to delegate the policy decision by defining the goto_next action for the next lower-level policy to be evaluated. Let's look at how hierarchical firewall policy evaluation works.

The rule evaluation for hierarchical firewall policies is fairly easy and follows three rules.

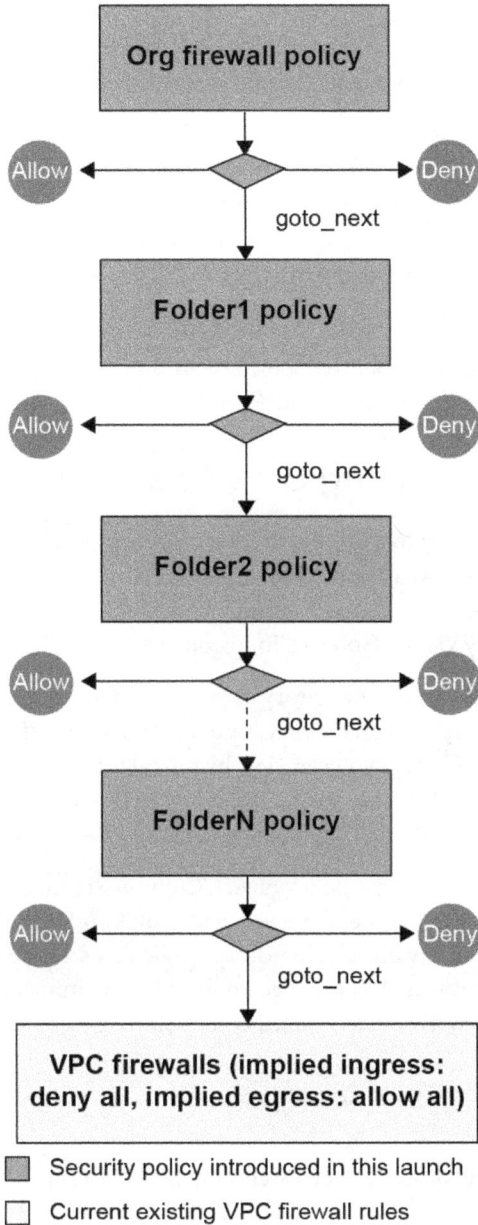

Figure 4.10 – Hierarchical firewall policy evaluation

Let's look at *Figure 4.10* and understand how the rules are applied and evaluated:

1. The first rule is that when you apply the firewall policy at the organization level, all policies are evaluated against an `allow` or `deny` action for a given virtual machine. You can further include the `goto_next` action to delegate the rule to be evaluated by the next lower-level policy.

2. The second rule is when firewall policies are applied at the folder level, the policies are evaluated and then they make their way to the child folders if they exist. Similar to organization policies, you can configure a `goto_next` action for the policy to be evaluated by a child folder.

3. The third rule is unless an `allow` or `deny` action was executed, no action is required. If the `goto_next` action was associated, then the VPC firewall rules will enforce the `allow` or `deny` action to a connection.

In this section, we looked at how hierarchical firewall policies work. Next, we will look at asset management in Google Cloud using the Cloud Asset Inventory service.

Asset management using Cloud Asset Inventory

Cloud Asset Inventory plays a key role in security as it gives you the ability to view your assets in near real time and also to detect the associated changes to the asset. Previously, Cloud Asset Inventory was accessible either via the CLI or Security Command Center, but with recent changes, you can now access Cloud Asset Inventory via the Google Cloud console.

Cloud Asset Inventory is a metadata inventory service that lets you search, export, monitor, and analyze metadata related to supported Google Cloud assets. All metadata information related to an asset is presented on a timeline where you can view historical information (the past five weeks) to get insights into changes to an asset. Before we look at some use cases that Cloud Asset Inventory can help with, let's understand some key concepts.

An asset is a Google Cloud resource or a policy object. Cloud Asset Inventory collects metadata about resources, such as for Compute Engine, storage buckets of App Engine, and so on. Policy-related metadata includes IAM policies, organization constraint policies, and Access Context Manager policies. The third type of metadata information is collected for runtime information such as OS inventory, which includes the operating system and installed and available packages for a given Compute Engine virtual machine.

> **Note**
> You can view the full list of all supported assets at `https://packt.link/GWLd3`.

Now let's look at some of the key attributes and features of Cloud Asset Inventory.

Asset search

The key advantage of Cloud Asset Inventory is its features that can help you search, export, monitor, and analyze information on different assets and provide useful insights. Let's take a look at each one of them.

With the Cloud Asset Inventory API, you can create a custom query to find IAM policies at the organization, folder, or project level. The following command is an example that you can use to list all IAM policies:

```
gcloud asset search-all-iam-policies \
  --scope=projects/12345678
```

You can detect risky policy settings using the Cloud Asset Inventory API by looking for service accounts that have an owner role. The following command is an example of such a query:

```
gcloud asset search-all-iam-policies \
  --scope=organizations/123456 \
  --query='policy roles/owner serviceAccoun')' \
  --page-size=50 \
  --flatte'='policy.bindings[].members']' \
  --forma'='table(resource.segment(3):label=RESOURCE_TYPE, resource.
basename():label=RESOURCE, policy.bindings.member')' \
  | grep serviceAccount
```

Using the Cloud Asset Inventory search function can help you answer questions such as these:

- What IAM policies contain `"foo@bar.com"`?
- Which resources are open to the world (containing `"allUsers"`)?
- Who has an owner role in my organization?
- Are there any `gmail.com` users with `*.setIamPolicy` permissions?

Besides searching policies, you can also search for resources, such as listing all the resources within your project, finding VMs located in the EU region, or finding BigQuery datasets labeled as sensitive. All these capabilities give you powerful access to reduce the time it takes and retrieve information to take corrective action. Next, let's take a look at how you can export asset-related information.

Asset export

With asset export, you can export all resources and policies using the Cloud Asset Inventory API. Using the `ExportAssets` API, you can export all assets at a given timestamp to a Cloud Storage file or BigQuery table. Further, you can use the `ListAssets` API to list all assets at a given timestamp and can use the `BatchGetAssetsHistory` API to retrieve change histories of specific assets for a given timeframe. Cloud Asset Inventory provides time series metadata on resources, IAM policies, organization policies, and access policies. A five-week history is available to export.

Asset monitoring

You can monitor your Google Cloud assets by using the real-time notification APIs, which can create feeds to receive asset changes in real time through Cloud Pub/Sub. This allows you to select interesting changes by specifying types, names, and **Common Expression Library** (**CEL**) conditions upon any data field. For example, in order to detect whether an `@gmail` account has been newly added to in IAM policy, you can use the following:

```
temporal_asset.asset.iam_policy.bindings.filter(b, b.members.exists(m,
endsWith("@gmail.com"))).size() > temporal_asset.prior_asset.iam_
policy.bindings.filter(b, b.members.exists(m, endsWith("@gmail.
com"))).size()
```

This provides a continuous monitoring capability for sensitive resources and policies such as firewalls and IAM policies.

Asset analyzer

Using a policy analyzer, you can get more details on the impact of policies on your cloud resources. You can answer questions such as *Who can access what and why?* You can find out who can read sensitive data from a BigQuery dataset or who has access to a Google Cloud Storage bucket and at what time.

This is an extremely useful and powerful capability to help you gain control and visibility of your Google Cloud environment. Another useful feature is **Asset Insights**, which can give you details on IAM policies that are applied to your resources and detect any risky policies so you can take corrective action.

Another key update to Cloud Asset Inventory, which is available now for use, is **Asset Relationships**. Some assets are related to each other; for instance, a web server may be connected via a firewall rule to access a MySQL database. In situations where a network administrator modifies a firewall rule that breaks the connectivity between the web application and the database, you can establish a relationship based on policies and resources to help you troubleshoot the issue and identify who (the user) did what (the action) to a resource(s) that led to an incident.

Cloud Asset Inventory is not part of the exam blueprint, but you may see indirect references to assets and policies, and it will benefit you as a Google Cloud Security engineer to have a foundational understanding of how asset management is done on Google Cloud and, more importantly, its relevance to security.

We will next look at some of the best practices and design considerations that you should know about and how they apply to the resources in your project.

Best practices and design considerations

Some of the design considerations are to understand how the resources will be managed inside the project. Using one project might be a good idea to keep it simple, but the isolation and separation of duties will not be achieved. On the flip side, if you use too many projects, there will be a lot of overhead to manage the projects, but you will achieve the separation of duties and the isolation required.

Some of the design considerations to follow when breaking down resources and workloads into projects are as follows. Bear in mind that all considerations are correlated:

- You don't want a misconfiguration or a compromise in one operating environment to impact the other. A key consideration is how to reduce the blast radius.

- Quotas and limits are applied at the project level. It's undesirable for a dev/test project to consume the quota required by a prod project, or that one app consumes the quota of another.

- You want to break down cloud resources in a way that will ensure ease of IAM management to achieve least-privilege access. A key consideration is reducing administrative complexity.

- It's easier to track billing at the project level.

- Ensure the separation of duties. For example, you might want to separate central networking projects from app projects to achieve the separation of duties between networking teams and development teams.

- You want to achieve all the above for different operating environments by separating accordingly (for example, prod, test, dev, staging, and user acceptance testing).

The preceding considerations help us understand how and what to consider when breaking down resources and workloads in projects. Further to this, some other key considerations for managing projects are having one project per application, using data classification as a way to keep sensitive data in separate projects and not mixing different data classifications, and finally, using consistent project ID naming conventions.

The best practice is to use workload- and environment-specific projects, and as project creation is a repetitive task, Infrastructure as Code and automation should be leveraged.

In terms of folder design considerations, try not to replicate your organization structure. Many examples cited here use that construct for the purpose of illustration. The key is to understand the workflow and access pattern. When designing your folder structure, the key questions to ask are these:

- What is the access pattern today?

- Does an entire team that works on an app need access to all of its components?

- Do you have separation of access policies between different operating environments?

This will help you understand how to organize your folder structure based on workflow and access control that fits your organization's needs.

There is almost never a need for multiple organizations. Usually, an organization can lump all of its data that's subject to compliance policies into a single folder structure to separate it from all other projects and ensure that the organization admins are trained in the handling of all types of compliant information.

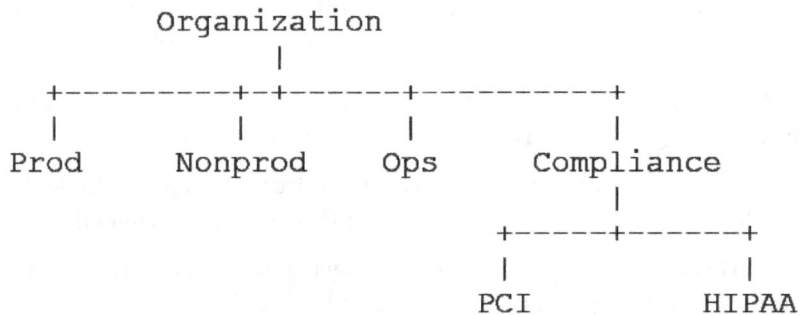

```
            Organization
                 |
    +---------+-+------+----------+
    |         |        |          |
  Prod     Nonprod    Ops      Compliance
                                   |
                              +----+------+
                              |           |
                             PCI        HIPAA
```

Figure 4.11 – Example organization structure

Let's consider this example: if you have to create multiple organizations, you can use folders to group projects based on business units, development environments, and teams to share common IAM permissions and organizational policies. The IAM permissions will use the inheritance model, and for organizational policies, you can make exceptions as required per project.

Use multiple organizations only if multiple teams handle data subject to mutually exclusive compliance policies (for example, **HIPAA** data needs to be separated from **PCI** data). Some key design considerations for managing multiple organizations include the following:

- Each organization should have its own Cloud Identity account and will need admin accounts provisioned and managed independently

- It requires managing multiple Cloud Identity directories (users, groups, domains)

- IAM policies should be decentralized

- Organization-level policies will need to be duplicated

- Any changes/updates to policies will need to be appropriated and applied to each organization

- Organization-level dashboards will only provide a view of their own environment

- Environments are separated by organizations

- Combining environments or restructuring is very difficult

- Projects cannot be easily moved between organizations

- Shared VPC can only be used to share network resources within the same organization

- Future org-wide GCP features may not be able to be fully leveraged or may require workarounds to apply to all environments

It's important to keep these considerations in mind when looking to deploy multiple organizations and avoid complexity. The best practice, wherever possible, is to use folders to separate business units.

Summary

In this chapter, we learned how to organize our Google Cloud infrastructure and manage our available resources. We discussed the basics of creating folders and projects, as well as the features available to you if you want to enforce organizational policy constraints on them. If you're planning on using IAM or firewall rules in your infrastructure, we also went over how policy inheritance works and how it might aid in your organizational structure. We wrapped up by reviewing Cloud Asset Inventory and some best practices for managing your resources.

In the next chapter, we will do a deep dive into Cloud Identity.

Further reading

For more information on GCP compliance, refer to the following links:

- Resource Manager how-to guides: `https://packt.link/RtxyV`

- Best Practices: GCP Resource Organization and Access Management (Cloud Next'19): `https://packt.link/Z35Ox`

- Creating and managing organization policies: `https://packt.link/OegQi`

- Cloud Asset Inventory how-to guides: `https://packt.link/MexmV`

- Understanding Cloud Asset Inventory: `https://packt.link/L91Io`

5

Understanding Google Cloud Identity

In this chapter, we will look at Google Cloud Identity, which is Google's **Identity as a Service** (**IDaaS**) and **Enterprise Mobility Management** (**EMM**) product. We will cover aspects such as directory management, how to create and manage user accounts and groups, and how to sync directory services such as Active Directory using **Google Cloud Directory Sync** (**GCDS**). There are other features and services that will be covered, including **Single Sign-On** (**SSO**) and device and application management.

Furthermore, we will look at how you can use Google Cloud Identity to enforce **2-step verification** (**2SV**), password management, session management, and reporting and admin log activity. As the topics within Cloud Identity are very broad and cover some aspects that are related to Google Workspace (formerly known as G Suite), we will limit our discussion in this chapter to the topics that are relevant to the Google Professional Cloud Security Engineer exam.

In this chapter, we will cover the following topics:

- Overview of Cloud Identity
- Account security, such as configuring users, two-factor authentication, session management, and SAML
- How to configure Google Cloud Directory Sync

Overview of Cloud Identity

Google Cloud Identity is different from some of the other cloud security products that we will cover in this book. What makes it different is that it covers two different platforms: **Google Workspace** and **Google Cloud**. Google Workspace is out of scope as it's not covered in the Google Professional Cloud Security Engineer exam; the features and aspects that we will cover will only pertain to the use of Cloud Identity with regard to Google Cloud.

First, let's understand a few aspects of Cloud Identity. Cloud Identity is accessed via a separate console (`admin.google.com`). Cloud Identity is also the first product that you will interact with when you configure your Google Cloud environment, as the super administrator account exists in Cloud Identity. There'll be more on the super administrator account later in this chapter. Cloud Identity only provides an authentication service and not authorization. The authorization aspect is covered by Google Cloud **Identity and Access Management (IAM)**, which is accessed via the Google Cloud console (`console.cloud.google.com`).

Before we get into the configuration and setup of Cloud Identity, let's look at some of the key features to better understand Cloud Identity. As mentioned earlier, Cloud Identity is the same IDaaS that powers Google Workspace, and it's available both as a free version and a premium version. The premium version has no cap on the number of users, although you can ask Google in the free version to increase the number of users from the default 50-user license. The other differences include the premium version's support for Secure LDAP, access to the Google security center, mobile device management, auto-exporting audit logs to BigQuery, and session length management, which lets you control the duration of the authentication tokens. Finally, the free version comes with no **service-level agreements (SLAs)**, whereas the premium version offers a 99.9% SLA.

Now that we know about the key differences between free and premium Cloud Identity, let's take a quick look at some of the features of Cloud Identity that we will cover in this chapter.

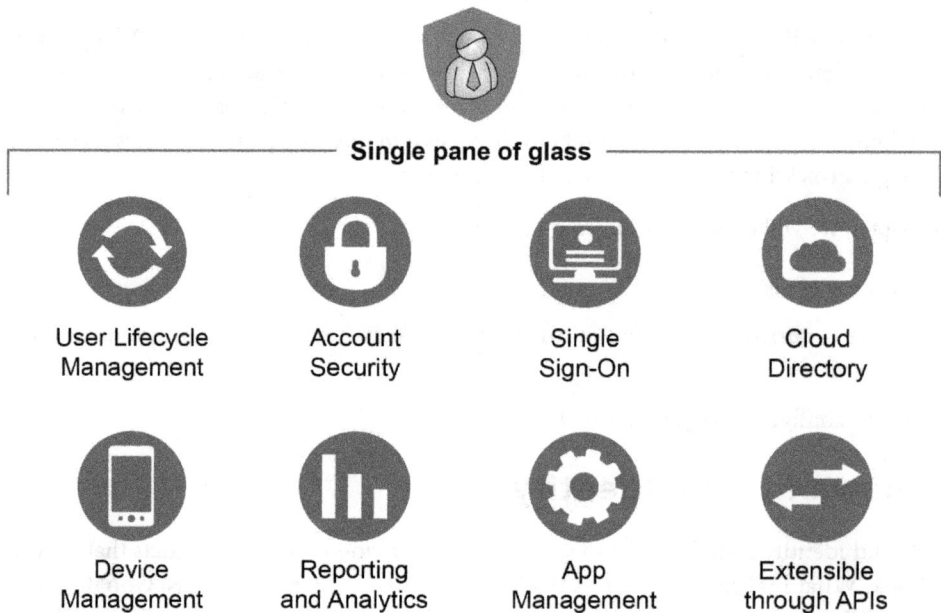

Figure 5.1 – Google Cloud Identity features

The preceding figure captures the key features of Google Cloud Identity. Let's look at some of the features that are more relevant to Google Cloud. In terms of user lifecycle management, you can create or import user accounts into a cloud-based directory. If you use Active Directory in your on-premises environment, you can use the GCDS tool to configure Active Directory and import users, groups, and memberships to Google Cloud Identity.

You can control the process of provisioning and de-provisioning as users join the organization, change roles, or leave. Account security lets you enforce the use of 2SV, apply password policies, and turn on/off access to the Google Cloud console. You can also use Google Authentication or SSO with an external **Identity Provider** (**IdP**), such as Okta or Ping Identity. We will look at SSO in more detail later in this chapter.

In the next section, we will cover how to get started with Cloud Identity, beginning with setting up your domain verification. Domain verification is *not* covered in the exam and is included here only for context.

Cloud Identity domain setup

Before we begin, remember that Cloud Identity is accessed via `admin.google.com`; for the purpose of segregation of the admin role, it is recommended to set up a different domain for Google Cloud if you already have a Workspace domain. Separating the Google Cloud account from the Google Workspace account is a good idea due to governance and compliance requirements.

Configuring a new domain includes the following steps:

1. Sign up for Cloud Identity. Provide your personal details, such as your name, email address, business, geographical region, and domain name.

2. The next step is to perform a domain verification, to ensure that you are the owner of the domain that you are trying to set up.

    If you know who your domain registrar is, you can select the name and then follow the guidance from the Cloud Identity web interface to verify the domain. There is registrar-specific guidance provided, which can be accessed from this link: `https://packt.link/QiqiK`.

    If you do not have your registrar listed and need generic guidance on how to verify your domain using the method of adding a TXT record with a verification code generated from Google Workspace, you can follow the instructions provided here: `https://packt.link/H2aNx`.

As mentioned earlier, these steps are listed for completeness so that you are aware of the Cloud Identity domain setup. Next, we will look at the super admin user role, how to secure access, and some best practices before we move on to understanding how users and groups can be created and managed.

Super administrator best practices

Cloud Identity has a super admin role, which is not the same as the Google Cloud IAM Organization Administrator, but the super admin is by default an Organization Administrator and has administrator privileges for both platforms. The super admin is managed via `admin.google.com` and has the access rights to manage users, groups, and security settings for Cloud Identity. It is also used to delegate access to the Cloud IAM Organization Administrator role. For all purposes, your super admin should create a Cloud IAM Organization Administrator role, but it should never be used to access `console.cloud.google.com` to provision or manage Google Cloud resources.

Given the importance of a super administrator, there are some best practices that should be followed. These best practices include the following:

- Always enable 2SV/multi-factor authentication for the super admin account.

- Keep a backup security key in a secure location.

- Disable device trust and limit the web session length.

- To ensure resilience and avoid over-reliance on a single individual, it is recommended to limit the usage of super admin accounts and keep the number of such accounts to a maximum of 4. This precautionary measure mitigates the risk associated with a single point of failure and ensures an adequate number of backup super admins in case of emergencies.

- Set recovery phone and email options, and ensure the recovery email is secure and protected with 2SV.

> **Note**
> Domain DNS access to verify domain ownership is needed in the event that you lose access to super admin accounts if a recovery email/phone was not set up.

- Create a dedicated super admin account and lock it away. This is a break-glass account to be used only in emergencies.

- Assign Cloud Identity admin roles for the delegated administration of users, groups, and so on.

- Delegate the setup and management of Google Cloud organization resources to other administrators and assign fundamental IAM roles to them to ensure the separation of duties.

- The Cloud Identity super admin will always bypass any SSO; they will always authenticate with Google Cloud Identity directly.

The topic of Google Cloud Identity is very broad and some areas overlap with Google Cloud Workspace features and functions. In this section, we only covered what is relevant from a Google Cloud Professional Security Engineer exam perspective. You can refer to the documentation for Cloud Identity if you wish to learn further. Next, we will cover some account-security-related features of Cloud Identity.

Securing your account

Google Cloud Identity provides a number of different options that can help you secure your account and enforce strong security controls. In this section, we will look at how to enforce 2SV using security keys, enforce a password policy and password recovery options, and configure user security settings such as session length, as well as doing a walk-through of the Google security center.

2-step verification

With 2SV, users log in to their accounts using their username and password (also referred to as *something the users know*) as well as a second factor (*something they have*), which could be a physical security token or a mobile phone that can generate a key. Google Cloud Identity supports a number of methods that can be used as a second factor for authentication. These methods include the following:

- **Security keys**: A physical security key, such as Google's Titan Security Key or a YubiKey.

- **Google prompt**: Users can set up their mobile phone (iOS or Android) to send a sign-in prompt. When a user attempts to sign in and successfully completes the first step of entering a username and password, the user then gets a sign-in prompt on their authorized device to confirm whether it's the user who has initiated a sign-in.

- **Code generators**: Another option is to use code generators, such as Google Authenticator, Authy, and so on. Users can use code generators to generate a one-time code to be used as a second factor.

- **Backup code**: An offline method can be used where the user does not have access to a mobile phone to generate a code. They can print backup codes and use them instead. Backup codes are often used for recovery.

- **Text or call**: You can also opt to have your one-time password sent to you via **Short Message Service** (**SMS**) on your mobile phone, or you can receive a phone call on your authorized device with the one-time code.

There are a variety of choices for what type of 2SV can be configured. You can use any combination of 2SV options. Next, we will take a look at how you enforce 2SV in the web interface.

Before you enforce 2SV, you have to ensure that users are aware that they need to enroll for 2SV and choose their verification methods.

Next, let's look at how you can enforce 2SV from the console:

1. Log in with your credentials to `admin.google.com`.

2. Navigate in the left-hand side menu to **Security | Authentication | 2-step verification** (see *Figure 5.2*). Once in the settings, select the organizational group from the left where you want to enforce the 2SV policy.

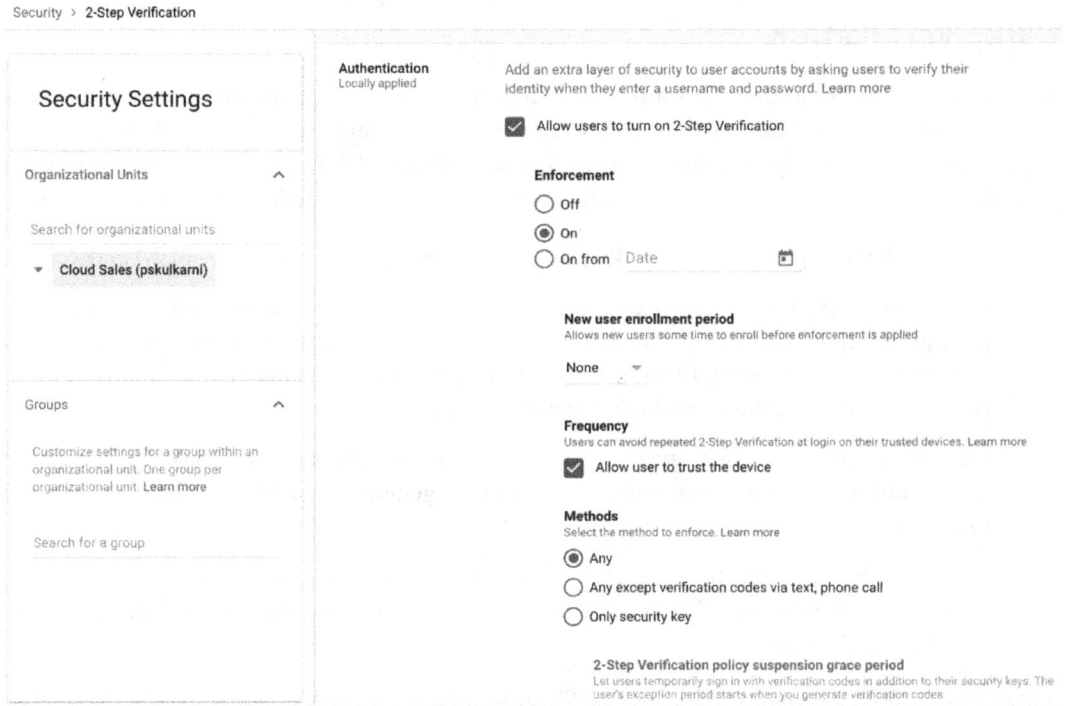

Figure 5.2 – Account security (2SV)

3. From the configuration options available here, you can set **Enforcement** to **On** or **Off** or schedule it to turn on for specific data. Selecting **On** will enforce it immediately.

4. The other important configuration is to let users specify whether the device they are logging in from is a trusted device. With this setting in place, when users first log in, they will be prompted with a username and password and will be asked whether they want to remember the device. If the user selects this option, then the next time they log in, they will not be prompted for 2SV. This will remain in place unless the user deletes the cookies or user access is revoked.

5. As part of your 2SV policy, you can also create an exception group for users to whom the policy may not apply. This can be done for a variety of users; although it is not recommended, you do have the option to configure this.

6. Next, you can give your users time to enroll in 2SV, from zero to six months. This helps you in rolling out 2SV if it's being done for the first time. Users will get time to configure their 2SV, and after that, they will be able to log in. If they do not do that by the enrollment deadline, they will be unable to log in.

7. Finally, you have the option to select the verification methods. As a best practice, selecting **Only security key** is recommended as it is the most secure option. But you are not limited to that and have the option to configure other options, such as **Any except verification codes via text, phone call**, which will enable all supported verification methods. Based on your organizational requirements, you can select these options.

8. Other configuration options include the ability to configure a suspension policy and the ability to use backup codes.

> **Note**
>
> You can read more about these settings using the following link:
> `https://packt.link/BVasl`. For the purpose of the exam, you should
> be able to configure a 2SV policy as explained earlier.

User security settings

As an administrator, you have the ability to view a user's settings and perform actions such as resetting passwords, adding or removing security keys, resetting user sign-in cookies, turning temporary challenges off, or viewing and revoking application-specific passwords or access to third-party applications. Let's take a quick look at where you can access these settings from:

1. Log in via admin.google.com.

2. Navigate to **Directory** | **Users** and select the username you want to view the security settings for, which can be done by clicking on the name.

3. Once you are on the user's details page, you can see multiple options, such as user details, groups, permissions, and security settings. For this exercise, we will be navigating to the security settings.

User information		∨
	This user profile is incomplete. Add contact information for Test, like a secondary email address and a phone number.	
User details		

Security		∨
2-step verification: OFF	**Application-specific password**	**Connected applications**
Enforced but not enabled for Test	0 application-specific passwords created	**0 applications** are connected with Test's account
Recovery information		
Add a recovery email		
Add a recovery phone		
Password settings | Application integrations		

Groups	∨
Test doesn't belong to any groups. Add Test to team and project groups, making it easier for this user to collaborate.	

Admin roles and privileges	∨
Test doesn't have any admin roles or privileges. **ASSIGN ROLES**	

Apps		∨
Google apps	**Other cloud apps**	
54 of 57 available Google services are on for Test. Turn apps on or off	No other cloud apps have been added to this organization. Browse for apps Turn apps on or off	

Managed devices	
Your organization doesn't have mobile device management.	

Figure 5.3 – Cloud Identity – user details

4. On the **User information** page, scroll to the **Security** section and click on it to be taken to the security settings for the selected user.

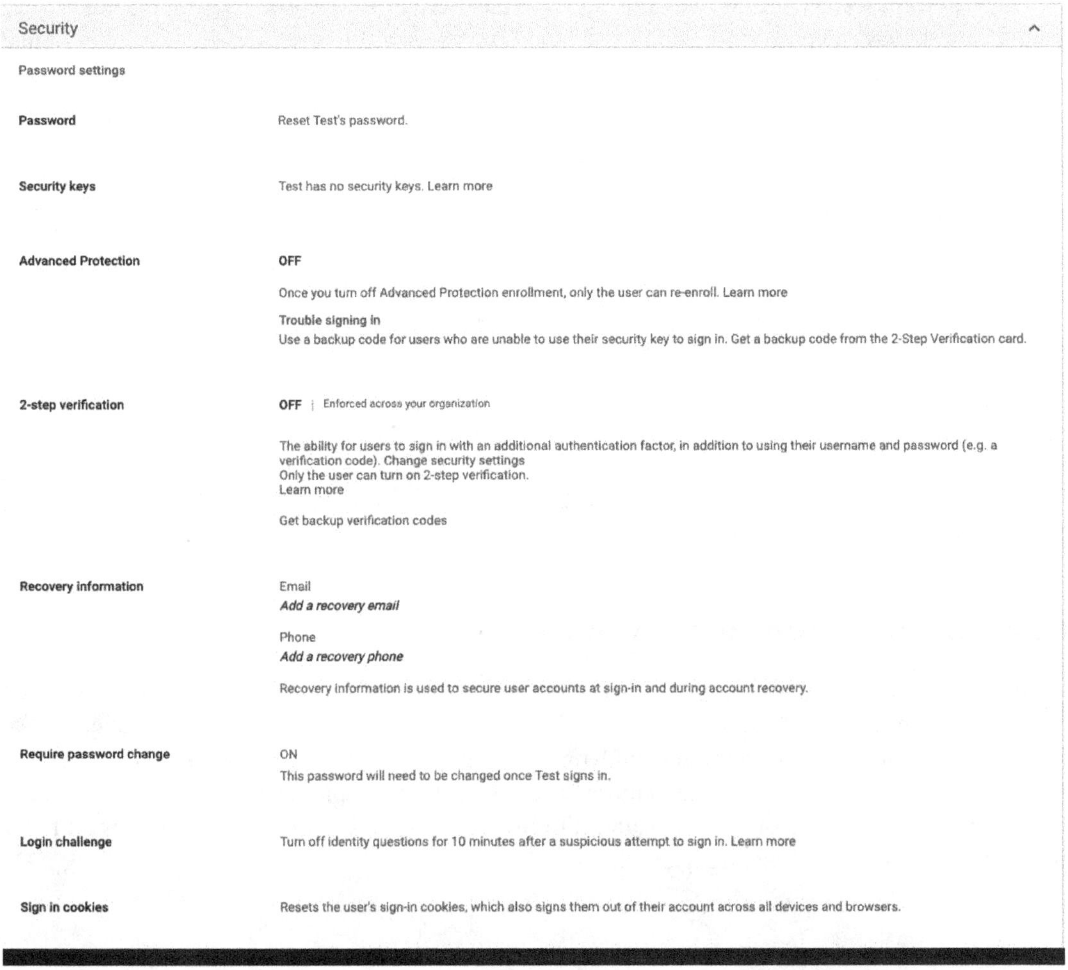

Security	^
Password settings	
Password	Reset Test's password.
Security keys	Test has no security keys. Learn more
Advanced Protection	**OFF**
	Once you turn off Advanced Protection enrollment, only the user can re-enroll. Learn more
	Trouble signing in
	Use a backup code for users who are unable to use their security key to sign in. Get a backup code from the 2-Step Verification card.
2-step verification	**OFF** ⋮ Enforced across your organization
	The ability for users to sign in with an additional authentication factor, in addition to using their username and password (e.g. a verification code). Change security settings
	Only the user can turn on 2-step verification.
	Learn more
	Get backup verification codes
Recovery information	Email
	Add a recovery email
	Phone
	Add a recovery phone
	Recovery information is used to secure user accounts at sign-in and during account recovery.
Require password change	ON
	This password will need to be changed once Test signs in.
Login challenge	Turn off identity questions for 10 minutes after a suspicious attempt to sign in. Learn more
Sign in cookies	Resets the user's sign-in cookies, which also signs them out of their account across all devices and browsers.

Figure 5.4 – Cloud Identity – user security settings

5.   From here, you can view and configure multiple security settings. We will briefly look at what each one of them does:

- **Reset password**: This lets you reset the user's password. You can create a password automatically and view the password. When you email the password to the user, you can set **Change password on next sign-in**. You can also copy and paste the password if needed, although that is not recommended; you should email the password from the console.

- **Security keys**: You can add or revoke security keys for the user.

- **2-step verification**: Only a user can turn this setting on. As an administrator, you can only check the 2SV settings or, if required, get a backup code for a user that has been locked out.

- **Require password change**: You can enforce a password change for a user.

Other settings include viewing or revoking application-specific passwords, and you can also revoke third-party application access.

> **Note**
>
> To read more about the user security settings, you can use this link:
> `https://packt.link/HUyYn`.

Session length control for Google Cloud

As an administrator, you can configure the session length of Google Cloud services. You do have the option to configure it for Google services as well, such as Gmail, but this is not in our scope, and we will only focus on configuring the session length for Google Cloud services. There are a variety of use cases for which you would want to enforce session length. Examples include access by privileged users or billing administrators who are subject to session length restrictions – you might want them to sign in more frequently by timing out their sessions.

You do have the option to create groups to which this policy will not apply. When enforced, this policy applies to Google Cloud console access, the `gcloud` command-line tool (the Google Cloud SDK), and any application, whether owned by you or a third party, that requires user authorization for Google Cloud scopes (`https://packt.link/Q1sR2`). Note that Google Cloud session length control does not apply to the Google Cloud mobile app. We will next see how you can enforce session length from the admin console:

1. Log in via `admin.google.com`.

2. Navigate to **Security | Access and Data Control | Google Cloud session control**.

    Refer to the following screenshot to see the multiple options that are available to us to configure.

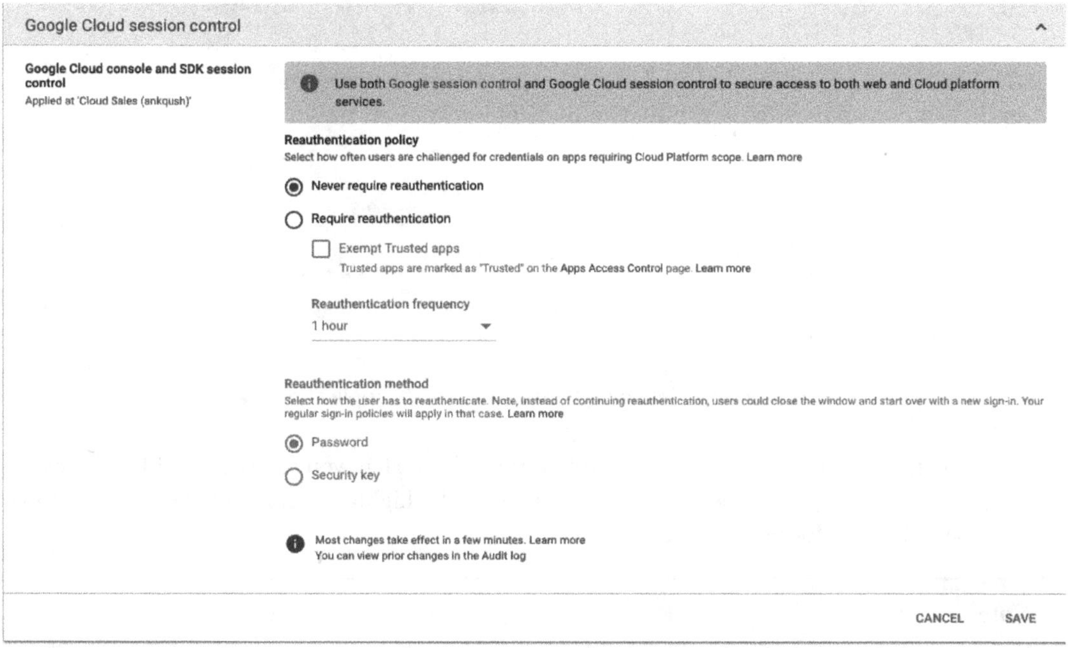

Figure 5.5 – Google Cloud session control

3. From the left-hand side menu, select the organizational unit and the user group to which you want this policy to apply. As mentioned earlier, you can apply this policy selectively to users in a certain group and not subject all users to session control, having different session control settings for standard users versus privileged users.

4. Let's take a look at other options available to us that we can configure:

   - **Reauthentication policy**: Here, you select **Require reauthentication** and then specify **Reauthentication frequency**. The minimum frequency is one hour and the maximum is 24 hours. There is an option to exempt trusted apps from the reauthentication policy. You can configure which applications are trusted by navigating to **Security | Access and Data Control | API controls**. From there, you can manage trust for third-party applications.

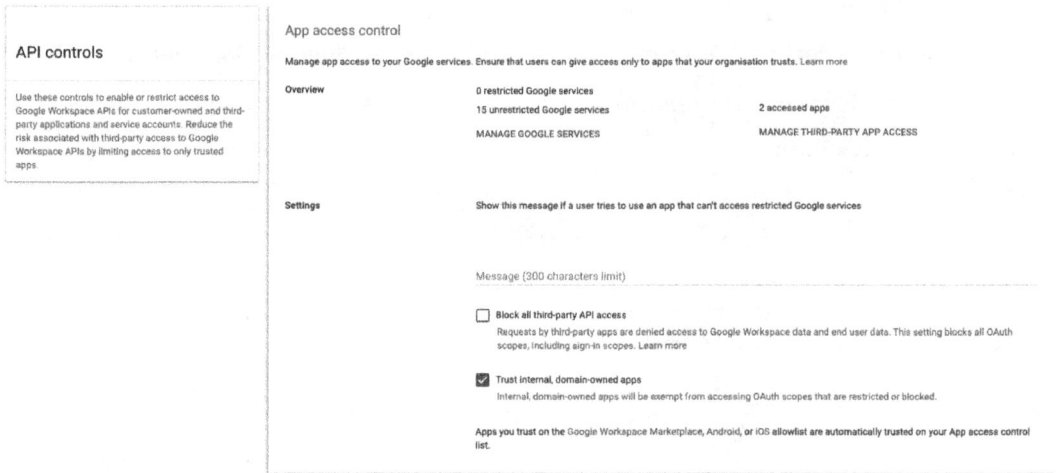

Figure 5.6 – Managing trusted third-party applications

   - Next, you can configure **Reauthentication method**. Here you can specify either password or security keys. This depends on your use case. It's highly recommended that you enforce security keys for privileged users.

> **Note**
> You can read more about Google Cloud session length here: `https://packt.link/B2wvT`.

SAML-based SSO

With **SSO**, you can configure your enterprise cloud applications to let users sign in using their Google-managed credentials; in other words, Google Workspace will act as an identity provider. There are two different options for you to configure SSO: pre-integrated or custom. With the pre-integrated option, Google supports over 300 pre-configured applications that you can deploy from the Cloud Identity console. The custom **Security Assertion Markup Language** (**SAML**) option can be used if you have custom applications or applications that are not pre-configured.

It is assumed that you understand how SAML 2.0 works. In this section, we will only look at how to configure SSO using SAML and not cover the foundational knowledge of how Google implements SAML. If you wish to understand more about how SSO using SAML works on Google Cloud, please refer to the *Further reading* section at the end of this chapter.

For the purpose of the exam, we will walk through the steps required to configure SSO using SAML for a custom application.

Before we begin, ensure that you have the **Assertion Consumer Service** (**ACS**) URL and the entity ID, as they will be required when you configure your external IdP and optionally a start URL. Also, determine at this stage whether your external IdP supports **multi-factor authentication** (**MFA**); if it does, you can configure the option to use MFA by external IdP, but if for some reason your custom application does not support MFA, you can configure Google Cloud Identity to enforce MFA.

Now let's look at the steps required to complete the SSO setup using SAML for a custom application:

1. Begin by logging in to the admin console at `admin.google.com`.

2. Navigate from the main console to **Apps** | **Web and mobile apps**.

3. From there, select **Add app** | **Add custom SAML app**.

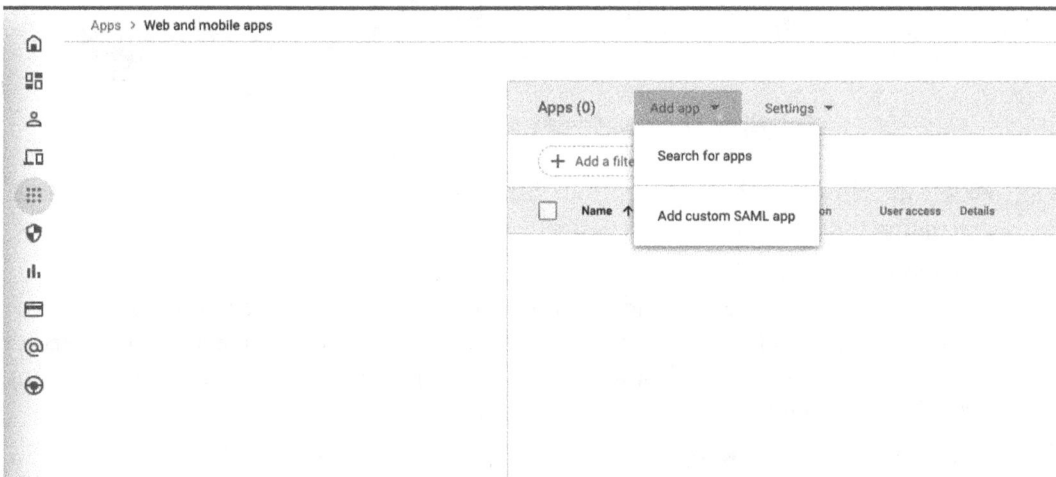

Figure 5.7 – Cloud Identity – Add custom SAML app

4. This will take you to a four-step wizard to configure your custom SAML app.

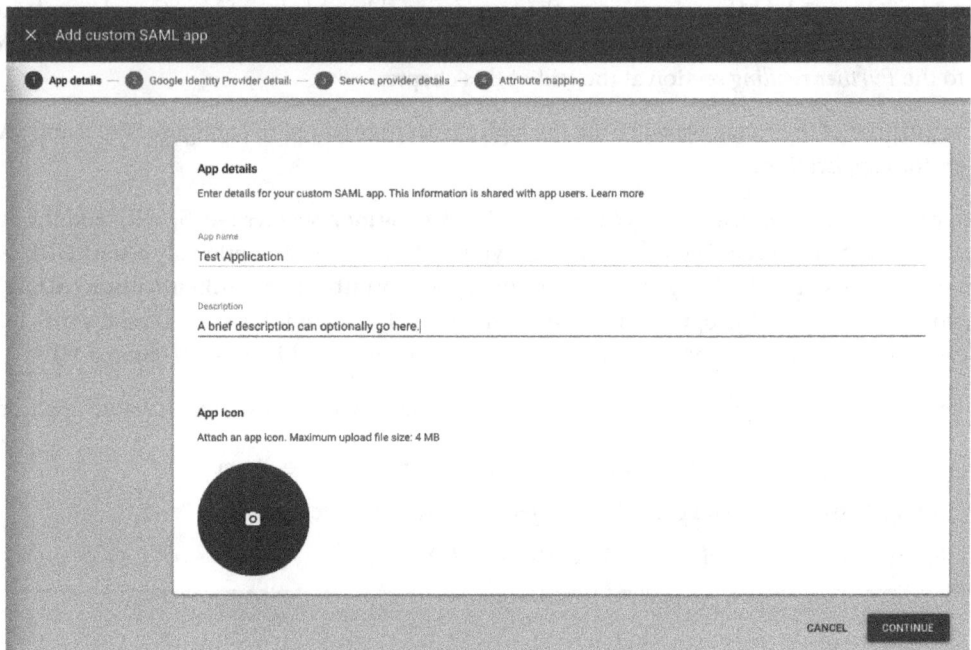

Figure 5.8 – Configure your custom SAML app

5. Follow the steps to give a name to your custom application and optionally provide a brief description and upload an icon. Once done, click **Continue**.

6. The next step will provide you with two options: either download the IdP metadata or copy and paste the SSO URL, entity, and certificate with an SHA-256 fingerprint. These are Google Identity Provider details that will be required by your service provider. Once you have decided either to download or copy and paste the information, you move on to the next step by clicking the **CONTINUE** button.

7. Optionally, you can now log in to your service provider console and copy and paste the information that was captured in *Step 6*.

8. In this step, you can fill in **ACS URL**, **Entity ID**, and optionally a start URL. The ACS URL is simply an endpoint at your service provider's end; this is where the IdP will redirect the authentication response. The **Entity ID** value is provided by your service provider. At this stage, you can also set the option to enable **Signed response**. This option enables you to sign the entire SAML authentication response instead of the default option, which only signs the assertion within the response. The default **Name ID** value is the primary email; however, you have the option to create the custom attributes that need to be created using the admin console before you start the **Add SAML custom app** process.

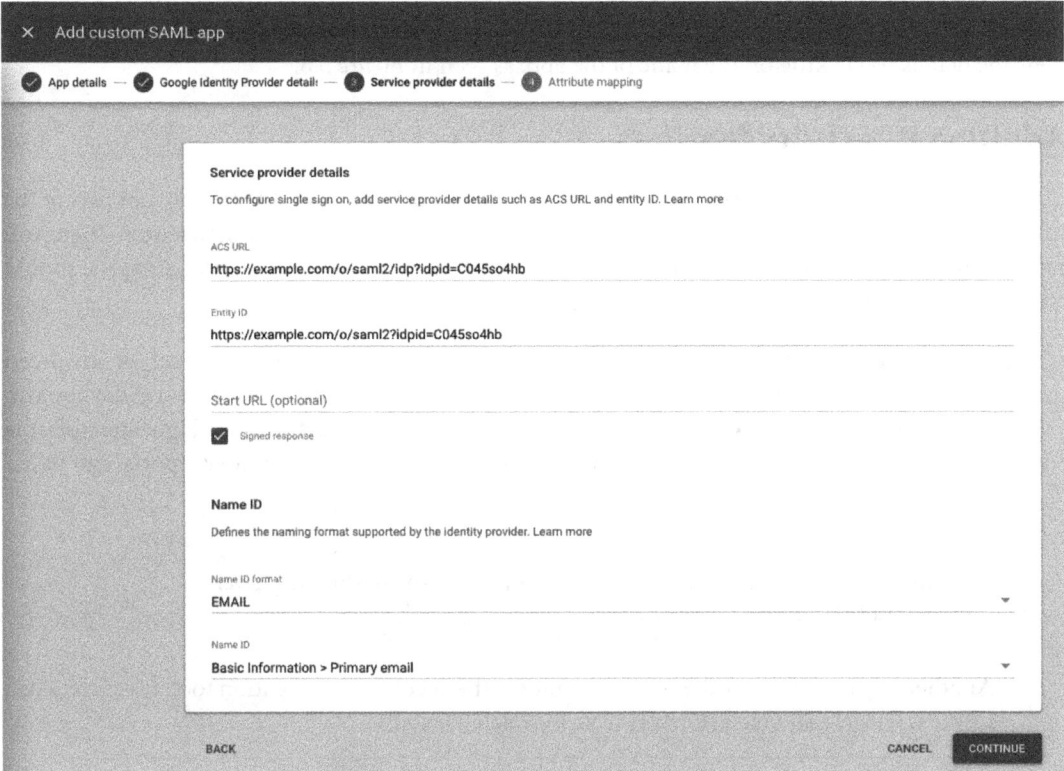

Figure 5.9 – SAML service provider details

9. The next step is optional, for you to create attribute mappings. If you don't have mappings, you can click **FINISH** to complete the setup process.

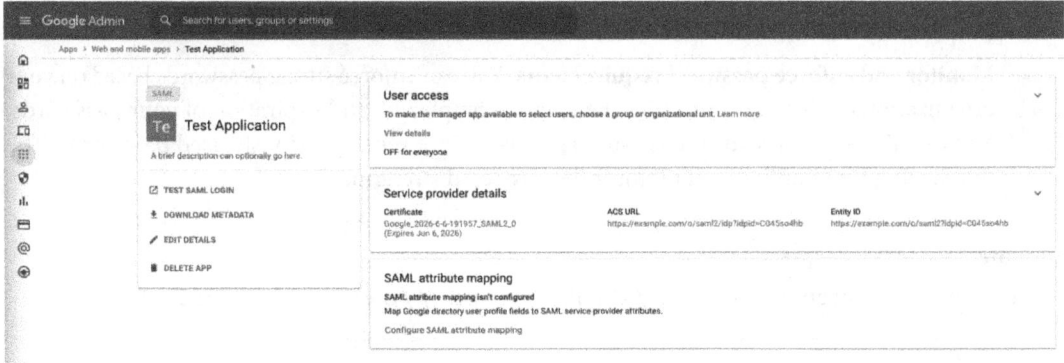

Figure 5.10 – App details page

You will be able to view the configured app on the **Apps | Web and mobile apps** page, and you can view the details by clicking on the name of the app, as seen in *Figure 5.8*.

Additional security features

There are some additional security features that are available in Cloud Identity that are not part of the exam's scope. Therefore, we will briefly cover them here for the purpose of completeness. There will be links in this section and in the *Further reading* section on some of these additional topics, should you need to refer to them. These features include the following:

- **Google Cloud security center**: The security center provides capabilities such as advanced security analytics and visibility into security-related issues, all from a central dashboard. From the security dashboard, you can view reports, such as reports on user login attempts, file exposure, DLP events, spam-related information, OAuth grant activity, user reports, and so on.

> **Note**
> You can find a full list of reports that you can view from the dashboard here:
> `https://packt.link/yGWLH`.

Another key capability of the security center is the security investigation tool, which lets you identify, triage, and take action on security-related events.

> **Note**
> You can learn more about the security investigation tool here:
> `https://packt.link/ovam0`.

Finally, the dashboard also provides you with an overview of your security health, which gives you visibility of the admin console and its related activities.

- **Monitor and enforce password requirements**: You can enforce strong passwords based on your organization's policy. This includes the length, complexity, and expiration of your passwords. You can also stop password reuse so that users cannot reuse previously used passwords. The monitoring function lets you monitor the password strength.

> **Note**
> You can read more about this topic at this link: `https://packt.link/Rol3H`.

- **Self-service password recovery**: You have two options for password recovery: either you can let users recover the password themselves or you can get users to contact an administrator to reset the password.

> **Note**
>
> You can read more details about this topic here: `https://packt.link/ccOZe`.

In this section, we covered some optional security features that are available for Google Cloud Identity. Next, we will cover directory management, which includes aspects of identity federation.

Directory management

This is one of the most important sections of the entire chapter. We will learn how to configure identity provisioning, in particular, how to integrate Microsoft **Active Directory** (**AD**) with Google Cloud Identity using the GCDS tool. We will look at some other directory management tasks, such as how to create users and groups and assign admin permissions and how we can provision and de-provision user access using Google Cloud Identity and third-party IdPs. Finally, we will have a look at how to automate user lifecycle management.

Google Cloud Directory Sync

This section will be a deep dive into GCDS. We will start by understanding what GCDS is, the benefits of using it, how it works, and how to configure it using Configuration Manager.

GCDS helps you to synchronize your Microsoft AD or LDAP objects, such as security users and groups, to your Google Cloud Identity account.

> **Note**
>
> To look at the entire list of content that is synced, you can check this link: `https://packt.link/rMBYS`. This content is synced as a one-way sync from your LDAP or AD. Your AD or LDAP is not modified in any way.

GCDS features and capabilities

Let's look at some of the capabilities that GCDS has to offer. It is important from an exam perspective to understand what GCDS can and cannot do:

- GCDS is available as a tool to download on your server. It comes packaged with all necessary components, and once installed, you can begin the setup process. There are also built-in security features in GCDS to help ensure your content is secure during the synchronization. Before any synchronization can begin, an OAuth token is created using Configuration Manager, which is used to connect to your Google account. You will further need to authorize GCDS with your Google account for authentication.

- GCDS lets you sync information such as organizational units, mailing lists, users and their related attributes (you have the option to specify this), extended user information (again, you can specify what to synchronize), and calendar information, such as rooms, contacts, and passwords.

- Using configuration management, you will be able to specify which attributes you want to include, exclude, or create exceptions for.

- To make the entire setup of using GCDS easy to use, you do have the option, if you are using Microsoft AD or Open LDAP, to use the default settings in Configuration Manager.

- With GCDS, you have the ability to create exclusion rules where you can specify what you want to include in your sync. All of this can be easily managed and configured from Configuration Manager, which we will see a bit later.

Now, let us understand how GCDS works.

How does GCDS work?

By using GCDS, your Google Cloud Identity domain's data can be automatically provisioned from your LDAP directory server by adding, editing, and deleting users, groups, and non-employee contacts. Your LDAP directory server's data is safe and secure.

Configuration Manager is a GUI-based wizard that walks you through the steps to configure synchronization. You set up your LDAP directory server settings and connection, configure the Google Cloud Identity domain settings, and select what LDAP data to synchronize and what to exclude.

The following steps explain how GCDS data flows:

1. Relevant data is exported in a list from your LDAP server. You can set up rules to specify how this list is generated.

2. GCDS connects to the Google Workspace domain and generates a list of users, groups, and shared contacts that you specify.

3. GCDS compares these lists and generates a list of changes.

4.   GCDS updates your Google Workspace directory to match the AD data.

5.   When the synchronization is complete, GCDS emails a report to any addresses that you specify.

Figure 5.11 illustrates how GCDS works and some of the best practices associated with it – for example, provisioning it from a single source of truth, such as your on-premises Active Directory, and running it on dedicated hardware.

Figure 5.11 – The workings of GCDS

All connections from GCDS to LDAP are secured using TLS, and you have the option to specify that in Configuration Manager. For standard LDAP, no encryption is used. All communications between Google and GCDS are done over HTTPS.

In the next section, we will walk through Configuration Manager. Configuration Manager is used to configure GCDS to work with your user directory and Cloud Identity.

Using GCDS Configuration Manager

In this section, we will look at how to configure a sync using Configuration Manager. As we look at each step, we will explain what you can and cannot do:

1.   To download and install GCDS on your server, make sure you select the correct version, such as 32-bit or 64-bit for Windows or Linux. GCDS can be downloaded from the following link: `https://packt.link/ZruGO`.

2. Once installed, you need to gather information related to your LDAP server, as that can help you configure the sync more quickly. To gather information on your LDAP structure, you can install a third-party browser such as JXplorer or Softerra LDAP Administrator. Besides information on the structure, you should also use the browser to capture information such as the LDAP base **Distinguished Name** (**DN**) and security groups. GCDS requires a base DN to search users and groups. You do have the ability to use multiple base DNs in your configuration. Similar to security groups, if you would like to synchronize them, you need to identify which ones you would like to synchronize.

3. Next, you will need to connect the following information to your LDAP server:

    I.   Hostname and IP address of the LDAP server.

    II.   Network-related information such as access and proxies.

    III. Whether you will be installing Secure LDAP using SSL or Standard LDAP with no encryption.

    IV.   User credentials of the LDAP server with read and execute permissions.

> **Note**
>
> You can only get data from a single LDAP directory; if you are using multiple Microsoft AD directories, then consider consolidating or syncing from a Global Catalog or using a virtual directory product.

4. You should next clean up your LDAP directory to identify users and mail-enabled groups and review the naming guidelines for names and passwords to ensure there are no unsupported characters.

5. Next, mark all Google users in your LDAP directory. This can be done using organizational units, groups, descriptive names, and custom attributes.

6. As mentioned earlier, before you can begin configuring, you need to authorize GCDS with your Google account. The following steps will authorize the account and generate an OAuth token that will be used by Configuration Manager to connect and synchronize:

    I.   Open **Configuration Manager** and then select **Google Domain Configuration**.

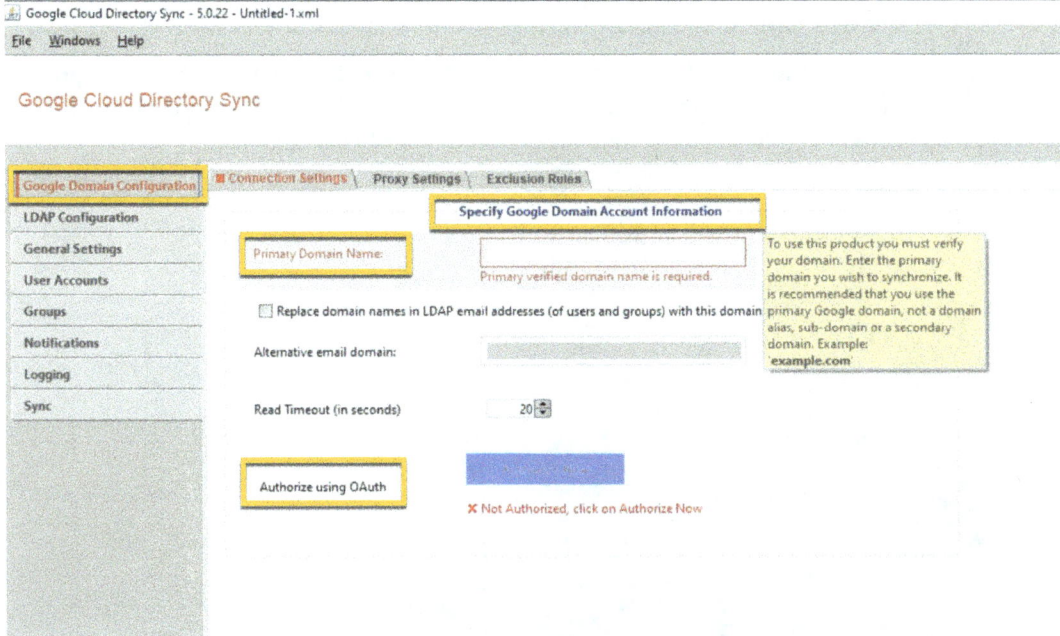

Figure 5.12 – Google Domain configuration

II. Click **Authorize Now**, which will prompt you to sign into your Google Account using your super admin credentials.

III. An OAuth token will be generated, which you will need to copy and paste into **Configuration Manager**; after that, click **Validate**.

7. In the next steps, we will configure the sync using Configuration Manager. For the purpose of this walk-through, we will be using the default settings. Configuration Manager uses a step-by-step process to set things up. The first step in preparing and planning includes identifying the information you want to synchronize, such as user accounts, groups, user profiles, organizational units, calendar resources, licenses, and so on.

8. Next, click the **Connection Settings** tab under **Google Domain Configuration** and specify **Primary Domain name** (if the domain is not verified, you will be directed to a domain verification process). Specify the alternate email address and, if applicable, authorize it by signing into your Google account using super admin credentials and the OAuth token to validate.

9. Under the **Proxy Settings** tab, specify whether you have a proxy in your network.

10. On the **LDAP Configuration** page, specify the LDAP server information. For the purpose of this exercise, we will assume that we are using Microsoft AD or Open LDAP. See the description link for examples of the accepted ways to connect to your LDAP server.

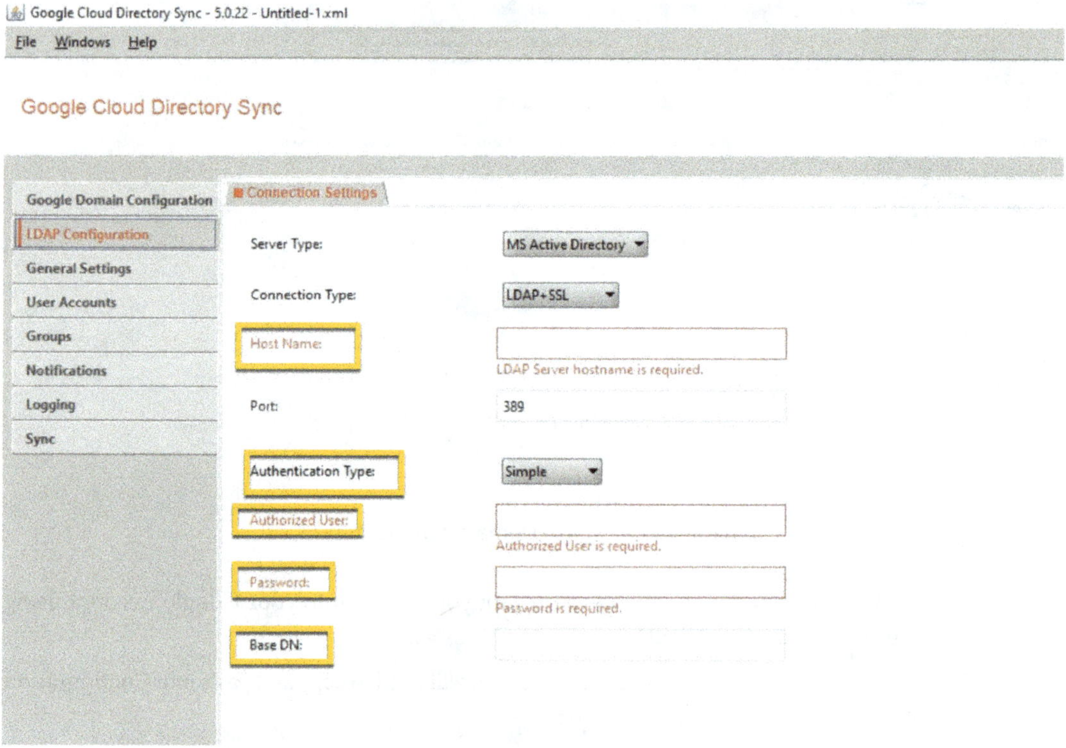

Figure 5.13 – LDAP configuration

The next few steps are for you to specify what you want to synchronize. Specify inclusions, exclusions, and any exceptions in the settings.

11. On the **Licenses** page, you can specify the license information, add the Google product, and specify the SKU and product.

> **Note**
>
> For further information on licenses, refer to this page: `https://packt.link/KbYfK`.

12. Next, you can configure your notification settings. Every time data is synchronized, GCDS will send an email.

13. Configure logging based on the detail you need.

14. Finally, verify your sync; at this stage, Configuration Manager will simulate and test the sync, and if there are any failures, it will ask you to address them. Once the simulation is successful, Configuration Manager will generate a report and you can then select **Sync and apply**.

This concludes the steps required to configure the GCDS tool. This lets you connect, configure, and synchronize your LDAP directory to Google Cloud Directory. We will now move on to the next section to see how user provisioning works.

User provisioning in Cloud Identity

Google Cloud requires users and groups to be pre-provisioned in Cloud Identity. There are multiple options available to help you do so. The following screenshot shows the various options, and we will briefly cover which options are recommended and why:

Method	Effort	Staff involved	Notes
Manual Provisioning	High	Google Admin	Easiest method, but not scalable
CSV Upload via Google Admin	Medium	Google Admin	More flexibility, but not scalable
Google Cloud Directory Sync (GCDS)	Medium	LDAP Admin	Integrates with LDAP, scalable, requires no programming
Third-Party Tools (Okta, Ping, etc.)	Medium	LDAP Admin	Scalable, may incur additional cost
Admin SDK Directory API	High	LDAP Admin Development Staff	Scalable, flexible, requires in-depth programming

Figure 5.14 – User provisioning options in Google Cloud Identity

Based on the methods listed in *Figure 5.14*, you can choose to manually add users to Cloud Identity as it's an easy option and requires little effort if you only have 5-10 users to add. The effort required increases if you have more users to add.

The next option is to use a CSV file where you can upload users in bulk; this is more convenient as you can add more users at once. You will, however, need to prepare your CSV file by listing the users' details, such as first name, last name, email address, password, and org path. Listing passwords in CSV files is not recommended, so many organizations choose not to select this option.

The third option is configuring Active Directory Federation using GCDS, which we discussed in detail in the previous section. The effort required is not low as it does require following a few steps, but once established, it's a very scalable and secure way to provision/de-provision users on Google Cloud Identity.

Another option, which many organizations choose, is to select a third-party provisioning solution that can be federated with Google Cloud Identity. This is very similar to using GCDS but offers a commercial third-party product. It's a scalable method but it does have costs involved.

The following architecture is a very common deployment scenario, where Google Cloud Identity is used to federate with either GCDS or a third-party IdP such as Okta or Ping Identity.

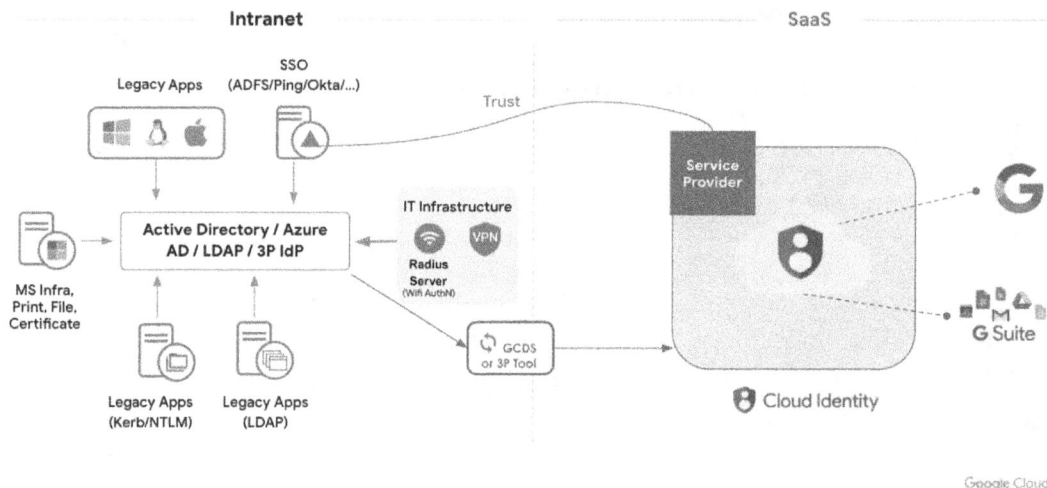

Figure 5.15 – Third party as an IdP

In the next section, we will look at how you can use Cloud Identity and federation to manage the user lifecycle.

Automating user lifecycle management with Cloud Identity as the IdP

User provisioning and de-provisioning in larger enterprises can become very complex. Users leaving the organization or moving within the organization can lead to changes in the scope of what applications a user has access to. In order to address this, Google Cloud Identity provides a catalog of automated provisioning connectors between third-party apps and Cloud Identity. In the *SAML-based SSO* section, we looked at how, by using Cloud Identity and SAML-based SSO, you can use more than 300 pre-configured applications and, if required, create custom applications as well. This option is typically used when Cloud Identity is your IdP and you want to integrate third-party apps with Cloud Identity. Let us look at this briefly.

Once your SSO using SAML has been configured, you can enable fully automated user provisioning, such as creating, deleting, or modifying a user's identity across cloud apps. Cloud Identity administrators can be configured to synchronize the subset of users and automate the entire user lifecycle management process, which further leads to a great user experience.

Let's look at an example of automated user provisioning flow. In *Figure 5.16*, we see an example of a user, Bob, who joins an organization. Even before the user's first day, the admin adds Bob to Cloud Identity as a user and adds him to the relevant organization. This gives Bob access to all the apps that particular organization's members have access to.

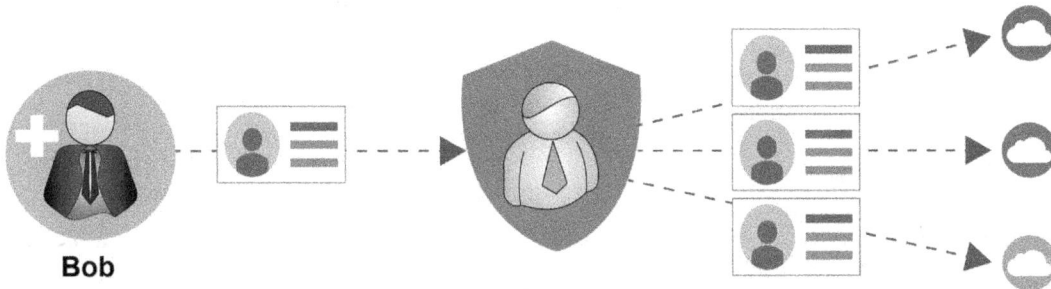

Figure 5.16 – Cloud Identity replicates Bob's identity to all allowed cloud apps

In *Figure 5.17* we see how Bob is able to sign in to all cloud apps using SSO.

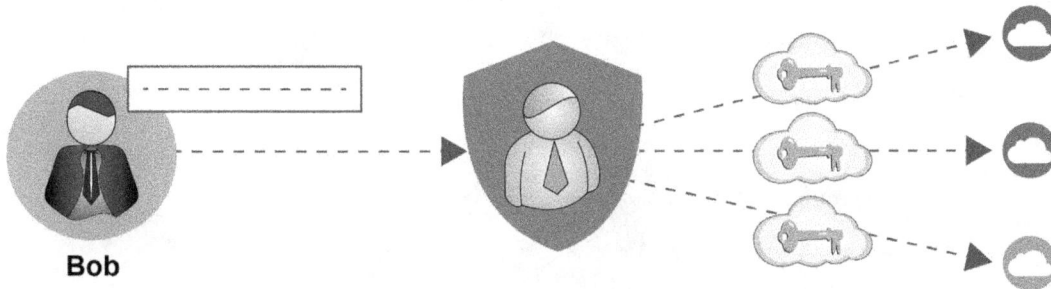

Figure 5.17 – On Bob's first day, he can sign in to all cloud apps using SSO

We have now covered the process of automating user lifecycle management. This helps large organizations to automatically provision and de-provision users and give them the right level of access to business applications. Let us now look at some of the APIs that are used by third-party products to manage users and groups in Cloud Identity.

Administering user accounts and groups programmatically

User and group accounts in Cloud Identity can be managed via the Directory API. This REST API is part of the Admin SDK. The following are a couple of the provisioning use cases that you can implement using this API. In fact, the third-party apps that we discussed in the previous section use this API:

- Creating and managing users and adding administrators
- Creating and managing groups and group memberships

The API can be accessed from this page: `https://packt.link/w0lbi`.

Some of the operations that the API allows you to do are as follows:

- User lifecycle operations:

  - Creating a user
  - Updating a user
  - Deleting a user
  - Granting an administrator role
  - Searching users
  - Adding a relationship between two user accounts, for example, setting manager-employee relations

- Group lifecycle operations:

  - Creating a group
  - Updating a group
  - Adding a group alias
  - Searching groups
  - Searching all groups for a member
  - Deleting a group

- Group membership operations:

  - Adding a member to a group
  - Updating a group membership
  - Retrieving a group's members
  - Deleting membership

This concludes our section covering the Directory API.

Summary

In this chapter, we covered Google Cloud Identity. We looked at what services and features are available and how to design and build your authentication strategy on Google Cloud using Cloud Identity. The topics covered included domain setup, super administrator best practices, account security, how to enforce 2SV, how to configure user security settings, session management, how to configure SSO using SAML, how to use GCDS to federate AD with Cloud Identity, user and group provisioning, automated user lifecycle management, identity federation, and SSO.

In the next chapter, we will cover Google Cloud Identity and Access Management, looking at the authorization aspect of Google Cloud.

Further reading

For more information on Google Cloud Identity, refer to the following links:

- Difference between Cloud Identity Free and Premium: `https://packt.link/oKxkl`

- The Google security center: `https://packt.link/f5yss`

- Active Directory user account provisioning: `https://packt.link/pWIUp`

- Automated user provisioning and deprovisioning: `https://packt.link/Rsnr2`

- Active Directory single sign-on: `https://packt.link/4e85k`

- Best practices for planning accounts and organizations: `https://packt.link/j8eod`

- Best practices for federating Google Cloud with an external identity provider: `https://packt.link/24owJ`

- GCDS FAQ: `https://packt.link/EcGwY`

- Google Cloud Identity training: `https://packt.link/TABqf`

- Google Cloud Identity license information: `https://packt.link/j03kr`

6

Google Cloud Identity and Access Management

In this chapter, we will explore Google Cloud **Identity and Access Management** (**IAM**), an essential service to comprehend for the exam. With IAM, you can authorize cloud services, and assign appropriate access to users and applications. Acquiring a good understanding of IAM is crucial to ensure that your cloud implementation follows the principle of least privilege, restricting access to only what is necessary.

In this chapter, we will cover the following topics:

- Overview of IAM
- IAM roles and permissions
- Service accounts
- IAM policy bindings
- IAM conditions
- Cloud Storage, IAM, and ACLs
- Logging and IAM APIs

Overview of IAM

In the previous chapter, we discussed Cloud Identity and its role in authentication, user management, and device management in Google Cloud and Google Workspace. Now, let us explore IAM, which focuses on authorization in Google Cloud. Authorization is a key principle of cloud computing, addressing various requirements and ensuring secure access to resources. Some of the problems it solves are the following:

- How do I grant access to people and workloads?
- How do I provide time-bound access?

- How do I create service accounts with the least privilege?

- How do I enable services in a particular project but not others?

- How do I grant just the right access to users?

- How do I operate in multi-cloud environments?

- How do I find over-provisioned access?

- How do I troubleshoot access issues?

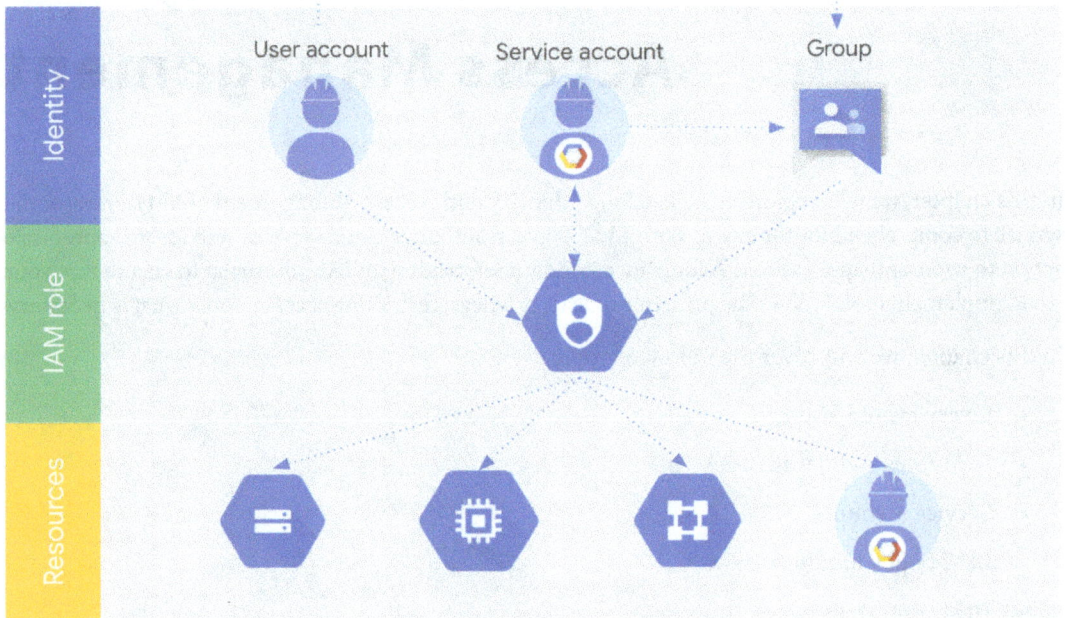

Figure 6.1 – IAM overview

In *Figure 6.1*, you can see how IAM works on the principle of *who* (identity) has *what* access (role) to *which* resource. The principal entity is usually a user, group, or service account. However, there are other principals, as explained later. The role is a set of fine-grained permissions. Permissions are predefined actions you can take on a particular resource (for example, BigQuery). Permissions for a given resource are fixed and cannot be created. We will talk about service accounts later in this chapter. At this point, the thing to remember is a service account represents a service or application identity in Google Cloud. It is one of the most important distinctions in how Google Cloud handles permissions for workloads.

In Cloud IAM, the following principals are supported:

- **Google account (a Gmail account is a form of Google account)**: Individuals who use a personal Google cloud have a Google account. This could be a developer, an administrator, or anyone else who works with the service. A person can be identified by any email address that is linked to a Google account. This can be gmail.com or any other domain.

- **Service account**: A service account is an identity for an application or VM instance instead of a person. Service accounts are principals as well as resources. We will see more on this later.

- **Google group**: A Google group is a group of Google accounts and service accounts. There is a unique email address for each Google group. Google groups provide a convenient way to apply IAM policies to a group of individuals. Instead of individually managing access controls for each person, you can apply or modify access controls for an entire group simultaneously. Additionally, you can easily add or remove members from a Google group, eliminating the need to modify IAM policies for user additions or removals.

- **Google Workspace account**: A Google Workspace account is a Google account linked to your organization-specific Google Workspace. It has your business email address. Google Workspace contains Google apps such as Docs, Slides, and Sheets in addition to a host of other apps that you may have licensed.

- **Cloud Identity domain**: Cloud Identity domains are like a Google Workspace account but without any of the Google apps. If your organization does not use Google Workspace, then you typically get a free edition of Cloud Identity with Google Cloud. Note that there are features that only a premium edition of Cloud Identity can offer. Refer to Google support documentation for a comparison between free and premium editions.

- **All authenticated users**: allAuthenticatedUsers is a unique identifier for all service accounts and all people on the internet who have signed in with their Google account, that is, *any authenticated Google Identity*. People who do not have a Google Workspace account or Cloud Identity domain can still use this identifier. For example, they can use their personal Gmail accounts. Users who have not been authenticated, such as anonymous visitors, are not on the list. Some types of resources do not work with this type of principal.

- **All users**: The default value is allUsers, which is a unique identifier that represents everyone who is on the internet, whether they are authenticated or not. Some types of resources do not work with this type of principal.

Now that you understand the types of principals, let us look at how they get access to cloud resources.

IAM roles and permissions

The *role* is a grouping of permissions in Google Cloud. Permissions cannot be granted to principals directly.

There are three types of roles possible within IAM:

- Basic roles or legacy roles
- Predefined roles
- Custom roles

Basic roles

There are three basic roles that exist in IAM. These are considered legacy now and were introduced prior to IAM:

- **Viewer**: Permissions for read-only actions that do not affect the state, such as viewing (but not modifying) existing resources or data

- **Editor**: All Viewer permissions, plus permissions for actions that modify state, such as changing existing resources

- **Owner**: All Editor permissions and the ability to manage roles and permissions for a project and all resources within the project

It is important to note that the basic roles are meant to make you productive in no time but are not recommended for production usage. In particular, the Editor and Owner roles grant a lot of permissions under the cover and will create over-permissive access in your Google Cloud environment. Enterprises usually should figure out a custom owner role that has just the right permissions to do the job and is not overly restrictive.

Predefined roles

IAM provides several service-specific predefined roles that are created by Google Cloud for easy assignment. These roles are usually product- or service-level roles based on a predefined set of permissions, for example, BigQuery Data Viewer. These roles are maintained by Google. In other words, any changes in permissions (addition/deprecation) are taken care of by Google, hence it is not recommended to create custom roles for services.

At any level of the resource hierarchy, you can grant the same user various roles. For instance, the same user can have the roles of Compute Network Admin and Logs Viewer on a project and simultaneously also have the role of BigQuery Editor on a particular BigQuery dataset within that project.

Now that you understand what predefined roles are, let us look at how to choose a predefined role for your workload. We will take the example of BigQuery roles.

Choosing predefined roles

There are a lot of predefined roles in IAM. Usually, these roles are tailored for a given cloud service. Let us take the example of BigQuery. Here are the predefined roles supplied by Google for BigQuery:

- BigQuery Admin
- BigQuery Connection Admin
- BigQuery Connection User
- BigQuery Data Editor
- BigQuery Data Owner
- BigQuery Data Viewer
- BigQuery Filtered Data Viewer
- BigQuery Job User
- BigQuery Metadata Viewer
- BigQuery Read Session User
- BigQuery Resource Admin
- BigQuery Resource Editor
- BigQuery Resource Viewer
- BigQuery User

How do you decide which predefined role to use? Consider the following steps:

1. Identify the necessary permissions.
2. Find the role/s that contain the permissions.
3. Choose the most appropriate roles *matching* the permissions. This could be one role or multiple roles making sure *least privileges* are granted.
4. Decide at which *level* of the resource hierarchy to grant the role.
5. Grant the role to a principal, and use conditions if needed.

It is also important to understand at what *level* (resource/project/folder/organization) the role should be granted to the principal. We make this point often since it is important to know the difference, as it impacts the ability of what the user can do.

Let us take an example of the *BigQuery User* role. Review the *permissions* it contains:

- `bigquery.bireservations.get`
- `bigquery.capacityComitments.get`

- `bigquery.capacityComitments.list`
- `bigquery.config.get`
- `bigquery.datasets.create`
- `bigquery.datasets.get`
- `bigquery.datasets.getIamPolicy`
- `bigquery.jobs.create`
- `bigquery.jobs.list`
- `bigquery.models.list`
- `bigquery.readsessions.*`
- `bigquery.reservationAssignments.list`
- `bigquery.reservationAssignments.search`
- `bigquery.reservations.get`
- `bigquery.reservations.list`
- `bigquery.routines.list`
- `bigquery.savedqueries.get`
- `bigquery.savedqueries.list`
- `bigquery.tables.list`
- `bigquery.transfers.get`
- `resourcemanager.projects.get`
- `resourcemanager.projects.list`

When you assign the *BigQuery User* role to a project or dataset, the following happens:

- This role allows the creation of a new dataset in a given project
- This role allows the principal to read the dataset's metadata and list the tables in that dataset
- This role allows the principal to run BigQuery tasks and SQL queries within the project
- This role also gives the principal the ability to list their own jobs and cancel the jobs they created
- This role also grants the BigQuery Data Owner role (`roles/bigquery.dataOwner`) to those who create new datasets within the project

Now that you understand how predefined roles work, let us look at some best practices for choosing a predefined role.

Best practices for predefined roles

Not every task requires a comprehensive list of permissions. Instead, prioritize the relevant permissions needed for the specific task. If a predefined role includes the required permissions, it is likely to include other permissions as well. Take this opportunity to identify the most impactful permissions needed. In general, fewer predefined roles provide more potent permissions.

The following types of IAM permissions are *considered* powerful:

- Resource creation and deletion permissions
- Permissions to gain access to confidential information, such as encryption keys or **Personal Identifiable Information (PII)**
- Permissions to configure a resource's IAM policy
- The ability to make changes to organizational structures, folders, and projects
- Permission to assign IAM policies

Compare these to the following permissions, which are less powerful:

- Resource listing permissions
- Access rights to non-sensitive data
- The ability to change settings that provide negligible risk, such as Compute Engine virtual machine instances' minimum CPU platform

Once you have discovered the required permissions, compile a list of roles that might be a good fit.

To assign permissions to a single Google Cloud service, you must identify as many specified roles as possible. For example, it is unlikely that a single specified role will contain the relevant permissions for both services if a principal needs to access Cloud Storage and administer Cloud SQL databases. If such a role exists, it may have unrelated permissions. Choosing a specific role that satisfies the requirements for Cloud Storage access and another one with Cloud SQL permissions can help reduce risk.

Let us look at some of the best practices for role assignments.

Assigning roles to resources

Select where you need to grant the predefined roles in the resource hierarchy. Here are a few points to consider:

- You can grant roles on lower-level resources (for example, a Compute Engine VM or a Cloud Storage bucket) if you just need access to them.
- To allow access to a project, folder, or organization's resources, grant the appropriate roles at that level. You can use IAM conditions to provide a role solely on a particular resource in the project, folder, or organization.

- You can use tags to define IAM policies for cloud services that support tags. Do not confuse labels and tags. Tags are an IAM construct and are defined at an organization level.

Let us take an example to demonstrate this.

If the principal needs access to a single Cloud Spanner database but several VM instances, you want to choose to grant the *Cloud Spanner admin* role on the database and the *Compute Admin* role on the project (in addition to the *Service Account User* role since some compute instances are preconfigured to use a service account).

You may verify which resources the principal can access and troubleshoot access difficulties using the IAM Policy Analyzer and Policy Troubleshooter (part of the Policy Intelligence tools, which are beyond the scope of this book).

You may have granted fewer permissions than the principal requires if the principal is unable to complete their tasks despite having the intended privileges on the relevant resources. The next step is to add more rights to the list, then search for predefined roles that have those permissions and pick the best ones. In some cases, you will have no choice but to create a custom role.

So far, we have looked at what predefined roles are and the best practices surrounding their assignment. Now let us look at custom roles.

Custom roles

In some instances, the predefined roles do not solve the purpose, or you would want to scale down the permissions the principal might get to a more appropriate level based on your requirements. In that case, you can create custom roles. The IAM Role Recommender (covered as part of IAM Policy Intelligence) also provides recommendations to create custom roles based on usage patterns. Please note that some IAM permissions (labeled TESTING and NOT_SUPPORTED) are not supported in custom roles. In fact, always use permissions with the SUPPORTED label.

Consider the following points while creating custom roles:

- Permissions that are only available in folders or organizations cannot be included in a custom role created at the project level. Because a project cannot contain other projects, for example, the resourcemanager.organizations.get permission cannot be used in a custom role at the project level; as a result, the permission is only applicable at the folder or organization level.

- If you create a custom role for a certain project or organization, you can only use that role there. Individuals in other projects and organizations, and resources within them, cannot be granted that role.

You will be able to manage all your organization's custom roles when you have the *Role Administrator* role.

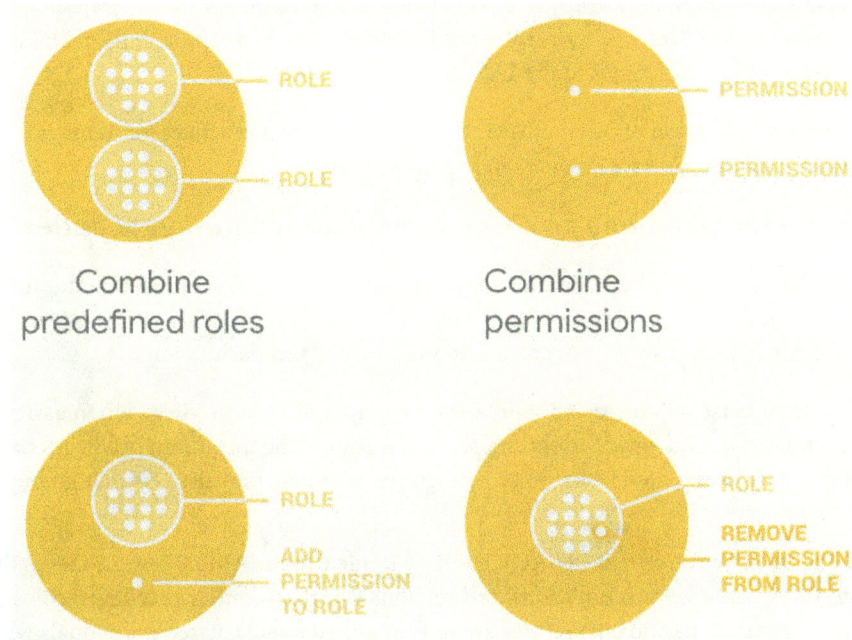

Figure 6.2 – IAM—custom roles

Figure 6.2 shows a few ways you can create custom roles:

- By combining predefined roles
- By combining permissions of predefined roles
- By combining a predefined role and adding additional permissions
- Starting with a predefined role but removing some permissions from that role

Lifecycle of a custom role

Consider the following permissions dependencies while creating custom roles:

- A predefined role or many predefined roles may exist for the service before you decide to establish your own custom role.
- TESTING and NOT_SUPPORTED permissions are ineligible for inclusion within a custom role.
- Even if a service's API is enabled, you may not be able to see or use certain permissions in a custom role. Consider checking out the Google Cloud documentation for custom role permissions.

- You can only use some permissions if you combine them with another related one. It is necessary to employ the *read-modify-write* permission while changing an IAM policy, for example. You will also need the `getIAMPolicy` permission for that service in addition to the `setIAMPolicy` permission to make changes to the IAM policy.

This concludes our discussion of roles in IAM. We will go over best practices for managing privileged roles and then move on to *service accounts* in the next section.

Best practices for managing privileged roles and separation of duties

Managing privileged roles and ensuring the separation of duties is crucial for maintaining a secure and compliant environment in Google Cloud. Here are some best practices for managing privileged roles and implementing separation of duties using IAM roles and permissions:

- **Principle of least privilege**: Adhere to the principle of least privilege when assigning roles and permissions. Only grant users and service accounts the minimum privileges necessary to perform their designated tasks. Avoid assigning excessive permissions that go beyond their job requirements.

- **Role-Based Access Control (RBAC)**: Utilize Google Cloud IAM's RBAC model to define and assign roles based on job functions and responsibilities. Identify privileged roles that have elevated permissions and ensure they are only assigned to authorized individuals who require those privileges for their specific tasks.

- **Segregation of duties**: Implement segregation of duties to prevent conflicts of interest and reduce the risk of abuse or unauthorized actions. Separate critical functions and assign them to different individuals or teams. This ensures that no single person has complete control over sensitive operations.

- **Predefined roles**: Leverage predefined roles provided by Google Cloud IAM. These roles are designed with specific responsibilities and permissions, making it easier to assign appropriate privileges based on common use cases. Regularly review and update roles to align with changes in job functions and responsibilities.

- **Custom roles**: Create custom roles when predefined roles do not meet your specific requirements. This allows for fine-grained control over permissions and ensures that privileged roles are tailored to your organization's needs. Exercise caution when defining custom roles and regularly review and audit them.

- **Role hierarchy**: Establish a role hierarchy to manage privileged roles effectively. Consider creating a tiered structure where higher-level roles inherit permissions from lower-level roles. This ensures a logical and controlled flow of permissions and allows for easier management of access control.

- **Dual control and approval processes**: Implement dual control mechanisms and approval processes for critical actions or changes that require privileged access. This involves requiring multiple authorized individuals to review and approve such actions, reducing the risk of unauthorized or accidental actions.

- **Regular reviews and audits**: Conduct regular reviews and audits of privileged roles and their assigned permissions. Validate that the permissions assigned are still necessary and appropriate. Remove any unnecessary or outdated permissions and ensure that roles align with current job functions and responsibilities.

- **Monitoring and logging**: Implement robust monitoring and logging mechanisms to track privileged activities and detect any unusual or unauthorized actions. Enable the logging of IAM role changes, permission modifications, and administrative activities to establish an audit trail and facilitate incident response if needed.

- **Continuous Education and Awareness**: Provide ongoing education and training to privileged users, administrators, and stakeholders regarding the importance of role management, separation of duties, and best practices in access control. Foster a culture of security awareness and accountability within your organization.

By implementing these best practices, organizations can effectively manage privileged roles, enforce separation of duties, and maintain a secure and compliant environment in Google Cloud. Regular reviews, defined processes, and continuous monitoring help ensure that access privileges remain aligned with business requirements and minimize the risk of unauthorized access or malicious actions.

Policy binding

IAM policy binding is how you assign roles to principals for them to be able to act on resources. The binding can exist at the resource level (not all resources may support this), project level, folder level, or organization node level. It is important to understand at what level the binding should be created to achieve the least privileged access while fulfilling business goals.

The higher in the Google Cloud resource hierarchy the binding is created, the larger the effect it has on downstream resources such as folders, projects, and actual workloads. For this reason, be careful where you define your IAM policy binding. We will see more on IAM policy binding later, in the *IAM policy bindings* section.

Service accounts

Google Cloud service accounts are a critical part of the platform. A cloud resource or workload uses a specific type of account. To make API calls, an application deployed (for example, Compute Engine, App Engine, or GKE) or a workload (Dataproc, Dataflow, and so on) utilizes service accounts. Using a service account as an identity, the application can access cloud resources (either in the same or a different project) based on the role it has been assigned.

There are some main differences between a service account and a user account:

- Service accounts have no ability to log in to the Cloud console like a normal user.

- Public and private RSA key pairs are used to authenticate the service account and sign the API request.

- A service account can be impersonated by a human or another service account.

- Service accounts are not visible in Cloud Identity because they belong to the Google Cloud managed domain. While service accounts can be added to a Google group, it is not recommended since groups are meant for specific purposes that service accounts don't fit into.

- A service account is not created in your Google Workspace domain. They are not under the control of your Google Workspace and Cloud Identity administrators. They live in Google Cloud and should be managed there.

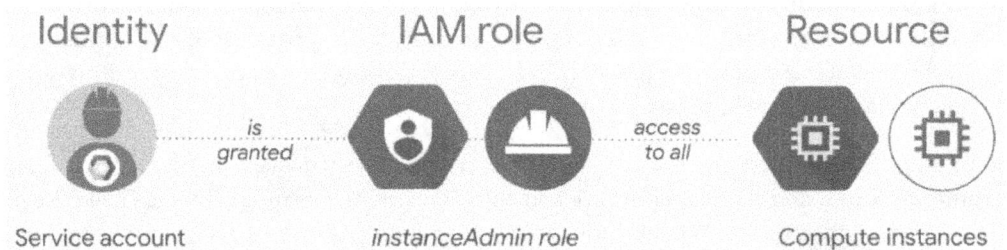

Figure 6.3 – Service account and resource

As depicted in *Figure 6.3*, service accounts get access to perform actions on a Google Cloud resource via an IAM role, just like users. Now we will see how to manage the lifecycle of service accounts.

Creating a service account

Service accounts can be created under the **IAM | Service accounts** menu in the Cloud console. Service accounts can also be created using gcloud, REST APIs, or client libraries.

To create a service account, the user should have the *Service Account Admin* role (`roles/iam.serviceAccountAdmin`).

It is recommended to wait for a minimum of 60 seconds before you use the service account post creation.

Disabling a service account

You can disable a service account either by using the Cloud console, *gcloud*, or APIs. However, note that if a resource is using a service account, after disabling it the resource can no longer access Google Cloud resources.

Deleting a service account

If a service account is deleted, its role bindings are not instantly eliminated; they are automatically purged from the system within 60 days. Do not include deleted service accounts in your quota. It is best practice to disable a service account before deleting it to make sure your production workloads are not negatively impacted.

Undeleting a service account

You can use the `undelete gcloud` command to undelete a deleted service account in some cases if it meets the following criteria:

- The service account was deleted less than 30 days ago
- There is no existing service account with the same name as the deleted service account

You will need the numeric ID of the service account to undelete it.

Now that we have looked at what service accounts are, let us look at how to use them. To be able to use a service account, you need a service account key or workload identity federation.

Service account keys

When you create a service account key, you are creating a private-public key pair. The public key is stored within Google Cloud, and you get a private part of that key pair. This is how you establish the identity of the service account. The key is used to authenticate that service account to Google Cloud from outside of Google Cloud. Within Google Cloud, you do not need keys (except for GKE). These keys need to be stored securely as leakage of the key in the wrong hands could cause unauthorized access to your Google Cloud environment. Crypto mining is one of the biggest misuses of such leaked keys.

Google Cloud, however, has introduced a more secure access method called **Workload Identity Federation** (**WIF**). WIF lets your workloads access resources directly, using a short-lived access token, and eliminates the maintenance and security burden associated with service account keys. WIF may be suitable in some scenarios such as multi-cloud authentication (for example, calling Google Cloud APIs from AWS or Azure) or, in some cases, hybrid cloud workloads. You will see more details on this in the *Configuring Workload Identity Federation using Okta* section.

Here is a decision tree that you can use to determine when you need to generate service account keys.

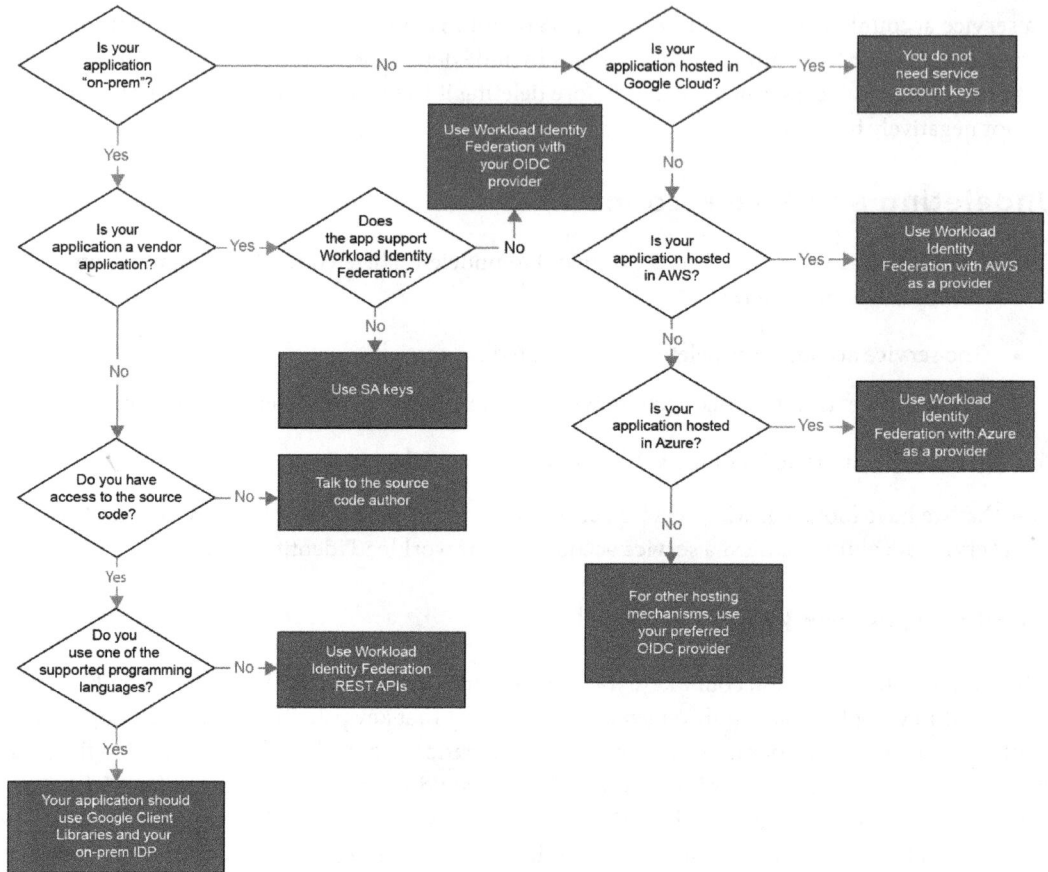

Figure 6.4 – Decision tree for service account keys

As you can see in *Figure 6.4*, you can select the right way to connect to Google Cloud APIs from hybrid workloads in a secure way. We recommend incorporating this decision tree in your organization process for development teams to refer to. Now, let us look at how to manage the lifecycle of service account keys.

Creating a service account key

Service account keys can be generated through the Cloud console, gcloud, using the APIs, or one of the client libraries. The key is either in the format of JSON or PKCS#12 (P12 for backward compatibility).

> **Note**
> There is a hard limit of 10 keys per service account. If you generate more than 10, the oldest key becomes invalid.

Keys for service accounts do not automatically expire. Using **Resource Settings**, you may set the validity period for a service account key. However, the certification exam may not reflect this new feature.

The service account JSON key looks like this:

```
{
  "type": "service_account",
  "project_id": "project-id",
  "private_key_id": "key-id",
  "private_key": "-----BEGIN PRIVATE KEY-----\private-key\n-----END
PRIVATE KEY-----\n",
  "client_email": " prod-service-account@project-id.iam.
gserviceaccount.com ",
  "client_id": "client-id",
  "auth_uri": "https://accounts.google.com/o/oauth2/auth",
  "token_uri": "https://accounts.google.com/o/oauth2/token",
  "auth_provider_x509_cert_url": "https://www.googleapis.com/oauth2/
v1/certs",
  "client_x509_cert_url": "https://www.googleapis.com/robot/v1/
metadata/x509/service-account-email"
}
```

In addition to creating a service account key, you can also upload the public part of your service account key to use with your workloads (thus bringing your own service account key to the cloud). Let us look at how to do this.

Bringing your own key to Google Cloud

Google Cloud allows you to bring your own private key. After creating a public-private key pair outside of Google Cloud, you will upload the public key portion of the key pair to the given service account.

For example, the following section generates a 2048-bit RSA key pair and wraps the public key in a self-signed certificate that is valid for 365 days. The following steps will also generate the service account JSON file for you:

1. Generate a private key:

    ```
    PROJECT_ID=$(gcloud config get-value project)
    SV_ACCT_EMAIL=sa-account-name@${PROJECT_ID}.iam.gserviceaccount.
    com
    SV_ACCT_ID=$(gcloud iam service-accounts \
            describe $SV_ACCT_EMAIL \
    ```

```
      --format 'value(uniqueId)')
PRIVATE_KEY=$(openssl genrsa 2048)
```

2. Create a self-signed certificate:

```
openssl req -x509 -new \
  -key - \
  -subj /CN=customer@acme.com \
  -out csr.pem <<< $PRIVATE_KEY

openssl x509 \
  -in csr.pem \
  -signkey - \
  -days 365 \
  -out certificate.pem <<< $PRIVATE_KEY
```

3. Upload the public part of the key to Google Cloud:

```
gcloud iam service-accounts keys \
  upload certificate.pem \
  --iam-account $SV_ACCT_EMAIL \
  --format json > uploaded.json
PRIVATE_KEY_ID=$(jq -r .name uploaded.json | \
  awk -F/ '{print $NF}')
```

4. Generate the service account key file using the private part of the key. Look at the following code snippet:

```
touch look-no-keys.json
chmod 0600 look-no-keys.json
jq -n \
  --arg PRIVATE_KEY "$PRIVATE_KEY" \
  --arg PROJECT_ID $PROJECT_ID \
  --arg SV_ACCT_EMAIL $SV_ACCT_EMAIL \
  --arg SV_ACCT_ID $SV_ACCT_ID \
  --arg PRIVATE_KEY_ID $PRIVATE_KEY_ID \
  '{
  "type": "service_account",
  "project_id": $PROJECT_ID,
  "private_key_id": $PRIVATE_KEY_ID,
  "private_key": $PRIVATE_KEY,
  "client_email": $SV_ACCT_EMAIL,
  "client_id": $SV_ACCT_ID,
  "auth_uri": "https://accounts.google.com/o/oauth2/auth",
  "token_uri": "https://oauth2.googleapis.com/token",
```

```
    "auth_provider_x509_cert_url": "https://www.googleapis.com/
oauth2/v1/certs",
    "client_x509_cert_url": @uri "https://www.googleapis.com/
robot/v1/metadata/x509/\($SV_ACCT_EMAIL)"
}' > sa-key.json
```

This should produce the `sa-key.json` key file, which you can use in your code.

Now that we have seen how to generate a service account key, let us look at some of the best practices associated with service account keys.

Best practices when managing service account keys

As a Google Cloud security practitioner, it is critical that you securely manage the key that grants access to your service account. Here are a few things to keep in mind:

- Determine whether you truly need to use service account keys or whether your application could use a more secure method such as WIF.

- The service accounts created for development purposes shouldn't have access to production resources.

- Have a procedure to rotate your service account keys. Rotate them often—daily, if possible—in development environments.

- Developers should download a new key every day, and enable this by developing a daily key rotation mechanism.

- You can develop an audit process by monitoring the usage of the service account keys. The `serviceAccount.keys.list()` API method will allow you to find all the keys associated with a given service account. You can match key IDs with audit logs. Any suspicious activity can be alerted for further investigation.

- Local development should always be done using the client libraries and Google Application Credentials.

- Make it impossible for developers to upload their private keys to external code repositories. There are several ways to achieve this, as we will see in the latter part of this chapter.

- Finally, perform periodic key scans on external repositories and correct any issues that are discovered. There are commercial products available on the market that will alert you to key leakage. Security Command Center Premium, a native Google Cloud offering, also has this capability. More on this in *Chapter 14, Security Command Center*.

Key rotation is one of the best practices we have mentioned. Now let us see how to do this.

Key rotation

Once you have conducted proper research and determined the necessity of using service account keys, it is crucial to prioritize regular rotation of the keys for development purposes. Implementing a key rotation process is essential to minimize the risk of any potential leaks or unauthorized access. The following outlines a recommended approach for effectively rotating service account keys:

1. Keyrotator is a simple CLI tool written in Python that you can use as is or as the basis for a service account rotation process. Run it as a cron job on an admin instance, say, at midnight, and write the new key to Cloud Storage for developers to download in the morning.

2. Create a dedicated project setup for shared resources.

3. Create a bucket in the dedicated project; do *NOT* make it publicly accessible.

4. Create a group for the developers who need to download the new daily key.

5. For additional security, you can have each developer use their own key. This will require you to provision a storage bucket for each developer in the project. This will also reduce the risk of non-repudiation.

6. Grant read access to the bucket using IAM by granting the `storage.objectViewer` role to your developer group for the project with the storage bucket.

A common issue in developing a process for key rotation is accidentally committing the key to the source repository. We will take an example of GitHub and show how to detect a key that has been committed to GitHub.

Preventing committing keys to external source code repositories

Your CI/CD pipeline should have the ability to detect a key being pushed to Git. If a key is found, the push should fail. A tool called `git secrets` can be used for this purpose. It will be invoked automatically when you run the `git commit` command.

You will need to configure `git secrets` to check for patterns that match the service account key file. For example, you can use the following command to detect private keys:

```
git secrets --add 'private_key'
git secrets --add 'private_key_id'
```

Now, when you try to run `git commit` and it detects these two keywords, you will receive an error message and be unable to do the commit unless you remove the key file.

Scanning external repositories for keys

There are various commercial products available that monitor service account key leakage in public source repositories. We will look at an open source tool called Trufflehog that you can use to scan your *private* Git repository.

Trufflehog is an open source tool you can use with `git secrets`. You can find it at `https://packt.link/uoyAx`. Trufflehog uses Shannon entropy to look through a repo's history for secrets. It does this by looking at the amount of entropy in the data.

Here is how you can use Trufflehog:

```
trufflehog git https://github.com/repot/trufflehog-testing
```

The output looks like this when it finds a service account key in the GitHub repo:

```
🐷🔍🐷  TruffleHog. Unearth your secrets. 🐷🔍🐷
Found verified result 🐷🔍
Detector Type: GCP
Decoder Type: PLAIN
Raw result: svc-acct-key-test@test-project-1231232.iam.
gserviceaccount.com
Repository: https://github.com/repo
Timestamp: 2022-11-04 09:41:04 -0700 PDT
Line: 6
Commit: 147d9d9e85555965f28f80cd45d1567c9947b98e
File: sa-key.json
Email: jdoe <jdoe@acme.com>

Found unverified result 🐷🔍?

Detector Type: PrivateKey

Decoder Type: PLAIN
```

As you can see, Trufflehog has found a private key in the Git repository. It also shows the email of the committer that committed the key.

So far, we have seen ways of managing security around service account keys. We will move on to understand a few more features of service accounts, such as how to create short-lived credentials.

Service account impersonation

One of the key features of IAM is that you can impersonate a service account. Impersonation is the ability to let other users and resources *act like* the service account. We will look at that later in the section:

- **Service Account User**: This role has the `iam.serviceAccounts.actAs` permission, which allows principals to access all the resources that the service account can access through their own account. Suppose the principal is a user and has the *Service Account User* role. The principal can then impersonate the service account to set up Cloud SQL on that service account's project.

  This role also lets people link a service account to a resource. However, this will not allow the principal to create a short-term OAuth token for the service accounts or use the Google Cloud CLI to impersonate service accounts. If you would like that ability, then you need to have the *Service Account Token Creator* role.

- **Service Account Token Creator**: This allows principals to impersonate service accounts to create OAuth 2.0 access tokens, which you can use to authenticate with Google APIs. It also allows principals to sign **JSON Web Tokens** (**JWTs**) and sign binary blobs so that they can be used for authentication.

  To impersonate service accounts from outside of Google Cloud or from GKE workloads, use the Workload Identity User role.

  There are a couple of considerations when granting impersonation capabilities to principals:

  - Be extra careful when granting the role on a project, folder, or organization. This will allow a principal to act on any service accounts created within that project, folder, or organization. This is *not* a customary practice.

  - Granting the role on a specific service account will allow a principal to act in the place of another user on that account. This is a customary practice.

Now let us see how to enable service account access across projects.

Cross-project service account access

When managing many service accounts in an enterprise environment, it can be managed in a single project. That way, you can provide greater control over service account governance and the lifecycle process, and monitor the activity for any threat vector. This design pattern can be quite useful when you have a project implementing automation or monitoring tasks that span multiple projects and need to have access to them. This requires the ability of a service account from one project to be able to call resources from other projects.

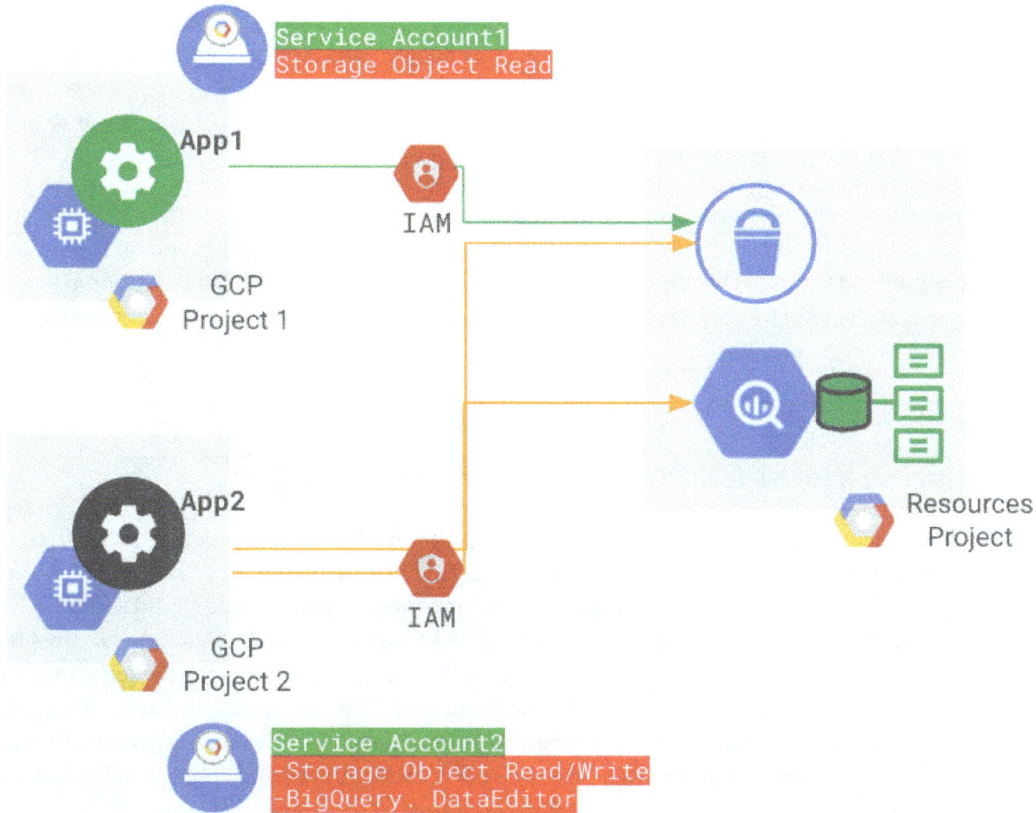

Figure 6.5 – Cross-project service account access

As depicted in *Figure 6.5*, to support this, Google Cloud has introduced the ability to allow access to service accounts to resources across projects. The default behavior is you can create a service account in one project and attach it to a resource in another project. If you do not want this behavior, you can set an organization policy to prevent it.

In the organization policy for the project where your service accounts are located, check the following Boolean constraints:

- Make sure that the `iam.disableCrossProjectServiceAccountUsage` Boolean constraint is not enforced for the project. When this constraint is not enforced, Cloud IAM adds a project lien that prevents the project from being deleted. This lien has the origin `iam.googleapis.com/cross-project-service-accounts`. It is strongly recommended that you do not delete this lien.

- It is recommended that the `iam.restrictCrossProjectServiceAccountLienRemoval` Boolean constraint is enforced for the project. This Boolean constraint ensures that principals can remove the project lien only if they have the `resourcemanager.projects.updateLiens` permission at the organization level. If this constraint is not enforced, principals can remove the project lien if they have this permission at the project level.

Before you take on enabling this feature, it is recommended that you create a proper design and understand all the dependencies that this process may bring across the enterprise, and make sure that you have considered the pros and cons of such a decision. After you update the organization policy, it is strongly recommended to not change it, especially in the production environment, as your Google Cloud resources might not work correctly.

Before we move on to service account activity, let us quickly go over how to configure WIF.

Configuring Workload Identity Federation with Okta

WIF enables access to Google Cloud services without the need for service account keys, thereby allowing access from on-premises or other cloud providers. In the following configuration, we assume the use of a third-party OIDC provider such as Okta for connecting to Google Cloud services. The client credentials flow, as defined in OAuth 2.0 RFC 6749, will be utilized. This flow requires the application to authenticate itself by passing the client ID and client Secret, after which a token is obtained. **Machine-to-Machine (M2M)** applications such as CLIs, batch jobs, or backend services authenticate and authorize as the application itself rather than a user. In such scenarios, typical authentication schemes such as username + password or social logins are not applicable. Instead, the OAuth client credentials flow is used.

> **Note**
> If your application requires a user context, consider using OAuth2.0 to access Google APIs on behalf of the user rather than WIF. You can find the details at `https://packt.link/UycpJ`.

Before we dive deeper into configurations, let us look at the data flow that happens in this scenario:

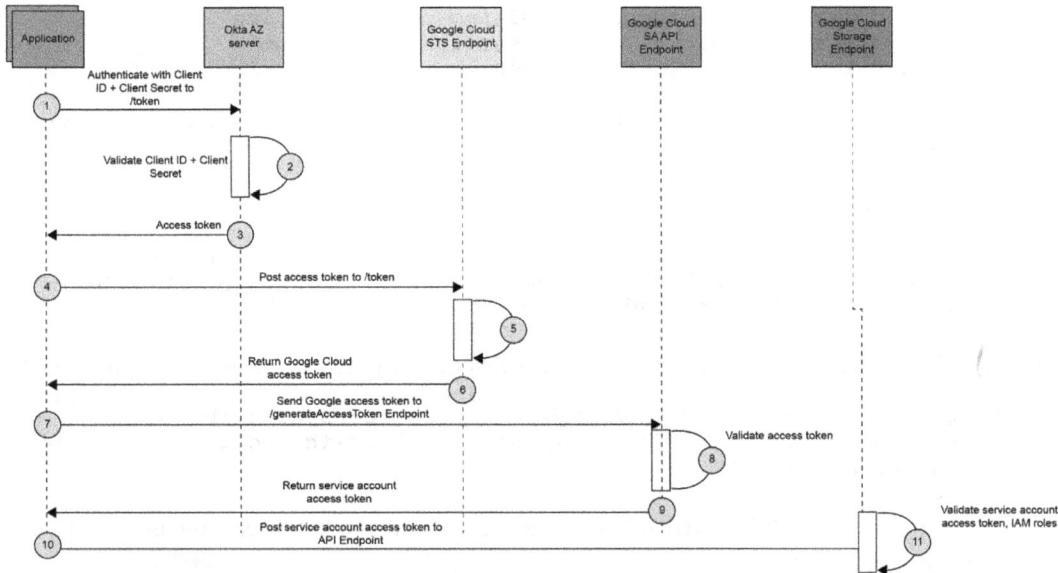

Figure 6.6 – Data flow for WIF with Okta

In the data flow shown in *Figure 6.6*, you will notice a call is made to the Okta authorization server using the client credentials to get an OIDC token. That token is then passed on to two Google Cloud endpoints before an access token can be obtained to call a Google Cloud service. Now let us go over the steps required to configure WIF:

1. Generate client credentials from Okta. Please refer to the Okta documentation on how to generate client credentials if you are not familiar with the process.

2. Create a workload identity pool using the following `gcloud` command:

    ```
    gcloud iam workload-identity-pools create workload-id-pool1
    - location="global" - description="Testing workload identity
    federation with Okta " - display-name="workload-id-pool1"
    ```

3. Create an OIDC provider for the pool we just created:

    ```
    gcloud iam workload-identity-pools providers create-oidc
    okta-provider - workload-identity-pool="workload-id-pool1"
    - issuer-uri="<okta-issuer-url>" - location="global" -
    attribute-mapping="google.subject=assertion.sub" - allowed-
    audiences="<ENTER CLIENT_ID>"
    ```

4. Add an IAM policy binding for the service account:

```
gcloud iam service-accounts add-iam-policy-binding
oktagcpsvacct@PROJECT_ID.iam.gserviceaccount.com —
role=roles/iam.workloadIdentityUser — member="principal://
iam.googleapis.com/projects/731056981369/locations/global/
workloadIdentityPools/workload-id-pool-1/subject/<authz-server-
sub>"
```

5. Update the provider with the allowed audience value as follows:

```
gcloud beta iam workload-identity-pools providers update-oidc
okta-provider — allowed-audiences="api://24wwds23" — workload-
identity-pool="workload-id-pool1" — location="global"
```

6. Use the following gcloud command to verify that the aud and sub values are set up correctly:

```
gcloud iam workload-identity-pools providers describe okta-
provider —workload-identity-pool="workload-id-pool1" —
location="global"
```

7. Now, download the JSON credentials configuration file and use it where you used the service account key before.

Service accounts pose a large threat vector to your Google Cloud organization, so it is pertinent that you monitor service account activity. In the next section, we will look at how to go about doing this.

Best practices for monitoring service account activity

It is important to understand service account activity to make sure that there is no threat actor or misuse of service accounts. Google Cloud provides Cloud Monitoring to view usage metrics for service accounts and service account keys.

These metrics will let you view and track usage patterns, which can help you identify anomalies.

Google APIs (for example, Google Maps and YouTube) that are not part of Google Cloud are included in these metrics if service accounts and service account credentials are used to call them. There are analytics for both successful and unsuccessful API requests. Using this example, the service account or key that was used for an API call failed because the caller was not permitted or because the request referenced a resource that does not appear in the metrics.

In these metrics, even if the system does not utilize the key to authenticate the request, service account keys appear if a system lists them while attempting to authenticate a request. Using signed URLs for Cloud Storage or authenticating third-party applications is the most prevalent cause of this problem. Usage statistics for non-authentication key pairs are therefore available.

To use Metrics Explorer to view the metrics for a monitored resource, follow these steps:

1. In the Google Cloud console, go to the **Metrics Explorer** page within **Monitoring**.

2. Go to **Metrics Explorer**.

3. In the toolbar, select the **Explorer** tab.

4. Select the **Configuration** tab.

5. Expand the **Select a metric** menu, enter `IAM Service Account` in the filter bar, and then use the submenus to select a specific resource type and metric (turn off **Show only active resources and metrics**):

    I.   In the **Active resources** menu, select **IAM Service Account**.

    II. In the **Active metric categories** menu, select **Service_account**.

6. In the **Active metrics** menu, select a service account metric. The following metrics are available within your selected time interval:

    I.   For service account usage metrics, select **Service account authentication events**.

    II. For service account key usage metrics, select **Service account key authentication events**.

7. Click **Apply**.

8. *Optional*: To configure how the data is viewed, use the **Filter, Group By, Aggregator**, and chart type menus.

9. *Optional*: Change the graph settings:

    I.   For quota and other metrics that report one sample per day, set the period to at least one week and set the plot type to **Stacked bar chart**.

    II. For distribution-valued metrics, set the plot type to **Heatmap chart**.

Monitoring metrics can be exported to BigQuery. Exporting metrics is necessary for performing in-depth analysis because Cloud Monitoring only saves data for a limited amount of time.

Here are a few more tips for tracking service account activity and keys that you should be aware of:

*   Use **Activity Analyzer** to keep track of service accounts and service account keys

*   Using the **Recommendation Hub**, you can see and manage all your project's proposals, including IAM recommendations

*   If you have not used a service account in the last 90 days, **Service Account Insights** usage can help you locate it

*   It is a good idea to disable accounts that have not been used in a while

So far, we have seen user-managed service accounts, but there are some service accounts that are created and managed by Google. We will take a brief look at them before moving on to IAM policy bindings.

Service agents

Google will create a service account for you in your project if you use one of the managed services (for example, Security Command Center or DLP). These are called **service agents**. Here are a couple of examples of what service agents look like:

- **Security Center Service Agent**: `service-53984177202@security-center-api-staging.iam.gserviceaccount.com`

- **Risk Manager Service Agent**: `organizations-720164443624@gcp-sa-riskmanager.iam.gserviceaccount.com`

The service agent typically has the following:

- The domain name used in the service agent's email address

- The role that the service agent is granted on the project

- After you activate an API that uses the service agent, Google grants the role automatically

There are some considerations when it comes to service agents:

- Service agent roles' permissions are subject to change at any time.

- Google can introduce new service agents at any time, both for existing services and for new services. In addition, the format of each service agent's email address is subject to change.

- Do not assign any principal impersonation ability to these service agents.

> **Note**
> Not all service agents can be impersonated but some allow impersonation.

- Keys for service agents cannot be created.

Now that we have covered service accounts in detail, we will move on and learn about IAM policy bindings in depth.

IAM policy bindings

In Google Cloud, access is managed through an IAM policy binding. An IAM policy is attached to a particular resource (remember, a resource could be a service account). An IAM policy contains a collection of role bindings that associate with one or more principals.

Recall that a principal could be one or more of the following:

- A Google account (a Gmail account is a form of Google account)

- A service account

- A Google group

- A Google Workspace account

- A Cloud Identity domain

- All authenticated users

- All users

IAM policy bindings (sometimes simply called bindings) associate a role to the principals both on the resource that the policy is attached to and on all the resource's descendants (for example, a policy attached to a folder is applicable to all the resources underneath that folder).

Policy structure

IAM policies consist of role definitions and additional details. A role binding determines the resources that can be accessed by specific users or groups. A role is associated with one or more principals, along with any applicable conditions. Metadata, including the etag and version, provides extra information about the policy.

Let us understand some guiding principles in creating IAM policies:

- There can be up to 1,500 principals in each IAM policy. Up to 250 unique groups can be specified in a single policy. Note that if you employ IAM conditions or grant roles to many principals with lengthy identifiers, then IAM may limit the policy to a smaller number of principals.

- IAM tracks the number of times each principal appears in the role bindings of the *allow policy*. No principals that exist in more than one role binding are deduplicated by this method. For example, the principal user `alice@acme.com` occurs in 50 role bindings in an allow policy, thus you could add 1,450 additional principals to the role bindings in the allow policy. Regardless of the number of individual members of a domain or Google group, the domain or group is counted as a single principal.

- Any additional information about the request, such as its origin or target resource, can be used as a condition to further restrict role binding. Conditional access is often used to determine whether a user's request can be granted. The term *conditional role binding* refers to a role binding that includes a condition. Some Google Cloud services do not accept conditions in IAM policies.

Now we understand the principles, let us look at the structure of the policy. The IAM policy includes the following fields:

- An `etag` field, which is used for concurrency control, ensures that policies are updated consistently. Concurrency control is supported by IAM via an `etag` field in the policy. Every time an IAM policy is updated, the value of the `etag` field is updated as well. As a result, an IAM policy with an `etag` field but no role bindings is ineffective.

- There is an optional `version` column that indicates the policy's schema version number.

- Additionally, the IAM policy can include an `auditConfig` field, which defines how each service logs activities for each service type, including organizations, folders, projects, and billing accounts.

Within 60 seconds of making an IAM policy modification, the new policy will take effect. The change can take up to seven minutes, however, to propagate across Google Cloud in some instances.

Here is an example of a simple policy:

```
{
  "bindings": [
    {
      "members": [
        "user:bob@acme.com"
      ],
      "role": "roles/owner"
    }
  ],
  "etag": " BwUjMhCsZpY =",
  "version": 1
}
```

The *Owner* basic role is provided to bob@acme.com without any restrictions in the simple policy example here. The access granted to bob@acme.com by this position is virtually limitless.

Here is an example of a policy that has multiple roles bound to it. Each role binding confers a distinct role to its recipient:

```
{
  "bindings": [
    {
      "members": [
        "user:bob@acme.com"
      ],
      "role": "roles/resourcemanager.organizationAdmin"
    },
```

```
    {
        "members": [
            "user:alice@acme.com",
            "user:bob@acme.com"
        ],
        "role": "roles/resourcemanager.projectCreator"
    }
    ],
    "etag": "BwUjMhCsZpY=",
    "version": 1
}
```

The Organization Admin predefined role (`roles/resourcemanager.organizationAdmin`) is granted to Jie (`jie@acme.com`) in the first role binding. Organizations, folders, and limited project operations are all included in this role's set of privileges. The Project Creator role (`roles/resourcemanager.projectCreator`) gives Jie (`jie@acme.com`) and Raha (`raha@acme.com`) the power to start new projects. Both Jie and Raha have access to fine-grained role bindings, but Jie has more access than Raha.

Example: Policy with conditional role binding

This example shows an IAM policy that binds principals to a predefined role and uses a condition expression to constrain the role binding:

```
{
    "bindings": [
        {
            "members": [
                "group:prod@acme.com",
                "serviceAccount:prod-example@acme-project-id.iam.
gserviceaccount.com"
            ],
            "role": "roles/appengine.deployer",
            "condition": {
                "title": "Expires_July_1_2022",
                "description": "Expires on July 1, 2022",
                "expression":
                    "request.time < timestamp('2022-07-01T00:00:00.000Z')"
            }
        }
    ],
    "etag": " BwUjMhCsZpY =",
    "version": 3
}
```

The `version` field is set to 3 in this example because of a condition expression in the policy. The policy's role binding only lasts until July 1, 2022, and only for the Google groups `prod-dev@acme.com` and `prod-example@acme-project-id.iam.gserviceaccount.com`.

Let us see an example now that shows a policy with conditional and unconditional role bindings.

In this example, an IAM policy contains both conditional and unconditional role bindings for the same role:

```
{
  "bindings": [
    {
      "members": [
        "serviceAccount:prod@acme-project-id.iam.gserviceaccount.com"
      ],
      "role": "roles/appengine.deployer"
    },
    {
      "members": [
        "group:prod@acme.com",
        "serviceAccount:prod@acme-project-id.iam.gserviceaccount.com"
      ],
      "role": "roles/appengine.deployer",
      "condition": {
        "title": "Expires_July_1_2024",
        "description": "Expires on July 1, 2024",
        "expression":
          "request.time < timestamp('2024-07-01T00:00:00.000Z')"
      }
    }
  ],
  "etag": " BwUjMhCsZpY =",
  "version": 3
}
```

The `serviceAccount:prod@acme-project-id.iam.gserviceaccount.com` service account is included in two role bindings for the same role in this case. No conditions are attached to the first binding. Until July 1, 2024, the second role binding grants the role.

In Google Cloud IAM, conditional role bindings take precedence over role bindings without conditions. When a conditional role binding is specified for a principal, it overrides any non-conditional role bindings for that principal. This means that the conditions defined in the conditional role binding will determine whether the principal is granted the specified role. If the conditions are not met, the non-conditional role bindings will not be considered for that principal.

The group:prod@acme.com Google group, on the other hand, is only included if the role binding conditions are met. As a result, it is only in effect until July 1, 2024.

Now let us look at how policy inheritance works in Google Cloud.

Policy inheritance and resource hierarchy

Policy inheritance describes how policies are applied to resources that are lower in the resource hierarchy. The term *effective policy* refers to a resource's policies being passed down through all its parents, all the way up the resource hierarchy. In that sequence, it is a combination of the following:

- The policy set on the resource

- The policies set on all of the resource's ancestry resource levels in the hierarchy

Each new role binding (acquired from parent resources) that has an impact on the resource's effective policy is assessed separately. If any of the higher-level role bindings provide access to the resource, a specific access request is granted. The access grant scope expands when a new role binding is added to any level of the resource's inherited policy.

To understand policy inheritance, let us consider a scenario where you grant a user, Bob, two different IAM roles at different levels in the resource hierarchy.

To grant Bob a role at the organization level, you set the following policy for your organization:

```
{
  "bindings": [
    {
      "members": [
        "user:bob@acme.com"
      ],
      "role": "roles/storage.objectViewer"
    }
  ],
  "etag": "BwUjMhCsNaY=",
  "version": 1
}
```

This policy grants Bob the Storage Object Viewer role (roles/storage.objectViewer). Since you set the policy at the organization level, Bob can use these permissions for all projects and all Cloud Storage objects in the organization.

To grant Bob a role at the project level, you set the following policy on the project:

```
{
  "bindings": [
    {
      "members": [
        "user:bob@acme.com"
      ],
      "role": "roles/storage.objectCreator"
    }
  ],
  "etag": " BwUjMhCsNaY =",
  "version": 1
}
```

This policy grants Bob the *Storage Object Creator* role (`roles/storage.objectCreator`), which lets him create Cloud Storage objects. Since this policy is set on the project level, Bob can create a cloud storage object only in the given project.

Let's summarize this particular example:

- A policy at the organization level grants the ability to list and get all Cloud Storage objects under this organization

- A policy at the project level, for the given project, grants the ability to create objects within that project

Now you have learned about how IAM policies work, let us look at some of the best practices.

IAM Conditions

You can provide access to principals only if certain requirements are met using IAM Conditions. A condition is part of the role binding. If a condition exists, access is only permitted if the condition expression evaluates to true. Each condition expression is made up of a series of logical statements that indicate which attributes should be checked. Let us take a look at the structure of IAM conditions.

The IAM policy binding structure looks like this. The `condition` object within that structure will have the conditions:

```
"bindings": [
  {
    "role": ...,
    "members": ...,
```

```
        "condition": ...
    },
    ...
]
```

The `condition` object has the following structure:

```
"condition": {
    "title": ...,
    "description": ...,
    "expression": ...
}
```

Let us go over the syntax of `condition`:

- `title` is required; however, `description` is optional.

- `expression` is required where you will define logic for conditional evaluation.

- You would use **Common Expression Language** (**CEL**) to define your logic using logical operators such as and (`&&`), or (`||`), or inverse (`!`) to define conditions. You can have up to 12 logical operators in each expression.

Check the Google Cloud documentation for a list of resources that accept condition role bindings and attributes supported by conditions.

Here are the different elements of conditions:

- **Variables**: These are attributes such as `request.time` (of type `Timestamp`) or `resource.name` (of type `String`). These variables are populated with values based on the context at runtime.

- **Operators**: Every data type (for example, `String` or `Timestamp`) supports a set of *operators* that can be used to create a logical expression, for example, `resource.service == "compute.googleapis.com"`. Operators are used for comparing values in a `resource.service` variable with a literal value. For example, `compute.googlepis.com`.

- **Functions**: These support more complex operations; for example, if you needed to match a part of a string, you would use `request.path.startsWith("/acmeBucket")`.

- **Logical operators**: Conditions support three logical operators: `&&`, `||`, and `!`. They make it possible to use multiple input variables in a condition expression. For example, `request.time.getFullYear() < 2020 && resource.service == "compute.googleapis.com"` joins two simple statements.

Policy best practices

The following best practices apply to organizations with many Google Cloud users:

- **Managing a large number of users**: When managing multiple user accounts with the same access, use Google groups. Each individual user account becomes a member of a group and the group is granted the required roles instead of individual user accounts.

- **Permissions granted at the organizational level**: Think about *which* principals have access permissions at the organizational level. Only a few *specific* teams (such as security and network teams) should have access to this level of the resource hierarchy in most organizations.

- **Grant permissions at the folder level**: When granting permissions at the folder level, consider using layers of folders to match your organization's operation structure, with each parent/child folder having various sets of access grants that are aligned with business and operation demands. A parent folder, for example, could represent a department, while one of its child folders could represent resource access and operation by a group, and yet another child folder could represent a small team. All folders may contain projects related to their team's operational requirements. This method of using folders ensures correct access isolation while adhering to policies inherited from the parent folder(s) and organization. When building and administering Google Cloud resources, this technique demands minimal policy maintenance.

- **Permissions provided at the project level**: When necessary, grant role bindings at the project level to adhere to the principle of least privilege. For example, if a principal requires access to three of the ten projects in a folder, you should grant access to each of the three projects separately; however, granting a role on the folder would grant the principal access to another seven projects that they do not require.

- **Granting permissions selectively**: You may also grant roles at the organization or folder level using IAM Conditions, but only for a subset of folders or projects.

- **Regularly review and audit IAM policies**: Conduct regular audits of IAM policies to identify any excessive or unnecessary permissions. Review the access granted to users, service accounts, and groups. Remove any outdated or unused permissions to minimize potential security risks.

- **Use IAM Conditions**: Leverage IAM Conditions to enforce additional security constraints based on contextual attributes such as IP address, time of day, or device status. IAM Conditions provides granular control over access to resources and can enhance security for specific use cases.

- **Implement monitoring and logging**: Enable monitoring and logging for IAM-related activities to detect and respond to any suspicious or anomalous behavior. Monitor and analyze logs to identify any unauthorized access attempts, policy violations, or unusual patterns of activity.

- **Educate and train users**: Provide regular training and awareness programs to educate users about IAM policies, best practices, and the importance of security. Promote a culture of security within the organization and encourage users to follow secure practices when managing IAM policies.

- **Use IAM Policy Intelligence tools**: As a part of the IAM Policy Intelligence portfolio, you have several tools to effectively manage permissions across your entire cloud organization. Use these tools effectively and train your developer community to utilize them.

In the next section, we will look at IAM Policy Intelligence briefly.

Policy Intelligence for better permission management

Policy Intelligence is a powerful feature of Google Cloud IAM that enables better permission management by providing insights, recommendations, and controls to optimize access control policies. With the ever-growing complexity of cloud environments and the need to balance security and productivity, Policy Intelligence offers valuable capabilities to enhance the overall governance and security posture of an organization. In this section, we will explore the various aspects of Policy Intelligence in Google Cloud IAM and how it can be leveraged for effective permission management. There are three main products in the Policy Intelligence suite:

- **IAM Recommender**: IAM Recommender is an AI-powered tool that helps optimize access control policies in Google Cloud. It provides recommendations for removing excessive or unnecessary permissions from IAM policies based on usage patterns, helping to ensure the principle of least privilege is followed.

- **Policy Analyzer**: Policy Analyzer is a feature within the Google Cloud console that analyzes IAM policies to identify potential security risks and violations. It scans policies for potential issues, such as overly permissive roles or resource-level permissions that can lead to security vulnerabilities.

- **Policy Troubleshooter**: Policy Troubleshooter is a feature of the Policy Intelligence suite that allows users to troubleshoot IAM permissions. It does this by comparing the requirements of resource permission to the permissions of a principal. This allows users to determine whether they have access to a resource based on their current IAM policy.

A critical aspect of Policy Intelligence is its ability to provide intelligent recommendations for permission changes. By analyzing historical data and access patterns, Policy Intelligence can identify over-permissive or under-permissive access policies and suggest modifications to align them with the principle of least privilege. These recommendations help organizations enhance their security posture by ensuring that access permissions are granted based on actual usage and business requirements. Implementing these recommendations can help reduce the attack surface, mitigate the risk of unauthorized access, and ensure that only the necessary permissions are granted to each user or service account.

Let us go over the best practices for permission management when using Policy Intelligence tools:

- **Analyze access patterns**: Utilize Policy Intelligence tools and features to analyze the collected access data. This analysis includes identifying access patterns, access frequencies, and potential security risks. By leveraging machine learning algorithms and advanced analytics, Policy Intelligence can provide valuable insights into access behaviors.

- **Review policy recommendations**: Policy Intelligence generates recommendations based on the analysis of access patterns and behaviors. Review these recommendations to identify areas where permissions can be optimized. The recommendations may include suggestions to remove excessive privileges, modify existing roles, or create new custom roles.

- **Implement recommended changes**: Apply the recommended changes to your access control policies. This may involve modifying existing roles, creating custom roles, or adjusting permission assignments for specific identities or groups. Follow the principle of least privilege to ensure that users and service accounts have only the necessary permissions required to perform their tasks.

- **Combine with other security best practices**: Remember that Policy Intelligence is a complementary feature within the Google Cloud IAM ecosystem. It should be used in conjunction with other security best practices, such as strong authentication mechanisms (for example, multi-factor authentication), regular security audits, and adherence to security frameworks and compliance standards.

By following these steps, organizations can effectively leverage Policy Intelligence in Google Cloud IAM for better permission management. This approach enables proactive identification of security risks, optimization of access control policies, and continuous monitoring of policy compliance, enhancing the overall security and governance of your cloud resources.

So far, we have looked at IAM policy best practices. Now let us briefly go over IAM tags and how they can be used for access control.

Tag-based access control

Tags are key-value pairs that can be attached to organizations, folders, or projects. They are an IAM construct and differ from labels and network tags. Tags follow an inheritance model, where a tag applied at the organization level is inherited by child objects, but this inheritance can be overridden if needed. Conditional IAM roles can be granted based on specific tags assigned to a resource.

In the resource hierarchy, tags are automatically inherited, but you can attach an additional tag to a resource to prevent it from inheriting a specific tag value. Essentially, each tag on an organization or folder sets a default value, which can be overridden by tags on lower-level resources such as folders or projects. Once tags are attached to a resource, you can define conditions to grant access based on those tags.

Tag structure

Here are how tags are structured in IAM:

- A *tag* is a key and value pair.

- A *permanent ID*, which is globally unique and can never be reused.

- A *short name* for each key must be unique within your organization, and the short name for each value must be unique for its associated key. For example, a tag key could have the short name `env`, and a tag value could have the short name `prod`.

- A *namespaced name*, which adds an organization ID to the short name of a tag key. For example, a tag key could have the namespaced name `123456789012/env`.

Best practices for tags

The following are some of the best practices when using tags:

- **Consistent tagging strategy**: Establish a consistent tagging strategy across your organization. Define clear guidelines for how tags should be structured and used. Consistency ensures that tags are meaningful, standardized, and easily understood by administrators and users.

- **Tag resource hierarchy**: Align your tag structure with your resource hierarchy. Consider organizing tags in a way that mirrors your project, folder, or organization structure. This helps in efficient management and makes it easier to associate tags with specific resources.

- **Use descriptive tags**: Use descriptive tags that accurately describe the purpose, ownership, or attributes of a resource. This helps in quickly identifying and categorizing resources, especially when dealing with a large number of assets.

- **Security and compliance tags**: Implement security- and compliance-related tags to identify resources that have specific security requirements or compliance obligations. These tags can help enforce access controls, ensure proper encryption, or track resources subject to specific regulations.

- **Tag resource owners**: Include tags to identify resource owners or responsible individuals or teams. This allows for better accountability and facilitates communication among stakeholders. It can be useful in managing permissions, delegating responsibilities, and streamlining resource management processes.

- **Automation and tagging policies**: Leverage automation tools and scripting capabilities to enforce tagging policies. Automate the application of specific tags based on predefined rules or criteria. This helps ensure consistency, reduces manual errors, and streamlines the process of managing tags across a large number of resources.

- **Regular tag reviews**: Conduct regular reviews of tags applied to resources. Remove unused or outdated tags and ensure that tags remain accurate and up to date. Regular reviews help maintain data integrity, optimize resource management, and avoid potential confusion or misinterpretation of tag meanings.

- **Tag-based IAM policies**: Utilize tag-based IAM policies to simplify access management. Assign IAM roles and permissions based on tags rather than individual resources. This allows for easier administration, especially when resources are dynamically created or changed frequently.

- **Monitor and audit tags**: Implement monitoring and auditing mechanisms to track changes to tags and associated resources. Monitor tag usage, modifications, and policy enforcement to ensure compliance and identify any unauthorized changes or deviations.

- **Education and training**: Educate and train your teams on the importance of using tags effectively. Provide guidelines and documentation to ensure that everyone understands the purpose and significance of tagging. Promote a culture of tag awareness and adherence to best practices.

So far, we have looked at IAM; now we will switch gears and look at access control for Cloud Storage. Cloud Storage is one of the original Google Cloud products and has evolved to have some fine-grained access policies (ACLs), so we will also look at those.

Cloud Storage ACLs

Cloud Storage provides separate access control in addition to IAM. There are two ways, in fact: a more uniform way of doing access control via IAM and a legacy way of doing access control via fine-grained ACLs. Object ACLs do not appear in the hierarchy of IAM policies, so be aware of how your Cloud Storage buckets are controlled. When evaluating who has access to one of your objects, make sure you check the ACLs for the object, in addition to checking your project- and bucket-level IAM policies. This could get very convoluted, so the recommendation is to use uniform access control using IAM in most cases.

Access Control Lists (ACLs)

You can use an ACL to determine who has access to your buckets and objects, as well as what level of access they have. ACLs are applied to specific buckets and objects in Cloud Storage. There are one or more entries in each ACL. An entry enables a certain user (or group) to carry out specific tasks. Each entry is made up of two bits of data:

- A *permission*, which defines *what* actions can be performed (for example, read or write)

- A *scope* (sometimes referred to as a *grantee*), which defines *who* can perform the specified actions (for example, a specific user or group of users)

Consider the following scenario: you have a bucket from which you want anonymous users to be able to access objects, but you also want your collaborator to be able to add and delete objects from the bucket. Your ACL would be made up of two entries in this case:

- In one entry, you would give `READER` permission to a scope of `allUsers`

- In the other entry, you would give `WRITER` permission to the scope of your *collaborator* (there are several ways to specify this person, such as by their email)

Here are some points to consider when using ACLs:

- You can only make up to 100 ACLs for a bucket or object.

- When the entry scope is a group or domain, it counts as one ACL entry, no matter how many users are in the group or domain.

- When a user tries to access a bucket or storage object, the Cloud Storage system looks at the bucket or object's ACL. If the ACL gives the user permission to do what is being asked, the request is granted. If not, the request fails, and a **403 Forbidden** error is sent back.

Let us look at ACL permissions now.

ACL permissions

Permissions describe *what* can be done to a given object or bucket. Cloud Storage lets you assign concentric permissions for your buckets and objects within the bucket.

What are concentric permissions?

You do not have to assign multiple scopes to ACLs in Cloud Storage to give more than one permission. When you give someone WRITER permission, you also give them READER permission, and when you give someone OWNER permission, you also give them READER and WRITER permission.

Based on how objects are uploaded, object ACLs are applied accordingly:

- **Authenticated uploads**: You (the person who uploaded the object) are listed as the object owner. Object ownership cannot be changed by modifying ACLs. You can change object ownership only by replacing an object. The project owners and project editor group have OWNER permission on the object.

- **Anonymous uploads**: If an anonymous user uploads an object, which is possible if a bucket gives the allUsers group WRITER or OWNER permission, the object gets the default bucket ACLs.

Best practices for Cloud Storage access while using ACLs

ACLs require active management, like other administrative settings. Before sharing a bucket or object with other users, consider who you want to share it with and what function each person will play. Changes in projects, usage patterns, and organizational ownership may need you to modify bucket and object ACL settings over time, especially if you manage them for a large organization or a large team. Consider these recommended practices when evaluating and planning your access control settings:

- Do not use sensitive information in the Cloud Storage bucket name.

- Follow the principle of least privilege when granting access to buckets and objects. This will make sure that data contained in the bucket is not accidentally exposed.

- Do not grant OWNER permission to anyone in the organization. Typically, you want the IaC service account to have ownership of the buckets.

- Be aware of how you grant permissions to anonymous users. The allUsers and allAuthenticatedUsers scopes provide access to everyone on the internet – be they anonymous users or users logged in with a Google account. You may not want this behavior.

- Avoid setting ACLs that result in inaccessible objects. An inaccessible object is an object that cannot be downloaded (read) and can only be deleted. This can happen when the owner of an object leaves a project without granting anyone else OWNER or READER permission on the object.

- Make sure to delegate administrative control of your buckets. By default, *project owners* have OWNER permissions. Make sure to not assign this role to individuals.

- Make sure you understand Cloud Storage's interoperable behavior before using it.

Uniform bucket-level access

Cloud Storage has uniform bucket-level access to support the system's uniform permissions. When you use this feature on a bucket, all ACLs for Cloud Storage resources in the bucket are disabled, and access to Cloud Storage resources is allowed solely through IAM. You have 90 days after enabling consistent bucket-level access to revoke your decision.

Please keep in mind that enabling uniform bucket-level access revokes access for users who get access purely through object ACLs and prevents users from managing rights through bucket ACLs. Before enabling consistent bucket-level access, read the Google Cloud product documentation when moving an existing bucket and consider whether it's the right thing to do in your situation.

Using uniform bucket-level access in practice

When should you use uniform bucket-level access? Uniform bucket-level access streamlines how you offer access to Cloud Storage resources. Using consistent bucket-level access also enables you to use features such as Domain Restricted Sharing and IAM Conditions.

You might not want to use uniform bucket level access and instead keep fine-grained ACLs in the following situations:

- You want legacy ACLs to control bucket object access

- You want an object's uploader to have full control over that object but others to have less access to the objects

- You want to use the XML API to view or set bucket permissions

IAM Conditions can only be used on buckets with uniform bucket-level access to prevent conflicts between policies and ACLs. So, note the following points when using it:

- Set IAM conditions on a bucket after enabling uniform bucket-level access

- Remove all IAM conditions from a bucket's policy to deactivate uniform bucket-level access

- Uniform bucket-level access cannot be disabled after 90 days of use

This concludes the section on IAM policies and storage bucket ACLs. Let us look at IAM APIs.

IAM APIs

IAM uses the following API endpoints (regular OAuth access tokens either for a user or service account can be used to access these APIs):

- Policies (v2)

- Roles (query and get/list)

- Organizations roles

- Permissions

- Projects

  - IAM policies (linting and querying)

  - Workload identity pools, operations, and providers

  - Permissions

  - Roles

  - Service accounts

  - Service account keys

- Service account credentials

- Security token services

Finally, let us look at various log files for IAM APIs. You will often start with these logs to troubleshoot an access issue.

IAM logging

Google Cloud IAM writes audit logs and admin logs to help with questions such as "*Who did what, where, and when?*" These logs are vitally important for audit and forensic capabilities.

For information on Admin Activity and Data Access read audit logs, please check the Google Cloud product documentation.

IAM audit logs use one of the following resource types:

- `api`: A request to list information about multiple IAM roles or policies
- `audited_resource`: A request to exchange credentials for a Google access token
- `iam_role`: An IAM custom role
- `service_account`: An IAM service account, or a service account key

Log name

Let us assume `project_id = acme-project-id`, `folder_id = acme-folder`, `billing_account_id = 123456`, and `organization_id = 987654321`:

```
projects/acme-project-id/logs/cloudaudit.googleapis.com%2Factivity
projects/acme-project-id/logs/cloudaudit.googleapis.com%2Fdata_access
projects/ acme-project-id/logs /cloudaudit.googleapis.com%2Fsystem_event
projects/acme-project-id/logs/cloudaudit.googleapis.com%2Fpolicy

folders/acme-folder/logs/cloudaudit.googleapis.com%2Factivity
folders/acme-folder/logs/cloudaudit.googleapis.com%2Fdata_access
folders/acme-folder/logs/cloudaudit.googleapis.com%2Fsystem_event
folders/acme-folder/logs/cloudaudit.googleapis.com%2Fpolicy

billingAccounts/987654321/logs/cloudaudit.googleapis.com%2Factivity
billingAccounts/987654321/logs/cloudaudit.googleapis.com%2Fdata_access
billingAccounts/987654321/logs/cloudaudit.googleapis.com%2Fsystem_event
billingAccounts/987654321/logs/cloudaudit.googleapis.com%2Fpolicy

organizations/987654321/logs/cloudaudit.googleapis.com%2Factivity
organizations/987654321/logs/cloudaudit.googleapis.com%2Fdata_access
organizations/987654321/logs/cloudaudit.googleapis.com%2Fsystem_event
organizations/987654321/logs/cloudaudit.googleapis.com%2Fpolicy
```

These are the logs that you should be familiar with for Cloud IAM. You should also understand service account-specific activities that get logged into these logs. Let us look at service account-specific information now.

Service account logs

One of the critical aspects of working with Google Cloud is to be able to identify service accounts' activities. The following service account activities are logged by the IAM API:

> **Note**
>
> For details on the relevant fields of log entries, please look at the Google Cloud product documentation. You might see log entries in which the `service-agent-manager@ system.gserviceaccount.com` service account grants roles to other Google-managed service accounts. This behavior is normal and expected.

- Creating service accounts

- Granting a service account a user role

- Granting access to a service account on a resource

- Setting up a Compute Engine instance to run as a service account

- Accessing Google Cloud with a service account key

- Creating a service account key

- Authenticating with a service account key

- Impersonating a service account to access Google Cloud

- Authenticating with a short-lived credential

This concludes various aspects of IAM logging. It's important to understand this very well as you might have to develop security alerts based on your security operations requirements.

Summary

In this chapter, we explored various powerful features of Cloud IAM, including principals, roles, IAM policies, and service accounts. We gained insights into effective service account key management and learned how to detect potential issues when keys are checked into Git. Additionally, we discovered the versatility of IAM conditions and adopted best practices for creating robust IAM policies. We also delved into Cloud Storage ACLs and their ability to provide fine-grained access control. Armed with this knowledge, you are now equipped to confidently set up IAM policies for any workloads in Google Cloud, troubleshoot access problems, and implement the recommended best practices we discussed. We even delved into advanced features such as IAM Policy Intelligence and WIF.

As we conclude this chapter on Google Cloud's IAM features, the upcoming chapters will focus on exploring the robust network security capabilities of Google Cloud.

Further reading

- Attribute reference for IAM Conditions: `https://packt.link/wMFb4`
- Predefined ACLs for Cloud Storage: `https://packt.link/jfhAt`
- IAM Relation to Cloud Storage ACLs: `https://packt.link/gQoHG`
- Cloud Storage ACL behavior: `https://packt.link/VgFY0`
- Cloud Storage interoperability with AWS S3: `https://packt.link/vqNy3`
- Tags using conditions: `https://packt.link/zzvld`

7

Virtual Private Cloud

In this chapter, we will look at Google Cloud **Virtual Private Cloud** (**VPC**). The chapter will focus on the network security concepts within Google Cloud, although we will cover some foundational networking concepts that are essential. We will begin by looking at how Google Cloud's global footprint is structured with regard to different regions and zones. Then, we will cover the key concepts of VPC, such as global VPC versus regional, how to create custom IP address subnets, micro-segmentation, custom routing, and the different types of firewall rules and their usage. We will look at some design patterns for VPC, focusing on shared VPC in particular and its importance from a security perspective, and we'll get an overview of the different types of connectivity options that are available to connect Google Cloud to your on-premises or third-party cloud provider using different options. Finally, we will look at DNSSEC and some load balancer options available to handle TLS.

In this chapter, we will cover the following topics:

- Introduction to VPC
- Google regions and zones
- VPC deployment models
- Micro-segmentation
- Cloud DNS
- Load balancers
- Hybrid connectivity options
- Best practices and design considerations

Overview of VPC

Google Cloud VPC is a virtual network built on Google's internal production network and is based on Andromeda, which is Google's implementation of its software-defined network. Andromeda is out of scope for the exam, but those who want to understand more about the underlying network and how it is built can read more about it by using the link in the *Further reading* section.

You can think of Google Cloud VPC as a virtual network, which is very similar to a physical environment but more powerful due to its software-defined nature. At a high level, VPC is responsible for providing underlying connectivity to your Google Cloud services, such as **Compute Engine (virtual machines)**, **Google Kubernetes Engine (GKE)**, **Google App Engine (GAE)**, and any other Google Cloud services that are built on top of these services. VPC also natively provides load balancing and proxy services, helps distribute traffic to backend services, and provides the capability to connect your Google Cloud to either your on-premises data center or other cloud service providers.

Let's understand some of the key features that VPC offers, as it will help you understand what capabilities are offered and how to use them in your network design:

- A VPC network is a global resource, including its components, such as the routes and the firewall rules. We will look at global/regional/zonal resources in the *Google Cloud regions and zones* section.

- With VPC, you have the ability to create IPv4-based subnets. These subnets are regional resources. IPv6 is also supported, where you can enable IPv6 on supported subnets; the only exception is that an auto-mode VPC network cannot have IPv6, but if you add a custom subnet to the auto mode VPC, you can enable IPv6 on that subnet. The important thing to note here is that auto mode VPC networks do not support dual-stack subnets.

- Firewall rules are used to control the traffic from the instances. When you create firewall rules for the network, although they control the network traffic, these rules are in fact applied to the VM interface. This then lets you control which VMs can communicate with each other on which ports. We will cover firewall rules in more detail in the *Micro-segmentation* section of this chapter.

- When you create a VPC network, all the resources inside the network with IPv4 addressing can communicate with each other without the need for any additional rules. Some restrictions may apply if you create firewall rules to control the traffic inside the VPC network.

- VM instances that are created inside the VPC network and have a private Ipv4 address can communicate with Google APIs and services. Google Cloud has private access, which we will cover later in this chapter, that lets instances communicate with Google APIs and services even if they don't have an external IP address.

- Fine-grained identity and access management policies are available for network administration. You can create custom roles to give the relevant privileges to your network team to manage VPC and its associated components.

- Shared VPC is a deployment model that can be used to centralize network functions in a common host project. Other services' projects can consume network services from the shared VPC host project, such as IP address, subnet, and hybrid connectivity, as long as they are part of the same organization.

- VPC peering is a concept used to connect a VPC network in one project to another or across two different organizations. Permissions are required at each end to authorize the creation of a VPC peer with no IP address overlaps.

- There are multiple options to create secure hybrid connectivity; you can connect your on-premises environment to Google Cloud using a VPN or a dedicated interconnect. We will look at hybrid connectivity in more detail later in the chapter, under the *Hybrid connectivity options* section.

- For use cases where you need to access Secure Access Service Edge and **Software Defined-Wide Area Network (SD-WAN)** and you require the use of **Generic Routing Encapsulation (GRE)**, you can use VPC, which supports GRE. Other options such as VPN and Interconnect support the same capability. You can terminate GRE on your instance and forward the traffic to its respective location.

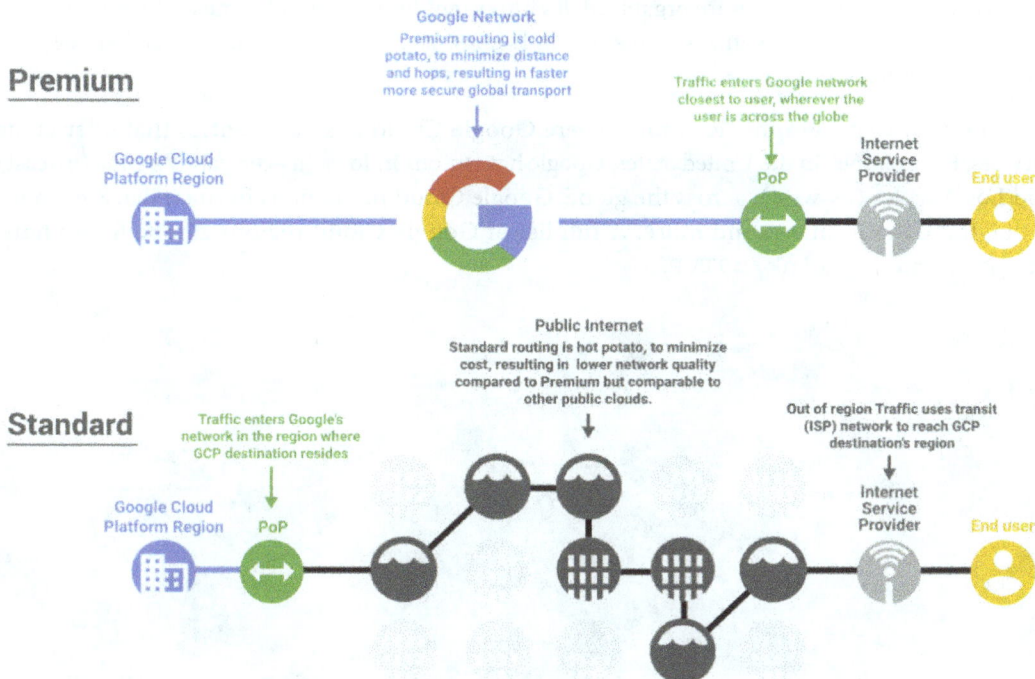

Figure 7.1 – Google Cloud network tiers

Figure 7.1 shows the network tiers that Google provides. Google offers two tiers, Standard Tier and Premium Tier, that can be configured at the VPC level. In a Premium Tier network, Google utilizes its own private network to route the traffic. From an end user perspective, if the user is trying to access services hosted on Google Cloud, the traffic will connect to the closest Google **point of presence (PoP)** location. Google has hundreds of PoP locations across the globe. From the PoP location, the traffic will not traverse the internet and will instead use Google's own operated and managed fully encrypted private network. This provides better reliability and security.

The Standard Tier option is what most service providers use, that is, *hot potato*, meaning when a user tries to access the services hosted on Google Cloud, the service will go via the internet, which is non-deterministic and will not use Google's private network. This, although a more cost-effective option, does not provide the reliability, security, and availability of a Premium Tier network.

In the *VPC deployment models* section, where we will walk through the setup of VPC, we will highlight where you can configure the network tiers.

Google Cloud regions and zones

This topic is not part of the exam blueprint. Due to the fact that this is related to the design and architecture and how services are organized, it's important to understand some of the foundational concepts of how Google organizes its regions and zones. We will also look at what global, regional, and zonal resources are.

Regions refer to geographic locations where Google Cloud has data centers that offer cloud services. For example, in the United States, Google has regions in Iowa (us-central), Virginia (us-east), and Los Angeles (us-west); across the globe, Google Cloud has regions in Australia, Singapore, India, the UK, Germany, and more. A full list of Google Cloud regions can be found here: `https://packt.link/b9TVP`.

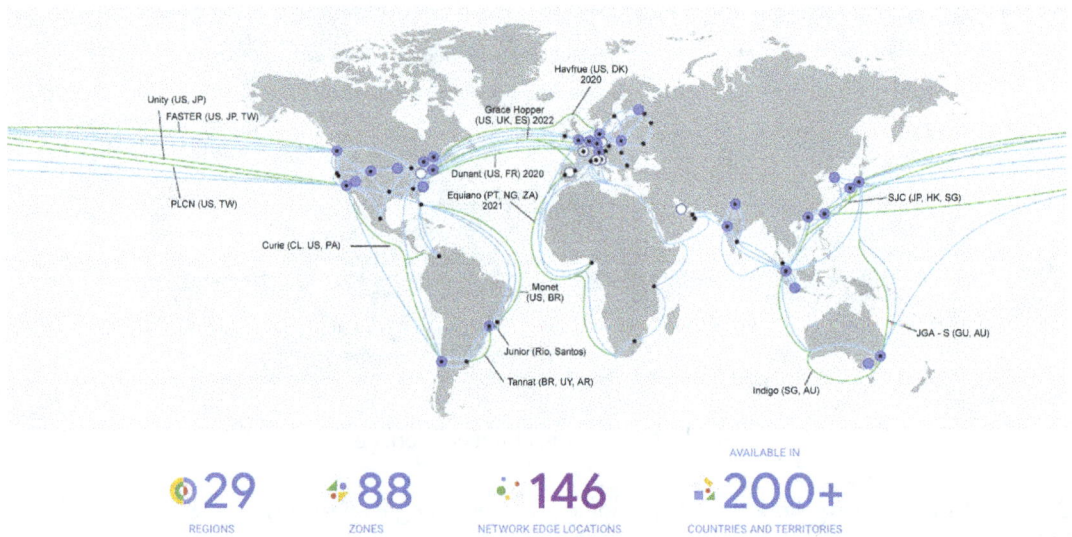

Figure 7.2 – Google Cloud region locations

At the time of writing, Google has a presence in more than 200 countries, with 29 regions, 88 zones, and 146 PoP or edge locations. As part of Google Cloud's strategy to expand, there are more regions announced every year.

Each region has at least two zones, and some have more than two zones to provide additional capacity and resilience. This is dictated by demand. As a rule of thumb, there are always two zones to provide fault tolerance and high availability. In order to address the resiliency and availability of your services, it is highly recommended to use multiple zones and regions. Both regions and zones have a standard naming convention to identify them, which is `<region>-<zone>`, for example, `us-central1`. Furthermore, a, b, or c is used to identify the zone, for example, `us-east1-a`. You can select any of these zones to deploy your cloud services, such as compute instances.

Google Cloud service availability is also region-specific. You can see whether the service you want is available in the region of your choice by navigating to `https://packt.link/ehHg8`.

We will now take a look at different types of resources that are either global, regional, or zonal in nature.

As the name suggests, global resources are global in nature, which means when configured inside a project, these resources can be accessed by any other resource in any zone as long as they are in the same project. VPC networks, firewall rules, routes, images, and snapshots are all examples of global resources.

Regional resources are only available in the region; for example, the subnets that you create are accessible only in the regions they are in and cannot cross a regional boundary. Some examples of regional resources include regional managed instance groups and cloud interconnects.

Zonal or per-zone resources are created in a zone and are available only within that zone. A compute instance that is created requires a zone to be specified where the resource will exist. This resource can access other global or regional resources but cannot access any other per-zone resource, such as a disk.

> **Note**
>
> For more details on which services are global, regional, or zonal, you can refer to `https://packt.link/41g8M`.

VPC deployment models

VPC can be deployed in different models based on your network architecture requirements. In this section, we will look at the different models that are available and how you can create them. We will look at the two VPC modes that can be used to create a VPC network: auto mode and custom mode. After that, we will look at Shared VPC networks, what they are, and how to create one. In the next section, will go over VPC peering, a technique for connecting two VPCs that are located in different organizations but can be considered peers.

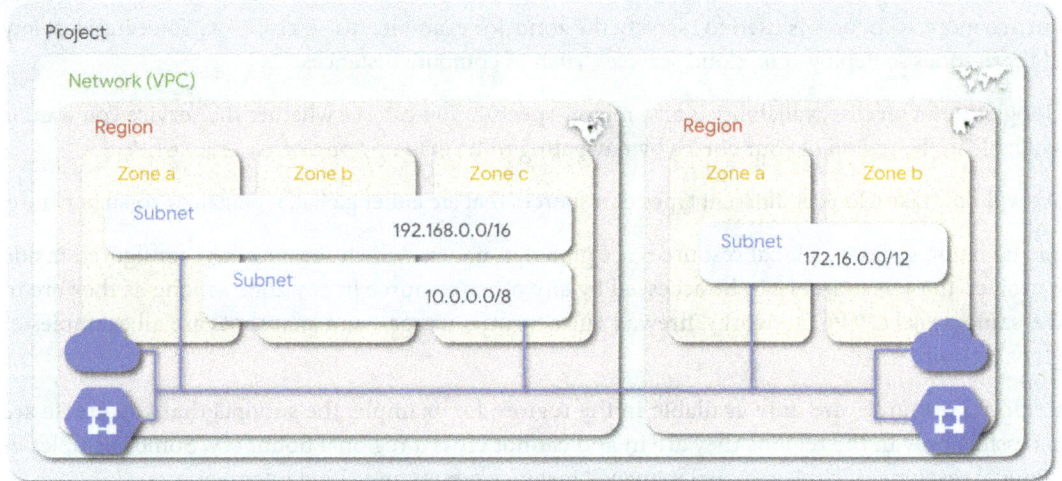

Figure 7.3 – Google network components

We will use the illustration shown in *Figure 7.3* to understand a few concepts before we jump into the deployment models. A VPC as a resource is created inside the project and is global in nature. Once you create the VPC network, you have the option to either create a global VPC with all regions in scope or customize things based on which region(s) you want to use. We will look at this in the next section on how to create a VPC using the two modes. Within each region, there are zones. You can select one, two, or three (if available) zones to create resources. For example, to create a compute instance, you need to specify which zone you want to use in which region. Furthermore, you can create subnets inside the zone. We will cover how to create subnets in the following sections, but in Google Cloud, subnets are regional resources; therefore, they can span across zones, as shown in *Figure 7.3*. In summary, you can create a single VPC network spanning multiple regions and provide connectivity to your cloud resources.

VPC modes

A VPC can be deployed in two different modes, as dictated by the subnet creation process.

Creating an auto mode VPC network

The first mode is auto mode, where the default network is created and one subnet per region is added automatically. In auto mode, all IP address ranges are pre-defined to `10.128.0.0/9`, and new subnets are also automatically added when new regions are made available. As the name suggests, auto mode essentially creates a global network in a project. You do have the option to create custom subnets for an auto mode VPC and, if required, you can also convert an auto mode VPC network to a custom VPC network as a one-way conversion, but you cannot convert a custom mode VPC network to auto mode. Auto mode VPC network creation is enabled by default when you create a project; if you want to disable the default behavior, you can do so by creating an organizational constraint policy called `compute.skipDefaultNetworkCreation`.

Let's take a look at how you can create an auto mode VPC network on Google Cloud:

1. Navigate to the **VPC networks** section from the Google Cloud menu: `https://packt.link/dYLnN`.

2. Next, click on **Create a VPC network**.

3. Fill in **Name**, following the naming convention.

4. Optionally, fill in **Description** as well for the network.

5. Next, under the **Subnets** section, select **Automatic** under **Subnet creation mode**.

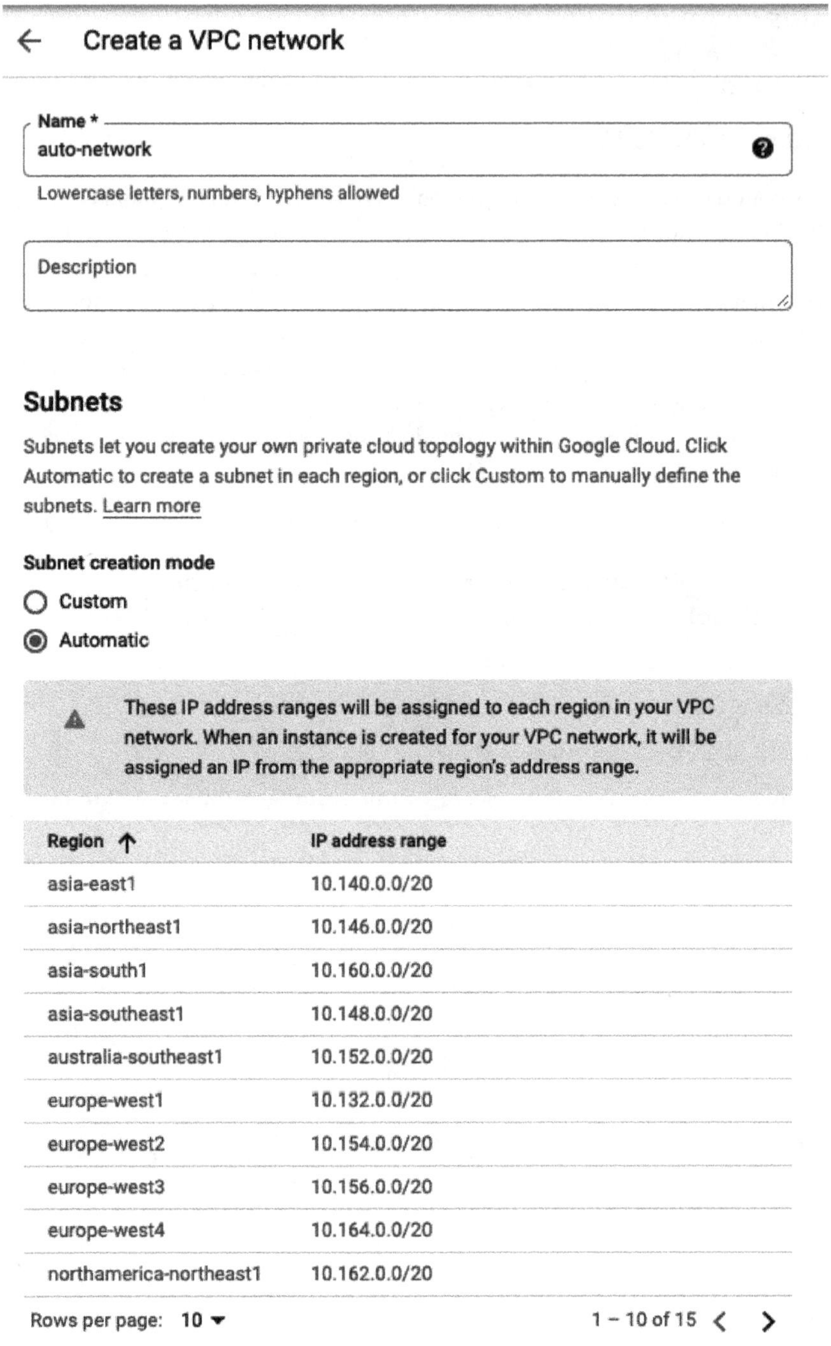

← **Create a VPC network**

Name *

auto-network   ❓

Lowercase letters, numbers, hyphens allowed

Description

Subnets

Subnets let you create your own private cloud topology within Google Cloud. Click
Automatic to create a subnet in each region, or click Custom to manually define the
subnets. Learn more

Subnet creation mode

○ Custom

◉ Automatic

> ⚠ These IP address ranges will be assigned to each region in your VPC
> network. When an instance is created for your VPC network, it will be
> assigned an IP from the appropriate region's address range.

Region ↑	IP address range
asia-east1	10.140.0.0/20
asia-northeast1	10.146.0.0/20
asia-south1	10.160.0.0/20
asia-southeast1	10.148.0.0/20
australia-southeast1	10.152.0.0/20
europe-west1	10.132.0.0/20
europe-west2	10.154.0.0/20
europe-west3	10.156.0.0/20
europe-west4	10.164.0.0/20
northamerica-northeast1	10.162.0.0/20

Rows per page: 10 ▾   1 – 10 of 15 ‹ ›

Figure 7.4 – VPC creation – auto mode

6. You can remove the default firewall rules established depending on the use case. There are two rules that prohibit all incoming traffic but permit all outgoing traffic; these rules cannot be deleted.

Firewall rules ❷

Select any of the firewall rules below that you would like to apply to this VPC network. Once the VPC network is created, you can manage all firewall rules on the Firewall rules page.

IPV4 FIREWALL RULES   IPV6 FIREWALL RULES

	Name	Type	Targets	Filters	Protocols / ports	Action	Priority ↑	
☐	auto-network-allow-custom ❷	Ingress	Apply to all	IP ranges: 10.128.0.0/9	all	Allow	65,534	EDIT
☐	auto-network-allow-icmp ❷	Ingress	Apply to all	IP ranges: 0.0.0.0/0	icmp	Allow	65,534	
☐	auto-network-allow-rdp ❷	Ingress	Apply to all	IP ranges: 0.0.0.0/0	tcp:3389	Allow	65,534	
☐	auto-network-allow-ssh ❷	Ingress	Apply to all	IP ranges: 0.0.0.0/0	tcp:22	Allow	65,534	
	auto-network-deny-all-ingress ❷	Ingress	Apply to all	IP ranges: 0.0.0.0/0	all	Deny	65,535	
	auto-network-allow-all-egress ❷	Egress	Apply to all	IP ranges: 0.0.0.0/0	all	Allow	65,535	

Figure 7.5 – Default firewall rules

7. Under **Dynamic routing mode**, select either **Regional** or **Global** based on your network requirements.

8. Leave the **Maximum Transmission Unit (MTU)** settings at their defaults, unless you need to change them.

9. Click **CREATE** for an auto mode VPC network to be created.

Creating a custom mode VPC network

Custom mode VPC creation gives you more control to select the regions where you want to have the network created and the flexibility to specify your own custom RFC1918-based IP address range for the subnets. For use cases where you need to create VPC peering, you need to create a custom network, as an auto mode network creates the same IP address range in every project. Therefore, to avoid IP address overlap, you need to be in control of the IP ranges when creating peering and hybrid connectivity with your on-premises network.

The steps to create a custom VPC network are as follows:

1. Navigate to the **VPC networks** section from the Google Cloud menu: `https://packt.link/ek0Sw`.

2. Next, click on **Create a VPC network**.

3. Provide a name following the naming convention.

4. Optionally, provide a description of the network.

5. Next, set the subnet creation mode to **Custom**.

6. Next, click on **New subnet** and provide the following information:

   I. The name of the subnet.

   II. An optional description of the subnet.

   III. Select the region you want to use.

   IV. Specify the RFC1918 subnet range. Refer to this link for the ranges that can be used: `https://packt.link/yko0P`.

   V. Create a secondary IP subnet range, if required. Secondary IP address ranges are used for allocating different IPs to multiple microservices running in a VM (for example, containers and GKE pods). You can change and extend a primary IP range but not a secondary IP range.

   VI. Specify whether you want to use **Private Google Access**. If you're not sure, you can always edit this and update it later.

   VII. Select whether you would like to turn the flow logs on or off. This attribute can again be changed by editing.

   VIII. Click on **DONE** when finished.

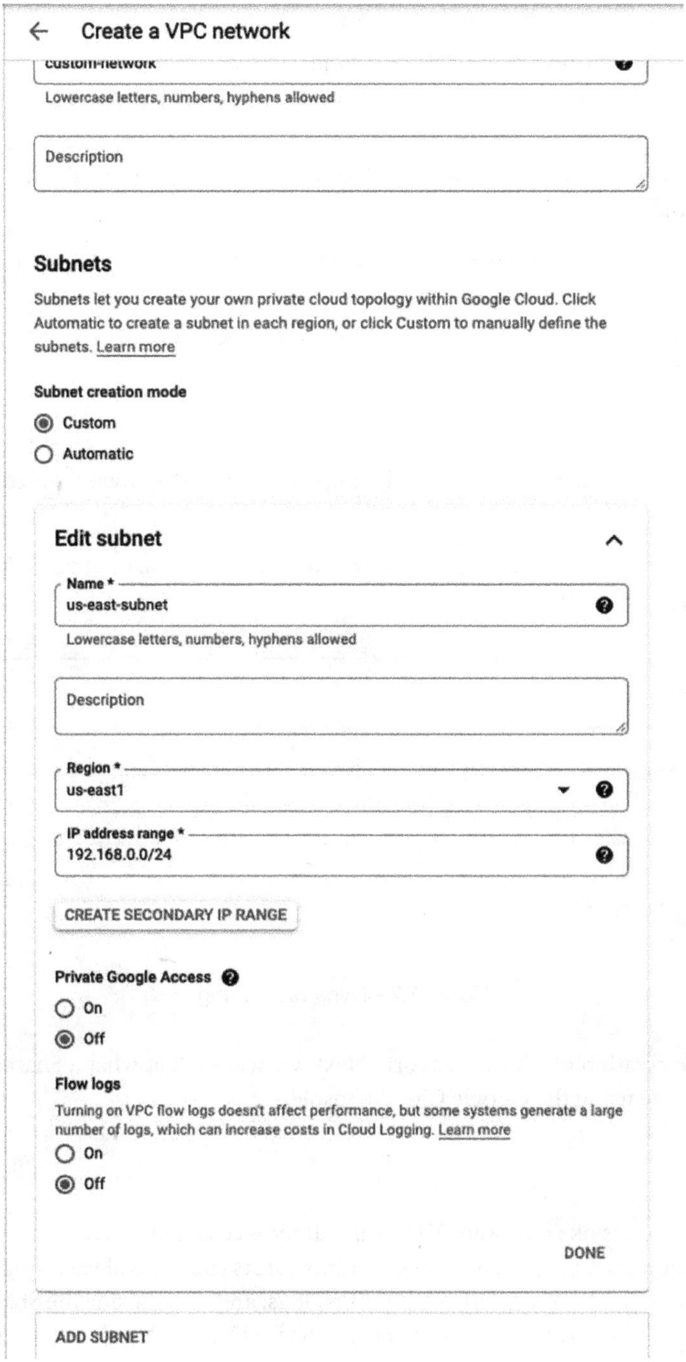

← **Create a VPC network**

custom-network

Lowercase letters, numbers, hyphens allowed

Description

Subnets

Subnets let you create your own private cloud topology within Google Cloud. Click
Automatic to create a subnet in each region, or click Custom to manually define the
subnets. Learn more

Subnet creation mode

⦿ Custom

◯ Automatic

Edit subnet   ︿

Name *
us-east-subnet   ❓

Lowercase letters, numbers, hyphens allowed

Description

Region *
us-east1   ▼ ❓

IP address range *
192.168.0.0/24   ❓

CREATE SECONDARY IP RANGE

Private Google Access ❓

◯ On

⦿ Off

Flow logs

Turning on VPC flow logs doesn't affect performance, but some systems generate a large
number of logs, which can increase costs in Cloud Logging. Learn more

◯ On

⦿ Off

DONE

ADD SUBNET

Figure 7.6 – Custom VPC creation

7. To add more subnets, you can repeat the preceding steps.

8. In the same way that auto mode default firewall rules are added based on typical use cases, you can also remove them. However, you cannot get rid of the two rules that block all incoming traffic and let all outgoing traffic through.

9. Under **Dynamic routing mode**, select either **Regional** or **Global** based on your network requirements.

10. Leave the **Maximum transmission unit (MTU)** settings at their defaults, unless you need to change them.

11. Click **CREATE** for a custom mode VPC network to be created.

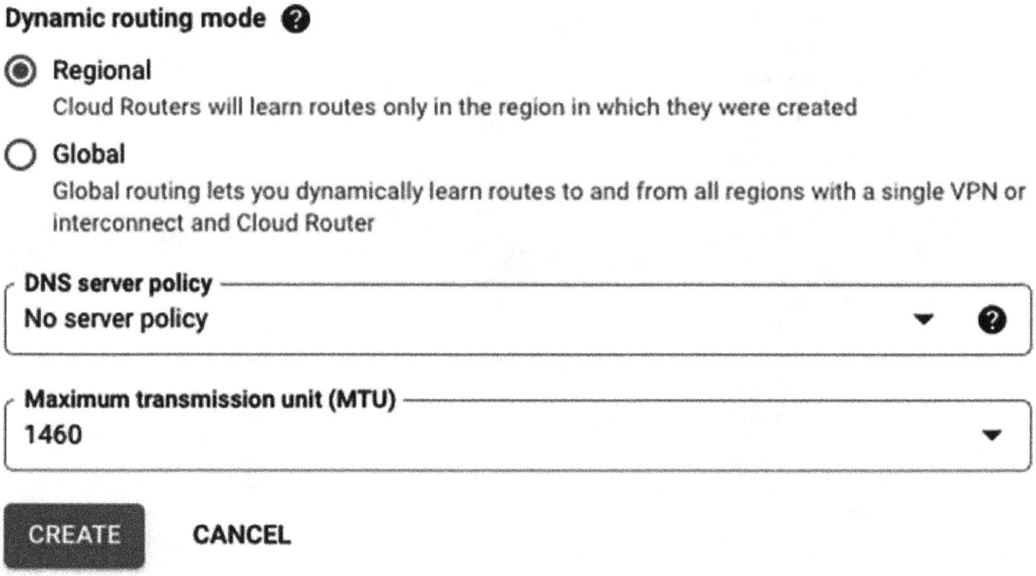

Dynamic routing mode ❓

⦿ Regional
Cloud Routers will learn routes only in the region in which they were created

◯ Global
Global routing lets you dynamically learn routes to and from all regions with a single VPN or interconnect and Cloud Router

DNS server policy
No server policy ▾ ❓

Maximum transmission unit (MTU)
1460 ▾

[CREATE]   **CANCEL**

Figure 7.7 – Dynamic routing

This concludes the creation of a VPC network. Next, we will look at what a Shared VPC network is and how to create one using the Google Cloud console.

Shared VPC

A Shared VPC network is like any other VPC – the difference is that it is shared. You create a Shared VPC network inside a **host project**. Network administrators can control via a single pane of glass all the routes, subnets, firewall rules, interconnect/VPN, logs, and more inside the Shared VPC network. You can also create an organizational policy to restrict Shared VPC networks to host projects. The point of a Shared VPC network is to centrally control and manage all the network services that are offered by VPC. **Service projects** can attach to a host project, and services such as VMs and the resources provisioned on them can allocate an IP from the Shared VPC network. Billing for resources that use the Shared VPC network is attributed to the service project. Permissions can be granted at the VPC or subnet level, as shown in *Figure 7*.8.

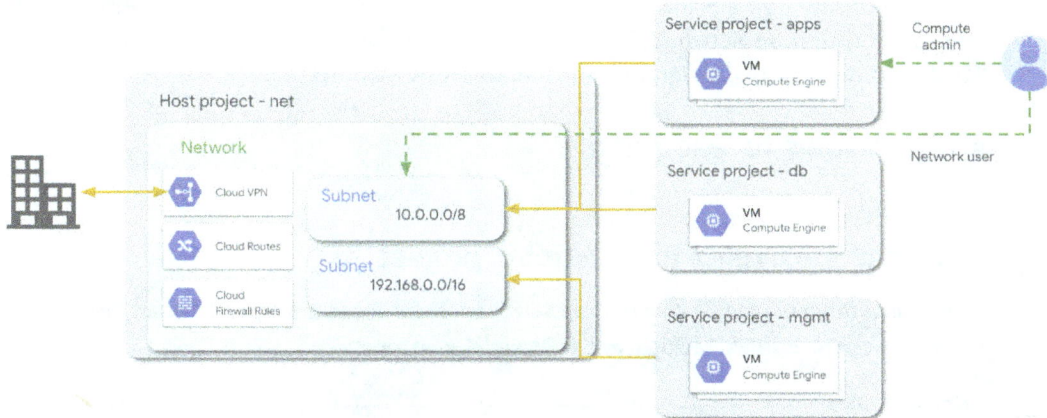

Figure 7.8 – Shared VPC network

Let us understand the IAM permissions for Shared VPC. You can use IAM roles for delegated administrator access. Organization admins can create Shared VPC Admin roles, and a Shared VPC Admin can further define and create Service Project VPC Admin roles. Shared VPC Admins have Compute Shared VPC Admin (`compute.xpnAdmin`) access and Project IAM Admin role (`resourcemanager.projectIAMAdmin`) permissions. A Service Project Admin can have service-project-wide scope and access to all host project subnets. The Shared VPC Admin can restrict access to particular subnets to make things more restrictive.

Shared VPC does have some limitations:

- You can have multiple Shared VPC networks in a host project, but you can only have one service project attached to a host project.

- You can have a maximum of 100 service projects attached to a host project.

Let us now look at how to configure IAM permissions before you create a Shared VPC network:

1. Before you can create the Shared VPC network, you need to make sure that the right IAM roles are assigned either at the organization level or at the folder level.

   We will now look at the steps to assign two roles; the first will be **Compute Shared VPC Admin** and the next is **Project IAM Admin**.

   Navigate to **IAM & admin** from the Google Cloud console navigation menu on the left and select **IAM**.

2. You must log in to the console as an organization administrator and then go to the **IAM** page to see the role.

3. Select your project, if not already selected. Refer to the following figure showing where to navigate to add the role for a new principal. In *Figure 7.9*, for the Shared VPC resource, **Project IAM Admin** and **Compute Network Viewer** roles have been assigned. Click on **ADD ANOTHER ROLE**, and you can then assign **Compute Shared VPC Admin**.

Add principals to "exomoon"

Add principals, roles to "exomoon" project

Enter one or more principals below. Then select a role for these principals to grant them access to your resources. Multiple roles allowed. Learn more

New principals
test@ankqush.altostrat.com ✕   ❓

Role *
Project IAM Admin   ▼   Condition
                                      Add condition   🗑

Access and administer a project IAM policies.

Role
Compute Network Viewer   ▼   Condition
                                      Add condition   🗑

Read-only access to Compute Engine networking resources.

Select a role
                           ▼   Condition
                                      Add condition   🗑

+ ADD ANOTHER ROLE

[SAVE]   [CANCEL]

Figure 7.9 – Assign IAM roles for Shared VPC

4. Once you have completed the settings, click on **SAVE**.

Once the IAM roles have been assigned, we can now create the Shared VPC network in the host project:

1. Navigate to the **Shared VPC** page from the Google Cloud console.
2. Ensure that you are logged in as **Shared VPC Admin**.
3. From the project picker, select the Shared VPC host project.
4. Click **SET UP SHARED VPC**.

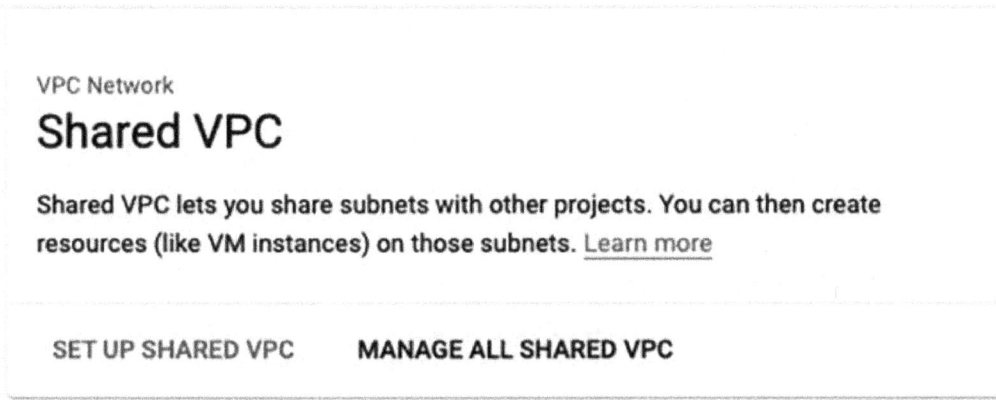

VPC Network
Shared VPC

Shared VPC lets you share subnets with other projects. You can then create resources (like VM instances) on those subnets. Learn more

SET UP SHARED VPC   **MANAGE ALL SHARED VPC**

Figure 7.10 – SET UP SHARED VPC

5. We will now move on to the next page, where we will click **SAVE & CONTINUE** under **Enable host project**. Here you will select your existing project as your host project. Once done, we will then move on to configuring subnets in the next step.

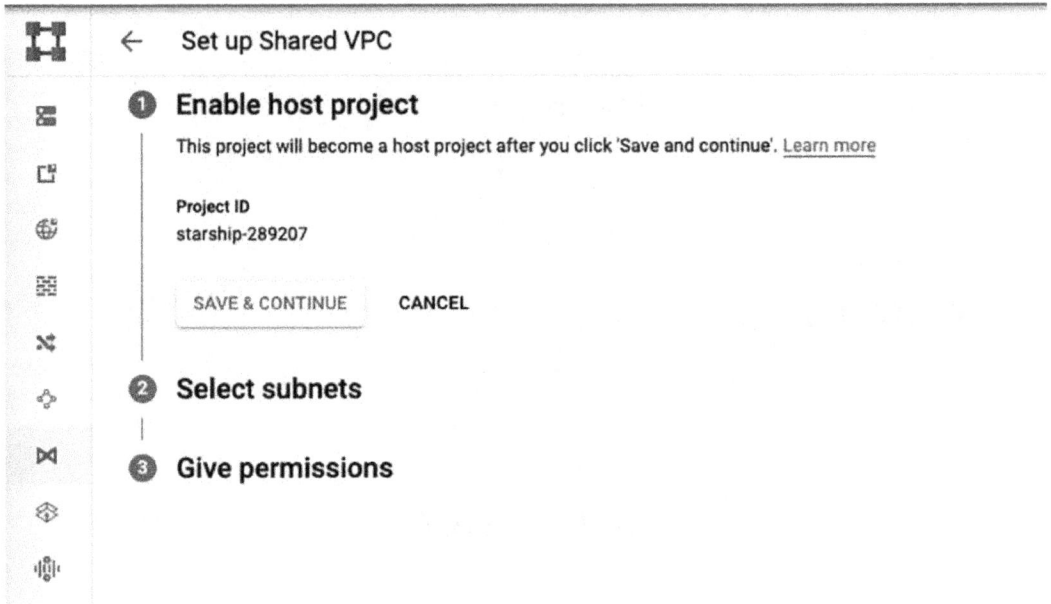

Figure 7.11 – Enable host project

6. There are two choices for selecting subnets in the **Select subnets** section. You can click **Share all subnets** if you want to share all the host project's VPC networks with the service projects and Service Project Admins listed below (project-level permissions). Alternatively, if you need to share some VPC network subnets with service projects and Service Project Admins, you can pick **Individual subnets** (subnet rights). Select the subnets you want to share first. Refer to *Figure 7.12* to see what options are available.

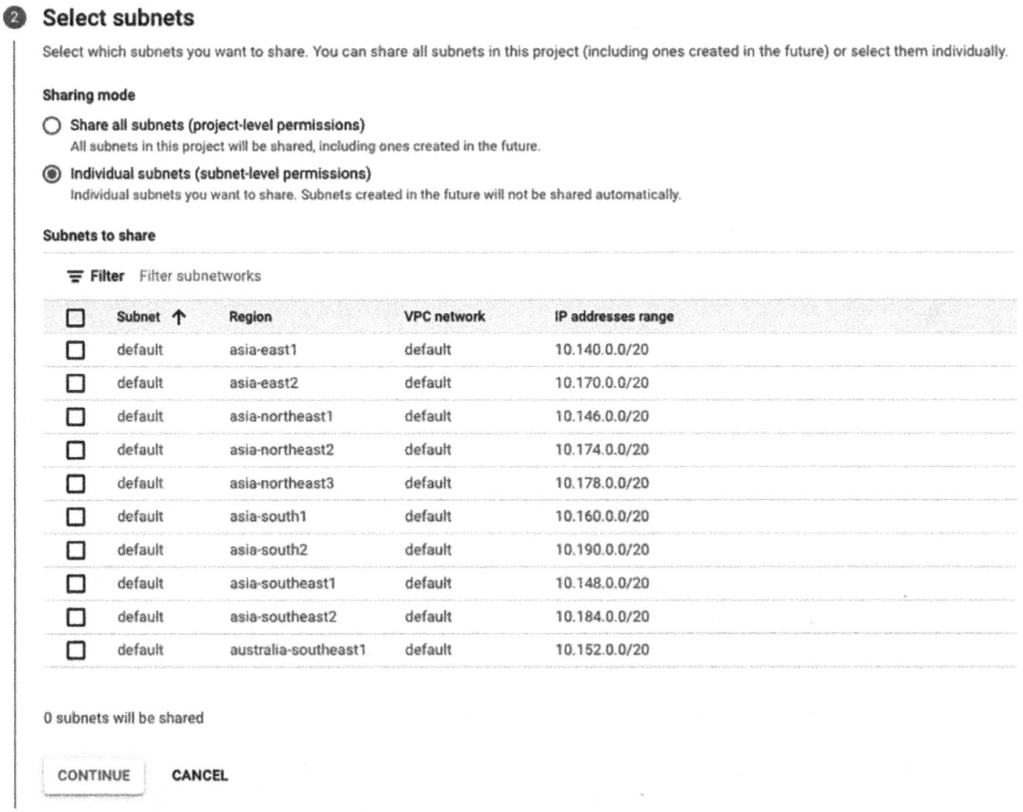

2 Select subnets

Select which subnets you want to share. You can share all subnets in this project (including ones created in the future) or select them individually.

Sharing mode

○ Share all subnets (project-level permissions)
  All subnets in this project will be shared, including ones created in the future.

◉ Individual subnets (subnet-level permissions)
  Individual subnets you want to share. Subnets created in the future will not be shared automatically.

Subnets to share

≡ **Filter** Filter subnetworks

	Subnet ↑	Region	VPC network	IP addresses range
☐	default	asia-east1	default	10.140.0.0/20
☐	default	asia-east2	default	10.170.0.0/20
☐	default	asia-northeast1	default	10.146.0.0/20
☐	default	asia-northeast2	default	10.174.0.0/20
☐	default	asia-northeast3	default	10.178.0.0/20
☐	default	asia-south1	default	10.160.0.0/20
☐	default	asia-south2	default	10.190.0.0/20
☐	default	asia-southeast1	default	10.148.0.0/20
☐	default	asia-southeast2	default	10.184.0.0/20
☐	default	australia-southeast1	default	10.152.0.0/20

0 subnets will be shared

[CONTINUE]   CANCEL

Figure 7.12 – Select subnets

7. Once done, you can then click **CONTINUE** to move to the next step to configure permissions.

8. In **Project names**, list the attached service projects. Using **Attach service projects** doesn't specify Service Project Admins; that's next.

9. Under the **Select users by role** section, you can add **Service Project Admins to Roles**. These users will have `compute.networkUser` for shared subnets. Only Service Project Admins can build Shared VPC subnet resources.

10. Once complete, you can hit the **Save** button.

Once the Shared VPC network is created, you can then attach projects using the following steps:

1. Click on the **Attached projects** tab; then, under this tab, click the **Attach projects** button.

2. When you click on **Attach projects**, you will navigate to a new page from where you can specify **Project names**. Here, check the service projects attached. Attaching service projects does not specify Service Project Admins; that is done in the next step.

3. Under **VPC network permissions**, select the role as `compute.networkUser`. Depending on the VPC network sharing mode, IAM principals are granted the Network User role for the entire host project or selected subnets. These principals are Service Project Admins.

4. In **VPC network sharing mode**, you have two options; first, there is **Share all subnets (project-level permissions)**. Selecting this option will share all current and future subnets in the VPC networks of the host project with all service projects and Service Project Admins. Alternatively, if you select **Individual subnets (subnet-level permissions)**, this will selectively share subnets from the VPC networks of the host project with service projects and Service Project Admins. Once you have made your selection, you can move on to the next step.

5. You can save and complete the process of attaching projects.

The Shared VPC Admin can also designate service accounts as Service Project Admins. Service Project Admins have two types of service accounts:

- The user-managed service account, with the following format: `USER_ID@SERVICE_PROJECT_ID.iam.gserviceaccount.com`

- The Google API service account, with the following format: `SERVICE_PROJECT_NUMBER@cloudservices.gserviceaccount.com`

For both types of service accounts, you do have the option to either give access to all subnets or only to limited subnets. In the following example, we will look at giving service account access to all subnets.

The steps to create a user-managed service account or a Google API service account as a Service Project Admin are the same. They are shown in the following steps, where you need to specify a service account principal based on whether you need a user-managed service account or Google API service account:

1. First, we will log in to the Google Cloud console as a Shared VPC Admin and then navigate to the **Settings** page. Here we will change the project to the service project that contains the service account that needs to be defined as a Service Project Admin:

2. Next, copy the project ID of the service project. For clarity, we will refer to the service project ID as `SERVICE_PROJECT_ID`.

3. Next, ensure that you change the project to the Shared VPC host project. Then, navigate to the **IAM** page in the Google Cloud console.

4. Next, we will add a new service account by clicking **Add**.

5. Specify the following details:

I.   Add `SERVICE_ACCOUNT_NAME@SERVICE_PROJECT_ID.iam.gserviceaccount.com` to the **Principals** field, replacing `SERVICE_ACCOUNT_NAME` with the name of the service account.

II. To make the Google API service account a Service Project Admin, add `SERVICE_PROJECT_NUMBER@cloudservices.gserviceaccount.com` to the **Members** field.

III. Select **Compute Engine | Compute Network User** from the **Roles** menu.

IV. Click **Add**.

This concludes the Shared VPC configuration. There are a few more aspects of Shared VPC that are more network-centric and not required as part of the Google Professional Cloud Security Engineer exam. In the following section, we will cover VPC peering and how you can enable the sharing of routing information by configuring peer networks in Google Cloud.

VPC peering

VPC peering allows you to exchange the internal IP addressing of one VPC network with another VPC network irrespective of whether the VPC network is in the same project or belongs to another organization. The two main use cases for VPC peering include allowing your applications in one VPC network to communicate with services in another VPC network without needing to traverse the internet and keeping traffic within the Google Cloud network. **Software as a Service (SaaS)** providers can also expose their services privately to their users on Google Cloud by configuring VPC peering.

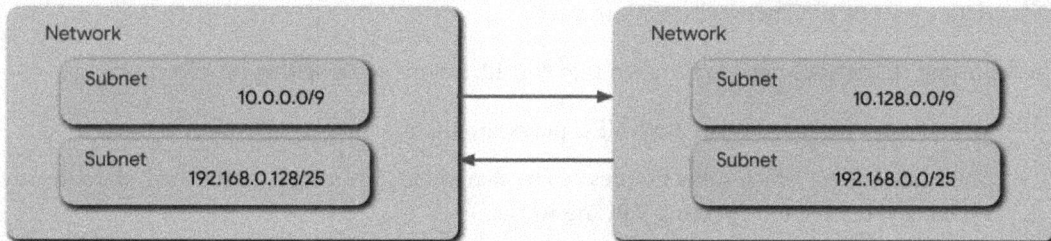

Figure 7.13 – VPC peering

Figure 7.13 shows two VPC networks that are peers and have subnet ranges in each of the networks that are exchanged once the peering is established.

Some of the key advantages of VPC peering are as follows:

- **Network latency**: As the traffic stays within the Google network and is local rather than traversing the internet, there is lower network latency.
- **Network security**: Application owners do not need to make their services publicly accessible, thereby reducing the attack surface.
- **Cost**: Egress traffic is charged, but when using VPC peering, your traffic stays within the Google network, hence no egress network charges will be applied, which helps in reducing the cost.

Next, we will look at some of the key properties of VPC peering:

- VPC peering supports Compute Engine, GKE, and GAE.
- Even though VPC networks are peered, they are administratively separate; that is, you can manage VPC attributes such as routing, firewall rules, and subnets per VPC and it has no impact on the peering.
- VPC peering requires setup on both sides. Administrators for the VPC networks have to complete the configuration on each side to complete the setup. We will look at this process in our VPC peering setup walk-through.
- Both static and dynamic routes can be exchanged.
- You can peer multiple VPCs together (limits apply).
- IAM permissions are required to have the ability to create and manage VPC peers.
- An organization policy administrator can apply the constraint to restrict VPC peering and define a set of VPC networks that can peer.

The following restrictions need to be taken into consideration before setting up VPC peering:

- IP addresses cannot overlap. Both VPC peers should have different IP address ranges.
- You cannot select which subnet routes can be shared; once peering is established, all routes are exchanged between the peering VPC networks.
- Dynamic routes can overlap with a peer network's subnet route, although overlapping destination ranges are silently dropped.

- Only direct peering is supported; you cannot have transit peers.

- Tags and service accounts cannot be used across the peering networks.

- Internal DNS names for compute engines are not accessible across the peering networks.

- Firewall rules are not exchanged across the peering networks, and you need to create rules to allow ingress traffic from compute instances. The default behavior is to block the ingress traffic to VMs by applying an implied deny ingress rule.

- Furthermore, you need to create firewall rules to restrict the access of your VMs to the services they shouldn't be able to access.

- If you are using an internal load balancer and need to restrict access, then you need to create ingress firewall rules that apply to the load balancer's backend VMs.

- Peering is permitted when establishing a peer with a Shared VPC network.

Next, we will look at how to configure a VPC peer:

1. Navigate to the **VPC Network Peering** page and click **Create connection**. Then, click **Continue**.

   Look at *Figure 7.14* for the fields that you need to complete in order to create a VPC network peer.

2. First, we will fill in **Name**; we will use the name `peer-from-starship`.

3. Next, we will select the network that is available under **Your VPC network**. Select a network you want to peer; in our example, we have selected `starshipnw`.

4. Now specify the network you want to peer with. This can be a network in your existing project, or it can be a network in a different project. If it is in another project, when you select that option, you must specify the project ID and the network name in that project. For our example and simplicity, we will select an existing project and then select the *default* network.

5. You also have the option to import or export custom routes. To do that, you can choose one or both of the following options. In our example, we will not import/export any custom routes:

    I.   Use **Import custom routes** to import custom routes exported by the other network.

    II.   Use **Export custom routes** to export custom routes to the other network. The other network must import the routes to see them.

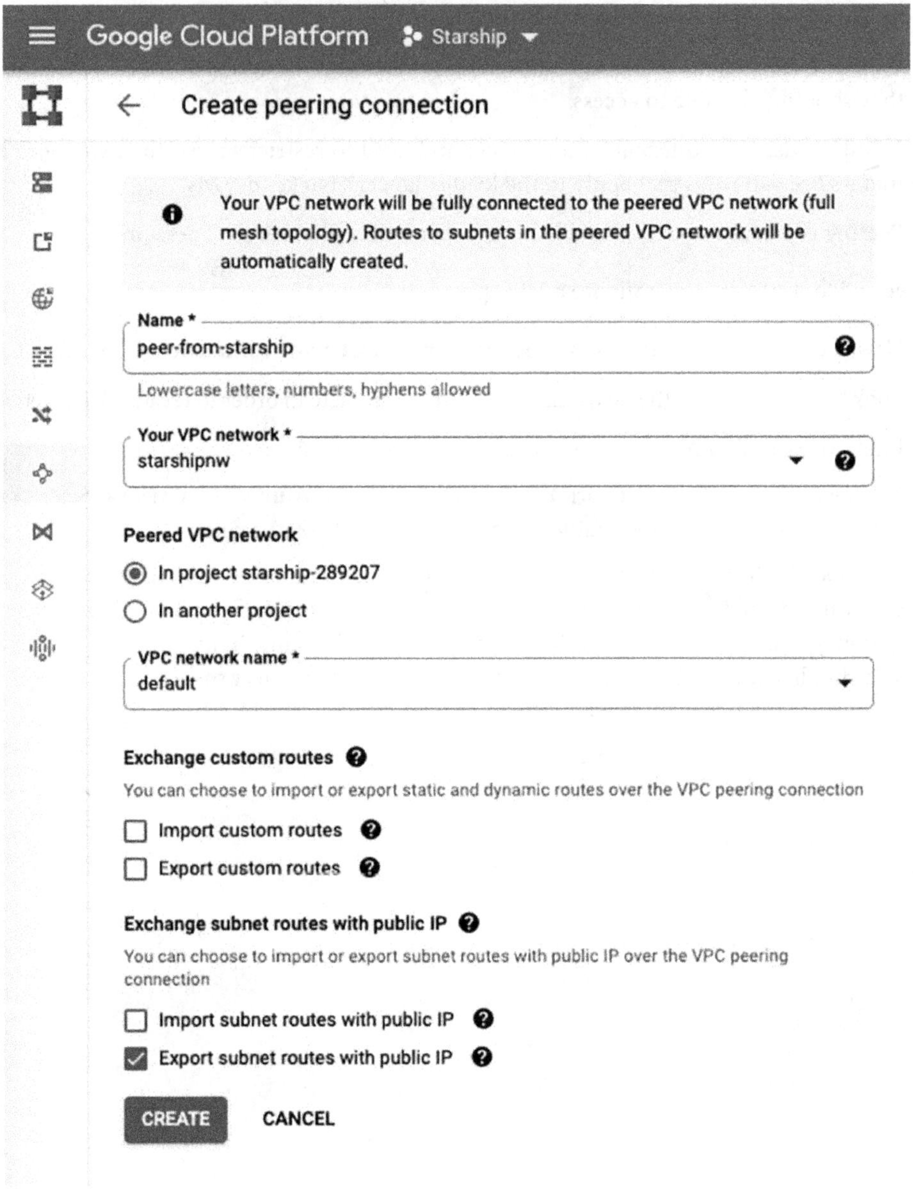

Figure 7.14 – Create peering connection

6. If your network or the partner network uses privately used public IP ranges, these routes are exported by default but not imported. Choose **Import subnet routes with public IP** to import privately used public IP subnet routes exported by the other network.

7. Click **Create**.

The peer configuration is only complete once you configure the peering on both sides. You can further modify the peers or delete them as required. The list of all VPC peers is found under the **VPC Peering** page on the Google Cloud console. Access to on-premises can be done using Cloud VPN. We will look at Cloud VPN in the *Hybrid connectivity options* section later in the chapter.

	Shared VPC	VPC Peering	Cloud VPN
Network services management (Firewalls, subnets, routes, VPN, DNS)	Central management of shared network resources	Clear network and security administrative boundaries	Clear network and security administrative boundaries
Transitivity	N/A	Non-transitive	Transitive
Scale	1000 service projects or more, depending on multiple factors	Up to 25 peered networks	Approximately 100 connected projects
Pricing	General network pricing	General network pricing	General network pricing. Excluding intra-zone traffic, which is <u>billed</u> as interzone.
Performance implication	None	None	Throughput limited based on number of tunnels (1.5 to 3 Gbps per tunnel)

Figure 7.15 – Cross-project communication options comparison

Figure 7.15 gives a quick snapshot of the different options available for cross-project communication across different dimensions, such as management, scale, pricing, and performance. You can use this to understand what options are available and, more importantly, which options align with your network architecture requirements.

We will now look at how micro-segmentation allows you to logically partition your network to have better control of traffic and security.

Micro-segmentation

In this section, we will look at some micro-segmentation techniques. We will cover topics such as how to create subnets, define custom routing, and use firewall rules that can help in creating segmentation in your network.

Subnets

Creating subnets for different types of workloads is a key micro-segmentation strategy. In this section, we will look at what types of subnets you can create and how to apply those subnets to your network design. Irrespective of what type of subnet you create, whether using auto mode or custom mode, on Google Cloud there are two types of **Classless Inter-Domain Routing (CIDR)** ranges: primary and secondary. Let us look at *Figure 7.16* to better understand the difference between the two and when to use one over the other.

	Primary	Secondary
Configuration	Mandatory – one per subnet	Optional – multiple ranges are supported
Used for	Allocation of VM primary IP reserved IPs	Allocating a different IP to multiple microservices running in a VM (e.g., containers, GKE pods).
Extendable	Range can be extended, but not shrunk	No

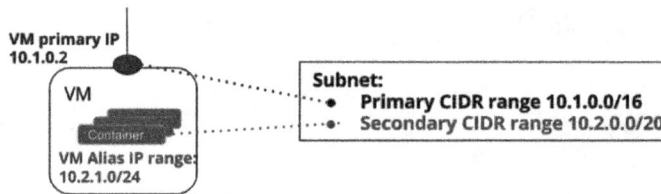

Figure 7.16 – Subnet CIDR ranges

The primary CIDR range is mandatory in a subnet; the secondary range is optional. The VMs, load balancers, and so on get IP addresses from the primary CIDR range. The secondary ranges are used for allocating IP addresses and microservices such as containers. You can extend the primary IP address range but cannot reduce the size of the IP range. Secondary IP address ranges cannot be extended and are fixed.

Custom routing

You can also use VPC routes to create custom routing to restrict and manage access to your services. Custom routing is a combination of both static and/or dynamic routing. In *Figure 7.15*, you can see different types of VPC routes that are supported, along with other attributes. Let us look at the different options available.

Route	Type	Created by	Next Hop	Restrictions	Exchanged with VPC Peering
Subnet route	System	System	VPC network	Cannot be removed	Automatic
Static route	Custom	User	Instance IP/name Cloud VPN	Must be broader than a subnet IP range	Flag controlled
Dynamic route	Custom	Cloud router (BGP session)	BGP peer	Must be broader than a subnet IP range	Flag controlled

Figure 7.17 – VPC routes

Google Cloud supports three different route types: system-generated routes, static custom routes, and dynamic custom routes. System-generated routes are created by the system and cannot be removed. These include routes added to allow communication between subnets, exchange routing information via VPC peering, and those exchanged using Cloud Router.

Static routes are added by the user manually and are also called custom routes. Using static routes, you can define a next hop, such as an internal TCP/UDP load balancer or Cloud VPN for connecting to on-premises services.

Dynamic routes are also classified as custom routes and are dynamically updated, such as creating a **Border Gateway Protocol (BGP)** peer via Cloud Router (we will cover Cloud Router in the *Hybrid connectivity options* section later in this chapter). The next hop is always a BGP peer, as this is configured point-to-point between two autonomous systems to dynamically exchange routing information.

You should not apply custom routes to instances as they will not persist once the instance reboots. You can, however, apply routes to all instances by using tags and service accounts.

Firewall rules

Firewall rules are one of the most important parts of network security. In this section, we will look at how firewall rules work, the evaluation criteria, the different types of firewall rules that you can create (ingress/egress), 5-tuple rules, and tag- service-account-based firewall rules.

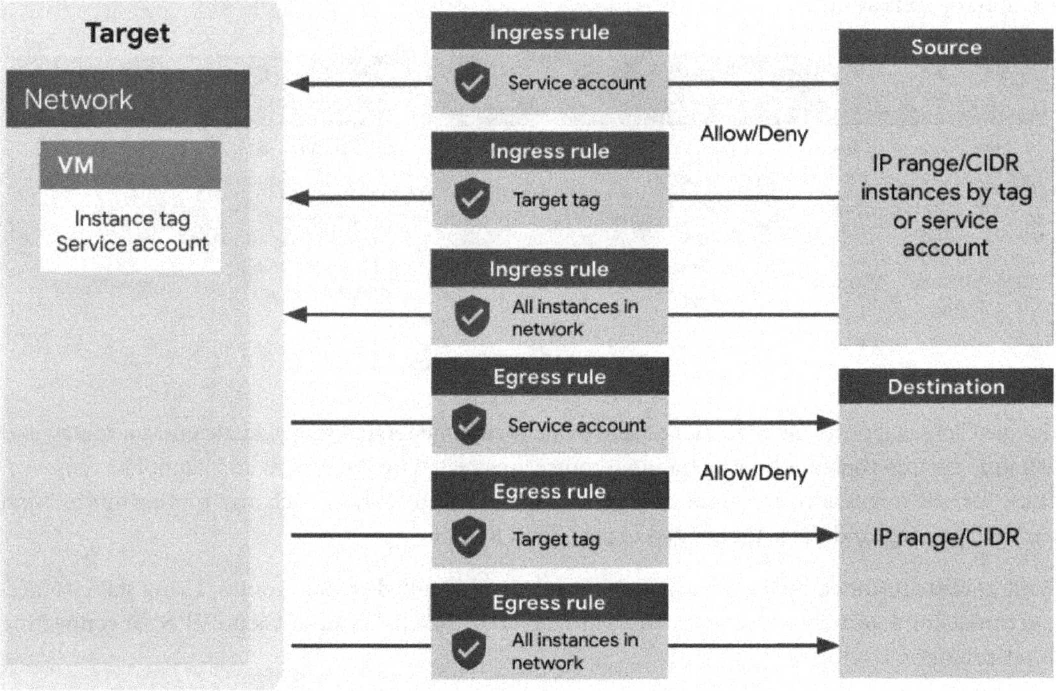

Figure 7.18 – VPC firewall rules

Let us look at some of the firewall rule features shown in *Figure 7.18*:

- Firewall rules are stateful in nature and are applied to a network inside a project. This means, for example, that if you create an ingress deny on port 22, you don't need to configure an equivalent egress deny rule.

- Enforcement is done on the host level, which means there is a negligible performance penalty.

- The control paths that you can manage using firewall rules are VM to VM, VM to the internet, and VM to on-premises.

- For every VPC, two implied rules for ingress/egress are created, which cannot be deleted: a rule to block all incoming connections and another rule to allow all outgoing connections.

- There are some other exceptions as well; egress traffic on port 25 **Simple Mail Transfer Protocol (SMTP)** is always denied.

- All communication between a VM and its corresponding metadata server (169.254.169.254) is allowed.

- Firewall rules support both IPv4 and IPv6 addresses, but a single firewall rule can only have either IPv4 or IPv6.

- Each firewall rule has an allow or deny associated with it, and you have the option to disable firewall rules.

- ICMP response traffic is allowed through the firewall rules.

- All firewall rules are tracked irrespective of the protocol used.

This concludes our coverage of the firewall features; it's good to remember these from an exam perspective. Next, we move on to look at the different components of firewall rules.

Components of firewall rules

There are a few key components of firewall rules that we need to understand as it's important for configuration. Let us look at what these components are:

- **Direction of the rule**: Ingress rules govern connections from specific sources to Google Cloud targets, while egress rules govern connections from targets to specific destinations.

- **Priority**: The rule that is used is based on a number of factors. Rules with lower priority that conflict are ignored and only the rules with the highest priority (the lowest priority number) and that match the traffic are used.

- **Action**: The action determines whether the rule allows or denies connections.

- **Enforcement status**: Firewall rules can be either enabled or disabled without you having to delete them.

- **Target**: The target specifies the instances to which a particular rule applies.

- **Source**: The source is a filter for ingress rules or a destination filter for egress rules.

- **Protocol**: The protocol might be TCP, UDP, or ICMP, and the destination port might be 22, 80, or 443, for instance.

- **Logs**: This option logs connections that match the rule to Cloud Logging.

Firewall rule evaluation

Figure 7.19 illustrates how sets of firewall rules are processed. The figure does not include implied rules or default rules for a default network, as the processing logic only cares about processing the rules and is not concerned with how the rules were inserted into the stack of rules to process.

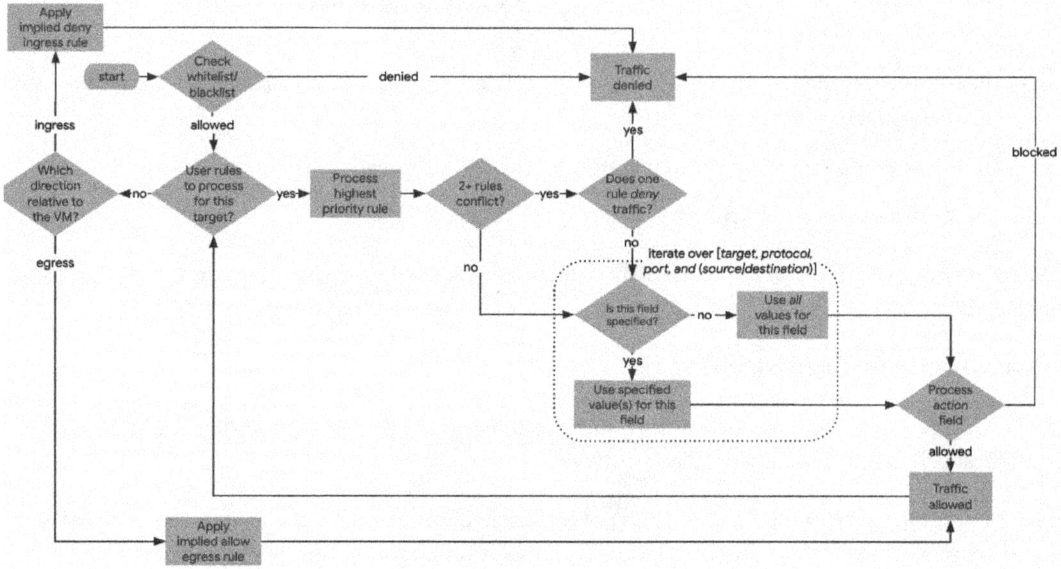

Figure 7.19 – Firewall rule evaluation logic

The evaluation logic is self-explanatory, so take some time to follow the rules and understand how the logic is applied. There are a few things to keep in mind: rule priority is rated from 0-65535, where the lowest integer indicates the highest priority. *Target* refers to the instance(s) to which the rule applies; it is not the target of the network connection. *Port* refers to only TCP and UDP traffic.

Firewall rule options

There are three different options for how to configure your firewall rules:

- **5-tuple-based firewall rules**: You can create firewall rules based on the **5-tuple**, which specifies the source and destination IP, the port and protocol, and an associated action to allow or deny, along with the direction ingress/egress. You also have the option to either allow or deny all TCP/UDP ports or specific ports.

- **Network-tag-based firewall rule**: You can create a rule that specifies a network tag under **Targets**. A network tag is an arbitrary attribute. Any IAM principal with edit permission on an instance can associate one or more network tags with it. IAM principals assigned to a project that have the Compute Engine Instance Admin role have permission to edit an instance and change its network tags, which can change the set of applicable firewall rules for that instance.

- **Service-account-based firewall rule**: You also have the option to create firewall rules where you can specify the target based on the service account.

Let us look at how you can create firewall rules based on the three options:

1. Go to the **Firewall** page in the Google Cloud console and click on **Create firewall** rule. This will then display a screen that will let you create a new firewall rule.

2. Next, we will configure the attributes in the relevant fields, such as filling in **Name** for the firewall rule. In our example, in *Figure 7.20*, we have the name `new-rule-tags`.

> **Note**
> The firewall rule name must be unique for the project.

3. Optionally, you can also enable firewall rule logging by toggling the option in the setting to **Logs | On**. To remove metadata, you can further expand **Logs** details and then clear **Include metadata**.

4. In the next step, we will fill in **Network** for the firewall rule. For example, our network is `vpca`.

5. You can now specify **Priority** for the rule. As we discussed earlier, the lower the number, the higher the priority. Refer to the *Firewall rules evaluation* section covered earlier to understand how the logic works.

6. We will next specify **Direction of traffic**, where you can choose to select either **ingress** or **egress**.

7. For **Action on match**, choose **allow** or **deny**.

8. Next, we have the three options that you can specify as the targets of the rule:

    I.   If you want the rule to apply to all instances in the network, choose **All instances in the network**.

II.   If you want the rule to apply to select instances by network (target) tags, choose **Specified target tags**, then type the tags to which the rule should apply into the **Target tags** field.

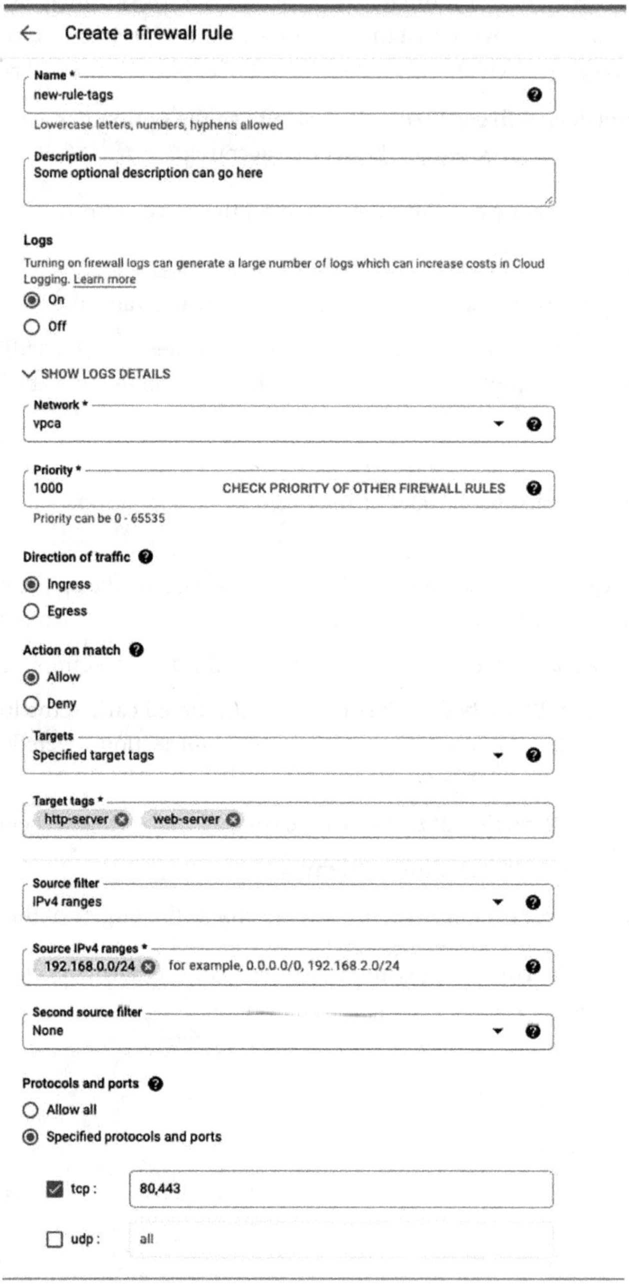

Figure 7.20 – Create a firewall rule using target tags

III.   If you want the rule to apply to select instances according to the associated service account, choose **Specified service account**, indicate whether the service account is in the current project or another one under **Service account scope**, and choose or type the service account name in the **Target service account** field.

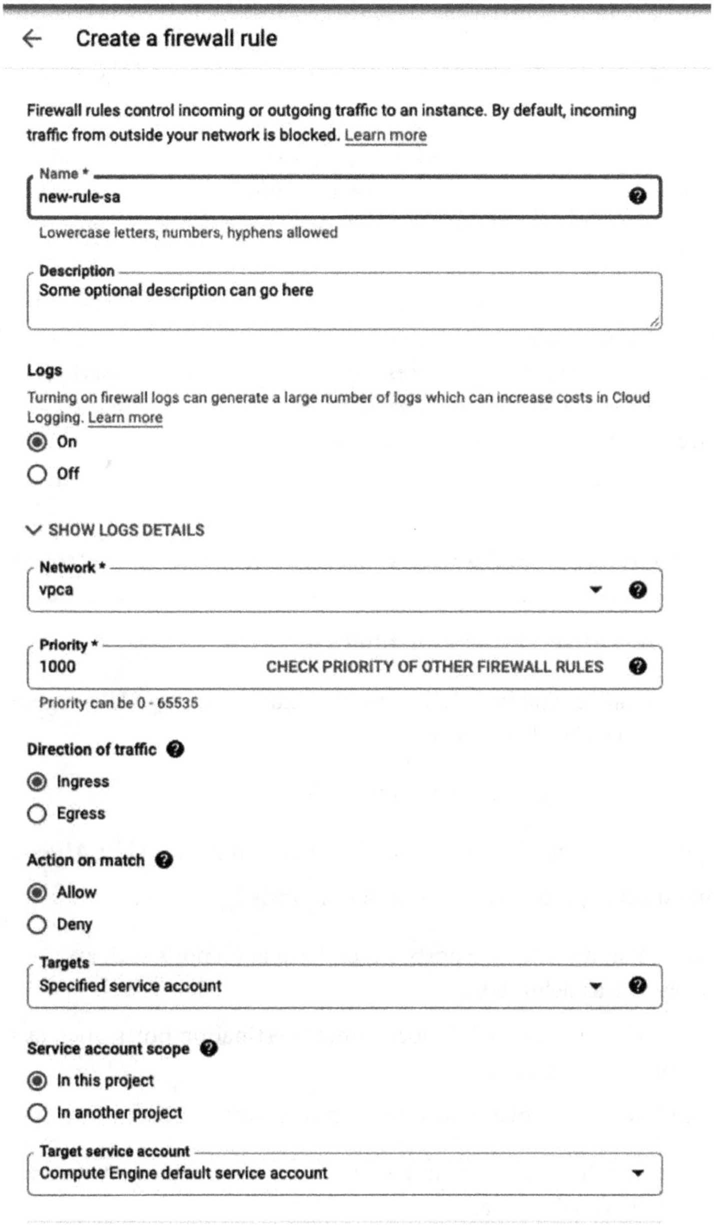

Figure 7.21 – Create a firewall rule using the service account

9. For an ingress rule, specify **Source filter**:

    I.   Choose IP ranges and type CIDR blocks into the source IP ranges to establish the incoming traffic sources. You can specify any network source by using the default IP range, that is, `0.0.0.0/0`.

    II.   To limit sources by network tag, from the options presented under **Source Filter**, select **Source tags** and enter the tags. Source tag filtering is only available if the target is not a service account.

    III.   To limit sources by service account, choose **Service account**, indicate whether the service account is in the current project or another, then type the service account name in **Source service account**. Source service account filtering is only accessible if the target is not tagged.

    IV.   Specify a second source filter. Secondary source filters cannot employ primary criteria. Source IP ranges work with source tags and source service accounts. An effective source set is the source range IP addresses plus the network tags or service accounts. The source is included in an effective source set if either the source IP range or source tags (or source service accounts) fulfill the filter requirements.

> **Note**
>
> Remember that **Source tags** and **Source service account** cannot be used together.

10. For an egress rule, specify **Destination filter**:

    I.   Choose IP ranges and type **CIDR blocks** into **Destination IP ranges** to create outgoing traffic destinations. *Everywhere* is `0.0.0.0/0`.

11. Define the protocols and ports to which the rule applies:

    I.   To apply the rule to all protocols and destination ports, select **Allow all** or **Deny all**.

    II.   Define specific protocols and destination ports:

        i.   Select **TCP** to include TCP ports. Enter destination ports such as `20-22`, `80`, and `8080`. Use commas as delimiters.

        ii.   Select **UDP** to include UDP ports. Enter destination ports, such as `67-69` and `123`. Use commas as delimiters.

        iii.   Select **Other protocols** to include protocols such as `icmp` or `sctp`.

12. To avoid enforcing the firewall rule, you can set the enforcement state to **Disabled**. Select **Disabled** from the **Disable** rule.

13. Click **Create**.

Firewall rules are referenced throughout the exam in network security questions, so do spend some hands-on time configuring firewall rules. There are additional links in the *Further reading* section that point to some labs that are available on Google Cloud Skills Boost to get more familiar with firewall rules and their implementation so you can better apply the concepts learned here.

Cloud DNS

In this section, we will look at Cloud DNS and how to configure it with some basics. For the exam, you only need basic knowledge of the Cloud DNS topics. We will look at an overview of Cloud DNS and some key components that you need to understand.

Cloud DNS is a highly scalable fully managed service offered by Google Cloud. You can create both public and private zones using Cloud DNS. Cloud DNS uses an internal metadata server that acts as the DNS resolver for both internal and external resolutions, such as resolving hostnames on the public internet. Every VM instance has a metadata server used for querying instance information – for example, name, ID, startup/shutdown scripts, custom metadata, service account, and so on – and the DNS resolver is set on VMs as part of default DHCP (Dynamic Host Configuration Protocol) leases. Overriding DHCP leases is possible by customizing the DHCP configuration; however, it is not a common pattern.

Cloud DNS also supports split-horizon, where VMs can be resolved within a private zone or public zone, depending on where the query comes from. For hybrid connectivity, you can use DNS forwarding zones, where you can forward requests to an on-premises resolver.

You can also create DNS peering, allowing you to query private zones in different VPC networks. Peering is one-way and no connectivity is required. It supports two levels of depth, meaning that transitive DNS peering across two DNS peering hops is supported. This is required in a hub-and-spoke model to allow spokes to query each other's private zones without creating a full-mesh peering topology.

With Cloud DNS, you can also create a managed reverse zone to prevent non-RFC 1918 address resolutions from being sent to the internet. **Domain Name System Security Extensions (DNSSEC)** is also supported, and we will cover DNSSEC in the next section. You can create resolver policies to configure access to private and restricted Google APIs from within a VPC-SC perimeter. We will cover VPC-SC in *Chapter 10, Cloud Data Loss Prevention*.

The internal DNS is where the records are automatically created for the VM's primary IP, such as `instance1.us-west1b.c.projectx.internal`. These are used for resolution within the same VPC and project.

Configuring Cloud DNS – create a public DNS zone for a domain name

Before you begin, please ensure that you have a valid domain name registered with the domain registrar. You will also need a Windows or Linux VM instance and the IP address to point to the A record of your zone. Next, check and enable the DNS API if it is not enabled. This can be done by navigating to **API & Services** from the menu in the Google Cloud console.

Take the following steps to configure and set up the DNS public zone:

1. In the Google Cloud console, go to the **Create a DNS zone** page.

2. For **Zone type**, select **Public**.

3. For **Zone name**, enter my-new-zone.

4. For **DNS name**, enter a DNS name suffix for the zone by using a domain name that you registered (for example, example.com).

5. For **DNSSEC**, ensure that the **Off** setting is selected.

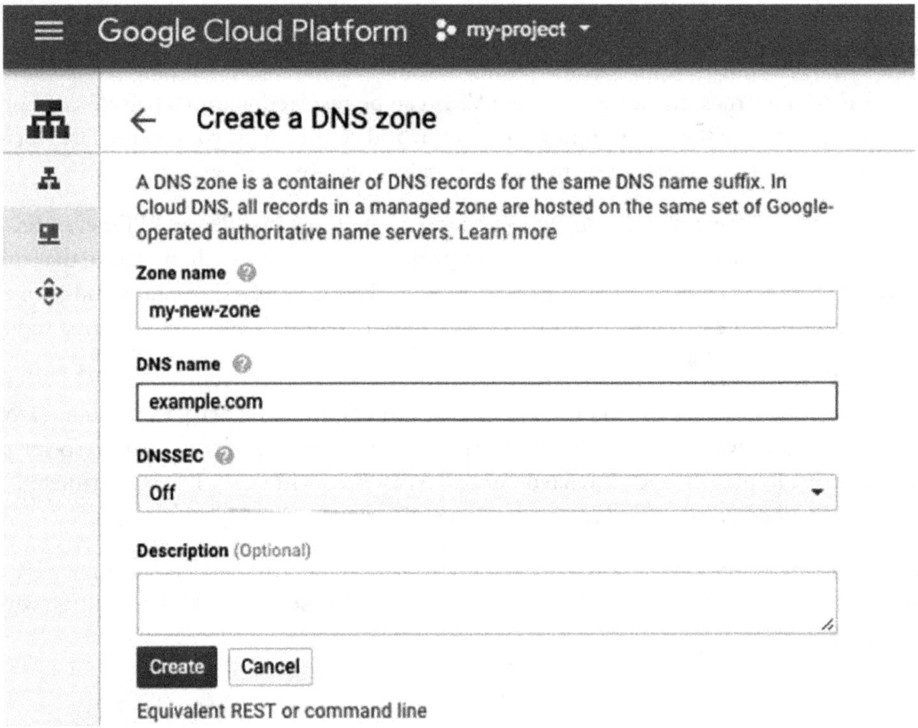

Figure 7.22 – Create a DNS zone

6. Click **Create**.

Next, we will look at the steps on how to create a record to point the domain to an external IP address:

1. In the Google Cloud console, go to the **Cloud DNS** page.

2. Click the zone where you want to add a record set.

3. Click **Add record set**.

4. For **Resource Record Type**, to create an A record, select **A**. To create an AAAA record, select **AAAA**.

5. For **IPv4 Address** or **IPv6 Address**, enter the IP address that you want to use with this domain.

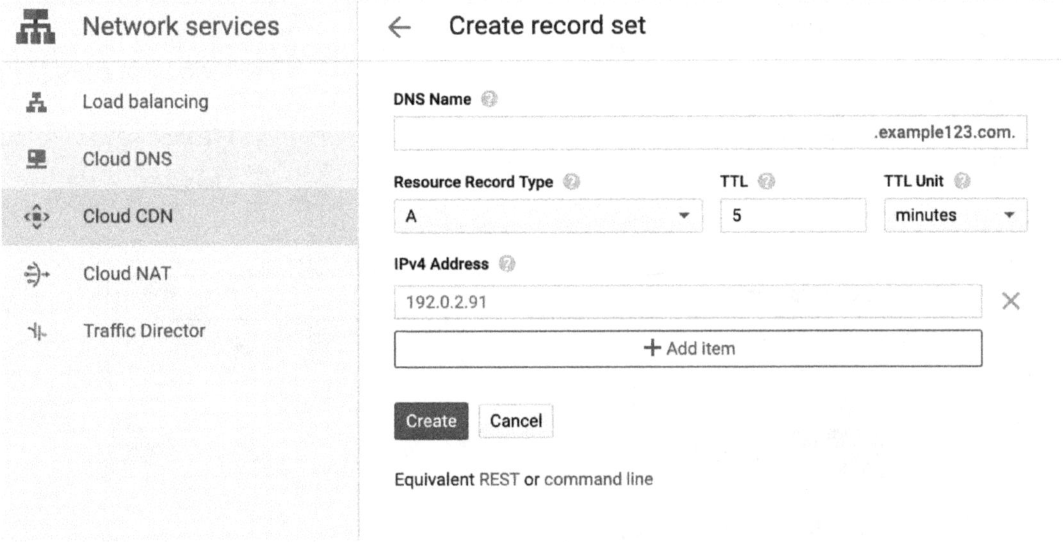

Figure 7.23 – Create a record set

6. Click **Create**.

In this last step, we will create a CNAME record for the WWW domain:

1. In the Google Cloud console, go to the **Cloud DNS** page.

2. Click the zone where you want to add a record set.

3. Click **Add record set**.

4. For **DNS Name**, enter www.

5. For **Resource Record Type**, select **CNAME**.

6. For **Canonical names**, enter the domain name, followed by a period (for example, `example.com.`).

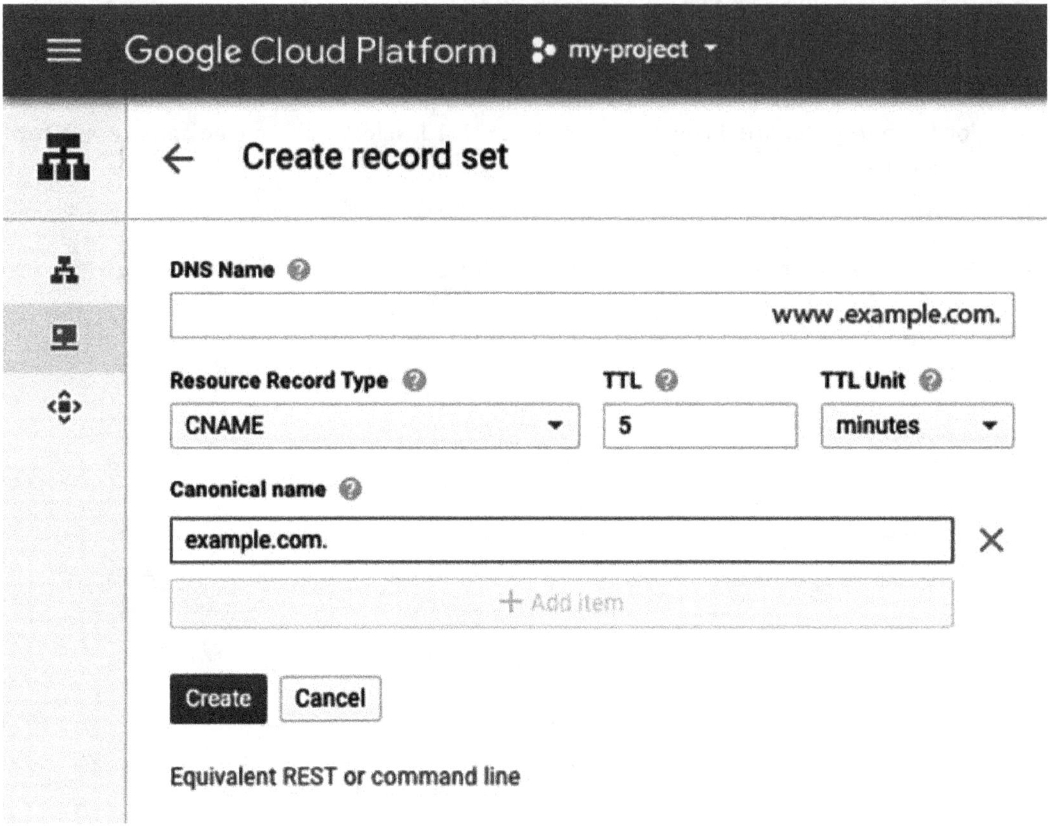

Figure 7.24 – Create a CNAME record

7. Click **Create**.

In the next section, we will take a look at DNSSEC. It is a set of protocols that are designed to increase the security of the DNS.

DNSSEC

DNSSEC is a security feature of DNS that helps prevent attackers from poisoning or manipulating DNS requests. The exam covers DNSSEC at an extremely basic level, so you should understand what DNSSEC is and how it works. From a Cloud DNS perspective, you can enable DNSSEC for your public zone by defining the parameters as shown in *Figure 7.25*.

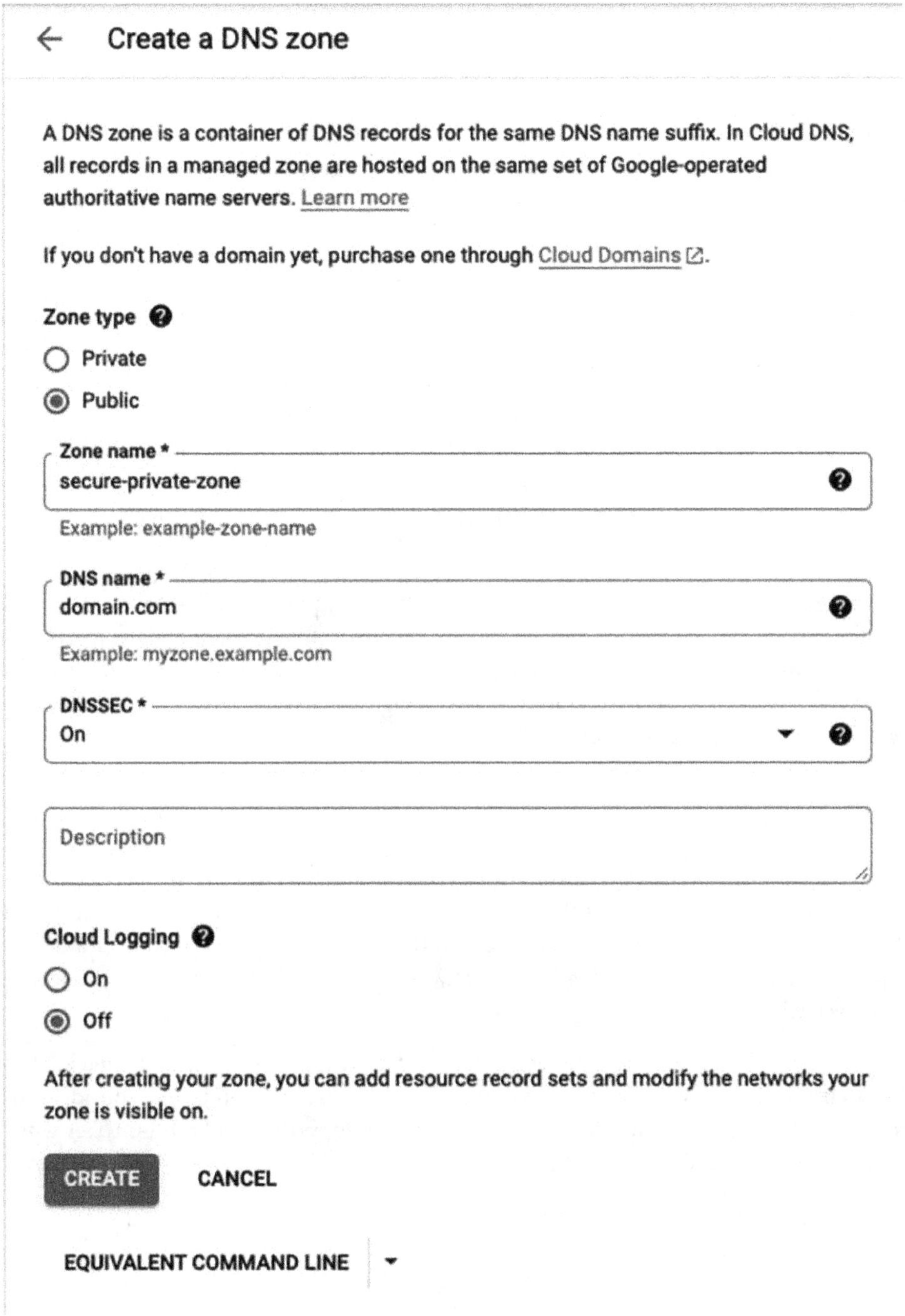

← Create a DNS zone

A DNS zone is a container of DNS records for the same DNS name suffix. In Cloud DNS, all records in a managed zone are hosted on the same set of Google-operated authoritative name servers. Learn more

If you don't have a domain yet, purchase one through Cloud Domains ↗.

Zone type ❓
- ⚪ Private
- ⦿ Public

Zone name *
```
secure-private-zone                                              ❓
```
Example: example-zone-name

DNS name *
```
domain.com                                                      ❓
```
Example: myzone.example.com

DNSSEC *
```
On                                                          ▼  ❓
```

```
Description

```

Cloud Logging ❓
- ⚪ On
- ⦿ Off

After creating your zone, you can add resource record sets and modify the networks your zone is visible on.

[CREATE]   CANCEL

EQUIVALENT COMMAND LINE   ▼

Figure 7.25 – Enable DNSSEC for a private DNS zone

In *Figure 7.25*, you first assign a name to your private zone in the **Zone name** field. Then, specify **DNS name**, which is the domain name, and then set the **DNSSEC** option to **On**. Once completed, click the **CREATE** button.

In the most basic form, DNSSEC works by including a digital signature in responses to DNS queries. So, for every DNS zone, public and private keys are created. Cloud DNS serves the public key (DSKEY), resource record signatures (RRSIG), and non-existence (NSEC) parameters to authenticate your zone's contents. All these are automatically managed by Cloud DNS once you have enabled DNSSEC.

An important thing to note is that for DNSSEC to work, both your registrar and registry should support DNSSEC for your top-level domain. This means that for DNSSEC to be effective, both the company that is responsible for registering the domain name (the registrar) and the company that is responsible for maintaining the database of domain names and their associated IP addresses (the registry) must support DNSSEC for the top-level domain (for example, `.com`, `.org`, and so on). If you are unable to add a **Delegation Signer** (**DS**) record through your domain registrar to enable DNSSEC, then enabling DNSSEC on Cloud DNS will have no effect. Another thing to be aware of is that DNSSEC is not encrypted; keys are used to authenticate the resolver, not to encrypt client-server queries and resolutions.

If you are migrating from your DNSSEC-signed zone to Cloud DNS, you can use the **Transfer** state when enabling DNSSEC for your public zone. The **Transfer** state lets you copy your relevant keys, such as the **key signing key** (**KSK**) and **zone signing key** (**ZSK**), from your old zone to Cloud DNS. You should keep the state as **Transfer** until all DNS changes have propagated to the authoritative DNS server and then change the state to **On**.

Load balancers

In this section, we will look at load balancing. There are many different load balancers that are available on Google Cloud. We will look at each of the different types of load balancers, what they are, and when to use which type of load balancer based on the traffic type. We will go over a decision tree that helps you decide what type of load balancer would meet your requirements, along with some limitations as well.

The other aspects that we will cover include the difference between external and internal load balancers and when to use which and why; regional versus global load balancers; and some considerations from a network tier perspective, as some load balancers are only supported by Premium Tier while others are also supported by Standard Tier. This can be an important thing to be aware of both from a cost and security perspective.

Let us start by looking at the different types of load balancers:

- **Global external HTTP(S) load balancer**: This load balancer handles both HTTP and HTTPS traffic and is a proxy-based Layer 7 function that caters to your services and is configured behind a single external IP address. It can service traffic to different types of Google Cloud services as backends, such as Google Compute Engine, Google GKE, and Cloud Storage. You can use an external HTTP(S) load balancer to distribute and manage traffic for your hybrid workloads in an on-premises environment as well. This load balancer is implemented on **Google Front End (GFE)** and is global when using Premium Tier but can be configured to be regional when using Standard Tier.

- **Regional external TCP/UDP load balancer**: This is also referred to as a regional network load balancer and is configured as a pass-through. It balances the traffic for VMs in the same region. This is offered as a managed service and can cater to any client on the internet, including Google Compute Engine, with an external IP address and clients using Cloud **Network Address Translation (NAT)**. This load balancer is not a proxy, and it distributes traffic for the backend VMs using the packet's source and destination IP address and protocol. The traffic is terminated at the VM and responses from the backend are sent directly to the client and not through the load balancer.

- **SSL proxy load balancer (global)**: This is a reverse proxy load balancer that distributes SSL traffic from the internet to the closest available backend VMs. The SSL proxy load balancer terminates the incoming TLS requests and forwards the traffic to the backend VM as TLS traffic or TCP. As with the HTTP(S) load balancer, based on the network tier, you can configure the SSL proxy load balancer to be global by using Premium Tier or configure it to be regional if using Standard Tier. Both IPv4 and IPv6 are supported, and the traffic is intelligently routed to the backends based on capacity. Both self-managed and Google-managed certificates are supported. You can also control the SSL features on the load balancer by configuring the SSL policies.

- **TCP proxy load balancer (global)**: This is a reverse proxy load balancer, and it distributes the traffic to the VMs configured as your backends inside the Google Cloud VPC network. It uses a single external IP address for all users globally. All TCP traffic coming from the internet is terminated at the load balancer and can then be routed to the VMs as TCP or SSL. With this load balancer, you can have global load balancing if using Premium Tier or regional load balancing if using Standard Tier.

- **Internal TCP/UDP load balancer**: This load balancer distributes traffic to your internal VMs within the region in a VPC network. A typical use case is using internal load balancers in a three-tier web architecture, where they can be deployed with an external load balancer. In this architecture, you will have an external HTTP(S) load balancer in front of your web servers and then have internal load balancers behind the web servers to cater and scale traffic to your VMs, which are private and only accessible within the VPC network.

- **Internal HTTP(S) load balancer**: An internal HTTP(S) load balancer is a regional proxy-based Layer 7 load balancer. Using this load balancer, you can distribute traffic to backend services such as Compute Engine and GKE. The internal load balancer is built on the open source Envoy proxy.

	Type	Geographical scope	Network tiers	Proxy/pass-through
Internal	TCP/UDP	Regional	Premium	Pass-through
	HTTP(s)			Proxy
External	TCP/UDP	Regional	Standard/Premium	Pass-through
	HTTP(s)			
	TCP proxy	Regional/Global depending on network tier	Standard/Premium	Proxy
	SSL proxy			

Figure 7.26 – Different types of Google Cloud load balancers

Figure 7.26 gives a quick overview of the different types of load balancers, their geographical scope, and network tiers.

The topic of load balancers is very broad, with a lot of features and capabilities that are more network-centric than security-related. Therefore, for the purpose of the exam, the content here is limited to the security scope. Understanding how load balancers work and how to configure different types of load balancers is important; therefore, it is highly recommended that you spend time reading about load balancers in more detail and spend some time on hands-on exercises using Google Cloud Skills Boost. Links in the *Further reading* section will take you to Google Cloud Skills Boost network labs and documentation on understanding Google Cloud load balancing.

Now we will look at some important distinctions, such as external versus internal, and when to use what load balancer based on the use case or traffic type.

Google Cloud load balancers are of two types: external or internal. You will use an external load balancer if you have traffic coming from the internet to access services that are in your Google Cloud VPC network. An internal load balancer, on the other hand, is only used when you need to load balance traffic to VMs that are private and only accessible from within the VPC network.

Another aspect to understand is when to use global versus regional load balancers. A global load balancer will manage and distribute traffic coming in from the internet to backends that are distributed across multiple regions. Your users only interact with one application using the same unicast IP address, and a global load balancer can distribute traffic to the closest backend location. Premium Tier is a requirement for global load balancers. Regional load balancers, however, are used when you have a requirement such as regulatory requirements to keep your traffic limited to backends in a particular region. For this type of load balancer, you can use Standard Tier.

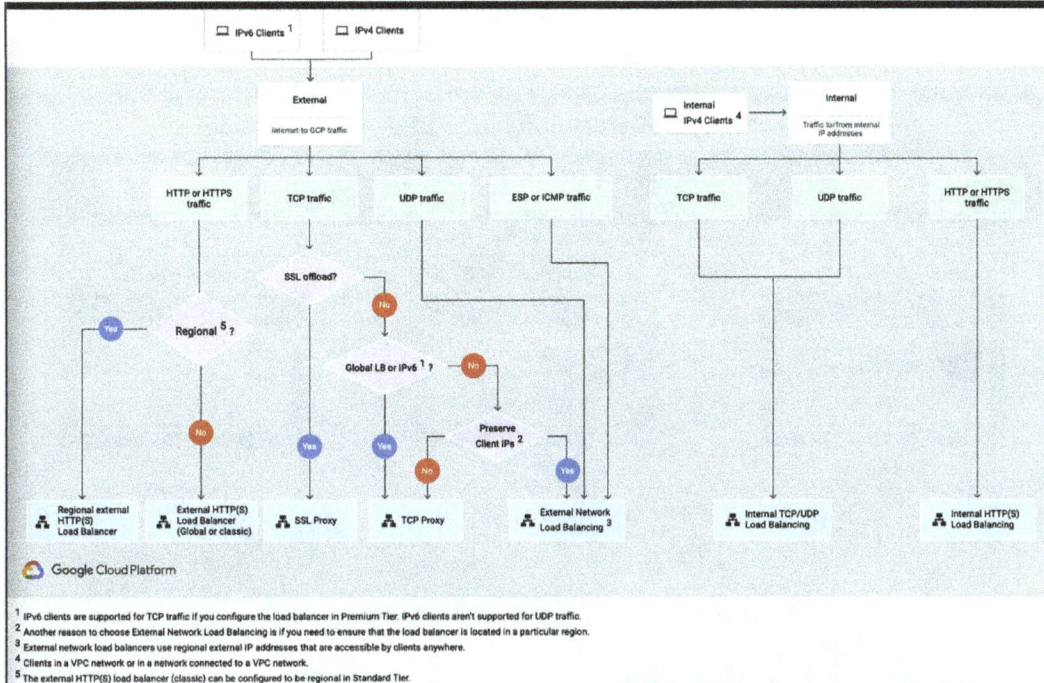

Figure 7.27 – Decision tree for choosing a load balancer

The next important thing to know is when to use which type of load balancer. You can use *Figure 7.27* as a decision tree to help you decide.

Configuring external global HTTP(S) load balancers

Let us look at the following architecture to better understand how the HTTP(S) load balancer accepts and distributes traffic. The following architecture (*Figure 7.28*) is only for illustrative purposes and is not relevant to the actual configuration.

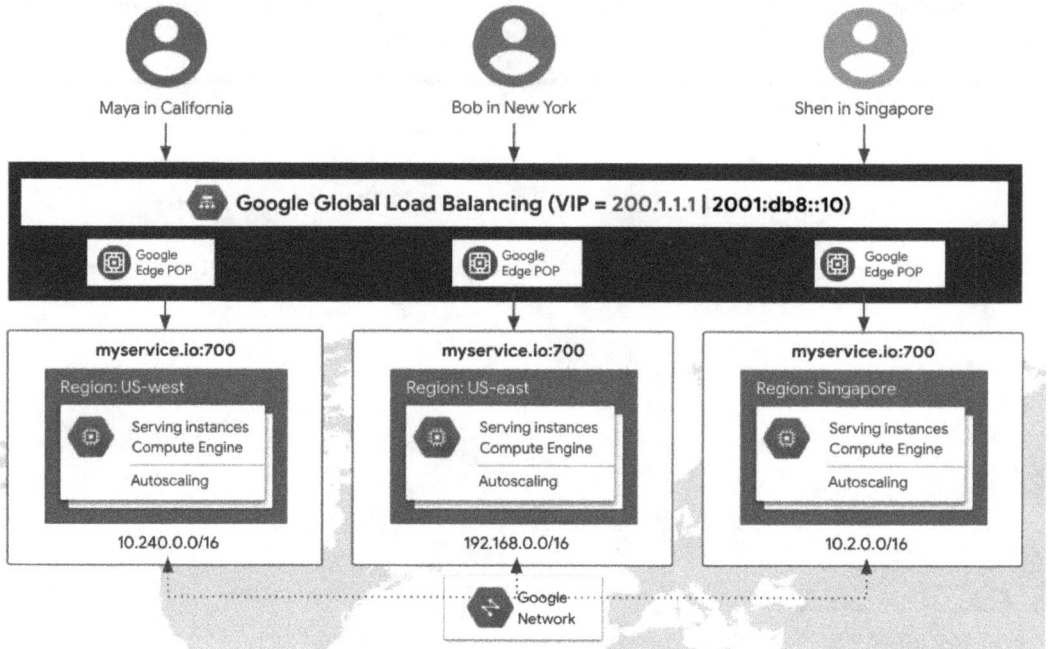

Figure 7.28 – External global HTTP(S) load balancing

Configuring an HTTP(S) load balancer is just one step. You will also need to configure your VMs, Compute Engine instances, and GKE nodes for the backend, as well as having a fixed static IP address and health check firewall rules. Refer to the links in *Further reading* to find a Google Cloud Skills Boost exercise on how to configure an HTTP(S) load balancer.

Hybrid connectivity options

Throughout this chapter, we have made references to hybrid connectivity. The term **hybrid connectivity** means that you can join your Google Cloud network to your on-premises network and a third-party cloud provider using multiple connectivity options. We will look at two options: Cloud VPN (IPSec) and Cloud Interconnect.

Before we look at the different connectivity options, it's important to understand what Cloud Router is, as it is a key component when creating a Google Cloud-based VPN. Cloud Router is a managed service and a regional resource. It is responsible for exchanging routes between your VPC and your on-premises network via BGP. Dynamic routing options include both regional and global. With regional routing, Cloud Router shares routes only for subnets in the region where Cloud Router is provisioned. With global routing, it shares routes for all subnets in the VPC network.

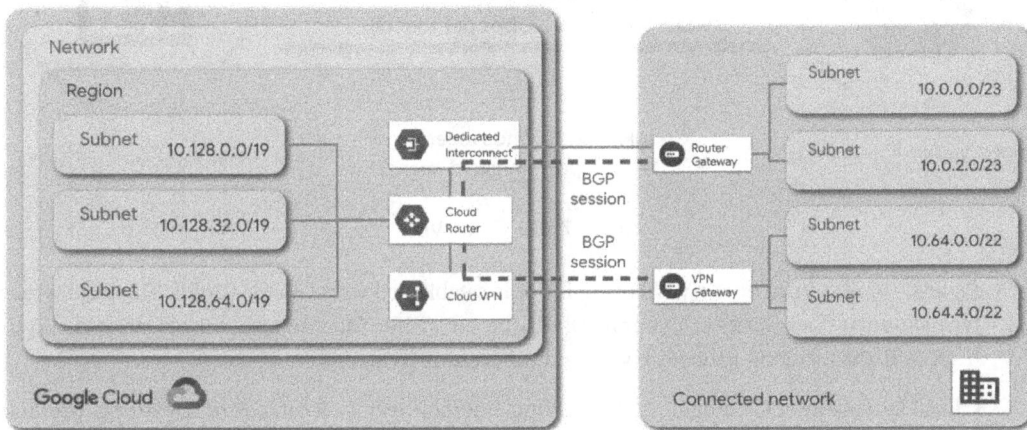

Figure 7.29 – Cloud Router

Figure 7.29 shows how Cloud Router exchanges routes using BGP with a connected network.

Let us now look at the connectivity options that are available for building hybrid connections with Google Cloud:

- **Cloud VPN** (**IPSec-based**): Creating a Cloud VPN instance, which is an IPSec-based VPN over the internet, is the fastest and easiest way to connect your cloud environment with other clouds or with your on-premises network. You can leverage your existing internet connection. This option supports a bandwidth of 1.5-3 Gbps per tunnel, depending on peer location (public or within Google Cloud/direct peer), with multi-tunnel support for higher bandwidth. A VPN device at the on-premises data center is required to support **IPSEC/IKE/Multi-tunnel** protocols.

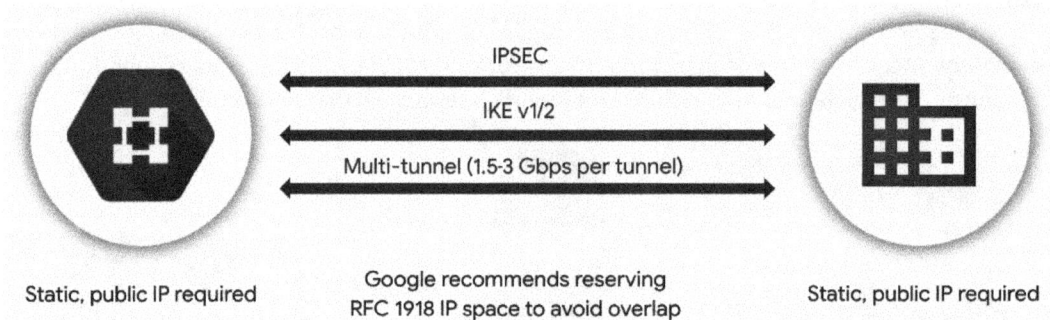

Figure 7.30 – Cloud VPN

Figure 7.30 illustrates how a VPN using IPSec is established with Google Cloud. This deployment type supports both static- or dynamic (BGP)-based VPNs. You also have the option to configure high availability using gateways with two different interfaces.

- **Cloud Interconnect**: Using dedicated Cloud Interconnect, you can connect your on-premises network with dedicated private links that do not traverse the public internet. The traffic takes fewer hops and gets a high level of reliability and security. Your VPC network internal (RFC 1918) IP addresses are directly accessible from your on-premises network.

There is no requirement for establishing a VPN or NAT. It supports high bandwidth from 8x10 Gbps, or 2x100 Gbps, depending on the need. You can further reduce your egress costs as traffic remains internal. It works with Private Google Access to allow Google API access through internal links. Although the traffic is unencrypted, you can use a self-managed IPSEC VPN if that's a requirement. Cloud VPN over Cloud Interconnect is not supported. You can create VLAN attachments and associate them with Cloud Router. You can also attach to multiple VPCs. Cloud Router is used to dynamically exchange routes.

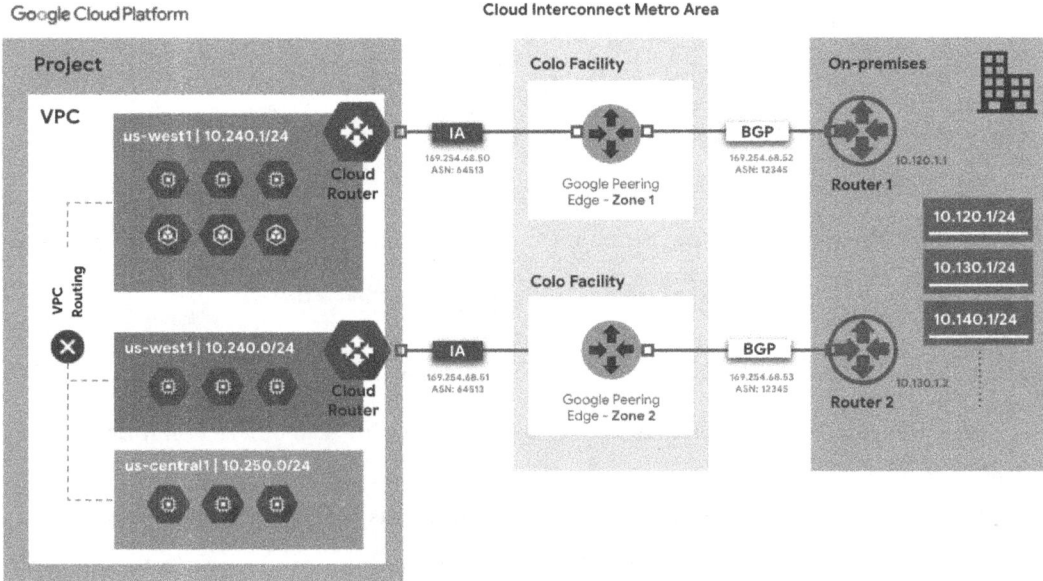

Figure 7.31 – Cloud Interconnect

In *Figure 7.31*, there are two routers in an on-premises location with links to two colo facilities in the same metro area for redundancy. There are `InterconnectAttachment` (**IA**)/VLAN attachments: one from each colo facility to a different Cloud Router instance. BGP sessions between Cloud Router and on-premises routers are used for route exchange. In this illustration, Cloud Router instances are in `us-west1`. To allow access from on-premises to resources in the `us-central1` subnet, global routing would be required.

Best practices and design considerations

In this section, we will look at some VPC best practices and design considerations that you need to factor in when designing and building your secure network on Google Cloud. From an exam perspective, it is important to understand these as you will find questions about best practices.

VPC best practices

For VPC, some of the best practices include the following:

- Prevent overlapping IPs and control subnet creation by creating VPC networks using custom subnet creation mode.
- Reduce management and topology complexity by making use of Shared VPC where possible.
- Group similar applications into fewer, more manageable, and larger subnets.

- Apply organization policies to do the following:

  - Skip the creation of default networks for new projects.

  - Restrict shared VPC host projects and subnets.

  - Restrict VPC peering usage.

- Ensure the design scales to your needs by considering the limitations of each network component.

Key decisions

Some of the key decisions you need to make include the following:

- How will your Google Cloud resources communicate with each other? Will it involve VPC design or Shared VPC?

- How will resources be segmented into networks and subnets? Will there be micro-segmentation?

- How will name resolution be solved among cloud resources and between the cloud and connected environments? Is Cloud DNS and DNSSEC to be factored into your public zones?

- What strategies will be used to connect Google Cloud with corporate networks? Will you use hybrid connectivity options?

- How will your resources communicate with the internet? Will you use external load balancing? Global or regional?

It is important not just to understand best practices but also to consider answering the preceding questions around design considerations, which will help you define requirements and build a resilient and secure network on Google Cloud and across your hybrid network.

Summary

In this chapter, we covered what VPC is and the concepts of regions and zones and how they are designed. We looked at VPC models such as Shared VPC and VPC peering. We covered micro-segmentation strategies such as custom routing, firewall rules, and subnets. We then looked at how to configure Cloud DNS and enable DNSSEC. We covered topics related to different options that are available for Google Cloud load balancing and hybrid connectivity, and finally, we looked at some VPC best practices and design considerations.

In the next chapter, we will cover Context-Aware Access and some more network security aspects, such as Identity-Aware Proxy, web application firewalls, distributed denial of service protection, and Google Private Access.

Further reading

For more information on Google Cloud VPC, refer to the following links:

- Andromeda: Performance, Isolation, and Velocity at Scale in Cloud Network Virtualization: `https://packt.link/y1soL`

- VPC Networks – Controlling Access: `https://packt.link/iQmOj`

- HTTP Load Balancer with Cloud Armor: `https://packt.link/Wi9Te`

- Cloud Load Balancing overview: `https://packt.link/Wm7kG`

- An overview of DNSSEC: `https://packt.link/D9PfM`

- Migrating DNSSEC zones to Cloud DNS: `https://packt.link/g8HmK`

- Networking in Google Cloud: Defining and Implementing Networks: `https://packt.link/YCEbn`

- Networking in Google Cloud: Hybrid Connectivity and Network Management: `https://packt.link/2BEqK`

8
Advanced Network Security

In this chapter, we will look at advanced network security. This chapter is an extension of the previous chapter and part of the overall network security domain. The chapter will focus more on how to secure your Google Cloud environment using the advanced network security features that are available on Google Cloud. In this chapter, we will be discussing context-aware security and its related topics, such as Identity-Aware Proxy and Private Google Access. We will explore their purpose and learn how to configure them for various use cases.

After that, we will look at Google Cloud **Virtual Private Cloud** (**VPC**), where you can define a context-aware approach to secure your cloud resources. To secure your web applications on Google Cloud, we will look at web application firewalls, followed by learning how you can use services such as Cloud Armor to protect your environment from distributed denial-of-service attacks. We conclude this chapter by looking at network logging and monitoring and some best practices and design considerations.

In this chapter, we will cover the following topics:

- Private Google Access
- Identity-Aware Proxy
- Cloud NAT
- Cloud Armor

Private Google Access

Private Google Access addresses the challenge where you want your **virtual machines** (**VMs**)/**Google Compute Engine** (**GCE**) instances that do not have external IP addresses but private addresses to access Google APIs. Instances without public IP addresses can't access Google Cloud's public API endpoints – but the Private Google Access service enables that capability. Let's look at some use cases on why Private Google Access is required before we learn how to configure the service.

VMs often have to communicate with managed services, for example, Google Cloud Storage, BigQuery, and GCE. Managed services have a public endpoint, for example, `storage.googleapis.com`. Assigning an external IP address to every VM that needs to communicate with a public API wouldn't be a practical or secure approach due to the shortage of valid IPv4 addresses. Private Google Access allows communication with Google API public endpoints without requiring an external IP. When interconnecting with on-premises Cloud **Virtual Private Network** (**VPN**) or Cloud Interconnect, it is possible to extend this so that access from on-premises to Google APIs remains internal. We will study more details on that when we discuss connectivity options.

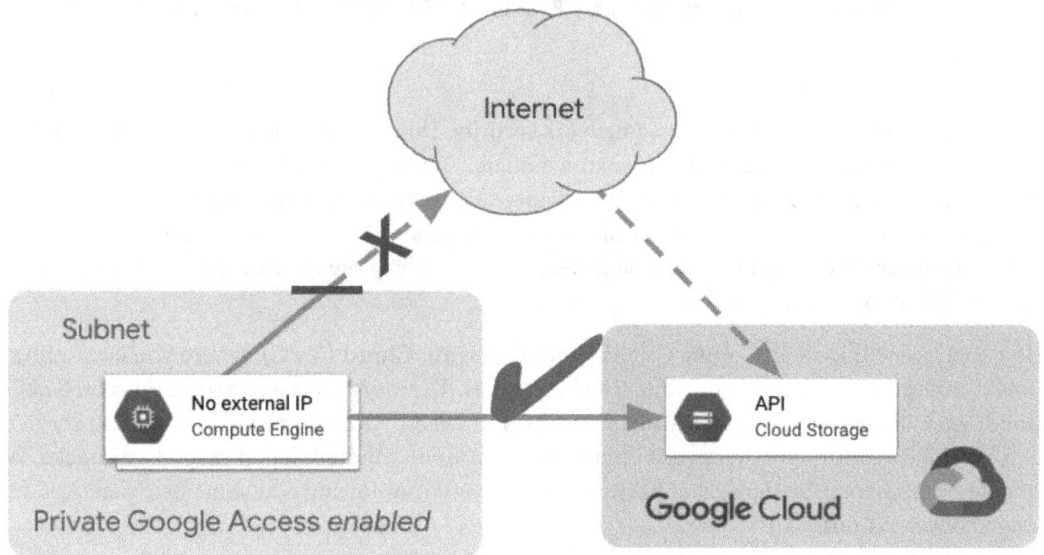

Figure 8.1 – Private Google Access

Figure 8.1 provides a high-level overview of how Private Google Access, when enabled, provides access to the public Google Cloud API securely via private connectivity.

Private Google Access is enabled on a subnet-by-subnet basis; this setting is available to you under the VPC subnet. Let's consider an example where you have two subnets (subnet-a and subnet-b) inside a VPC with four VMs. Subnet-a has Private Google Access enabled and subnet-b does not have Private Google Access. VM1 and VM2 are in subnet-a and VM3 and VM4 are in subnet-b. VM1 and VM3 have private addresses and VM2 and VM4 have external IP addresses. Based on these settings, the following is the case:

- VM1 can access Google APIs as it is part of subnet-a with Private Google Access.
- VM3, on the other hand, has a private IP address but is inside subnet-b, which does not have Private Google Access enabled; therefore, it cannot access Google APIs.

- Finally, VM2 and VM4 both have an external IP address and therefore are able to access Google APIs irrespective of whether they are in a subnet with Private Google Access enabled.

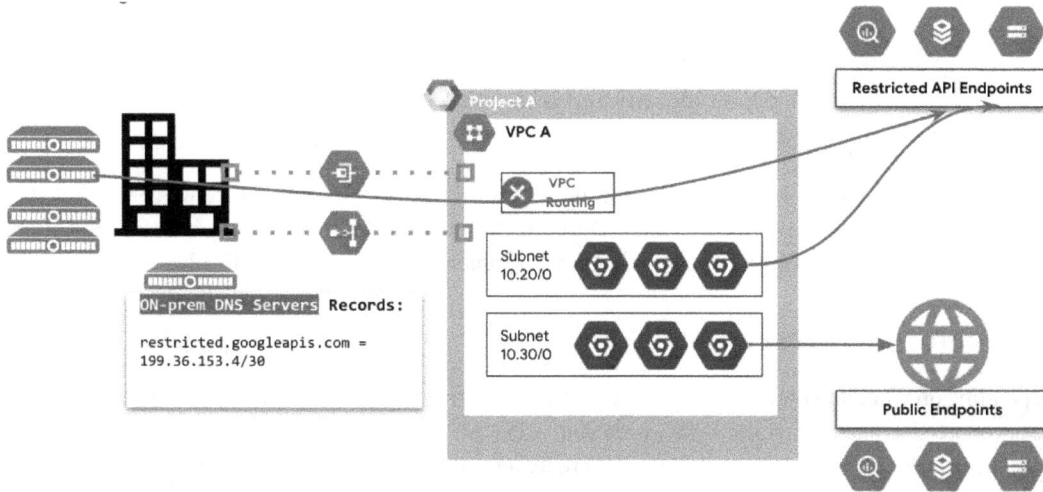

Figure 8.2 – Private Google Access for on-premises services

In *Figure 8.2*, we have an example architecture of how you can use Private Google Access to allow your on-premises services to access Google APIs over Cloud VPN. This same design principle applies if you have Cloud Interconnect instead of Cloud VPN.

Next, we will look at how you can configure Private Google Access for your subnets. But first, we will look at some prerequisites before you do so:

- The VM interface should be in a subnet that has Private Google Access enabled.

- An external IP address should not be assigned to the VM.

- The source IP address of the packet from which the traffic is sent must match the IP address of the primary interface of the VM. Alternatively, it can match an internal IP address that is from an alias IP range.

- The following network requirements must also be met:

  - Private Google Access can only be enabled on VPC networks; legacy networks are not supported as you cannot create subnets in a legacy network.

  - Enabling Private Google Access does not automatically enable it for all APIs. You have to individually select which APIs you need to enable Private Google Access for.

  - If you will be using either of the `private.googleapis.com` or `restricted.googleapis.com` domain names, you will need to create DNS records to direct the traffic to the IP address that is associated with these domains.

- You will need to configure a route to the public endpoints with the default internet gateway as the next hop.

- You will need the *egress firewall* rules to permit traffic to the IP address ranges used by Google APIs and services.

- Correct network admin **identity and access management (IAM)** permissions are required for the configuration.

Enabling Private Google Access is a very straightforward thing to do. But before we get to that step, it's important to look at how Google Cloud **Domain Name System (DNS)** service and routing options can be configured based on the options that are available as well as the firewall rules.

DNS configuration

Depending on whether you choose `restricted.googleapis.com` or `private.googleapis.com`, you need to ensure that the VMs inside your VPC can resolve DNS requests to `*.googleapis.com`. In this example, look at how you can create a private DNS zone for `*.googleapis.com` and also `*.gcr.io`:

1. Create a private DNS zone for `googleapis.com`. For this, you can use a Cloud DNS private zone.

2. When creating an A record in the `googleapis.com` zone, select one of the following domains:

   - An A record for `private.googleapis.com` pointing to the following IP addresses: `199.36.153.8`, `199.36.153.9`, `199.36.153.10`, and `199.36.153.11`

   - An A record for `restricted.googleapis.com` pointing to the following IP addresses: `199.36.153.4`, `199.36.153.5`, `199.36.153.6`, and `199.36.153.7`

3. Using Cloud DNS, add the records to the `googleapis.com` private zone.

4. In the `googleapis.com` zone, create a CNAME record for `*.googleapis.com` that points to whichever A record you created in the previous step.

Some of the Google APIs are provided using different domain names, such as `*.gcr.io`, `*.gstatic.com`, `*.pkg.dev`, and `pki.goog`. You can follow the same process of creating a DNS private zone using Cloud DNS and creating an A record and CNAME for the respective domains.

Routing options

Routing is important to understand as you do have two different ways to configure this:

- You can use the **default internet gateway**

- You can create a custom route

Based on your requirements, you can choose either of them. VPC comes configured with routing where you have the next hop already configured, and that is the default internet gateway. The VMs have the default internet gateway, where the packets are sent when the VM inside VPC sends a request to the Google APIs. Although the term default internet gateway suggests that all internet traffic is sent to the internet, this is not true. The default internet gateway routes the traffic sent from VMs to Google APIs within Google's network. Google does not allow routing traffic to Google APIs and services through other VM instances or custom next hops.

If your VPC has a default route pointing toward the default internet gateway, you can route all requests from your VM to the Google APIs and services without configuring custom routes.

You can create a custom route and define the next hop in use cases where you want to direct the traffic to Cloud VPN or an internal load balancer. In those cases, you can define a custom route with the next relevant hop.

Routing using a default route

Follow these steps to route using a default route:

1. Go to the **Routes** page in the Google Cloud console.
2. Select **Network Menu** and then **Routes** under the VPC sub-menu.

    Here you have the ability to filter the list of routes to show just the routes for the network you need to inspect (*Figure 8.3*).

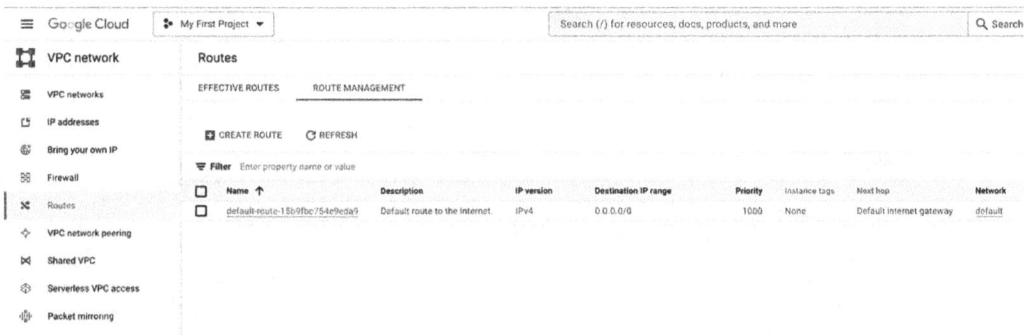

Figure 8.3 – Default internet gateway route

3. Look for a route whose destination is 0.0.0.0/0 and whose next hop is **Default Internet gateway**.

Routing using custom routes

Follow these steps to route using custom routes:

1. On the same **Routes** page in the Google Cloud console, use the **Filter table** text field to filter the list of routes using the following criteria:

- **Network**: YOUR_NETWORK_NAME. Here, replace YOUR_NETWORK_NAME with the name of your VPC network

- **Next hop**: Choose **Default Internet gateway**

2. Look at the **Destination IP range** column for each route. If you choose the default domains, check for several custom static routes, one for each IP address range used by the default domain. If you choose private.googleapis.com or restricted.googleapis.com, look for that domain's IP range.

3. You can create a custom route by clicking on **Create a route** and completing the details as indicated in *Figure 8.4*.

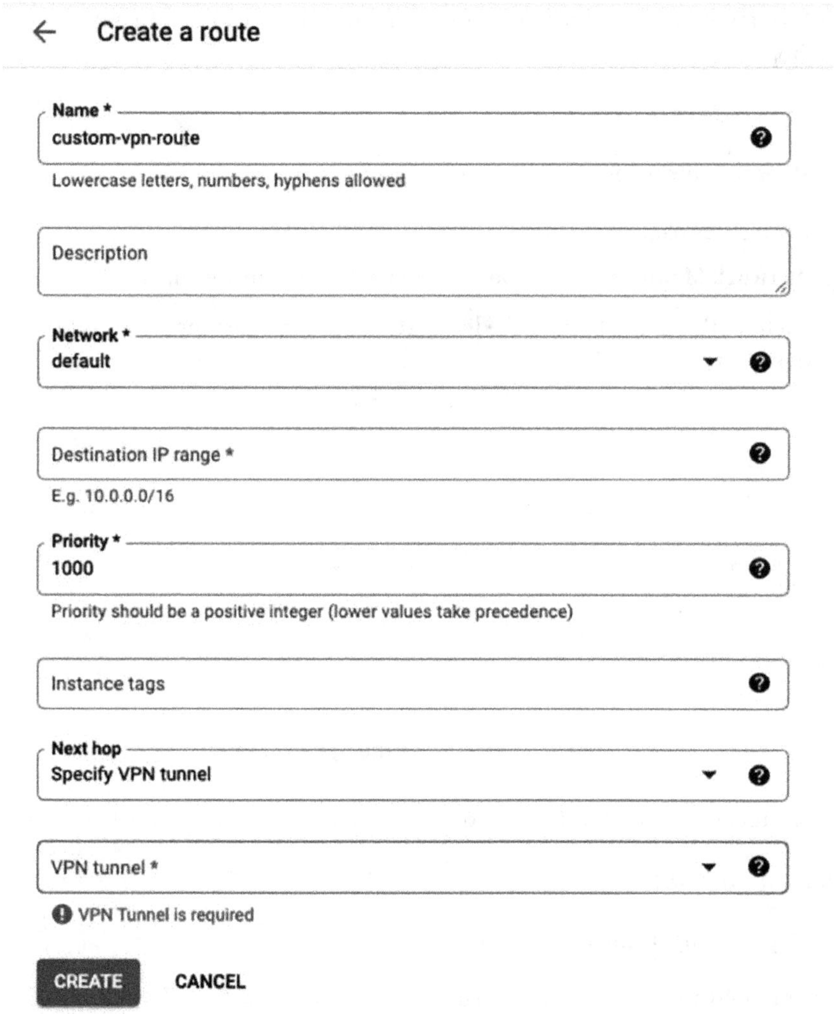

Figure 8.4 – Create a route for the VPN tunnel

4. In *Figure 8.4*, you can specify the name of the route you want to create, the **Network** name, **Destination IP range**, and **Priority**. Specify **Next hop** as the VPN tunnel and select the VPN tunnel that you have already created.

    Instance tags is optional. Also, note that the VPN tunnel name will only appear if you have already created a tunnel.

Firewall rules

Your VPC instance must have firewall rules for your VMs that allow access from VMs to the IP addresses used by Google APIs and services. Every VPC has two implied firewall rules that permit outgoing connections and block incoming connections. The implied allow egress rule satisfies this requirement.

Enabling Private Google Access for your VPC subnet

Follow these steps:

1. Go to the **VPC networks** page in the Google Cloud console.
2. From here, you can click the name of the network that contains the subnet for which you need to enable Private Google Access.
3. If you want to enable Private Google Access for an existing subnet, follow these steps:

    I.   Click the name of the subnet. In *Figure 8.5*, you can see the subnet name is **holodeck**.

    II.   Once you click on that, you will be taken to the **Subnet** details page.

    III. Here you can edit the details by clicking on **EDIT**.

    IV.   Then go to the **Private Google Access** section, set the option to **On**, and click **SAVE**.

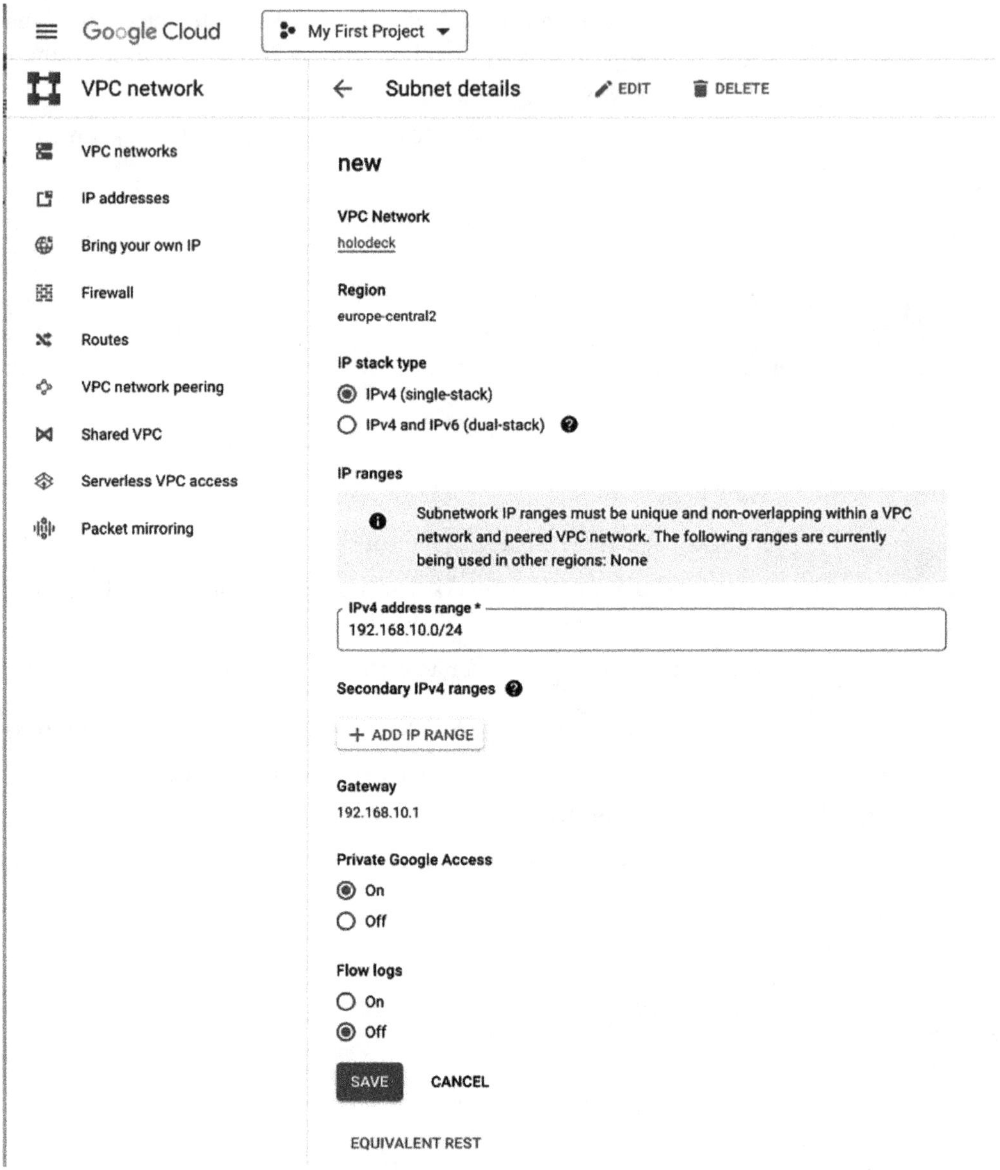

Figure 8.5 – Enable Private Google Access for the subnet

4. If you want to enable Private Google Access for a new subnet, the process is similar:

   I.   First, you will need to create the subnet.

   II.   While you are on the **VPC Networks** page, click **Add subnet**.

   III. Then specify **Name** and **Region** for the new subnet.

IV.   Next, you will need to specify **IP address range** for the subnet. Remember that this range cannot overlap with any subnets in the current VPC network or any networks connected through VPC network peering or VPN.

V.   Once you have made changes to the remaining selections on the subnet settings, such as turning on VPC flow logs, you can turn on **Private Google Access** and click **SAVE**.

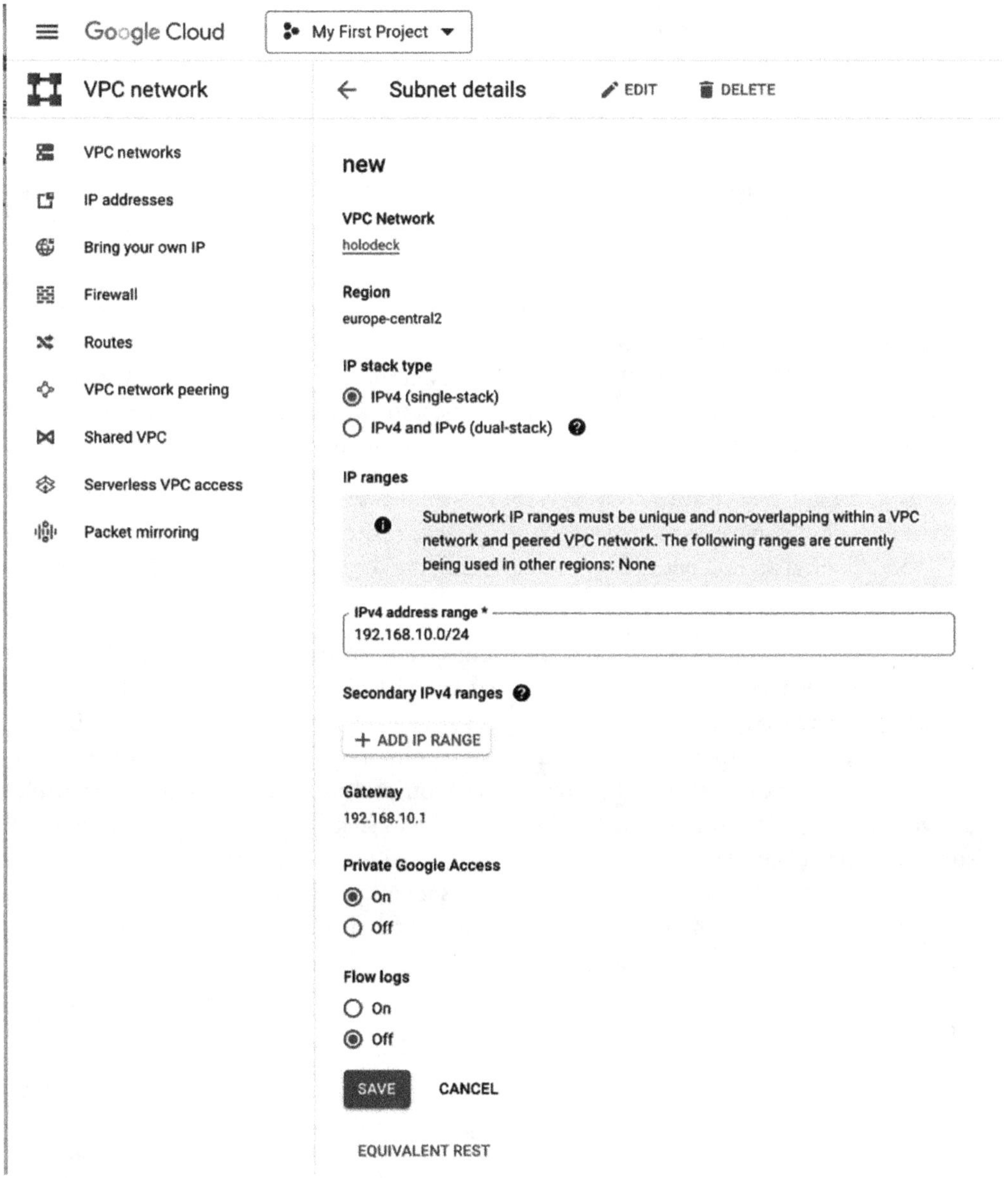

Figure 8.6 – Configuring subnet for Private Google Access

In *Figure 8.6*, the subnet has Private Google Access turned on. You can edit the subnet and turn the setting on or off.

In this section, we looked at how you can enable Private Google Access for subnets that can allow your VMs—either on-premises or on Google Cloud—to secure access to Google APIs.

Identity-Aware Proxy

IAP lets you configure centralized authorization to manage secure remote access to your VMs and applications. IAP and load balancers are in front of all your data requests. This provides a much simpler administration process, with less operational overhead, than more traditional VPN solutions. There is no VPN to implement and no VPN clients to install and maintain. It also makes the end user experience more streamlined as the user no longer has to launch the VPN client and sign in to the VPN.

In comparison to a traditional VPN, IAP takes the approach of application-based access control instead of network-based access control. Access is only possible through IAP by users who have been configured with the right IAM role. Authentication is done via Google Cloud Identity or a federated identity provider, including 2FA. To configure authorization using Cloud IAM, users need the IAP-secured Web App User role on the resource project to be configured. We will look at the steps on how to configure that in the *Enabling IAP for on-premise* section later in this chapter.

Using IAP, you can not only secure access to resources on Google Cloud, such as GCE, Google App Engine, and GKE, but you can also create secure access for your on-premises or third-party cloud provider. We will look at an example of how you can configure secure access using IAP for on-premises resources later in this section.

IAP has tight integration with some other Google Cloud products, such as Cloud IAM, Cloud Identity, and Access Context Manager. You can configure Access Context Manager to enforce additional security checks when giving access to a user. For example, you can check for geo-location, enforce IP address whitelisting, and also do endpoint device checks, such as checking for an allowed operating system, checking for X.509 certificates, checking for disk encryption, and so on. These additional controls not only give you visibility of the user context and aspects such as single and multi-factor authentication but also perform device checks before access is granted. The authentication server utilizes the request credentials, if they are legitimate, to determine the user's identity (email address and user ID). When a user is authenticated, the authentication server examines their IAM role to see whether they are allowed to access the resource in question.

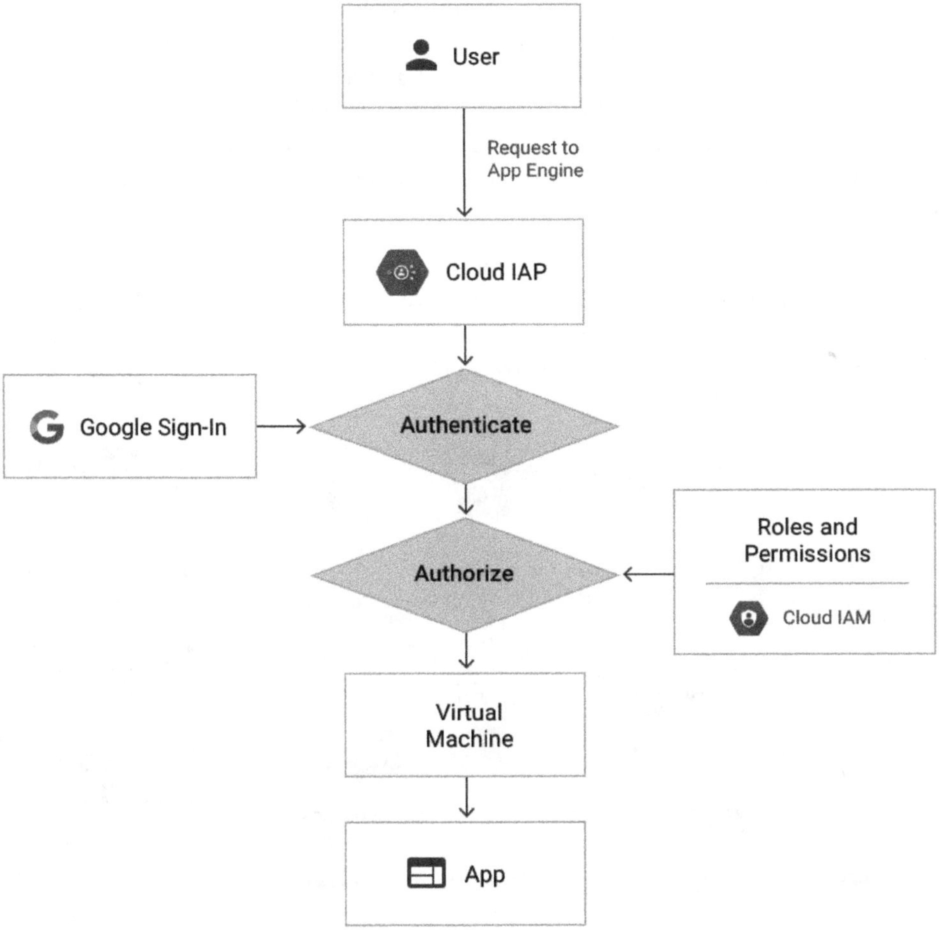

Figure 8.7 – How IAP works with App Engine

Let's look at *Figure 8.7* to understand how IAP works with App Engine. When an application or resource is protected by IAP, only users with the appropriate IAM rights (the IAP-secured Web App User role) can access it. In order to access protected resources, IAP runs both authentication and authorization checks on the requesting user.

IAP intercepts the request to access the resource and checks to see whether IAP is enabled for the service. If this option is enabled, any IAP credentials that appear in the request headers or cookies are submitted to an IAP authentication server. An OAuth 2.0 Google account sign-in flow that stores a token for future sign-ins is redirected to the user if they do not have browser credentials.

For GKE and GCE, users can bypass IAP authentication if they can access the VM's application-serving port. IAP-secured applications can't be protected from code executing on a different VM since firewall restrictions can't stop it. A similar aspect applies to Cloud Run, where, if a user has an auto-assigned URL, they can bypass the IAP authentication. In order to safeguard against traffic that does not originate from the serving infrastructure, you must implement firewall rules and a load balancer. Other alternatives, such as using ingress controls for Cloud Run and App Engine, can be used to sign headers.

Next, we will cover how IAP can work to support your on-premises applications' access. There is a new component that will be introduced in the setup, which is the IAP connector. We will understand what this connector is and also look under the hood of the IAP connector. From an exam perspective, you will not be tested on your knowledge of how an IAP connector works, but it's good to understand it anyway.

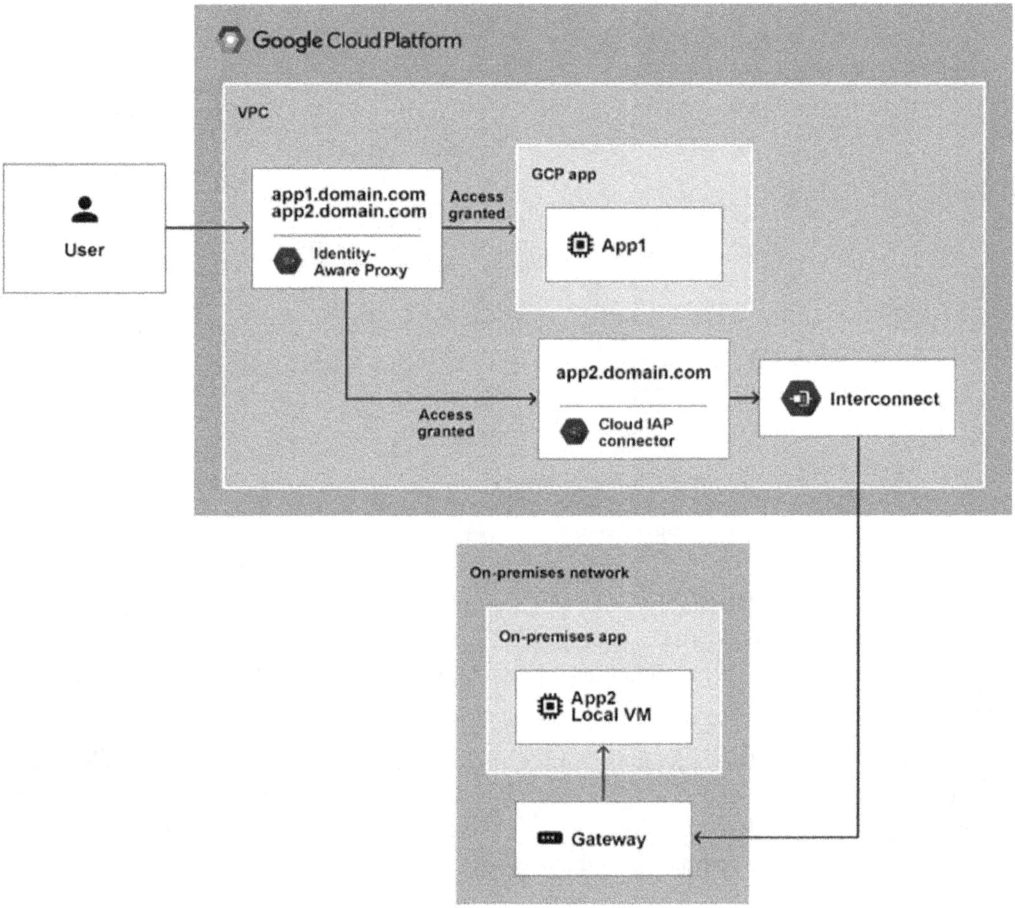

Figure 8.8 – How IAP for on-premises works

We will use the illustration given in *Figure 8.8* to understand the flow and the key components of IAP for on-premises. We will then look at how secure access is given to applications that are connected via a hybrid connector from Google Cloud to on-premises.

The initial part of the workflow is similar to how IAP works for App Engine, as explained earlier. There is no difference between the authentication and authorization checks that are performed for the user. The request is then sent to the IAP connector, which forwards the request to the on-premises network over a site-to-site connection established by Interconnect.

IAP targets on-premises applications with the use of an IAP connector. You can create an IAP connector from the IAP dashboard of the Google Cloud console. An IAP connector is deployed using a configurable Google Cloud Deployment Manager template. This template creates the resources that are needed to host and run the IAP connector. Inside your Google Cloud project, the template deploys an Ambassador proxy on a GKE cluster. This proxy is responsible for routing the traffic that is secured by Cloud IAP to your on-premises applications, by indirectly applying Google **Cloud Identity and Access Management (Cloud IAM)** access policies.

You have to define the routing parameters for the IAP connector. Every routing name must correspond to an ambassador-created GCE backend resource. The mapping parameter has to define the routing rules with the source and destination. This is to ensure that the requests can be routed from the source to the correct destination, which could be an application on the on-premises network. The following example shows what a mapping should look like:

```
routing:
    - name: crm
      mapping:
        - name: host
          source: www.crm-domain.com
          destination: crm-internal.domain.com
        - name: sub
          source: customer.hr-domain.com
          destination: customer.hr-internal.domain.com
    - name: billing
      mapping:
        - name: host
          source: www.billing-domain.com
          destination: billing-internal.domain.com
```

In this example, we route the incoming requests coming from www.crm-domain.com to crm-internal.domain.com and therefore create a mapping for both the host and subdomain as well. Later, we will look at the steps to enable IAP for on-premises applications.

An important point to note here is that IAP by default is integrated with Google identities and uses services such as Google Cloud Identity and Cloud IAM. However, you do have the option to use external identities instead of Google Cloud Identity Platform, which is Google's customer IAM solution. Google Cloud Identity Platform can be used with IAP. Google Cloud Identity Platform is a completely different product and is not in scope for the exam.

Next, we will look at how you can use TCP forwarding with IAP. IAP use cases are limited to supporting applications that use HTTP or HTTP(S). At the time of writing this book, there is no support for thick clients. But you can use TCP forwarding to support both **Secure Shell (SSH)** and **Remote Desktop Protocol (RDP)**. It is possible for users to connect to any TCP port on GCE via TCP forwarding. IAP opens a listening port and sends all the traffic to the chosen instance. IAP uses HTTPS to encrypt all client-side traffic. The `gcloud compute ssh` IAP encapsulates SSH in HTTPS and passes it to the remote instance, eliminating the need for a listening port when using SSH with `gcloud`. TCP forwarding only works with GCE using IAP and not with on-premises apps.

Enabling IAP for on-premises

There are four different configurations that you should be familiar with: enabling IAP for on-premises apps, enabling IAP for App Engine, enabling IAP for GKE, and enabling IAP for GCE. In the following example, you will see how Cloud IAP for App Engine is enabled and how access policies for your app are added.

IAP lets you manage access to services hosted on App Engine, GCE, or an HTTPS load balancer. Perform the following steps to configure IAP for App Engine:

1. Open the menu on the left side of the Google Cloud console.
2. Click **Security**.
3. Select **Identity-Aware Proxy**. All the resources of a project are listed on the **Identity-Aware Proxy** page. If you haven't already, make sure you've configured your **OAuth Consent** screen.
4. After doing that, come back to the **Identity-Aware Proxy** page. Follow the steps to configure the consent screen:

    I.   Go to the **OAuth consent** screen.
    II. Under **Support email**, select the email address that you want to display as a public contact. The email address must belong to the currently logged-in user account or a Google Group to which the currently logged-in user belongs.

III.   Enter the application name you want to display.

IV.   Add any optional details you'd like.

V.   Click **Save**.

5.   Navigate back to the **Identity-Aware Proxy** page and select an app that you want to secure. If you don't see your app here, ensure you have App Engine configured. In the case of GCE and GKE, ensure you have a load balancer configured with backends. We covered the ways to create load balancers in *Chapter 7, Virtual Private Cloud*.

> **Note**
> By enabling IAP for your selected app, only the authenticated and authorized members can access it.

6.   Select an app by clicking the checkbox on the left side of a row.

7.   Turn on the IAP toggle switch for the app that you have selected.

8.   To confirm that you want your resource to be secured by IAP, click **Turn on** in the **Turn on IAP** window that appears.

    To control who has access to the app, members need to be given access. In the following step, you will specify the members and assign them appropriate roles to access your app.

9.   Click on the **Add Member** button in the info panel. This opens the **Add Member** panel. This panel temporarily hides the example shared here.

10. In the **Add Member** panel, enter the users and/or groups in the **New members** field.

11. Select one of the IAP roles that you want to grant to each new member. These roles are as follows:

    I.   **IAP Policy Admin**: Grants administrator rights over Cloud IAP permissions

    II.   **IAP-secured Web App User**: Grants access to HTTPS resources that use Cloud IAP

12. Click **Save**.

Using Cloud IAP for TCP forwarding

In this section, we will look at how you can use IAP for TCP forwarding. When you create GCE instances, they appear on the **Identity-Aware Proxy** page under **SSH AND TCP RESOURCES**.

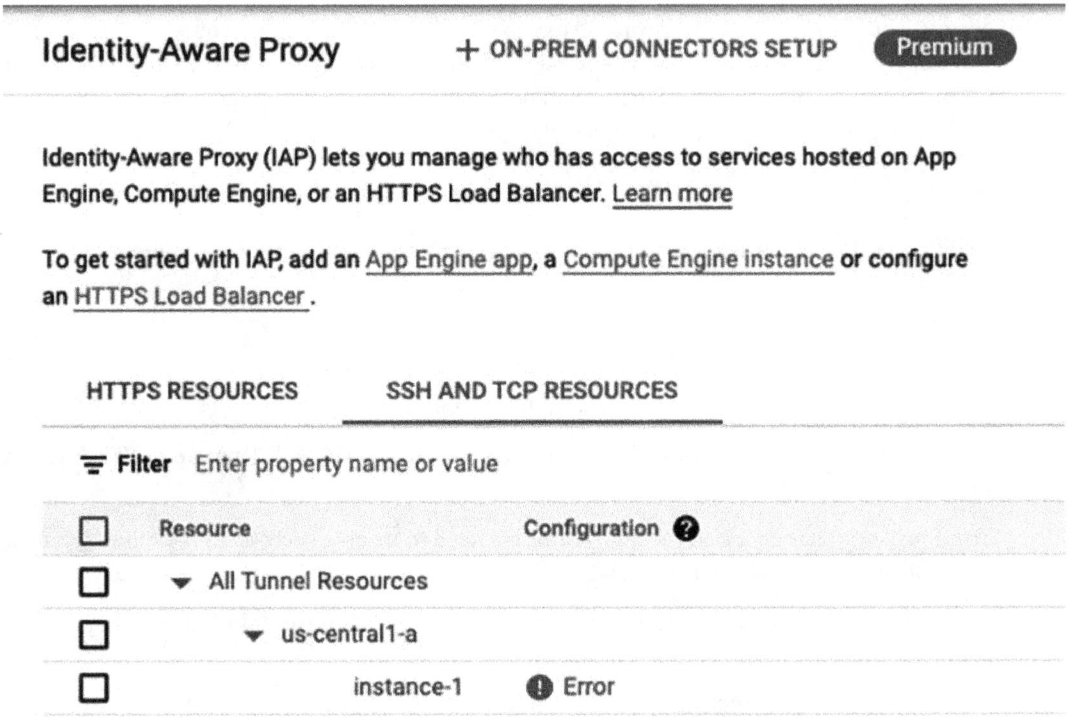

Identity-Aware Proxy   + ON-PREM CONNECTORS SETUP   Premium

Identity-Aware Proxy (IAP) lets you manage who has access to services hosted on App Engine, Compute Engine, or an HTTPS Load Balancer. Learn more

To get started with IAP, add an App Engine app, a Compute Engine instance or configure an HTTPS Load Balancer .

HTTPS RESOURCES   SSH AND TCP RESOURCES

Filter   Enter property name or value

	Resource	Configuration ❓
☐	▼ All Tunnel Resources	
☐	▼ us-central1-a	
☐	instance-1	❗ Error

Figure 8.9 – The Identity-Aware Proxy dashboard

Figure 8.9 illustrates where you will see the GCE instances appear after they are created. You can see an Error message (in red) displayed in the figure. The error message appears because a corresponding firewall rule – one that will allow this instance to be accessible using IAP – does not exist.

So, let's create the firewall rule and revisit this page and see the error message disappear. Let's look at how you can create the firewall rule:

1. Click on the error message and it will take you to a page that provides details of the missing access level with the source IP address range that you need to add to your firewall rule.

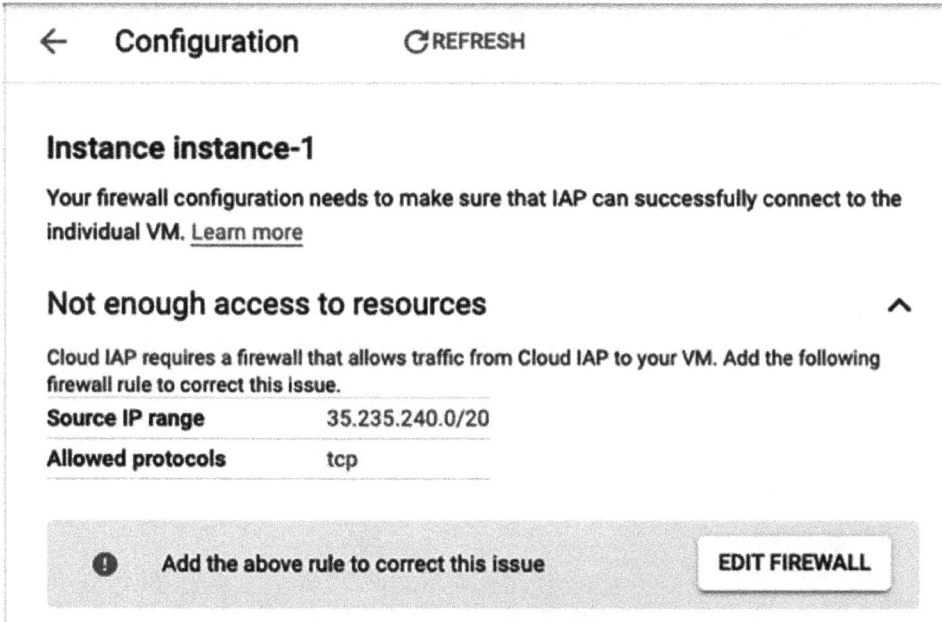

Figure 8.10 – Correcting a firewall configuration for IAP

Figure 8.10 shows the message when you click on the error.

2. From here, you can click on **EDIT FIREWALL** and it will take you directly to the firewall settings page. Here you can configure the firewall rule.

Let's look at the rule that we need to create for the VM to be accessed using IAP. To grant RDP and SSH access to all your VMs, perform the following steps:

1. Open the **Firewall Rules** page and click **Create a firewall rule**.

2. Configure the following settings:

    I.   **Name**: `allow-ingress-from-iap`

    II. **Direction of traffic**: `Ingress`

    III. **Target**: `All instances in the network`

    IV. **Source filter**: `IP ranges`

    V.   **Source IP ranges**: `35.235.240.0/20`

VI.   **Protocols and ports:** Select TCP and enter 22,3389 to allow both RDP and SSH.

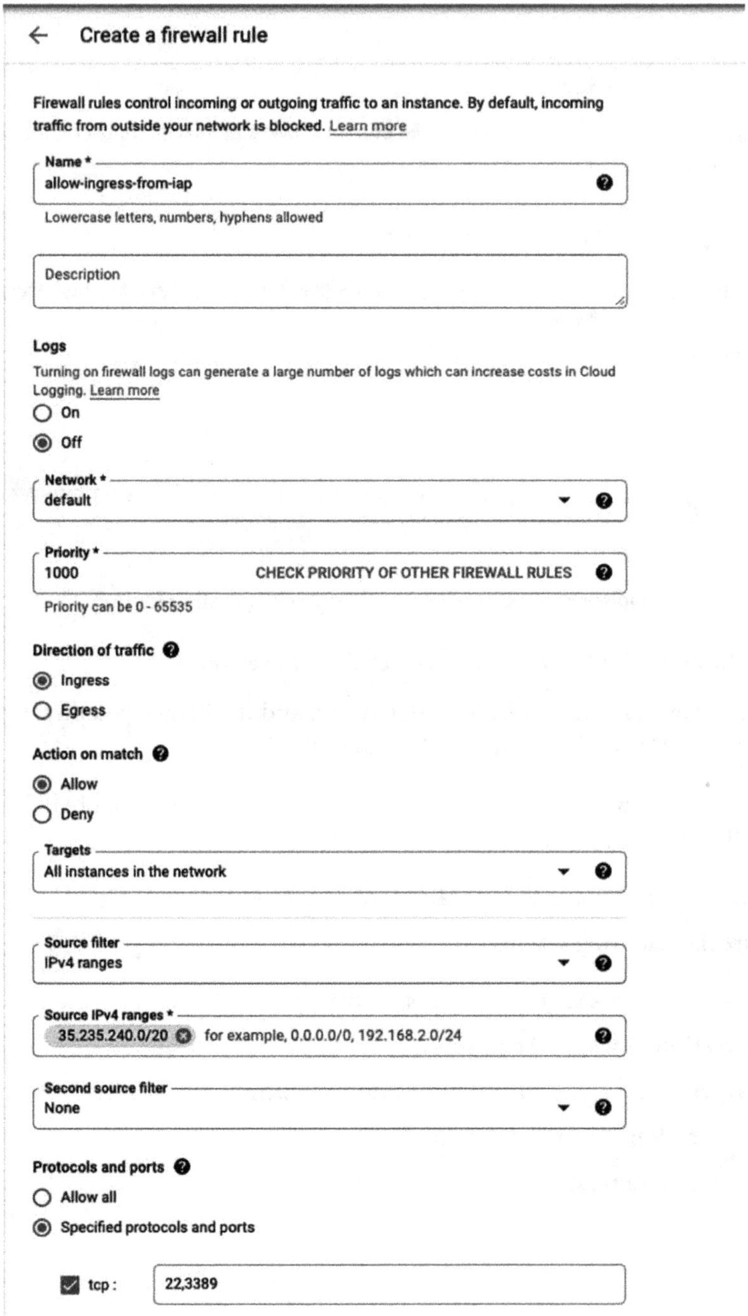

Figure 8.11 – Creating a firewall rule to enable IAP access

3. Click **Create**.

    Figure 8.12 shows how your configuration should look once you have populated the firewall rule settings as per the preceding example. You only specify 22 or 3380 if required under **Protocols and ports**. The example illustrates how you can open both SSH and RDP ports.

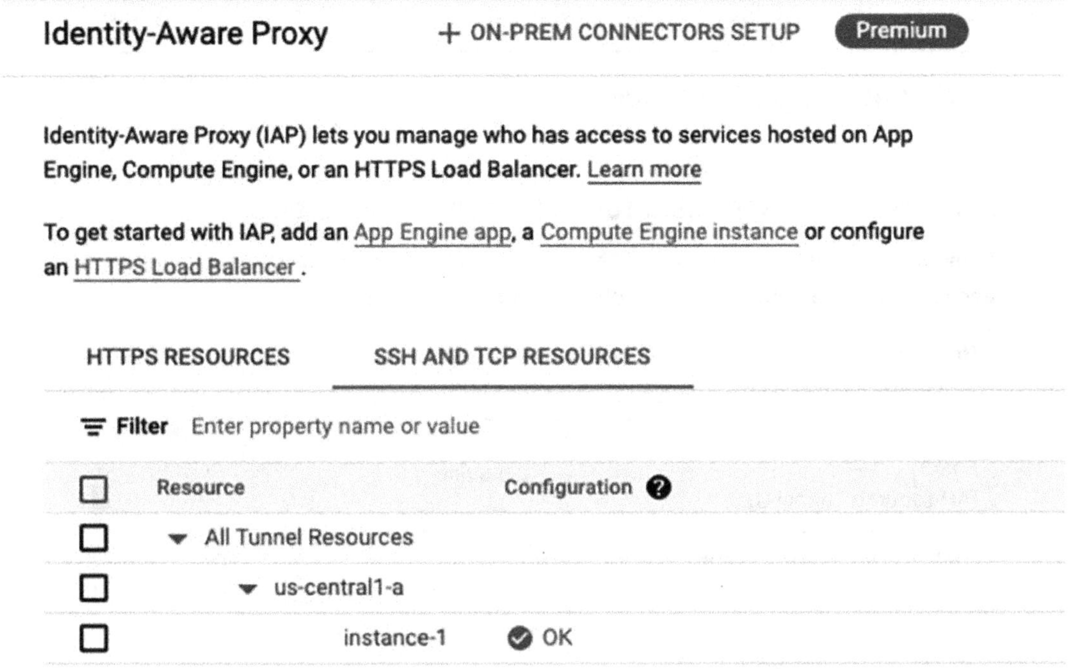

    Identity-Aware Proxy   + ON-PREM CONNECTORS SETUP   Premium

    Identity-Aware Proxy (IAP) lets you manage who has access to services hosted on App Engine, Compute Engine, or an HTTPS Load Balancer. Learn more

    To get started with IAP, add an App Engine app, a Compute Engine instance or configure an HTTPS Load Balancer .

HTTPS RESOURCES	SSH AND TCP RESOURCES

    ⇛ **Filter**   Enter property name or value

	Resource	Configuration ❓
☐	▼ All Tunnel Resources	
☐	▼ us-central1-a	
☐	instance-1	✅ OK

    Figure 8.12 – SSH and TCP resources after creating the firewall rule successfully

    In *Figure 8.12*, observe that after applying the firewall rule, when we navigate back to **SSH AND TPC RESOURCES** under the IAP settings, an OK message is presented. The Error message is no longer displayed.

    Next, we need to give access permissions to the users. You can offer access to all VMs in a project – to a user or a group – by establishing IAM permissions at the project level. Let's take a look at what's involved:

4. Navigate to the IAP admin page from the left menu under the **Security** sub-menu.

5. From there, you can select the **SSH and TCP Resources** tab.

6. Then, you need to select the VM instances that you want to configure. You can click on **Show info panel** if the info panel is not visible. This panel comes up on the right-hand side of the console.

7. We will next look at how you can add a member and configure them. Refer to *Figure 8.13* on how to add a new member and apply the relevant role.

8. We add a new member that can either be an email address or a group email address that you have the option to configure in Google Cloud Identity.

9. Once you have added the user or group, you can set **Role** to IAP-secured Tunnel User.

Add principals to "instance-1"

Add principals and roles for "instance-1" resource

Enter one or more principals below. Then select a role for these principals to grant them access to your resources. Multiple roles allowed. Learn more

New principals
testt@google.com ❌   ❓

Role *   Condition   🗑
IAP-secured Tunnel User   ▼   Add condition

Access Tunnel resources which use
Identity-Aware Proxy

+ ADD ANOTHER ROLE

SAVE   CANCEL

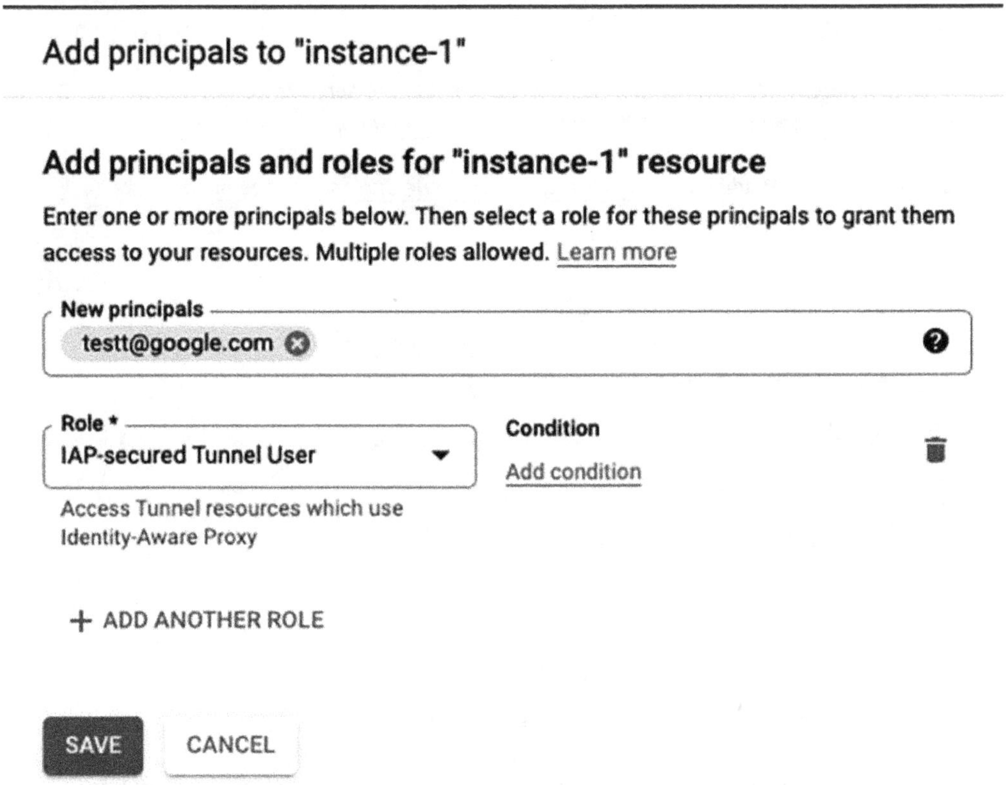

Figure 8.13 – Adding a principal and applying the IAP-secured Tunnel User role

You can also optionally create more fine-grained permissions by using the **Add condition** feature and configure a member restriction.

> **Note**
>
> You can refer to *Chapter 6, Google Cloud Identity and Access Management*, to learn more about how to add conditions to an IAM principal.

10. Once finished, you can click **SAVE**.

> **Note**
>
> In the preceding step, *Step 9*, we are referring to the access levels that can be created using Access Context Manager. Within Access Context Manager (which is a different product), you have the option of configuring policies based on access levels. For example, you can create an access policy for all privileged users called `PrivAccess`. Here you can specify certain parameters – you might want to restrict access to users only coming from a certain IP range or geo-location, for example. With the advanced features that you can get as part of Access Context Manager using the Beyond Corp Enterprise solution, you can also configure a policy that can do endpoint checks, such as checking for X.509 certifications, ensuring the operating system is approved and patched, hard disk encryption is enforced, and so on. This is part of Access Context Manager and is outside the scope of the Google Cloud Professional Security Engineer exam.

TCP forwarding requires different permissions based on how the user plans to utilize it. On the other hand, the user would need the following rights in order to connect to an unauthenticated VM using `gcloud compute ssh`:

- `iap.tunnelInstances.accessViaIAP`
- `compute.instances.get`
- `compute.instances.list`
- `compute.projects.get`
- `compute.instances.setMetadata`
- `compute.projects.setCommonInstanceMetadata`
- `compute.globalOperations.get`
- `iam.serviceAccounts.actAs`

If you don't have an external IP address, you can connect to Linux instances through IAP. The `gcloud compute ssh` command can be used to establish a secure connection to your instance. For TCP tunneling to work, your instance's access settings (specified by IAM permissions) must permit it:

```
gcloud compute ssh instance-1
```

IAP TCP tunneling is used automatically if an external IP address is not provided by the instance. If the instance has an external IP address, IAP TCP tunneling is bypassed in favor of the external IP address. You can use the `--tunnel-through-iap` flag so that `gcloud compute ssh` always uses IAP TCP tunneling.

RDP traffic can be tunneled using IAP to connect to Windows instances that do not have an external IP address.

In order to connect to a VM's remote desktop, you can use IAP TCP forwarding with IAP Desktop:

1. In the application, select **File | Add Google Cloud project**.

2. Enter the ID or name of your project and click **OK**.

3. In the **Project Explorer** window, right-click the VM instance you want to connect to and select **Connect**.

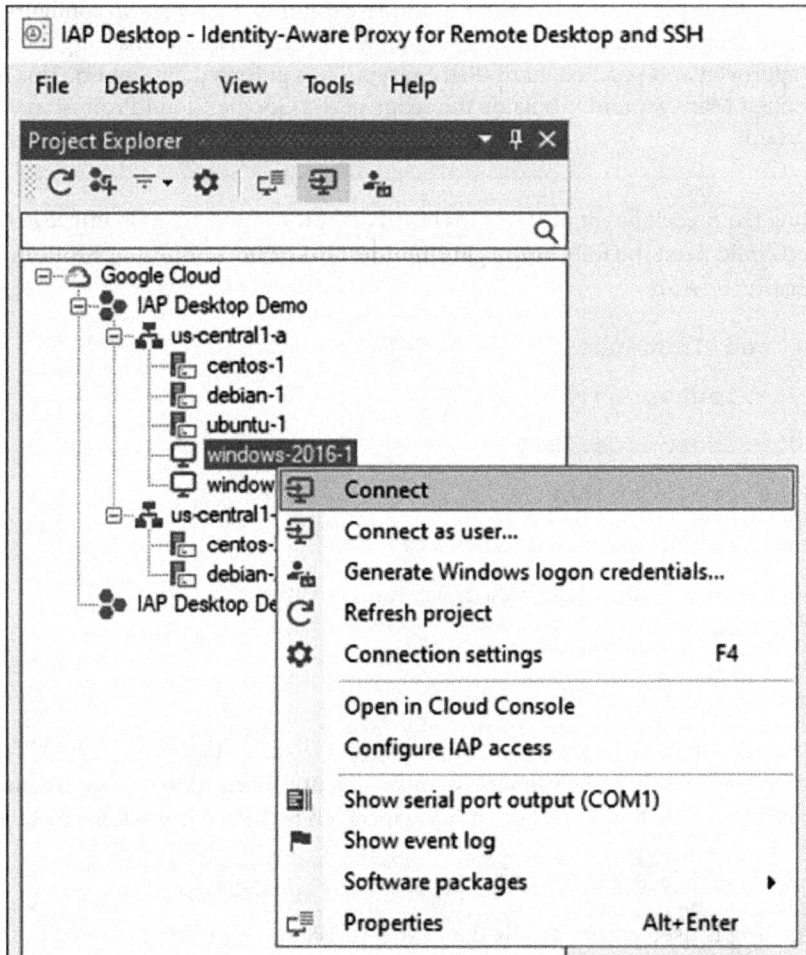

Figure 8.14 – Configuring IAP Desktop for IAP

Figure 8.14 is a screenshot of the IAP Desktop tool, which can be used to establish RDP connections for your Windows instances.

> **Note**
> You can find more information about IAP Desktop from its GitHub page at
> `https://packt.link/1Zh5q`.

We will next move on to the topic of Cloud NAT. Here we will look at how NAT is used with some examples and gain a better understanding of the topic.

Cloud NAT

Cloud NAT is a topic that does not appear a lot in the exam. However, it is important to know how it works and the use cases for why you would need NAT. We will also look at the Google Cloud implementation of NAT architecture, which is different from the traditional NAT architecture.

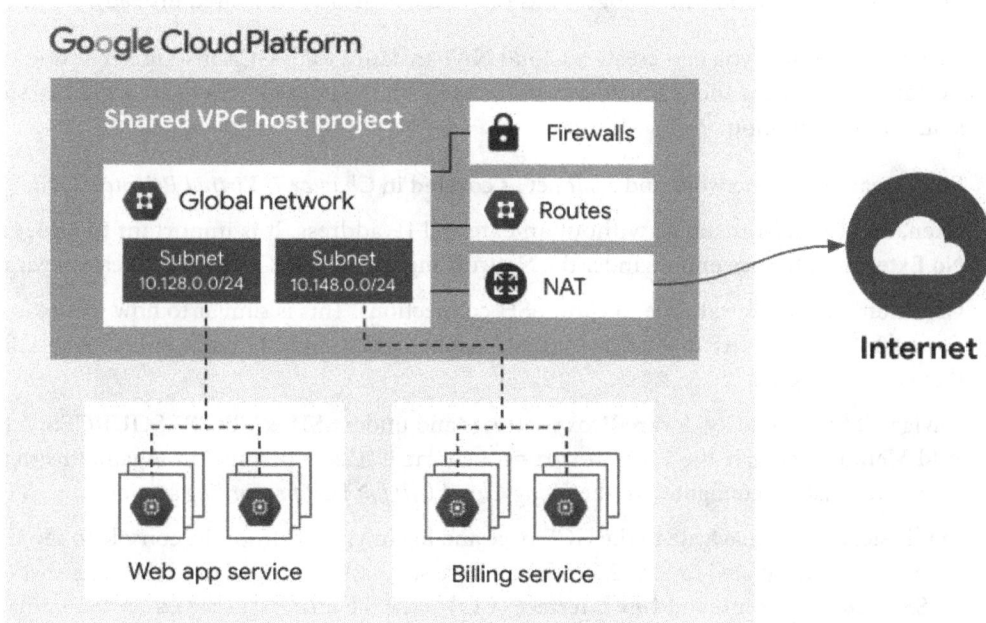

Figure 8.15 – Cloud NAT allowing outbound connections only to the internet

Figure 8.15 shows how Google Cloud NAT works. Cloud NAT is offered as a managed service that provides high availability and seamless scalability. It allows outbound connections only to the internet, whereas inbound traffic is allowed only if it is in response to a connection initiated by an instance. Cloud NAT is a regional resource, fully distributed and software-defined. There are no intermediate NAT proxies in the data path. NAT configuration is stored in the control plane and is pushed to the hosts; this means NAT keeps working regardless of the control plane state, and there are no choke points or performance penalties. Cloud NAT also supports alias IPs on VMs and relies on the default internet route in VPC.

It is important to note that there are cases when NAT is not performed even when configured. They are as follows:

- The VM has an external IP.

- The default internet route has changed.

- There's communication between backend VMs and the load balancer proxy.

- There's communication with Google APIs (Private Google Access is used instead).

Next, we will look at how you can create a Cloud NAT instance for a GCE instance that does not have an external IP address and wants to communicate with the internet. There are eight key steps involved in the configuration:

1. First, create a VPC network and a subnet as covered in *Chapter 7, Virtual Private Cloud*.

2. Then, create a VM instance without an external IP address. It is important to select the **No External Interface** option under the **Networking** tab of the GCE instance creation wizard.

3. Create an ingress firewall rule to allow SSH connections. This is similar to how we created a firewall rule to allow IAP in the IAP section. Ensure that the source IP range for IAP is specified, that is, the range `35.235.240.0/20`.

4. Navigate to the **Identity-Aware Proxy** settings and under **SSH & TPC RESOURCES**, select **Add Member** and give the `IAP-secured Tunnel User` permission. Again, this step is similar to what we configured in the *Using Cloud IAP for TCP forwarding* section.

5. In this step, we will navigate to the GCE page and log in via SSH from the console to the GCE instance that we created in *Step 2*. Once you have successfully logged in to the GCE instance via SSH, from the **command-line interface** (**CLI**), issue the `curl example.com` command. This should not result in any output.

6. Next, we will create a NAT configuration using Cloud Router. The NAT configuration is very straightforward. Once you have logged in to your Google Cloud console and the project is selected, you can go to the **Cloud NAT** page (**Networking | Network Services | Cloud NAT**). Once there, click on **Get started** or **Create NAT gateway**. You may see a welcome message if you are accessing this page for the first time. If you have already visited the page in the past, you will not see the welcome message; do not be confused if you don't see the following message. You should see a screen similar to the one shown in *Figure 8.16*.

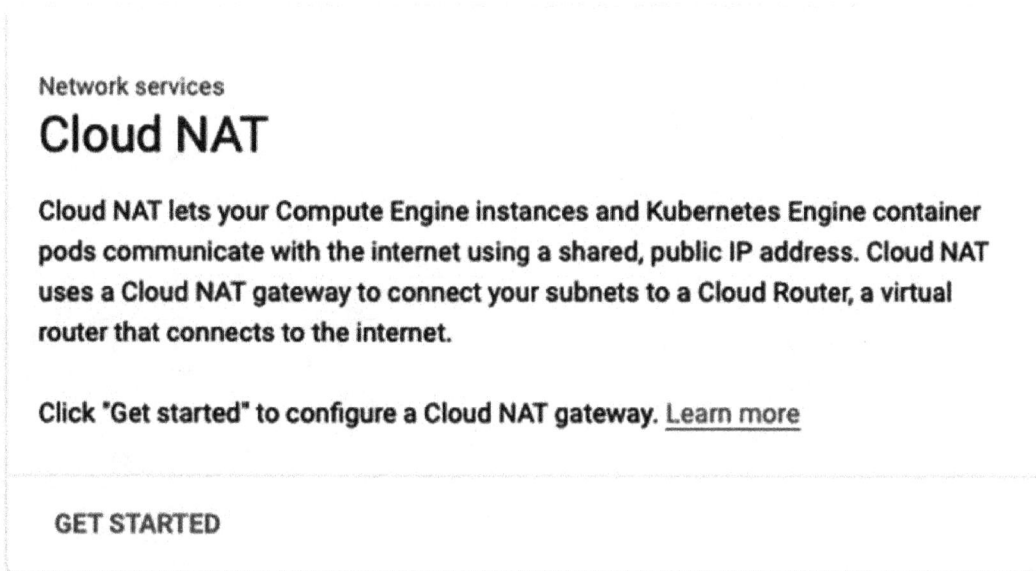

Network services

Cloud NAT

Cloud NAT lets your Compute Engine instances and Kubernetes Engine container pods communicate with the internet using a shared, public IP address. Cloud NAT uses a Cloud NAT gateway to connect your subnets to a Cloud Router, a virtual router that connects to the internet.

Click "Get started" to configure a Cloud NAT gateway. Learn more

GET STARTED

Figure 8.16 – Getting started with Cloud NAT

7. Refer to *Figure 8.17*, where you see the various properties you can configure when you create a Cloud NAT gateway. Here enter the name for your gateway; for this example, we are using the name nat-config. Then, specify your network; for this example, we have set **VPC network** to startshipnw. In your configuration, it will be the network that you have created, or you can even use the default network. Next, set **Region** to us-east1 (your region). For **Cloud Router**, select Create new router. Then, enter the name of your preference; in our example, we have used the name my-router. Once finished, click **CREATE**.

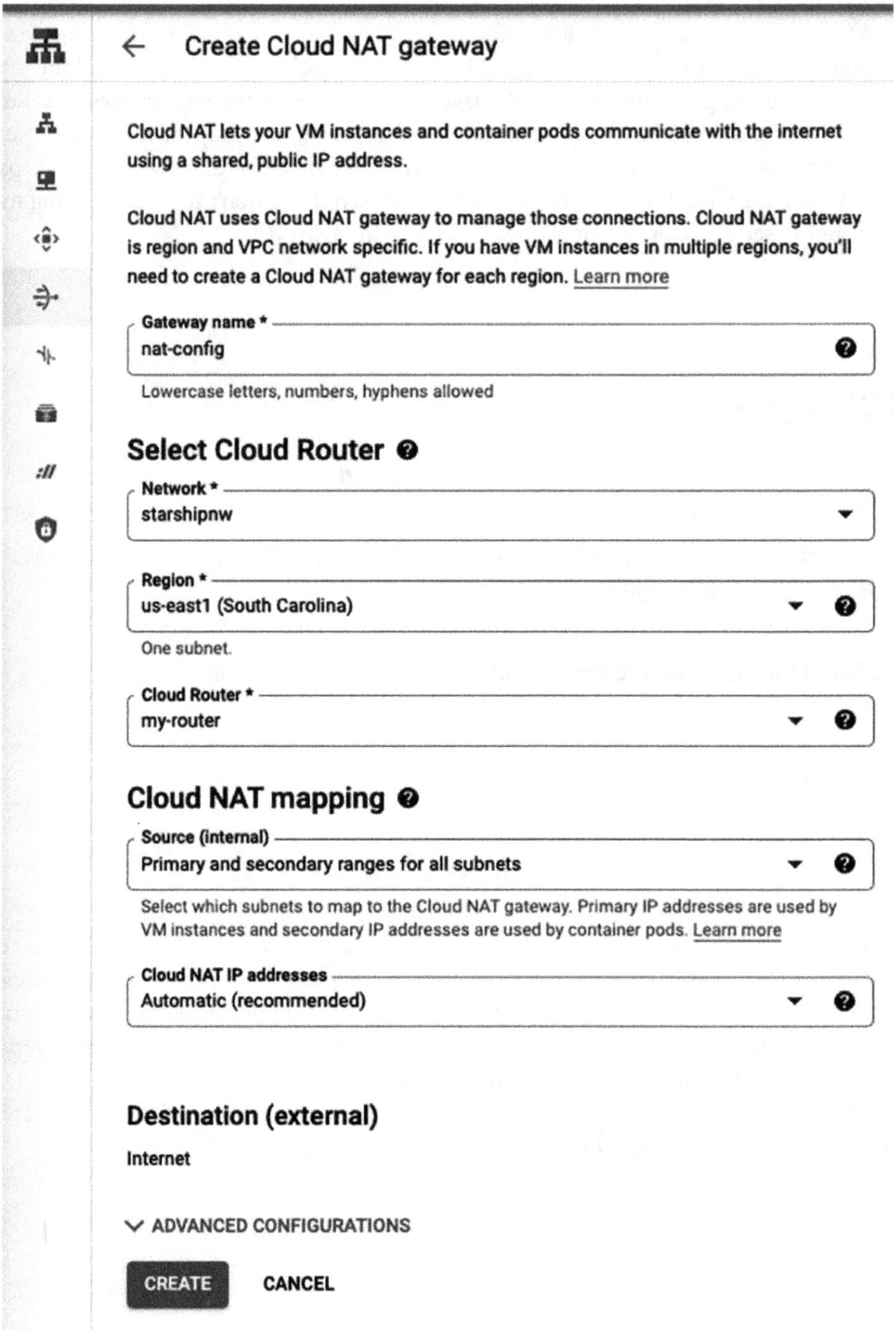

Figure 8.17 – Configuration to create a Cloud NAT gateway

8. Once the steps are completed, we can now go back to our instance under GCE, repeat the test, and issue the `curl example.com` command. This time, we will see an output similar to the following:

```
<html>

<head>

<title>Example Domain</title>

...

...

...

</head>

<body>

<div>

<h1>Example Domain</h1>
<p>This domain is established to be used for illustrative
examples in documents. You can use this domain in examples
without prior coordination or asking for permission.</p>

<p><a href="http://www.iana.org/domains/example">More
information...</a></p></div>

</body>

</html>
```

This concludes the process to create a Cloud NAT instance, which will now allow your VM that was configured with no internet access to access the internet. We will now move on to learn about Cloud Armor, which provides DDoS mitigation and a WAF function.

Google Cloud Armor

This section covers DDoS protection and the use of WAFs to provide safety for your web-based infrastructure. You can protect your Google Cloud workloads from a wide range of threats, including DDoS attacks and application attacks, such as XSS and SQL injection, with Cloud Armor (SQLi). Some capabilities are built in to provide automated protection, while others require manual configuration. We will look at those capabilities of WAFs in more detail in this section:

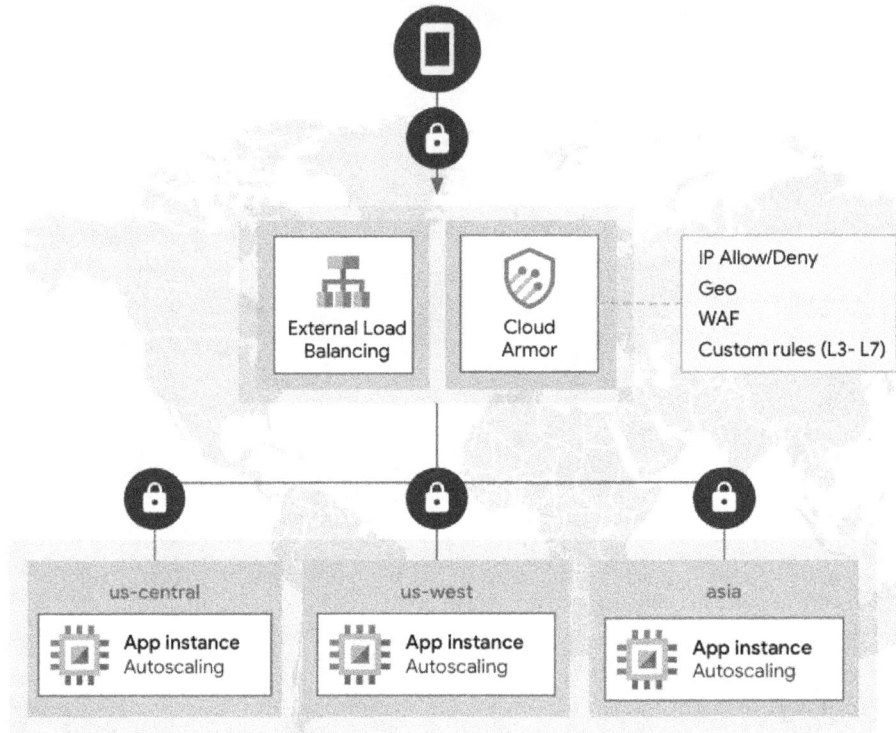

Figure 8.18 – How Google Cloud Armor secures your infrastructure

Cloud Armor leverages Google's global and distributed infrastructure to detect and absorb attacks and filter traffic through configurable security policies at the edge. It should be kept in mind that several aspects of Google Cloud Armor are only available for applications running behind an external HTTP(S) load balancer. *Figure 8.18* illustrates the placement of Cloud Armor, which is in line with the external load balancer, providing the ability to create IP allow and deny lists, enforce geo-location-based rules, and configure the WAF and custom rules from Layer 3 to Layer 7.

There are some Layer 3 and Layer 4 protections built into Cloud Armor that do not require any user configuration. These pre-built rules provide protection against volumetric attacks such as DNS amplification, SYN floods, Slowloris, and so on.

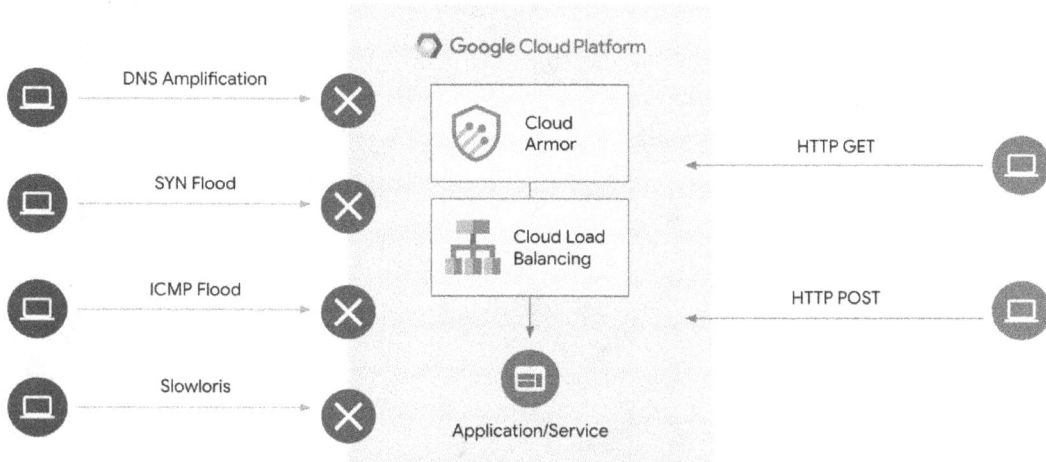

Figure 8.19 – DDoS protection against volumetric attacks

Figure 8.19 illustrates the built-in security policies for Cloud Armor that provide protection against these common types of volumetric attacks.

Next, we will look at how Cloud Armor works and some deployment models that will help you understand the use cases. As mentioned earlier, Google Cloud Armor is always in line and scales to match Google's global network. It protects applications and services behind external HTTP(S) load balancers, SSL proxy load balancers, or TCP proxy load balancers from volumetric DDoS attacks on the network or protocol. Because it can detect and counteract network threats, Cloud Armor's load balancing proxies will only allow properly formatted requests. Custom Layer 7 filtering policies, including preconfigured WAF rules to limit OWASP Top 10 web application vulnerability risks, are also available to backend services behind an external HTTP(S) load balancer. Google Cloud Edge can be used to define rules that enable or restrict access to your external HTTP(S) load balancer, as near as is feasible to the source of incoming traffic, through the use of security policies. A firewall can be set up to block unwanted traffic from accessing or consuming resources in your private cloud.

Cloud Armor is available in two tiers, called **Managed Protection Standard** and **Managed Protection Plus**. The key difference between them is the DDoS response team and cost protection that Plus provides compared to the Standard edition. There is no difference in the capabilities of the product.

Let's take a look at the Cloud Armor deployment models before we deep dive into some technical aspects such as security policies and WAF rules.

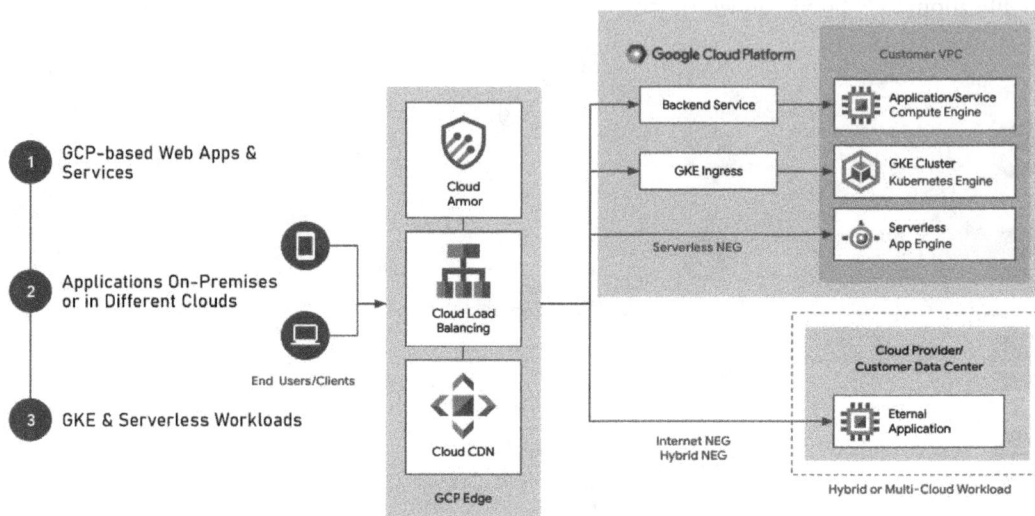

Figure 8.20 – Cloud Armor deployment models

We will use *Figure 8.20* to look at the deployment models:

- Cloud Armor supports the protection of Cloud **Content Delivery Network** (**CDN**) origin servers by enforcing Cloud Armor security policies on dynamic requests as well as cache misses destined for the CDN origin server. Most applications are often complex, serving both cacheable static content as well as dynamic requests from the same services. Cloud Armor is a security service that can help protect websites and applications from malicious attacks. It is able to inspect and filter requests that are sent to the origin servers of CDN. This helps to prevent so-called *cache-busting* attacks, which are attempts to bypass the cache and force the origin servers to send updated content. Additionally, Cloud Armor can help protect dynamic portions of websites and applications from the 10 most common security vulnerabilities as defined by OWASP.

- There is often a need to enforce a consistent set of security controls to applications no matter where they are deployed, whether they are migrating to Google Cloud or running in a hybrid configuration. With internet **Network Endpoint Groups** (**NEGs**), you can leverage all of Google's edge infrastructure, including global load balancers, Cloud CDN, and Cloud Armor, to protect your website or applications no matter where they are hosted. Cloud Armor can help protect your applications, whether from DdoS attacks or other common web attacks, without you having to deploy your applications on Google Cloud.

> **Note**
> NEGs do not fall within the scope of the exam. You can refer to the *Further reading* section to read more about NEGs and how to configure them.

- With GKE Ingress support for Cloud Armor, you can help protect your containerized workloads by placing them behind Google's global load balancers and configuring Cloud Armor security policies for Layer 7 filtering and WAF use cases.

We will now look at the key components of Cloud Armor in more detail, with examples of how to configure them.

Security policies

In Cloud Armor, you can build security policies that can help you defend applications operating behind a load balancer against DDoS and other web-based assaults, regardless of whether the apps are deployed on Google Cloud or in a hybrid or multi-cloud architecture. It is possible to stop traffic before it reaches your load-balanced backend services or backend buckets using security policies that filter Layer 3 and Layer 7 requests for common web exploits. An IP address, an IP range, a region code, and request headers are only a few examples of the conditions used to filter traffic by security policies.

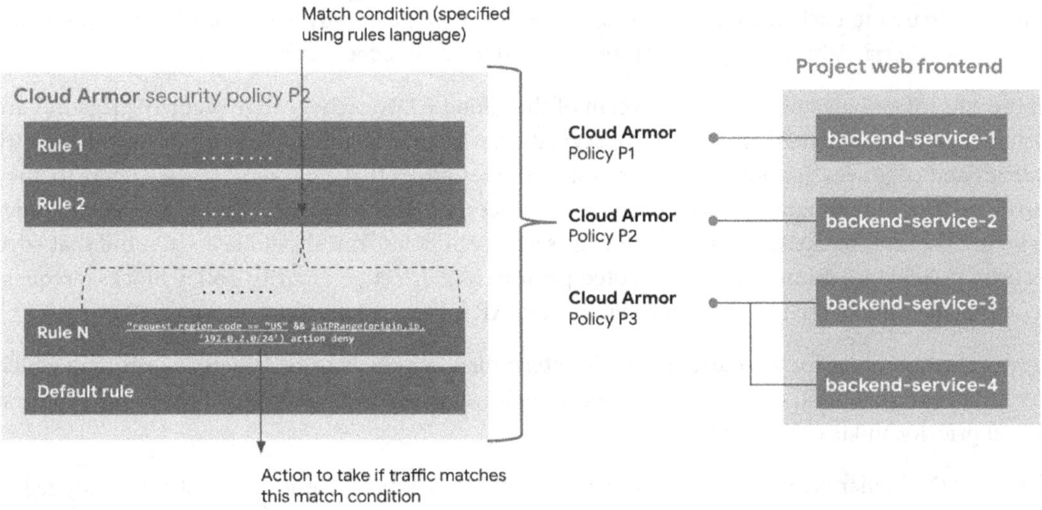

Figure 8.21 – Cloud Armor security policies

This section will take a closer look at security policies, looking at factors such as the requirements before you develop a policy and some of security policies' most important features (as depicted in *Figure 8.21*). Backend services behind an external load balancer are only able to access the security policies available to those services. Instance groups, serverless NEGs, internet NEGs for external services, and Google Cloud Storage buckets are all supported backend services for Google App Engine, Cloud Run, and Cloud Functions. You must employ internet NEGs for all of your hybrid or multi-cloud protection needs.

Security policies cannot be applied until the load balancer is an external HTTP(S) load balancer and the backend service's external load balancing scheme and the backend service's protocol are met – that is, the protocol must be either HTTP, HTTPS, or HTTP/2.

There are two categories of security policies that you can configure – **backend security policies** and **edge security policies**. Instance groups or NEGs, including internet, zonal, and serverless NEGs, can be used to filter and protect backend services. The actions associated with backend security policies are allow, deny, redirect (to Google reCAPTCHA), throttle, and rate-based ban for each source IP range or geography. You can also create WAF rules and named IP lists, including Layer 7 filtering and adaptive protection (adaptive protection is a new feature and currently out of scope for the exam).

For edge security policies, you can create and allow or deny based on source IP and source geography. These policies allow users to establish access control and filtering policies for cached information. When compared to backend security rules, edge security policies only allow for filtering based on a handful of criteria. A backend policy cannot be used to set an edge security policy.

At the edge of Google's network – upstream of the Cloud CDN cache – edge security measures are installed and implemented. Two levels of security can be provided by coexisting backend security policies and edge security policies. Regardless of the resources that a backend service refers to, they can all be applied simultaneously (for example, instance groups or network endpoint groups). In order to secure backend buckets, you must use edge security policies. You should keep in mind that edge security policies are examined and executed prior to IAP. An edge security policy blocks a request before the identity of the requestor is evaluated by IAP.

Rule evaluation order for a security policy is determined by rule priority. When determining which rules are examined first, look at the rule with the lowest numeric value. This rule has the highest logical priority and is evaluated first.

If none of the higher priority rules is met, or if no other rules are present, a default rule is applied to all security policies. A priority of 2147483647 is automatically assigned to the default rule, which is always included in the policy.

Although the default rule cannot be deleted, you can change the default action associated with the rule. It is possible to change the default rule's action from allow to deny.

Use the Google Cloud Armor custom rules language to define expressions in the match condition of one or more rules. When Cloud Armor receives a request, it analyzes it against the following expressions. Depending on whether the rules are met, inbound traffic is either denied or allowed. The following are some instances of Google Cloud Armor expressions written in the **Common Expression Language** (**CEL**):

- To define expressions in a rule, use the `gcloud --expression` flag or the Google Cloud console.

- In the following example, requests from `2001:db8::/32` in the `AU` region match the following expression:

```
origin.region_code == "AU" && inIpRange(origin.ip,
'2001:db8::/32')
```

- The following example matches with requests from `192.0.2.0/24` and with a user agent that contains the string `WordPress`:

```
inIpRange(origin.ip, '192.0.2.0/24') && has(request.
headers['user-agent']) && request.headers['user-agent'].
contains('WordPress')
```

WAF rules

In this section, we will look at the different types of rules that you can create. There are some WAF rules that come pre-configured, but you do have the option of creating custom rules to meet your requirements. Let's take a look at the options available.

You can create IP-address-based rules both at the edge and for your backend services. These rules are the IP address `allowlist-` and `denylist`-based rules. Both Ipv4 and Ipv6 are supported. HTTP `403` (Unauthorized), `404` (Access Denied), or `502` (Bad Gateway) responses are all possible outcomes of deny rules. An HTTP `429` error is an error code that is returned when an application has exceeded a set number of requests. This is usually caused by an action rule that limits the number of requests that can be made in a given period of time.

There are pre-configured rules based on the OWASP ModSecurity core rule set version 3.0. These rules can provide you with protection from the following types of attack:

- SQL injection
- **Cross-site scripting** (**XSS**) attacks
- **Local file inclusion** (**LFI**) attacks
- **Remote file inclusion** (**RFI**) attacks
- **Remote code execution** (**RCE**) attacks

Use rate-limiting rules to restrict requests per client based on the threshold you define, or temporarily ban clients who exceed the request threshold for the duration you set.

There are bot management rules as well (in preview only), which are out of the scope of the exam. Pre-configured rules also exist for named IP lists; we will cover them in more detail in the *Named IP lists* section.

> **Note**
>
> You can fine-tune the pre-configured WAF rules or write custom rules. For the purpose of the exam, you need to know what types of rules exist and how they work. You are not tested on writing custom WAF rules.

Named IP lists

Using the named IP list feature in Cloud Armor, you can reference third-party maintained IP ranges and IP addresses within a security policy. You don't have to specify individual IP addresses. Instead, you can reference an entire list containing multiple IP addresses that you would like to allow or deny. It is important to note that named IP lists are not security policies, but they can be specified in a policy.

It's possible to build security rules that allow all IP addresses that are in the provider list and reject all IP addresses that are not in the provider list: `ip1, ip2, ip3....ipN`:

```
gcloud beta compute security-policies rules create 1000 \
    --security-policy POLICY_NAME \
    --expression "evaluatePreconfiguredExpr('provider-a')" \
    --action "allow"
```

Custom named IP address lists are not possible to construct. Only third-party providers who work with Google and maintain named IP address lists can use this capability. CloudFlare and Imperva are a couple of the providers who partner with Google Cloud to supply named IP lists for Google's named IP list service.

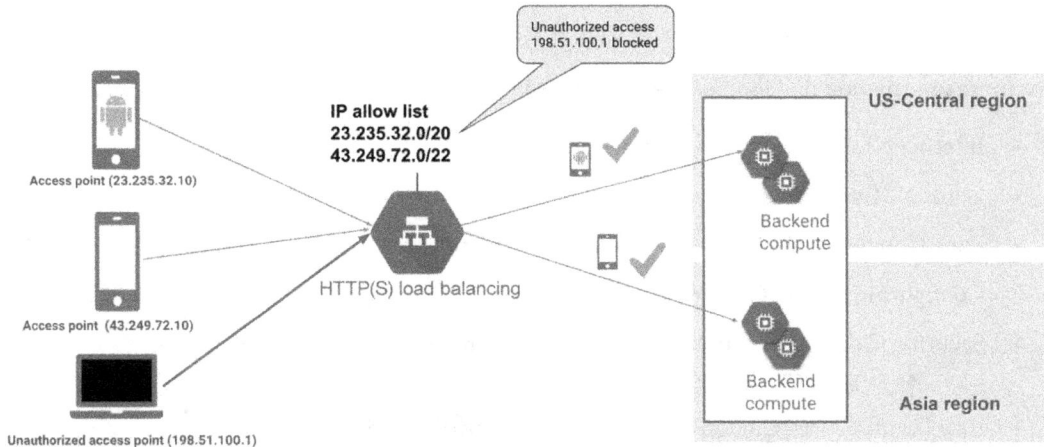

Figure 8.22 – Cloud Armor named IP list

In *Figure 8.22*, you can see how named IP lists work. CDN provides a list of IP addresses, such as 23.235.32.0/20, 43.249.72.0/22, and so on. Only communication coming from these IP addresses is permitted by this security rule. This means that the traffic of two CDN providers can be accessed (the access points are 23.235 32 10 and 43.249 72 10), while unapproved traffic from 198.51.100.1 is banned.

Summary

In this chapter, we looked at some advanced network security concepts. We covered the usage and configuration of Private Google Access, IAP and its use cases, and Cloud NAT. Finally, we looked at Cloud Armor and how it provides protection against DDoS and web-application-based attacks. We also covered additional details related to Cloud Armor, such as security policies, WAF rules, and named IP lists.

In the next chapter, we will cover data security, which is an important topic for the exam. We will look at the Google Cloud Key Management system and then cover data loss prevention and Secret Manager in the subsequent chapters.

Further reading

For more information on Google Cloud advanced network security, refer to the following links:

- Internet NEGs: `https://packt.link/DlCXS`
- Zonal NEGs: `https://packt.link/IlB39`
- Tune Google Cloud Armor preconfigured WAF rules: `https://packt.link/YEScF`
- Configuring Private Google Access and Cloud NAT: `https://packt.link/JyutC`
- Securing Cloud Applications with Identity-Aware Proxy (IAP) using Zero-Trust: `https://packt.link/bM1OX`
- Rate Limiting with Cloud Armor: `https://packt.link/rmCAn`

9

Google Cloud Key Management Service

In this chapter, we will look at Google Cloud **Key Management Service** (**KMS**). Cloud KMS is a foundational service for all cryptographic operations in Google Cloud. Every workload that you deploy on Google Cloud is going to need the ability to encrypt data and use it for authorized purposes. There are various options presented by Cloud KMS, and it's essential to understand them and make an informed choice to help with regulatory and audit requirements.

In this chapter, we will cover the following topics:

- Overview of Cloud KMS
- Encryption and key management in Cloud KMS
- Key management options
- Customer-supplied encryption key
- Symmetric and asymmetric key encryption
- Bringing your own key to the cloud
- Key lifecycle management
- Key IAM permissions
- Cloud HSM
- Cloud External Key Manager
- Cloud KMS best practices
- Cloud KMS APIs and logging

Let us start by learning about the capabilities of Cloud KMS.

Overview of Cloud KMS

With Cloud KMS, Google's focus is to provide a scalable, reliable, and performant solution with a wide spectrum of options that you can control on a platform that is straightforward to use. Let us start with a quick overview of the Cloud KMS architecture.

Cloud KMS Platform

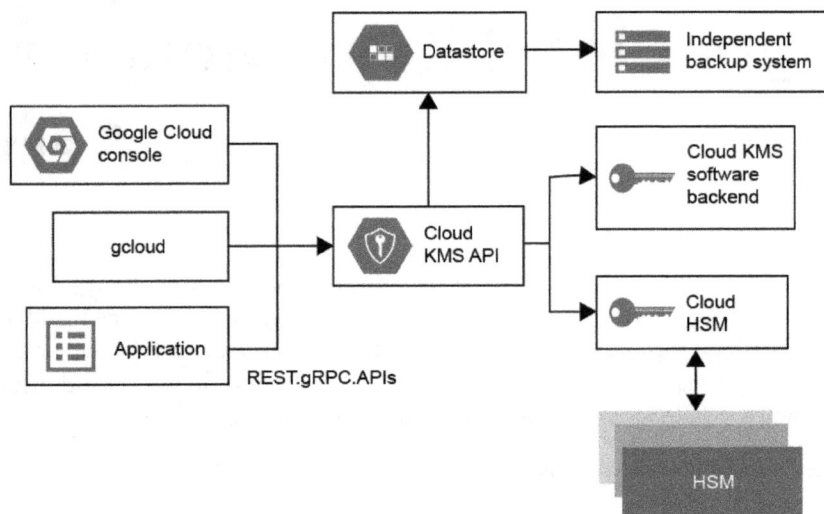

Figure 9.1 – The Cloud KMS architecture

The key components of the Cloud KMS platform are depicted in *Figure 9.1*. Administrators can access key management services through the Google Cloud console or CLI, as well as through the REST or gRPC APIs. A REST API or gRPC is used by applications to access key management services.

When creating a key on the Cloud KMS platform, you can select a protection level to define which key backend the key should use. The Cloud KMS platform has two backends (excluding Cloud EKM): the **software** and **HSM** protection levels. The software protection level is for keys that are protected by the **software security module**. HSM refers to keys that are protected by **hardware security modules (HSMs)**.

Cloud KMS cryptographic operations are performed by FIPS 140-2-validated modules. Keys with the software protection level, and the cryptographic operations performed with them, comply with FIPS 140-2 Level 1. Keys with the HSM protection level, and the cryptographic operations performed with them, comply with FIPS 140-2 Level 3.

Let us now see the current offerings of Cloud KMS.

Current Cloud KMS encryption offerings

In this section, we will look at various KMS offerings. The offerings are based on the source of the key material, starting from Google-managed encryption and going up to where the key material is managed externally.

Current Google Cloud portfolio

DEFAULT ENCRYPTION	CLOUD KMS	CLOUD HSM	KEY IMPORT	CUSTOMER-SUPPLIED ENCRYPT. KEYS	EXTERNAL KEY MANAGER
Google's default data-at-rest encryption. Customer has no access to keys or control of key rotation.	Customer can manage keys generated and stored by Google.	Customer can manage keys generated by Google and stored in a Google-owned and operated HSM.	Customer can import keys used and managed outside of Google, and use key material in a Google HSM.	Keys owned by customer and provided on each API call to be used ephemerally to access data.	Keys stored in a management system of customer's choice, even outside of Google Cloud.

Source of key material

Google controls key material

Customer controls key material

Figure 9.2 – Google Cloud encryption offerings

Figure 9.2 shows different offerings of encryption on Google Cloud.

Cloud KMS is supported by five design pillars:

1. **Customer control**: You can use Cloud KMS to handle software and hardware encryption keys, or you can provide your own via the key import functionality.

2. **Control and monitoring of access**: You can manage permissions on individual keys and see how they are used.

3. **Regionality**: Regionalization is built into Cloud KMS. Only the Google Cloud location you choose is used to produce, store, and process software keys in the service.

4. **Durability**: Cloud KMS meets the most stringent durability requirements. Cloud KMS checks and backs up all key material and metadata on a regular basis to protect against data corruption and ensure that data can be correctly decrypted.

5. **Security**: Cloud KMS is fully linked with **Identity and Access Management** (**IAM**) and **Cloud Audit Logs** controls, providing robust protections against unwanted access to keys. Cloud Audit Logs helps you understand who used a key and when.

Now that you understand the underlying principles of the Cloud KMS offerings, let us learn the basics of key management.

Encryption and key management in Cloud KMS

In this section, we will learn the basics of key management as it relates to Cloud KMS.

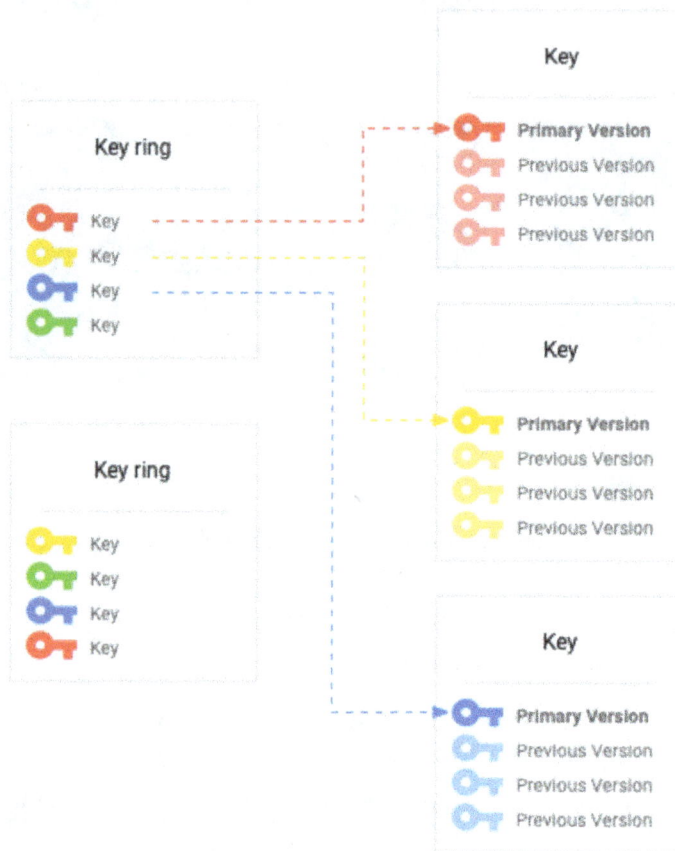

Figure 9.3 – Key structure

Figure 9.3 shows the structure of keys in Cloud KMS. Let us learn about the terms of key management:

- **Key**: A named object representing a cryptographic key that is used for a specific purpose. The key material—the actual bits used for cryptographic operations—can change over time as you create new key versions. Key purpose and other attributes of the key are connected with and managed using the key. Thus, the key is the most important object for understanding Cloud KMS usage. Cloud KMS supports both asymmetric keys and symmetric keys. A symmetric key is used for symmetric encryption to protect some corpus of data—for example, using AES-256 in GCM mode to encrypt a block of plaintext. An asymmetric key can be used for asymmetric encryption, or for creating digital signatures.

- **Key ring**: A grouping of keys for organizational purposes. A key ring belongs to a Google Cloud project and resides in a specific location. Keys inherit IAM policies from the key ring that contains them. Grouping keys with related permissions in a key ring lets you grant, revoke, or modify permissions to those keys at the key ring level without needing to act on each key individually. Key rings provide convenience and categorization, but if the grouping of key rings is not useful to you, you can manage permissions directly on keys. To prevent resource name collisions, a key ring cannot be deleted. Key rings and keys do not have billable costs or quota limitations, so their continued existence does not affect costs or production limits.

- **Key metadata**: Resource names, properties of Cloud KMS resources such as IAM policies, key type, key size, key state, and any data derived from them. Key metadata can be managed differently than the key material.

- **Key version**: Represents the key material associated with a key at some point in time. The key version is the resource that contains the actual key material. Versions are numbered sequentially, beginning with version 1. When a key is rotated, a new key version is created with new key material. The same logical key can have multiple versions over time, thus limiting the use of any single version. Symmetric keys will always have a primary version. This version is used for encrypting by default. When Cloud KMS performs decryption using symmetric keys, it automatically identifies which key version is needed to perform the decryption. A key version can only be used when it is enabled. Key versions in any state other than destroyed incur costs.

- **Purpose**: A key's purpose determines whether the key can be used for encryption or for signing. You choose the purpose when creating the key, and all versions have the same purpose. The purpose of a symmetric key is always symmetric encrypt/decrypt. The purpose of an asymmetric key is either asymmetric encrypt/decrypt or asymmetric signing. You create a key with a specific purpose in mind and it cannot be changed after the key is created.

- **State**: A key version's state is always one of the following:

  - Enabled

  - Disabled

  - Scheduled for destruction

  - Destroyed

Let us now move on to understand the key hierarchy in Cloud KMS.

Key hierarchy

The following diagram shows the key hierarchy of Cloud KMS. Cloud KMS uses Google's internal KMS in that Cloud-KMS-encrypted keys are wrapped by Google's KMS. Cloud KMS uses the same root of trust as Google's Cloud KMS.

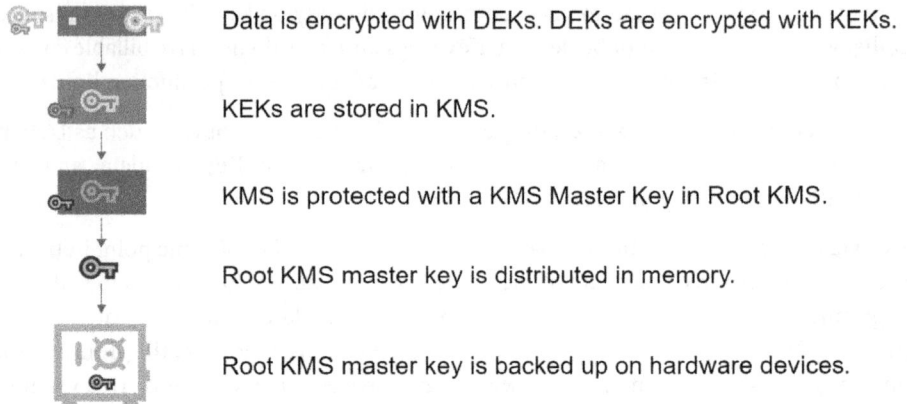

Data is encrypted with DEKs. DEKs are encrypted with KEKs.

KEKs are stored in KMS.

KMS is protected with a KMS Master Key in Root KMS.

Root KMS master key is distributed in memory.

Root KMS master key is backed up on hardware devices.

Figure 9.4 – Key hierarchy

Figure 9.4 shows the key hierarchy in Cloud KMS. There are several layers in the hierarchy:

- **Data encryption key (DEK)**: A key used to encrypt actual data. DEKs are managed by a Google Cloud service on your behalf.

- **Key encryption key (KEK)**: A key used to encrypt, or wrap, a data encryption key. All Cloud KMS platform options (software, hardware, and external backends) let you control the KEK.

- **KMS master key**: The key used to encrypt the KEK. This key is distributed in memory. The KMS master key is backed up on hardware devices. This key is responsible for encrypting KEKs.

- **Root KMS master key**: Google's internal KMS key.

Now that you understand how key hierarchy works, let us go over the basics of encryption.

Envelope encryption

As depicted in *Figure 9.5*, the process of encrypting data is to generate a DEK locally, encrypt data with the DEK, use a KEK to wrap the DEK, and then store the encrypted data and the wrapped DEK together. The KEK never leaves Cloud KMS. This is called **envelope encryption**. This section is more about understanding how Google handles envelope encryption, which is not something Google Cloud customers need to manage.

Figure 9.5 – Envelope encryption

Here are the steps that are followed to encrypt data using envelope encryption:

1. A DEK is generated locally, specifying a cipher type and a key material from which to generate the key.

2. This DEK is now used to encrypt the data.

3. A new KEK is either generated or an existing KEK from Cloud KMS is used—based on user preference. This KEK is used to encrypt (wrap) the DEK.

4. The wrapped DEK is stored with the encrypted data.

Now let us see the steps that are followed to decrypt data using envelope encryption.

As depicted in *Figure 9.6*, the process of decrypting data is to retrieve the encrypted data and the wrapped DEK, retrieve the KEK that wrapped the DEK, use the KEK to unwrap the DEK, and then use the unwrapped DEK to decrypt the data. The KEK never leaves Cloud KMS.

Figure 9.6 – Envelope decryption

To decrypt data using envelope encryption, you do the following:

1. Retrieve the encrypted data and the wrapped DEK.

2. Use the KEK stored in Cloud KMS to unwrap the encrypted DEK.

3. Use the plaintext DEK to decrypt the encrypted data.

Now that we understand the basics of keys and envelope encryption, let us look at key management options within Cloud KMS.

Key management options

In this section, we will cover several aspects of key management that are either Google-managed or customer-managed. It is important to know which option is best suited to which scenario so that you can make the right decision for a given use case.

Google Cloud's default encryption

Google Cloud stores all data encrypted at rest using a Google-managed default encryption key. The key is the AES-256 symmetric encryption key. There is no setup of keys or configuration required to turn on this option; all data by default uses this type of encryption. Google manages the keys and the rotation period of those keys. Google Cloud's default encryption is best suited for those customers who do not have specific requirements related to compliance or regional requirements for cryptographic key material. It is simple to use and does not require additional configuration to create keys, hence there is no cost to use it.

Customer-managed encryption keys (CMEKs)

Some customers of Google Cloud have stringent regulatory and compliance requirements to have control over the keys used to encrypt data at rest. To help with these requirements, Google Cloud offers the ability to encrypt data related to those services using an encryption key managed by the customer within Cloud KMS. CMEKs just mean that the customer decides the key type (software versus hardware), algorithm strength, and key rotation period when creating a key in Cloud KMS.

CMEKs give you control over aspects of the key lifecycle, including (but not limited to) the following:

- Customers can disable the keys used to safeguard data at rest, limiting Google's ability to decode it

- Customers can protect their data by utilizing a key that is personal to their location

- Customers can rotate the keys used to protect the data either automatically or manually

- Customers can use a Cloud HSM key, a Cloud **External Key Manager** (**EKM**) key, or an existing key that they import into Cloud KMS to protect their data

Customer-Managed Encryption Keys (**CMEKs**) are a supported feature in certain Google Cloud services. Let's explore what it entails for services to have CMEK support.

CMEK integrations

When a service supports CMEKs, it is said to have a CMEK integration. Some services, such as GKE, have multiple CMEK integrations for protecting several types of data related to the service.

For the exact steps to enable CMEKs, see the documentation for the relevant Google Cloud service. You can expect to follow steps like these:

1. You create or import a Cloud KMS key, selecting a location as geographically near as possible to the location of the service's resources. The service and the key can be in the same project or different projects. This is the CMEK.

2. You grant the CryptoKey Encrypter/Decrypter IAM role (`roles/cloudkms.cryptoKeyEncrypterDecrypter`) on the CMEK to the service account for that service.

3. You configure the service to use the CMEK to protect its data. For example, you can configure a GKE cluster to use a CMEK to protect data at rest on the boot disks of the nodes.

    *   If a service account has a `cryptoKeyEncrypterDecrypter` role, the service can encrypt and decrypt its data. If you revoke the role, or if you disable or destroy the CMEK, that data cannot be accessed.

> **Note**
>
> The rotation of the CMEK will not impact data availability since the service keeps track of which CMEK version was used to encrypt the data and will use that version to decrypt it.

CMEK compliance

Some services do not directly store data, or store data for only a brief period as an intermediate step in a long-running operation. For this type of workload, it is not practical to encrypt each write separately. These services do not offer CMEK integrations but can offer CMEK compliance, often with no configuration on your part.

A CMEK-compliant service encrypts temporary data by using an ephemeral key that only exists in memory and is never written to disk. When the temporary data is no longer needed, the ephemeral key is flushed from memory, and the encrypted data cannot be accessed, even if the storage resource still exists.

A CMEK-compliant service might offer the ability to send its output to a service with a CMEK integration, such as Cloud Storage.

Customer-supplied encryption key

You can provide your own AES-256 key, encoded in standard Base64, as an additional layer on top of Google-managed encryption keys. This key is known as a **customer-supplied encryption key (CSEK)**.

The CSEK is currently supported by only two services: Cloud Storage and Compute Engine.

CSEKs with Cloud Storage

If you provide a CSEK, Cloud Storage does not permanently store your key on Google's servers or otherwise manage your key.

Instead, you provide your key for each Cloud Storage operation, and your key is purged from Google's servers after the operation is complete. Cloud Storage stores only a cryptographic hash of the key so that future requests can be validated against the hash. Your key cannot be recovered from this hash, and the hash cannot be used to decrypt your data. Here are the best practices when using CSEKs:

- You should back up each key to a secure location and take precautions to ensure that keys are not shared with untrusted parties

- If any file or machine containing the encryption key is compromised, you should immediately perform key rotation for all objects encrypted with the compromised key

When you apply a customer-supplied encryption key to an object, Cloud Storage uses the key when encrypting:

- The object's data

- The object's CRC32C checksum

- The object's MD5 hash

Cloud Storage uses standard server-side keys to encrypt the remaining metadata for the object, including the object's name. This allows you to read and update general metadata, as well as list and delete objects, without needing the CSEK. However, to perform any of these actions, you must have sufficient permission to do so.

For example, if an object is encrypted with a CSEK, the key must be used to perform operations on the object such as downloading or moving it. If you attempt to read the object's metadata without providing the key, you receive metadata, such as the object name and content type, but not the object's CRC32C checksum or MD5 hash. If you do supply your key with the request for the object metadata, the object's CRC32C checksum and MD5 hash are included with the metadata.

The following restrictions apply when using CSEKs:

- Cloud Storage Transfer Service and Cloud Dataflow do not currently support objects encrypted with CSEKs.

- You cannot use the Google Cloud console to download objects that are encrypted with a CSEK. Similarly, when you use the Google Cloud console to upload an object, you cannot encrypt the object with a CSEK.

- You can only set CSEKs on individual objects. You cannot set a default CSEK for a bucket.

- If you are performing a composition operation on objects encrypted by CSEKs, the component objects must be encrypted by the same key, and you need to provide the key with the compose request. The resulting composite object is encrypted by the same key.

Now that you understand the restrictions of using CSEKs with Google Cloud Storage, here is how you can use CSEKs with `gsutil`.

CSEKs with gsutil

To use a CSEK with `gsutil`, add the `encryption_key` parameter to the `[GSUtil]` section of your boto configuration file. `encryption_key` is an RFC 6848 Base64-encoded string of your AES-256 encryption key.

You can optionally specify one or more decryption keys, up to 100. While the `encryption_key` option is used by `gsutil` as both an encryption and decryption key, any `decryption_key` options you specify are used only to decrypt objects. Multiple decryption keys must be listed in the boto configuration file as follows:

```
decryption_key1 = ...
decryption_key2 = ...
decryption_key3 = ...
```

If you have encryption or decryption keys in your boto configuration file, they are used for all `gsutil` commands. When decrypting, `gsutil` calculates the SHA256 hash of the supplied encryption and decryption keys and selects the correct key to use for a particular object by matching the SHA256 hash in the object's metadata.

Objects encrypted with CSEKs require the matching decryption key during **encryption key rotation**. If an object is encrypted using a CSEK, you can rotate the object's key by rewriting the object. Rewrites are supported through the JSON API, but not the XML API.

Now that we have seen how CSEKs are used with Cloud Storage, let us see how they can be used with Compute Engine.

CSEKs with Compute Engine

Compute Engine encrypts all data at rest by default on the persistent disks by using Google default encryption keys. You can bring your own encryption key if you want to control and manage this encryption yourself.

If you provide your own encryption key, Compute Engine uses your key to protect the Google-generated keys used to encrypt and decrypt your data. Only users who can provide the correct key can use resources protected by a CSEK.

Google does not store your keys on its servers, and it cannot access your protected data unless you provide it to them. This also implies that if you forget or lose your key, Google will be unable to recover it, as well as any data encrypted with it.

Google discards the cryptographic keys when you destroy a persistent disk, making the data unrecoverable. This is an irreversible procedure.

There are some technical restrictions in using CSEKs with Compute Engine:

- You can only encrypt new persistent disks with your own key. You cannot encrypt existing persistent disks with your own key.

- You cannot use your own keys with local SSDs because local SSDs do not persist beyond the life of a VM. Local SSDs are already protected with an ephemeral encryption key that Google does not retain.

- Compute Engine does not store encryption keys with instance templates, so you need to store your own keys in Cloud KMS to encrypt disks in a managed instance group.

Now you understand the restrictions of using CSEKs with Compute Engine, please look at the Google Cloud documentation on how to use CSEKs with Compute Engine. Try out a few of these use cases on your own to get a fair idea of how a CSEK is used:

- Encrypt a new persistent disk with a CSEK

- Create a snapshot from a disk encrypted with a CSEK

- Create a new image from a disk or custom image encrypted with a CSEK

- Encrypt an imported image with a CSEK

- Create a persistent disk from a resource encrypted with a CSEK

- Attach a disk encrypted with a CSEK to a new VM

- Start or restart VMs that have disks encrypted with a CSEK

So far, we have seen different types of keys and where you can use them. Let us move on now to understand symmetric and asymmetric key operations.

Symmetric key encryption

Recall that symmetric keys are used for encryption to protect some data—for example, using AES-256 in GCM mode to encrypt a block of plaintext.

Creating a symmetric key

To create a symmetric key, you will first need to create a key ring. The key ring determines the location of the key. Let us start with creating that.

Step 1: Creating a key ring

Here is a `gcloud` command to create a key ring:

```
gcloud kms keyrings create key-ring-name \
    --location location
```

Replace `key-ring-name` with a name for the key ring to hold the key. Replace `location` with the Cloud KMS location for the key ring and its keys.

Step 2: Creating a key

Use the following command to create a key in an existing key ring:

```
gcloud kms keys create key \
    --keyring key-ring-name \
    --location location \
    --purpose "encryption"
```

Replace `key` with the name of the key you would like to use and `key-ring-name` with the name of the key ring you created in the previous step. Replace `location` with the Cloud KMS location of the key ring. Note the *purpose* of this key.

Step 3: Setting a key rotation period and starting time

Once the key is created, you can set a rotation period with a starting time. Here is the command that will allow you to do so:

```
gcloud kms keys create key \
    --keyring key-ring-name \
    --location location \
    --purpose "encryption" \
    --rotation-period rotation-period \
    --next-rotation-time next-rotation-time
```

Replace `key` with a name for the key. Replace `key-ring-name` with the name of the existing key ring where the key will be located. Replace `location` with the Cloud KMS location for the key ring. Replace `rotation-period` with an interval, such as `30d` to rotate the key every 30 days. Replace `next-rotation-time` with a timestamp at which to begin the first rotation, such as `1970-01-01T01:02:03`.

Now that you have created a key for symmetric encryption, let us see how to use it to encrypt content.

Encrypting content with a symmetric key

Here is a command to use an existing key for encryption:

```
gcloud kms encrypt \
    --key key \
    --keyring key-ring-name \
    --location location  \
    --plaintext-file file-with-data-to-encrypt \
    --ciphertext-file file-to-store-encrypted-data
```

Replace key with the name of the key to use for encryption. Replace key-ring-name with the name of the key ring where the key is located. Replace location with the Cloud KMS location for the key ring. Replace file-with-data-to-encrypt and file-to-store-encrypted-data with the local file paths (include the actual filename as well) for reading the plaintext data and saving the encrypted output.

This command will produce a file containing encrypted data. The name of the file is the one you provided for the ciphertext-file argument.

Now that you have seen how to encrypt the content, let us see how to decrypt it.

Decrypting content with a symmetric key

Here is a command to use an existing key for decryption:

```
gcloud kms decrypt \
    --key key \
    --keyring key-ring-name \
    --location location  \
    --ciphertext-file file-path-with-encrypted-data \
    --plaintext-file file-path-to-store-plaintext
```

Replace key with the name of the key to use for encryption. Replace key-ring-name with the name of the key ring where the key is located. Replace location with the Cloud KMS location for the key ring. Replace file-path-with-encrypted-data and file-path-to-store-plaintext with the local file paths (include the actual filename as well) for reading the plaintext data and saving the encrypted output.

This command will produce a file containing decrypted data. The name of the file is the one you have provided for plaintext-file.

Now that you have seen symmetric key encryption and decryption using Cloud KMS, let us move on to see how to use asymmetric key encryption.

Asymmetric key encryption

The following section describes the flow for using an asymmetric key to encrypt and decrypt data. Asymmetric key encryptions involve a key pair (public and private key pair). As the name suggests, the private key is not shared while the public key is shared. There are two participants in this workflow—a sender and a recipient. The sender creates a ciphertext using the recipient's public key, and then the recipient decrypts the ciphertext using the private key it holds. Only someone with knowledge of the private key can decrypt the ciphertext.

Cloud KMS provides the following functionality as it relates to asymmetric encryption:

- The ability to create an asymmetric key with the key purpose of `ASYMMETRIC_DECRYPT`. For information about which algorithms Cloud KMS supports, see asymmetric encryption algorithms in the Google Cloud documentation.

- CloudKMS asymmetric keys also support `ASYMMETRIC_SIGN` (ECC and RSA).

- The ability to retrieve the public key for an asymmetric key. You use the public key to encrypt data. Cloud KMS does not directly provide a method to asymmetrically encrypt data. Instead, you encrypt data using openly available SDKs and tools, such as `OpenSSL`. These SDKs and tools require the public key that you retrieve from Cloud KMS.

- The ability to decrypt data with an asymmetric key.

Now let us look at the steps to be able to do asymmetric encryption and signing. Similar to symmetric key creation, in order to create an asymmetric key, you will first need to create a key ring. The key ring determines the location of the key. Let us start.

Step 1: Creating a key ring

Use the following command to create a key ring for your asymmetric key:

```
gcloud kms keyrings create key-ring-name \
    --location location
```

Replace `key-ring-name` with a name for the key ring. Replace `location` with the Cloud KMS location for the key ring and its keys.

Step 2: Creating an asymmetric decryption key

Follow these steps to create an asymmetric decryption key on the specified key ring and location. These examples use the software protection level and an rsa-decrypt-oaep-2048-sha256 algorithm. When you first create the key, the key's initial version has a state of pending generation. When the state changes to enabled, you can use the key:

```
gcloud kms keys create key \
    --keyring key-ring-name \
    --location location \
    --purpose "asymmetric-encryption" \
    --default-algorithm "rsa-decrypt-oaep-2048-sha256"
```

Replace key with a name for the new key. Replace key-ring-name with the name of the existing key ring where the key will be located. Replace location with the Cloud KMS location for the key ring.

Step 3: (Optional) Creating an asymmetric signing key

Follow these steps to create an asymmetric signing key on the specified key ring and location. The following command uses the software protection level and the rsa-sign-pkcs1-2048-sha256 algorithm. When you first create the key, the key's initial version has a state of pending generation. When the state changes to enabled, you can use the key:

```
gcloud kms keys create key \
    --keyring key-ring-name \
    --location location \
    --purpose "asymmetric-signing" \
    --default-algorithm "rsa-sign-pkcs1-2048-sha256"
```

Now let us move on to understand how to use an asymmetric key.

Encrypting data with an asymmetric key

This section provides examples that run at the command line. We use OpenSSL to encrypt data. Cloud Shell is pre-installed with OpenSSL, so go ahead and try this in Cloud Shell.

> **Note**
>
> You cannot follow this procedure with a key that has a purpose of ASYMMETRIC_SIGN.
>
> The version of OpenSSL installed on macOS does not support the flags used to decrypt data in this topic. To follow these steps on macOS, install OpenSSL from Homebrew.

Step 1: Downloading the public key

Run the following command to download the public key part of the asymmetric key that you created in *Step 2* in the previous section:

```
gcloud kms keys versions get-public-key key-version \
    --key key \
    --keyring key-ring-name \
    --location location  \
    --output-file public-key-path
```

Replace key-version with the key version that has the public key. Replace key with the name of the key. Replace key-ring-name with the name of the key ring where the key is located. Replace location with the Cloud KMS location for the key ring. Replace public-key-path with the location to save the public key on the local system.

Now encrypt the data with the public key you downloaded from Cloud KMS:

```
openssl pkeyutl -in cleartext-data-input-file \
    -encrypt \
    -pubin \
    -inkey public-key-path \
    -pkeyopt rsa_padding_mode:oaep \
    -pkeyopt rsa_oaep_md:sha256 \
    -pkeyopt rsa_mgf1_md:sha256 \
    > encrypted-data-output-file
```

Replace cleartext-data-input-file with the path and filename to encrypt. Replace public-key-path with the path and filename where you downloaded the public key. Replace encrypted-data-output-file with the path and filename to save the encrypted data.

Now let us see how to decrypt the data using an asymmetric key.

Decrypting data with an asymmetric key

We will use the private key part of the asymmetric key to decrypt the encrypted data. Run the gcloud command for decryption:

```
gcloud kms asymmetric-decrypt \
    --version key-version \
    --key key \
    --keyring key-ring-name \
    --location location  \
    --ciphertext-file file-path-with-encrypted-data \
    --plaintext-file file-path-to-store-plaintext
```

Replace `key-version` with the key version or omit the `--version` flag to detect the version automatically. Replace `key` with the name of the key to use for decryption. Replace `key-ring-name` with the name of the key ring where the key will be located. Replace `location` with the Cloud KMS location for the key ring. Replace `file-path-with-encrypted-data` and `file-path-to-store-plaintext` with the local file paths for reading the encrypted data and saving the decrypted output, respectively.

The decrypted text will be in `plaintext-file`.

We looked at some common operations with a key generated by KMS. Now let us look at an advanced option to bring your own key to the cloud, which some organizations may prefer to achieve compliance.

Importing a key (BYOK)

Google allows you to bring your own cryptographic key material. You can import that using the Software or Cloud HSM protection level. We will see step-by-step instructions on how to do this. But before we do that, let us understand the reasons you want to import a key:

- You may be using existing cryptographic keys that were created on your premises or in an external KMS.

- If you migrate an application to Google Cloud or if you add cryptographic support to an existing Google Cloud application, you can import the relevant keys into Cloud KMS.

- As part of key import, Cloud KMS generates a wrapping key, which is a public/private key pair, using one of the supported import methods. Encrypting your key material with this wrapping key protects the key material in transit.

- This Cloud KMS public wrapping key is used to *encrypt*, on the client, the key to be imported. The private key matching this public key is stored within Google Cloud and is used to unwrap the key after it reaches the Google Cloud project. The import method you choose determines the algorithm used to create the wrapping key.

Before we begin to go over instructions on how to bring your key, make sure of the following prerequisites:

- Prepare the local system by choosing *one* of the following options. Automatic key wrapping is recommended for most users.

  - **If you want to allow gcloud to wrap your keys automatically** before transmitting them to Google Cloud, you must install the Pyca cryptography library on your local system. The Pyca library is used by the import job that wraps and protects the key locally before sending it to Google Cloud.

  - **If you want to wrap your keys manually**, you must configure OpenSSL for manual key wrapping.

- In addition to these options, make sure you follow these guidelines as well:

  - Verify that your key's algorithm and length are supported by Google Cloud KMS. Allowable algorithms for a key depend on whether the key is used for symmetric encryption, asymmetric encryption, or asymmetric signing, and whether it is stored in software or an HSM. You will specify the key's algorithm as part of the import request.

  - Separately, you must also verify how the key is encoded, and adjust if necessary.

Now let us start with the instructions on importing keys to Google Cloud. For simplicity, we will be using `gcloud`.

Step 1: Creating a blank key

1. Create a project in the Google Cloud console, and enable Cloud KMS.

2. If you do not have a key to import but want to test importing keys, you can create a symmetric key on the local system, using the following command:

   ```
   openssl rand 32 > ${HOME}/test.bin
   ```

> **Note**
> Use this key for testing only. A key created this way might not be appropriate for production use.

3. Create a new key ring in a region of your choice.

4. Create a new key of type imported key by using the following parameters:

   I.   **Name**: ext-key-3

   II.   **Protection Level**: Software

   III. **Purpose**: Symmetric encrypt/decrypt

   IV.   **Rotation Period**: Manual

5. An empty key is created with no version; you will be redirected to create a key version.

6. Use the following `gcloud` command to create the key version. We will be creating a symmetric key:

   ```
   gcloud kms keys create ext-key-4 --location us-central1
   --keyring external-central-key-ring-name --purpose encryption
   --skip-initial-version-creation
   ```

7. Create a new import job.

8. Download the wrapping key.

    This key will not be available for use yet since it is an empty shell to hold the key material that you will import in the following steps. Now, you have two options:

    - Upload your pre-wrapped encryption key.

    - Use the `gcloud` command to provide your key to the job, which will automatically wrap it. You will use different flags to make the import request, depending on whether you want the `gcloud` command-line tool to wrap your key automatically or you have wrapped your key manually. We will use the `gcloud` option here as it is simple to understand.

Step 2: Importing the key using an import job

1. Set `export CLOUDSDK_PYTHON_SITEPACKAGES=1`, otherwise, you will see the following error:

    ```
    Cannot load the Pyca cryptography library. Either the library is
    not installed, or site packages are not enabled for the Google
    Cloud SDK. Please consult https://cloud.google.com/kms/docs/
    crypto for further instructions
    ```

2. Make sure the preceding environment variable is set by using this command:

    ```
    echo $CLOUDSDK_PYTHON_SITEPACKAGES
    ```

3. Execute the following command to upload your key to Cloud KMS:

    ```
    user@cloudshell:~ $ gcloud kms keys versions import    --import-
    job ext-key-import-job    --location us-central1    --keyring
    external-central-key-ring-name    --key ext-key-4    --algorithm
    google-symmetric-encryption    --target-key-file ${HOME}/test.bin
    --public-key-file /home/user/ext-key-import-job.pub --verbosity
    info
    ```

    You will see an output similar to what is shown here:

    ```
    INFO: Display format: "default"
    algorithm: GOOGLE_SYMMETRIC_ENCRYPTION
    createTime: '2020-04-08T22:25:46.597631370Z'
    importJob: projects/PROJECT_ID/locations/us-central1/keyRings/
    external-central-key-ring-name/importJobs/ext-key-import-job
    name: projects/PROJECT_ID/locations/us-central1/keyRings/
    external-central-key-ring-name/cryptoKeys/ext-key-1/
    cryptoKeyVersions/1
    protectionLevel: SOFTWARE
    state: PENDING_IMPORT
    ```

4. Wait until the key version is in the **ENABLED** state, then set it to primary using the following `gcloud` command:

```
gloud kms keys set-primary-version ext-key-1 --version=1
--keyring=external-central-key-ring-name --location=us-central1
```

Cloud KMS will only use the primary version of the key. Now that you have set it, let us move on to using it.

Step 3: Verifying key encryption and decryption

1. Create a `secrets.txt` file with some plain text in it. Encrypt that file using `gcloud`:

```
gcloud kms encrypt --ciphertext-file=secrets.txt.enc
--plaintext-file=secrets.txt --key=ext-key-4 --keyring=external-
central-key-ring-name --location=us-central1
```

2. Now use the following command to decrypt it. Decrypt the file using the same key:

```
gcloud kms decrypt --ciphertext-file=secrets.txt.
enc --plaintext-file=secrets.txt.dec --key=ext-key-1
--keyring=external-central-key-ring-name --location=us-central1
```

Verify the text you have decrypted is the same as the plain text. This tutorial demonstrated that you can bring your own key material and use it for encryption and decryption.

Now that we understand several types of keys you can use in Cloud KMS, let us understand the lifecycle of keys.

Key lifecycle management

While operating your workloads, you need to manage the lifecycle of your keys. The US **National Information Standards Institute** (**NIST**) **special publication** (**SP**) *800-57, Part 1* describes a key management lifecycle that is divided into four phases: pre-operational, operational, post-operational, and destroyed.

The following section provides a mapping of the NIST lifecycle functions from the publication to Google Cloud KMS lifecycle functions.

1. The **Pre-operational** lifecycle phase is mapped to the following:

    I.   **NIST section 8.1.4 Keying-Material Installation Function**: The equivalent Cloud KMS operation is **Key import**.

    II. **NIST section 8.1.5 Key Establishment Function**: The equivalent Cloud KMS operation is **Key creation (symmetric, asymmetric)**.

2.   The **Operational** lifecycle phase is mapped to the following:

    I.   **NIST section 8.2.1 Normal Operational Storage Function**: The equivalent Cloud KMS operation is **Key creation in SOFTWARE, HSM, or EXTERNAL protection levels (symmetric, asymmetric).**

    II. **NIST section 8.2.3 Key Change Function**: The equivalent Cloud KMS operation is **Key rotation.**

3.   The **Post-operational** lifecycle phase is mapped to the following:

    I.   **NIST section 8.3.4 Key Destruction Function**: The equivalent Cloud KMS operation is **Key destruction (and recovery).**

In addition, Cloud KMS offers the capability to disable a key. Typically, you disable the old key after rotating to a new key. This gives you a period to confirm that no additional data needs to be re-encrypted before the key is destroyed. You can re-enable a disabled key if you discover data that needs to be re-encrypted. When you are sure that there is no more data that was encrypted by using the old key, the key can be scheduled for destruction.

Key IAM permissions

When considering key permissions, think about the hierarchy in which the key exists. A key exists in a key ring, a project, a folder in another folder, or under "Cloud Organization".

Recall that there are two fundamental security principles IAM enforces:

- Principle of separation of duties
- Principle of least privilege

A primary role a principal can play is the Cloud KMS CryptoKey Encrypter/Decrypter role at various levels of the hierarchy. There are several other roles Cloud KMS has based on how you structure it. Please refer to the Google Cloud KMS documentation for the list of other IAM roles: `https://packt.link/RyY17`.

We have looked at various IAM roles and permissions for Cloud KMS; let us now look at some best practices on how to manage access:

- Key management roles can be granted based on the culture and process of your enterprises. Traditionally, this role is played by the IT security team.
- For a large or complex organization, you might decide on an approach such as the following:

- Grant members of your IT security team the Cloud KMS Admin role (`roles/cloudkms.admin`) across all projects. If different team members handle various aspects of a key's lifecycle, you can grant those team members a more granular role, such as the Cloud KMS Importer role (`roles/cloudkms.importer`).

- Grant the Cloud KMS Encrypter/Decrypter role (`roles/cloudkms.cryptoKey EncrypterDecrypter`) to users or service accounts that read or write encrypted data.

- Grant the Cloud KMS Public Key Viewer role (`roles/cloudkms.publicKeyViewer`) to users or service accounts that need to view the public portion of a key used for asymmetric encryption.

- For a small organization, each project team can manage its own Cloud KMS and grant the IT security team access to audit the keys and usage.

- Consider hosting your keys in a separate Google Cloud project from the data protected by those keys. A user with a basic or highly privileged role in one project, such as an editor, cannot use this role to gain unauthorized access to keys in a different project.

- Avoid granting the owner role to any member. Without the owner role, no member in the project can create a key and use it to decrypt data or for signing, unless each of these permissions is granted to that member. To grant broad administrative access without granting the ability to encrypt or decrypt, grant the Cloud KMS Admin (`roles/cloudkms.admin`) role instead.

- To limit access to encrypted data, such as customer data, you can restrict who can access the key and who can use the key for decryption. If necessary, you can create granular custom roles to meet your business requirements.

- For projects using the VPC Service Controls perimeter, we recommend that you have a separate Cloud KMS project for the perimeter.

Now that we have looked at various IAM roles and best practices for key management, let us look at Cloud HSM offerings next.

Cloud HSM

Cloud HSM is a cloud-hosted HSM service that allows you to host encryption keys and perform cryptographic operations in a cluster of FIPS 140-2 Level 3 certified HSMs. The Cloud HSM cluster is managed by Google for you; you do not get access to the physical device. You also do not need to patch or scale it for multi-regional applications. Cloud HSM uses Cloud KMS as its frontend; you use Cloud KMS APIs to interact with the Cloud HSM backend. This abstracts the communication with Cloud HSM, so you do not need to use Cloud HSM-specific code.

When you use HSM-backed keys and key versions, the Google Cloud project that makes the cryptographic request incurs cryptographic operation quota usage, and the Google Cloud project that contains the HSM keys incurs HSM QPM quota usage.

> **Note**
> You can find more information on Cloud KMS in the Google Cloud documentation for quotas.

Here are some architectural characteristics of Cloud HSM that you should be aware of:

- The Cloud HSM service provides hardware-backed keys to Cloud KMS. It offers Google Cloud customers the ability to manage and use cryptographic keys that are protected by fully managed HSMs in Google data centers.

- The service is available and auto-scales horizontally. It is designed to be extremely resilient to the unpredictable demands of workloads.

- Keys are cryptographically bound to the Cloud KMS region in which the key ring was defined. You can choose to make keys global or enforce strict regional restrictions.

- With Cloud HSM, the keys that you create and use cannot be exported outside of the cluster of HSMs belonging to the region specified at the time of key creation.

- Using Cloud HSM, you can verifiably attest that your cryptographic keys are created and used exclusively within a hardware device.

- No application changes are required for existing Cloud KMS customers to use Cloud HSM: the Cloud HSM services are accessed using the same API and client libraries as the Cloud KMS software backend.

- If you choose to, you can use a PKCS#11-compliant C++ library, `libkmsp11to.so`, to interact with Cloud HSM from your application. You use this library typically for the following purposes:

  - Creating signatures, certifications, or **certificate signing requests** (**CSRs**) using the command line

  - TLS web session signing in web servers such as Apache or NGINX backed by Cloud HSM keys

  - Migrating your application to a Google Cloud project that uses PKCS#11 APIs

  This library authenticates Google Cloud using a service account. The library uses a YAML file to store the Cloud KMS configurations. Use the following link to learn more about this: `https://packt.link/H53BX`.

Let us look at the HSM key hierarchy now.

HSM key hierarchy

In *Figure 9.7*, Cloud KMS is the proxy for HSM. Cloud HSM root keys wrap customer keys, and then Cloud KMS wraps the HSM keys that are passed to Google Datastore for storage.

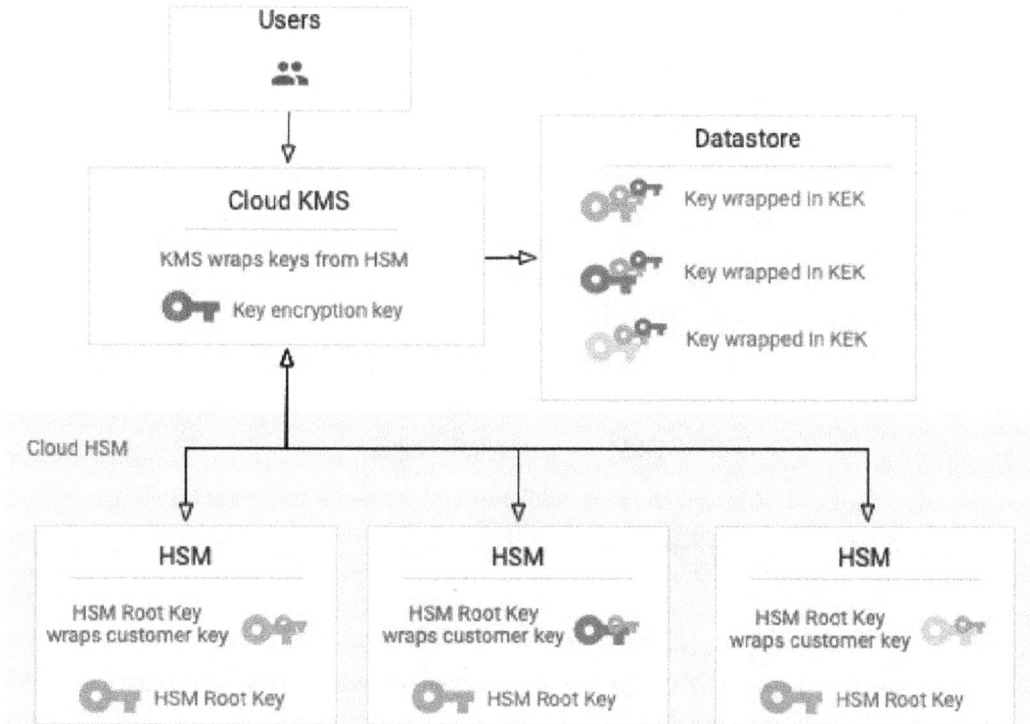

Figure 9.7 – HSM key hierarchy

Cloud HSM has a key (not shown) that controls the migration of material inside the Cloud HSM administrative domain. A region might have multiple HSM administrative domains.

The HSM root key has two characteristics:

- Customer keys wrapped by HSM root keys can be used on the HSM, but the HSM never returns the plaintext of the customer key
- The HSM only uses the customer key for operations

Datastore protection

HSMs are not used as permanent storage for keys; they store keys only while they are being used. Because HSM storage is constrained, the HSM keys are encrypted and stored in the Cloud KMS key datastore.

Rotation policy

Several types of keys are involved in Cloud HSM's key protection strategy. Customers rotate their own keys and rely on Cloud KMS to rotate the HSM keys.

Provisioning and handling process

The provisioning of HSMs is carried out in a lab equipped with numerous physical and logical safeguards, including, for example, multi-party authorization controls to help prevent single-actor compromise.

The following are Cloud HSM system-level invariants:

- The key is generated on an HSM and, throughout its lifetime, never leaves the well-defined boundaries of HSMs

- It may be replicated on other HSMs, or on backup HSMs

- It can be used as a KEK to directly or indirectly wrap customer keys that HSMs use

- Customer keys cannot be extracted as plaintext. Customer keys cannot be moved outside the region of origin

- All configuration changes to provisioned HSMs are guarded through multiple security safeguards

- Administrative operations are logged, adhering to the separation of duties between Cloud HSM administrators and logging administrators

- HSMs are designed to be protected from tampering (such as by the insertion of malicious hardware or software modifications, or unauthorized extraction of secrets) throughout the operational lifecycle

Vendor-controlled firmware

HSM firmware is digitally signed by the HSM vendor. Google cannot create or update the HSM firmware. All firmware from the vendor is signed, including development firmware that is used for testing.

Regionality

Customer keys are assigned to specific geographic regions because of their binding to a specific HSM root key. For example, a key created specifically in the us-west1 region cannot migrate into the us-east1 region or the US multi-region. Similarly, a key created in the US multi-region cannot migrate into or out of the us-west1 region.

Strict security procedures safeguard HSM hardware

As mandated by FIPS 140-2 level 3, HSM devices have built-in mechanisms to help protect against and provide evidence of physical tampering.

In addition to the assurances provided by the HSM hardware itself, the infrastructure for Cloud HSM is managed according to Google infrastructure security design.

> **Note**
> You can find more information at the following link: `https://packt.link/B8pgP`.

Documented, auditable procedures protect the integrity of each HSM during provisioning, deployment, and in production:

- All HSM configurations must be verified by multiple Cloud HSM **site reliability engineers (SREs)** before the HSM can be deployed to a data center
- After an HSM is put into service, configuration change can only be initiated and verified by multiple Cloud HSM SREs
- An HSM can only receive firmware that is signed by the HSM manufacturer
- HSM hardware is not directly exposed to any network
- Servers that host HSM hardware are prevented from running unauthorized processes

Service and tenant isolation

The Cloud HSM architecture ensures that HSMs are protected from malicious or inadvertent interference from other services or tenants.

An HSM that is part of this architecture accepts requests only from Cloud HSM, and the Cloud HSM service accepts requests only from Cloud KMS. Cloud KMS enforces that callers have appropriate IAM permissions on the keys that they attempt to use. Unauthorized requests do not reach HSMs.

Key creation flow in HSM

When you create an HSM-backed key, the Cloud KMS API does not create the key material but requests that the HSM creates it.

An HSM can only create keys in locations it supports. Each partition on an HSM contains a wrapping key corresponding to a Cloud KMS location. The wrapping key is shared among all partitions that support the Cloud KMS location. The key-creation process looks like this:

1. The KMS API **Google Front End Service** (**GFE**) routes the key creation request to a Cloud KMS server in the location that corresponds to the request.

2. The Cloud KMS API verifies the caller's identity, the caller's permission to create keys in the project, and that the caller has a sufficient write request quota.

3. The Cloud KMS API forwards the request to Cloud HSM.

4. Cloud HSM directly interfaces with the HSM. The HSM does the following:

    I.   Creates the key and wraps it with the location-specific wrapping key.

    II. Creates the attestation statement for the key and signs it with the partition signing key.

5. After Cloud HSM returns the wrapped key and attestation to Cloud KMS, the Cloud KMS API wraps the HSM-wrapped key according to the Cloud KMS key hierarchy, then writes it to the project.

This design ensures that the key cannot be unwrapped or used outside of an HSM, cannot be extracted from the HSM, and exists in its unwrapped state only within locations you intend.

Key attestations

In cryptography, an attestation is a machine-readable, programmatically provable statement that a piece of software makes about itself. Attestations are a key component of trusted computing and may be required for compliance reasons.

To view and verify the attestations, you request a cryptographically signed attestation statement from the HSM, along with the certificate chains used to sign it. The attestation statement is produced by the HSM hardware and signed by certificates owned by Google and by the HSM manufacturer (currently, Google uses Marvell HSM devices).

After downloading the attestation statement and the certificate chains, you can check its attributes or verify the validity of the attestation using the certificate chains.

Google has developed an attestation script, an open source Python script that you can use to verify the attestations. You can view the source code for the script to learn more about the attestation format and how verification works, or as a model for a customized solution, at the following link: `https://packt.link/AN1oU`.

> **Note**
>
> To learn more about how to view and verify attestations, see the following Google Cloud documentation: `https://packt.link/2A5Er`.

Cryptographic operation flow in HSM

When you perform a cryptographic operation in Cloud KMS, you do not need to know whether you are using an HSM-backed or software key. When the Cloud KMS API detects that an operation involves an HSM-backed key, it forwards the request to an HSM in the same location:

1. The GFE routes the request to a Cloud KMS server in the appropriate location. The Cloud KMS API verifies the caller's identity, the caller's permission to access the key and perform the operation, and the project's quota for cryptographic operations.

2. The Cloud KMS API retrieves the wrapped key from the datastore and decrypts one level of encryption using the Cloud KMS master key. The key is still wrapped with the Cloud HSM wrapping key for the Cloud KMS location.

3. The Cloud KMS API detects that the protection level is HSM and sends the partially unwrapped key, along with the inputs to the cryptographic operation, to Cloud HSM.

4. Cloud HSM directly interfaces with the HSM. The HSM does the following:

    I.   Checks that the wrapped key and its attributes have not been modified.

    II.   Unwraps the key and load it into its storage.

    III. Performs the cryptographic operation and returns the result.

5. The Cloud KMS API passes the result back to the caller.

Cryptographic operations using HSM-backed keys are performed entirely within an HSM in the configured location, and only the result is visible to the caller. Now that we have looked at Cloud HSM, let us move on and understand Cloud **External Key Manager** (**EKM**). This is the newest offering from Google for cloud key management.

Cloud EKM

Cloud EKM is one of the newest offerings for data protection. With Cloud EKM, you use the keys that you manage within an EKM partner.

Cloud EKM provides several benefits:

*   **Key provenance**: You control the location and distribution of your externally managed keys. Externally managed keys are never cached or stored within Google Cloud. Instead, Cloud EKM communicates directly with the external key management partner for each request.

- **Access control**: You manage access to your externally managed keys. Before you can use an externally managed key to encrypt or decrypt data in Google Cloud, you must grant the Google Cloud project access to use the key. You can revoke this access at any time.

- **Centralized key management**: You can manage your keys and access policies from a specific location and user interface, whether the data they protect resides in the cloud or on your premises.

In all cases, the key resides on the external system and is never sent to Google. The following partners are supported for EKM hosting:

- Fortanix

- Futurex

- Thales

- Virtu

Google Cloud supports several cloud services for Cloud EKM for CMEK encryption. Please refer to the Google Cloud documentation for currently supported services.

The architecture of Cloud EKM

Figure 9.8 shows the architecture of Cloud EKM.

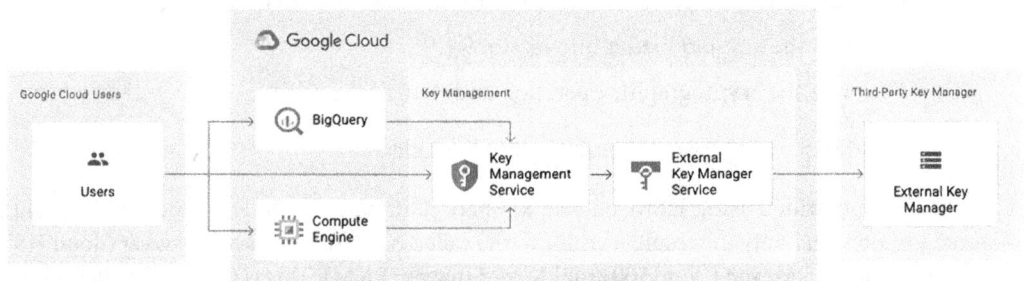

Figure 9.8 – Cloud EKM architecture

The EKM key creation flow is as follows:

1. Establish an account with the partner. They have their own portal where you manage the keys.

2. Create a key or use an existing key. This key has a unique URI or key path. Copy this path to use in *Step 4*.

3. Next, you grant your Google Cloud project workload's service account access to use the key in the external key management partner system.

4. In your Google Cloud project, you create a Cloud EKM key, using the URI or key path for the externally managed key.

While Cloud EKM seems like a great option to use, there are some considerations you should be aware of:

- Cloud EKM can be used with Hosted Private HSM to create a single-tenant HSM solution integrated with Cloud KMS. Choose a Cloud EKM partner that supports single-tenant HSMs.

- When you use a Cloud EKM key, Google has no control over the availability of your externally managed key in the partner system. Google cannot recover your data if you lose keys you manage outside of Google Cloud.

- Review the guidelines about external key management partners and regions when choosing the locations for your Cloud EKM keys.

- Review the Cloud EKM **service-level agreement (SLA)**.

- Communicating with an external service over the internet can lead to problems with reliability, availability, and latency. For applications with a low tolerance for these types of risks, consider using Cloud HSM or Cloud KMS to store your key material.

- You will need a support contract with the external key management partner. Google Cloud support can only provide support for issues in Google Cloud services and cannot directly assist with issues on external systems. You may need to work with support on both sides to troubleshoot interoperability issues.

Restrictions

Here are some general restrictions you should be aware of while using Cloud EKM:

- Automatic rotation is not supported.

- When you create a Cloud EKM key using the API or the Google Cloud CLI, it must not have an initial key version. This does not apply to Cloud EKM keys created using the Cloud console.

- Cloud EKM operations are subject to specific quotas in addition to the quotas on Cloud KMS operations.

When it comes to *symmetric encryption keys*, be aware of these restrictions:

- Symmetric encryption keys are only supported for the following:

  - CMEKs in supported integration services

  - Symmetric encryption and decryption using Cloud KMS directly

- Data that is encrypted by Cloud EKM using an externally managed key cannot be decrypted without using Cloud EKM

When it comes to *asymmetric signing keys*, be aware of these restrictions:

- Asymmetric signing keys are limited to a subset of Cloud KMS algorithms

- Asymmetric signing keys are only supported for the following:

  - Asymmetric signing using Cloud KMS directly

  - Custom signing key with Access Approval

- Once an asymmetric signing algorithm is set on a Cloud EKM key, it cannot be modified

- Signing must be done on the `data` field

Now that you understand various Cloud KMS offerings, let us look at some of the best practices for Cloud KMS.

Cloud KMS best practices

Key access and key ring access are managed by organizing keys into key rings and projects, and by granting IAM roles on the keys, key rings, and projects. As you build out your cloud environment, follow the guidance in the following list for how to design your key resource hierarchy to reduce risk:

1. Create a dedicated project for Cloud KMS that is separate from workload projects.

2. Add key rings into the dedicated Cloud KMS project. Create key rings as needed to impose a separation of duties.

3. Monitor privileged admin operations: key deletion operations for out-of-band key creation are considered a privileged operation.

4. Review CMEK-related findings in Security Command Center.

5. Use encryption keys with the appropriate key strength and protection level for data sensitivity or classification. For example, for sensitive data, use keys with a higher strength. Additionally, use encryption keys with different protection levels for different data types.

The following list provides guidance on how to apply IAM roles to support your security and administrative needs:

- Avoid the basic project-wide roles, such as owner, editor, and viewer, on projects that host keys or on enclosing folders or organizations. Instead, designate an organization administrator that is granted at the organization level, as noted on the Cloud KMS separation of duties page.

- The Organization Admin functions as the administrator for all the organization's cryptographic keys. Grant other IAM roles at the project level. If you have further concerns about the separation of duties, grant IAM roles at the key ring level or key level.

- Use Cloud KMS predefined roles for least privilege and separation of duties. For example, do the following:

  - Separate administration roles (`roles/cloudkms.admin` and `roles/cloudkms.importer`) and usage roles for keys

  - Limit the use of `roles/cloudkms.admin` to members of the security administration team and to service accounts that are responsible for creating key rings and key objects through tools such as Terraform

  - For asymmetric keys, grant roles that need private key access (`roles/cloudkms.cryptoKeyDecrypter` and `roles/cloudkms.signer`) separately from roles that do not need private key access (`roles/cloudkms.publicKeyViewer` and `roles/cloudkms.signerVerifier`)

  - In general, grant the most limited set of permissions to the lowest object in the resource hierarchy

Now that you are familiar with the best practices for key management, let us understand some important decisions for key management that you must make for your cloud infrastructure.

Cloud KMS infrastructure decisions

When you are setting up Cloud KMS for a project, you must make several decisions regarding your keys. The following table provides you with guidance on what factors to consider when you create keys and key rings.

Key attribute	Key attribute guidance
Key location	Choose the location that is geographically closest to the data on which you will be performing cryptographic operations. Use the same ring location for CMEKs used for the data they are encrypting. For more information, see choosing the best type of location in the Cloud KMS documentation.

Key attribute	Key attribute guidance
Key protection level	Use protection level EXTERNAL when your workloads require keys to be maintained outside of the Google Cloud infrastructure in a partner system.
	Use protection level HSM when your workloads require keys to be protected in FIPS 140-2 Level 3-certified hardware security modules (HSMs).
	Use protection level SOFTWARE when your workload does not require keys to be maintained outside of Google Cloud and does not require keys to be protected with FIPS 140-2 Level 3-certified hardware.
	Choose appropriate protection levels for development, staging, and production environments. Because the Cloud KMS API is the same regardless of the protection level, you can use different protection levels in different environments, and you can relax protection levels where there is no production data.
Key source	Allow Cloud KMS to generate keys unless you have workload requirements that require keys to be generated in a specific manner or environment. For externally generated keys, use Cloud KMS key import to import them as described in the *Importing keys into Cloud KMS* section.
Key rotation	For symmetric encryption, configure automation key rotation by setting a key rotation period and starting time when you create the key.
	For asymmetric encryption, you must always manually rotate keys, because the new public key must be distributed before the key pair can be used. Cloud KMS does not support automatic key rotation for asymmetric keys.
	If you have indications that keys have been compromised, manually rotate the keys and re-encrypt data that was encrypted by the compromised keys as soon as possible. To re-encrypt data, you typically download the old data, decrypt it with the old key, encrypt the old data using the new key, and then re-upload the re-encrypted data.
Key destruction	Destroy old keys when there is no data encrypted by those keys.
Key attribute	Key attribute guidance

Table 9.1 – KMS infrastructure decision

Now let us look at a few other factors involved in decision-making.

Application data encryption

Your application might use Cloud KMS by calling the API directly to encrypt, decrypt, sign, and verify data. Applications that handle data encryption directly should use the envelope encryption approach, which provides better application availability and scaling behavior.

> **Note**
> In order to perform application data encryption in this way, your application must have IAM access to both the key and the data.

Integrated Google Cloud encryption

By default, Google Cloud encrypts all your data at rest and in transit without requiring any explicit setup by you. This default encryption for data at rest, which is transparent to you, uses Cloud KMS behind the scenes and manages IAM access to the keys on your behalf.

CMEKs

For more control over the keys for encrypting data at rest in a Google Cloud project, you can use several Google Cloud services that offer the ability to protect data related to those services by using encryption keys managed by the customer within Cloud KMS. These encryption keys are called CMEKs.

Google Cloud products that offer CMEK integration might require the keys to be hosted in the same location as the data used with the key. Cloud KMS might use different names for some locations than other services use. For example, the Cloud KMS multi-regional location Europe corresponds to the Cloud Storage multi-region location EU. Cloud KMS also has some locations that are not available in all other services. For example, the Cloud KMS dual-regional location eur5 has no counterpart in Cloud Storage. You need to identify these requirements before you create the Cloud KMS key ring so that the key ring is created in the correct location. Keep in mind that you cannot delete a key ring.

Importing keys into Cloud KMS

Your workloads might require you to generate the keys outside of Cloud KMS. In this case, you can import key material into Cloud KMS. Furthermore, you might need to provide assurance to reliant parties on the key generation and import processes. These additional steps are referred to as a **key ceremony**.

You use a key ceremony to help people trust that the key is being stored and used securely. Two examples of key ceremonies are the DNSSEC root **key signing key** (**KSK**) ceremony and the ceremony used by Google to create new root CA keys. Both ceremonies support high transparency and high assurance requirements because the resulting keys must be trusted by the entire internet community.

During the key ceremony, you generate the key material and encrypt known plaintext into ciphertext. You then import the key material into Cloud KMS and use the ciphertext to verify the imported key. After you have successfully completed the key ceremony, you can enable the key in Cloud KMS and use it for cryptographic operations.

Because key ceremonies require a lot of setup and staffing, you should carefully choose which keys require ceremonies.

> **Note**
> This is a high-level description of the key ceremony. Depending on the key's trust requirements, you might need more steps.

Cloud KMS API

The Cloud KMS service has an endpoint of `cloudkms.googleapis.com`. Here are a few widely used endpoints that you should be aware of:

- `projects.locations`
- `projects.locations.ekmConnections`
- `projects.locations.keyRings`
  - `create`
  - `list`
  - `get`
  - `getIamPolicy`
  - `setIamPolicy`
- `projects.locations.keyRings.cryptoKeys`
  - `create`
  - `decrypt`
  - `encrypt`
  - `get`

- `getIamPolicy`

- `list`

- `setIamPolicy`

- `updatePrimaryVersion`

- `projects.locations.keyRings.cryptoKeys.cryptoKeyVersions`

- `Projects.locations.keyRings.ImportJobs`

When interacting with Cloud KMS via a programmatic method, you should have a good understanding of these endpoints. Let us move on and understand the Cloud KMS logging components now.

Cloud KMS logging

The following types of audit logs are available for Cloud KMS:

- **Admin Activity audit logs**: Include `admin write` operations that write metadata or configuration information. You cannot disable Admin Activity audit logs.

  Admin Activity audit logs cover the following Cloud KMS operations:

  ```
  cloudkms.projects.locations.keyRings.create
  cloudkms.projects.locations.keyRings.setIamPolicy
  cloudkms.projects.locations.keyRings.cryptoKeys.create
  cloudkms.projects.locations.keyRings.cryptoKeys.patch
  cloudkms.projects.locations.keyRings.cryptoKeys.setIamPolicy
  cloudkms.projects.locations.keyRings.cryptoKeys.
  updatePrimaryVersion
  cloudkms.projects.locations.keyRings.cryptoKeys.
  cryptoKeyVersions.create
  cloudkms.projects.locations.keyRings.cryptoKeys.
  cryptoKeyVersions.destroy
  cloudkms.projects.locations.keyRings.cryptoKeys.
  cryptoKeyVersions.patch
  cloudkms.projects.locations.keyRings.cryptoKeys.
  cryptoKeyVersions.restore
  cloudkms.projects.locations.keyRings.importJobs.create
  cloudkms.projects.locations.keyRings.importJobs.setIamPolicy
  ```

- **Data Access audit logs**: These include `admin read` operations that read metadata or configuration information. They also include `data read` and `data write` operations that read or write user-provided data. To receive Data Access audit logs, you must explicitly enable them.

Data Access audit logs cover the following Cloud KMS operations:

- `ADMIN_READ` for the following API operations:

```
cloudkms.projects.locations.get
cloudkms.projects.locations.list
cloudkms.projects.locations.keyRings.get
cloudkms.projects.locations.keyRings.getIamPolicy
cloudkms.projects.locations.keyRings.list
cloudkms.projects.locations.keyRings.testIamPermissions
cloudkms.projects.locations.keyRings.cryptoKeys.get
cloudkms.projects.locations.keyRings.cryptoKeys.getIamPolicy
cloudkms.projects.locations.keyRings.cryptoKeys.list
cloudkms.projects.locations.keyRings.cryptoKeys.
testIamPermissions
cloudkms.projects.locations.keyRings.cryptoKeys.
cryptoKeyVersions.get
cloudkms.projects.locations.keyRings.cryptoKeys.
cryptoKeyVersions.list
cloudkms.projects.locations.keyRings.importJobs.get
cloudkms.projects.locations.keyRings.importJobs.getIamPolicy
cloudkms.projects.locations.keyRings.importJobs.list
cloudkms.projects.locations.keyRings.importJobs.
testIamPermissions
kmsinventory.organizations.protectedResources.search
kmsinventory.projects.cryptoKeys.list
kmsinventory.projects.locations.keyRings.cryptoKeys.
getProtectedResourcesSummary
```

- `DATA_READ` for the following API operations:

```
cloudkms.projects.locations.keyRings.cryptoKeys.decrypt
cloudkms.projects.locations.keyRings.cryptoKeys.encrypt
cloudkms.projects.locations.keyRings.cryptoKeys.
cryptoKeyVersions.asymmetricDecrypt
cloudkms.projects.locations.keyRings.cryptoKeys.
cryptoKeyVersions.asymmetricSign
cloudkms.projects.locations.keyRings.cryptoKeys.
cryptoKeyVersions.getPublicKey
```

This concludes the logging section and the chapter.

Summary

In this chapter, we went over the details of Cloud KMS, its supported operations, and how to use them. We also looked at bringing your own encryption key to the cloud. We went over advanced options such as Cloud HSM and Cloud EKM. In addition to this, we saw the best practices and Cloud KMS infrastructure decisions while setting up your project on Google Cloud. As a security engineer, you should be able to define the right architecture for key management for your organization and recommend the right compliance options for project teams.

In the next chapter, we will look at data security, specifically how to use Google Cloud's **Data Loss Prevention** (**DLP**) services. Cloud KMS and DLP should bring you one step closer to creating the right strategy for data security.

Further reading

For more information on Google Cloud KMS, refer to the following link:

- Key attestations and verifications: `https://packt.link/V0Fki`

10
Cloud Data Loss Prevention

In this chapter, we will look at Google Cloud data loss protection products and capabilities. **Data Loss Prevention** (DLP) is a strategy for detecting and preventing the exposure and exfiltration of sensitive data. Google's DLP strategy involves a layered approach. In addition to a proper organizational hierarchy, network security, IAM access, and **VPC Service Controls** (**VPC-SC**), DLP plays a key role in data protection.

Cloud DLP is quite widely used in data pipelines, especially for data warehouses. Protecting confidential data is one of the critical aspects of data workloads, so Cloud DLP helps customers gain visibility of sensitive data risks across the organization. We will look at several features of Cloud DLP, how to configure the product to do inspection and de-identification, and some best practices. There are few tutorials in the chapter, so try out examples to get a solid understanding.

In this chapter, we will cover the following topics:

- Overview of Cloud DLP
- DLP architecture
- How DLP discovery works
- De/re-identification of data
- How to create a DLP scan job
- DLP use cases
- How to mask and tokenize sensitive data
- Best practices and design considerations
- Data exfiltration controls

Overview of Cloud DLP

Cloud DLP offers some key features for Google's customers:

- BigQuery-based data warehouses can be profiled to detect sensitive data, allowing for automated sensitive data discovery. You can scan through the entire Google Cloud organization or choose folders or projects with the profiler's flexibility.

- Over 150 built-in information detectors are available in Cloud DLP. Because DLP is API-based, it can be used to swiftly scan, discover, and classify data from anywhere.

- Support for Cloud Storage, Datastore, and BigQuery is built in: Cloud DLP comes with built-in support for these storage options.

- You can calculate the level of risk to your data privacy: quasi-identifiers are data elements or combinations of data that can be linked to a single individual or a small group of people. Cloud DLP gives you the option to examine statistical features such as k-anonymity and l-diversity, allowing you to assess the risk of data re-identification.

- DLP classification results can be delivered straight to BigQuery for more thorough analysis or exported to your analytical instrument of choice. BigQuery and Data Studio can be used to create bespoke reports.

- Cloud DLP secures your data by storing it in memory. The data in the backend is not persistent. In addition, the product is subjected to various independent third-party audits to ensure data confidentiality, privacy, and safety.

- Cloud DLP may be swiftly deployed using reusable templates, with periodic scans monitoring the data and Pub/Sub notifications for integration into serverless architectures.

- To suit your company's needs, you can add your own custom info types, alter detection levels, and establish detection rules.

Now that you understand Cloud DLP's capabilities at a high level, let us understand the DLP architecture.

DLP architecture options

Cloud DLP primarily is seen in three architecture patterns: the content/streaming and storage methods and a hybrid architecture that combines these two patterns.

Content methods

In this architecture option, the data is streamed to the Cloud DLP APIs for inspection/classification or de-identification/transformation. A synchronous API response is received from Cloud DLP. In this case, the client application is expected to process the response. This architecture is typically seen in data pipelines or call center applications where real-time response is needed.

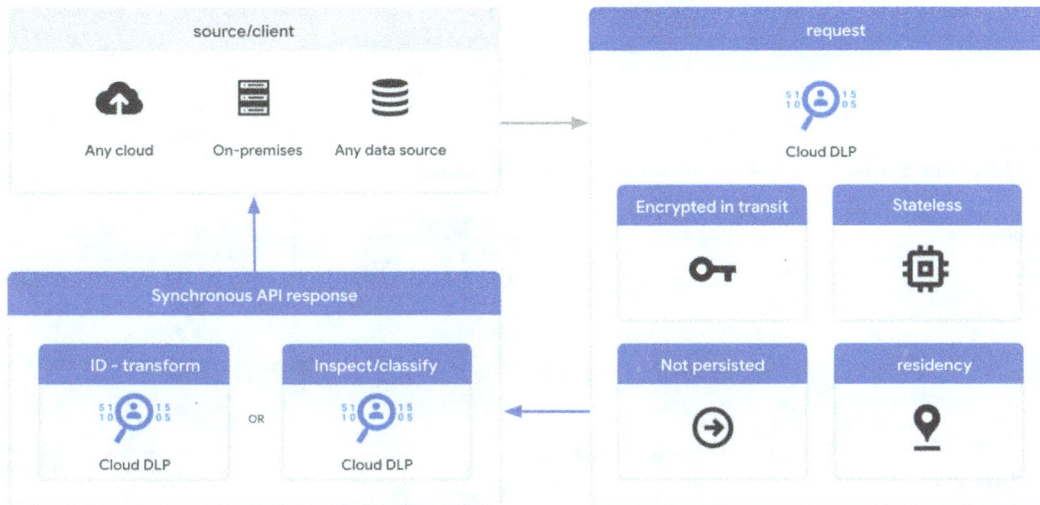

Figure 10.1 – Content method architecture

As shown in *Figure 10.1*, using content inspection, you stream small payloads of data to Cloud DLP along with instructions about what to inspect for. Cloud DLP then inspects the data for sensitive content and **personally identifiable information (PII)** and returns the results of its scan back to you.

Storage methods

In this architecture option, a job is set up based on a trigger to scan for sensitive data. The results of the scans are published so that action can be taken based on the results. The results can be pushed to **Security Operations Center (SOC)** tools such as Security Command Center so security responders can take action or an automated response detection can be built using Cloud Functions or a more sophisticated product such as SOAR.

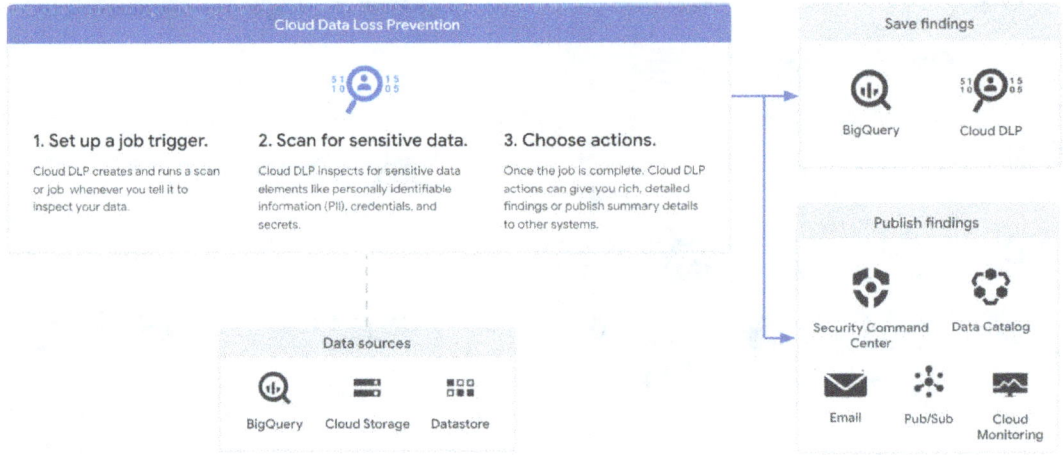

Figure 10.2 – Storage method architecture

As shown in *Figure 10.2*, in this architecture option, you tell Cloud DLP what to inspect and then Cloud DLP runs a job that scans the repository. After the scan is complete, Cloud DLP saves a summary of the results of the scan back to the job. You can additionally specify that the results are sent to another Google Cloud product for analysis, such as a separate BigQuery table or Security Command Center.

The type of scan typically involves those Google Cloud projects where you do not expect to have sensitive data. For projects that are meant to have sensitive data such as cardholder data or PII, you should also invest in data exfiltration controls such as VPC Service Controls for DLP.

Hybrid methods

Hybrid jobs and job triggers enable you to broaden the scope of protection that Cloud DLP provides beyond simple content inspection requests and **Google Cloud Storage (GCS)** repository scanning.

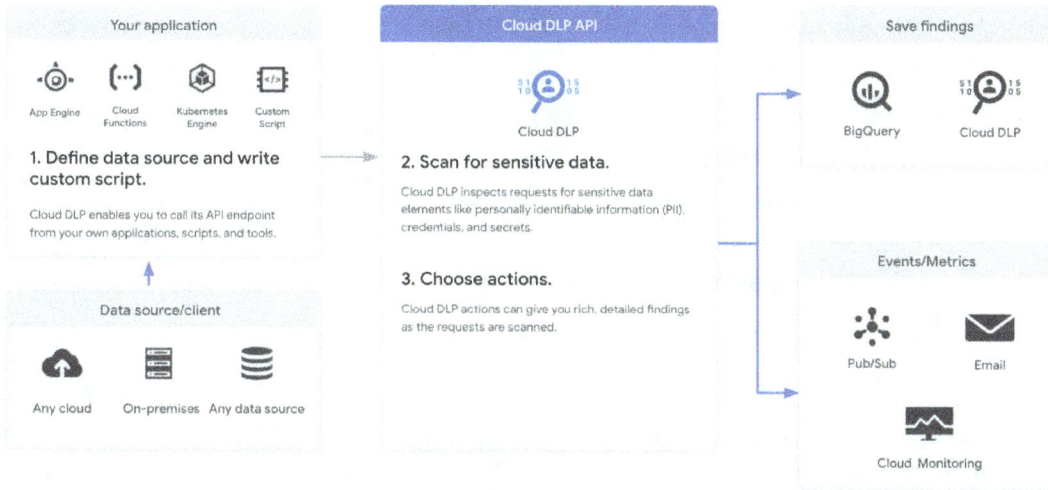

Figure 10.3 – Hybrid inspection architecture

As shown in *Figure 10.3*, you may feed data from practically any source—including sources outside Google Cloud—directly to Cloud DLP via hybrid jobs and job triggers, and Cloud DLP will analyze the data for sensitive information and automatically record and aggregate the scan results for further analysis.

Hybrid jobs and *job triggers* encompass a set of asynchronous API methods that allow you to scan payloads of data sent from virtually any source for sensitive information, and then store the findings in Google Cloud. Hybrid jobs enable you to write your own data crawlers that behave and serve data similarly to the Cloud DLP storage inspection methods.

Hybrid environments are common in enterprises. Many organizations store and process sensitive data using some combination of the following:

- Other cloud providers
- On-premises servers or other data repositories
- Non-native storage systems, such as systems running inside a virtual machine
- Web and mobile apps
- Google Cloud-based solutions

Using hybrid jobs, Cloud DLP can inspect data sent to it from any of these sources. Example scenarios include the following:

- Inspect data stored in Amazon **Relational Database Service (RDS)**, MySQL running inside a virtual machine, or an on-premises database
- Inspect and tokenize data as you migrate from on-premises to the cloud, or between production, development, and analytics
- Inspect and de-identify transactions from a web or mobile application before storing the data at rest

The basic workflow for using hybrid jobs and job triggers is as follows:

1. You write a script or create a workflow that sends data to Cloud DLP for inspection along with some metadata.
2. You configure and create a hybrid job resource or trigger and enable it to activate when it receives data.
3. Your script or workflow runs on the client side and sends data to Cloud DLP. The data includes an activation message and the job trigger's identifier, which triggers the inspection.
4. Cloud DLP inspects the data according to the criteria you set in the hybrid job or trigger.
5. Cloud DLP saves the results of the scan to the hybrid job resource, along with the metadata that you provide. You can examine the results using the Cloud DLP UI in the Cloud console.
6. Optionally, Cloud DLP can run post-scan actions, such as saving inspection results data to a BigQuery table or notifying you by email or Pub/Sub.

A hybrid job trigger enables you to create, activate, and stop jobs so that you can trigger actions whenever you need them. By ensuring that your script or code sends data that includes the hybrid job trigger's identifier, you don't need to update your script or code whenever a new job is started.

Now that you understand the different inspection methods, let us get started with some foundational aspects of DLP.

Cloud DLP terminology

Before we jump into defining Cloud DLP inspection templates, let us go over some important terminology that you will see in the templates.

DLP infoTypes

Information types, also known as infoTypes, are sensitive data kinds that Cloud DLP is preconfigured to scan and identify—for instance, US Social Security numbers, credit card numbers, phone numbers, zip codes, and names. Both built-in and custom InfoTypes are supported by Cloud DLP.

There is a detector for each infoType defined in Cloud DLP. To identify what to look for and how to transform findings, Cloud DLP employs infoType detectors in its scan configuration. When showing or reporting scan findings, infoType names are also used. Cloud DLP releases new infoType detectors and groups regularly. Call the Cloud DLP REST API's `infoTypes.list` method to receive the most up-to-date list of built-in infoTypes.

Please keep in mind that the built-in infoType detectors aren't always reliable. Google suggests that you evaluate your settings to ensure that they comply with your regulatory requirements.

Here are some examples of infoType detectors (this is not an exhaustive list):

- `ADVERTISING_ID`: Identifiers used by developers to track users for advertising purposes. These include Google Play **Advertising IDs**, Amazon **Advertising IDs**, Apple's **Identifier For Advertising (IDFA)**, and Apple's **Identifier For Vendor (IDFV)**.

- `AGE`: An age measured in months or years.

- `CREDIT_CARD_NUMBER`: A credit card number is 12 to 19 digits long. They are used for payment transactions globally.

- `CREDIT_CARD_TRACK_NUMBER`: A credit card track number is a variable-length alphanumeric string. It is used to store key cardholder information.

- `DATE`: A date. This infoType includes most date formats, including the names of common world holidays.

- `DATE_OF_BIRTH`: A date that is identified by context as a date of birth. Note that this is not recommended for use during latency-sensitive operations.

- `DOMAIN_NAME`: A domain name as defined by the DNS standard.

- `EMAIL_ADDRESS`: An email address identifies the mailbox that emails are sent to or from. The maximum length of the domain name is 255 characters, and the maximum length of the local part is 64 characters.

- `US_SOCIAL_SECURITY_NUMBER`: A United States **Social Security number** (**SSN**) is a nine-digit number issued to US citizens, permanent residents, and temporary residents. This detector will not match against numbers with all zeros in any digit group (that is, `000-##-####`, `###-00-####`, or `###-##-0000`), against numbers with 666 in the first digit group, or against numbers whose first digit is nine.

Now we have seen the overview of the Cloud DLP info types, let us understand the technical terms that you will frequently come across while working with Cloud DLP.

Data de-identification

De-identification is a term used to represent a process that removes personal information from a dataset. You will also come across the term *redaction* in relation to Cloud DLP. Redaction in general refers to the removal or masking of information, while de-identification refers to a process of changing it so you no longer identify the original text or are able to derive meaning from it. De-identified data is considered suitable for applications since it doesn't contain any PII that can be used to trace the results back to the user. There are several ways data can be de-identified:

- Masking sensitive data by partially or fully replacing characters with a symbol, such as an asterisk (*) or hash (#)

- Replacing each instance of sensitive data with a token, or surrogate, string

- Encrypting and replacing sensitive data using a randomly generated or pre-determined key

Cloud DLP supports the following methods of de-identification:

- **Masking**: Replaces the original data with a specified character, either partially or completely.

- **Replacement**: Replaces original data with a token or the name of the infoType if detected.

- **Date shifting**: Date-shifting techniques randomly shift a set of dates but preserve the sequence and duration of a period of time. Shifting dates is usually done in relation to an individual or an entity. That is, each individual's dates are shifted by an amount of time that is unique to that individual.

- **Generalization and bucketing**: Generalization is the process of taking a distinguishing value and abstracting it into a more general, less distinguishing value. Generalization attempts to preserve data utility while also reducing the identifiability of the data. One common generalization technique that Cloud DLP supports is bucketing. With bucketing, you group records into smaller buckets in an attempt to minimize the risk of an attacker associating sensitive information with identifying information. Doing so can retain meaning and utility, but it will also obscure the individual values that have too few participants.

- **Pseudonymization**: This is a de-identification technique that replaces sensitive data values with cryptographically generated tokens:

  - **Two-way tokenization pseudonymization**: Replaces the original data with a token that is deterministic, preserving referential integrity. You can use the token to join data or use the token in aggregate analysis. You can reverse or de-tokenize the data using the same key that you used to create the token. There are two methods for two-way tokenization:

- **Deterministic Encryption (DE) using AES-SIV: Advanced Encryption Standard-Synthetic Initialization Vector (AES-SIV)** is a cryptographic mode of operation designed to provide secure and authenticated encryption of data. It is based on the **Advanced Encryption Standard (AES)** block cipher and is intended for applications that require both data confidentiality and data integrity. It is commonly used for protecting data stored in databases, files, or other forms of persistent storage. AES-SIV also provides a way to protect data against replay attacks and can be used to construct secure communication protocols. Using AES-SIV, an input value is replaced with a value that has been encrypted using the AES-SIV encryption algorithm with a cryptographic key, encoded using base64, and then prepended with a surrogate annotation, if specified. This method produces a hashed value, so it does not preserve the character set or the length of the input value. Encrypted, hashed values can be re-identified using the original cryptographic key and the entire output value, including surrogate annotation. Learn more about the format of values tokenized using AES-SIV encryption.

- **Format Preserving Encryption (FPE) with Flexible Format-Preserving Encryption (FFX)**: This is an encryption technique that encrypts data while preserving the format of the original data. This means that FFX encryption can be used to encrypt data such as credit card numbers, SSNs, and other sensitive data without changing the format of the original data. FFX is used to protect data while it is stored or transmitted and to prevent unauthorized access to the data. Using FPE-FFX, an input value is replaced with a value that has been encrypted using the FPE-FFX encryption algorithm with a cryptographic key, and then prepended with a surrogate annotation, if specified. By design, both the character set and the length of the input value are preserved in the output value. Encrypted values can be re-identified using the original cryptographic key and the entire output value, including the surrogate annotation.

- **One-way tokenization using cryptographic hashing pseudonymization**: An input value is replaced with a value that has been encrypted and hashed using **Hash-Based Message Authentication Code Secure Hash Algorithm** 256 or **HMAC-SHA56** on the input value with a cryptographic key. The hashed output of the transformation is always the same length and can't be re-identified. Learn more about the format of values tokenized using cryptographic hashing.

Refer to the following table for a comparison of these three pseudonymization methods.

	Deterministic encryption using AES-SIV	Format preserving encyption	Cryptographic hashing
Encryption type	AES-SIV	FPR-FFX	HMAC-SHA256
Supported input values	At least 1 char long; no character set limitations.	At least 2 chats long; must be encoded as ASCII.	Must be a string or an integer value.
Surrogate annotation	Optional	Optional	N/A
Context tweak	Optional	Optional	N/A
Character set and length preserved	No	Yes	No
Reversible	Yes	Yes	No
Referential integrity	Yes	Yes	Yes

Table 10.1 – Comparison of the pseudonymization methods

Method selection

Choosing the best de-identification method can vary based on your use case. For example, if a legacy app is processing the de-identified records, then format preservation might be important. If you're dealing with strictly formatted 10-digit numbers, FPE preserves the length (10 digits) and character set (numeric) of an input for legacy system support.

However, if strict formatting isn't required for legacy compatibility, as is the case for values in the cardholder's name column, then DE is the preferred choice because it has a stronger authentication method. Both FPE and DE enable the tokens to be reversed or de-tokenized. If you don't need de-tokenization, then cryptographic hashing provides integrity but the tokens can't be reversed.

Other methods—such as masking, bucketing, date-shifting, and replacement—are good for values that don't need to retain full integrity. For example, bucketing an age value (for example, 27) to an age range (20-30) can still be analyzed while reducing the uniqueness that might lead to the identification of an individual.

Token encryption keys

A cryptographic key, also known as a token encryption key, is necessary for cryptographic de-identification transformations. The same token encryption key that is used to de-identify the original value is also used to re-identify it. This book does not cover the secure development and maintenance of token encryption keys.

However, there are a few key aspects to keep in mind that will be applied later in the lessons:

- In the template, avoid using plaintext keys. Instead, build a wrapped key with Cloud KMS.

- To limit the danger of keys being compromised, use different token encryption keys for each data element.

- Token encryption keys should be rotated. Although the wrapped key can be rotated, the token encryption key cannot be rotated because it compromises the tokenization's integrity. You must re-tokenize the entire dataset when the key is rotated.

Now that we are familiar with the basics of de-identification and which method is better suited for our use case, let us walk through how to create an inspection template. Later we will look at how to use de-identification.

Remember that Cloud DLP requires an inspection of the data before de-identification can be performed. The Cloud DLP inspection process identifies the infoTypes that further can be used in de-identification. The inspection step is *not* optional.

Creating a Cloud DLP inspection template

The first step in using classification capabilities is to create an inspection template. The inspection template will store all the data classification requirements:

1. In the Cloud console, open **Cloud DLP**.

2. From the **CREATE** menu, choose **Template**.

Data Loss Prevention	CREATE ▾	EXPLORE FINDINGS	JOBS & JOB TRIGGERS	CONFIGURATION	SHOW PREVIEW PANEL

Job or job trigger

TEMPLATES   INFOTYPES   Template

Stored infoType

INSPECT   DE-IDENTIFY

Template ID	Display name	Resource location	Creation time	Last updated ↓	Actions
pii-template	PII Template	Global (any region)	Jul 9, 2019, 6:07:10 PM	Jul 9, 2019, 6:07:10 PM	⋮
ssn-template	US & CAN Soc Security numbers	Global (any region)	Mar 13, 2019, 4:20:58 PM	Jun 3, 2019, 12:49:37 PM	⋮
credit-card-template	Credit cards	Global (any region)	Apr 14, 2019, 3:11:05 PM	Jun 3, 2019, 12:49:05 PM	⋮
mildly_naughty_words	Finds gently naughty words	Global (any region)	May 31, 2019, 9:57:35 AM	May 31, 2019, 9:57:35 AM	⋮

Rows per page: 30 ▾   1 – 30 of many   ‹   ›

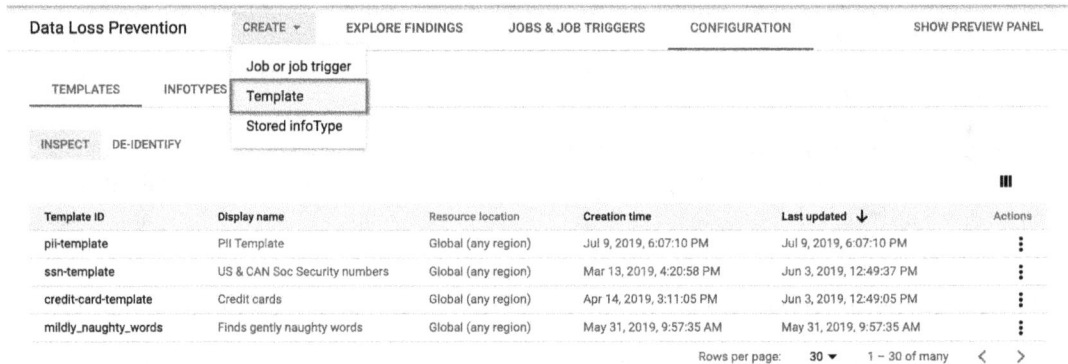

Figure 10.4 – Creating a DLP inspection template

3. Alternatively, click the following button: **Create new template**.

This page contains the following sections:

- **Define template**
- **Configure detection**

Defining the template

Under **Define template**, enter an identifier for the inspection template. This is how you'll refer to the template when you run a job, create a job trigger, and so on. You can use letters, numbers, and hyphens. If you want, you can also enter a more human-friendly display name, as well as a description to better remember what the template does.

Configuring detection

Next, you configure what Cloud DLP detects in your content by choosing an infoType and other options.

Under **InfoTypes**, choose the infoType detectors that correspond to a data type you want to scan for. You can also leave this field blank to scan for all default infoTypes. More information about each detector is provided in the *Further reading* section at the end of this chapter.

You can also add custom infoType detectors in the **Custom infoTypes** section, and customize both built-in and custom infoType detectors in the **Inspection rulesets** section.

Custom infoTypes

Be aware that any custom infoType detector you create here is specific to this workflow and can't be reused elsewhere. The one exception is *Stored infoType*, which requires that you create the stored custom infoType detector before specifying it here.

To add a custom infoType detector, do the following:

1. Click **Add custom infoType**.
2. Choose the type of custom infoType detector you want to create:

    *   **Words or phrases**: Matches on one or more words or phrases that you enter into the field. Use this custom infoType when you have just a few words or phrases to search for. Give your custom infoType a name, and then type the word or phrase you want Cloud DLP to match. To search for multiple words or phrases, press *Enter* after each one.

    *   **Dictionary path**: Searches your content for items in a list of words and phrases. The list is stored in a text file in Cloud Storage. Use this custom infoType when you have anywhere from a few to several hundred thousand words or phrases to search for. This method is also useful if your list contains sensitive elements and you don't want to store them inside of a job or template. Give your custom infoType a name, and then, under **Dictionary location**, enter or browse to the Cloud Storage path where the dictionary file is stored.

    *   **Regular expression** (**regex**): Matches content based on a regular expression. Give your custom infoType a name, and then, in the **Regex** field, enter a regex pattern to match words and phrases. See the supported regex syntax in Google Cloud documentation at `https://packt.link/dRR06`.

    *   **Stored infoType**: This option adds a stored custom dictionary detector, which is a kind of dictionary detector that is built from either a large text file stored in Cloud Storage or a single column of a BigQuery table. Use this kind of custom infoType when you have anywhere from several hundred thousand to tens of millions of words or phrases to search for. Be aware that this is the only option in this menu for which you must have already created the stored infoType to use it. Give your custom infoType a name (different from the name you gave the stored infoType), and then, in the **Stored infoType** field, enter the name of the stored infoType.

3. Click **Add custom infoType** again to add additional custom infoType detectors.

Now let us see how to use rulesets to customize the infoTypes to match your requirements. This helps you to avoid false positives.

Inspection rulesets

Inspection rulesets allow you to customize both built-in and custom infoType detectors using context rules. The two types of inspection rules are as follows:

- **Exclusion rules**, which help exclude false or unwanted findings
- **Hotword rules**, which help adjust the likelihood of the finding based on how near the hotword is to the finding

To add a new ruleset, first, specify one or more built-in or custom infoType detectors in the infoTypes section. These are the infoType detectors that your rulesets will be modifying. Then, do the following:

1. Click in the **Choose infoTypes** field. The infoType or infoTypes you specified previously will appear below the field in a menu, as shown in *Figure 10.5*.

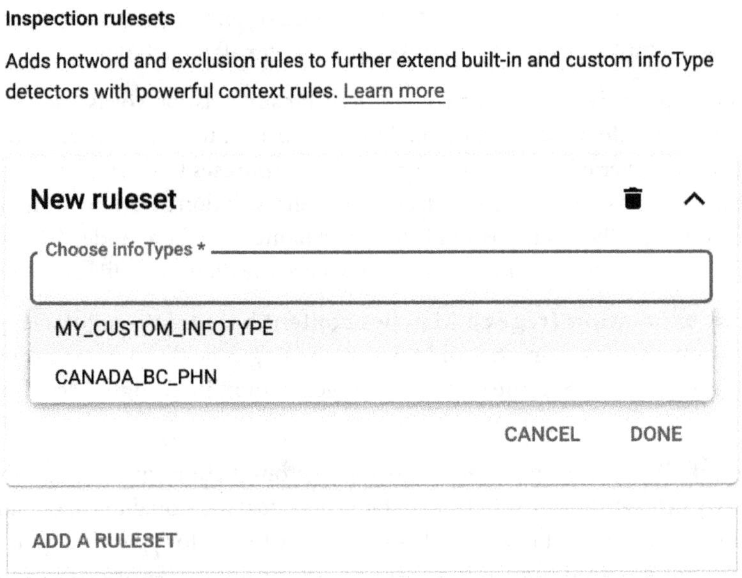

Inspection rulesets

Adds hotword and exclusion rules to further extend built-in and custom infoType detectors with powerful context rules. Learn more

New ruleset

Choose infoTypes *

MY_CUSTOM_INFOTYPE

CANADA_BC_PHN

CANCEL   DONE

ADD A RULESET

Figure 10.5 – Choosing infoTypes for Inspection rulesets

2. Choose an infoType from the menu, and then click **Add rule**. A menu appears with two options: **Hotword rule** and **Exclusion rule**.

For hotword rules, choose **Hotword rule**. Then, do the following:

I. In the **Hotword** field, enter a regular expression that Cloud DLP should look for.

II. From the **Hotword proximity** menu, choose whether the hotword you entered is found before or after the chosen infoType.

III. In **Hotword distance from infoType**, enter the approximate number of characters between the hotword and the chosen infoType.

IV. In **Confidence level adjustment**, choose whether to assign matches to a fixed likelihood level or to increase or decrease the default likelihood level by a certain amount.

For exclusion rules, choose **Exclusion rules**. Then, do the following:

V. In the **Exclude** field, enter a regular expression (regex) that Cloud DLP should look for.

VI. From the **Matching type** menu, choose one of the following:

- **Full match**: The finding must completely match the regex.
- **Partial match**: A substring of the finding can match the regex.
- **Inverse match**: The finding doesn't match the regex.

You can add additional hotword or exclusion rules and rulesets to further refine your scan results.

Confidence threshold

Every time Cloud DLP detects a potential match for sensitive data, it assigns it a likelihood value on a scale from `Very unlikely` to `Very likely`. When you set a likelihood value here, you are instructing Cloud DLP to only match data that corresponds to that likelihood value or higher.

The default value of `Possible` is sufficient for most purposes. If you routinely get matches that are too broad, move the slider up. If you get too few matches, move the slider down.

When you're done, click **Create** to create the template. The template's summary information page appears.

Let us discuss some of the best practices for inspection.

Best practices for inspecting sensitive data

There are several things that you need to consider before starting an inspection. We will go over them now:

- **Identify and prioritize scanning**: It's important to identify your resources and specify which have the highest priority for scanning. When just getting started, you may have a large backlog of data that needs classification, and it'll be impossible to scan it all immediately. Choose data initially that poses the highest risk—for example, data that is frequently accessed, widely accessible, or unknown.

- **Reduce latency**: Latency is affected by several factors: the amount of data to scan, the storage repository being scanned, and the type and number of infoTypes that are enabled. To help reduce job latency, you can try the following:

  - Enable sampling.

  - Avoid enabling infoTypes you don't need. While useful in certain scenarios, some infoTypes—including PERSON_NAME, FEMALE_NAME, MALE_NAME, FIRST_NAME, LAST_NAME, DATE_OF_BIRTH, LOCATION, STREET_ADDRESS, and ORGANIZATION_NAME—can make requests run much more slowly than requests that do not include them.

  - Always specify infoTypes explicitly. Do not use an empty infoTypes list.

  - Consider organizing the data to be inspected into a table with rows and columns, if possible, to reduce network round trips.

- **Limit the scope of your first scans**: For the best results, limit the scope of your first scans instead of scanning all of your data. Start with a few requests. Your findings will be more meaningful when you fine-tune what detectors to enable and what exclusion rules might be needed to reduce false positives. Avoid turning on all infoTypes if you don't need them all, as false positives or unusable findings may make it harder to assess your risk. While useful in certain scenarios, some infoTypes such as DATE, TIME, DOMAIN_NAME, and URL detect a broad range of findings and may not be useful to turn on.

- **Limit the amount of content inspected**: If you are scanning BigQuery tables or Cloud Storage buckets, Cloud DLP includes a way to scan a subset of the dataset. This has the effect of providing a sampling of scan results without incurring the potential costs of scanning an entire dataset.

> **Note**
> Due to the need to scan the entire image for sensitive data, sampling is not supported for image file types. Any images scanned will be billed according to the size of the image file.

- **Inspect data on-premises or in other clouds**: If the data to be scanned resides *on-premises or outside of Google Cloud*, use the API methods `content.inspect` and `content.deidentify` to scan the content to classify findings and pseudonymized content without persisting the content outside of your local storage.

We have seen how to inspect data and best practices around data inspection. Let us now understand how to de-identify sensitive data.

Inspecting and de-identifying PII data

To de-identify sensitive data, use Cloud DLP's `content.deidentify` method.

There are three parts to a de-identification API call:

- **The data to inspect**: A string or table structure (`ContentItem` object) for the API to inspect.

- **What to inspect for**: Detection configuration information (`InspectConfig`) such as what types of data (or infoTypes) to look for, whether to filter findings that are above a certain likelihood threshold, whether to return no more than a certain number of results, and so on. Not specifying at least one infoType in an `InspectConfig` argument is equivalent to specifying all built-in infoTypes. Doing so is not recommended, as it can cause decreased performance and increased cost.

- **What to do with the inspection findings**: Configuration information (`DeidentifyConfig`) that defines how you want the sensitive data de-identified. This argument is covered in more detail in the following section.

The API returns the same items you gave it, in the same format, but any text identified as containing sensitive information according to your criteria is *de-identified*. Now let us look at various de-identification transformations.

De-identification transformations

We saw how to inspect data but many times you want to inspect and de-identify the data. Now we will see how to do that using various transformations supported by DLP. You must specify one or more transformations when you set the de-identification configuration (`DeidentifyConfig`). There are two categories of transformations:

- **InfoTypeTransformations**: Transformations that are only applied to values within the submitted text that are identified as a specific infoType.

- **RecordTransformations**: Transformations that are only applied to values within submitted tabular text data that are identified as a specific infoType, or on an entire column of tabular data.

Now let us go over each deidentification configuration.

replaceConfig

`replaceConfig` will replace any sensitive data with a string you specify.

redactConfig

`redactConfig` redacts a given value by removing it completely.

characterMaskConfig

Setting `characterMaskConfig` to a `CharacterMaskConfig` object partially masks a string by replacing a given number of characters with a fixed character. Masking can start from the beginning or end of the string.

cryptoHashConfig

Setting `cryptoHashConfig` to a `CryptoHashConfig` object performs pseudonymization on an input value by generating a surrogate value using cryptographic hashing.

This method replaces the input value with an encrypted *digest*, or hash value. The digest is computed by taking the SHA-256 hash of the input value. The method outputs a base64-encoded representation of the hashed output. Currently, only string and integer values can be hashed.

dateShiftConfig

Setting `dateShiftConfig` to a `DateShiftConfig` object performs date shifting on a date input value by shifting the dates by a random number of days.

Date-shifting techniques randomly shift a set of dates but preserve the sequence and duration of a period of time. Shifting dates is usually done in relation to an individual or an entity. You might want to shift all of the dates for a specific individual using the same shift differential but use a separate shift differential for each other individual.

Now that you have understood different methods of de-identification, let us go over a tutorial on how to do this in practice. Make sure you have a Google Cloud project ready to execute the steps covered next.

Tutorial: How to de-identify and tokenize sensitive data

Cloud DLP supports both reversible and non-reversible cryptographic methods. In order to re-identify content, you need to choose a reversible method. The cryptographic method described here is called deterministic encryption using **Advanced Encryption Standard in Synthetic Initialization Vector mode (AES-SIV)**. We recommend this among all the reversible cryptographic methods that Cloud DLP supports because it provides the highest level of security.

In this tutorial, we're going to see how to generate a key to de-identify sensitive text into a cryptographic token. In order to restore (re-identify) that text, you need the cryptographic key that you used during de-identification and the token.

Before you begin, make sure you have the following roles in your Google Cloud project:

- Service account admin, to be able to create service accounts
- Service usage admin, to be able to enable services
- Security admin, to be able to grant roles

Once you have the right roles, follow these steps. The steps walk you through the process of creating an AES key to be able to de-identify sensitive text into a cryptographic token:

1. In the Google Cloud console, on the project selector page, select or create a new Google Cloud project.
2. Make sure that billing is enabled for your cloud project.
3. Enable the Cloud DLP and Cloud KMS APIs.
4. Create a service account by following the next steps:

    I.   In the Cloud console, navigate to the **Create service account** page.

    II.   In the **Service account name** field, enter a name. The Cloud console fills in the **Service account ID** field based on this name. In the **Service account description** field, enter a description.

    III. Click **Create** and continue.

    IV.   To provide access to your project, grant the following role(s) to your service account: **Project > DLP Administrator**.

> **Note**
>
> In production environments, do not grant the Owner, Editor, or Viewer roles. Instead, grant a predefined role or custom role that meets your needs.

    V.   Click **Continue**.

    VI.   Click **Done** to finish creating the service account.

Do not close your browser window. You will use it in the next step.

5. Create a service account key:

    I.   In the Cloud console, click the email address for the service account that you just created.

    II.   Click **Keys**.

    III. Click **Add key**, then click **Create new key**.

    IV.   Click **Create**. A JSON key file is downloaded to your computer.

Note

It is against security practice to create a key and keep it forever. You should delete this key as soon as this tutorial is finished.

    V.   Click **Close**.

6. Set the GOOGLE_APPLICATION_CREDENTIALS environment variable to the path of the JSON file that contains your service account key. This variable only applies to your current shell session, so if you open a new session, set the variable again.

Now that you have the right service account, we will create a KMS key that will be used to wrap the AES key used for the actual encryption of the DLP token.

Step 1: Creating a key ring and a key

Before you start this procedure, decide where you want Cloud DLP to process your de-identification and re-identification requests. When you create a Cloud KMS key, you must store it either globally or in the same region that you will use for your Cloud DLP requests. Otherwise, the Cloud DLP requests will fail.

You can find a list of supported locations in Cloud DLP locations. Take note of the name of your chosen region (for example, us-west1).

This procedure uses global as the location for all API requests. If you want to use a different region, replace global with the region name.

Create a key ring:

```
gcloud kms keyrings create "dlp-keyring" --location "global"
```

Create a key:

```
gcloud kms keys create "dlp-key" --location "global"   --keyring
"dlp-keyring" --purpose "encryption
```

List your key ring and key:

```
gcloud kms keys list --location "global" --keyring "dlp-keyring"
```

You will get the following output:

```
NAME: projects/PROJECT_ID/locations/global/keyRings/dlp-keyring/
cryptoKeys/dlp-key
PURPOSE: ENCRYPT_DECRYPT
ALGORITHM: GOOGLE_SYMMETRIC_ENCRYPTION
PROTECTION_LEVEL: SOFTWARE
LABELS:
PRIMARY_ID: 1
PRIMARY_STATE: ENABLED
```

In this output, PROJECT_ID is the ID of your project.

The path under NAME is the full resource name of your Cloud KMS key. Take note of it because the de-identify and re-identify requests require it.

Step 2: Creating a base64-encoded AES key

This section describes how to create an **Advanced Encryption Standard (AES)** key and encode it in base64 format. This key shall be used to encrypt the actual sensitive data. As you can see, you have complete control over the generation and maintenance of this key.

> **Note**
> These steps use the openssl and base64 commands, but there are a few other ways to perform this task based on your security policies.

Now use the following command to create a 256-bit key in the current directory:

```
openssl rand -out "./aes_key.bin" 32
```

The aes_key.bin file is added to your current directory.

Encode the AES key as a base64 string:

```
base64 -i ./aes_key.bin
```

You will get an output similar to the following:

```
uEDo6/yKx+zCg2cZ1DBwpwvzMVNk/c+jWs7OwpkMc/s=
```

> **Warning**
>
> Do not use this example key to protect actual sensitive workloads. This key is provided only to serve as an example. Because it's shared here, this key is not safe to use.

Step 3: Wrapping the AES key using the Cloud KMS key

This section describes how to use the Cloud KMS key that you created in *Step 1* to wrap the base64-encoded AES key that you created in *Step 2: Creating a base64-encoded AES key*.

To wrap the AES key, use `curl` to send the following request to the Cloud KMS API `projects.locations.keyRings.cryptoKeys.encrypt`:

```
curl "https://cloudkms.googleapis.com/v1/projects/PROJECT_ID/
locations/global/keyRings/dlp-keyring/cryptoKeys/dlp-key:encrypt"
--request "POST"
   --header "Authorization:Bearer $(gcloud auth application-default
print-access-token)" --header "content-type: application/json" --data
"{\"plaintext\": \"BASE64_ENCODED_AES_KEY\"}"
```

Replace the following:

- PROJECT_ID: The ID of your project.
- BASE64_ENCODED_AES_KEY: The base64-encoded string returned in *Step 2: Creating a base64-encoded AES key*.

The response that you get from Cloud KMS is similar to the following JSON:

```
{
   "name": "projects/PROJECT_ID/locations/global/keyRings/dlp-keyring/
cryptoKeys/dlp-key/cryptoKeyVersions/1",
   "ciphertext":
"CiQAYuuIGo5DVaqdE0YLioWxEhC8LbTmq7Uy2G3qOJlZB7WXBw0SSQAj
dwP8ZusZJ3Kr8GD9W0vaFPMDksmHEo6nTDaW/
j5sSYpHalym2JHk+1UgkC3Zw5bXhfCNOkpXUdHGZKou189308BDby/82HY=",
   "ciphertextCrc32c": "901327763",
   "protectionLevel": "SOFTWARE"
}
```

In this output, PROJECT_ID is the ID of your project.

Take note of the value of ciphertext in the response that you get. That is your wrapped AES key.

Step 4: Sending a de-identify request to the Cloud DLP API

This section describes how to de-identify sensitive data in text content.

To complete this task, you need the following:

- The full resource name of the Cloud KMS key that you created in *Step 1: Creating a key ring and a key*

- The wrapped key that you created in *Step 3: Wrapping the AES key using the Cloud KMS key*

To de-identify sensitive data in text content, follow these steps:

1. Create a JSON request file with the following text:

```
{
  "item": {
    "value": "My name is Alicia Abernathy, and my email address
is aabernathy@example.com."
  },
  "deidentifyConfig": {
    "infoTypeTransformations": {
      "transformations": [
        {
          "infoTypes": [
            {
              "name": "EMAIL_ADDRESS"
            }
          ],
          "primitiveTransformation": {
            "cryptoDeterministicConfig": {
              "cryptoKey": {
                "kmsWrapped": {
                  "cryptoKeyName": "projects/PROJECT_ID/
locations/global/keyRings/dlp-keyring/cryptoKeys/dlp-key",
                  "wrappedKey": "WRAPPED_KEY"
                }
              },
              "surrogateInfoType": {
                "name": "EMAIL_ADDRESS_TOKEN"
              }
            }
          }
        }
      ]
    }
  }
}
```

```
    },
    "inspectConfig": {
      "infoTypes": [
        {
          "name": "EMAIL_ADDRESS"
        }
      ]
    }
  }
```

2. Replace the following:

*   PROJECT_ID: The ID of your project.

*   WRAPPED_KEY: The wrapped key that you created in *Step 3: Wrapping the AES key using the Cloud KMS key.*

    Make sure that the resulting value of cryptoKeyName forms the full resource name of your Cloud KMS key.

3. Save the file as deidentify-request.json.

Step 5: Sending a de-identity request to the Cloud DLP API

Now let us send the de-identification request to the DLP API based on the file you created in the previous step:

```
curl -s -H "Authorization: Bearer $(gcloud auth application-
default print-access-token)" -H "Content-Type: application/json"
https://dlp.googleapis.com/v2/projects/dlp-tesing/locations/global/
content:deidentify -d @deidentify-request.json
```

You should see output similar to this:

```
{
  "item": {
    "value": "My name is Alicia Abernathy, and my email
address is EMAIL_ADDRESS_TOKEN(52):ARa5jvGRxjop/UOzU9DZQA1CT/
yoTOjcOws7I/2IrzxrZsnlnjUB."
  },
  "overview": {
    "transformedBytes": "22",
    "transformationSummaries": [
      {
        "infoType": {
          "name": "EMAIL_ADDRESS"
        },
```

```
        "transformation": {
          "cryptoDeterministicConfig": {
            "cryptoKey": {
              "kmsWrapped": {
                "wrappedKey": "CiQAolK1/0r6aNktZPVngvs2ml/
ZxWAMXmjssvZgzSTui4keEgQSSQBaC4itVweyjdz5vdYFO3k/gh/
Kqvf7uEGYkgmVF98ZIbSffI3QRzWtR6zwLK8ZpXaDuUaQRgOuhMZJR2jf9Iq2f68aG0y
WKUk=",
                "cryptoKeyName": "projects/PROJECT_ID/locations/
global/keyRings/dlp-keyring/cryptoKeys/dlp-key"
              }
            },
            "surrogateInfoType": {
              "name": "EMAIL_ADDRESS_TOKEN"
            }
          }
        },
        "results": [
          {
            "count": "1",
            "code": "SUCCESS"
          }
        ],
        "transformedBytes": "22"
      }
    ]
  }
}
```

A couple of things to note in this output are as follows:

- wrappedKey is the KMS-wrapped key used to encrypt the token.

- EMAIL_ADDRESS_TOKEN is the encrypted token of the sensitive data (email address in our example). This is the data that you will store as well as the wrapped key, so if needed you can re-identify it later. We will see how to do that in the next step.

Step 6: Sending a re-identify request to the Cloud DLP API

This section describes how to re-identify tokenized data that you de-identified in the previous step.

To complete this task, you need the following:

- The full resource name of the Cloud KMS key that you created in *Step 1: Creating a key ring and a key.*
- The wrapped key that you created in *Step 3: Wrapping the AES key using the Cloud KMS key.*
- The token that you received in *Step 4: Sending a de-identify request to the Cloud DLP API.*

To re-identify tokenized content, follow these steps:

1. Create a JSON request file with the following text:

```
{
  "reidentifyConfig":{
    "infoTypeTransformations":{
      "transformations":[
        {
          "infoTypes":[
            {
              "name":"EMAIL_ADDRESS_TOKEN"
            }
          ],
          "primitiveTransformation":{
            "cryptoDeterministicConfig":{
              "cryptoKey":{
              "kmsWrapped": {
                "cryptoKeyName": "projects/PROJECT_ID/locations/
global/keyRings/dlp-keyring/cryptoKeys/dlp-key",
                "wrappedKey": "WRAPPED_KEY"
              }
            },
              "surrogateInfoType":{
                "name":"EMAIL_ADDRESS_TOKEN"
              }
            }
          }
        }
      ]
    }
  },
  "inspectConfig":{
```

```
        "customInfoTypes":[
          {
            "infoType":{
              "name":"EMAIL_ADDRESS_TOKEN"
            },
            "surrogateType":{

            }
          }
        ]
      },
      "item":{
        "value": "My name is Alicia Abernathy, and my email address
      is TOKEN."
      }
    }
```

2. Replace the following:

    - PROJECT_ID: The ID of your project

    - WRAPPED_KEY: The wrapped key that you created in *Step 3*

    - TOKEN: The token that you received in *Step 4*—for example, EMAIL_ADDRESS_
      TOKEN(52):AVAx2eIEnIQP5jbNEr2j9wLOAd5m4kpSBR/0jjjGdAOmryzZbE/q

    Make sure that the resulting value of cryptoKeyName forms the full resource name of your
    Cloud KMS key.

3. Save the file as reidentify-request.json. Now we will use this file to send a request
    to DLP API via curl.

4. Use curl to make a projects.locations.content.reidentify request:

    ```
    curl -s \
    -H "Authorization: Bearer $(gcloud auth application-default
    print-access-token)" \
    -H "Content-Type: application/json" \
    https://dlp.googleapis.com/v2/projects/PROJECT_ID/locations/
    global/content:reidentify \
    -d @reidentify-request.json
    ```

5. Replace PROJECT_ID with the ID of your project.

6. To pass a filename to `curl`, you use the `-d` option (for data) and precede the filename with an @ sign. This file must be in the same directory where you execute the `curl` command.

> **Note**
>
> This example request explicitly targets the global location. This is the same as calling the `projects.content.reidentify` API, which defaults to the global location.

The response that you get from Cloud DLP is similar to the following JSON:

```json
{
  "item": {
    "value": "My name is Alicia Abernathy, and my email address
is aabernathy@example.com."
  },
  "overview": {
    "transformedBytes": "70",
    "transformationSummaries": [
      {
        "infoType": {
          "name": "EMAIL_ADDRESS"
        },
        "transformation": {
          "cryptoDeterministicConfig": {
            "cryptoKey": {
              "kmsWrapped": {
                "wrappedKey":
"CiQAYuuIGo5DVaqdE0YLioWxEhC8LbTmq7Uy2G3qOJlZB7WXBw0SSQAjdwP
8ZusZJ3Kr8GD9W0vaFPMDksmHEo6nTDaW/
j5sSYpHa1ym2JHk+lUgkC3Zw5bXhfCNOkpXUdHGZKou189308BDby/82HY=",
                "cryptoKeyName": "projects/PROJECT_ID/locations/
global/keyRings/dlp-keyring/cryptoKeys/dlp-key"
              }
            },
            "surrogateInfoType": {
              "name": "EMAIL_ADDRESS_TOKEN"
            }
          }
        }
      },
      "results": [
        {
          "count": "1",
          "code": "SUCCESS"
        }
      ],
```

```
            "transformedBytes": "70"
        }
    ]
  }
}
```

In the `item` field, `EMAIL_ADDRESS_TOKEN` from the previous step is replaced with the plain email address from the original text.

You've just de-identified and re-identified sensitive data in text content using deterministic encryption. Now let us move on and understand a few use cases of workloads where DLP can be used.

DLP use cases

You have seen how DLP can be used to inspect, identify, and re-identify sensitive data in your workloads. Now let us understand various use cases to see how DLP fits:

- **Automatically discover sensitive data**: With Cloud DLP, you can automatically understand and manage your data risk across your entire enterprise. Continuous data visibility can assist you in making more informed decisions, managing and reducing data risk, and being compliant. Data profiling is simple to set up on the Cloud console, and there are no jobs or overhead to worry about, so you can focus on the results and your business.

- **Classify data across your enterprise**: Cloud DLP can help you categorize your data, whether it's on or off the cloud, and provide the insights you need to ensure correct governance, management, and compliance. Publish summary findings to other services such as Data Catalog, Security Command Center, Cloud Monitoring, and Pub/Sub or save comprehensive findings to BigQuery for study. In the Cloud console, you may audit and monitor your data, or you can use Google Data Studio or another tool to create custom reports and dashboards.

- **Protect sensitive data as you migrate to the cloud**: You can evaluate and classify sensitive data in both structured and unstructured workloads with Cloud DLP.

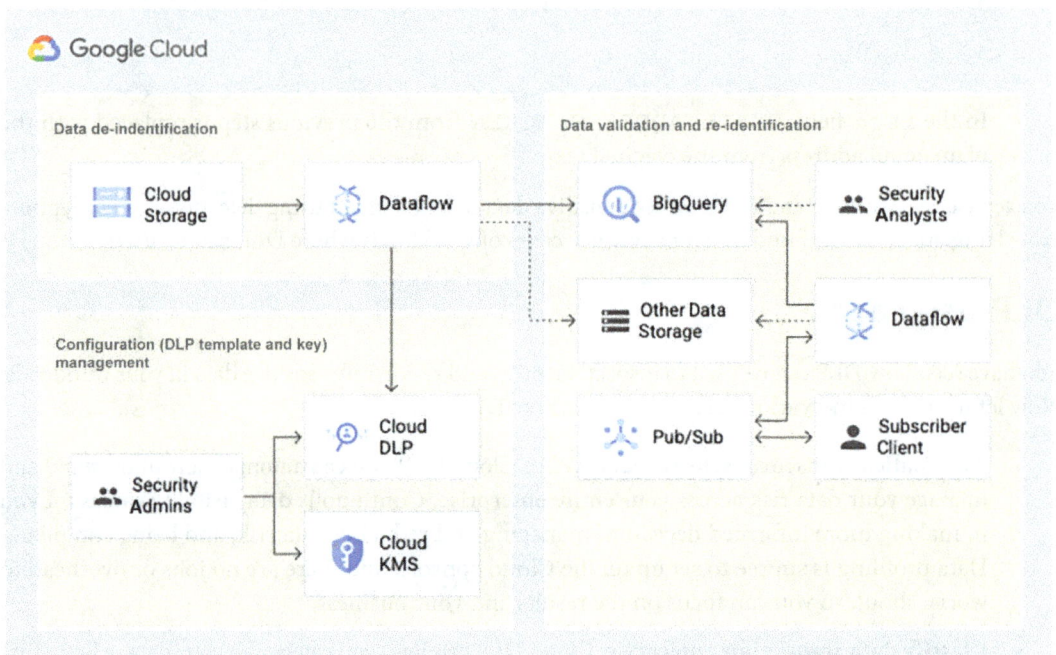

Figure 10.6 – DLP pattern for Dataflow and Data Fusion pipeline

As in *Figure 10.6*, here are a couple of patterns that you can employ to use Cloud DLP:

- Use Cloud DLP + Dataflow to tokenize data before loading it into BigQuery

- Use Cloud DLP + Cloud Data Fusion to tokenize data from Kafka Streams

By obfuscating the raw sensitive identifiers, de-identification techniques such as tokenization (pseudonymization) preserve the utility of your data for joining or analytics while decreasing the danger of handling the data. If you don't want the data to end up in the data warehouse, you can create a quarantine pipeline to send it to a sensitive dataset (with very limited permissions).

- **Use Cloud DLP in contact center chats to de-identify PII**: Cloud DLP can be used to mask any PII in customer support chats to make sure the agent doesn't get hold of any customer data.

We have seen some examples of workloads that you can use DLP for; now let us learn some best practices while using DLP.

Best practices for Cloud DLP

It can be difficult to figure out where Cloud DLP fits in your architecture or to identify requirements for Cloud DLP. Here are some best practices for you to understand how to use Cloud DLP in various scenarios:

- **Use data profiling versus inspection jobs**: Data profiling allows you to scan BigQuery tables in a scalable and automated manner without the need for orchestrating jobs. Considering the growth of data and the increasing number of tables, leveraging profiling features is recommended as it takes care of orchestration and running inspection jobs behind the scenes without any overhead. The inspection jobs can complement profilers when deeper investigation scans are needed. For example, if there are around 25,000 tables to be scanned, the recommendation is to scan all the tables with a profiler and then do a deep scan of 500 tables to flag sensitive/unstructured data that needs a more exhaustive investigation.

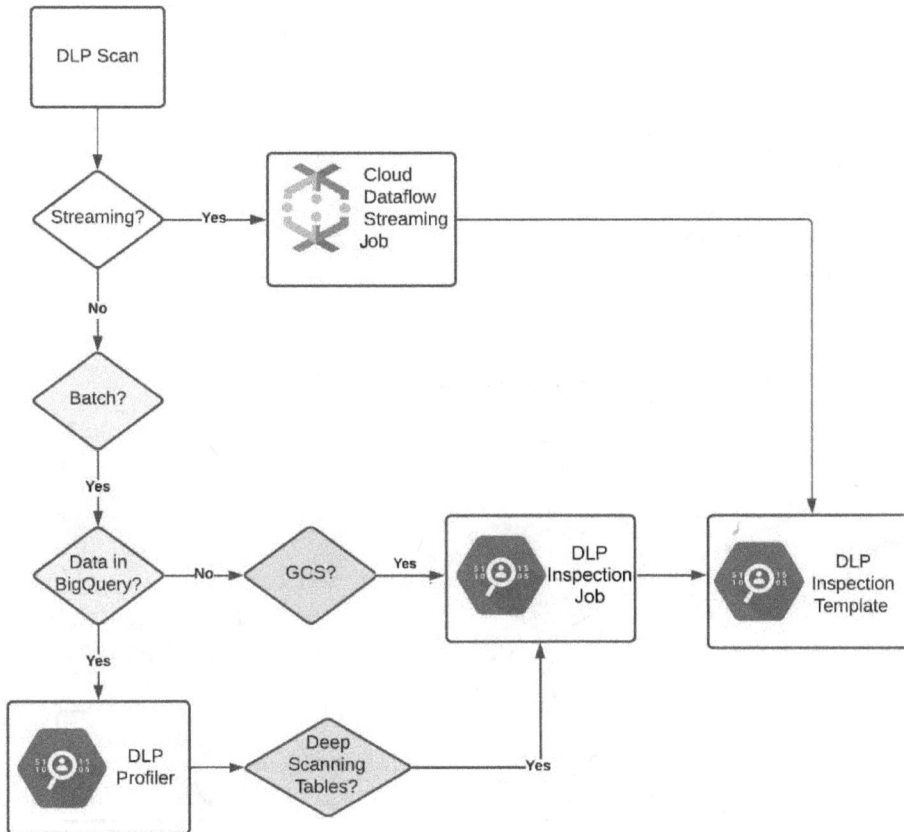

Figure 10.7 – Decision tree for inspection

Figure 10.7 shows a decision tree on when to use inspection jobs versus data profiling services.

- **Leverage built-in rules wherever possible**: Cloud DLP's built-in inspection templates should be used wherever possible. With over 150 built-in templates, Cloud DLP allows us to detect and classify data with speed and scale. For example, the US_HEALTHCARE_NPI tag can detect the 10-digit national provider number used for Medicare services. The use of built-in infoTypes saves the time and effort needed to create and maintain custom rules for standard infoTypes.

- **Trigger Cloud DLP scans based on events**: Cloud DLP's data profiling capability allows the automated scanning of all BigQuery tables and columns in your organization, folders, and projects. However, there might be a need to automate triggers that will enable the scan to run on new files that get uploaded to Cloud Storage or a new message that's added to Pub/Sub topics. To support this use case, Eventarc API or other BigQuery sink listeners can be configured to identify the change events that will eventually trigger a Cloud DLP scan.

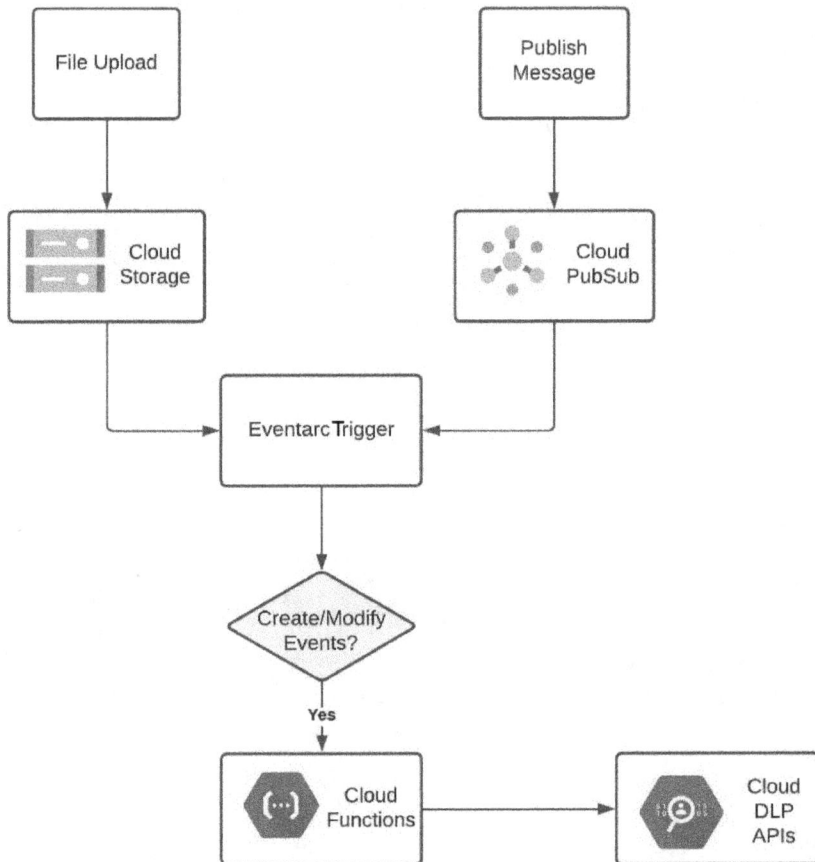

Figure 10.8 – Pattern for new updates

As shown in *Figure 10.8*, the pattern shows an example of a file upload or a Pub/Sub message triggering an Eventarc trigger. Based on the event, a cloud function will be triggered that will start the Cloud DLP scan.

- **Provide necessary permissions to the service account**: Cloud DLP creates service account agent accounts by default, which will have the necessary permissions to run Cloud DLP scan jobs. If you are scanning a highly restricted table or file, the relevant IAM roles must be added to the Cloud DLP service agent. Alternatively, if you are using a Cloud Function or Cloud Run applications to trigger Cloud DLP jobs, those service accounts must have the `dlp.jobTriggers.create` permission to successfully start the Cloud DLP scan job.

- **Publish Cloud DLP tags to Data Catalog**: Once the classification is complete, the results can be sent to Data Catalog so that the tables are tagged, only the right people get access to the data, and any sensitive data is protected. Cloud DLP allows native integration with the Data Catalog, so once we scan the BigQuery tables, it can send the tagging results into Data Catalog in the form of tag templates. The findings will be included in the summary form for the table in Data Catalog.

- **Restrict access prior to running Cloud DLP scans**: Access to any new BigQuery tables must be restricted until the Cloud DLP profiling is complete. To achieve this goal, the Cloud DLP profiler must be enabled, and only after it passes the policy checks should the data assets be moved to a state where end users can start accessing them. A quarantine state can be added to policy tags for all new tables so that users won't have access. Once Cloud DLP identifies sensitive data, a policy tag can be created in the form of a hierarchy of high, medium, and low to further restrict access depending on the content Cloud DLP identifies.

We have seen best practices for how to use Cloud DLP in various scenarios. Now let us switch gears and look at how to control data exfiltration and the best practices to prevent it.

Data exfiltration and VPC Service Controls

In the public cloud, there are several threats that organizations need to understand before deploying critical workloads. Here are a few threats that would lead to data exfiltration:

- Misconfigured IAM policies
- Malicious insiders copying data to an unauthorized destination
- Compromised code copying data to an unauthorized destination
- Access to data from unauthorized clients using a stolen credential

Here are various paths via which data can be exfiltrated in the cloud:

- Internet <-> service (stolen credentials)

  - Copy to internet

- Service <-> service (insider threat)

  - Copy from one storage service to another

- VPC <-> service (compromised VM)

  - Copy to consumer Google services
  - Copy to public GCS buckets/BigQuery dataset/GCR repo

Google Cloud offers some excellent offerings to stop the exfiltration of data as a part of its data loss prevention portfolio of products. VPC Service Controls extends a logical security perimeter around multi-tenant Google Cloud services such as **Google Cloud Storage (GCS)**, **BigQuery**, and **Google Container Registry (GCR)**. VPC Service Controls isolates Google Cloud-managed resources from the internet, unauthorized networks, and unauthorized Google Cloud resources. VPC Service Controls allows you to configure a security perimeter around the data resources of your Google-managed services (such as GCS, BigQuery, and Cloud BigTable) and control the movement of data across the perimeter boundary.

Let us look at the architecture of VPC Service Controls now.

Architecture of VPC Service Controls

Let us see a common VPC Service Controls architecture.

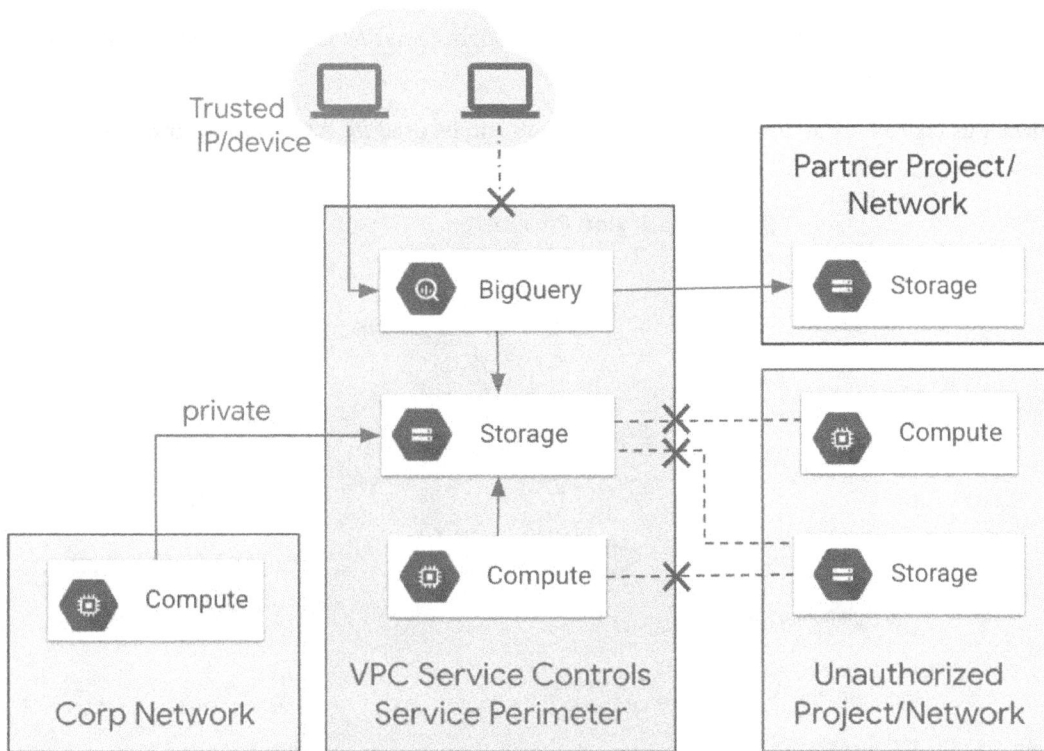

Figure 10.9 – VPC Service Controls architecture

As seen in *Figure 10.9*, the service perimeter provides a unified policy construct to isolate managed GCP resource access across the following three network interfaces:

- Internet-to-Google Cloud resource
- VPC network-to-Google Cloud resource
- Google Cloud resource-to-resource (on Google backend)

VPC Service Controls also allows you the following:

- The ability to run the configuration in dry run mode to evaluate the impact of a policy change before enforcing it.
- Fine-grained ingress and egress rules for secure data exchange between projects and other Google Cloud organizations.
- To create an access level with IP address and device attributes to enable secure access from outside the perimeter. Device attributes are typically used to establish organization trust to make sure the requests are coming from a trusted device (device attributes require BeyondCorp Enterprise).

- VPC accessible services to constrain which Google Cloud APIs (services) are accessible from a VPC network.

Now let us take a look at how VPC Service Controls can be used for API access restriction.

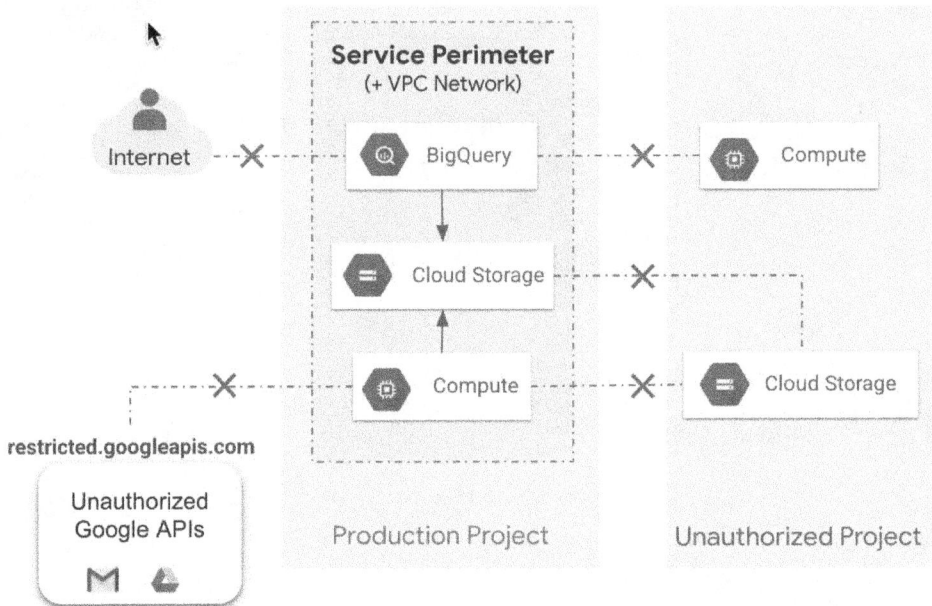

Figure 10.10 – Control APIs

As shown in *Figure 10.10*, VPC Service Controls allows you to control which APIs can be accessed from within the service perimeter:

- **Private Google Access or Private Service Connect**: Privately access Google Cloud APIs using Private Google Access.

- `restricted.googleapis.com`: Limit access to Google Cloud services that can be isolated with VPC Service Controls using the restricted **Virtual IP** (**VIP**) address range. To allow access to Cloud and Developer APIs protected by VPC Service Controls, use `restricted.googleapis.com`. The `restricted.googleapis.com` domain resolves to the `199.36.153.4/30` VIP range. The internet does not have access to this IP address range. The VIP `restricted.googleapis.com` denies access to Google APIs and services that are not supported by VPC Service Controls.

- **VPC accessible services**: Specify the exact list of APIs that can be accessed from a VPC.

Now we have seen how to restrict API access, let us see how can we allow access to the APIs within the perimeter.

Allowing access to protected resources within the VPC Service Controls perimeter

Use access levels to allow access to protected Google Cloud resources within service perimeters from outside a perimeter. An access level specifies a set of requirements that must be met in order for a request to be honored. Various variables, such as IP address and user identity, can be used to determine access levels.

To configure access levels, you'd use **Access Context Manager**. Let's take a look at it in more detail next.

Access Context Manager

Access Context Manager is a policy engine that allows administrators to create access control policies based on factors such as user geolocation and source IP address. These policies can be used as part of VPC Service Controls to ensure that a set of controls is applied to protect data in the project from adversaries.

Here are some rules when defining access levels:

- Only requests from outside a perimeter for resources of a protected service inside a perimeter are allowed.

- Access levels allow ingress only. Use an egress policy to allow access from a protected resource inside a perimeter to resources outside the boundary.

- The ingress and egress rules define which identities and resources are granted access to and from the perimeter. Use cases that formerly needed one or more perimeter bridges can be replaced and simplified with ingress and egress rules. A perimeter bridge is a feature of Google Cloud VPC Service Controls that allows users to securely and reliably connect two Google Cloud VPC networks. With this feature, users are able to create a secure connection between two VPC networks, allowing them to securely share resources, such as applications and databases, across the two networks. This provides an additional layer of security to protect resources from unauthorized access. Additionally, the perimeter bridge makes it easier to manage traffic between the two networks.

- Even though an access level normally accepts the external request, requests for a protected resource in a perimeter that originate from another perimeter are denied. You will need to add appropriate rules to get the desired action by applying ingress/egress rules.

- For IP-based allowlists, you can only utilize public IP address ranges in the access levels. Internal IP addresses are not allowed in these allowlists at the time of writing. A VPC network has internal IP addresses, and VPC networks must be referenced by its containing project via an entrance or egress rule, or a service boundary.

Now let us look at how to configure a VPC Service Controls perimeter.

Configuring a VPC Service Controls perimeter

To configure a VPC Service Controls perimeter, you should follow these high-level steps:

1. Set up access levels.

2. Create an access policy (aka perimeter).

3. Secure Google-managed resources with service perimeters.

4. Set up VPC-accessible services to add additional restrictions to how services can be used inside your perimeters (optional).

5. Set up private connectivity from a VPC network (optional).

6. Allow context-aware access from outside a service perimeter using ingress rules (optional).

7. Configure secure data exchange using ingress and egress rules (optional).

You also have the option to create an access level that will determine how your perimeter will be accessed. Let us look at that now.

Creating an access level

The following examples explain how to create an access level using different conditions:

1. Open the **Access Context Manager** page in the Cloud console and then open the **Access Context Manager** page.

2. If you are prompted, select your organization.

3. At the top of the **Access Context Manager** page, click **New**.

4. In the **New Access Level** pane, do the following:

    I.   In the **Access level title** box, enter a name for the access level.

    II. Click **Add Attribute** and then select **IP Subnetworks**. The supported access level attributes are as follows:

        i.   IP subnetworks

        ii.   Regions

        iii. Access level dependency

        iv.   Principals

        v.   Device policy

    III. In the **IP Subnetworks** box, enter an IPv4 or IPv6 CIDR block—for example, **93.184.216.0/32**.

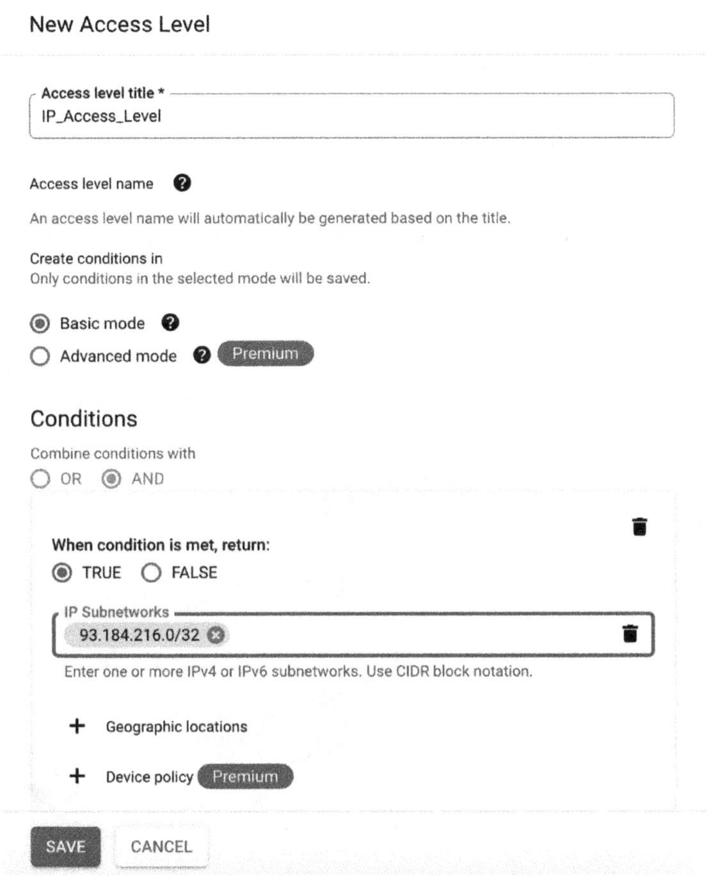

New Access Level

Access level title *

IP_Access_Level

Access level name   ❓

An access level name will automatically be generated based on the title.

Create conditions in
Only conditions in the selected mode will be saved.

◉ Basic mode   ❓
◯ Advanced mode   ❓ `Premium`

Conditions

Combine conditions with

◯ OR   ◉ AND

🗑

When condition is met, return:

◉ TRUE   ◯ FALSE

IP Subnetworks

`93.184.216.0/32 ✕`   🗑

Enter one or more IPv4 or IPv6 subnetworks. Use CIDR block notation.

➕ Geographic locations

➕ Device policy `Premium`

`SAVE`   `CANCEL`

Figure 10.11 – Creating access level

Figure 10.11 shows the **New Access Level** pane.

5. Click **SAVE**.

6. The access level is saved and appears in the grid on the **Access Context Manager** page.

That's it—you just created an access level that can be used in the access policy. Now let us look at how to create an access policy.

Creating a service perimeter

Access policies are always created at an organizational level. Access policies have the following components:

- **Resources you want to include in the policy**: These are folders or projects that the perimeter will protect

- **An administrator**: This is the administrative principal (a user or a service account) that either has access to view or manage the policy

- **VPC-accessible services**: This is a service that is allowed to be accessed by other VPCs

- **Access levels**: These are, as defined in the previous sections, endpoints that will have access to the perimeter

- **Ingress policy**: A rule that allows clients outside of the service perimeter to call a protected service within the perimeter

- **Egress policy**: A rule that allows services or clients within the perimeter to call a service outside of the perimeter

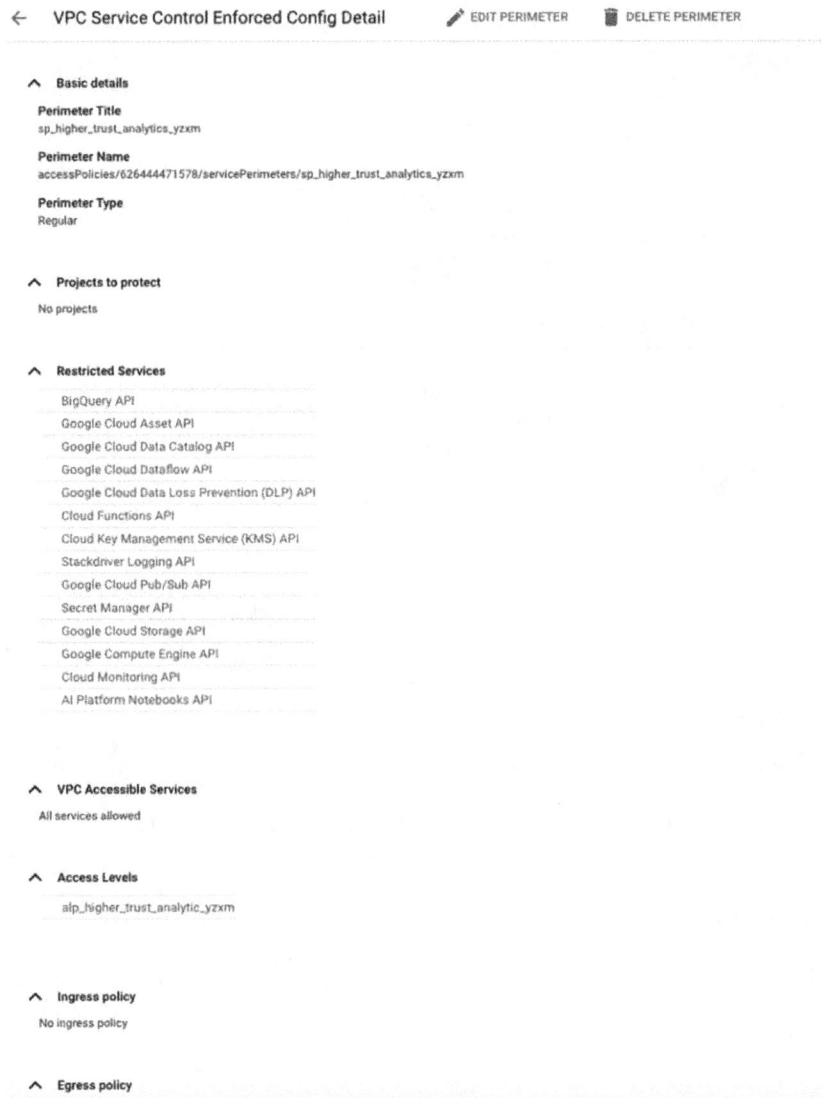

Figure 10.12 – Defining a service perimeter

As shown in *Figure 10.12*, the service perimeter will contain all the components necessary to create a perimeter.

Next, we will take a look at some of the best practices for VPC Service Controls.

Best practices for VPC Service Controls

Now that you understand the higher-level details of VPC Service Controls perimeters, let us go over some best practices:

- A single large perimeter is the simplest to implement and reduces the total number of moving parts requiring additional operational overhead, which helps to prevent complexity in your allowlist process.

- When data sharing is a primary use case for your organization, you can use more than one perimeter. If you produce and share lower-tier data such as de-identified patient health data, you can use a separate perimeter to facilitate sharing with outside entities.

- When possible, enable all protected services when you create a perimeter, which helps to reduce complexity and reduces potential exfiltration vectors. Make sure that there isn't a path to the private VIP from any of the VPCs in the perimeter. If you allow a network route to `private.googleapis.com`, you reduce the VPC Service Controls protection from insider data exfiltration. If you must allow access to a non-supported service, try to isolate the use of unsupported services in a separate project, or move the entire workload off the perimeter.

- An enterprise has many projects representing different workloads and applications. It is recommended that you organize these projects into folders.

- Allow ample time to gather data, conduct tests, and analyze violation logs. Make sure that stakeholders from your network, operations, and applications team are available for the task.

- Configure Private Google Access or Private Service Connect with `restricted.googleapis.com`.

- Move any applications using services not on `restricted.googleapis.com` to a separate project.

- Use dry run mode when configuring VPC Service Controls to an existing production environment. Make sure you understand the exceptions and errors produced by the dry run mode and see whether they match your design expectations. For example, certain service accounts such as an organization-level log sink will need to be allowed to collect logs. The dry run mode will catch these exceptions that you may not have considered in your design.

- Use the VPC Service Controls troubleshooting tool to analyze VPC Service Controls error codes.

- Set VPC-accessible services to restricted services to prevent access to unrestricted services.

- Ideally, do not include on-premises corp networks with user devices within a very secure service perimeter configuration.

- Document the following for every use case you use VPC Service Controls for:

  - The access pattern

  - The actors that can trigger the use case

  - Conditions that trigger the use case

  - Whether the use case is a valid access pattern and should be allowed

  - Any assumptions that pertain to the use case

  - Treat VPC Service Controls logically the same way you would a firewall; in the network, you need to "know your flows" to successfully secure the environment with the required ingress and egress flows enabled

VPC Service Controls is an important part of your cloud security strategy, so make sure you spend enough time understanding it.

Summary

We have covered a lot of things in this chapter. We went over various DLP definitions, use cases, and architecture options. We went over in detail how to use DLP for inspection and de-identification. We also saw examples of how to call DLP APIs and how to interpret the response. Last but not least, we went over data exfiltration strategies such as VPC Service Controls and their best practices. In the next chapter, we will go over the features of Secret Manager and how it can be used to store your application secrets securely.

Further reading

For more information on Cloud DLP and VPC Service Controls, refer to the following links:

- InfoType detector reference: `https://packt.link/cVC5r`

- Access level design: `https://packt.link/ZAEk4`

- Creating device-based access levels for VPC Service Controls: `https://packt.link/MpHwV`

- Ingress and egress rules for VPC Service Controls: `https://packt.link/3bBkP`

11
Secret Manager

In this chapter, we will look at Google Cloud Secret Manager. A secret is any piece of data that needs to be protected, such as passwords, encryption keys, API keys, certificate private keys, and other sensitive information. Secrets can be stored in a secure and encrypted format using Google Cloud Secret Manager. Applications that run on the cloud platform often need to be able to securely store secrets and rotate them as needed. The secrets should also provide redundancy in the event that a region goes down. Traditionally, secrets were stored in configuration files embedded within the application using some form of encryption or in clear text. However, a secure way of storing secrets is by using Secret Manager. Secret Manager is a native offering on Google Cloud to store application secrets such as database passwords or API keys. It provides a single place to store application secrets and be able to manage access and audit who did what.

In this chapter, we will cover the following topics:

- Overview of Secret Manager
- Managing secrets and versions
- Accessing a secret
- Secret rotation policy
- CMEKs for Secret Manager
- Best practices for secret management

Overview of Secret Manager

Secret Manager allows you to store and access secrets as binary blobs. It uses IAM permissions to grant access to the secrets and be able to manage them. Secret Manager is used for applications running on Google Cloud to store information such as database passwords, API keys, or certificates.

> **Note**
> Cryptographic keys should not be stored in Secret Manager. Cloud KMS is a better service since it allows you to encrypt the key material.

Before we start using Secret Manager, let us go over some core concepts. This will help you understand how Secret Manager works so you can make the right decision for your workloads.

Secret Manager concepts

Let us look at some key definitions related to Secret Manager as defined in the Google Cloud documentation:

- **Secret**: A secret is an object at the project level that stores a collection of metadata and secret versions. The metadata includes replication locations, labels, and permissions.

- **Version**: A secret version stores the actual confidential information, such as API keys, passwords, and certificates. You cannot modify a secret once you create it, but you can delete it and create a new version.

- **Rotation**: Secret Manager supports rotational schedules for secrets. This, however, doesn't create a new secret version automatically but merely sends a message to a Pub/Sub topic configured for that secret based on the rotational frequency and time.

- **Replication policy**: Secrets have global names and globally replicated metadata. The replication policy can only determine where the secret payload data is stored. Upon the creation of each secret, it will have its own replication policy. You cannot modify the location in the replication policy.

- **Resource consistency**: Adding a secret version and then immediately accessing that secret version is an example of a consistent operation in Secret Manager. Consistent operations usually synchronize in minutes but may take a few hours. You should take consistency into consideration when designing your applications.

Managing secrets and versions

Now let us look at some basic operations you can perform in Secret Manager. These operations can either be performed using `gcloud`, the Cloud console, or APIs. We have used the console to keep it simple.

Creating a secret

Follow these steps to create a secret using the Google Cloud console:

1. Go to **Console | Security | Secret Manager**.
2. Click on **Create secret**.

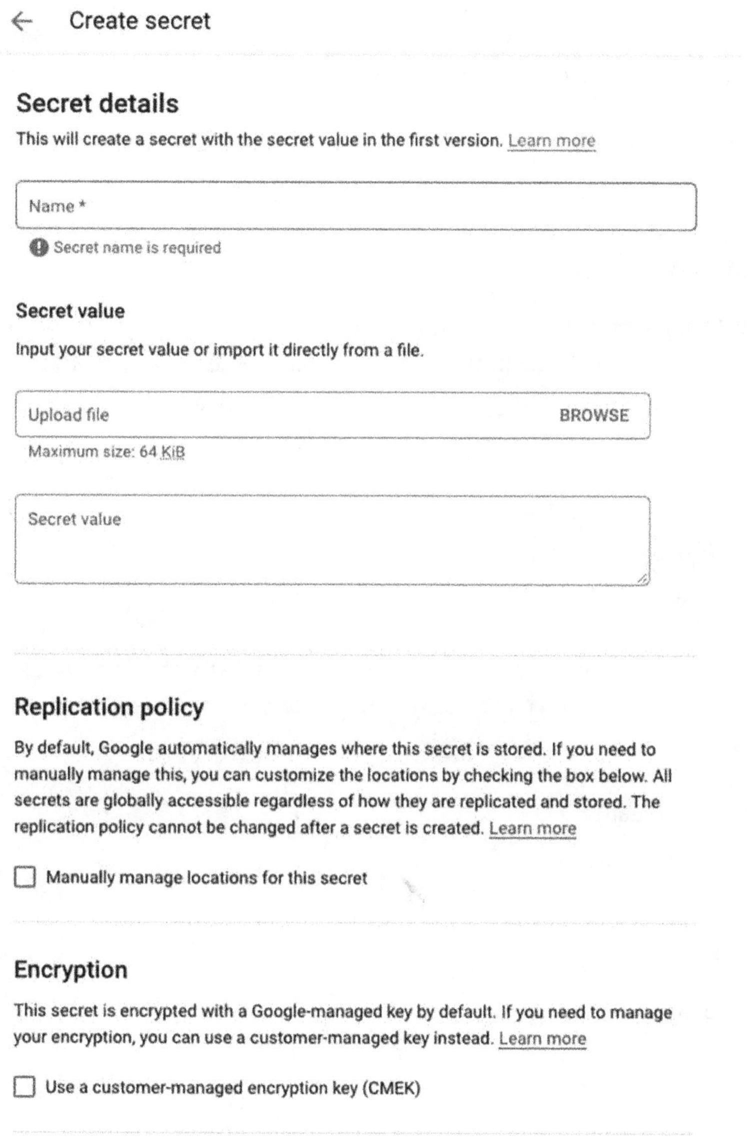

Figure 11.1 – Creating a new secret

As shown in *Figure 11.1*, a secret value can be copied directly into the console or provided via a file. Typically, binary secrets are provided via a file.

3.   Choose the desired *rotation* period (**Set rotation period**). Note that this will only set a notification but not rotate the secret automatically.

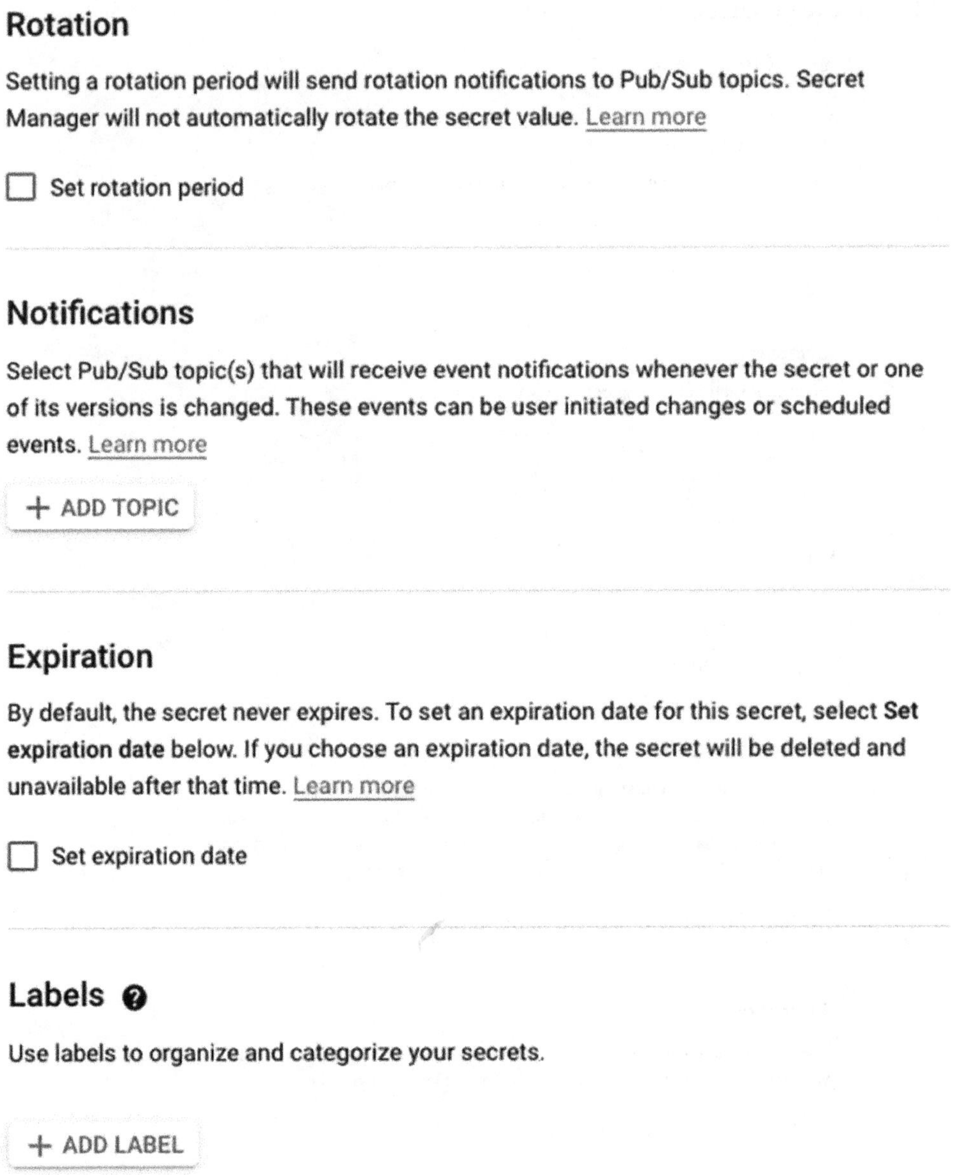

Rotation

Setting a rotation period will send rotation notifications to Pub/Sub topics. Secret Manager will not automatically rotate the secret value. Learn more

☐ Set rotation period

Notifications

Select Pub/Sub topic(s) that will receive event notifications whenever the secret or one of its versions is changed. These events can be user initiated changes or scheduled events. Learn more

+ ADD TOPIC

Expiration

By default, the secret never expires. To set an expiration date for this secret, select **Set expiration date** below. If you choose an expiration date, the secret will be deleted and unavailable after that time. Learn more

☐ Set expiration date

Labels ❷

Use labels to organize and categorize your secrets.

+ ADD LABEL

Figure 11.2 – Creating a new secret—rotation period

As shown in *Figure 11.2*, there are additional properties you can set on a secret. We recommend that you do not set **Expiration** since this can cause some unintended behavior. You can set **Labels** to organize secrets.

4. Alternatively, you can use the following `gcloud` command to create a secret:

```
gcloud secrets versions add secret-id --data-file="/file path/
to/setcret.txt"
```

Adding a new secret version

We will now see how to add a new secret version to an existing secret:

1. Select the secret and click on +**NEW VERSION**.

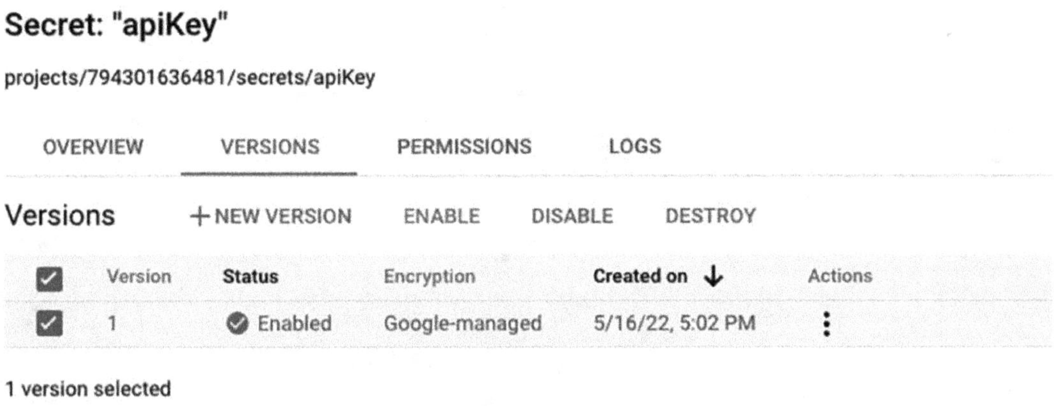

Secret: "apiKey"

projects/794301636481/secrets/apiKey

OVERVIEW	VERSIONS	PERMISSIONS	LOGS

Versions	+ NEW VERSION	ENABLE	DISABLE	DESTROY

	Version	Status	Encryption	Created on ↓	Actions
☑	1	✅ Enabled	Google-managed	5/16/22, 5:02 PM	⋮

1 version selected

Figure 11.3 – Adding a new secret version

It should show a popup to allow you to add a secret either from a file or by copying directly into the **Secret value** field.

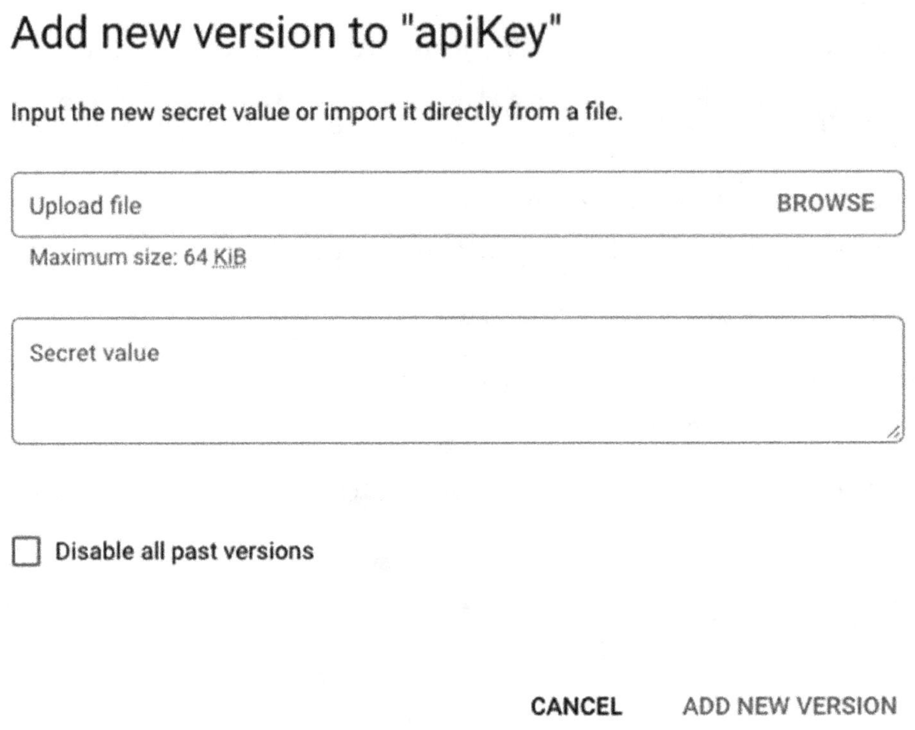

Add new version to "apiKey"

Input the new secret value or import it directly from a file.

Upload file	BROWSE

Maximum size: 64 KiB

Secret value

☐ Disable all past versions

CANCEL   ADD NEW VERSION

Figure 11.4 – Adding a new secret version (continued)

As shown in *Figure 11.4*, you have an option to disable all past secret versions (see the **Disable all past versions** check box), so make sure to choose this option carefully as disabling a secret version currently used by your application could cause an outage.

Disabling a secret

Now let us look at how to disable a secret that you no longer want to use:

1. Click on the secret you want to disable and click **DISABLE**.

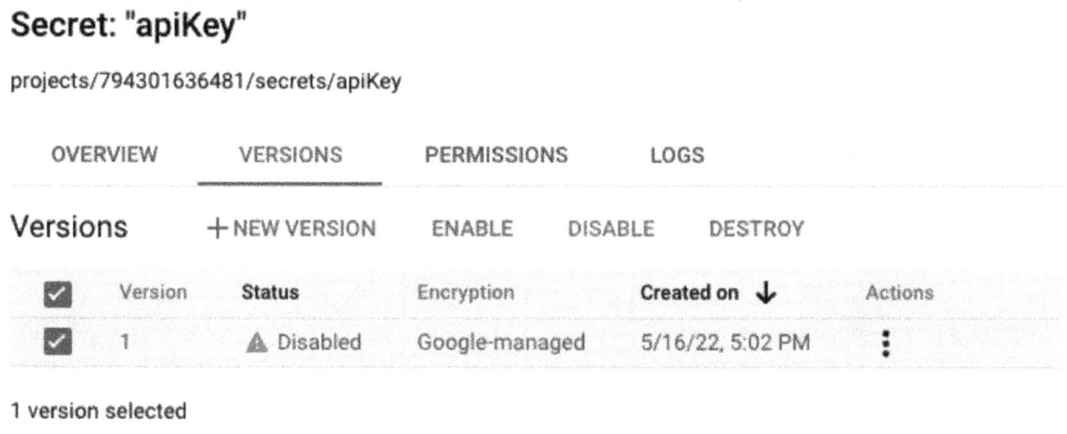

Secret: "apiKey"

projects/794301636481/secrets/apiKey

| OVERVIEW | VERSIONS | PERMISSIONS | LOGS |

Versions   + NEW VERSION   ENABLE   DISABLE   DESTROY

✓	Version	Status	Encryption	Created on ↓	Actions
✓	1	⚠ Disabled	Google-managed	5/16/22, 5:02 PM	⋮

1 version selected

Figure 11.5 – Disabling a secret

As seen in *Figure 11.5*, the secret will be disabled, and you will also see **Status** changed to **Disabled** on the console.

Enabling a secret

This operation will enable a secret that is in the **Disabled** state:

1. Click on the secret you want to enable and click **ENABLE**.

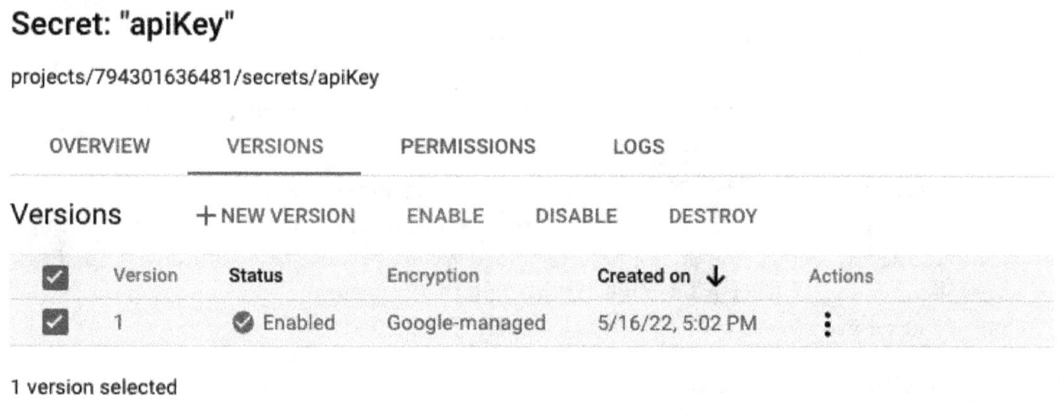

Secret: "apiKey"

projects/794301636481/secrets/apiKey

| OVERVIEW | VERSIONS | PERMISSIONS | LOGS |

Versions   + NEW VERSION   ENABLE   DISABLE   DESTROY

✓	Version	Status	Encryption	Created on ↓	Actions
✓	1	✅ Enabled	Google-managed	5/16/22, 5:02 PM	⋮

1 version selected

Figure 11.6 – Enabling a secret

As seen in *Figure 11.6*, the secret will be enabled, and you will also see **Status** changed to **Enabled** on the console.

Accessing a secret

Accessing a secret version returns the secret contents as well as additional metadata about the secret version. When you access a secret version, you specify its `version-id`. You can also access the latest version of a secret by specifying `latest` as the version.

Accessing a secret version requires the `secretmanager.secretAccessor` IAM role. Typically, this role is granted to the service account used by your application.

The following is a `gcloud` command that can be used to access a particular version of the secret. However, a common method is to use application libraries for access, as you will see later in the section:

```
gcloud secrets versions access version-id --secret="secret-id"
```

You can also use the `latest` keyword to get the current version, but this is *not* a recommended best practice.

Accessing a binary secret version

You can access binary secrets directly but note that Cloud SDK formats the output as UTF-8, which can corrupt binary secrets. To get the raw bytes, Cloud SDK prints the response as base64-encoded, which you can then decode:

```
gcloud secrets versions access version-id --secret="secret-id"
--format='get(payload.data)' | tr '_-' '/+' | base64 -d
```

Accessing secrets from your application

You can access secrets from Google Cloud services such as Compute Engine, Application Engine, GKE, and Cloud Run.

Secret Manager has a REST and gRPC API for using and managing secrets. However, a convenient way to get access to secrets is by using client libraries. You can use these client libraries bundled with your application to access secrets. You do not need to embed service account keys within your application to access Secret Manager APIs. All you need is the right IAM role for the service account used by the Google Cloud service of your choice, such as GCE, GAE, or Cloud Functions:

- In Cloud Build, you can access secrets using environment variables in the build step of the build YAML config file by referring a field called `availableSecrets` to a specific secret version.

- For Cloud Run, you can use Secret Manager in two ways:

  - Mount the secret as a volume, which will make the secret available to the container as files. Reading the volume will read the secret from Secret Manager. You can use the `latest` keyword to fetch the secret using this method.

- Access the secret using a traditional environment variable. Environment variables are resolved by Cloud Run at the start of the container. When you use this method, do not use the `latest` keyword, use a particular version.

- For GKE, you can use Workload Identity in conjunction with Secret Manager client libraries to access secrets. You can also use the Secret Store CSI driver in conjunction with the Google Secret Manager provider for this driver. This allows you to access secrets as files mounted in Kubernetes pods. The provider is an open source project supported by Google that uses the workload identity of the pod that a secret is mounted onto when authenticating to the Google Secret Manager API. For this to work, the workload identity of the pod must be configured and appropriate IAM bindings must be applied. This plugin is built to ensure compatibility between Secret Manager and Kubernetes workloads that need to load secrets from the filesystem. The plugin also enables syncing secrets to Kubernetes-native secrets for consumption as environment variables. When evaluating this plugin, consider the following threats:

  - When a secret is accessible on the filesystem, application vulnerabilities such as **directory traversal** (`https://packt.link/wYWmj`) attacks can become higher severity as the attacker may gain the ability to read the secret material.

  - When a secret is consumed through environment variables, misconfigurations such as enabling a debug endpoint or including dependencies that log process environment details may leak secrets.

  - When syncing secret material to another data store (such as Kubernetes Secrets), consider whether the access controls on that data store are sufficiently narrow in scope.

- For multi-cloud application deployments, consider using workload identity federation on other platforms, such as Amazon Web Services or Microsoft Azure, that use current identity protocols to authenticate to Google Cloud APIs. Typically, you would want to use the native offering of the cloud providers for the secrets where your application is deployed.

Let us look at how you can achieve multi-region redundancy of secrets by using a secret rotation policy. This strategy supports the application redundancy you would need for high availability and failover.

Secret replication policy

Secrets are a global resource entity; however, secret payloads (the underlying secret material) are stored locally within a region. Some regulated customers such as financial and healthcare institutions may have strict regionalization requirements, while other customers may want to store the secret near the data. A replication policy allows control over where secret payloads are stored.

There are two replication policy types: automatic and user-managed.

Automatic

With the automatic policy type, the replication of the secret is managed by Google. This policy provides the highest level of availability:

- When a secret has an automatic replication policy, its payload data is copied as many times as needed. This is the easiest way to set things up, and most users should choose it. This is the policy that is used by default when a secret is created using the Google Cloud CLI or the web UI.

- A secret that is automatically replicated is stored in a single place for billing purposes.

- For a resource location organization policy evaluation, you can only make a secret with an automatic replication policy if you can make resources global.

User-managed (user-selected)

With the user-managed replication policy type, the secret is replicated to only locations selected by users:

> **Note**
> The secret version addition will be impacted if one of the regions you selected is unavailable.

- The payload data of a secret with a user-managed replication policy is duplicated to a user-configured list of locations. The secret can be duplicated to as many supported locations as you choose. If there are regulations on where the secret payload data can be stored, this could be useful.

- Each location in the user-managed replication policy is treated as a separate location for billing reasons.

- A secret with a user-managed replication policy can only be created if the organization policy allows the creation of resources in all selected locations.

- As a rule, choose between two and five locations for replication. Having a large number of replication locations results in longer replication delays as well as increased latency in accessing the new secret payload.

Let us look at some of the encryption options, namely Google default encryption and customer-managed encryption, for Secret Manager.

CMEKs for Secret Manager

By default, secrets are encrypted with Google default encryption. However, some highly regulated customers require control of keys, so Secret Manager supports **customer-managed encryption keys (CMEKs)** (within Cloud KMS) for encrypting:

> **Note**
> However, if you disable or permanently destroy the CMEK, the secret encrypted with that key cannot be decrypted.

- Secret payloads are encrypted by Google-managed keys before being written to persistent storage with no additional configuration required.

- Secret Manager encrypts data with a unique **data encryption key** (**DEK**) before writing it to persistent storage in a specific location. The Secret Manager service owns a replica-specific key called a **key encryption key** (**KEK**), which is used to encrypt the DEK. This is commonly referred to as envelope encryption.

- The CMEK is a symmetric key that you control within Cloud KMS when using CMEKs with Secret Manager. The CMEK must be stored in the same GCP region as the secret. This makes sure that the Secret Manager has access to the key in the event of a zone or region failure.

- Customers who desire complete control over encryption keys can use the Cloud **External Key Manager** (**EKM**) key in the CMEK policy for encryption and decryption. This completely removes Google's management of the encryption key for your secrets as the encryption key is controlled outside of Google Cloud.

- CMEKs are also supported when using user-managed replication. When you create a CMEK in Cloud KMS, make sure the location of the key matches the location of the secret if you are using a user-managed replication policy.

So far, we have seen how to set up secrets in Google Cloud. Let us now go over some of the best practices for managing secrets in production and development environments.

Best practices for secret management

Here are some general best practices that Google recommends when it comes to managing secrets:

- As with pretty much all services in Google Cloud, access to the Secret Manager API is protected by IAM. Follow the principle of least privilege when granting permissions to secrets to your applications.

- Divide applications and environments (staging/production) into independent projects. This can assist in segregating environments with IAM binding at the project level and guarantee that quotas are implemented independently.

- If necessary, establish a custom role or choose an existing role with the bare minimum of access. Think about who manages the secret (creates the secret, disables/enables it, or creates a new version) and who uses it, such as developers. You should have a separation of duties between these two roles, especially in production.

- Use secret-level IAM bindings or IAM conditions to limit access to the necessary subset of secrets when numerous services' secrets are in a single project.

- Use `gcloud auth application-default login` when developing locally. This produces a file with credentials that client libraries will immediately recognize.

Let us look at some of the best practices that you should consider while specifically developing your application.

Best practices for development

Here are some best practices for working with Secret Manager during the development of an application that will ultimately be deployed in Google Cloud:

- To use secrets within your development IDEs such as Visual Studio Code or IntelliJ, use the Secret Manager integration plugin. Please see the Google Cloud documentation on how to enable Secret Manager for your choice of IDE (`https://packt.link/XRAGF`).

- For deployments in a single project, consider creating secrets in the project where the workload will be deployed. This makes the management of secrets much easier.

- Do not use slashes, `/`, when naming a secret as this violates Google Cloud's resource naming convention.

- Secret data stored in secret versions must fit within the quotas and limits specified in the Secret Manager specification. Apart from this, Secret Manager has no restrictions on the format of the secret material.

- Secrets such as API keys, SSH keys, and cryptographic keys are generated in external systems with formatting requirements.

- Use randomly generated, large, complicated values and cryptographically strong random number generators for secrets such as passwords when the format and length are not constrained.

Best practices for deployment

Here are some best practices for Secrets Manager while deploying applications on Google Cloud:

- Use a separate project for secrets that are used by workloads in many projects, separate from the workload projects.

- Instead of granting Cloud IAM roles at the organization, folder, or project level, grant them directly on secrets. This will prevent over-grants and misuse.

- Managing secret-level IAM role grants can be easier using an **infrastructure-as-code (IaC)** approach such as Terraform. You can typically embed this in the given application CI/CD pipeline.

- The expiration date feature shouldn't be used for production workloads. This feature is best used to clean up transitory situations automatically. Consider using time-based IAM conditional access to secrets instead of secrets that expire.

- On projects that contain secrets or enclosing folders or organizations, avoid utilizing basic project-wide roles such as owner, editor, and viewer.

- Create distinct key administration and access roles according to the following guidelines:

  - Most applications require secret versions for specific secrets. For those specific secrets, grant these accounts `roles/secretmanager.secretAccessor`.

  - Grant `roles/secretmanager.secretVersionAdder` to processes that add new secret versions, for example, a CI/CD pipeline or administrator that owns the secret.

  - Grant `roles/secretmanager.secretVersionManager` to processes that handle timed disabling and destruction of secret versions.

- Rotate your secrets periodically to minimize the impact of leaked secrets.

- Exercise the rotation flow on a regular basis to lessen the chances of an outage.

- Unless your workload has specified location requirements, use the automatic replication policy. Most workloads' availability and performance requirements are met by the automated policy.

- To obtain and analyze `AccessSecretVersion` requests, enable data access logs at the folder or organization level.

- Automatically rotate secrets and have emergency rotation processes ready in case of a compromise.

- Instead of utilizing the most recent alias, refer to secrets by their version number. Create a hidden version of your program that is read at launch. Use your existing release methods to deploy updates to version numbers. Although using the most recent alias can be easy, if the latest version of the secret has an issue, your workload may be unable to use the secret version. The configuration can be evaluated and rolled back using your regular release processes if you pin it to a version number.

- Before deleting or destroying secret versions, disable them. This helps prevent outages by putting the secret in a reversible state that looks like destruct. That is, before permanently deleting data, you can disable it and wait a week to ensure there are no lingering dependencies.

- Secret Manager should not be used to store Google Cloud service account keys.

- In addition to IAM controls, you can set up a VPC Service Controls perimeter for your organization to limit access to the Secret Manager API from outside of Google Cloud using network-based controls such as IP address range and service accounts.

- The organization policy `PolicyMemberDomains` can be used to limit the identities that can be added to IAM policies for secrets.

- Estimate your peak secret usage (taking into account a *thundering herd* of queries owing to concurrent application deployments or service autoscaling) and make sure your project has enough quota to accommodate it. Request an increase in quota if more is required.

- Using Cloud Asset Inventory, keep track of secrets across your business to do the following:

  - Assist in the discovery of secrets throughout your company.

  - Identify non-conformance with organizational standards such as rotation, encryption setup, and location.

Having discussed the best practices for production, we now turn our attention to troubleshooting and auditing Secret Manager operations.

Secret Manager logs

You can consult Cloud Logging to audit or troubleshoot the operation of Secret Manager.

Let us assume `project_id` = `acme-project-id`, `folder_id` = `acme-folder`, `billing_account_id` = `123456`, and `organization_id` = `987654321`. The logs of interest would have the names listed as follows:

```
projects/acme-project-id/logs/cloudaudit.googleapis.com%2Factivity
projects/acme-project-id/logs/cloudaudit.googleapis.com%2Fdata_access
projects/acme-project-id/logs /cloudaudit.googleapis.com%2Fsystem_
event
projects/acme-project-id/logs/cloudaudit.googleapis.com%2Fpolicy

folders/acme-folder/logs/cloudaudit.googleapis.com%2Factivity
folders/acme-folder/logs/cloudaudit.googleapis.com%2Fdata_access
folders/acme-folder/logs/cloudaudit.googleapis.com%2Fsystem_event
folders/acme-folder/logs/cloudaudit.googleapis.com%2Fpolicy

billingAccounts/987654321/logs/cloudaudit.googleapis.com%2Factivity
```

```
billingAccounts/987654321/logs/cloudaudit.googleapis.com%2Fdata_
access
billingAccounts/987654321/logs/cloudaudit.googleapis.com%2Fsystem_
event
billingAccounts/987654321/logs/cloudaudit.googleapis.com%2Fpolicy

organizations/987654321/logs/cloudaudit.googleapis.com%2Factivity
organizations/987654321/logs/cloudaudit.googleapis.com%2Fdata_
access
organizations/987654321/logs/cloudaudit.googleapis.com%2Fsystem_
event
organizations/987654321/logs/cloudaudit.googleapis.com%2Fpolicy
```

This concludes the logging part of the Secret Manager application.

Summary

In this chapter, we reviewed Secret Manager, its operations, and some critical aspects of setting secrets for your requirements. We also discussed best practices for the development and deployment of secrets. It is important to follow these best practices so that your application is designed optimally and to reduce the risk of outages. As a member of the application development team or information security team, you should be able to design your applications to leverage Secret Manager.

In the next chapter, we will look at the logging features of Google Cloud. Cloud Logging is one of the critical aspects of cloud deployment. We will also go over the best practices of Cloud Logging.

Further reading

- Secret Manager IAM roles: https://packt.link/wgzCw

- Secret Manager rotation: https://packt.link/slcoa

- Creating and managing expiring secrets: https://packt.link/js5eW

- Analyzing secrets with Cloud Asset Inventory: https://packt.link/v7w8z

- Secret Manager data integrity assurance: https://packt.link/8AmOG

12
Cloud Logging

Logging provides visibility into your environment and aids in troubleshooting and incident response. In this chapter, we will discuss what Cloud Logging is, how it works, the different types of logs and their applications, and how to collect, store, analyze, and export logs. We will also look at who log producers and consumers are and how to export logs to a centralized logging solution or a **Security Information and Event Management** (**SIEM**) system running either on-premises or in the cloud. Finally, we will discuss how to securely store and keep logs to meet regulatory requirements.

In this chapter, we will cover the following topics:

- Overview of Google Cloud Logging
- Understanding log categories
- Log management
- Logging and auditing best practices

Introduction to Google Cloud logging

Cloud Logging is a managed service on Google Cloud. It gives you the ability to collect, store, search, analyze, monitor, and set alerts based on logs that are collected. You can use Cloud Logging to collect log data from over 150 applications, Google Cloud components, third-party cloud providers, and any combination of cloud platforms (hybrid environments). Cloud Logging, formerly known as Stackdriver, is part of Google Cloud's operations suite. It includes a console interface called the Logs Explorer, query logs, and an API to manage logs programmatically.

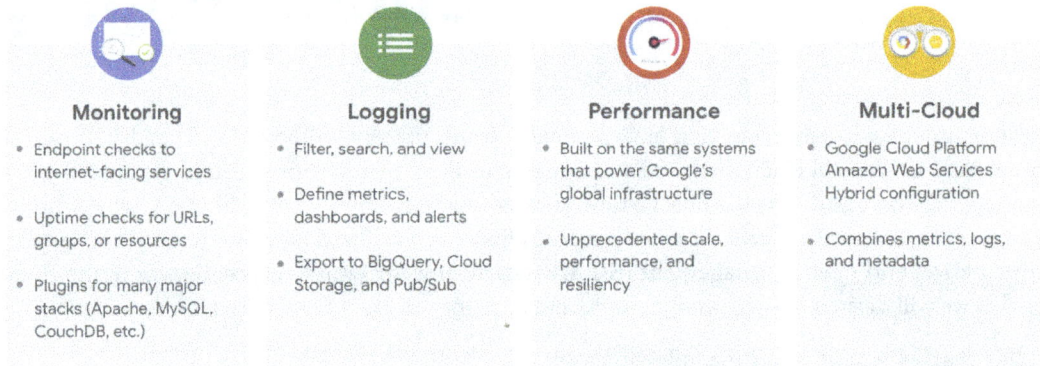

Monitoring	**Logging**	**Performance**	**Multi-Cloud**
• Endpoint checks to internet-facing services	• Filter, search, and view	• Built on the same systems that power Google's global infrastructure	• Google Cloud Platform Amazon Web Services Hybrid configuration
• Uptime checks for URLs, groups, or resources	• Define metrics, dashboards, and alerts	• Unprecedented scale, performance, and resiliency	• Combines metrics, logs, and metadata
• Plugins for many major stacks (Apache, MySQL, CouchDB, etc.)	• Export to BigQuery, Cloud Storage, and Pub/Sub		

Figure 12.1 – Google Cloud's operations suite

Cloud Logging is one of the four components of Google Cloud's operations suite, as shown in *Figure 12.1*. Let's explore each of these components in more depth. Cloud Logging captures all logs and provides searching and filtering capabilities. Cloud Logging derives metrics from logs, creates dashboards, autoscales instances, and provides the ability to export logs for retention and analytics. We will cover these topics in more depth later in this chapter.

Application Performance Management (**APM**) combines the monitoring and troubleshooting capabilities of Cloud Logging and Cloud Monitoring with Cloud Trace, Cloud Debugger, and Cloud Profiler, to help you reduce latency and cost so you can run more efficient applications. This is out of the scope of the Google Cloud Professional Security Engineer exam.

Additionally, the Google Cloud operations suite offers multi-cloud capabilities in its support of both Google Cloud and Amazon Web Services and can also monitor on-premises resources and integrate with partner solutions.

By default, the operations suite monitors all system metrics, including Google **Compute Engine** (GCE) and **Google Kubernetes Engine** (GKE). The operations suite also monitors applications and managed services, such as Datastore and BigQuery. You can utilize the operations suite's Monitoring API to interact with users and collect business metrics. You can also deploy a monitoring agent on compute instances to collect lower-level and third-party tool metrics, such as disk latency/IO, for supported services. *Figure 12.2* illustrates the capabilities of the operations suite and how cloud resources generate signals and telemetry that are then consumed by different operations suite functions.

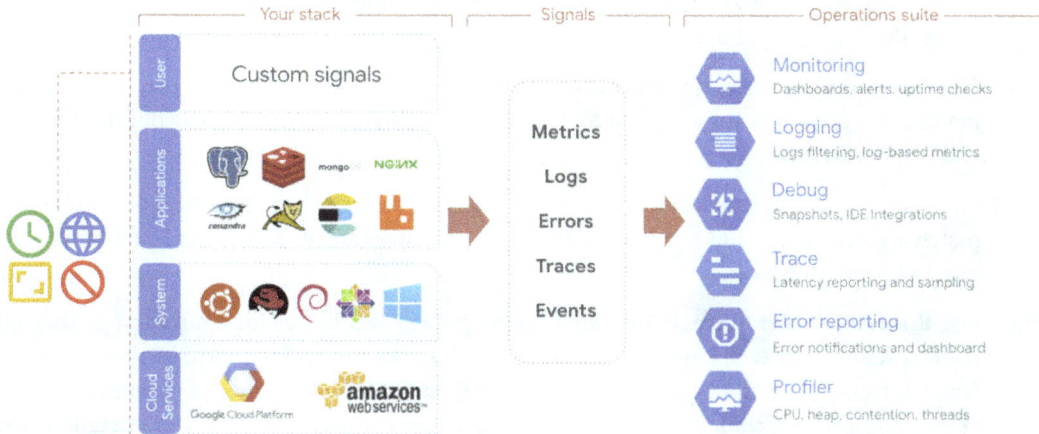

Figure 12.2 – Operations suite layers

We will now go over some fundamental Cloud Logging principles, as well as a few significant terms. It is important to understand them as they will be used throughout the chapter and assessed in the exam:

- **Log entries**: A log entry is a record of the state of a computer system or a description of specific events or transactions. Each log entry includes different types of data based on the service generating the log. Most log entries contain these attributes:

  - A timestamp to indicate when the event took place or when it was received by Cloud Logging.

  - The resource that produced the log entry.

  - A payload, also known as a message, is either provided as unstructured textual data or as structured textual data in JSON format.

  - The name of the log to which it belongs. Some logs also have metadata associated with them, such as the severity of each associated log entry.

- **Logs**: In Google Cloud resources, such as a Google Cloud project, a log is a named collection of log entries. There can be no logs unless there are log entries. A log's name is identified by the full path of the resource to which the log entries belong, followed by a simple log ID, such as **syslog**, or a structured ID that includes the log's writer, such as `compute.googleapis.com/activity`.

- **Retention period**: Log entries are stored in Cloud Logging for a specific period of time known as the retention period. Each log type has a different default retention period. You have the ability to create custom retention periods to store logs for longer periods than the defaults that are available in Cloud Logging.

- **Queries and filters**: Queries are written in the Logging query language. Queries return the matching log entries. The Logs Explorer and the Logging API both employ queries to select and display log entries.

  Filters are queries in the Logging query language that are used by log sinks to direct logs that match a given expression to a storage destination. Filters are also used to redirect matching logs to Cloud Monitoring.

- **Log Router**: In order to reach the Cloud Logging API, all collected logs must first go through the Log Router. For each log entry, the Log Router checks against pre-existing rules to identify which log entries should be ingested (stored) and routed to a destination, as well as which log entries should be excluded (discarded). We will cover the Log Router in more detail later in this chapter.

- **Sinks**: A sink consists of a filter and a storage destination. The filter logs entries to send to the sink.

- **Log-based metrics**: You can define metrics for the logs and then create alerts and triggers based on those metrics.

- **Access control**: You can control who has access to the logs using Cloud IAM permissions.

Each of the log types is categorized based on the log type, such as security, user, or platform. We will look at all these categories in more detail in the next section.

Log categories

In this section, we broadly divide logs into three categories. We will look at each category from the perspective of security.

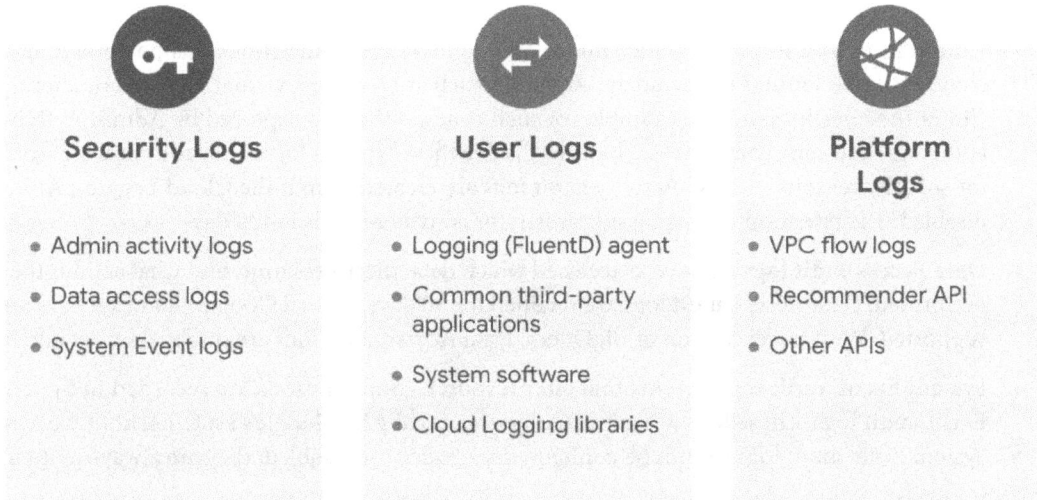

Security Logs	User Logs	Platform Logs
• Admin activity logs	• Logging (FluentD) agent	• VPC flow logs
• Data access logs	• Common third-party applications	• Recommender API
• System Event logs	• System software	• Other APIs
	• Cloud Logging libraries	

Figure 12.3 – Log categories

Figure 12.3 illustrates the different types of log categories: security logs, user logs, and platform logs. Security logs consist of admin activity logs, data access logs, system event logs, and transparency logs. User logs are generated by user software, services, or applications and are written to Cloud Logging using a logging agent, the Cloud Logging API, or the Cloud Logging client libraries. Google Cloud Platform logs are service-specific logs that can help you better understand the Google Cloud services you're using. VPC flow logs, firewall logs, and other API logs are examples of platform logs.

Our focus will be only on logs that are useful from a security perspective. That doesn't necessarily mean that we will only look at the security logs category. We will also look at user logs and platform logs, specifically the subordinate log types within these categories that pertain to security.

Security logs

Cloud Logging offers two forms of security logs: **Cloud Audit Logs** and **Access Transparency Logs**. Cloud Audit Logs generates the following types of audit logs for each cloud project, folder, and organization:

- **Admin Activity audit logs** include information on API calls and actions that potentially alter cloud resource settings or metadata. Activities such as creating a virtual machine or altering Cloud IAM permissions are examples of such changes that are captured by Admin Activity audit logs. You can't configure, exclude, or disable these types of logs. They're always recorded for security reasons. Admin Activity audit logs are created even if the Cloud Logging API is disabled. The retention period for administrator activity records is 400 days.

- **Data Access audit logs** show who accessed which data, the access time, and what actions they performed. Data Access audit logs are retained for 30 days. Not all Google Cloud services are supported. With the exception of BigQuery, Data Access audit logs are disabled by default.

- **System Event audit logs**: Events that alter resource configurations are recorded in System Event audit logs. These logs are generated automatically by Google's systems, not by users. System Event audit logs cannot be configured, excluded, or disabled; they are always written.

- **Policy Denied audit logs**: Policy Denied audit logs are created when a Google Cloud service rejects a user or service account access for a security policy violation. VPC Service Controls determines security policies and sends Cloud Logging Policy Denied audit logs. Your Google Cloud project gets charged for Policy Denied audit log storage. You can't disable Policy Denied audit logs, but you can exclude them from Cloud Logging.

The next type of security log is **Access Transparency**. Access Transparency provides logs based on the actions taken by Google staff when accessing your Google Cloud content. Access Transparency logs can help you track the compliance posture of your organization with regard to your legal and regulatory requirements. We covered Access Transparency in depth in *Chapter 3, Trust and Compliance*.

User logs

As mentioned earlier, user logs, sometimes referred to as user-written logs, are written to Cloud Logging using an agent, the Cloud Logging API, or client libraries. Let's take a look at the user-agent-based log type:

- **Cloud Logging agent**: An agent can be installed to stream logs from instances to Cloud Logging. The Cloud Logging agent is based on Fluentd and is preconfigured by default to send syslogd logs and common third-party tools' logs (for example, MySQL, PostgreSQL, MongoDB, Cassandra, and Apache). It is possible to customize the pre-configured Fluentd agent configurations as required.

Platform logs

Next, we will look at examples of platform logs:

- **VPC flow logs**: VPC flow logs contain granular VM flow-level network telemetry from Google Cloud. VPC flow logs provide insights into VPC traffic and can help with performance, traffic planning, a better understanding of networking costs, and forensics in the case of security-related incidents. VPC flow logs are aggregated collections of packets for a given interval and for a given connection. These logs are by default retained for 30 days and they do not lead to any performance degradation. The VPC flow log format includes a 5-tuple—for the source IP address, destination IP address, source port number, destination port number, and protocol (TCP or UDP)—and the timestamp. The metrics include packets, bytes (throughput), RTT for TCP flows, VPC annotations (region, zone, and VM name), and geographic annotations (country, region, and city). Logs are collected on each VM connection and aggregated at 5-second intervals. Google samples about one out of every 10 packets.

- **Firewall logs**: You can enable firewall rule logging individually for each firewall rule. Firewall rule logging only records TCP and UDP connections. Log entries are written from the perspective of VM instances.

- **NAT logs**: You can enable NAT logging on a NAT gateway instance. You can choose to generate logs for the creation of NAT connections and when packets are dropped because no port was available for NAT. Cloud NAT logs both TCP and UDP, including dropped egress packets. Dropped ingress packets (for example, if an inbound reply to an egress request was dropped) are not logged.

We have covered the different types of logs and their relevant examples. We will now consider the retention of logs. Defining a retention period gives you the ability to change the log period to match your compliance or regulatory requirement. Let's take a look at some of the key log types and their associated log retention periods in the following section.

Log retention

Cloud Logging retention is critical for many organizations due to compliance requirements. The default retention period is often not sufficient; therefore, many customers configure custom retention periods for their logs. Longer retention periods come at a higher cost.

	Retention	Cost
Admin Activity audit logs	13 months (400 days)	Free
System Event audit logs	13 months (400 days)	Free
Access Transparency logs	13 months (400 days)	Free
Data Access audit logs	30 days	$0.50 per GB over 50GB/Month
All other logs	30 days	$0.50 per GB over 50GB/Month
Workspace admin console logs	6 months	Free
Log sink	Indefinite	Based on service option (GCS, BQ, Pub/Sub)

Figure 12.4 – Cloud Logging default retention periods and costs

Figure 12.4 shows the default retention periods and the associated costs for the different types of logs that we have covered. The costs are correct at the time of writing and may change.

Next, we'll explore the topic of log management. We will learn about log producers and consumers and understand how a log router works. We will also discuss exporting logs and creating log sinks in detail.

Log management

A key component of logging is the ability to export logs so they can be consumed by a service running on the cloud or by a third-party solution. You will also learn how to aggregate logs, build log pipelines, perform log analysis, and deliver logs to SIEM solutions.

Log producers

All resources that generate logs, such as products, services, and applications, whether they are in the cloud or a hybrid environment, are classified as log producers. These could be Google Cloud services or services running in your on-premises data center or a third-party cloud service provider.

Log consumers

Log consumers are services such as centralized logging solutions and SIEM solutions. Any service that has the ability to consume logs and provide functions such as alerting, troubleshooting applications, and business intelligence is considered a log consumer. Cloud Logging on Google Cloud is an example of such a service.

Log Router

The term Log Router has been used a few times in the chapter; we will now look at the workings of the Log Router in more detail to understand what it is and how it works. A Log Router ensures that logs are collected from producers and delivered to the consumer.

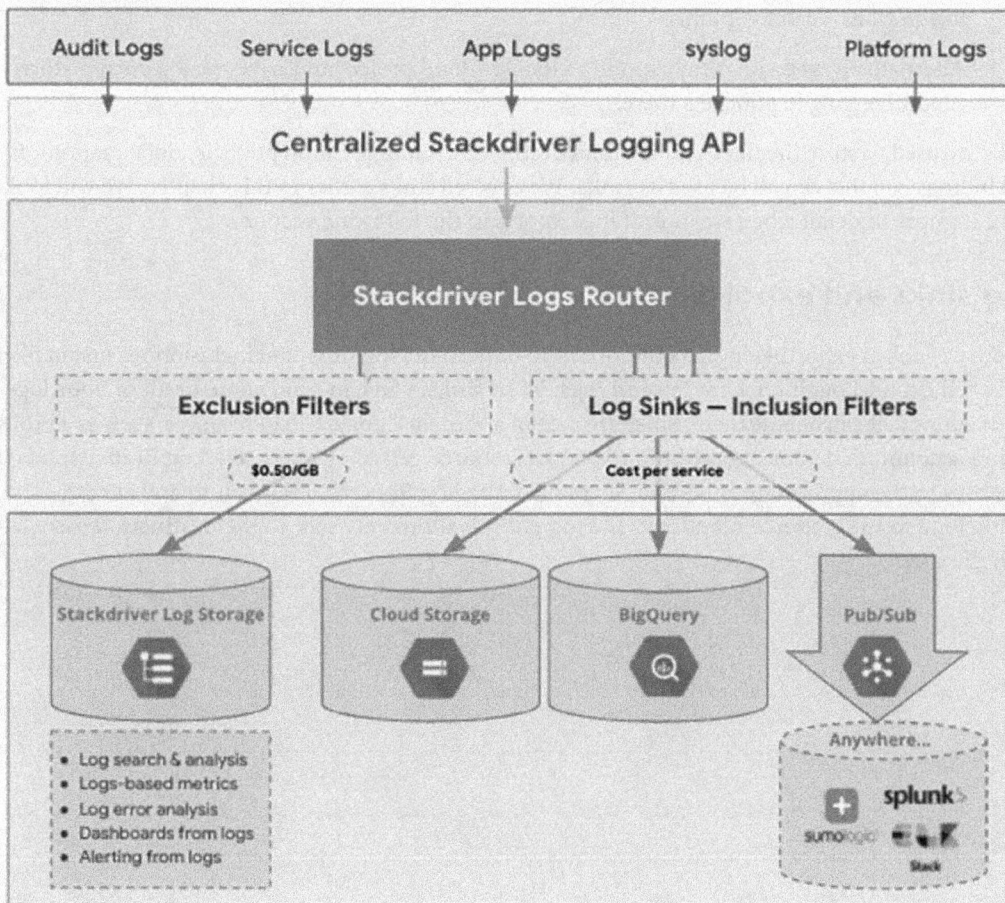

Figure 12.5 – Log Router

Figure 12.5 shows how a Log Router works. Logs are transmitted to the Cloud Logging API, where they are processed by the Log Router. These logs include audit logs, platform logs, and user-written logs. The Log Router compares each log entry to the rules that are already in place to determine which log entries should be ingested and stored, which log entries should be included in exports, and which log entries should be discarded.

To export logs, create a filter that selects the relevant log entries to export, and then select a destination. You can choose from these options:

- JSON files can be stored in Google Cloud Storage buckets.

- Tables can be created in BigQuery datasets.

- JSON messages can also be delivered via Pub/Sub topics. This option also supports third-party integrations, such as Splunk.

  Alternatively, you can create another Google Cloud project and have the log entries stored in Cloud Logging log buckets there.

Sinks are used to store the filter and the final destination. Google Cloud projects, organizations, files, and billing accounts can all be used as sinks. We covered sinks earlier in this chapter. We will look at them in more in detail when we look at log exports in the following section.

Log sinks and exports

Before we look at exporting logs, it's important to understand log sinks and inclusion/exclusion filters. Sinks tell Cloud Logging where to send logs. With sinks, you can send some or all of your logs to destinations that can handle them. Sinks are part of a specific Google Cloud resource, such as a project, billing account, folder, or organization. When a resource gets a log entry, the Log Router sends the log entry to the appropriate sinks and, if enabled, the Log Router forwards it to any ancestral sinks that belong to the resource hierarchy. The log entry is ultimately sent to the destination associated with the sink.

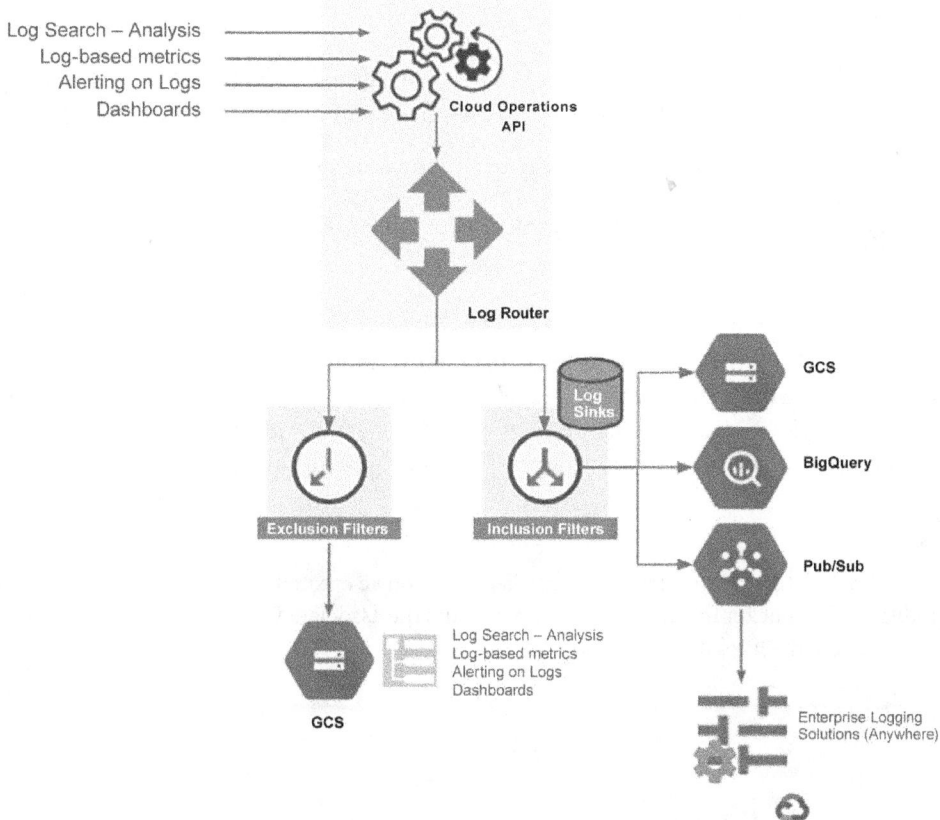

Figure 12.6 – Log exports and sinks

Figure 12.6 shows the relationships between sinks, filters, and exports. By defining one or more sinks that have a log query and an export destination, you can easily export logs from a database. New log entries are compared to each sink as they are received by Cloud Logging. When an entry matches a sink's filter, the entry is written to the sink's destination.

If no filters are attached to a sink, all logs will match and be forwarded to their final destination. The inclusion filter can be used to choose specific logs for the sink. Alternatively, you can use exclusion filters to keep unwanted logs out of the sink altogether. Filters are defined using the Logging query language.

Log buckets are containers used by Cloud Logging to store and organize log data in your Google Cloud projects, billing accounts, folders, and groups. Using Cloud Logging, you can study your logs in real time by having them indexed, optimized, and provided to you. Cloud Logging buckets are distinct from Cloud Storage buckets, despite the similarity of their names. Log buckets should be considered a local resource. You can pinpoint the location of the servers and storage facilities that handle your logs.

Next, we will look at the steps for how to create a log export.

Creating a log export

In this section, you will learn how to create a log export sink. You will build a centralized logging solution by creating log buckets that are bound to specified regions with retention policies.

You can create 100 log buckets per project. Follow these steps to create user-defined log buckets:

1. From the **Logging** menu, select **Logs Storage**.

2. Click **Create Logs Bucket**.

3. Fill out **Name** and **Description** for your bucket.

4. (*Optional*) To set the region in which you want your logs to be stored, click the **Select log bucket region** drop-down menu and select a region. If you don't select a region, the global region is used, which means that the logs could be physically located in any of the regions. In our demonstration, in *Figure 12.6*, we have used a region in Australia.

> **Note**
>
> You can't change the region of your log bucket once you've created it. You can, however, create an additional log bucket in a different region, reroute the associated sinks to the new log bucket, and then delete the log bucket.

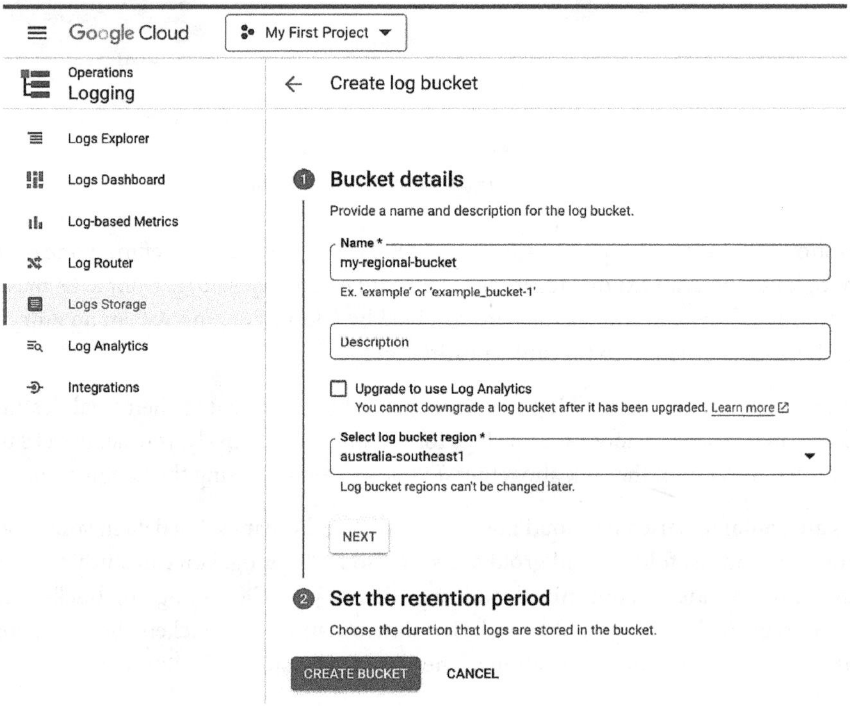

Figure 12.7 – Create log bucket

Figure 12.7 shows how to configure a log bucket. Once you have specified the name of the bucket as per the naming convention, you can then either set the bucket region to global or select the region of your choice.

5. (*Optional*) To set a custom retention period for the logs in the bucket, click **NEXT**.

6. In the **Retention period** field, enter the number of days that you want Cloud Logging to retain your logs. Google Cloud lets you define that period in seconds, days, and years, with a maximum period of retention of 100 years. If you don't customize the retention period, the default is **30** days. In *Figure 12.8*, we have kept the retention period set to its default value. You can also update your bucket to apply custom retention after you create it. Keep in mind that longer retention periods will result in higher charges.

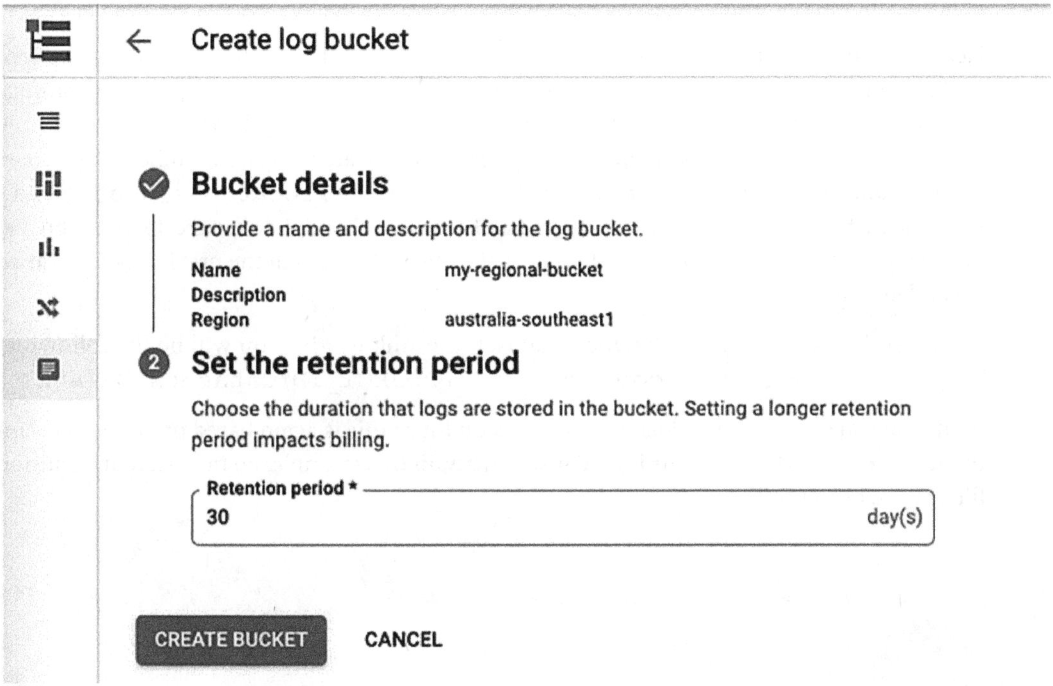

Figure 12.8 – Set the retention period for the log bucket

7. Click **CREATE BUCKET**. Your new bucket will appear in the **Log bucket** list.

You can also lock the bucket. When you stop updates to a bucket, you also stop updates to the bucket's retention policy. After you lock a retention policy, you can't delete a bucket until every log in it has been kept for as long as the policy dictates.

Next, we will cover the steps on how to create a log sink:

1. In the Cloud console, go to the Log Router, and select the Cloud project where you want to create the log sink.

2. Next, from the top left, select the **CREATE SINK** button and you will be presented with options as per *Figure 12.9*.

3. Here you can specify the details of the log sink, such as the sink name and its description; the name used in the example is `my-log-sink`.

4. Next, you can specify the destination where you want logs to be stored. There are different options available here, and based on your requirements, you can either select Google Cloud Storage (as per the example), create a new dataset in BigQuery or an existing dataset, specify Pub/Sub, or use **Splunk integration** as an option. In the example, we are using a Cloud Logging bucket, and the name of the bucket is `projects/Project_name/locations/australia-southeast1/buckets/my-regional-bucket`. You can either create a new bucket or use one that's already been created, such as the one we created in the previous step with an Australian region.

    If your sink destination is a BigQuery dataset, the sink destination will be the following: `bigquery.googleapis.com/projects/PROJECT_ID/datasets/DATASET_`.

5. Next, you can specify the inclusion and exclusion filter; this is again based on what you want to include or exclude from your logs. For simplicity, in this example, no inclusion or exclusion filters have been used.

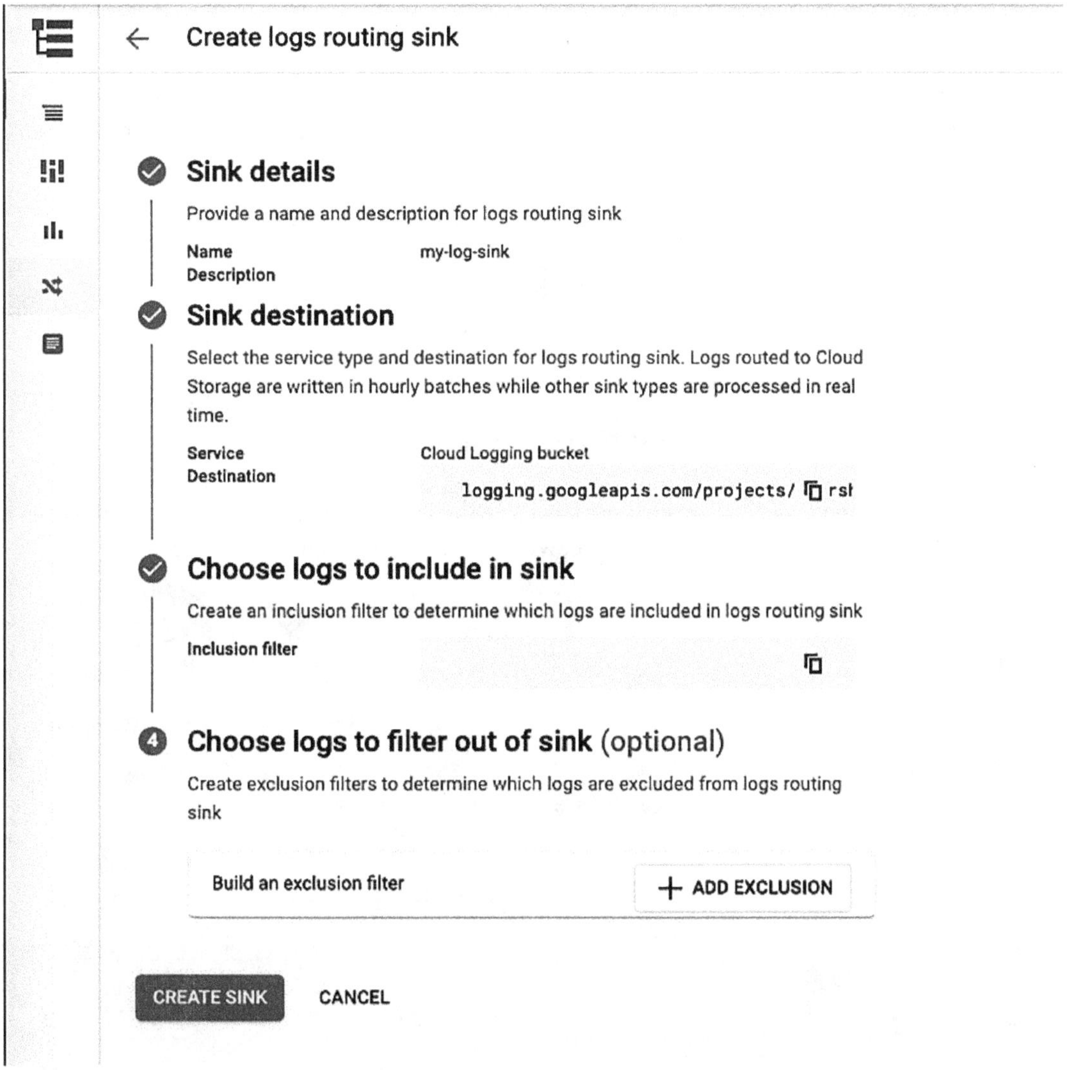

Figure 12.9 – Create a log sink

6. In *Figure 12.9*, we created a log sink named my-log-sink and selected the sink destination, its associated project, and geographical location, for example, starbase155 and australia-southeast1, respectively. If you are routing logs between Google Cloud projects, you will need the appropriate destination permissions.

7. Finally, when all options are completed, click **CREATE SINK**.

Here we learned how to create an export and a log sink to send logs to the destination of your choice. Next, we will look at archiving and aggregating logs.

Log archiving and aggregation

The process of archiving logs is like the process outlined in the previous section. You create a log sink, specify the inclusion and exclusion criteria, and choose the Google Cloud Storage bucket as the destination.

Figure 12.10 – Log archiving pipeline

Figure 12.10 shows an illustration of what the log archiving pipeline looks like. You collect the events using Cloud Logging and then create a log sink with Cloud Storage as the destination.

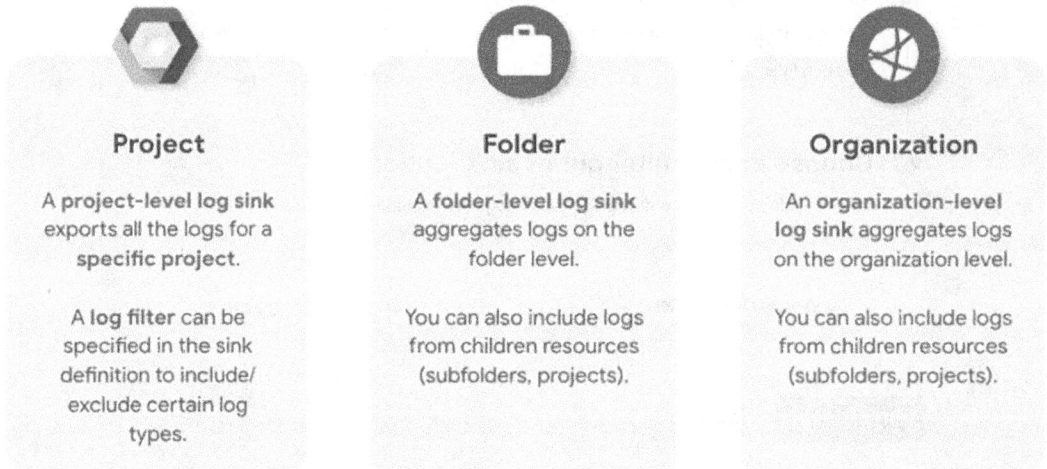

Project	Folder	Organization
A project-level log sink exports all the logs for a specific project.	A folder-level log sink aggregates logs on the folder level.	An organization-level log sink aggregates logs on the organization level.
A log filter can be specified in the sink definition to include/exclude certain log types.	You can also include logs from children resources (subfolders, projects).	You can also include logs from children resources (subfolders, projects).

Figure 12.11 – Log aggregation

Log centralization is a typical requirement for auditing, archiving, and ensuring the non-repudiation of data and is considered a best practice. In order to achieve it, it is possible to configure aggregate exports at the organization level. This ensures that all logs on all projects (new and existing) in the organization are exported to a central location. *Figure 12.11* shows how you can configure log aggregation based on your requirements. You can aggregate logs at the project, folder, or organization level.

Real-time log analysis and streaming

As mentioned earlier, Cloud Logging is a collection of different components. We have the Cloud Logging API, where all the logs are delivered. We also have the Log Router, where you can create your inclusion and exclusion filter and redirect the logs to a log sink. We also looked at several storage choices for logs after they've been removed from a log sink. With Google Cloud Storage, you can store the logs and apply lifecycle management rules to them based on your retention policy. If you wish to analyze the collected logs, you can do so with BigQuery.

In this section, we will look at storing logs in BigQuery for analytics. At the time of writing, there is a built-in feature that Google Cloud has called Log Analytics. As this feature is still in preview, it will not feature in the exam. In addition to Log Analytics, you can also create a pipeline that streams logs to BigQuery.

Figure 12.12 – Log streaming pipeline

Figure 12.12 illustrates a log streaming pipeline using Cloud Logging, Pub/Sub, and a DataFlow pipeline that triggers a Cloud **Data Loss Prevention** (**DLP**) template. DLP inspects sensitive data such as **personally identifiable information** (**PII**) to remove sensitive data before storing it for analytics in BigQuery. In our example, we're exporting through Pub/Sub, then through Dataflow, and lastly to BigQuery. Dataflow is very useful for processing logs in real time and at scale. However, we don't need to stream logs; we can simply create a log sink and deliver logs to BigQuery.

BigQuery enables you to store data in a secure and cost-effective manner. Its easy-to-use SQL interface can provide a solid foundation for creating AI data models and simplifying data operations. Data Studio and Looker are two tools that can be used to visualize BigQuery results. Visualization is out of scope for our discussion. BigQuery offers an easy-to-use and powerful capability to run queries to help you with analytics that you can use for troubleshooting and security incident response. In the next section, we will discuss an example of exporting logs to address compliance requirements. We will also cover the configuration aspects of the log pipeline discussed here.

The Logs Dashboard displays the severity and error data for the resources in your Cloud project. The Logs Dashboard allows you to spot patterns in your systems' activity, keep track of your workloads, and diagnose and address issues. All the log-based metrics are preconfigured and cannot be modified. The Logs Dashboard only shows statistics for resources that generate log data.

You can also use Logs Explorer to analyze logs. With Logs Explorer, you can run queries using the Logging query language based on your criteria, which can include logical operations such as AND and OR on the resource type.

Log Analytics can reduce the need to send logs to different systems to address separate use cases. We will briefly cover three common use cases. The first is for DevOps, where resolving issues quickly is critical to maintaining reliability. Log Analytics can help uncover patterns and correlate data across services. Faster troubleshooting can also help improve the speed of software development by reducing the time spent on debugging.

The second is for security. Investigations are a critical part of understanding and remediating security threats. Log Analytics can identify logs across large time ranges, which often means large data volumes.

The third is for IT operations, where managing a fleet of different services is a core part of IT operations. It's important to understand the events and trends across the whole fleet. Log Analytics can help identify patterns and fleet performance over time.

There are many other ways that Log Analytics helps enable business decisions, including analyzing business data reported in the logs. By unlocking valuable insights, Log Analytics brings new value to your logs.

We have covered Log Analytics and how you can use BigQuery and third-party applications for analytics. The next section will cover how to meet your compliance and regulatory requirements using log exports.

Exporting logs for compliance

In this section, we will look at exporting logs to meet compliance requirements. Configuring log exports is an important topic in the exam. There are some advanced export configurations that you can practice, such as exporting logs for security and analytics and configuring logs to go to Elastic or Splunk when you are using a third-party SIEM tool.

In this example, we will export logs to a Cloud Storage bucket. We will then look at how to limit access to the logs. Logs can be moved to Nearline or Coldline storage classes and then deleted using Cloud Storage's object lifecycle management capability.

There are five steps to the configuration of log exports:

1. First, we will begin the setup by creating a logging export bucket in Cloud Storage.

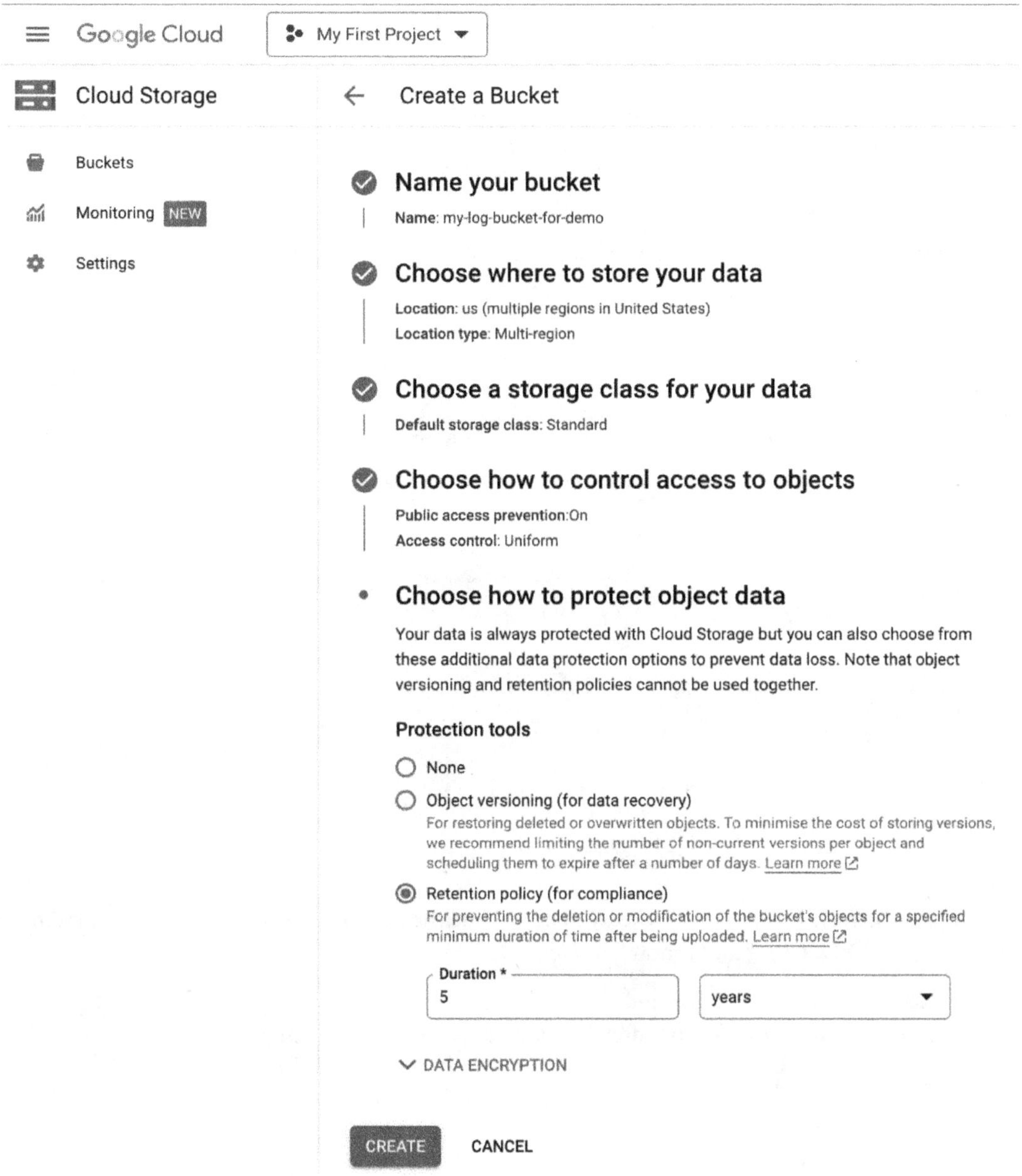

Figure 12.13 – Create a Cloud Storage bucket for logs

In this step, we create a storage bucket and specify the details based on our requirements. Refer to *Figure 12.13*, where we have selected a globally unique name: my-log-bucket-for-demo.

2. Next, you can specify the location, which can be **Regional** or **Multi-region**, based on your requirements.

3. We then set **Default storage class**, select **Uniform** access control, and finally set **Retention policy (best for compliance)**, which is the best option for compliance when storing logs. You can specify a log retention period in seconds, days, hours, months, or years. In our example, we set it to 5 years.

4. Next, we configure object lifecycle management for the Cloud Storage bucket.

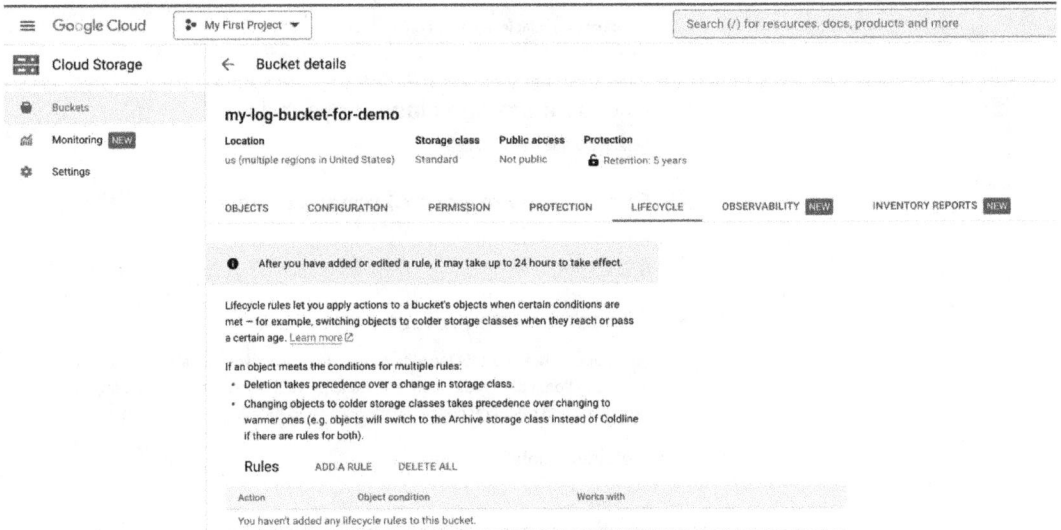

Figure 12.14 – The LIFECYCLE tab

Once you have created the bucket, you can define the object lifecycle rule. You can then move to the **LIFECYCLE** tab, as shown in *Figure 12.14*.

5. Next, click on **ADD A RULE** and specify your policy. We will add two rules: after 60 days, move logs to **Nearline storage**, and after 120 days, move logs to **Coldline storage**.

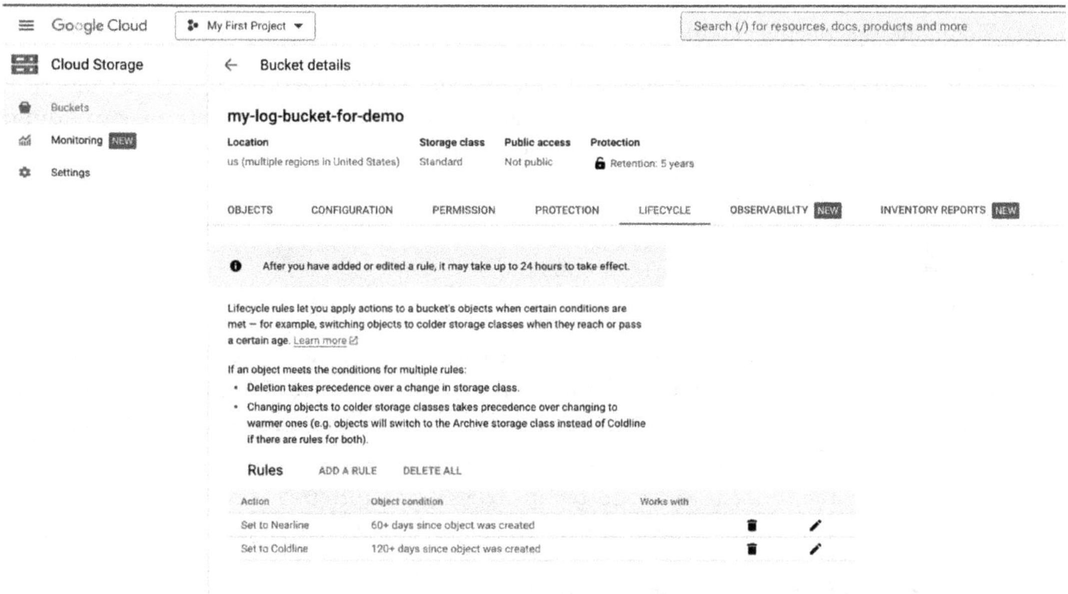

Figure 12.15 – Add a rule for lifecycle management

Figure 12.15 illustrates what your rules look like once you have defined the criteria.

6. Turn on audit logging for all Google Cloud services.

    Using the following, you can turn on audit logging for all your services:

```
"auditConfigs": [
    {
        "service": "allServices",
        "auditLogConfigs": [
            { "logType": "ADMIN_READ" },
            { "logType": "DATA_READ"  },
            { "logType": "DATA_WRITE" },
        ]
    },
]
```

7. Configure the logging export.

Next, we'll create aggregated exports and fine-tune the logging filters to export audit logs, data about virtual machines, data about storage, and data about databases. There are also Admin Activity and Data Access logs, as well as logs for certain types of resources:

```
logName:"/logs/cloudaudit.googleapis.com" OR
resource.type:gce OR
resource.type=gcs_bucket OR
resource.type=cloudsql_database OR
resource.type=bigquery_resource
```

You can create a sink either using the Google Cloud CLI or the Cloud console. We looked earlier at the Console option to configure a sink and the respective filters. Now we will look at the Google Cloud CLI version to demonstrate how you can create a sink and the filters:

```
gcloud logging sinks create gcp_logging_sink_gcs \
    storage.googleapis.com/gcp-logging-export-000100011000 \
    --log-filter='logName: "/logs/cloudaudit.googleapis.com" OR
\
    resource.type:\"gce\" OR \
    resource.type=\"gcs_bucket\" OR    \
    resource.type=\"cloudsql_database\" OR   \
    resource.type=\"bigquery_resource\"' \
    --include-children    \
    --organization=324989855333
```

8. Set up an IAM policy and permissions for the bucket.

Now we will add a service account to the logging export bucket with storage object creator permissions:

- In the Cloud console, open **Buckets**.

- Select the **my-log-bucket-for-demo** bucket.

- Click **Show info panel**, and then select the **Storage Object Creator** permissions.

You have now successfully created a log export using a Google Cloud Storage bucket with object lifecycle rules based on your compliance requirements.

Log compliance

Log compliance is an important topic, and we are going to briefly discuss it here as it is also relevant to the certification exam. It is important to make sure logs are centrally located, secure, and can only be accessed by the right resources (by applying the principle of least privilege). Log compliance is critical for customers who are regulated. Here are some ways to achieve log compliance.

Separation of duties:

- Use aggregated exports to a different project that is owned by a different team
- Cloud Storage is recommended for log archival

Least privilege:

- Grant the minimum required permissions on a project, so users cannot remove the logs
- Enforce the Bucket Policy Only feature (effectively disabling object-level permissions)

Non-repudiation:

- In the case of Cloud Storage, configure Bucket Lock to ensure the retention of objects within the bucket. This prevents deletion of the bucket or underlying objects by anyone until all objects have reached the end of their retention period.
- Additionally, enable object versioning on the bucket.

Google Cloud provides a comprehensive set of solutions to ensure your organization's logs are secured, monitored, and compliant with industry regulations.

Logging and auditing best practices

In this last section, we will cover some logging and auditing best practices. From an exam perspective, you are not really tested with questions on these practices, but you may find indirect references to them. Since Data Access audit logs are not enabled by default, it's important that you review and enable Data Access audit logs for relevant services.

> **Note**
> You can find more details on how to enable these logs at `https://packt.link/w0ZWY`.

Let's look at some best practices for logging and auditing:

- Ensure that you specify the correct log storage destination—Google Cloud Storage for archival and retention and BigQuery for analytics and forensics
- Configure appropriate permissions for the access of your logs
- Ensure that sensitive data is stripped from the logs before they are stored
- Periodically review your audit logs that are stored in Cloud Logging, BigQuery, or your third-party SIEM solutions

As the volume of logs grows over time, managing them well and having appropriate controls is required early on. Logs play a key role in incident response and meeting regulatory requirements. Therefore, it is essential to demonstrate these best practices as you build your logging and auditing capabilities.

Summary

In this chapter, we looked at the different categories of logs and what types of logs are available in each of those categories. We also looked at key properties of the different types of logs, such as whether they are enabled by default and the default retention period associated with each category. We also looked at the key components of Cloud Logging, such as the Cloud Logging API, the Log Router, log producers, and log consumers. Then, we looked at how to create log exports, how to specify the filters on what you want to exclude or include, and the different destinations that are available to store your logs. We covered the use of logging pipelines for analytics and storage. Finally, we looked at how to address compliance needs through logging and discussed best practices for logging and auditing.

In the next chapter, we will learn about Cloud Monitoring. That chapter will build on top of the knowledge gained in this one and introduce the topics of log-based metrics and alerting policies.

Further reading

For more information on logging, refer to the following links:

- Design patterns for exporting Cloud Logging data: `https://packt.link/glqqx`
- Logging, Monitoring, and Observability in Google Cloud: `https://packt.link/1EnJt`
- Exporting Cloud Logging data for security and analytics: `https://packt.link/mF2Tg`
- Exporting Cloud Logging data to Elasticsearch: `https://packt.link/dvg2g`
- Exporting logging data to Splunk: `https://packt.link/t9ipu`
- Using BigQuery and Cloud Logging to analyze BigQuery usage: `https://packt.link/tmCSd`
- Monitor and Log with Google Cloud Operations Suite: `https://packt.link/0v0dh`

13

Image Hardening and CI/CD Security

In this chapter, we will look at Google's approach to Compute Engine image hardening and DevOps pipeline security. One of the most critical issues facing industries today is software supply chain attacks. To address this matter in the cloud, we need to be able to build secure infrastructure, monitor operations, and fix vulnerabilities. This is a very broad topic. We will only cover the topics required for the exam in this chapter.

In this chapter, we will cover the following topics:

- Overview of image management
- Custom images for Compute Engine
- Image management pipeline
- Controlling access to images
- Image lifecycle
- Enforcing lifecycle policies
- Secure CI/CD pipeline
- Best practices for a CI/CD pipeline
- Shielded VMs
- Confidential computing

Overview of image management

A Google Compute Engine image is a pre-configured **virtual machine** (**VM**) image that can be used to quickly deploy applications and services to Google Compute Engine. An image includes the operating system, configuration settings, and any other software required for the application or service to run. Securing a Google Compute Engine image is important to be able to prevent unauthorized users and malicious software from accessing applications and services. This can be done by setting up strong access control measures with **identity and Access Management** (**IAM**) tools, creating secure user accounts, and using encryption and authentication measures. Regularly updating the image with the latest security patches and using intrusion detection and prevention systems can also help protect the image from potential security threats. Let's understand the concept of image management used for hardening a Compute Engine image.

An image in Compute Engine refers to an immutable disk image. This is not to be confused with a container or Docker image. We will cover container image security in *Chapter 15, Container Security*. The disk image is used to create a VM. Let's take a look at *Figure 13.1*.

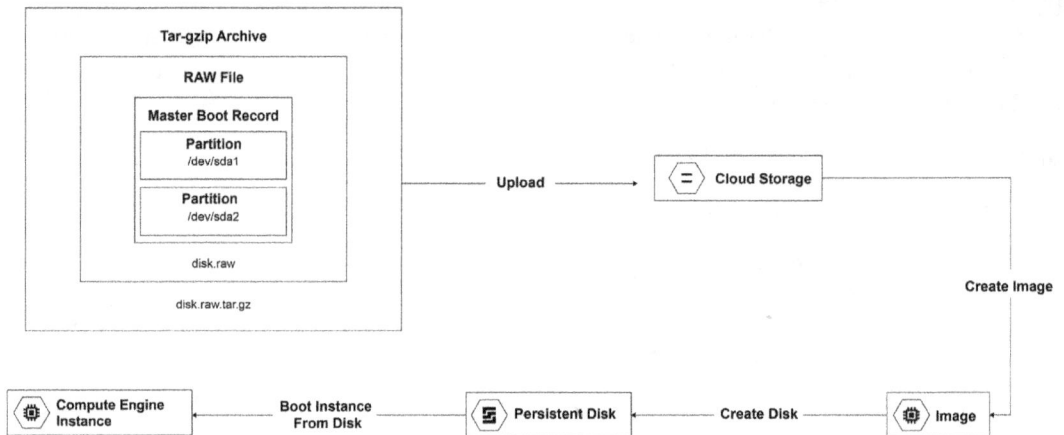

Figure 13.1 – A pipeline for creating a VM image

A machine image includes all of the configuration, metadata, permissions, and data from multiple disks of a VM instance. This information may be retrieved quickly and easily. Performing system maintenance, creating backups and recoveries, and cloning instances are just some of the many uses for machine images.

The following data from the source instance is captured by a machine image:

- Type of machine
- Metadata of instance

- Labels

- Network tags

- Preventative maintenance plan

- Volume mapping

- Hard drive information that persists across reboots

- Where relevant, **Unified Extensible Firmware Interface** (**UEFI**) settings

- A machine image does not capture data in memory and in the local SSD. However, local SSD device mapping and information about the original instance, such as its name or IP address, can be captured.

There are two types of image options available within the Google Cloud environment:

- **Public images**: Google, some open source groups, or third-party businesses produce and maintain these images. These images are accessible to all Google projects; no further IAM permissions are required. These can be downloaded for free. Some of the images are premium, for which you must pay. A list of public and premium images can be found in the Google Cloud documentation.

- **Custom images**: These are your images, and they are only accessible through the cloud project in which you created them. By granting appropriate IAM permissions, you can share these with other cloud projects. These incur a cloud storage fee, but there is no usage fee in Compute Engine.

Let's next explore more details about custom images and the options available, both manual and automated, to bake images.

Custom images for Google Compute Engine

It is possible to customize your Compute Engine instance by way of a startup script, which allows you to install the necessary software components and harden the image. An efficient method is to create a custom image with your specific needs of security configurations and image standards. There are three ways you can customize an image. The process of customization is generally referred to as image baking:

- Manual baking

- Automated baking

- Import an existing image

The images needs to be encrypted and that can be achieved either by using Google's default encryption keys or by using your own encryptions keys (customer-managed encryption keys).

Changing or baking images offers the following benefits:

- Shorter boot time for applications to be ready

- A more stable environment for applications to be installed

- Easier to go back to older versions of the image

- During application startup, there are fewer external services that need to be used

- Scaling up compute instances that have identical software versions

Manual baking

When you start the process of establishing a new VM instance from a public image, you will have the opportunity to generate a custom image for that instance. You are then able to customize the newly created instance with the applications and settings of your choosing once the new instance has been created. After you have finished configuring those features, you will be able to create a custom image based on that instance.

Automated baking

If you only have a few images that need to be managed, manual baking is an easy method to get started. If you have many custom images, however, employing the manual technique of management becomes more challenging and difficult to audit. HashiCorp Packer is a free and open source program that makes the process of creating images reproducible, auditable, and configurable.

To learn more about creating an automated image-creation pipeline, visit the link provided in the *Further reading* section. It explains how to use Jenkins, Packer, and Kubernetes to build images. You can also use Packer as part of a Spinnaker pipeline to generate images.

Importing existing images

You can migrate images by exporting them from your existing cloud infrastructure and moving them to Google Cloud Compute Engine. Another way to get your old images onto your new computer is to use Google Cloud Migrate for Compute Engine.

Migrate for Compute Engine is a suite of tools and a service that streamlines the process of migrating machines from one platform to another with minimal disruption. This is made possible via continuous replication at the block level. Creating images can be done by manually baking on Compute Engine after migrating your VMs there.

Encrypting images

By default, Google's encryption keys are used to encrypt all Compute Engine disks. Disk images are likewise encrypted during creation. You also have the option of using your own encryption keys throughout the disk creation process. If you want to produce an encrypted image after you've made the disk, you'll need to supply the relevant command with the encryption keys. **Encryption at rest** in the Google Cloud documentation has more details about using customer-supplied encryption keys. Images that are made from disks are also protected by encryption. Alternatively, you can provide your own encryption keys when you create the disks. Then, after you create the disk, you can create an encrypted image by giving the image command the encryption keys you want.

Please refer to the encryption at rest documentation link in the *Further reading* section. This document provides an overview of encryption at rest features available in Google Cloud. It explains why encryption is important, how it works, and what tools are available to make encryption easier to manage.

Image management pipeline

In this section, we will look at the process of creating an image management pipeline. The process involves a few procedures, and we will look at the high-level steps, including prerequisites that you need to meet before you build your image factory. Let's now look at the steps:

1. Create a strategy for managing image lifecycles, such as golden image promotion, versioning, deprecation, and deletion.

2. Bake a golden image, and use an automated compliance check, such as Chef InSpec.

3. Ensure that an organization policy is in place to limit the compute images available to individuals working on specific projects.

You will also need to meet a couple of prerequisites:

*   Ensure you have a Google Cloud account.

*   You either need to have Project Editor access for an existing project, or you need organization permissions to be able to create a new project under the organization.

The process of creating an image is quite similar to the process of creating source code. You will have access to a repository that stores the base image as well as the templates that you will need to construct an image build. The following is a tutorial that will walk you through the process of building an image.

Creating a VM image using Packer and Cloud Build

In this section, we will go over how to create a Google Cloud VM image using HashiCorp Packer. This process will allow you to set up automation. We will go over the process and how the pieces fit together. You do not need to use Cloud Build or third-party products such as Packer for the exam, but it is important to know how to create an automated VM image pipeline.

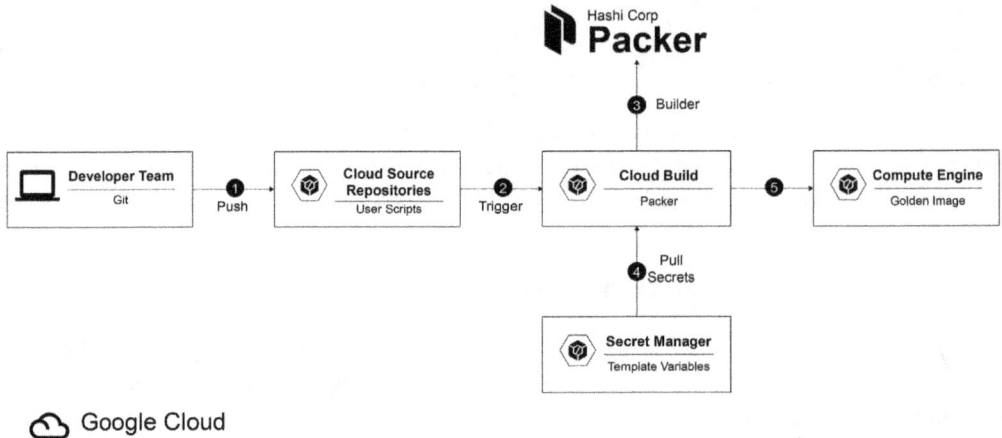

Figure 13.2 – VM image creation using Packer

Let us analyze the components of the architecture seen in *Figure 13.2*, and then outline the steps required to build an automated image factory with Packer. Prior to starting, it is important to have an understanding of Packer. The exam does not include Packer, yet these steps are included to explain the automated VM image creation process.

Before you begin, there are the following prerequisites:

- A Google Cloud account
- A Packer template
- The Packer binary
- The Google Cloud SDK

Step 1: Creating an infrastructure for the image creation

First, you need to create an infrastructure for the image creation, and for that, we need to follow these steps:

1. Create a Compute Engine instance to use as a builder.
2. Create a Cloud Storage bucket to store the image.
3. Create a service account with the necessary permissions.

Step 2: Creating the Packer template

Now that your infrastructure is in place, you can create the Packer template. The Packer template is a JSON file that defines the configuration of your image. It should include the following information:

- Builder type: `googlecompute`
- Source image
- Zone
- Machine type
- Boot commands
- Post-processing

Here is an example of a JSON Packer template:

```
{
    "variables": {
        "project": "{{ env `GCE_PROJECT` }}",
        "zone": "{{ env `GCE_ZONE` }}",
        "machine_type": "{{ env `GCE_MACHINE_TYPE` }}",
        "disk_image_name": "{{ env `GCE_DISK_IMAGE_NAME` }}",
        "disk_image_project": "{{ env `GCE_DISK_IMAGE_PROJECT` }}"
    },
    "builders": [
        {
            "type": "googlecompute",
            "project_id": "{{ user `project` }}",
            "source_image_family": "{{ user `disk_image_name` }}",
            "zone": "{{ user `zone` }}",
            "disk_size": "10",
            "disk_type": "pd-ssd",
            "image_family": "{{ user `disk_image_name` }}",
            "image_project": "{{ user `disk_image_project` }}",
```

```
            "machine_type": "{{ user `machine_type` }}"
        }
    ],
    "provisioners": [
        {
            "type": "shell",
            "script": "install.sh"
        }
    ]
}
```

The JSON Packer template is provided as an illustration only; the intent is to give a simplistic example. For an individual use case, you will need to modify a template or create a new template.

Step 3: Installing the Packer binary

Once you have the Packer template ready, you need to install the Packer binary. This is a command-line utility that you can use to create images with Packer. To install the Packer binary, follow these steps:

1. Download the Packer binary from the official download site.
2. Extract the binary and copy it to the preferred location.
3. Add the binary to your PATH environment variable.

Step 4: Creating the image

Once you have the Packer binary installed, you can use it to create the image. To do this, you need to run the following command:

```
packer build -var-file=<variable-file> <packer-template>
```

This command will use the Packer template and the variable file to create the image. Once the image is created, it will be stored in the Cloud Storage bucket you created in *Step 1*.

Step 5: Automating image creation with Cloud Build

The last step is to automate image creation with Cloud Build. Cloud Build is a managed build service on Google Cloud that can be used to automate your build process. To use Cloud Build to automate image creation, you need to create a build configuration file. The configuration file should specify the following information:

*   **Source repository**: The location of the Packer template and the variable file
*   **Steps**: The commands that Cloud Build should execute
*   **Trigger**: The events that will trigger the build process

Once you have the configuration file ready, you can upload it to Cloud Build and configure the triggers. After that, Cloud Build will take care of the image creation process and you will have a fully automated VM image creation pipeline.

Using this image factory, you can now automatically create new images from a Cloud Source repository every time a new tag is pushed to that repository.

> **Note**
>
> The full tutorial can be obtained from the Google Cloud community:
> `https://packt.link/qTlcv`. A corresponding tutorial can also be
> found on GitHub: `https://packt.link/02Rgp`.

Controlling access to the images

To split workloads, environments, and user access, you will usually need different Google Cloud projects. Although most cloud workloads do not require sharing between projects, images are an excellent choice for doing so. You can follow a consistent approach to distributing images with best practices for security, permission, package management, and operations pre-configured for the rest of the company by using a shared collection of images.

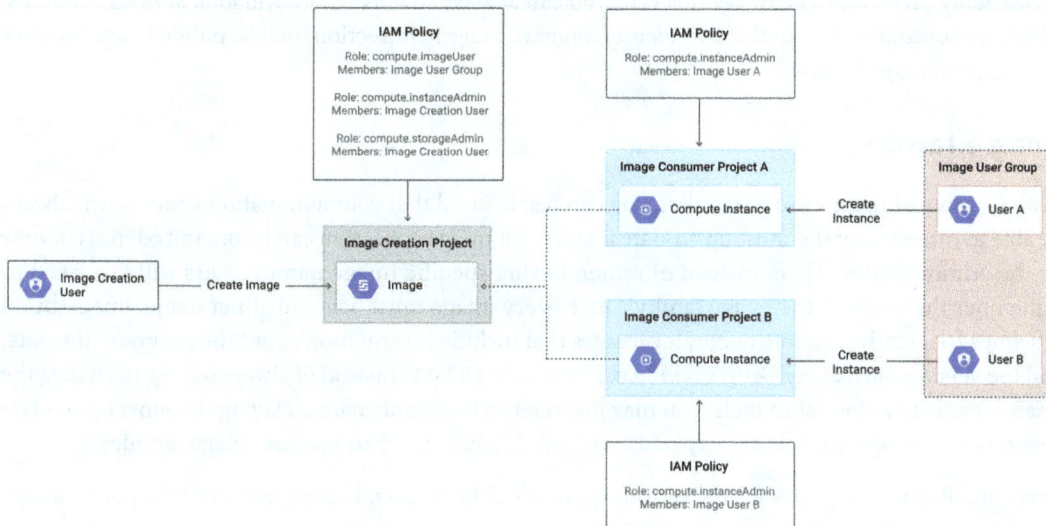

Figure 13.3 – Sharing images between projects

You can share images by giving different IAM roles to different projects inside an organization. **Image Creation Project**, represented in *Figure 13.3*, is the project that holds the images that you want to share with other projects, and it must have the following IAM roles and policies applied to it:

- Allow users of **Image User Group** to create instances from these images by granting them the `compute.imageUser` role

- Allow **Image Creation User** to create instances in this project by granting them the `compute.instanceAdmin` role

- Allow **Image Creation User** to create images and disks in this project by granting them the `compute.storageAdmin` role

In order for your projects to be able to use the shared images, you will need to ensure that users have access to the `compute.image` API. The `compute.imageUser` role allows other users to create instances by giving them the `compute.instanceAdmin` role.

Image lifecycle

After you've built up an image build pipeline, you'll need to keep the images up to date. While the pipeline creates the images, you must make sure that your deployment techniques use the most recent versions. You'll also need a method for curating images so that no outdated or obsolete images are accidentally used. With the image lifecycle, you can achieve that. Next, we will look at image families, which we covered earlier, in the *Overview of image management* section, that is, public image families and custom image families.

Image families

With Compute Engine's image families, you can rest assured that your automation systems will always be able to make use of the most up-to-date images. An image collection can be organized into a *family* by the administrator. Then, instead of remembering specific image names, users will just need to remember the name of the image family. Since every image must have a distinct name, image-build pipelines frequently generate names for images that include information about the program, the date, and the version, such as `my-application-v3-20210101`. Instead of always having to change the image's name in automation tools, you may just refer to the family name. Having the most up-to-date version of an image, such as `my-application`, is a breeze when you use image families.

There are distinct categories for the various types of public images. Every member of the public image family always links to the most up-to-date version of an image in their respective region. The zonal fault tolerance of your workflows is improved by the fact that newly released images are made available in image families at different times across different zones upon their initial global release.

Using a custom image family, you can create your own images. The image used to create the image family is linked to the most up-to-date version of that image. Deprecating the most up-to-date image in a family is one way to revert to an older version of the family's images (if the previous image is not deprecated).

You may more easily manage the images in your project with the assistance of image families, which help group images that are related together and allow you to roll ahead and back between specific image versions.

Deprecating an image

You also have the ability, as an administrator, to roll back the image to which the image family is pointing by deprecating the image and entering the following command:

```
gcloud compute images deprecate nginx-v3-20191019 --state DEPRECATED
```

The following table shows the various stages of deprecation you can choose from:

State	Description
DEPRECATED	Although the image is marked as DEPRECATED, it can still be used for creating a VM. However, new links to this image are not allowed. Additionally, image families no longer refer to this image, even if it is the most up-to-date image within the family.
OBSOLETE	The image has been deemed obsolete and is no longer available for use. Attempts to use this image in a request will result in an error message. Links to this image that already exist are still valid.
DELETED	If you try to use a deleted image, an error message will be returned.

Table 13.1 – States of image deprecation

We will now move on to the next section and look at how to enforce the lifecycle policies for your VM images.

Enforcing lifecycle policies

Lifecycle policies for VM images are necessary to ensure that images are updated regularly with the latest security patches and features. By enforcing lifecycle policies, organizations can ensure that their VMs remain secure and up to date, thereby reducing the risk of security breaches and other problems due to outdated software. Additionally, regular updates can help improve the performance and reliability of VMs, thus increasing their overall efficiency and cost-effectiveness.

Google Cloud VM lifecycle policies allow administrators to define a set of rules for how their VMs should be handled over time. These policies are important for ensuring that images are regularly updated, properly configured, and can be easily identified for deletion or obsolescence.

The most basic policy is the image deletion policy, which sets the time frame for when an image should be deleted. This helps to keep images up to date and avoid any potential security vulnerabilities caused by outdated images.

The image retirement policy allows administrators to set a time frame for when an image should be retired and no longer used. This helps to avoid any potential problems caused by outdated images. Additionally, administrators can use the image deprecation policy to mark images that they no longer use, allowing them to easily identify these images for deletion or obsolescence.

These policies are important for helping administrators to keep their VMs up to date and ensure that they can easily identify images for deletion or obsolescence.

Let's look at an example where you can mark an image for deletion or obsolescence; you can do so by using the following command:

```
gcloud compute images deprecate
```

You can also attach metadata to images to mark them for future deletion by providing one of the `--delete-in` or `--delete-on` flags.

To attach metadata to mark images for future obsolescence, provide the `--obsolete-in` or `--obsolete-on` flags.

You may also use this command as part of an image-build process to implement an image lifecycle policy that prevents your project from accumulating stale or expired images. You could, for example, implement an additional check for images that need to be deprecated or destroyed at the conclusion of your image-build process, and then conduct those actions directly.

While deprecated and deleted images are no longer visible through the API and UI by default, the `--show-deprecated` parameter allows you to see them. You must explicitly use the `delete` command for that image to entirely erase it and its data.

Securing a CI/CD pipeline

The Continuous Integration and Continuous Delivery (CI/CD) pipeline is a set of procedures that software developers follow in order to work on smaller chunks of code and increase overall productivity and efficiency. Its goal is to expose errors as early as possible in the process, allowing for faster failures. Developers typically activate CI processes by pushing code changes. Linting, testing, and building are all processes in the pipeline that validate the modifications. Typically, a CI pipeline produces an artifact that may be deployed later in the deployment process. The CI/CD pipeline is the DevOps processes' foundational infrastructure. It is critical to secure the CI/CD pipeline at every step to ensure that the applications, services, and data in the cloud are secure and protected. Securing your CI/CD pipeline helps to reduce the risk of malicious attacks, data breaches, and other security vulnerabilities. Additionally, it can help organizations to improve the overall efficiency of their cloud deployments by ensuring that only necessary code changes, configurations, and updates are applied.

CI/CD security

Securing your CI/CD pipeline is essential for ensuring the integrity, availability, and confidentiality of the application and its data. Without proper security controls in place, a pipeline can be vulnerable to malicious attacks, which can lead to data breaches and other security incidents. Implementing secure configuration guidelines, automating security testing, implementing role-based access controls, and monitoring and auditing logs are all important steps that can help protect the pipeline and its components. Let us look at some guidelines for incorporating security into CI/CD:

- Secure configuration guidelines should be established to ensure that security settings are properly configured and maintained across all components in the CI/CD pipeline. These guidelines should include requirements for authentication, authorization, encryption, logging, and other security-related settings.

- Automated security testing should be integrated into the CI/CD pipeline to detect and address security vulnerabilities. This can include static and dynamic analysis, penetration testing, and vulnerability scanning.

- Role-based access controls should be implemented to restrict access to the CI/CD pipeline and its components. This should include access control policies that define who can access and modify the pipeline and its components.

- Logs should be monitored and audited regularly to detect any suspicious activity. This includes monitoring access to and modification of the pipeline and its components, as well as any errors or exceptions that occur.

The primary focus in safeguarding a CI/CD pipeline should be to ensure that all potential security flaws are addressed at every step the code takes from inception to deployment.

CI/CD security threats

CI/CD are powerful tools for increasing the speed and efficiency of software development. However, as with any technology, there are security threats that must be taken into consideration when using these tools. These threats can range from unauthorized access to data leakage and malware injection. In addition, poorly configured CI/CD pipelines can introduce security risks, as can insufficient logging and monitoring, and inadequate change management. By understanding these threats and taking the appropriate steps to protect against them, organizations can ensure that their CI/CD processes remain secure and reliable. Here are a few examples:

- Unauthorized access to the CI/CD pipeline can lead to malicious code being injected and confidential information, such as credentials, being stolen.

- Without proper testing and security scanning, malicious code can be deployed and security threats can be introduced into the system.

- Without patching, vulnerabilities can be exploited to gain access to the system, leading to data loss and system disruption.

- Poor user access controls can lead to users being able to access more than they should, resulting in malicious code being injected or confidential information being stolen.

- Poorly configured CI/CD pipelines can lead to insecure code being deployed or private information being exposed.

- Data leakage can occur when sensitive information such as credentials, tokens, or passwords is exposed to unauthorized individuals.

- Malware can be injected into the system and can be used to steal confidential information or disrupt the system.

This is not an exhaustive list of CI/CD security concerns—there are certainly more—but the goal here is to identify a few key ones. Let's take a look at how you can further secure your CI/CD pipeline.

How to secure a CI/CD pipeline

Securing a CI/CD pipeline is essential to ensure the safety and reliability of code. Access control policies and encryption algorithms should be applied to the source code repository. Authentication and authorization mechanisms should be used to protect the delivery pipeline. Firewalls and network segmentation should be used to secure the infrastructure. Secure scripting and testing tools should be used to check for any malicious code. Logging and analytics tools should be used to monitor the whole pipeline. All these measures help to ensure that the CI/CD pipeline is secure and reliable.

Source Composition Analysis (SCA)

Source Composition Analysis (SCA) is a process used in CI/CD pipelines to assess the security posture of the source code used in development. SCA runs scans on the source code to identify vulnerabilities and security issues. SCA is often used to detect any malicious or unauthorized code that may have been introduced into the development process. SCA should be placed near the beginning of the CI/CD pipeline, ideally before the code is even checked in, in order to get an initial assessment of the security posture of the code before it is released to the public.

Static Application Security Testing (SAST)

Static Application Security Testing (SAST) is a process of analyzing the source code of an application for potential security vulnerabilities. It is typically done before the application is deployed, and it is the first step of the security testing process. It can detect security issues in the source code, such as missing input validation, hardcoded credentials, SQL injection, and cross-site scripting vulnerabilities.

SAST can be used to identify vulnerabilities in any application, regardless of the technology used or the development methodology.

SAST should be included in the CI/CD pipeline in order to ensure that vulnerabilities are discovered and addressed prior to the application being deployed. It should be done at the beginning of the pipeline, before any integration or deployment steps, and should be repeated after any code changes are made. This will ensure that any newly introduced vulnerabilities are identified and addressed before the application is made available to users.

CI/CD IAM controls

IAM controls are an essential part of ensuring the security of a CI/CD pipeline. They are responsible for protecting access to the systems and resources within the CI/CD pipeline, as well as providing secure authentication and authorization for users. IAM controls can be used to ensure that only authorized users have access to the necessary systems and resources to ensure a secure CI/CD pipeline. Additionally, IAM controls can help to ensure that only users with the correct permissions are able to make changes to the pipeline. By providing secure access control and authentication, IAM controls can help to reduce the risk of unauthorized access and malicious activity within the CI/CD pipeline.

To mitigate the risks posed by a lack of IAM controls in a CI/CD pipeline, it is important to ensure that all users and systems within the pipeline are adequately authenticated and authorized. This can be done by implementing strong access control and authentication measures, such as multi-factor authentication and role-based access control. Additionally, it is important to ensure that all users are assigned to the appropriate roles based on their access needs and that all access is regularly monitored and reviewed. Finally, it is important to ensure that all users are routinely trained on best practices for security and that all security policies are regularly updated and enforced.

Secrets management and CI/CD

Passwords and access keys are frequently required at many phases of the CI/CD process, such as when integrating or building code, deploying apps in testing or production, and so on.

Hardcoded secrets are easily accessible to anyone with access to configuration files or **Infrastructure as Code (IaC)** templates, posing a serious security concern.

A preferable method is to keep sensitive data in Google Cloud Secret Manager and communicate it as needed throughout CI/CD operations using variables.

Container registry scanning

Container registry scanning is an important part of the CI/CD pipeline security process. It is the process of scanning container images in a container registry to detect and prevent the introduction of any malicious code that could lead to a security breach. By scanning the container images and ensuring their integrity, organizations can ensure that only trusted images are deployed in their environment, helping to protect their application and infrastructure from malicious code injection.

Container registry scanning also enables organizations to detect and identify any vulnerabilities in the images, allowing them to take corrective action before any malicious code is deployed. In addition, it can help to detect any changes made to the images over time, allowing organizations to track the source of any changes and take appropriate action if necessary.

Container runtime security

The security of a container runtime is an essential element of a CI/CD pipeline. Containers are an efficient way to package and deploy applications and offer numerous advantages over traditional virtualization. Containers must be secured to protect applications from malicious actors, unauthorized access, and other security risks.

Container runtime security ensures that the container environment is secure and that any malicious code or malicious actors do not have access to the underlying host system. Container security also helps to ensure that applications are not exposed to a variety of potential threats, such as data breaches, denial-of-service attacks, and more. Furthermore, it also ensures that applications are running in an optimal environment, with all necessary security measures in place. By incorporating container runtime security into a CI/CD pipeline, organizations can maximize their security posture while also ensuring that applications are being deployed quickly and efficiently.

Establishing trust in CI/CD

Trust is when your business believes that someone or something is reliable, honest, able, or strong. You can keep track of both implicit and explicit trust. Both implicit and explicit trust have different weights in terms of confidence when they are talked about outside of the pipeline. Because implicit trust can't be checked, an artifact in a repository might or might not have been pushed through a security-aware CI/CD pipeline. If trust is explicitly conveyed, an audit trail can be made for each item that can be checked. This makes it possible to build trust outside of the pipeline environment.

An example of implicitly recorded trust is when a **quality assurance** (**QA**) team confirms the quality of a software release version and tells others that they validated the build, but doesn't document the validation. An example of explicitly recorded trust is when a QA team checks the quality of a software release version and then writes down what they did. They could, for example, send an email or make a digital note of the date, time, and situation of a successful operation. Trust must be written down so that you can confidently rebuild the series of stages. Getting more trust is the same as keeping track of trust. Over time, trust is built by going through a series of steps. As an item moves from a lower-level environment into production, its trust increases. Each stage of the pipeline includes tasks such as running an automated test suite or manually validating code through exploratory testing. After the successful completion of these tasks, digital evidence that has been cryptographically signed to prove its authenticity can be linked to the resulting artifacts.

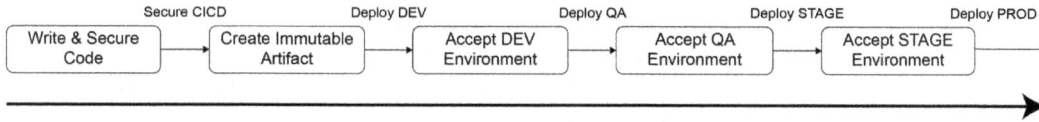

Figure 13.4 – Artifact trust

As illustrated in the preceding diagram, trust is seen as follows:

- When feature development is complete, trust is implicit.
- When code security tools are complete, trust is stated explicitly.
- When DEV members accept the DEV environment, trust is implicit.
- When QA approves one or more releases, trust is stated explicitly.
- When stakeholders accept the staging environment, trust is stated explicitly.

Next, we will look at binary authorization, which is a security control that enables organizations to verify the integrity of their container images prior to deployment. It is an important security measure that allows organizations to ensure that only trusted, approved images are being used in their production environments.

Binary authorization

Attestations of successful events can be combined to show the quality, security, and functionality of the artifact. The Binary Authorization service from Google is a security control that can be used when a program is being deployed in **Google Kubernetes Engine (GKE)**. It helps ensure that only trusted container images are used.

The Binary Authorization toolset is made up of a GKE cluster, an admission controller, a structured policy document protocol, and programmatic access to the digital attestations that go with a given container.

Policies can be developed to allow or reject deployment based on the presence or lack of attestations. Diverse policies can be developed for different contexts because policies are applied at the cluster level. As environments come closer to production, each cluster can require a higher level of attestation.

CI/CD pipelines can automate the process, codify trust, and increase confidence, but they are not risk-free. Because artifacts are pulled from a repository outside of the pipeline, a hacked item could be sent out without any more security checks. The goal of binary permission policies is to reduce this risk. They should be used to restrict deployments to files from a known set of repositories.

Establishing confidence with attestations in the items traveling through pipelines is important to pipeline security. Docker image attestation is the process used for verifying the provenance and integrity of Docker images in the pipeline. It is a secure process used to confirm the contents of a Docker image. It works by verifying that the contents of the image are approved and safe to use. The process begins by scanning the image for known vulnerabilities and malware. If any issues are found, they are reported to the user, and the image is marked as not approved. Next, the image is compared to a list of approved images and verified to be the same version. Finally, a signature is generated to ensure that all the contents of the image are unaltered. This signature is then used to verify the integrity of the image at any point during its lifetime. Obtaining these attestations creates a verifiable chain of trust, allowing you to make an informed decision about deploying an artifact to a certain cluster or environment.

Best practices for CI/CD security

The foundation of DevOps is CI/CD. Through automated monitoring and processes throughout the development cycle, CI/CD provides value to software production. In this rapidly evolving, technology-driven environment, security must be balanced with the need for flexibility. To prevent data breaches, the best approach is to build security into the development process.

Here are some of the best practices for securing CI/CD pipelines:

- Use IaC to manage and provision IT resources on Google Cloud. IaC uses configuration files and automation tools to manage resources to ensure that resources are set up correctly and efficiently.

- Automate builds and deployments with tools such as Jenkins, CircleCI, and Spinnaker to define and execute the necessary steps in the process. These automation tools make it easy to quickly deploy code changes and reduce the risk of potential bugs and are essential for a successful CI/CD pipeline.

- Using Git for version control is essential to the success of a project. Git is the most commonly used version control system and helps to keep track of changes and maintain consistency throughout the project's lifecycle. By using Git, teams are able to easily collaborate, share their work, and resolve conflicts quickly. Additionally, Git allows for easy rollbacks and provides a secure environment for all stakeholders involved.

- Use notifications and alerts to identify any problems in the CI/CD pipeline and notify team members of any significant changes or updates. This is particularly essential when rolling out to production.

- Track performance regularly by using monitoring tools such as Google Cloud's operations suite to make sure your pipeline runs efficiently. With these tools, you can detect any potential issues and take the necessary steps to solve them.

- Perform testing frequently throughout the CI/CD pipeline to ensure the code is functioning as expected. Automated and manual tests should be used to validate the application code and confirm whether the application is working properly.

- Use cloud-native tools such as Kubernetes and Cloud Build to simplify deploying applications and managing the CI/CD pipeline on Google Cloud.

- Adopting containerization can help make application deployment more efficient and reliable. It isolates applications into containers, enabling them to be quickly and easily deployed to multiple cloud environments. This reduces the time and resources needed to deploy applications, while also making it simpler to manage and scale applications. Additionally, containerization leads to increased resource utilization, making it possible to get more out of existing resources.

- Ensure that changes to the CI/CD pipeline are reversible to support automated rollbacks. If any issues arise, changes that have been made can be quickly reverted.

- Enable authentication and authorization in the CI/CD pipeline using a centralized authentication system such as Google Cloud IAM. This will ensure efficient management of access to the CI/CD pipeline.

- Implement a security monitoring system to audit all CI/CD activities and detect any suspicious behavior. This will enable the organization to be aware of any potential threats and react accordingly.

- Implement the principle of least privilege access by utilizing Google Cloud IAM to define roles and assign users with the minimum necessary access level to the CI/CD pipeline. This will help ensure that only authorized personnel can make changes to the environment, and any unauthorized access attempts can be readily identified.

- Ensure the security of your configuration by utilizing Google Cloud Security Command Center to detect any misconfigurations and enforce secure configurations.

- Monitoring and patching of vulnerable components should be done using Google Cloud Security Scanner or any other security scanners to identify and fix any weak points in the CI/CD pipeline. Doing so will ensure that the pipeline remains secure and free from any potential risks.

- It is important to regularly back up the CI/CD pipeline so that any modifications can be undone if needed. This will help to ensure that any mistakes or issues that arise can be easily rectified.

- Encryption is a must for safeguarding data, both when it's in motion and when it's at rest. Encrypting data will prevent unauthorized access and protect it from potential cyber-attacks. Doing so will also help to ensure that any information that is shared is kept confidential and secure.

- Utilize containers to separate the CI/CD pipeline and its elements. Containers are a great way to ensure that the pipeline and its components are adequately isolated from each other. This helps to guarantee that the pipeline runs smoothly and provides a stable environment for the components. Additionally, using containers makes it easier to troubleshoot any issues that may arise during the CI/CD process.

- Set up a threat detection system. Establish a system to detect potential threats and trigger notifications when malicious activity is identified.

- Take advantage of Google Cloud's security offerings to secure your CI/CD pipeline. These include Cloud Armor, Cloud Security Scanner, and Cloud IAM.

This concludes the best practices for CI/CD security. Next, we'll look at Shielded VMs, what they are, and how and where to use them.

Shielded VMs

Shielded VMs on Google Cloud are protected against rootkits and bootkits by a set of security safeguards. Shielded VMs safeguard company workloads from dangers such as remote attacks, privilege escalation, and hostile insiders.

Shielded VMs' verifiable integrity is achieved using the following features:

- Secure Boot

- **Virtual trusted platform module (vTPM)**-enabled Measured Boot

- Integrity monitoring

Let us look at each of them in more detail.

Secure Boot

Secure Boot checks all boot components' digital signatures and stops the booting process if the signature verification fails. Let's look at how Secure Boot for Shielded VMs works.

Shielded VM instances run software that has been certified and confirmed by Google's Certificate Authority Service. This makes sure that the firmware of the instance hasn't been changed and gives Secure Boot its foundation of trust. The UEFI 2.3.1 firmware protects the certificates that include the keys that software vendors use to sign the system firmware, the system boot loader, and any binaries they load. Shielded VM instances use UEFI firmware.

The UEFI firmware checks each boot component's digital signature against a secure repository of permitted keys at each boot. Any boot component that isn't signed properly, or at all, isn't allowed to run.

If this happens, an entry will appear in the VM instance's serial console log with the strings **UEFI: Failed to load image** and **Status: Security Violation**, as well as a description of the boot option that failed.

Now that we understand how Secure Boot works, let's take a look at Google's secure chip called a **virtual Trusted Platform Module (vTPM)**.

Virtual Trusted Platform Module (vTPM)

A vTPM is a specialized computer chip that can be used to protect assets used to authenticate access to your system, such as keys and certificates. Let's look at some key aspects of vTPMs:

- The BoringSSL library is used by the Shielded VM vTPM, which is fully compatible with the **Trusted Computing Group** (**TCG**) library specification 2.0. The BoringCrypto module is used by the BoringSSL library.

Note

You can refer to NIST Cryptographic Module Validation Program Certificate #3678 for FIPS 140-2 (`https://packt.link/x1N4p`) data on the BoringCrypto module.

- Measured Boot is enabled by the Shielded VM vTPM, which performs the measurements required to generate a known good boot baseline, called the integrity policy baseline. To see if anything has changed, the integrity policy baseline is compared to measurements from successive VM boots.

- The vTPM can also be used to secure secrets by shielding or sealing them.

We will now look at the importance of integrity monitoring and how it helps in understanding the security state of the VM.

Integrity monitoring

Integrity monitoring assists in understanding and making decisions regarding the state of your VMs. Let's look at how the process of integrity monitoring works:

- Measured Boot uses **Platform Configuration Registers** (**PCRs**) to hold information about the components and component load order of both the integrity policy baseline (a known good boot sequence) and the most recent boot sequence for integrity monitoring.

- Integrity monitoring compares the most recent boot measurements to the integrity policy baseline and returns two pass/fail outcomes, one for the early boot sequence and the other for the late boot sequence, depending on whether they match or not:

  - The boot sequence from the start of the UEFI firmware until it delivers control to the bootloader is known as early boot.

  - The boot sequence from the bootloader to the operating system kernel is known as late boot.

- An integrity validation failure occurs if any section of the most recent boot sequence does not match the baseline.

In summary, integrity monitoring for VMs is a service that uses multiple layers of intelligence to help identify and respond to potential security threats. It is an important tool for protecting cloud-hosted VMs from malicious actors, malicious software, and potential configuration vulnerabilities.

IAM authorization

Shielded VM uses Cloud IAM for authorization. The following Compute Engine permissions are used by Shielded VMs:

- `compute.instances.updateShieldedInstanceConfig`: Allows the user to change the Shielded VM options on a VM instance
- `compute.instances.setShieldedInstanceIntegrityPolicy`: Allows the user to update the integrity policy baseline on a VM instance
- `compute.instances.getShieldedInstanceIdentity`: Allows the user to retrieve endorsement key information from the vTPM

Shielded VM permissions are granted to the following Compute Engine roles:

- `roles/compute.instanceAdmin.v1`
- `roles/compute.securityAdmin`

You can also grant Shielded VM permissions to custom roles.

Organization policy constraints for Shielded VMs

You can set the `constraints/compute.requireShieldedVm` organization policy constraint to `True` to require that Compute Engine VM instances created in your organization be Shielded VM instances.

Confidential computing

Confidential computing involves the use of hardware-based **Trusted Execution Environments** (TEEs) to protect data while it is being used. TEEs are secure and isolated environments that keep applications and data from being accessed or changed while they are in use. A group called the **Confidential Computing Consortium** came up with this security standard.

The three states of end-to-end encryption are as follows:

- **Encryption at rest**: This protects your data while it is being stored
- **Encryption in transit**: This protects your data when it is moving between two points
- **Encryption in use**: This protects your data while it is being processed

Confidential computing gives you the last piece of end-to-end encryption: encryption in use.

Key features of Google Cloud Confidential Computing

When you use a Confidential VM, your data and applications stay private and encrypted even when they are being used. This is a type of Compute Engine VM. It runs on hosts that have AMD EPYC processors that have AMD **Secure Encrypted Virtualization** (**SEV**). Confidential VMs run on these hosts. Adding SEV to a Confidential VM has the following benefits and features:

- **Isolation**: Encryption keys are made by the AMD **Secure Processor** (**SP**) when a VM is created, and they only live on the AMD **System-on-Chip** (**SOC**). These keys can't even be found by Google, which makes them more private.

- **Attesting**: Confidential VMs use the vTPM. Whenever an AMD SEV-based confidential VM starts up, an event is made that says *launch attestation report*.

- **High performance**: AMD SEV has a lot of power for a lot of complicated tasks. Allowing Confidential VMs has little or no effect on most applications, with a performance loss of only zero to 6% when it is turned on for most applications.

In addition to Compute Engine, the following Google Cloud Confidential Computing services are also available:

- Confidential Google Kubernetes Engine nodes require all of your GKE nodes to use Confidential VMs

- Dataproc Confidential Compute uses Confidential VMs in Dataproc clusters

Benefits of Confidential Computing

Let us look at some of the key benefits of using Google Cloud Confidential Computing:

- Google Cloud's customers shouldn't have to choose between usability, performance, and confidentiality. Google's goal is to make confidential computing easy. The transition to Confidential VMs is seamless—all workloads you run today can run as a Confidential VM without the need to change anything.

- With Confidential VMs, customers do not need to make any changes to their applications. Entire VMs can be run in a confidential manner.

- The VM memory is encrypted by a key per VM and generated in hardware (AMD). The keys are ephemeral and not extractable by anyone, including Google.

- Finally, customers can protect their data end to end, from data-in-transit to data-at-rest, and finally to data-in-use.

With Google Cloud Confidential Computing, organizations can securely process and store data in the cloud without having to worry about it being exposed to third parties. Additionally, it helps organizations comply with regulations such as GDPR, as well as providing an added layer of security when it comes to protecting sensitive data. As more organizations move to the cloud, Google Cloud Confidential Computing provides an important security layer that helps protect their data from unauthorized access.

Summary

This chapter highlights the need for hardening images for both VMs and containers. It outlines the steps for managing images, securing and hardening them, and building image management pipelines. In addition, we discussed the use of cloud-native tools on Google Cloud to build security scanning of the CI/CD pipeline. To further secure applications running in the cloud environment, we explored Google Compute Engine security capabilities such as Shielded VMs, vTPMs, and Confidential Computing. Finally, we discussed various measures for securing containers and applications running inside them, such as network policies to control traffic flow and key management systems for encryption key security and management.

In the next chapter, we will cover Security Command Center, which is used to monitor the security posture of your Google Cloud organization.

Further reading

For more information on Google Cloud image hardening and CI/CD security, refer to the following links:

- Creating a Cloud Build image factory using Packer: `https://packt.link/tr8ks`
- Shifting left on security: `https://packt.link/BWbBN`
- vTPMs: `https://packt.link/JiQqG`
- AMD SEV-SNP: Strengthening VM Isolation with Integrity Protection and More: `https://packt.link/28XiO`
- Default encryption at rest: `https://packt.link/jcUlr`

Security Command Center

In this chapter, we will look at the capabilities of Google's Security Command Center. The exam typically has questions on how to configure and use **Security Command Center** (**SCC**) to monitor the security posture of your Google Cloud organization. You may also get questions on how to detect threats and vulnerabilities in your cloud environment and workloads. This is one of the critical aspects of security operations, so make sure you understand it very well.

In this chapter, we will cover the following topics:

- Overview of SCC
- Core services:
  - Cloud Asset Inventory
  - Detecting security misconfiguration using Security Health Analytics
  - VM Manager
- Rapid vulnerability detection
- Threat detection
- Continuous compliance monitoring using SCC
- Exporting SCC findings
- Automating findings response

Overview of SCC

Google introduced SCC in mid-2018. SCC provides many features to monitor your organization's security controls, detect threats, and use alerts to automate security responses.

Here are some of the key features of SCC:

- **Gain centralized visibility and control over your Google Cloud data and resources**:

  - SCC gives enterprises centralized visibility of their cloud assets across App Engine, BigQuery, Cloud SQL, Cloud Storage, Compute Engine, **Identity and Access Management (IAM)** policies, **Google Kubernetes Engine (GKE)**, and more.

  - SCC enables enterprises to quickly find out the number of projects in their environment, what resources are deployed, where sensitive data is located, and which service accounts have been added or removed. You can leverage the SCC REST API to access assets and findings and make it easier to integrate with existing systems.

  - You can view your Google Cloud asset history to understand exactly what changed in your environment and respond to the most pressing issues first.

  - You can receive notifications about new findings or updates to existing findings. The notifications are typically delivered within six to twelve minutes, ensuring that you stay informed and can take appropriate actions promptly.

- **Find and fix risky misconfigurations**:

  - **Security Health Analytics (SHA)** is a built-in service in SCC that helps you identify security misconfigurations in your Google Cloud assets and resolve them by following actionable recommendations.

  - **Web Security Scanner (WSS)** is a built-in service in SCC that can automatically detect web applications running in Google Cloud and scan them for web app vulnerabilities. This can help you catch web application vulnerabilities before they hit production and reduce your exposure to risks.

- **Report on and maintain compliance**:

  - SCC Premium helps you identify compliance violations in your Google Cloud assets and resolve them by following actionable recommendations.

  - You can review and export compliance reports to help ensure all your resources are meeting their compliance requirements.

- **Detect threats targeting your Google Cloud assets**:

  - Event Threat Detection is a built-in service in SCC Premium that helps customers detect threats using logs running in Google Cloud at scale:

    - Uncover suspicious cloud-based activity using Google's unique threat intelligence

- Use kernel-level instrumentation to identify potential compromises of containers, including suspicious binaries

- Combine threat intelligence from first- and third-party providers, such as Palo Alto Networks, to better protect your enterprise from costly and high-risk threats

- Detect whether your **virtual machines** (**VMs**) are being used for abuse cases, such as coin mining

- Respond to threats by using a Cloud Pub/Sub event or Cloud Functions and reduce your time to resolution

- **Container Threat Detection** (**KTD**) is a built-in service in SCC that detects the most common container runtime attacks and alerts you to any suspicious activity

Now that you have a brief idea of what SCC can do, let us dive deep into the core services of SCC.

Core services

Core services contribute to various parts of the security architecture of your Google Cloud organization for detection and alerting. The following diagram shows the core services offered by SCC.

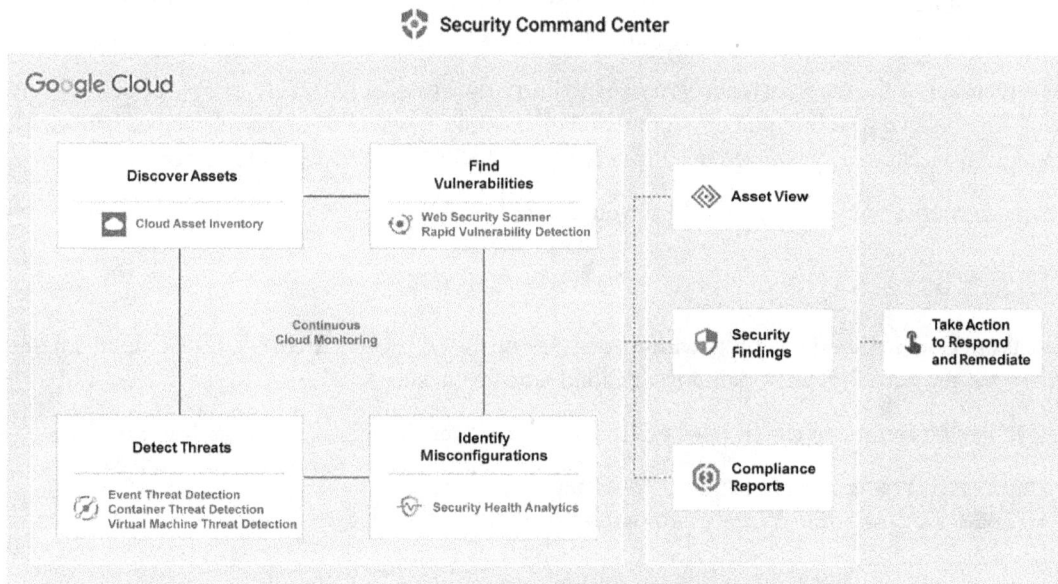

Figure 14.1 – SCC core services

As shown in *Figure 14.1*, SCC is a collection of various modules providing detection and alerting capability:

- **Cloud Asset Inventory (CAI)**: CAI provides full visibility of all assets in your Google Cloud organization. You can search by type of resources, projects, and locations. CAI also provides all IAM policies in your Google Cloud organization.

- **Vulnerability Findings**: You can detect misconfigurations and vulnerabilities in your Google Cloud organization using SHA, VM Manager, WSS, and Rapid Vulnerability Detection.

- **Event Threat Detection (ETD)**: ETD is a collection of threat detection capabilities that provides alerts on threats to your Google Cloud organization. It will also alert threats to containers and VMs.

Now let us go over each of these capabilities and understand the details of how SCC generates findings.

Cloud Asset Inventory

CAI provides a list of asset metadata for your cloud resources based on when they were created and/or updated. Note that the roles in SCC are assigned at various levels of your Google Cloud resource hierarchy. The amount of access you have determines your ability to see, edit, create, or change findings, assets, and security sources. Typically, security operations have access to see findings at the organization level, while project teams have access to see findings at the individual project level.

As a member of the security team, you need to know how to query assets to be able to quickly find what has changed in your cloud environment. For example, it would be highly suspicious behavior if you found accelerator-optimized machines (GPUs and HPC) being unexpectedly provisioned.

Let us go over various features of CAI so you can understand how it works and how to use it.

Listing assets

Assets are Google Cloud resources within your Google Cloud organization, such as Compute Engine instances, projects, BigQuery datasets, or Cloud Storage buckets.

The following command can be used to list assets for a given Google Cloud organization:

```
ORGANIZATION_ID=12344321
gcloud scc assets list $ORGANIZATION_ID
```

The output will look like this:

```
asset:
  createTime: '2021-10-05T17:55:14.823Z'
  iamPolicy:
    policyBlob: '{"bindings":[{"role":"roles/
owner","members":["serviceAccount:SERVICE_ACCOUNT@PROJECT_ID.iam.
```

```
gserviceaccount.com","user:USER_EMAIL@gmail.com"]}]}'
  name: organizations/ORGANIZATION_ID/assets/ASSET_ID
  resourceProperties:
    createTime: '2021-10-05T17:36:17.915Z'
    lifecycleState: ACTIVE
    name: PROJECT_ID
    parent: '{"id":"ORGANIZATION_ID","type":"organization"}'
    projectId: PROJECT_ID
    projectNumber: 'PROJECT_NUMBER'
  securityCenterProperties:
    resourceDisplayName: PROJECT_ID
    resourceName: //cloudresourcemanager.googleapis.com/projects/
PROJECT_NUMBER
    resourceOwners:
    - serviceAccount:SERVICE_ACCOUNT@PROJECT_ID.iam.gserviceaccount.
com
    - user:USER_EMAIL@gmail.com
    resourceParent: //cloudresourcemanager.googleapis.com/
organizations/ORGANIZATION_ID
    resourceParentDisplayName: ORGANIZATION_NAME
    resourceProject: //cloudresourcemanager.googleapis.com/projects/
PROJECT_NUMBER
    resourceProjectDisplayName: PROJECT_ID
    resourceType: google.cloud.resourcemanager.Project
  securityMarks:
    name: organizations/ORGANIZATION_ID/assets/ASSET_ID/securityMarks
  updateTime: '2021-10-05T17:55:14.823Z'
```

As you can see, you are going to get a very large list of assets, so it is imperative to understand how to filter them based on your requirements. Let us look at that now.

Filtering assets

An organization may have many assets. Because there are no filters in the preceding example, all assets are returned. You can utilize asset filters in SCC to get information about certain assets. Filters, like where clauses in SQL queries, only apply to objects returned by the API instead of columns.

The previous example's sample output displays certain fields and subfields, as well as their characteristics, that can be utilized in asset filters. The SCC API accepts complete JSON arrays and objects as potential property types. You can refine your results by using the following filters:

- Array elements

- Full JSON objects with partial string matches within the object

- JSON object subfields

Filter expressions must use the following comparison operators and sub-fields must be numbers, strings, or Booleans:

- Strings:

  - Full equality, =

  - Partial string matching, :

- Numbers:

  - Inequalities, <, >, <=, >=

  - Equality, =

- Booleans:

  - Equality, =

Now let us see how to create a filter and use it in a command to filter assets:

```
ORGANIZATION_ID=12344321
FILTER="security_center_properties.resource_type=\"google.cloud.
resourcemanager.Project\""
 gcloud scc assets list $ORGANIZATION_ID -filter="$FILTER"
```

Let us see some examples of how to construct a filter.

To find a project with a specific owner, you can form a filter like this:

```
"security_center_properties.resource_type = \"google.cloud.
resourcemanager.Project\" AND security_center_properties.resource_
owners : \"$USER\""
```

In this example, $USER is typically in the format user:someone@domain.com. This compares the $USER using the substring operator :, so an exact match is not necessary.

To find firewall rules with open HTTP ports, you can create a filter like this:

```
"security_center_properties.resource_type = \"google.compute.
Firewall\" AND resource_properties.name =\"default-allow-http\""
```

Now let us see a few examples of filters based on time conditions. To find project assets created at or before a specific time, create a filter as follows.

Let us say our requirement is for querying assets that were generated on or before July 18, 2019 at 8:26:21 PM GMT.

You can express time with the `create_time` filter in the following forms and types:

```
Unix time (in milliseconds) as an integer literal
"create_time <= 1563481581000"
RFC 3339 as a string literal
"create_time <= \"2019-07-18T20:26:21+00:00\""
```

Listing assets at a point in time

The previous examples demonstrate how to create a list of an organization's current assets. You can also view a historical snapshot of an organization's assets using SCC.

The following sample retrieves the current state of all assets at a given point in time. Millisecond time resolutions are supported by SCC:

```
# ORGANIZATION_ID=12344321
# READ_TIME follows the format YYYY-MM-DDThh:mm:ss.ffffffZ
READ_TIME=2019-02-28T07:00:06.861Z
gcloud scc assets list $ORGANIZATION_ID -read time=$READ_TIME
```

Listing assets that changed state

A prime requirement is to be able to find assets that changed state after a certain time. You can compare an asset at two points in time to see whether it was added, removed, or present at the specified time using SCC.

The following example compares projects that exist at READ_TIME to a previous point in time specified by COMPARE_DURATION. Note that COMPARE_DURATION is provided in seconds.

When COMPARE_DURATION is set, the `stateChange` attribute in the result of the list asset query is updated with one of the following values:

- ADDED: The asset was not present at the start of `compareDuration`, but was present at `readTime`

- REMOVED: The asset was present at the start of `compareDuration`, but was not present at `readTime`

- ACTIVE: The asset was present at both the start and the end time defined by `compareDuration` and `readTime`

Now let us see how to form the filter for this condition:

```
# ORGANIZATION_ID=12344321
# READ_TIME follows the format YYYY-MM-DDThh:mm:ss.ffffffZ
READ_TIME=2019-02-28T07:00:06.861Z
  FILTER="security_center_properties.resource_type=\"google.cloud.
resourcemanager.Project\""
COMPARE_DURATION=86400s
```

Now execute the following command using the preceding filter:

```
gcloud scc assets list $ORGANIZATION_ID --read-time=$READ_TIME
--filter="$FILTER" \
--compare-duration=$COMPARE_DURATION
```

We will take a bit of a detour and look at an important aspect of asset analysis: BigQuery exports. You can export assets to BigQuery and run queries using SQL. Let us see how to do that.

Exporting assets to BigQuery

In this section, we will quickly see how to export assets to BigQuery and then run data analysis on your asset inventory. BigQuery provides a SQL-like experience for users to analyze data and produce meaningful insights without the use of custom scripts.

Before you execute the queries, follow this URL to set up the BigQuery export of assets: https://packt.link/wvqQq.

Let us look at some of the most run queries for assets. Replace PROJECT_ID, DATASET_ID, and TABLE_NAME with the appropriate values for your project:

1. Find the quantity of each asset type by using the following query:

    ```
    SELECT asset_type, COUNT(*) AS asset_count
    FROM `PROJECT_ID.DATASET_ID.TABLE_NAME`
    GROUP BY asset_type
    ORDER BY asset_count DESC
    ```

2. To find an organization, folder, or project that allows creating using a public IP, run the following query. This query is useful because allowing public IPs with Cloud SQL instances can introduce vulnerabilities unless SSL or a proxy is configured:

    ```
    SELECT name
    FROM `PROJECT_ID.DATASET_ID.TABLE_NAME`
    JOIN UNNEST(org_policy) AS op
    WHERE
      op.constraint = "constraints/sql.restrictPublicIp"
      AND (op.boolean_policy IS NULL OR op.boolean_policy.enforced =
    FALSE);
    ```

The preceding two queries are for general cloud assets; however, one of the important aspects of asset inventory is to find out IAM policies that potentially violate your organization's security policies. Let us look at these now. Replace PROJECT_ID, DATASET_ID, and TABLE_NAME with the appropriate values for your project.

3. To find IAM policies that grant access to Gmail accounts, run the following query. This query is useful to see whether there has been any exfiltration from your Google Cloud organization to consumer accounts:

```
SELECT name, asset_type, bindings.role
FROM `PROJECT_ID.DATASET_ID.TABLE_NAME`
JOIN UNNEST(iam_policy.bindings) AS bindings
JOIN UNNEST(bindings.members) AS principals
WHERE principals like %@gmail.com
```

4. To find IAM policies that grant access to direct users rather than groups (as you know this is an anti-pattern for IAM access control), run the following query:

```
SELECT name, asset_type, bindings.role, members
FROM `asset-inventory-api.iam_asset_inventory.iam_policy_
inventory`
JOIN UNNEST(iam_policy.bindings) AS bindings
JOIN UNNEST(bindings.members) AS members
WHERE members like "%@acme.com"order by name
```

5. To find IAM policies containing all service accounts, run the following query. This query is important to find out whether any service accounts are being granted privileged roles:

```
SELECT name, asset_type, bindings.role, members
FROM `asset-inventory-api.iam_asset_inventory.iam_policy_
inventory`
JOIN UNNEST(iam_policy.bindings) AS bindings
JOIN UNNEST(bindings.members) AS members
WHERE members like "serviceAccount%"
order by name
```

6. To find IAM policies that are granted using groups, execute a query like this:

```
SELECT name, asset_type, bindings.role, members
FROM `asset-inventory-api.iam_asset_inventory.iam_policy_
inventory`
JOIN UNNEST(iam_policy.bindings) AS bindings
JOIN UNNEST(bindings.members) AS members
WHERE members like "group%"
order by name
```

Now that you have a solid understanding of how to query assets either by using SCC commands or BigQuery, we will move on to another module of SCC for detecting security misconfigurations.

Detecting security misconfigurations and vulnerabilities

Most of the cloud threats that you will find will be due to security misconfigurations or a lack of understanding of how the cloud works. So, it is critical to understand how to find misconfigurations and how to quickly analyze and fix them. SCC reports findings from four categories of detectors:

- Security Health Analytics

- Rapid Vulnerability Detection

- Web Security Scanner

- VM Manager vulnerabilities

Now let us look at each of them to understand the details.

Security Health Analytics

SHA is a service within SCC that has built-in detectors to identify misconfigurations. SHA automatically scans your Google Cloud organization for known vulnerable configurations against compliance benchmarks such as CIS, PCI DSS, NIS 800-53, ISO 27001, and the OWASP Top 10. SHA scans begin around an hour after SCC is turned on and can be done in one of two modes: batch mode, which conducts scans twice a day, 12 hours apart; and real-time mode, which executes scans in response to asset configuration changes.

SHA scans are available in three different modes:

- **Batch scan**: All detectors are set to run two or more times per day for all enrolled organizations. Detectors run on various schedules to satisfy **service-level objectives (SLOs)**. Detectors execute batch scans every 6 or 12 hours to meet 12- and 24-hour SLOs, respectively. Interim batch scan resources and policy changes are not immediately collected and applied in the next batch scan.

> **Note**
> Batch scan timetables are performance goals rather than service assurances.

- **Real-time scan**: When CAI reports a change in an asset's configuration, supported detectors begin scanning. The findings are sent to SCC right away.

- **Mixed mode**: Some detectors that offer real-time scans may not be able to detect changes in all supported assets in real time. Configuration updates for some assets are caught immediately, while batch scans capture changes for others. In the tables on this page, exceptions are highlighted.

> **Note**
> There are some detectors that do not support real-time scanning mode. For detector latency information, check out the Google Cloud documentation at `https://packt.link/TeQlR`.

SCC Premium must use most SHA detectors. The Standard tier provides the following finding types:

- `DATAPROC_IMAGE_OUTDATED`
- `LEGACY_AUTHORIZATION_ENABLED`
- `MFA_NOT_ENFORCED`
- `NON_ORG_IAM_MEMBER`
- `OPEN_CISCOSECURE_WEBSM_PORT`
- `OPEN_DIRECTORY_SERVICES_PORT`
- `OPEN_FIREWALL`
- `OPEN_GROUP_IAM_MEMBER`
- `OPEN_RDP_PORT`
- `OPEN_SSH_PORT`
- `OPEN_TELNET_PORT`
- `PUBLIC_BUCKET_ACL`
- `PUBLIC_COMPUTE_IMAGE`
- `PUBLIC_DATASET`
- `PUBLIC_IP_ADDRESS`
- `PUBLIC_LOG_BUCKET`
- `PUBLIC_SQL_INSTANCE`
- `SSL_NOT_ENFORCED`
- `WEB_UI_ENABLED`

The following SHA detectors are not enabled by default:

- `BIGQUERY_TABLE_CMEK_DISABLED`
- `BUCKET_CMEK_DISABLED`
- `DATASET_CMEK_DISABLED`

- `DISK_CMEK_DISABLED`

- `DISK_CSEK_DISABLED`

- `NODEPOOL_BOOT_CMEK_DISABLED`

- `PUBSUB_CMEK_DISABLED`

- `SQL_CMEK_DISABLED`

- `SQL_NO_ROOT_PASSWORD`

- `SQL_WEAK_ROOT_PASSWORD`

To turn on a detector, also known as a module, run the following commands in the Google Cloud CLI:

```
gcloud alpha scc settings services modules enable \
    --organization=ORGANIZATION_ID \
    --service=SECURITY_HEALTH_ANALYTICS \
    --module=DETECTOR_NAME
```

In addition to SHA findings, SCC also reports on VM Manager and Rapid Vulnerability Detection. Let us go over those now.

VM Manager

VM Manager is a suite of tools that can be used to manage the OS for VMs running Windows and Linux on Compute Engine. This is a paid service and you will need to enable it. The findings are reported to SCC only for the SCC Premium version. Findings simplify the process of using VM Manager's patch compliance feature, which is in preview at the time of writing this book. The feature lets you conduct patch management at the organization level across all of your projects. Note that VM Manager supports patch management at the single project level.

VM Manager reports findings in SCC. Here are some features of the findings that you should be aware of:

- VM Manager's vulnerability reports detail vulnerabilities in installed OS packages for Compute Engine VMs, including **common vulnerabilities and exposures (CVEs)**.

- Assets excluded from scans: **SUSE Linux Enterprise Server (SLES)**, Windows OSs.

- Findings appear in SCC shortly after vulnerabilities are detected.

- Vulnerability reports in VM Manager are generated as follows:

  - For most vulnerabilities in the installed OS package, the OS Config API generates a vulnerability report within a few minutes of the change

  - For CVEs, the OS Config API generates the vulnerability report within three to four hours of the CVE being published to the OS

VM Manager also provides a nice graphical interface for visualization of the findings. Let us look at Rapid Vulnerability Detection.

Rapid Vulnerability Detection

Rapid Vulnerability Detection detects weak credentials, incomplete software installations, and other critical vulnerabilities that have a high likelihood of being exploited. The service automatically discovers network endpoints, protocols, open ports, network services, and installed software packages.

Rapid Vulnerability Detection findings are early warnings of vulnerabilities that Google recommends you fix immediately.

Here is a list of findings generated by Rapid Vulnerability Detection:

> **Note**
> Please refer to the Google Cloud documentation to find out the details of the findings and the remediation.

Weak credential findings:

- `WEAK_CREDENTIALS`

Exposed Interface findings:

- `ELASTICSEARCH_API_EXPOSED`
- `EXPOSED_GRAFANA_ENDPOINT`
- `EXPOSED_METABASE`
- `EXPOSED_SPRING_BOOT_ACTUATOR_ENDPOINT`
- `HADOOP_YARN_UNAUTHENTICATED_RESOURCE_MANAGER_API`
- `JAVA_JMX_RMI_EXPOSED`
- `JUPYTER_NOTEBOOK_EXPOSED_UI`
- `KUBERNETES_API_EXPOSED`
- `UNFINISHED_WORDPRESS_INSTALLATION`
- `UNAUTHENTICATED_JENKINS_NEW_ITEM_CONSOLE`

Software findings for remote code execution vulnerabilities:

- `APACHE_HTTPD_RCE`
- `APACHE_HTTPD_SSRF`
- `CONSUL_RCE`
- `DRUID_RCE`
- `DRUPAL_RCE`
- `FLINK_FILE_DISCLOSURE`
- `GITLAB_RCE`
- `GoCD_RCE`
- `JENKINS_RCE`
- `JOOMLA_RCE`
- `LOG4J_RCE`
- `MANTISBT_PRIVILEGE_ESCALATION`
- `OGNL_RCE`
- `OPENAM_RCE`
- `ORACLE_WEBLOGIC_RCE`
- `PHPUNIT_RCE`
- `PHP_CGI_RCE`
- `PORTAL_RCE`
- `REDIS_RCE`
- `SOLR_FILE_EXPOSED`
- `SOLR_RCE`
- `STRUTS_RCE`
- `TOMCAT_FILE_DISCLOSURE`
- `VBULLETIN_RCE`
- `VCENTER_RCE`
- `WEBLOGIC_RCE`

Now that we have looked at Rapid Vulnerability Detection, let us move on to web security vulnerabilities.

Web Security Scanner

WSS scans your App Engine, GKE, and Compute Engine web apps for security flaws. It crawls your apps, following all links that fall within the scope of your application's entry URLs, and tries to test as many user inputs and event handlers as possible. WSS only works with public URLs and IP addresses that are not behind a firewall.

App Engine standard and flexible environments, Compute Engine instances, and GKE resources are presently supported by WSS.

WSS works with your secure design and development procedures. It uses a combination of automated and manual techniques to scan web applications and services for common vulnerabilities such as SQL injection, cross-site scripting, and other security issues. It works by sending a series of requests to the target application or service and then analyzing the responses for possible vulnerabilities. WSS can also be used to conduct manual security reviews by providing detailed reports on potential issues. Additionally, WSS also provides remediation advice and steps to address any identified vulnerabilities.

The **OWASP Top Ten**, a publication that ranks and provides remedial assistance for the top 10 most critical online application security vulnerabilities, is supported by WSS.

There are two types of scans WSS supports:

- **Managed scans**: Managed scans detect and scan public web endpoints once a week automatically:

  - These scans do not employ authentication and perform GET-only queries, so no forms are submitted on live websites.

  - Managed scans are done independently of custom scans defined at the project level. Managed scan findings are automatically available on the SCC **Vulnerabilities** tab and related reports when you enable WSS as a service.

  A managed scan is especially useful without involving individual project teams, as you can utilize managed scans to centrally manage basic web application vulnerability detection for projects in your organization. You can work with those teams later to set up more comprehensive bespoke scans after the discoveries are made.

- **Custom scans**: WSS custom scans provide detailed information on application vulnerabilities such as obsolete libraries, cross-site scripting, and mixed content usage.

Here is a list of all the findings generated by WSS:

> **Note**
>
> For a description of these findings and remediation, look up the relevant Google Cloud documentation.

- `ACCESSIBLE_GIT_REPOSITORY`
- `ACCESSIBLE_SVN_REPOSITORY`
- `CACHEABLE_PASSWORD_INPUT`
- `CLEAR_TEXT_PASSWORD`
- `INSECURE_ALLOW_ORIGIN_ENDS_WITH_VALIDATION`
- `INSECURE_ALLOW_ORIGIN_STARTS_WITH_VALIDATION`
- `INVALID_CONTENT_TYPE`
- `INVALID_HEADER`
- `MISMATCHING_SECURITY_HEADER_VALUES`
- `MISSPELLED_SECURITY_HEADER_NAME`
- `MIXED_CONTENT`
- `OUTDATED_LIBRARY`
- `SERVER_SIDE_REQUEST_FORGERY`
- `SESSION_ID_LEAK`
- `SQL_INJECTION`
- `STRUTS_INSECURE_DESERIALIZATION`
- `XSS`
- `XSS_ANGULAR_CALLBACK`
- `XSS_ERROR`
- `XXE_REFLECTED_FILE_LEAKAGE`

While WSS is easy enough to use, there are some best practices that you should follow while using it. We will go over those now.

Best practices for WSS

You should use WSS with caution because it populates fields, pushes buttons, clicks links, and performs other user actions. This is especially true if you are scanning production resources. WSS may trigger features that alter the condition of your data or system, resulting in unfavorable outcomes. Here are some best practices:

- **Use a test environment for scanning**: Create a separate App Engine project and load your application and data there to create a test environment. When you upload your app using the Google Cloud CLI, you can provide the target project as a command-line argument.

- **Create a test account**: Create a user account with no access to sensitive data or potentially dangerous operations and use it to scan your app. When users log in for the first time, many applications need them to go through a unique process, such as accepting terms and creating a profile. A test account for an initial user may have different scan results than an established user account due to the different workflow. After the first-time flow is complete, scan using an account that is in the typical user state.

- **Deactivate some UI elements**: Apply the `no-click` CSS class to individual user interface elements that you do not wish to activate. Regardless of whether they are inline JavaScript, attached using `addEventListener`, or attached by specifying the appropriate event handler property, event handlers attached to this element are not enabled during crawling and testing.

- **Use backup data**: Before scanning, consider making a backup of your data.

- **Exclude URLs**: You can exclude URL patterns from being crawled or tested. See the following link for further details on the syntax: `https://packt.link/n1dwr`.

- **Scope of the scan**: Before you scan, check your app for any features that could affect data, users, or systems in ways that go beyond the scope of your scan.

So far, we have seen vulnerability detection findings when using SCC. Now we will look at the threat detection capabilities of SCC.

Threat detection

Google Cloud provides several types of threat detection via SCC Premium:

- Event Threat Detection
- Container Threat Detection
- VM Threat Detection
- Anomaly Detection

Let us start with ETD.

Event Threat Detection

Event Threat Detection (**ETD**) is a built-in feature of the SCC Premium tier that watches your Google Cloud environment in real time and detects threats within your systems. New detectors are added to ETD regularly to discover emerging threats at cloud scale.

ETD produces security findings by matching events in your Cloud Logging and Google Workspace log streams to known **indicators of compromise** (**IoCs**). IoCs, developed by internal Google security sources, identify potential vulnerabilities and attacks. ETD also detects threats by identifying known adversarial tactics, techniques, and procedures in your logging stream, and by detecting deviations from the historically observed behavior of your Google Cloud organization.

Here are some ETD features that you should be aware of:

- Project-specific logs are consumed when they become accessible by ETD. Cloud Logging records API calls and other operations that create, read, or modify resource configuration or metadata. Google Workspace logs keep track of user sign-ins to your domain and actions taken in the Google Workspace Admin console.

- ETD leverages log entries to swiftly detect threats. It uses Google's proprietary threat intelligence and detection technology to identify threats in near-real time.

- ETD also logs threats to SCC and Cloud Logging projects.

- You can use Cloud Functions to process data from Cloud Logging and Google Workspace Logging to automate responses to threats.

- You can also utilize Chronicle to explore findings. Chronicle is a Google Cloud service that lets you investigate threats and track them over time.

Now that you know what ETD is, let us see what it needs to detect threats.

Unsafe IAM changes

ETD finds external group members and examines each affected group's IAM roles using Cloud Audit Logs to see whether the groups have been granted sensitive responsibilities. This data is used to detect the following list of potentially dangerous modifications in privileged Google groups.

Unsafe changes in Google groups that involve high- or medium-sensitivity roles result in findings. The severity grade attributed to findings is influenced by the sensitivity of the roles:

- Billing, firewall settings, and logging are all controlled by high-sensitivity roles in businesses. Findings that correspond to these responsibilities are given a high severity rating.

- Editing permissions on Google Cloud resources, as well as viewing and executing permissions on data storage services that often hold sensitive data, are available to principals in medium-sensitivity positions. The severity of discoveries is determined by the resource:

  - Findings are categorized as *High* severity if medium-sensitivity roles are awarded at the organizational level

  - Findings are categorized as *Medium* severity if medium-sensitivity responsibilities are provided at lower levels in your resource hierarchy (folders, projects, and buckets, for example)

Look at Google Cloud's documentation for information on all highly privileged IAM role changes. The link is provided at the end of this chapter.

Let us look at the types of logs ETD needs to be able to detect threats.

Various log types for ETD

Admin Activity logs, which are part of Cloud Audit Logs, are automatically consumed by ETD (see the following list). Admin Activity logs are created automatically and do not require any configuration. Furthermore, turning on extra logs, which the service analyzes to detect specific threats, improves the performance of ETD. Here are various logs that you will need to enable specifically:

- SSH logs/syslog
- Data Access logs (part of Cloud Audit Logs)
- VPC flow logs
- Cloud DNS logs
- Firewall rules logs
- Cloud NAT logs
- **GKE** Data Access audit logs
- HTTP(S) load balancing backend service logs
- MySQL Data Access audit logs
- PostgreSQL Data Access audit logs
- Resource Manager Data Access audit logs
- SQL Server Data Access audit logs

> **Note**
>
> With frequent sampling and short aggregation periods, ETD works best. There may be a delay between the occurrence and detection of an event if you use lower sample rates or longer aggregation intervals. This lag can make evaluating any malware, cryptomining, or phishing traffic more difficult.

Before you turn on a log for ETD to scan, make sure you understand how Cloud Logging charges for the log data. After turning on a log, monitor the log for a couple of days to ensure that the log doesn't incur any unexpected Cloud Logging costs.

Although the scanning of logs by ETD does not incur any additional costs, depending on the volume of log data that your organizations and projects produce, Cloud Logging may charge you for the ingestion and storage of the log data.

Here are various Admin Activity logs that ETD scans automatically – you do not need to turn on or configure these:

- BigQueryAuditMetadata Data Access logs
- Cloud DNS Admin Activity audit logs
- GKE Admin Activity audit logs
- IAM Admin Activity audit logs
- MySQL Admin Activity logs
- PostgreSQL Admin Activity logs
- SQL Server Admin Activity logs
- VPC Service Controls Audit logs

Now that we have looked at Google Cloud logs, let us quickly understand the Workspace logs that ETD uses.

Google Workspace audit logs

These are enabled and maintained in your Google Workspace environment, although they must be shared with Google Cloud for ETD to access and detect Google Workspace threats:

- Login Audit logs (for Data Access audit logs)
- Admin Audit logs (for Admin Activity audit logs)

Now you know which logs ETD uses to detect threats, let us look at the findings ETD generates.

ETD findings

Here are some examples of findings generated by ETD:

- Evasion: Access from Anonymizing Proxy
- Exfiltration: BigQuery Data Exfiltration
- Exfiltration: Cloud SQL Data Exfiltration
- Brute Force: SSH
- Credential Access: External Member Added To Privileged Group
- Credential Access: Privileged Group Opened To Public
- Credential Access: Sensitive Role Granted To Hybrid Group
- Crypto Mining
- Initial Access: Log4j Compromise Attempt
- Active Scan: Log4j Vulnerabilities To RCE
- Leaked Credentials
- Malware
- Outgoing DOS
- Persistence: IAM Anomalous Grant
- Persistence: New Geography
- Persistence: New User Agent
- Phishing
- Service Account Self-Investigation
- Compute Engine Admin Metadata detections
- Persistence: Compute Engine Admin Added Startup Script

Refer to the Google Cloud documentation for a list of all findings and how to build a response.

Google Workspace threat detection

Let us look at various detectors available in Google Workspace now:

- Initial Access: Disabled Password Leak
- Initial Access: Suspicious Login Blocked
- Initial Access: Account Disabled Hijacked

- Impair Defenses: Two-Step Verification Disabled

- Initial Access: Government-Based Attack

- Persistence: SSO Enablement Toggle

- Persistence: SSO Settings Changed

- Impair Defenses: Strong Authentication Disabled

This concludes the section on ETD. Let us look at KTD now.

Container Threat Detection

KTD is another built-in service within SCC Premium that supports threat detection on the GKE platform. Please verify the version of the GKE cluster you are running to make sure it is supported. Refer to the Google Cloud documentation for supported versions. KTD gathers and analyzes low-level observable behavior in the guest kernel of your containers to generate insights.

Here are the findings generated by KTD:

- **Added Binary Executed**: A binary that was not part of the original container image was executed. Attackers commonly install exploitation tooling and malware after the initial compromise.

- **Added Library Loaded**: A library that was not part of the original container image was loaded. Attackers might load malicious libraries into existing programs to bypass code execution protections and hide malicious code.

- **Malicious Script Executed**: A machine learning model identified an executed Bash script as malicious. Attackers can use Bash to transfer tools and execute commands without binaries.

- **Reverse Shell Attack**: A process started with stream redirection to a remote-connected socket. With a reverse shell, an attacker can communicate from a compromised workload to an attacker-controlled machine. The attacker can then command and control the workload to perform desired actions, for example, as part of a botnet.

Now that we understand how KTD works, let us move on to learning how VM Threat Detection works.

VM Threat Detection

VM Threat Detection (**VMTD**) is a built-in feature of SCC Premium that detects threats at the hypervisor level. VMTD detects coin mining software, which is one of the most typical forms of software found in exploited cloud environments.

VMTD is a part of the SCC Premium threat detection suite, and it is meant to work alongside ETD and KTD. This feature is now in **general availability** (**GA**) as of July 2022. The certification exam will not have any questions on it at the time of publication of this book; it may be added in the future.

The service executes scans from the hypervisor into the guest VM's live memory regularly without halting the guest's activity. VMTD analyzes information about software running on VMs, such as a list of application names, per-process CPU usage, hashes of memory pages, CPU hardware performance counters, and information about executed machine code, using Google Cloud's threat detection rules to see whether it matches known crypto mining signatures.

Because VMTD operates from outside the guest VM instance, it does not require guest agents or specific guest OS configuration, and it is immune to complex malware countermeasures. Inside the guest VM, no CPU cycles are used, and network access is not required. Signatures do not need to be updated, and the service does not need to be managed. VMTD is not supported on confidential computing since it operates with hardware encryption of memory.

The capabilities of Google Cloud's hypervisor are required for VMTD; it cannot be used in on-premises or other public cloud settings.

Here are the threats it will alert you to:

- **Execution: Cryptocurrency Mining Hash Match**: Matches memory hashes of running programs against known memory hashes of cryptocurrency mining software.

- **Execution: Cryptocurrency Mining YARA Rule**: Matches memory patterns, such as proof-of-work constants, known to be used by cryptocurrency mining software.

- **Execution: Cryptocurrency Mining Combined Detection**: Combines multiple categories of findings detected within a one-hour period. The threats are rolled into a single finding.

You have seen how VMTD can be used; now let us look at the last topic of threat detection, anomaly detection.

Anomaly detection

Anomaly detection is a built-in feature that uses external behavior signals to detect anomalies. It shows granular details about security abnormalities found in your projects and VM instances, such as potential credential leaks and currency mining. When you subscribe to the SCC Standard or Premium tier, anomaly detection is turned on immediately, and the results are displayed on the SCC dashboard.

This feature is available for the Standard and Premium versions of SCC. Here are the findings detected by anomaly detection. They are generated in the following two categories:

- **Potential for compromise**:

    - `account_has_leaked_credentials`: Credentials for a Google Cloud service account are accidentally leaked online or are compromised.

    - `resource_compromised_alert`: Potential compromise of a resource in your organization.

- **Abuse scenarios**:

  - `resource_involved_in_coin_mining`: Behavioral signals around a VM in your organization indicate that a resource might have been compromised and could be getting used for crypto mining.

  - `outgoing_intrusion_attempt`: One of the resources or Google Cloud services in your organization is being used for intrusion activities, such as an attempt to break into or compromise a target system. These include SSH brute force attacks, port scans, and FTP brute force attacks.

  - `resource_used_for_phishing`: One of the resources or Google Cloud services in your organization is being used for phishing.

Now that we understand various abilities of threat detection, let us move on to look at the SCC feature for compliance monitoring.

Continuous compliance monitoring

In a regulated organization, compliance takes precedence as it is mandated by regulations; however, compliance is now generally enforced by all security-conscious organizations, regardless of regulations. SCC provides the ability to continuously monitor your Google Cloud compliance posture by doing the following:

- Identifying compliance violations in your Google Cloud assets helps you resolve them by following actionable suggestions

- Reviewing and exporting compliance reports to ensure all your resources are meeting their compliance requirements

- Supporting compliance standards, such as these:

  - **Payment Card Industry Data Security Standard (PCI DSS v3.2.1)**

  - **International Organization for Standardization (ISO 27001)**

  - **National Institute of Standards and Technology (NIST 800-53)**

  - **Center for Internet Security (CIS)** 1.0 and 1.1 benchmarks

Now let us look at how SCC supports these standards.

CIS benchmarks

SCC supports the following CIS benchmarks for Google Cloud. CIS 1.0 and CIS 1.1 are still supported, but eventually, they will be deprecated. It is recommended to use or transition to using the latest benchmark, CIS 1.2:

- CIS Google Cloud Computing Foundations Benchmark v1.2.0 (CIS Google Cloud Foundation 1.2)
- CIS Google Cloud Computing Foundations Benchmark v1.1.0 (CIS Google Cloud Foundation 1.1)
- CIS Google Cloud Computing Foundations Benchmark v1.0.0 (CIS Google Cloud Foundation 1.0)

Additional standards

The PCI DSS and the OWASP Foundation do not supply or approve additional compliance mappings, which are included for reference only. To manually check for these violations, consult the PCI Standard 3.2.1 (PCI-DSS v3.2.1), OWASP Top Ten, NIST 800-53, and ISO 27001.

Note that this feature is exclusively for customers to use to check for violations of compliance regulations. The mappings are not intended to be used as the foundation for, or as a substitute for, an audit, certification, or report of compliance with any regulatory or industry benchmarks or standards for your products or services.

So far, we have seen how SCC generates the finding by using various modules. Let us now move on to see how we can export the findings for analysis. The findings can also be sent for remediation in SOAR tools such as Google Chronicle SOAR.

Exporting SCC findings

SCC allows you to export SCC data, including assets, findings, and security marks to another system of your choice:

- Exports of current discoveries, assets, and security markings on a one-time basis
- Continuous exports, which automatically export new discoveries to Pub/Sub SCC for Premium users, and allow you to export data using the SCC API or the Google Cloud console
- You may also export your results to BigQuery

Let us look at these now.

One-time exports

You can manually transmit and download current and historical findings and assets in JSON or JSONL format via one-time exports using the Google Cloud console. You can upload data to a Cloud Storage bucket and then download it to your local machine. You need to take security measures to ensure all locally stored findings are stored safely.

Exporting data using the SCC API

Using the SCC API, you may export assets, results, and security marks to a Cloud Storage bucket. The API results for discoveries or assets can be retrieved or exported once they have been listed:

- The `ListFindings` and `ListAssets` API methods are used to list findings or assets with any connected security markings. The methods return assets or findings in JSON format, complete with all their characteristics, attributes, and related marks. If you need data in a different format for your application, you will need to develop additional code to convert the JSON output.

- The `GroupAssets` or `GroupFindings` methods are utilized if the `groupBy` field is set to a value. The `GroupAssets` and `GroupFindings` methods deliver a list of assets or findings for an organization, grouped by properties.

Continuous exports

SCC Premium clients can use continuous exports to automate the process of exporting SCC findings to Pub/Sub:

- New discoveries are immediately exported to selected Pub/Sub topics in near-real time when they are written, allowing you to integrate them into your existing process

- Using the SCC API, you may set up Pub/Sub finding notifications in SCC

- To set up Pub/Sub topics, construct finding filters, and create `NotificationConfig` files (files that contain notification configuration options), you must utilize the Google Cloud CLI

Now let us go over how to use Pub/Sub for continuous exports.

Configuring Pub/Sub exports

Continuous exports let you automate the export of all future findings to Pub/Sub or create filters to export future findings that meet specific criteria. You can filter findings by category, source, asset type, security marks, severity, state, and other variables. Let us see how to set up an export now.

Creating continuous exports

Your organization can create a maximum of 500 continuous exports. To create an export for Pub/Sub, do the following:

1. Go to the SCC **Findings** page in the Cloud console. In the **Filter** field, select the attributes, properties, or security marks you want to use to filter findings and enter the desired variables. A blank filter is evaluated as a wildcard and all findings are exported.

2. Click **Export**, and then, under **Continuous**, click **Pub/Sub**.

3. Review your filter to ensure it is correct and, if necessary, return to the **Findings** page to modify it.

4. Under **Continuous export name**, enter a name for the export.

5. Under **Continuous export description**, enter a description for the export.

6. Under **Export to**, select a project for your export.

7. Under **Pub/Subtopic**, select the topic where you want to export findings. To create a topic, do the following:

    I.   Select **Create a topic**.

    II.   Fill out **Topic ID**, and then select other options as needed.

    III. Click **Create Topic**.

8. Click **Save**. You will see a confirmation and are returned to the **Findings** page.

9. Follow the guide to create a subscription for your Pub/Sub topic.

The Pub/Sub export configuration is complete. To publish notifications, a service account is created for you in the form of `service-org-ORGANIZATION_ID@gcp-sa-scc-notification.iam.gserviceaccount.com`. This service account is automatically granted the `securitycenter.notificationServiceAgent` role at the organization level. This service account role is required for notifications to function.

BigQuery is a popular tool for the analysis of vast amounts of data. Now let us look at how to export findings to BigQuery for analysis.

Exporting findings to BigQuery

Any new discoveries written to SCC can be immediately exported to a BigQuery table. The data can then be integrated into current workflows and a unique analysis can be created. You can use this functionality to export findings based on your needs at the organization, folder, and project levels.

Because it is fully managed and does not need manual procedures or custom code, this feature is the ideal solution for exporting SCC findings to BigQuery.

Here are a few points that you need to know before you can export your findings to BigQuery:

- You create an export configuration to export findings to BigQuery. You can create export configurations at the project, folder, or organization level. For example, if you want to export findings from a project to a BigQuery dataset, you create an export configuration at the project level to export only the findings related to that project. Optionally, you can specify filters to export certain findings only.

- You can create a maximum of 500 export configurations to BigQuery for your organization. You can use the same dataset for multiple export configurations. If you use the same dataset, all updates will be made to the same findings table.

- When you create your first export configuration, a service account is automatically created for you. This service account is required to create or update the findings table within a dataset and to export findings to the table. It has the form `service-org-ORGANIZATION_ID@ gcp-sa-scc-notification.iam.gserviceaccount.com` and is granted the `BigQuery Data Editor (roles/bigquery.dataEditor)` role at the BigQuery dataset level.

Now let us go over the steps for exporting the SCC findings to BigQuery:

1. Go to the Google Cloud console.
2. Select the project for which you enabled the SCC API.
3. Click **Activate Cloud Shell**.
4. To create a new export configuration, run the following command:

```
gcloud scc bqexports create BIG_QUERY_EXPORT \
   --dataset=DATASET_NAME \
   --folder=FOLDER_ID | --organization=ORGANIZATION_ID |
 --project=PROJECT_ID \
   [--description=DESCRIPTION] \
   [--filter=FILTER]
```

Replace the following in the preceding command:

- Replace `BIG_QUERY_EXPORT` with a name for this export configuration.

- Replace `DATASET_NAME` with the name of the BigQuery dataset; for example, `projects/<PROJECT_ID>/datasets/<DATASET_ID>`.

- Replace `FOLDER_ID`, `ORGANIZATION_ID`, and `PROJECT_ID` with the name of your folder, organization, or project. You must set one of these options. For folders and organizations, the name is the folder ID or the organization ID. For projects, the name is the project number or the project ID.

- Replace DESCRIPTION with a human-readable description of the export configuration. This variable is optional.

- Replace FILTER with an expression that defines what findings to include in the export. For example, if you want to filter on the XSS_SCRIPTING category, type "category=\"XSS_SCRIPTING\". This variable is optional.

5. To verify the details of the export configuration, run the following command:

```
gcloud scc bqexports get BIG_QUERY_EXPORT \   --folder=FOLDER_ID
| --organization=ORGANIZATION_ID | --project=PROJECT_ID
```

Replace the following:

- Replace BIG_QUERY_EXPORT with the name for this export configuration.

- Replace FOLDER_ID, ORGANIZATION_ID, and PROJECT_ID with the name of your folder, organization, or project. You must set one of these options. For folders and organizations, the name is the folder ID or the organization ID. For projects, the name is the project number or the project ID.

You should see the findings in your BigQuery dataset about 15 minutes after you create the export configuration. After the BigQuery table is created, any new and updated findings that match your filter and scope will appear in the table in near-real time. Check out the Google Cloud documentation for useful queries to view the findings.

We have seen how to export findings via Pub/Sub. These findings can be sent to SOAR tools to build an automated response. We will quickly go over that workflow now.

Automating a findings response

Google provides procedures for the following four types of SOAR products for exporting SCC alerts and findings:

- Palo Alto Cortex XSOAR

- Elastic Stack

- Splunk

- IBM QRadar

However, you can set up an integration using Pub/Sub to any other product if it can ingest and parse the Pub/Sub message.

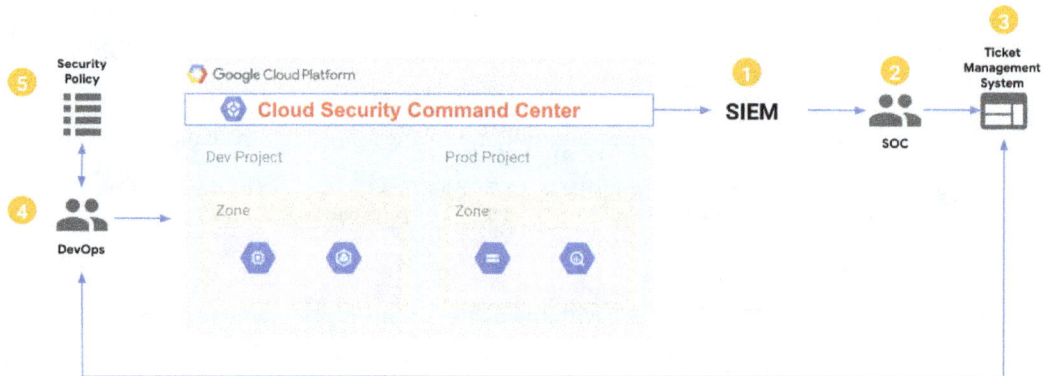

Figure 14.2 – Automating SCC response

Figure 14.2 shows an architecture of a simple workflow to automate a response based on SCC alerts and findings. The steps in the workflow are listed as follows. Each of these steps represents an action that can be taken either manually or automated. Understanding the various categories of threats and vulnerability findings is critical before building such a workflow.

Let us quickly run through these steps:

1. SCC alerts and findings are exported to the SIEM tool of your choice. As you saw in the previous section, you can export alerts and findings using continuous exports.

2. An SIEM alert is generated based on a pre-defined criterion. Your SIEM tool will have some logic for how to interpret the alert categories and what severity they are.

3. The SOC analyst collects information, understands the context, and classifies the incident.

4. The SOC analyst opens an IT service management ticket and assigns it to the appropriate operations team.

5. The operations team remediates the issue or contacts the project team that owns the asset that generated the alert for remediation.

6. If the alert is new, the security team creates preventative controls and updates the security policy.

Summary

In this chapter, we went over several capabilities of SCC. We learned how to use CAI, set up an export to BigQuery, and run SQL queries to understand your environment. We also went over how to detect security misconfigurations using SHA, VM Manager, WSS, and Rapid Vulnerability Detection. These are all critical capabilities before a security misconfiguration vulnerability becomes a threat. We learned about the threat detection capabilities of SCC in the form of ETD, CTD, VMTD, and anomaly detection. We also covered continuous compliance monitoring to understand how to apply industry standards to your cloud environment. Finally, we explored a simple architecture pattern for alerting.

In the next chapter, we will cover container security and look at how security measures are taken to protect containers and the applications and data that reside in them. This includes preventing unauthorized access and mitigating the risk of malicious code or attacks, as well as ensuring that your containers are configured in accordance with industry best practices.

Further reading

For more information on Google Cloud Security Command Center, refer to the following links:

* Event Threat Detection rules: `https://packt.link/Oeyqd`

* Sensitive IAM roles and permissions: `https://packt.link/5V1TK`

* Useful BigQuery queries for SCC findings: `https://packt.link/n8rwU`

* Creating charts in Google Looker Studio for findings: `https://packt.link/esxM2`

15

Container Security

In this chapter, we will look at container security. Container security is critical for today's enterprises because containers have become the go-to technology for deploying applications in modern IT environments. As a result, they have become a target for attackers who seek to exploit vulnerabilities in container infrastructure and applications to gain access to sensitive data or cause harm to the organization. Without proper security measures in place, containers can create significant risks for enterprises, including data breaches, system downtime, and compliance violations. By prioritizing container security and implementing best practices, enterprises can protect their applications, data, and infrastructure from cyber threats and ensure the safe and secure deployment of their workloads. Container security is considered a critical aspect of cloud security. It is a broad topic, so we will try to cover it from the exam point of view.

In this chapter, we will cover the following topics:

- Overview of containers
- Container basics
- Kubernetes and Google's GKE platform
- Threats and risks in containers
- GKE security features such as namespaces, RBAC, and service meshes
- Container image security
- Container vulnerability scanning
- Binary authorization
- Cluster certification authority
- Container security best practices

Overview of containers

A container is a lightweight, standalone executable package that contains everything needed to run an application, including the code, runtime, libraries, and dependencies. Containers are designed to be easily portable between different computing environments, making them an ideal solution for modern application deployment. Everything at Google runs in containers, from Gmail to YouTube to Search. Development teams can now move quickly, distribute software efficiently, and operate at unprecedented scale thanks to containerization.

Containers come with security advantages inherent to their architecture:

- Containers are short-lived and frequently re-deployed

- Containers are intentionally immutable; a modified container is a default security alert

- Good security defaults are one-line changes; setting secure configurations is easy

- With isolation technologies, you can increase security without adding resources

Google invests massively in container security. Here is Google's container security philosophy:

- **Prioritize security by default**: Google believes in giving users the power of Kubernetes without making them security experts.

- **Integrate the best of Google Cloud Platform security**: Integrations with IAM, audit logging, VPCs, encryption by default, and Security Command Center.

- **Strong security culture**: Google dedicates a large amount of resources to securely designing and running systems. Security is an integral part of Google's culture, products, and operations.

But before we dive deeper into container security, let us first understand what containers are.

Container basics

Traditionally, applications used to be deployed on dedicated servers. To run an application, you would do the following:

1. Purchase hardware.
2. Install the OS.
3. Install dependencies.
4. Deploy application code.
5. Make sure the application is the same across all environments.

This took a lot of time and resources to deploy and maintain. It was not portable and was difficult to scale. VMware popularized running multiple servers and operating systems (OSs) on the same hardware using a hypervisor. Each virtual machine (VM) has its own dedicated resources, including memory, CPU, and storage, which are allocated by the hypervisor that manages them. VMs are isolated from each other and from the host machine, providing greater security and flexibility but also requiring more resources and longer startup times. Containers share the host machine's OS kernel and use containerization technology to isolate the application from other processes running on the host. Because they don't need to emulate an entire OS, containers are much smaller and faster to start up than VMs.

Now let us see how containers are structured.

What are containers?

Containers are a method of *packaging an application executable and its dependencies* (runtime, system tools, system libraries, configuration, and so on) and running the package as a set of resource-isolated processes.

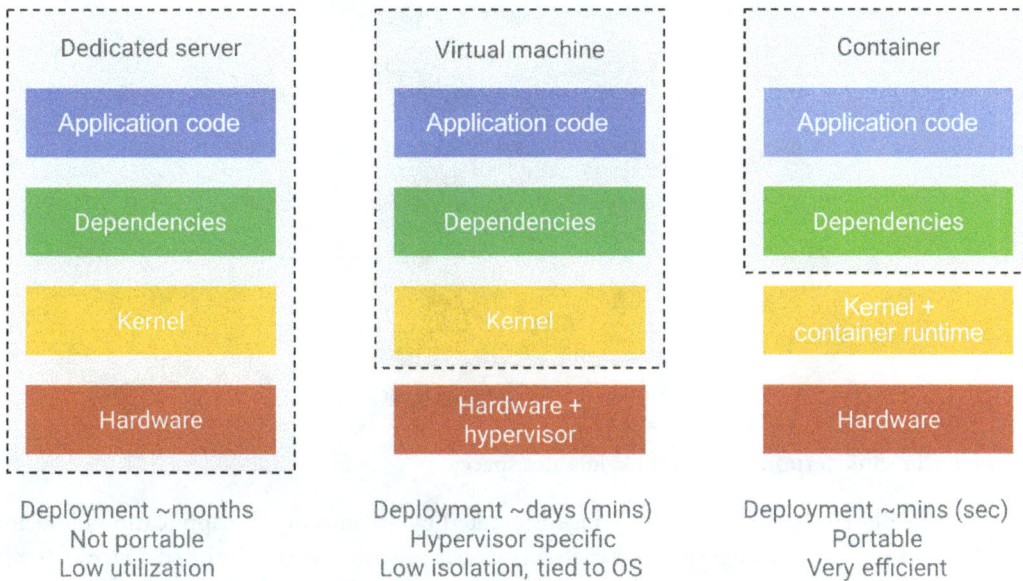

Dedicated server	Virtual machine	Container
Application code	Application code	Application code
Dependencies	Dependencies	Dependencies
Kernel	Kernel	Kernel + container runtime
Hardware	Hardware + hypervisor	Hardware
Deployment ~months Not portable Low utilization	Deployment ~days (mins) Hypervisor specific Low isolation, tied to OS	Deployment ~mins (sec) Portable Very efficient

Figure 15.1 – Container structure

Containers raise the abstraction one more level and virtualize the OS. They are extremely portable and can be run locally or in the cloud without any changes. Lightweight containers do not carry a full OS and can be packed tightly onto available resources. Fast startup is no more than starting a process on the OS.

Containers use the concept of a **layered filesystem**. The base image layers are all read-only. Updates are made to a small read-write layer built on top of a base image. Each container has its own writable container layer. All changes are stored in this layer.

Multiple containers share the same underlying read-only image. Any changes to lower levels are first copied to the container layer where changes are then overlaid only for that container. The base image is shared across containers, taking less disk space and enabling fast container start times.

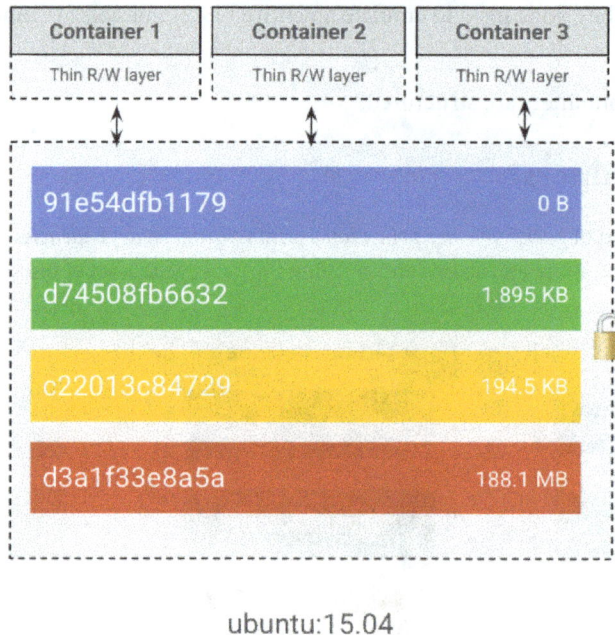

Figure 15.2 – Container layers

Let us go over some terminology in the container space:

- **Container image**: A container image is created by assembling the application code and dependencies into a single package that can be easily distributed and deployed. Once an image is created, it can be stored in a container registry, such as Docker Hub or Google Container Registry, and then used to spin up one or more containers on a Kubernetes cluster.

- **Container**: A container running in a pod is an instantiated container image.

- **Container host**: The container host is the computer that runs the containerized processes, commonly called containers.

- **Registry server**: A registry server is just a fancy file server where container images are stored.

- **Container orchestrator**: This is software that manages containers. Google GKE, AWS EKS, Azure AKS, and Red Hat OpenShift are examples of container orchestrators. A container orchestrator serves two purposes:

  - Container workloads are dynamically scheduled in a cluster of machines.

  - It uses a uniform application definition file to set up the cluster.

- **Kubernetes**: Kubernetes is an open source container orchestrator, developed by Google.

- **Namespaces**: Think of a namespace as a virtual mechanism to group containers within your Kubernetes cluster. You can have multiple namespaces inside a single cluster.

- **Docker**: Docker is the container runtime that builds, runs, and monitors containers. Other runtimes include LXC, systemd-nspawn, CoreOS rkt, and others.

- **Cgroups**: Control groups, or cgroups, is a feature of Linux that constrains the resources (CPU, memory, and so on) allocated to processes. The kubelet and the underlying runtime, such as Docker, use cgroups to enforce resource management for pods and containers.

- **Container registry**: A container registry is a repository that holds container images not yet deployed. Cloud providers including Google will provide a registry service in the cloud. For example, Google has Artifact Registry and Container Registry (deprecated) for container images.

Now that we understand the basic terminology of containers, let us understand the advantages of using containers.

Advantages of containers

There are many advantages of running containerized applications. Here are some:

- **Separation of code and computing**:

  - Consistency across dev, test, and production

  - Consistency across bare-metal, VMs, and the cloud

  - No more *it worked on my computer*

- **Packaged applications**:

  - Agile application creation and deployment

  - Containers aid massively in a Continuous Integration/Delivery/DevOps process

- **Conducive for microservices**:

  - Container deployments are introspectable

  - Isolated/loosely coupled, conducive to distributed systems, and elastic

- **Faster time to market**:

  - Small features can be rolled out multiple times a day rather than waiting weeks to deploy

  - Containers are easy to roll back, so if a feature fails in canary deployment, it can be quickly rolled back without impacting customers

Now that you understand the basics of containers and why to use containers, we will look at how to run containers in a scalable fashion using a container orchestrator such as Kubernetes.

What is Kubernetes?

Kubernetes, also known as **K8s**, is an open source system for automating the deployment, scaling, and management of containerized applications. The name Kubernetes originates from Greek, meaning helmsman or pilot. In simple terms, think of K8s as the orchestrator for your container fleet. It tracks how many containers are needed, which one is performing well, and how to direct your traffic, among other things.

Here are some features provided by K8s:

- **Load balancing and service discovery**: Kubernetes exposes a container using an independent IP address or a DNS name. Kubernetes may load balance and spread the traffic to keep the deployment stable.

- **Storage management**: Kubernetes can allow you to mount storage, also called volume, that containers in the pods can read and write to; for example, on GKE you can mount volumes such as **emptyDir**, **ConfigMap**, **Secret**, and so on.

- **Rollouts and rollbacks**: Kubernetes does an automated rollout and rollback for you. All you need to do is define the desired state of your application.

- **Packing**: Bin packing is done automatically for you. Bin packing is a scheduling strategy used by the Kubernetes scheduler to optimize the allocation of resources across nodes in a cluster. The goal of bin packing is to maximize the utilization of available resources while minimizing waste.

- **Self-healing**: This is a feature of Kubernetes implemented as auto-repair in GKE. Auto-repair makes periodic checks on the health of cluster nodes. If a node fails a health check, Kubernetes will try to repair that node.

- **Management of secrets and configurations**: Kubernetes will let you deploy secrets, such as OAuth tokens, passwords, and so on, securely. These are stored unencrypted in the K8S database. Secrets are kept separately from the pods that use them. That way, you do not need to embed secrets within your application code. GKE provides many advanced features for secret management.

Now that you understand what Kubernetes is, we should also understand what Kubernetes is not:

- Kubernetes doesn't impose restrictions on supported applications. Kubernetes promises to serve stateless, stateful, and data-processing workloads. Anything that runs in a container should run well on Kubernetes.

- Kubernetes does not build or deploy source code. CI/CD procedures are driven by organizational cultures and preferences and technical constraints.

- Kubernetes does not include application-level services such as middleware (message buses), data processing frameworks (Spark), databases (MySQL), caches, or cluster storage systems (Ceph). Applications running on Kubernetes can access such components via portable interfaces such as the Open Service Broker API. The Kubernetes **Open Service Broker (OSB)** is a component that allows Kubernetes users to easily provision and manage services from a variety of providers.

- Kubernetes has no configuration language/system (for example, Jsonnet). It exposes a declarative API that can target any declarative specification.

- Kubernetes has no extensive machine configuration, maintenance, management, or self-healing systems.

- Kubernetes isn't just an orchestration platform. Orchestration is the execution of a defined workflow: first, do A, then B, then C. Kubernetes, on the other hand, is a collection of *independent, composable control processes that continuously strive to achieve the desired state*. So, it does not matter how you go from state A to C. It also removes the need for centralized control. This makes the system more powerful, robust, resilient, and extensible.

Everything at Google runs on containers, such as Gmail, Search, Maps, and even **Google Cloud Platform (GCP)**. Google is said to deploy over 4 billion containers every week.

Now let us look at Google Cloud's managed Kubernetes platform, called GKE.

GKE

Google Kubernetes Engine (GKE) is a managed platform for Kubernetes on Google Cloud. It provides the following additional features on top of K8s:

- Kubernetes clusters as a service

- It runs Kubernetes on GCE

- It is integrated with GCP

- It supports heterogeneous and multi-zone clusters

- It manages Kubernetes (auto-upgrades, scaling, healing, monitoring, backup, and so on)

Let us now look at the architecture of GKE.

GKE architecture

In GKE, the master is the control plane that manages the entire lifecycle of a cluster. The cluster master is responsible for deciding what runs on all the cluster's nodes and acts as a unified endpoint that provides the Kubernetes API Server for the cluster. The project that holds the control plane is managed by Google for you. You do not get access to this project.

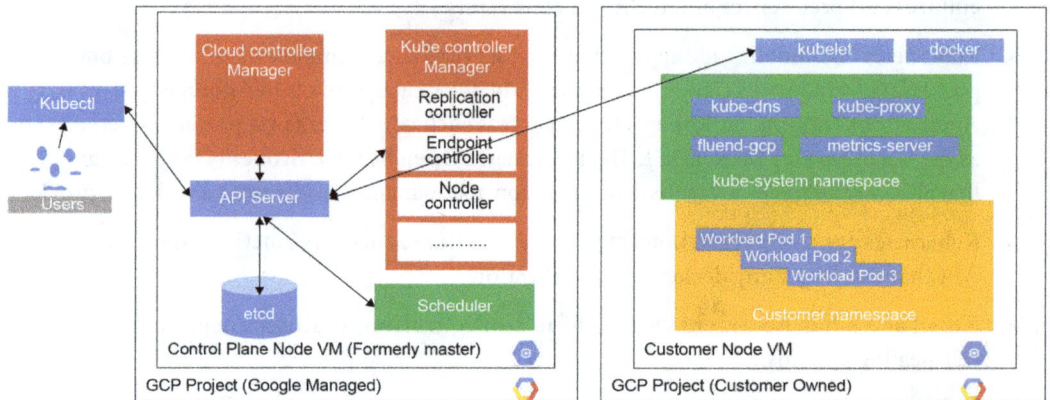

Figure 15.3 – GKE architecture

Here are the key components of GKE:

- **Control plane**: The control plane is the central management component of GKE. It includes various services that handle cluster management, scheduling, and communication between different components. The control plane manages the state of the cluster and ensures that the desired configuration is maintained. The control plane is managed by Google in a Google managed project. Customers do not have access to this project. The control plane in GKE is designed for high availability and fault tolerance. It runs across multiple compute instances (VMs) distributed across different availability zones within a region. The control plane consists of several master components, including the following:

  - **kube-apiserver**: This provides the API endpoint for interacting with the cluster. It handles authentication, authorization, and validation of API requests.

  - **etcd**: This is a distributed key-value store used to store the cluster's configuration data and state.

  - **kube-scheduler**: This assigns pods to nodes based on resource requirements, constraints, and availability.

  - **kube-controller-manager**: This runs various controllers responsible for maintaining the desired state of the cluster, handling replication, scaling, and other cluster-level operations.

- **cloud-controller-manager**: This interacts with GCP APIs to manage resources such as load balancers, disks, and network routes.

- **Customer node VM**: Nodes are the worker machines in a GKE cluster in a customer project. Each node runs the Kubernetes components necessary for managing containers, such as the kubelet, kube-proxy, and container runtime (for example, Docker). Nodes are responsible for running the containerized applications and scaling resources based on demand.

- **Cluster**: A GKE cluster is a set of compute instances (nodes) that run containerized applications. The cluster is managed by the control plane and provides the underlying infrastructure to deploy and manage containers. It can span multiple availability zones for high availability and resilience.

- **Pods**: Pods are the smallest deployable units in Kubernetes. They encapsulate one or more containers and share the same network namespace and storage volumes. Pods are scheduled and managed by Kubernetes, and they provide an isolated environment for running applications.

- **Services**: Services provide network connectivity and load balancing for the pods within a GKE cluster. They define a stable endpoint that can be used to access the application running inside the pods. Services can be exposed internally within the cluster or externally to the internet.

- **Load balancers**: GKE integrates with Google Cloud Load Balancing to distribute traffic across multiple nodes and services. Load balancers help distribute incoming requests to pods within the cluster and provide scalability and high availability for applications.

- **Persistent storage**: GKE supports various options for persistent storage. It integrates with Google Cloud Storage, Persistent Disk, and other storage solutions to provide durable and scalable storage for applications running in the cluster. Persistent volumes can be dynamically provisioned and attached to pods as needed.

- **Container Registry**: GKE integrates with Google Container Registry, which is a private container image registry. It allows you to store and manage your container images securely. Container Registry provides an easy way to store, share, and deploy container images for your applications.

- **kubectl**: kubectl is a command-line tool used to interact with Kubernetes clusters. It is part of the official Kubernetes distribution and provides a convenient interface for managing and controlling Kubernetes resources. With kubectl, you can deploy and manage applications, inspect and modify cluster resources, view logs, execute commands within containers, and perform various other administrative tasks within a Kubernetes environment. It supports a wide range of commands and options to interact with the Kubernetes API server and control the desired state of your cluster.

These are the key components of GKE that work together to enable the efficient deployment and management of containerized applications using Kubernetes. GKE abstracts away all the complexities of managing the underlying infrastructure, allowing developers to focus on building and deploying their applications. Now that we understand GKE architecture at a high level, it is imperative to understand Google's shared responsibility model.

GKE shared responsibility model

Google is responsible for the following aspects of GKE security:

- The hardware, firmware, kernel, OS, storage, network, and other components of the underlying infrastructure. This includes encrypting data at rest by default, encrypting data in transit, custom-designed hardware, private network connections, physical access protection for data centers, and secure software development methods.

- The OS for the nodes, such as **Container-Optimized OS** (**COS**) or Ubuntu. GKE makes any changes to these images available as soon as possible. These images are automatically installed if you have auto-upgrade enabled. This is the foundation of your container; it is different from the operating system that runs inside it.

- Kubernetes is a container orchestration system. GKE provides the most recent Kubernetes upstream versions and supports numerous minor versions. It is Google's responsibility to provide updates to these, including patches.

- The control plane, which comprises the master VMs, the API server, and other components that run on those VMs, as well as the etcd database, is managed by GKE. This includes upgrades and patches, scalability, and repairs, all of which are backed up by a **Service-Level Agreement** (**SLA**).

- IAM, Cloud Audit Logging, Cloud Logging, Cloud Key Management Service, Cloud Security Command Center, and other Google Cloud integrations. These controls are also accessible for IaaS workloads on GKE in Google Cloud.

Now let us see what Google Cloud customers are responsible for:

- The nodes on which your workloads are executed. Any additional software installed on the nodes, as well as any configuration changes made to the default, are your responsibility.

- Customers are also in charge of keeping their nodes up to date. Google automatically supplies hardened VM images and configurations, maintains the containers required to run GKE, and gives OS patches—all they need to do is upgrade. If they use node auto-upgrade, Google will upgrade these nodes for them.

- The workloads themselves, which include your application code, Dockerfiles, container images, data, RBAC/IAM rules, and running containers and pods. To help safeguard your containers, you can use GKE security features and other Google Cloud products such as **Container Threat Detection** (**KTD**), part of Security Command Center. Sometimes Google customers also use third-party products such as Twistlock for runtime protections.

Now that you understand GKE architecture and the shared responsibility model, let us see what are the challenges for container security.

Container security

Container security is about making sure that a container-based system or workload is protected by using different security methods and technologies. This includes securing the container image during creation, securing the deployment of the image, and making sure that the container environment is secure during runtime.

Let us look at threats and risks in containers.

Threats and risks in containers

NIST defines cybersecurity risks as relating to the loss of confidentiality, integrity, and availability of information and data and its potential adverse impact on an organization or business. The NIST definition of container security risks includes the following:

- **Image risks**: Image configuration defects, embedded malware, embedded clear text secrets, the use of untrusted images

- **Registry risks**: Insecure registry connections, stale images, and inadequate authentication and authorization to the registry are common risks

- **Orchestrator risks**: Unrestricted administrative access, unauthorized access, poorly separated inter-container network traffic, and the mixing of workload sensitivity levels

- **Container risks**: Vulnerabilities within the runtime software, unbounded network access from containers, insecure container runtime configurations, app vulnerabilities, and rogue containers

- **Host OS risks**: Large attack surface, shared kernel, vulnerabilities in host OS components, unauthorized user access permissions, manipulation with the host OS file system, and unauthorized hosts joining the cluster and running containers

Considering these risks, at a high level, the container threats in the cloud can be separated into three categories:

- **Container infrastructure security**: Is your infrastructure secure for deploying containers? The threats in this category include the following:

  - Privilege escalation

  - Credential compromise

  - Kubernetes API compromise

  - Overprivileged users

- **Software supply chain threats**: Is your container image secure to build and deploy? The threats in this category include the following:

  - Unpatched vulnerability

  - Supply chain vulnerability

  - Exploiting a common library

- **Runtime security**: Is your container secure to run? The threats in this category include the following:

  - DDoS

  - Node compromise and exploitation

  - Container escape

Now let us look at the GKE security features to understand how GKE protects container workloads from these threats.

GKE security features

The contents of your container image, the container runtime, the cluster network, and access to the cluster API server all play a role in protecting workloads in GKE. Let us understand a few security features in GKE.

Namespaces

In Kubernetes, namespaces are used to separate groups of resources in a cluster. Resources within a namespace must have unique names, but this requirement doesn't apply across namespaces. It's important to note that namespace-based scoping only applies to resources that are specific to a namespace, such as Deployments and Services, and doesn't apply to objects that are used across the entire cluster, such as Nodes, StorageClass, and PersistentVolume.

Namespaces in Kubernetes are intended for situations where there are multiple users spread across different teams or projects. If your cluster only has a small number of users, you may not need to worry about namespaces.

Namespaces allow you to group resources together by providing a unique scope for their names. Each resource can only be in one namespace, and namespaces cannot be nested inside each other. They also enable multiple users to share cluster resources through resource quotas.

If you only need to identify slightly different resources, such as different versions of the same software, you don't necessarily need to use multiple namespaces. Instead, you can use labels to differentiate resources within the same namespace.

Let us look at how GKE provides access control.

Access control

GKE supports two options for managing access to resources within the Google Cloud project and its clusters:

- **Kubernetes Role-Based Access Control (RBAC)**
- **Identity and Access Management (IAM)**

These two methods are similar in function, but they are focused on different types of resources. Let us look at them now.

Kubernetes RBAC

This is a built-in feature of Kubernetes that grants granular permissions to Kubernetes cluster objects. Within the cluster, permissions are represented by ClusterRole or Role objects. Roles in Kubernetes RBAC provide permissions at the namespace level, while ClusterRoles offer cluster-wide permissions. Proper usage of Roles and ClusterRoles is crucial for maintaining security by adhering to the principle of least privilege and enabling the separation of duties. Regular review and auditing of assigned Roles and ClusterRoles are essential to ensure that permissions align with security requirements. RoleBinding objects allow Kubernetes users, Google Cloud users, Google Cloud service accounts, and Google groups to have access to roles.

Kubernetes RBAC is the ideal choice if you primarily utilize GKE and need fine-grained rights for every item and operation in your cluster. GKE has built-in support for RBAC that allows you to create fine-grained Roles that exist within the GKE cluster. A role can be scoped to a specific Kubernetes object or a type of Kubernetes object and defines which actions (called verbs) the role grants in relation to that object. A **RoleBinding** is also a Kubernetes object, which grants roles to users. In GKE, the subject can be any of the following principals:

- Cloud Identity user
- Google Cloud IAM service account
- Kubernetes service account
- Cloud Identity Google group

Now, let us understand IAM for GKE.

IAM

IAM oversees Google Cloud resources, such as clusters and the types of things that can be accessed within them. GKE permissions/roles are assigned to IAM principals.

Within IAM, there is no way to provide permissions to individual Kubernetes objects. For example, you can give a user permission to create **Custom Resource Definitions (CRDs)**, but you cannot give them permission to create only one CustomResourceDefinition or to confine creation to a specific namespace or project cluster. If an IAM role is applied at the folder level, it grants rights to all clusters in the project or all clusters in all child projects.

IAM is a suitable choice if you use different Google Cloud components and do not need to maintain detailed Kubernetes-specific rights.

IAM and Kubernetes RBAC collaborate to help you manage cluster access. RBAC regulates access at the cluster and namespace levels, whereas IAM manages access at the project level. To work with resources in your cluster, an entity must have proper rights at both levels.

Now let us see how GKE manages secrets.

Secrets

Secrets are Kubernetes objects that store sensitive data in your clusters, such as passwords, OAuth tokens, and SSH keys. Secrets are more secure than plaintext ConfigMaps or Pod specs for storing sensitive data. Secrets provide you control over how sensitive data is utilized and decrease the chance of unauthorized persons accessing it. You can create a secret using the kubectl CLI or a YAML file.

Now let us understand how GKE tracks changes and activity.

Auditing

According to the Kubernetes documentation, Kubernetes auditing provides a security-relevant, chronological set of records documenting the sequence of actions in a cluster. The cluster audits the activities generated by users, by applications that use the Kubernetes API, and by the control plane itself.

Auditing allows cluster administrators to answer the following questions:

- What happened?
- When did it happen?
- Who initiated it?
- Where was it observed?
- From where was it initiated?
- To where was it going?

Audit records begin their lifecycle inside the `kube-apiserver` component. Each request on each stage of its execution generates an audit event, which is then pre-processed according to a certain policy and written to a backend. The policy determines what's recorded and the backends persist the records. The current backend implementations include log files and webhooks.

The Kubernetes documentation goes on to say that each request can be recorded with an associated stage. The defined stages are as follows:

- `RequestReceived`: The stage for events generated as soon as the audit handler receives the request, and before it is delegated down the handler chain.

- `ResponseStarted`: Once the response headers are sent, but before the response body is sent. This stage is only generated for long-running requests (for example, watch).

- `ResponseComplete`: The response body has been completed and no more bytes will be sent.

- `Panic`: Events generated when a panic occurred.

The Kubernetes audit policy defines rules about what events should be recorded and what data they should include. GKE receives the log entries from the Kubernetes API server, and it applies its own policy to determine which entries get written to the project's admin logs. For the most part, GKE applies the following rules to log entries that come from the Kubernetes API server:

- Entries that represent `create`, `delete`, and `update` requests go to the Admin Activity log

- Entries that represent `get`, `list`, and `updateStatus` requests go to the Data Access log

Admin Activity logs are turned on by default in your Google Cloud project. They can't be turned off; however, you must turn on Data Access logs. Let us move on to understanding the features of GKE logging.

Logging

By default, GKE clusters are natively integrated with Cloud Logging (and Monitoring). When you create a GKE cluster, both Monitoring and Cloud Logging are enabled by default. That means you get a monitoring dashboard specifically tailored for Kubernetes and your logs are sent to Cloud Logging's dedicated, persistent datastore and indexed for both searches and visualization in the Cloud Logs Viewer.

There are several ways to access your logs in Cloud Logging depending on your use case.

You can access your logs using the following:

- **Cloud Logging console**: You can see your logs directly from the Cloud Logging console by using the appropriate logging filters to select Kubernetes resources such as cluster, node, namespace, pod, or container logs. Here are some sample Kubernetes-related queries to help get you started.

- **GKE console**: In the **Kubernetes Engine** section of the Google Cloud console, select the Kubernetes resources listed in **Workloads**, and then the **Container** or **Audit Logs** link.

- **Monitoring console**: In the **Kubernetes Engine** section of the Monitoring console, select the appropriate cluster, nodes, pods, or containers to view the associated logs.

- **gcloud command line tool**: Using the `gcloud logging read` command, select the appropriate cluster, node, pod, and container logs.

These are all the methods of logging that you should be conversant with. Here are some best practices for containerized applications when it comes to logging:

- Use the native logging mechanisms of containers to write the logs to `stdout` and `stderr`.

- If your application cannot be easily configured to write logs to `stdout` and `stderr`, you can use a sidecar pattern for logging.

- Log directly with structured logging with different fields. You can then search your logs more effectively based on those fields.

- Use severities for better filtering and reducing noise. By default, logs written to the standard output are on the `INFO` level and logs written to the standard error are on the `ERROR` level. Structured logs with a JSON payload can include a severity field, which defines the log's severity.

- Use the links to the logs directly from the **Kubernetes Engine** section of the Cloud console for containers, which makes it quick to find the logs corresponding to the container.

Now that we have auditing and logging out of the way, let us move on to understand how GKE does network isolation.

Network Policies

You use Kubernetes NetworkPolicies for certain applications in your cluster if you wish to manage traffic flow at the IP address or port level (OSI layer 3 or 4). **Network policies** are an application-centric construct that allows you to declare how a pod can communicate across the network with various network *entities* (we use the term *entity* here to avoid overusing terms like *endpoints* and *services*, which have unique Kubernetes implications). Other connections are not affected by NetworkPolicies since they have a pod on one or both ends.

To manage communication between your cluster's pods and services, you can utilize GKE's network policy enforcement. Pod-level firewall rules are created using the Kubernetes Network Policy API to construct a network policy. These firewall rules control which pods and services in your cluster can communicate with one another.

When your cluster is hosting a multi-level application, defining a network policy allows you to enable things such as defense in depth. For example, you can set up a network policy to prevent a compromised frontend service from communicating directly with a billing or accounting server many tiers down.

A network policy can also help your application host data from several users at the same time. You can, for example, define a tenant-per-namespace paradigm to provide secure multi-tenancy. Network policy rules can ensure that pods and services in one namespace cannot access pods and services in another namespace in such a model.

Another form of network isolation is by using a feature called GKE private clusters, whereby you can host a private cluster, that is, a cluster with no public IP address. Let us understand this.

GKE private clusters

In private clusters, nodes only have internal IP addresses to isolate nodes from inbound and outbound connectivity to the internet.

Worker nodes in a private cluster only have internal IP addresses. The control plane, on the other hand, has both a private and a public destination. When creating a private cluster, you can disable access to the public endpoint. An internal load balancer provides access to the private endpoint. If you wish to reach the control plane from a GCP region other than where it is deployed, you will need to allow global access. Let us look at the architecture of private clusters now:

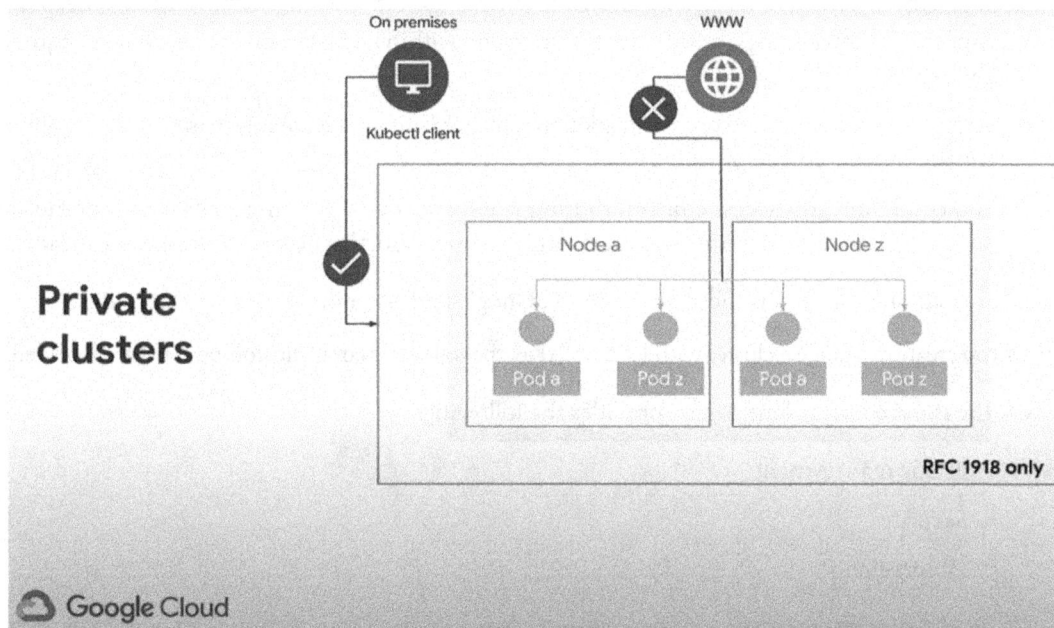

Figure 15.4 – Private clusters

As seen in *Figure 15.4*, using a private cluster has the additional security benefit that nodes are not exposed to the internet. As with public clusters, you can also use GKE's authorized networks feature with private clusters to restrict access to the master API.

A service mesh is an increasingly popular method of implementing network policies for GKE. We will understand that now.

Service mesh

A service mesh is a Layer 7 proxy. Microservices can use this service mesh to abstract the network. This effectively abstracts how inter-process and service-to-service communications are handled in the K8S cluster. In Kubernetes, the service mesh is usually implemented as a set of network proxies. These proxies, which are deployed as a *sidecar* of an application, serve as an entry point for service mesh functionality and manage communication between microservices. Istio is a popular open service mesh that connects, manages, and secures microservices in a consistent manner. It allows you to manage traffic flows between services, enforce access controls, and aggregate telemetry data without modifying the microservice code. The following are the benefits that Istio offers:

- Automatic load balancing for HTTP, gRPC, WebSocket, MongoDB, and TCP traffic
- Fine-grained control of traffic behavior with rich routing rules, retries, failovers, and fault injection
- A configurable policy layer and API that supports access controls, rate limits, and quotas
- Automatic metrics, logs, and traces for all traffic within a cluster, including cluster ingress and egress
- Secure service-to-service communication in a cluster with strong identity-based authentication and authorization
- You configure Istio access control, routing rules, and so on by using a custom Kubernetes API, either via kubectl or the Istio command-line tool istioctl, which provides extra validation

Google recommends using Anthos Service Mesh, Google's full-supported distribution of Istio.

When you create or update a cluster with Istio on GKE, the following core Istio components are installed:

- The *istiod* control plane, which provides the following:
  - Traffic management
  - Security
  - Observability
- The Istio ingress gateway, which provides an ingress point for traffic from outside the cluster

The installation also lets you add the Istio sidecar proxy to your service workloads, allowing them to communicate with the control plane and join the Istio mesh.

So far, we have understood the GKE security features. Now, we will look at how to secure a container image, which can be a source of vulnerability.

Container image security

Container images are *baked* by a pipeline, a series of steps that add the required components on top of each other. The application is deployed on the very top, as a last step. The following figure shows the process of a container pipeline published by NIST.

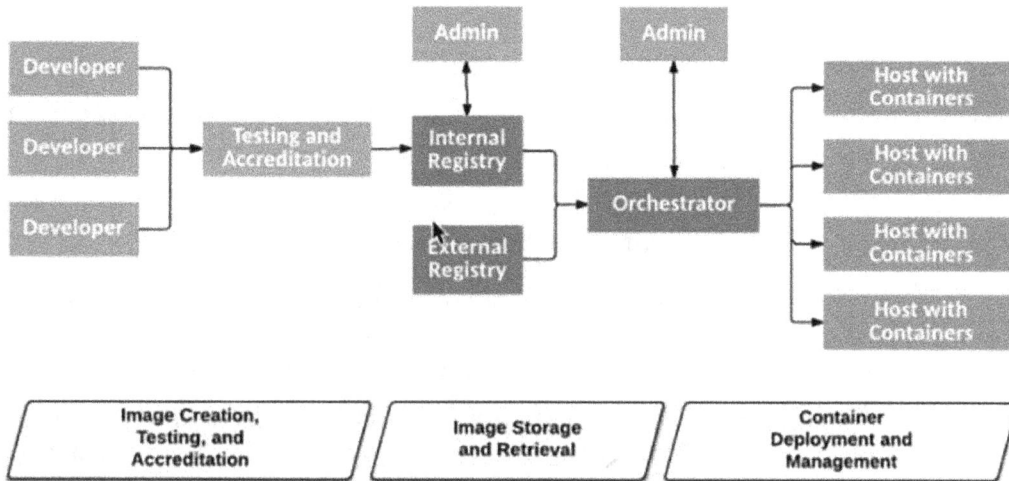

Figure 15.5 – Container pipeline

In *Figure 15.5*, as recommended by NIST (https://packt.link/luNhB), the container pipeline follows a controlled process for image generation:

1. Developer systems generate images and send them for testing and accreditation.
2. Testing and accreditation systems validate and verify the contents of images, sign images, and send images to the registry.
3. Registries store images and distribute images to the orchestrator upon request.
4. Orchestrators convert images into containers and deploy containers to hosts.
5. Hosts run and stop containers as directed by the orchestrator.

Now that you understand what the pipeline does, here are some best practices for container image security as recommended by Google:

- Use Google-maintained base images
- Do not rely on packages in third-party repositories (if possible, host an internal repository of the packages that are scanned for vulnerability)
- Do not include secrets in images

- Scan images for vulnerabilities

- Stop the deployment of the container if the images do not pass attestations (see the *Binary Authorization* section later in the chapter)

Now that you understand the best practices for image security, let us see how to scan an image for vulnerabilities on Google Cloud.

Container vulnerability scanning on Google Cloud

Container scanning is a service on Google Cloud that identifies known vulnerabilities in Debian, Ubuntu, Alpine, Red Hat, and CentOS packages inside the container on GCP. This feature can be enabled in Artifact Registry.

There are two types of scans supported by container scanning:

- **On-demand scanning**: Using the gcloud CLI, you may scan container images locally on your PC or in your registry on demand. This gives you the freedom to tailor your CI/CD pipeline to your specific needs, for example, when you need to obtain vulnerability results.

- **Automated scanning**: Container Analysis searches container images in Artifact Registry and Container Registry for vulnerabilities and keeps the vulnerability information up to date. Scanning and continuous analysis are the two major jobs in this technique.

When new images are uploaded to Artifact Registry or Container Registry, Container Analysis examines them. This scan extracts information on the container's system packages. Based on the image's digest, the images are only scanned once. This means that adding or changing tags will not result in new scans; only changing the image's content would. Here is what happens when you enable scanning:

- When you upload an image, Container Analysis creates occurrences for vulnerabilities found. It continually checks the information for scanned images in Artifact Registry and Container Registry for additional vulnerabilities after the initial scan.

- Container Analysis changes the metadata of the scanned images as new and updated vulnerability information is received from vulnerability sources, establishing new vulnerability occurrences for fresh images, and eliminating vulnerability occurrences that are no longer valid.

- Container Analysis only updates vulnerability metadata for images pushed or pulled in the previous 30 days. Vulnerability metadata older than 30 days is archived by Container Analysis. To re-scan an image with archived vulnerability metadata, push or pull that image.

You can also utilize **manifest lists** to scan for vulnerabilities. A manifest list is a collection of links to manifest files for various platforms. They allow a single image to work with numerous operating system architectures or variations. Only Linux amd64 images are supported by Container Analysis vulnerability scanning. Please note that if your manifest list points to more than one Linux amd64 image, only the first one will be scanned.

Container scanning uses the following severity levels:

- Critical

- High

- Medium

- Low

- Minimal

There are two types of *severity* associated with a vulnerability:

- **Effective severity**: The Linux distribution's designated severity level. Container scanning employs the severity level supplied by the provider if distribution-specific severity levels are not available.

- **CVSS score**: The **Common Vulnerability Scoring System** (**CVSS**) score and associated severity level, with two scoring versions:

  - **CVSS 2.0**: Available when using the API, the Google Cloud CLI, and the GUI

  - **CVSS 3.1**: Available when using the API and the gcloud CLI

Now that you understand container vulnerability scanning, let us see how to gate your deployment in case there are vulnerabilities or a critical step in the container pipeline is missing.

Binary Authorization

You can utilize Binary Authorization to construct a vulnerability allowlist as part of your Cloud Build workflow based on the vulnerability information provided by Container Analysis. The build will fail if the vulnerabilities contradict the allowlist's policy.

Container Analysis and Binary Authorization can be combined to provide attestations, which can prohibit known security vulnerabilities in container images from running in your production environment. Let us look at a process flow of how Binary Authorization can be incorporated into your pipeline:

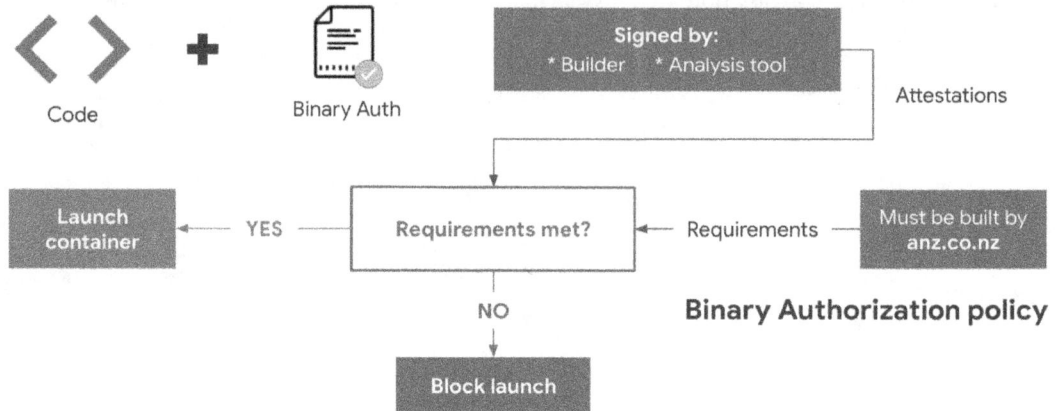

Figure 15.6 – Binary Authorization

As in *Figure 15.6*, Binary Authorization works by doing the following:

- Ensuring that only trusted code is deployed to your environment.

- Enforcing that certain signatures are on images deployed to production.

- Signing the build using Private PGP. **PGP** stands for **Pretty Good Privacy**. The public key is uploaded to the GKE admission controller for verification.

> **Note**
>
> PGP is a widely used encryption software program that allows users to encrypt and decrypt electronic messages, files, and data. PGP uses a combination of symmetric-key and public-key cryptography to provide strong encryption and digital signatures.

Here are the components that make up Binary Authorization:

- **Policies** govern the deployment of container images to GKE through a set of rules:

  - **Rules** are part of a policy that defines constraints that container images must pass before they can be deployed. Most often, a rule will require one or more digitally signed attestations. An **attestation** is a digitally signed record that signifies that the associated container image was built by the successful execution of a specific, required process. This is a *Continuous Integration* stage artifact.

- A **verified attestation** is a statement by an attestor that a container image is ready for deployment. This is a *Continuous Deployment* stage artifact.

- A **signer** is a person or an automated process that creates an attestation by signing a unique container image descriptor with a private key.

- Binary Authorization uses an **attestor** to verify the attestation at container deploy time with a public key.

Under the hood, Binary Authorization acts as a **Kubernetes admission controller**.

In GKE, this is implemented with the pod creation API, using the `ImagePolicy` admission controller. Binary Authorization supports using breakglass to override an authorization policy.

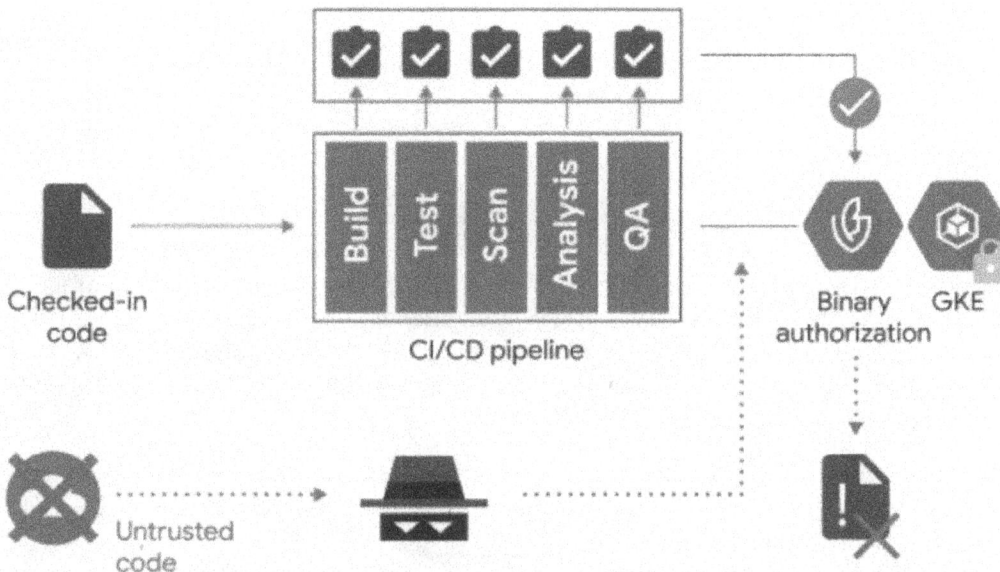

Figure 15.7 – Binary Authorization in the CI/CD pipeline

In *Figure 15.7*, you can see how Binary Authorization can stop untrusted code from deploying in the production GKE cluster.

Now that you understand the basics of the container pipeline and what Google Cloud products you can use for image vulnerability and to stop the deployment of untrusted code, let us move on to understand the certificate services of GKE.

Cluster Certificate Authority (CA)

A GKE cluster communicates with various components to keep the cluster healthy. The intracluster communication happens over **mutual TLS (mTLS)**. Here are various components of the cluster that uses mTLS:

- Control plane to node
- Node to node
- Pod to pod
- etcd to etcd (multiple instances of etcd)
- Control plane to etcd

Now let us understand the various components of the GKE **Public Key Infrastructure (PKI)** system that help with mTLS. We will start with the cluster root CA.

The cluster root CA

In GKE, the cluster root CA is used by the API server and `kubelet` to establish trust. Each cluster has its own CA, so if one CA is compromised, it doesn't affect other clusters. The API server and kubelet's client certificates are verified by the cluster root CA, ensuring a shared trust between control planes and nodes. A non-exportable root key managed by an internal Google service handles the CA and signs certificate requests from `kubelet`. Even if the API server is compromised, the CA remains secure, safeguarding other clusters. Additionally, a separate per-cluster etcd CA is used to validate etcd's certificates.

In Kubernetes, there is an API called `certificates.k8s.io` that allows you to create TLS certificates that are signed by your own CA (if required). You can then use these certificates and CA to establish trust in your workloads.

Let us understand the role of the API server and kubelet now.

The API server and kubelet

The API server and kubelet rely on the cluster root CA for trust. In GKE, the control plane API certificate is signed by the cluster root CA. Each cluster runs its own CA so that if one cluster's CA is compromised, no other cluster's CA is affected. Let us see some more details here:

- An internal Google service manages root keys for this CA, which are non-exportable. This service accepts certificate signing requests, including those from the kubelets in each GKE cluster. Even if the API server in a cluster were compromised, the CA would not be compromised, so no other clusters would be affected.

- Each node in the cluster is injected with a shared secret at creation, which it can use to submit certificate signing requests to the cluster root CA and obtain kubelet client certificates. These certificates are then used by the kubelet to authenticate its requests to the API server. This shared secret is reachable by pods on the node, unless you enable Shielded GKE nodes, Workload Identity, or metadata concealment.

- The API server and kubelet certificates are valid for five years but can be manually rotated sooner by performing credential rotation.

Let us understand etcd certificate exchange now.

etcd

In GKE, etcd relies on a separate per-cluster etcd certifying authority for trust. Let us see how etcd makes a cluster safe:

- Root keys for the etcd CA are distributed to the metadata of each VM on which the control plane runs.

- Any code executing on control plane VMs, or with access to compute metadata for these VMs, can sign certificates as this CA. Even if etcd in a cluster were compromised, the CA would not be shared between clusters, so no other clusters would be affected.

- The etcd certificates are valid for five years.

It is recommended that you perform certificate rotation to rotate all your cluster's API server and kubelet certificates. There is no need for you to initiate certificate rotation in etcd; this is handled by GKE.

Now that you understand GKE requirements and methods for the certificates, let us move on to understand the Workload Identity feature of GKE. This is different from the service account Workload Identity you studied earlier.

GKE Workload Identity

Workload Identity is an identity federation mechanism that allows K8s workloads to securely access Google Cloud services. On Autopilot clusters, Workload Identity is enabled by default. Workload Identity maps a pod to a **K8s Service account (KSA)** and KSA to an IAM service account.

Without using Workload Identity, this is what you need to do to access a Google Cloud service:

1. Create an IAM service account.
2. Create keys for a service account.
3. Import service account keys as a K8s secret.

On a K8s workload, you would usually follow the following steps for your application (running on a pod) to communicate with Google Cloud services, for example, Cloud Storage:

1. Define a volume with the secret.
2. Mount the volume inside the container.
3. Point $GOOGLE_APPLICATION_CREDENTIALS at the key file.
4. The workload can now authenticate to Google Cloud APIs as that service account.

This is toilsome to set up and hard to secure. A better option is to use Workload Identity. With Workload Identity, you can do the following:

1. Enable Workload Identity for a GKE cluster.
2. Run a workload using a dedicated KSA.
3. Grant KSA access to desired Google Cloud resources using IAM roles.
4. The workload can now access Google Cloud Storage APIs by presenting (short-lived, auto-rotated) KSA tokens.

You can see Workload Identity removes a lot of steps and makes your GKE workloads more secure than when using service account keys.

So far, we have seen various security features of GKE. Now let us look at the best practices recommended by CIS.

Center for Internet Security (CIS) best practices

Here are some security best practices to harden your GKE cluster security. These are presented in detail in the Google Cloud documentation as well as CIS GKE benchmarks, so make sure to understand them:

- Upgrade your GKE infrastructure in a timely fashion
- Restrict network access to the control plane and nodes
- Consider managing Kubernetes RBAC users with Google Groups for RBAC
- Enable Shielded GKE nodes
- Choose a hardened node image with the containerd runtime
- Enable Workload Identity
- Harden workload isolation with GKE Sandbox
- Enable security bulletin notifications
- Use least-privilege Google service accounts
- Restrict access to cluster API discovery

- Use namespaces and RBAC to restrict access to cluster resources

- Restrict traffic among pods with a network policy

- Consider encrypting Kubernetes secrets using keys managed in Cloud KMS

- Use admission controllers to enforce policies

- Restrict the ability of workloads to self-modify

- Audit your cluster configurations for deviations from your defined settings

- Ensure legacy Compute Engine instance metadata APIs are disabled and also ensure the GKE metadata server is enabled

- Ensure Basic Authentication using static passwords is disabled

- Ensure authentication using Client Certificates is disabled

- Leave Cloud Logging enabled

- Leave the Kubernetes web UI (dashboard) disabled

- Disable **Attribute-Based Access Control (ABAC)**, and instead use **RBAC** in GKE

- Do not disable the `DenyServiceExternalIPs` admission controller

Now let us see some best practices for containers in general.

Container security best practices

Here are a few general security best practices when using containers for your application development process. We will look at these in three parts: the build phase, the distribution/deployment phase, and the production/run phase. These go hand in hand with your CI/CD security:

- **Security in the container build phase**: This is where the container build starts:

  - **Source image control**: In this phase, you write the code to create a container. Follow these best practices for this phase:

    i. Avoid retrieving/using source images with unknown/untrusted publishers.

    ii. If a third-party image is used, it is strongly recommended to identify and document detailed information, such as the version/build of code included and information about the creator of the image.

    iii. Never include code from unverified/untrusted sources in an image.

    iv. Use digital signature/checksum verification services on images whenever possible.

    v. Prior to completing image creation, all dependencies and libraries in source images should contain the latest security updates.

vi. Less is more—include only core, necessary software/code in a base image. This alleviates future work and maintenance load from a security perspective.

vii. Never include code from unverified/untrusted sources in an image.

- **Security/vulnerability scanning**: In this phase, you have the container image ready. Follow these best practices for scanning containers:

  i. It is recommended to perform security and vulnerability scanning on images regularly. Most security scanning services can be integrated with the container environment and batched to automatically perform security scanning.

  ii. It is recommended to leverage security scanning tools. Clair is an open source security scanner developed by CoreOS and is widely used for container security scanning. There are other commercial security scanners available on the market as well.

  iii. Use both static scanning (for example, package integrity verification) and dynamic scanning (for example, binary-level code analysis and/or application behavior analysis) in the security scanning program.

- **Security in the container distribution phase**: In this phase, your container is scanned and ready for deployment. Follow these best practices:

  - **Container registry security**:

    i. Access to the registry should go through proper authentication and authorization processes.

    ii. Always connect to the registry through securely encrypted channels. Images usually contain confidential business components and applications—in some cases, they even contain user data. Connecting to the registry through secure channels can ensure data confidentiality and avoid data leakage through successful man-in-the-middle attacks.

    iii. Data security protection mechanisms offered by the registry provider should be closely reviewed and evaluated prior to container deployment.

  - **Version control**:

    iv. Proper tooling, such as change management, audit, and continuous delivery and integration tools are critical for image version control. Good version control tools are essential in urgent situations, such as when an emergency rollback is needed.

- **Security in the container run phase**: Now we are ready to deploy the container on GKE. Follow these best practices for production:

  - **Authentication/account management**: Here are the best practices when it comes to authentication:

    i. Access to the container runtime environment should go through proper authentication and authorization processes.

    ii. Many authentication issues happen when users' credentials are poorly managed (for example, username/password leakage through social engineering or phishing, or credentials are not properly terminated/transferred when a user leaves the organization). We recommend using the organization's account management system for container account management/authentication/authorization and performing regular audits and account privilege reviews.

    iii. Use RBAC to regulate access to container resources. The least privilege principle should be applied.

  - **Attack surface reduction**: Here are best practices on production clusters to minimize the risk of compromising your cluster:

    i. To minimize the risk of being targeted and attacked, critical features in container images, such as root access and kernel capabilities, should be activated/enabled only when needed under monitoring.

    ii. As part of the best practices, grant cluster-level permissions only to trusted administrators and restrict access based on the principle of least privilege.

  - **Patch management**: It's recommended to keep your images up to date with the latest version. Here are some best practices:

    i. Subscribe to relevant system/library update feeds and apply the latest patches to container images.

    ii. Use version control features from the container registry (or other tools) to maintain an audit trail of container image updates. Critical information, such as timestamps, patch details, and known issues (such as side effects) should be documented for compliance purposes.

- **Secret management**: Secret management is one of the largest attack planes. Follow these best practices to minimize the risk due to secret leaks:

  i. Secrets, or sensitive data, should not be stored within an image. They should be stored outside of the image and be called dynamically at runtime.

  ii. Major orchestration platforms, such as Kubernetes and Docker Swarm, provide native secret management features. Configure the settings properly so that the sensitive data is handled securely when it is stored in a container and when it is transmitted between different services.

  iii. If the organization has an existing secret management system, it should be integrated with the container environment by providing secrets from the non-container environment, through a secure/encrypted channel.

This concludes the best practices for container pipelines, from building to running.

Summary

We covered a lot of ground in this and the previous chapter when it comes to container security. We went over the basics of CI/CD security and then we understood what containers are. Kubernetes paved the way for modernizing applications. The deployments that used to take hours are now deployed in minutes and it's also done several times a day. Kubernetes also makes it easy to scale deployments. GKE is Google's managed offering for Kubernetes, which takes away the pain of management and the complexity. GKE is headed toward more robust, self-healing features. Granted, container and Kubernetes security can be quite challenging to understand, but our hope is that these last two chapters made it easy for you to get a solid foundation.

Congratulations! You have reached the end of this book. We hope you've enjoyed reading it as much as we enjoyed putting it together. We have covered a lot of ground on the different security offerings in Google Cloud, and we hope you feel confident in your knowledge of them. Our ultimate goal is to help you become a certified Google Cloud security engineer and a trusted practitioner in your everyday work. So go out there and ace those exams! Best of luck to you!

Further reading

For more information on container security, refer to the following links:

- A simple IAP proxy for accessing a private GKE master control plane: `https://packt.link/1XbwP`

- Best practices for building containers: `https://packt.link/UUz4G`

Google Professional Cloud Security Engineer Exam – Mock Exam I

1. In the context of Google Cloud's shared responsibility model, which of the following is the responsibility of the customer?

   A. Implementing network security measures

   B. Ensuring the physical security of data centers

   C. Managing Google hypervisor security

   D. Maintaining the server hardware

2. Which compliance standard does Google Cloud adhere to in its commitment to protecting customer data privacy and security?

   A. Health Insurance Portability and Accountability Act (HIPAA)

   B. ISO/IEC 27001

   C. Payment Card Industry Data Security Standard (PCI DSS)

   D. All of the above

3. What is the purpose of Google Cloud Access Transparency?

   A. To provide customers with real-time visibility into the status of their cloud resources

   B. To monitor and track user access and activity within Google Cloud environments

   C. To ensure transparency and accountability by providing customers with logs of Google Cloud's access to their data

   D. To enable seamless integration between Google Cloud and third-party access management systems

4.   Which of the following services is supported by Access Approval?

   A.   Secret Manager

   B.   Identity and Access Management (IAM)

   C.   Cloud Key Management Service (KMS)

   D.   All of the above

5.   Which of the following is a feature of Google Cloud Virtual Private Cloud (VPC)?

   A.   Automatic scaling of compute resources

   B.   High-performance global load balancing

   C.   Managed database services

   D.   Serverless function execution

6.   Which of the following statements is true regarding Google Cloud VPC auto mode?

   A.   In auto mode, you can specify a custom IP address range for your VPC

   B.   Subnets in auto mode are manually created by the user

   C.   Routing tables in auto mode are managed by the user

   D.   Google automatically configures default firewall rules in auto mode

7.   Which Google Cloud IAM permissions are required to create a Shared VPC network?

   A.   roles/compute.networkAdmin

   B.   roles/compute.instanceAdmin

   C.   roles/compute.sharedVpcAdmin

   D.   roles/iam.serviceAccountAdmin

8.   Which of the following statements is true regarding custom route export in Google Cloud VPC?

   A.   Custom route export is only available in VPC auto mode

   B.   Custom route export allows routes to be advertised from a VPC to other networks

   C.   Custom route export requires the use of Cloud Router

   D.   Custom route export is limited to a single region within a VPC network

9. Which of the following statements is true regarding the use of service accounts in Google Cloud VPC firewall rules?

   A. Service accounts cannot be used as a source or destination in firewall rules

   B. Service accounts can be used as a source or destination in firewall rules

   C. Service accounts can only be used as a source but not as a destination in firewall rules

   D. Service accounts can only be used as a destination but not as a source in firewall rules

10. Which of the following load balancer types are available in Google Cloud (select all that apply)?

    A. Internal Load Balancer and External Load Balancer

    B. Regional Load Balancer and Global Load Balancer

    C. TCP Load Balancer and HTTP Load Balancer

    D. Network Load Balancer and Application Load Balancer

11. True or false: Private Google Access can be enabled at the subnet level within a VPC network.

    A. True

    B. False

12. Which of the following authentication methods is supported by Google Cloud Identity-Aware Proxy (IAP)?

    A. OAuth 2.0 tokens

    B. Usernames and passwords

    C. Public/private key pairs

    D. Security Assertion Markup Language (SAML)

13. Which of the following scenarios would benefit from using Google Cloud NAT with multiple NAT IP configurations?

    A. A high-traffic web application with distributed users worldwide

    B. A small-scale development environment with limited outgoing traffic

    C. A local network connecting to a single Google Cloud region

    D. A scenario that requires complex load balancing configurations

14. Which of the following statements is true about Google Cloud NAT logs?

   A. NAT logs cannot be stored in Cloud Storage for long-term retention

   B. NAT logs provide detailed information about inbound traffic flows

   C. NAT logs can be exported to third-party logging and monitoring systems

   D. NAT logs are automatically enabled and cannot be disabled

15. Which of the following types of attacks can Google Cloud Armor help protect against?

   A. Denial-of-Service (DoS) attacks

   B. SQL injection attacks

   C. Cross-Site Scripting (XSS) attacks

   D. All of the above

16. Which of the following types of logs are available in Google Cloud Logging?

   A. Performance logs

   B. Network logs

   C. Security logs

   D. All of the above

17. What is the role of a log router in Google Cloud Logging?

   A. To aggregate logs from multiple projects into a single view

   B. To apply filters and transformations to log entries before storage

   C. To manage log retention policies and the archiving of log data

   D. To provide real-time streaming of logs for near-instant analysis

18. Which of the following statements is true regarding custom images in Google Compute Engine?

   A. Custom images can only be created from scratch using the Compute Engine API

   B. Custom images are automatically backed up and replicated across multiple regions

   C. Custom images can be created from existing boot disks or other custom images

   D. Custom images are limited to a maximum size of 10 GB per image

19. Which of the following methods can be used to control access to compute images on Google Cloud?

    A. Setting up IAM roles and permissions for specific users or service accounts

    B. Configuring firewall rules to restrict inbound and outbound traffic to the compute images

    C. Enforcing network tags and labels to regulate access to compute images

    D. Implementing Identity-Aware Proxy (IAP) to authenticate and authorize users accessing the compute images

20. Which of the following is considered a best practice for securing a CI/CD pipeline on Google Cloud?

    A. Regularly updating and patching the CI/CD tools and dependencies

    B. Disabling Multi-Factor Authentication (MFA) for pipeline service accounts to streamline the deployment process

    C. Storing sensitive credentials and secrets in plain text within the pipeline configuration files

    D. Allowing unrestricted access to the CI/CD pipeline from any external IP address

21. Which security concept is relevant for Static Code Analysis (SCA) in a CI/CD pipeline on Google Cloud?

    A. Analyzing code for vulnerabilities and security flaws

    B. Encrypting sensitive data during the code deployment process

    C. Enforcing strong IAM roles for pipeline administrators

    D. Disabling automated testing and quality checks

22. Which security feature helps enhance container runtime security on Google Cloud?

    A. Enforcing container runtime isolation through the use of lightweight Virtual Machines (VMs)

    B. Disabling container sandboxing to improve application performance

    C. Running containers with elevated privileges to ensure system compatibility

    D. Ignoring container image scanning and vulnerability assessment

23. Which statement accurately describes the concept of a container in Google Cloud?

    A. Containers are virtual machines that provide isolated environments for running applications

    B. Containers are lightweight, standalone executable packages that include everything needed to run an application

    C. Containers are graphical user interfaces used to manage virtual machine instances in Google Cloud

    D. Containers are physical servers that are partitioned into multiple isolated environments

24. Which security measure can help mitigate the risk of a container breakout attack in a Kubernetes environment?

    A.   Regularly updating the host operating system of the Kubernetes cluster

    B.   Disabling network policies to allow unrestricted communication between containers

    C.   Running containers with privileged access and unrestricted capabilities

    D.   Ignoring container image vulnerabilities and not performing vulnerability scans

25. True or false: Containers running in Kubernetes clusters are automatically isolated from each other by default, preventing unauthorized access between containers.

    A.   True

    B.   False

26. Which security measure can help mitigate the risk of a container breakout attack in a Kubernetes environment?

    A.   Regularly updating the host operating system of the Kubernetes cluster

    B.   Disabling network policies to allow unrestricted communication between containers

    C.   Running containers with privileged access and unrestricted capabilities

    D.   Ignoring container image vulnerabilities and not performing vulnerability scans

27. A customer has several business units that want to use Google Cloud products. Each has its own team that handles development, QA, and product support. The customer wants to give enough independence to the business teams but still wants to control the security aspects of Google Cloud to privilege escalation and avoid security incidents. What is the right approach for the customer to implement such controls?

    A.   Set up organization policies, create a project for the business unit, provide the development and QA team owner role to the project, and grant the production support team an Organization admin role so they can manage organization policies.

    B.   Set up organization policies, create a folder for the business unit, and provide the ability to create a new project under that folder for the production support team.

    C.   Set up organization policies, create a few projects for the business unit, and provide owner permission to all projects to the production support team.

    D.   Set up organization policies, create a folder for the business unit, and provision projects for each environment. Only enable services that the team needs in that project. Provide a limited role based on the job responsibilities.

28. A customer needs to implement workloads that comply with PCI and HIPAA regulations. What is the best approach to implement such controls with Google Cloud, provide strict requirements for data segregation, and implement access control among multiple teams while reducing the toil of management?

   A. Implement organization policies and provide access to the team using centralized SSO, create folders and provision projects underneath to segregate the development, QA, and production environments, and grant the development team access to the projects.

   B. Create two Organization Units (OUs) in Cloud Identity, provision users to those OUs based on the requirements, and create multiple SAML profiles.

   C. Create three Google Cloud organizations. One organization will host projects for HIPAA, the second will host projects for PCI, and the third will host all other projects. Provision users and groups for each organization and set up a separate SSO for all three.

   D. Create two Google Cloud organizations. One organization will host projects that do not need strict data and access segregation. Provision users from the same source to both organizations and separate SSO.

29. You are implementing Google Cloud. Your identities are synchronized from your on-premises Active Directory to Azure Active Directory. Your business rules are set in Azure. What is the best approach to provide access to Google Cloud?

   A. Use Google Cloud Identity Sync to provision users and groups from on-premises Active Directory and create SSO using Azure.

   B. Use Azure to provision users and groups into Cloud identity. Create another application in Azure to provide federated access to Google Cloud.

   C. Use Google Cloud Identity Sync to provision users and groups from on-premises Active Directory and use Active Directory Federation Services (ADFS) to provide SSO.

   D. Use Google Cloud Identity Sync to provision users and groups from on-premises Active Directory, use Azure to provision partners to Cloud Identity, and use Azure to provide SSO.

30. A customer needs to rely on their existing user directory and have native authentication when developing solutions in Google Cloud. They want to leverage their existing tooling and functionality to gather insights into user activity using a familiar interface. Which action should you take to meet the customer's requirements?

   A. Provision users to Cloud Identity using Just-in-Time SAML 2.0 user provisioning with the customer user directory as the source

   B. Configure Cloud Identity as a SAML 2.0 service provider, using the customer's user directory as the identity provider

   C. Configure and enforce 2-Step Verification (2SV) in Cloud Identity for all super admins

   D. Configure a third-party identity provider (Okta or PingFederate) to manage authentication

31. A customer wants to use Cloud Identity as their primary identity provider. The customer wants to use other non-Google Cloud SaaS products for CRM, messaging, and customer ticketing management. The customer also wants to improve employee experience with Single Sign-On (SSO) capabilities to securely access Google Cloud and non-Google Cloud applications. Only authorized individuals should be able to access these third-party applications. What action should the customer take to meet these requirements?

    A. Remove the employee from Cloud Identity, set the correct license for the individuals, and resync them to Cloud Identity for the changes to take effect

    B. Configure third-party applications to federate authentication and authorization to the Google Cloud identity provider

    C. Remove the individuals from the third-party applications, add the license to Cloud Identity, and resync the individuals back to the third-party applications

    D. Copy user personas from Cloud Identity to all third-party applications for the domain

32. All of the following are best practices for super admin accounts except:

    A. Create a dedicated super admin account and store it away in vault systems. Use this account only when break-glass access is required.

    B. Delegate the ability to manage Google Cloud organization resources to other users in the organization and assign fundamental Cloud IAM roles to ensure the separation of duties.

    C. Make sure you require Google Cloud super admins to use your organization's SSO system so their activities can be monitored for auditing.

    D. Make sure you have multiple super admins in your organization.

33. All of the following are best practices while setting up Multi-Factor Authentication (MFA) in a Google Cloud organization except (select all that apply):

    A. All users are to turn on 2-Step Verification (2SV)

    B. Do not turn on enforcement of 2SV since users may lock themselves out

    C. Allow new users enough time to enroll

    D. Allow users to trust the device

    E. Turn on any 2SV method

    F. Allow security codes with remote access

34. The data team needs to use service accounts to interact with BigQuery. Their project requires a Cloud Storage bucket that holds data feeds. The project transforms the data in the data feeds to BigQuery. What is the right approach for the data team to implement this?

    A. Grant each member of the data team access to Cloud Storage buckets and BigQuery datasets.

    B. Create a Google group with all developers of the data team and grant the Cloud Storage bucket and BigQuery Dataset access to the Google group.

    C. Create a Google group with all data team developers. Assign the group the IAM role of Service Account User.

    D. Create a Google group with all developers. Assign the group the IAM role of Service Account Admin and have developers generate and download their own keys.

35. A three-tier application is running on Google Cloud. The application's middle tier is running on Compute Engine and needs read access to a dataset in Google BigQuery. How should you grant access?

    A. Create a service account for the application and grant the BigQuery User role at the project level

    B. Create a service account for the application and grant the BigQuery User role at the dataset level

    C. Create a service account for the application and grant the BigQuery Admin role at the dataset level

36. A cloud development team needs to use service accounts extensively in their local development. You need to provide the team with the keys for these service accounts. You want to follow Google-recommended practices. What should you do?

    A. Implement a daily key rotation process that generates a new key and commits it to the source code repository every day.

    B. Implement a daily key rotation process and provide developers with a Cloud Storage bucket from which they can download the new key every day.

    C. Create a Google group with all developers. Assign the group the IAM role of Service Account User and have developers generate and download their own keys.

    D. Create a Google group with all developers. Assign the group the IAM role of Service Account Admin and have developers generate and download their own keys.

37. A hybrid application is running on AWS and Google Cloud. The application part on AWS needs to query Google BigQuery. How do you implement this approach securely?

    A. Create a service account for the application, and grant the BigQuery User role at the dataset level. The team managing the AWS side will have ownership of the keys that they will provision with the application.

    B. Create a workforce pool and an AWS workforce provider, and grant impersonation access to the AWS account to the service account at the project level.

    C. Create a workload pool and an AWS workload provider, and grant impersonation access to the AWS account to the service account for the BigQuery dataset.

    D. Create a workload pool and an AWS workload provider, and grant impersonation access to the AWS role to the service account for the BigQuery dataset.

38. You are implementing a control whereby the SRE team needs to get access to Google Cloud only when the condition arises. How do you implement this approach with the least privilege?

    A. Create a Google group for the SRE team, and grant access to the SRE team at the organization level with a condition that allows access only between 8:00 AM and 5:00 PM and with an on-premises IP range.

    B. Create a group for the SRE team, and grant access to the SRE team at the project level with a condition that allows access only between 8:00 AM and 5:00 PM.

    C. Create a group for the SRE team; pre-approve them for access to this group. Ask them to request access to this group, stating the amount of time in minutes that they need access to the Google Cloud project.

    D. Create a group for the SRE team and add the users to this group. Ask them to request access for the amount of time in minutes that they need access to the Google Cloud project.

39. A Google Cloud customer wants to implement segregation of duties. The SRE team should have the ability to generate the keys but shouldn't have the ability to use the key to encrypt or decrypt the data. What is the right method to achieve this?

    A. The SRE team and the service account used by the application should be granted a Cloud KMS Admin role in the project keys that are generated

    B. The SRE team and the service account used by the application should be granted a Cloud KMS Admin role in the project keys that are used

    C. The SRE team should be granted a KMS Admin role for the project and the service account should be granted the role of Cloud KMS CryptoKey Encrypter/Decrypter in the project keys that are generated

D. The SRE team should be granted a KMS Admin role for the project and the service account should be granted the role of Cloud KMS CryptoKey Encrypter/Decrypter in the project keys that are used

E. None of the above

40. What is the primary purpose of Google Cloud Key Management Service (KMS)?

A. Encrypting data at rest

B. Managing access control for Google Cloud resources

C. Generating and managing cryptographic keys

D. Monitoring and auditing cloud security events

41. Which of the following statements about Google Cloud KMS keys is true?

A. Google Cloud KMS generates and stores Customer-Managed Keys (CMKs) for encryption

B. Google Cloud KMS uses only pre-defined keys provided by Google for encryption

C. Google Cloud KMS keys can be used for authentication purposes

D. Google Cloud KMS keys are automatically rotated by the service

42. How does Google Cloud KMS handle key versioning?

A. It automatically generates and manages multiple versions of a key

B. It allows users to manually create and manage multiple versions of a key

C. It only supports a single version of a key at a time

D. It doesn't support key versioning

43. What is the role of Identity and Access Management (IAM) in Google Cloud KMS?

A. IAM is used to encrypt and decrypt data using KMS keys

B. IAM provides access control for managing KMS resources and operations

C. IAM is responsible for automatically rotating KMS keys

D. IAM enforces encryption policies for data stored in Google Cloud Storage

44. How can you list all keys within a key ring in Google Cloud KMS using the gcloud command-line tool?

    A. gcloud kms keys list

    B. gcloud kms keyrings list-keys

    C. gcloud kms keyrings keys list

    D. gcloud kms list-keys

45. A company wants to ensure compliance with data protection regulations by identifying and redacting sensitive information in its cloud storage. Which feature of Google Cloud DLP can help achieve this?

    A. Data classification

    B. Data de-identification

    C. Data discovery

    D. Data masking

46. An organization needs to analyze large volumes of data for patterns and trends without exposing any Personally Identifiable Information (PII). Which Google Cloud DLP technique can be applied to achieve this?

    A. Tokenization

    B. Redaction

    C. Masking

    D. Anonymization

47. A development team wants to securely store API keys and database credentials for their microservices deployed on Google Kubernetes Engine (GKE). They also need to rotate these secrets regularly. Which Google Cloud Secret Manager feature can help achieve this?

    A. Secret versioning

    B. Secret replication

    C. Secret auditing

    D. Secret scanning

48. A financial institution wants to grant granular access control to different teams within their organization for managing secrets. They want to ensure that only authorized individuals can create, access, and update specific secrets. Which Google Cloud Secret Manager feature provides this capability?

    A. IAM integration

    B. Secret rotation

    C. Secret monitoring

    D. Secret access controls

49. A large organization wants to have centralized visibility and monitoring of security risks and vulnerabilities across its Google Cloud infrastructure. Which feature of Google Cloud Security Command Center can help achieve this?

    A. Asset Inventory

    B. Security findings

    C. Security Health Analytics

    D. Security policies

50. A company wants to assess the compliance of its Google Cloud resources with industry-specific security standards and regulations. Which feature of Google Cloud Security Command Center can assist in this evaluation?

    A. Security Health Analytics

    B. Security policies

    C. Security findings

    D. Asset Inventory

Answer Key

1. A

2. D

3. C

4. D

5. B

6. D

7. C

8. B

9. B

10. A and B

11. A

12. A

13. A

14. C

15. D

16. D

17. B

18. C

19. D

20. A

21. A

22. A

23. B

24. A

25. B

26. A

27. D

28. D

29. B

30. B

31. B
32. C
33. B, E, and F
34. C
35. B
36. B
37. D
38. D
39. C
40. C
41. A
42. A
43. B
44. B
45. A
46. C
47. A
48. D
49. B
50. B

Google Professional Cloud Security Engineer Exam – Mock Exam II

1. Which of the following options can be configured for Google Cloud Access Transparency?

    A. Granular access control policies for individual users

    B. Real-time monitoring and alerting of access activities

    C. Logging and retention settings for access logs

    D. Integration with third-party identity providers

2. Which of the following statements is true regarding Google Cloud Access Approval?

    A. Access Approval allows administrators to grant automatic access to all users within a Google Cloud project

    B. Access Approval provides real-time monitoring and tracking of user access and activity within Google Cloud environments

    C. Access Approval streamlines and controls Google user access to sensitive resources and data within Google Cloud

    D. Access Approval is used to authenticate user identities for secure access to Google Cloud services

3. Which of the following options allows you to create hybrid connectivity between your on-premises network and Google Cloud?

    A. Google Cloud VPN

    B. Cloud Dataflow

    C. Google Cloud Storage

    D. Google Cloud Spanner

4. Which of the following statements accurately describes the default firewall rules in Google Cloud VPC auto mode?

   A. The default firewall rules allow incoming connections from any source to the instances within the VPC network

   B. The default firewall rules block all incoming and outgoing connections for instances within the VPC network

   C. The default firewall rules allow incoming connections from the internet to instances within the VPC network while blocking outgoing connections

   D. The default firewall rules allow outgoing connections from instances within the VPC network while blocking incoming connections

5. Which of the following requirements apply when establishing VPC peering in Google Cloud, depending on the VPC mode?

   A. In VPC auto mode, VPC networks must be located in the same region

   B. In VPC custom mode, VPC networks must have non-overlapping IP address ranges

   C. In both VPC auto mode and VPC custom mode, VPC peering can only be established within the same project

   D. In both VPC auto mode and VPC custom mode, VPC peering requires specific IAM roles to be assigned to the user

6. How are Google Cloud VPC firewall rules evaluated for incoming traffic?

   A. Firewall rules are evaluated in ascending order based on their creation timestamp

   B. Firewall rules are evaluated in descending order based on their priority value

   C. Firewall rules are evaluated randomly to ensure fair traffic distribution

   D. Firewall rules are evaluated based on their assigned project ID

7. Which of the following describes the different types of tags that can be used in Google Cloud VPC firewall rules?

   A. Network tags and service account tags

   B. Ingress tags and egress tags

   C. Source tags and destination tags

   D. Priority tags and action tags

8. Which of the following statements is true regarding Google Cloud Private Google Access?

    A. It provides access to Google APIs and services through the public internet

    B. It allows instances in a VPC network to access Google services using internal IP addresses

    C. It is only available for VPC networks located in the same region as the Google service

    D. It requires the creation of VPN tunnels for secure communication with Google services

9. What is the primary purpose of Google Cloud Identity-Aware Proxy (IAP)?

    A. To provide secure access to Google Cloud Virtual Machines (VMs) and applications

    B. To manage user identities and access permissions within Google Cloud

    C. To encrypt and secure data during transit between Google Cloud services

    D. To monitor and detect potential security threats within Google Cloud

10. What is the role of Cloud Identity-Aware Proxy (IAP) in protecting applications deployed on Google Cloud?

    A. It allows easy access management and authorization of users

    B. It provides encryption of data at rest and in transit

    C. It monitors application performance and uptime

    D. It automatically scales applications based on traffic demand

11. In Google Cloud NAT, what is the purpose of using the Manual NAT mapping option?

    A. To allow the automatic scaling of NAT configurations based on traffic demands

    B. To assign specific IP addresses for source and destination NAT mapping

    C. To enable fine-grained control over port allocation for NAT translations

    D. To integrate NAT configurations with Cloud Router for advanced routing capabilities

12. What is the primary purpose of Google Cloud Armor?

    A. To provide load balancing capabilities for Google Cloud resources

    B. To secure and protect applications against web-based attacks

    C. To monitor and analyze network traffic for performance optimization

    D. To manage user identities and access permissions within Google Cloud

13. What is the role of security policies in Google Cloud Armor?

    A. Security policies define rules for access control to Google Cloud resources

    B. Security policies enforce encryption of data at rest and in transit

    C. Security policies enable the configuration of firewall rules and network ACLs

    D. Security policies specify the behavior of Google Cloud Armor for incoming requests

14. What is the purpose of log sinks in Google Cloud Logging?

    A. To collect logs from various Google Cloud services and store them in Cloud Storage

    B. To analyze log data and generate insights using machine learning algorithms

    C. To export logs to third-party logging and monitoring systems

    D. To manage access controls and permissions for log data

15. What is the benefit of enabling log-based metrics in Google Cloud Logging?

    A. It allows you to visualize log data using custom dashboards and charts

    B. It enables you to monitor specific events and trigger alerts based on log entries

    C. It provides real-time analysis of log data to detect security threats

    D. It helps you automatically manage log storage and retention policies

16. What is the purpose of instance templates in Google Cloud Compute Engine?

    A. Instance templates are used to create snapshots of Compute Engine instances

    B. Instance templates allow for the management of machine types and sizes

    C. Instance templates enable the creation of custom images from scratch

    D. Instance templates define the configuration settings for creating VM instances

17. Which statement accurately describes the image lifecycle management for Compute Engine on Google Cloud?

    A. Compute Engine provides automatic image lifecycle management, including regular backups and versioning for all compute images

    B. Users have full control over the image lifecycle, including the ability to create and manage custom image snapshots and metadata

    C. Compute Engine automatically deletes all unused images after a specific period of inactivity to optimize storage usage

    D. Image lifecycle management is only available for Google-managed images and cannot be applied to custom images

18. Which Google Cloud feature provides enhanced security for Virtual Machines (VMs) by enabling Secure Boot, virtual Trusted Platform Module (vTPM), and integrity monitoring?

    A. Shielded VM

    B. Virtual Private Cloud (VPC)

    C. Google Cloud Armor

    D. Cloud Security Scanner

19. Which security measure should be implemented to secure the artifacts produced by a Google Cloud CI/CD pipeline?

    A. Storing artifacts in a publicly accessible storage bucket

    B. Encrypting the artifacts at rest and in transit

    C. Granting broad read access to all pipeline service accounts

    D. Disabling the logging and auditing of artifact access

20. Which Google Cloud feature helps enforce a secure software supply chain by allowing organizations to define and enforce custom policies for container image deployment based on metadata and attributes?

    A. Binary Authorization

    B. Container Registry

    C. Cloud Build

    D. Google Kubernetes Engine (GKE)

21. Which security feature in Google Kubernetes Engine (GKE) helps protect container workloads by automatically managing and rotating encryption keys for data at rest?

    A. Google Cloud Armor

    B. Cloud Identity-Aware Proxy (IAP)

    C. Binary Authorization

    D. GKE Data Encryption using Cloud Key Management Service (KMS)

22. Which statement accurately describes the purpose of namespaces in Google Kubernetes Engine (GKE)?

    A. Namespaces are used to control network traffic between different GKE clusters

    B. Namespaces provide logical isolation within a single GKE cluster by partitioning resources

    C. Namespaces are responsible for automatically scaling the number of nodes in a GKE cluster

    D. Namespaces ensure secure access to the GKE API server through token-based authentication

23. What is the primary purpose of Role-Based Access Control (RBAC) in Google Kubernetes Engine (GKE)?

    A.   RBAC enables fine-grained control over permissions and access to Kubernetes resources

    B.   RBAC automatically scales the number of GKE nodes based on the workload demand

    C.   RBAC manages containerized applications' network traffic within a GKE cluster

    D.   RBAC ensures secure communication between GKE clusters using a service mesh

24. Which statement accurately describes the role of a service mesh in Google Kubernetes Engine (GKE)?

    A.   A service mesh provides additional encryption layers for securing data at rest within a GKE cluster

    B.   A service mesh is responsible for managing network policies and ingress control for GKE services

    C.   A service mesh enhances observability, traffic management, and security for microservices in a GKE cluster

    D.   A service mesh automatically scans container images for vulnerabilities and security risks in GKE

25. Which security measure helps ensure the integrity and security of container images in Google Cloud?

    A.   Container Registry vulnerability scanning

    B.   Disabling image scanning for faster image deployment

    C.   Running containers with elevated privileges for system compatibility

    D.   Sharing container images publicly without any access controls

26. True or false: Container vulnerability scanning in Google Cloud automatically identifies and alerts users about security risks and vulnerabilities in container images.

    A.   True

    B.   False

27. Your Google Cloud organization policies provide guardrails for security controls for all organizations. Which of these are not best practices to follow when setting up organization policies (select all that apply)?

    A.   Organization policies should be implemented over a period of time as your requirements become clear

    B.   Delegate control of organization policies to the SRE teams

C. Prior to enforcing policies, thoroughly test and validate their impact on your resources and applications

D. It is usually not required to monitor and audit policies as they provide a robust framework to implement security controls right from the start

E. Since organization policies are set at the organizational level, it is often not required to implement them at the folder or project level

F. You should not version control policies via infrastructure as code

28. When creating projects in Google, which of the following are not best practices (select all that apply)?

A. Implement consistent naming conventions for your projects to ensure clarity and ease of identification

B. Use the default project controls since it allows you to get up and running quickly

C. Enable audit logs and monitoring for your projects to track and analyze activities within your environment

D. Google doesn't place a cap on the number of projects in a Google Cloud organization so it is safe to just leave the project and create a new one

E. Use IAM roles that are broad enough to grant more access than is needed so development is not hindered

F. Utilize Google Cloud's resource hierarchy, including folders and projects, to organize and manage resources effectively

29. A customer has a team that exclusively manages user identity and access. A cloud engineering team manages Google Cloud and has an intimate knowledge of organization policies. What is the right permission model for this company to manage Google Cloud securely?

A. Assign the super admin role to the cloud engineering team so they can manage users and groups for the entire organization.

B. Restrict the super admin role. Assign the user and group management roles to the identity access team. Assign the organization administrator role to the cloud engineering team.

C. Assign the super admin role to the identity access team and assign the organization administrator role to the cloud engineering team.

D. Assign the super admin and organization administrator roles to the identity access team so they can effectively manage access to the entire organization.

30. A Google Workspace customer is investigating the use of Google Cloud. They have called you to help with planning. They would like to set up Google Cloud in such a way that the roles and responsibilities in Cloud and Workspace are seperated while minimizing the effort required to set up Google Cloud. What approach would you recommend?

   A. Set up Google Cloud in the same organization as Google Workspace. Assign the organization administrator role to the cloud engineering team. Since identities are already provisioned, you can get up and running quickly.

   B. Create a subdomain in the Google Workspace domain and use that to set up Google Cloud.

   C. Create a new domain for Google Cloud. Provide access to users and groups from the Workspace domain to the Google Cloud domain.

   D. Create a new domain for Google Cloud, and provision users and groups to the Google Cloud domain.

31. Developers in an organization are prototyping a few applications on Google Cloud and are using their personal/consumer Gmail accounts to set up and manage their projects within Google Cloud. A security engineer raises this practice as a concern to the leadership team because of the lack of centralized project management and access to the data being stored in these accounts. Which solution should be used to resolve this concern?

   A. Enforce the setup of security keys using the 2-Step Verification (2SV) method for those Gmail accounts

   B. Set up Cloud Identity and require the developers to use those accounts for Google Cloud work

   C. Require the developers to log/store their Gmail passwords with the security team

   D. Enable logging on all Google Cloud projects to track all developer activity

32. It is a security best practice to set a session length for Google Cloud. Which of the following are not best practices when setting the session length (select all that apply)?

   A. Set the same session length for all Google applications (such as Gmail), including Google Cloud

   B. Exempt trusted apps from requiring session reauthentication

   C. Set a reauthentication policy to not require reauthentication

   D. Set a uniform session control for all users irrespective of their roles and responsibilities in your organization

   E. Set policies to limit long sessions

   F. Session length should apply to any application, including third-party applications that require user authorization for Google Cloud

33. You are setting up Google Cloud Directory Sync to provision users and groups to Cloud Identity. What should you not do (select all that apply)?

    A. Set a read-only account to your LDAP server to query users and groups

    B. Query all users and groups from your LDAP server and provision them to Cloud Identity

    C. Just select a few key attributes to sync to Cloud Identity

    D. Set a base distinguished name so Google Cloud Directory Sync (GCDS) can see all users and groups from your directory

34. In a large organization with multiple subsidiaries, each subsidiary has its own Google Cloud project. The organization wants to ensure that the IAM policies for each subsidiary's project are managed independently, but they also need a centralized view of IAM policies across all projects for auditing purposes. Which IAM feature can fulfill these requirements?

    A. IAM custom roles

    B. IAM conditions

    C. IAM service accounts

    D. IAM resource hierarchy

35. A company wants to grant access to specific resources in Google Cloud based on user attributes such as department, location, and job title. They also want to automate access provisioning and deprovisioning based on changes to user attributes. Which IAM feature can help accomplish this?

    A. IAM roles

    B. IAM Group membership

    C. IAM policies

    D. IAM service accounts

    E. IAM conditions

36. A multinational company wants to delegate administrative responsibilities for specific Google Cloud projects to regional IT teams. However, they want to ensure that the centralized IT team retains overall control and visibility of all projects. Which IAM feature can facilitate this delegation while maintaining centralized control?

    A. IAM service accounts

    B. IAM custom roles

    C. IAM policies

    D. IAM resource hierarchy

37. A company wants to grant a third-party consultant temporary access to their Google Cloud project to perform a security assessment. They want to ensure that the consultant has the necessary access rights for the assessment, and they want to make sure the consultant has access to the environment during working hours and gets a minimum privileged role. What can help achieve this (select all that apply)?

    A.   Assign project viewer roles

    B.   Assign IAM conditions in the IAM policies

    C.   Create an IAM service account for the consultant

    D.   Create a service account key for the consultant so they can execute queries

38. A company wants to implement fine-grained access control for a specific Google Cloud resource, allowing only specific actions to be performed by specific users. They want to ensure that users can perform only authorized actions and nothing beyond that. Which IAM feature can provide this level of granularity in access control?

    A.   IAM custom roles

    B.   IAM conditions

    C.   IAM policies

    D.   IAM service accounts

39. Google Cloud Key Management Service (KMS) supports all of the following purposes of encryption algorithm, except:

    A.   Symmetric encryption

    B.   Asymmetric signing

    C.   Asymmetric encryption

    D.   MAC signing

    E.   Symmetric signing

40. A cloud customer has an on-premises key management system and wants to generate, protect, rotate, and audit encryption keys with it. How can the customer use Cloud Storage with their own encryption keys?

    A.   Declare usage of default encryption at rest in the audit report on compliance

    B.   Upload encryption keys to the same Cloud Storage bucket

    C.   Use Customer-Managed Encryption Keys (CMEKs)

    D.   Use Customer-Supplied Encryption Keys (CSEKs)

41. Which encryption algorithm is used with default encryption in Cloud Storage?

    A. AES-256

    B. SHA512

    C. MD5

    D. 3DES

42. A cloud customer wants to use the same encryption keys in two projects. What are the possible options for customers to do this?

    A. Call the encrypt and decrypt methods of the KMS API in the project where the key exists

    B. Export the encryption from the first project and encrypt in the other project

    C. Use Cloud HSM in both projects and import the key there

    D. Bring the key from on-premises for both workloads

43. How can you create a new key ring in Google Cloud KMS using the gcloud command-line tool?

    A. gcloud kms keyrings create

    B. gcloud kms keyrings add

    C. gcloud kms keyrings insert

    D. gcloud kms keyrings generate

44. A financial institution wants to audit and monitor the usage of encryption keys across its Google Cloud projects. They need visibility into key usage, including key creation, deletion, and key operations. Which feature of Google Cloud KMS provides this capability?

    A. Key labels

    B. Key rings

    C. Key rotation

    D. Key usage logs

45. A healthcare organization wants to detect and protect sensitive health information stored in different languages, including English, Spanish, and Mandarin. Which feature of Google Cloud DLP can be used to achieve language-agnostic data detection?

    A. Custom infoType

    B. Predefined infoType

    C. Inspect Templates

    D. Entity Extraction

46. A financial institution wants to prevent the accidental sharing of sensitive data through a data warehouse. Which Google Cloud DLP feature can help accomplish this?

    A. Data discovery

    B. Job configuration

    C. Content redaction

    D. Inspect templates

47. An organization wants to grant different teams within their company granular access control over secrets stored in Google Cloud Secret Manager. They want to ensure that each team can only access and manage secrets specific to their projects. Which feature of Google Cloud Secret Manager enables this?

    A. Secret monitoring

    B. Secret replication

    C. Secret access controls

    D. Secret auditing

48. A company wants to integrate its existing on-premises secrets management system with Google Cloud Secret Manager to have a unified solution. Which feature of Google Cloud Secret Manager allows this integration?

    A. Secret import

    B. Secret monitoring

    C. Secret auditing

    D. Sync secrets using APIs

49. An organization wants to detect and respond to potential security incidents in real time within their Google Cloud environment. Which feature of Google Cloud Security Command Center can facilitate this proactive monitoring?

    A. Security findings

    B. Security Health Analytics

    C. Security policies

    D. Asset Inventory

50. A company wants to track and manage the security posture of its Google Cloud projects individually. Which feature of Google Cloud Security Command Center provides project-specific security insights and recommendations?

    A. Security Health Analytics

    B. Security findings

    C. Security policies

    D. Asset Inventory

Answer Key

1. C
2. C
3. A
4. D
5. C
6. B
7. A
8. B
9. A
10. A
11. C
12. B
13. D
14. C
15. B
16. D
17. B
18. A
19. B
20. A
21. D
22. B
23. A

24. C

25. A

26. A

27. A, B, D, E, and F

28. B, D, and E

29. B

30. C

31. B

32. A, B, C, and D

33. B and C

34. D

35. B

36. B

37. A and B

38. B

39. C

40. D

41. A

42. A

43. A

44. D

45. A

46. C

47. C

48. A

49. A

50. A

Index

B

‹packt›

www.packtpub.com

Subscribe to our online digital library for full access to over 7,000 books and videos, as well as industry leading tools to help you plan your personal development and advance your career. For more information, please visit our website.

Why subscribe?

- Spend less time learning and more time coding with practical eBooks and Videos from over 4,000 industry professionals

- Improve your learning with Skill Plans built especially for you

- Get a free eBook or video every month

- Fully searchable for easy access to vital information

- Copy and paste, print, and bookmark content

At www.packtpub.com, you can also read a collection of free technical articles, sign up for a range of free newsletters, and receive exclusive discounts and offers on Packt books and eBooks.

Other Books You May Enjoy

If you enjoyed this book, you may be interested in these other books by Packt:

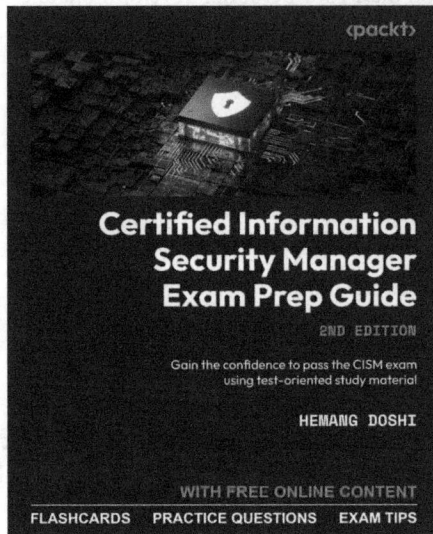

Certified Information Security Manager Exam Prep Guide – Second Edition

Hemang Doshi

ISBN: 978-1-80461-063-3

- Understand core exam objectives to prepare for the CISM exam with confidence
- Get to grips with detailed procedural guidelines for effective information security incident management
- Execute information security governance in an efficient manner
- Strengthen your preparation for the CISM exam using interactive flashcards and practice questions
- Conceptualize complex topics through diagrams and examples
- Find out how to integrate governance, risk management, and compliance functions

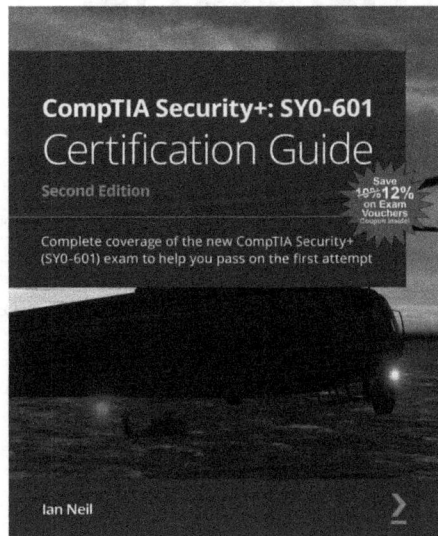

CompTIA Security+: SY0-601 Certification Guide - Second Edition

Ian Neil

ISBN: 978-1-80056-424-4

- Master cybersecurity fundamentals, from the CIA triad through to IAM
- Explore cloud security and techniques used in penetration testing
- Use different authentication methods and troubleshoot security issues
- Secure the devices and applications used by your company
- Identify and protect against various types of malware and viruses
- Protect yourself against social engineering and advanced attacks
- Understand and implement PKI concepts
- Delve into secure application development, deployment, and automation

Share your thoughts

Now you've finished *Official Google Cloud Certified Professional Cloud Security Engineer Exam Guide*, we'd love to hear your thoughts! Scan the QR code below to go straight to the Amazon review page for this book and share your feedback or leave a review on the site that you purchased it from.

https://packt.link/r/1835468861

Your review is important to us and the tech community and will help us make sure we're delivering excellent quality content.